ADVANCED MACROECONOMICS

ADVANCED MACROECONOMICS

Second edition

David Romer

University of California, Berkeley

Boston   Burr Ridge, IL   Dubuque, IA   Madison, WI   New York
San Francisco   St. Louis   Bangkok   Bogotá   Caracas   Kuala Lumpur
Lisbon   London   Madrid   Mexico City   Milan   Montreal   New Delhi
Santiago   Seoul   Singapore   Sydney   Taipei   Toronto

McGraw-Hill Higher Education

*A Division of The **McGraw-Hill** Companies*

ADVANCED MACROECONOMICS
Published by McGraw-Hill/Irwin, an imprint of The McGraw-Hill Companies, Inc. 1221
Avenue of the Americas, New York, NY, 10020. Copyright ©2001, 1996, by The
McGraw-Hill Companies, Inc. All rights reserved. No part of this publication may be
reproduced or distributed in any form or by any means, or stored in a data base or
retrieval system, without the prior written consent of The McGraw-Hill Companies,
Inc., including, but not limited to, in any network or other electronic storage or
transmission, or broadcast for distance learning. Some ancillaries, including electronic
and print components, may not be available to customers outside the United States.

This book is printed on acid-free paper.

1 2 3 4 5 6 7 8 9 0 FGR/FGR 0 9 8 7 6 5 4 3 2 1 0

ISBN 0-07-231855-4

Publisher: *Gary Burke*
Executive editor: *Paul Shensa*
Developmental editor: *Erin Strathmann*
Marketing manager: *Marty W. Quinn*
Project manager: *Scott Scheidt*
Production supervisor: *Susanne Riedell*
Designer: *Pam Verros*
Supplement coordinator: *Nate Perry*
Cover design: *JoAnne Schopler*
Compositor: *Techsetters, Inc.*
Typeface: *9.25/12 Lucida Bright*
Printer: *Quebecor Printing Book Group/Fairfield*

Library of Congress Cataloging-in-Publication Data

Romer, David.
   Advanced macroeconomics / David Romer.-2nd ed.
     p. cm.
   Includes index.
   ISBN 0-07-231855-4 (alk. paper)
   1. Macroeconomics. I. Title.
HB172.5.R66 2001
339-dc21   00-059456

http://www.mhhe.com

ABOUT THE AUTHOR

David Romer is the Royer Professor in Political Economy at the University of California, Berkeley, where he has been on the faculty since 1988. He received his A.B. from Princeton University, where he was valedictorian, and his Ph.D. from the Massachusetts Institute of Technology. He has been on the faculty at Princeton and has been a visiting faculty member at M.I.T. and Stanford University. He is also a Research Associate of the National Bureau of Economic Research. At Berkeley he has received both the Graduate Economics Association Distinguished Teaching Award and its Distinguished Advising Award. His main research interests are monetary policy, the foundations of price stickiness, empirical evidence on economic growth, and asset-price volatility. He is married to Christina Romer, who is also an economist, and has three children, Katherine, Paul, and Matthew.

To Christy

CONTENTS IN BRIEF

Introduction		1
Chapter 1	THE SOLOW GROWTH MODEL	5
Chapter 2	INFINITE-HORIZON AND OVERLAPPING-GENERATIONS MODELS	47
Chapter 3	NEW GROWTH THEORY	98
Chapter 4	REAL-BUSINESS-CYCLE THEORY	168
Chapter 5	TRADITIONAL KEYNESIAN THEORIES OF FLUCTUATIONS	217
Chapter 6	MICROECONOMIC FOUNDATIONS OF INCOMPLETE NOMINAL ADJUSTMENT	265
Chapter 7	CONSUMPTION	330
Chapter 8	INVESTMENT	367
Chapter 9	UNEMPLOYMENT	410
Chapter 10	INFLATION AND MONETARY POLICY	468
Chapter 11	BUDGET DEFICITS AND FISCAL POLICY	530
References		588
Indexes		626

CONTENTS

Preface to the Second Edition   xix

Introduction   1

Chapter 1 THE SOLOW GROWTH MODEL   5

1.1	Some Basic Facts about Economic Growth	5
1.2	Assumptions	9
1.3	The Dynamics of the Model	14
1.4	The Impact of a Change in the Saving Rate	17
1.5	Quantitative Implications	22
1.6	The Solow Model and the Central Questions of Growth Theory	26
1.7	Empirical Applications	28
1.8	The Environment and Economic Growth	35
	Problems	43

Chapter 2 INFINITE-HORIZON AND OVERLAPPING-GENERATIONS MODELS   47

Part A THE RAMSEY–CASS–KOOPMANS MODEL   47

2.1	Assumptions	47
2.2	The Behavior of Households and Firms	49
2.3	The Dynamics of the Economy	55
2.4	Welfare	60
2.5	The Balanced Growth Path	61
2.6	The Effects of a Fall in the Discount Rate	63
2.7	The Effects of Government Purchases	68

Part B THE DIAMOND MODEL   75

2.8	Assumptions	75
2.9	Household Behavior	76

2.10	The Dynamics of the Economy	78
2.11	The Possibility of Dynamic Inefficiency	85
2.12	Government in the Diamond Model	89
	Problems	91

Chapter 3 NEW GROWTH THEORY   98

Part A RESEARCH AND DEVELOPMENT MODELS   99

3.1	Framework and Assumptions	99
3.2	The Model without Capital	101
3.3	The General Case	107
3.4	The Nature of Knowledge and the Determinants of the Allocation of Resources to R&D	115
3.5	Endogenous Saving in Models of Knowledge Accumulation: An Example	122
3.6	Models of Knowledge Accumulation and the Central Questions of Growth Theory	125
3.7	Empirical Application: Population Growth and Technological Change since 1 Million B.C.	126

Part B CROSS-COUNTRY INCOME DIFFERENCES   132

3.8	Extending the Solow Model to Include Human Capital	133
3.9	Empirical Application: Accounting for Cross-Country Income Differences	138
3.10	Social Infrastructure	143
3.11	A Model of Production, Protection, and Predation	150
3.12	Differences in Growth Rates	156
	Problems	160

Chapter 4 REAL-BUSINESS-CYCLE THEORY   168

4.1	Introduction: Some Facts about Economic Fluctuations	168
4.2	Theories of Fluctuations	172
4.3	A Baseline Real-Business-Cycle Model	174
4.4	Household Behavior	176
4.5	A Special Case of the Model	180
4.6	Solving the Model in the General Case	186
4.7	Implications	190
4.8	Empirical Application: The Persistence of Output Fluctuations	196
4.9	Additional Empirical Applications	201
4.10	Extensions and Limitations	205
	Problems	212

Chapter 5 TRADITIONAL KEYNESIAN THEORIES OF FLUCTUATIONS 217

5.1 Review of the Textbook Keynesian Model of Aggregate
Demand 218
5.2 The Open Economy 225
5.3 Alternative Assumptions about Wage and Price Rigidity 234
5.4 Output-Inflation Tradeoffs 242
5.5 Empirical Application: Money and Output 252
5.6 The Cyclical Behavior of the Real Wage 258
Problems 260

Chapter 6 MICROECONOMIC FOUNDATIONS OF INCOMPLETE NOMINAL ADJUSTMENT 265

Part A THE LUCAS IMPERFECT-INFORMATION MODEL 266

6.1 The Case of Perfect Information 267
6.2 The Case of Imperfect Information 270
6.3 Implications and Limitations 274

Part B STAGGERED PRICE ADJUSTMENT 279

6.4 A Model of Imperfect Competition and Price-Setting 281
6.5 Predetermined Prices 285
6.6 Fixed Prices 288
6.7 The Caplin-Spulber Model 296

Part C NEW KEYNESIAN ECONOMICS 299

6.8 Are Small Frictions Enough? 301
6.9 The Need for Real Rigidity 304
6.10 Empirical Applications 313
6.11 Coordination-Failure Models and Real Non-Walrasian
Theories 316
6.12 Limitations 322
Problems 324

Chapter 7 CONSUMPTION 330

7.1 Consumption under Certainty:
The Life-Cycle/Permanent-Income Hypothesis 331
7.2 Consumption under Uncertainty: The Random-Walk
Hypothesis 337

7.3   Empirical Application: Two Tests of the Random-Walk
           Hypothesis   340
7.4   The Interest Rate and Saving   344
7.5   Consumption and Risky Assets   349
7.6   Beyond the Permanent-Income Hypothesis   353
           Problems   362

Chapter 8   INVESTMENT   367

8.1   Investment and the Cost of Capital   367
8.2   A Model of Investment with Adjustment Costs   370
8.3   Tobin's q 375
8.4   Analyzing the Model   376
8.5   Implications   380
8.6   The Effects of Uncertainty: An Introduction   387
8.7   Financial-Market Imperfections   392
8.8   Empirical Applications   402
           Problems   406

Chapter 9   UNEMPLOYMENT   410

9.1   Introduction: Theories of Unemployment   410
9.2   A Generic Efficiency-Wage Model   412
9.3   A More General Version   417
9.4   The Shapiro-Stiglitz Model   421
9.5   Implicit Contracts   432
9.6   Insider-Outsider Models   436
9.7   Hysteresis   440
9.8   Search and Matching Models   444
9.9   Empirical Applications   453
           Problems   461

Chapter 10   INFLATION AND MONETARY
                    POLICY   468

10.1   Introduction   468
10.2   Inflation, Money Growth, and Interest Rates   469
10.3   Monetary Policy and the Term Structure of Interest
           Rates   474
10.4   The Dynamic Inconsistency of Low-Inflation Monetary
           Policy   478
10.5   Addressing the Dynamic-Inconsistency Problem   483
10.6   What Can Policy Accomplish?   492
10.7   The Conduct of Policy   497

10.8	Seignorage and Inflation	510
10.9	The Costs of Inflation	519
	Problems	524

Chapter 11 BUDGET DEFICITS AND FISCAL POLICY 530

11.1	The Government Budget Constraint	531
11.2	The Ricardian Equivalence Result	535
11.3	The Ricardian Equivalence Debate	537
11.4	Tax-Smoothing	541
11.5	Political-Economy Theories of Budget Deficits	547
11.6	Strategic Debt Accumulation	551
11.7	Delayed Stabilization	561
11.8	Empirical Application: Politics and Deficits in Industrialized Countries	567
11.9	The Costs of Deficits	572
11.10	A Model of Debt Crises	576
	Problems	582

References 588

Name Index 626

Subject Index 634

EMPIRICAL APPLICATIONS

Section 1.7	Growth Accounting	28
	Convergence	30
	Saving and Investment	34
Section 2.7	Wars and Real Interest Rates	72
Section 2.11	Are Modern Economies Dynamically Efficient?	88
Section 3.7	Population Growth and Technological Change since	
	1 Million B.C.	126
Section 3.9	Accounting for Cross-Country Income Differences	138
Section 4.8	The Persistence of Output Fluctuations	196
Section 4.9	Calibrating a Real-Business-Cycle Model	201
	Productivity Movements in the Great Depression	203
Section 5.5	Money and Output	252
Section 5.6	The Cyclical Behavior of the Real Wage	258
Section 6.3	International Evidence on Output-Inflation Tradeoffs	276
Section 6.10	The Average Inflation Rate and the Output-Inflation	
	Tradeoff	313
	Microeconomic Evidence on Price Adjustment	315
Section 6.11	Experimental Evidence on Coordination-Failure	
	Games	319
Section 7.1	Understanding Estimated Consumption Functions	333
Section 7.3	Campbell and Mankiw's Test of the Random-Walk	
	Hypothesis Using Aggregate Data	340
	Shea's Test of the Random-Walk Hypothesis Using	
	Household Data	343
Section 7.5	The Equity-Premium Puzzle	351
Section 7.6	Liquidity Constraints and Aggregate Saving	359
Section 8.8	The Investment Tax Credit and the Price of Capital	
	Goods	402
	Cash Flow and Investment	403
Section 9.9	Contracting Effects on Employment	453
	Interindustry Wage Differences	456
	Survey Evidence on the Sources of Wage Rigidity	458
Section 10.3	The Response of the Term Structure to Changes in the	
	Federal Reserve's Federal-Funds-Rate Target	476
Section 10.5	Central-Bank Independence and Inflation	489
Section 11.8	Politics and Deficits in Industrialized Countries	567

PREFACE TO THE SECOND EDITION

Macroeconomics is an exciting field. New theories are constantly being proposed, new tests devised and implemented, and existing theories and evidence reconsidered. For the author of a book like this one, which tries to provide an introduction to the current state of the field, this is both a blessing and a curse. It is a blessing because there has been a great deal of work since I wrote the first edition that provides important new insights into many of the central questions of macroeconomics. It is a curse because a substantial amount of what was in the first edition needed to be changed.

Readers who are familiar with the first edition of this book will see many changes. There is a completely new chapter on fiscal policy. In addition to discussing the main issues in this area, this chapter provides an introduction to the burgeoning research on political economy. The second half of Chapter 3, which examines cross-country income differences, bears no resemblance to the corresponding material in the first edition: the evidence and ideas developed in the five years since I wrote the first edition have caused me to completely rethink my views on that subject. In other chapters, there are new sections on the environment and economic growth, the cyclical behavior of the real wage, and the conduct of monetary policy. I have also rewritten a great deal of material to reflect recent developments and changing views, or simply to make the presentation clearer.

At the same time, I have tried hard to maintain what readers perceived to be the main virtues of the first edition. I have tried to keep the focus on substantive questions rather than models, to concentrate on the essentials, to have a good balance between theoretical and empirical work, and to be concise.

This book owes a great deal to many people. The book is an outgrowth of courses I have taught at Princeton University, the Massachusetts Institute of Technology, Stanford University, and especially the University of California, Berkeley. I want to thank the many students in these courses for their feedback, their patience, and their encouragement.

Four people provided detailed, thoughtful, and constructive comments on almost every aspect of the first and second editions: Laurence Ball, A. Andrew John, N. Gregory Mankiw, and Christina Romer. Each significantly improved the book, and I am deeply grateful to them for their efforts.

In addition, Susanto Basu, Robert Chirinko, Matthew Cushing, Charles Engel, Mark Gertler, Robert Gordon, Mary Gregory, A. Stephen Holland, Hiroo Iwanari, Frederick Joutz, Gregory Linden, Maurice Obtsfeld, Stephen Perez, Robert Rasche, Peter Skott, and Peter Temin made valuable comments and suggestions concerning some or all of the book. Jeffrey Rohaly prepared the superb *Solutions Manual.* Teresa Cyrus and Ryan Edwards helped with the preparation of some of the tables and figures, and both Jeffrey Rohaly and Ryan Edwards provided invaluable help with proofreading and checking the manuscript. Finally, the editorial and production staff at McGraw-Hill did an excellent job of turning the manuscript into a finished product. I thank all these people for their help.

INTRODUCTION

Macroeconomics is the study of the economy as a whole. It is therefore concerned with some of the most important questions in economics. Why are some countries rich and others poor? Why do countries grow? What are the sources of recessions and booms? Why is there unemployment, and what determines its extent? What are the sources of inflation? How do government policies affect output, unemployment, inflation, and growth? These and related questions are the subject of macroeconomics.

This book is an introduction to the study of macroeconomics at an advanced level. It presents the major theories concerning the central questions of macroeconomics. Its goal is to provide both an overview of the field for students who will not continue in macroeconomics and a starting point for students who will go on to more advanced courses and research in macroeconomics and monetary economics.

The book takes a broad view of the subject matter of macroeconomics; it views it as the study not just of aggregate fluctuations but of other features of the economy as a whole. A substantial portion of the book is devoted to economic growth, and separate chapters are devoted to the natural rate of unemployment, inflation, and budget deficits. Within each part, the major issues and competing theories are presented and discussed. Throughout, the presentation is motivated by substantive questions about the world. Models and techniques are used extensively, but they are treated as tools for gaining insight into important issues, not as ends in themselves.

The first three chapters are concerned with growth. The analysis focuses on two fundamental questions: Why are some economies so much richer than others, and what accounts for the huge increases in real incomes over time? Chapter 1 is devoted to the Solow growth model, which is the basic reference point for almost all analyses of growth. The Solow model takes technological progress as given and investigates the effects of the division of output between consumption and investment on capital accumulation and growth. The chapter presents and analyzes the model and assesses its ability to answer the central questions concerning growth.

Chapter 2 relaxes the Solow model's assumption that the saving rate is exogenous and fixed. It covers both a model where the set of households in the economy is fixed (the Ramsey model) and one where there is turnover (the Diamond model).

Chapter 3 presents the new growth theory. The first part of the chapter explores the sources of the accumulation of knowledge, the allocation of resources to knowledge accumulation, and the effects of that accumulation on growth. The second part focuses specifically on the sources of the enormous differences in average incomes across countries.

Chapters 4 through 6 are devoted to short-run fluctuations—the year-to-year and quarter-to-quarter ups and downs of employment, unemployment, and output. Chapter 4 investigates models of fluctuations where there are no imperfections, externalities, or missing markets and where the economy is subject only to real disturbances. This presentation of real-business-cycle theory considers both a baseline model whose mechanics are fairly transparent and a more sophisticated model that incorporates additional important features of fluctuations.

Chapters 5 and 6 then turn to Keynesian models of fluctuations. These models are based on sluggish adjustment of nominal wages and prices, and emphasize monetary as well as real disturbances. Chapter 5 takes the existence of sluggish adjustment as given. It first reviews the closed-economy and open-economy versions of the traditional *IS-LM* model. It then investigates the implications of alternative assumptions about price and wage rigidity, market structure, and inflationary expectations for the cyclical behavior of real wages, productivity, and markups, and for the relationship between output and inflation.

Chapter 6 examines the fundamental assumption of Keynesian models that nominal wages and prices do not adjust immediately to disturbances. The chapter covers the Lucas imperfect-information model, models of staggered adjustment of prices or wages, and new Keynesian theories of small frictions in price-setting. The chapter concludes with a brief discussion of theories of fluctuations based on coordination failures and real non-Walrasian features of the economy.

The analysis in the first six chapters suggests that the behavior of consumption and investment is central to both growth and fluctuations. Chapters 7 and 8 therefore examine the determinants of consumption and investment in more detail. In each case, the analysis begins with a baseline model and then considers alternative views. For consumption, the baseline is the life-cycle/permanent-income hypothesis; for investment, it is q theory.

Chapter 9 turns to the labor market. It focuses on the determinants of an economy's natural rate of unemployment. The chapter also investigates the impact of fluctuations in labor demand on real wages and employment. The main theories considered are efficiency-wage theories, contracting and insider/outsider theories, and search and matching models.

The final two chapters are devoted to macroeconomic policy. Chapter 10 investigates monetary policy and inflation. It begins by explaining the central role of money growth in causing inflation and by investigating the effects of money growth on inflation, interest rates, and the real money stock. The remainder of the chapter considers two sets of theories of the sources of high money growth: theories emphasizing output-inflation tradeoffs (particularly theories based on the dynamic inconsistency of low-inflation monetary policy) and theories emphasizing governments' need for revenue from money creation.

Chapter 11 is concerned with fiscal policy and budget deficits. The first part of the chapter describes the government's budget constraint and investigates two baseline views of deficits: Ricardian equivalence and tax-smoothing. Most of the remainder of the chapter investigates theories of the sources of deficits. In doing so, it provides an introduction to the use of economic tools to study politics.[1]

Macroeconomics is both a theoretical and an empirical subject. Because of this, the presentation of the theories is supplemented with examples of relevant empirical work. Even more so than with the theoretical sections, the purpose of the empirical material is not to provide a survey of the literature; nor is it to teach econometric techniques. Instead, the goal is to illustrate some of the ways that macroeconomic theories can be applied and tested. The presentation of this material is for the most part fairly intuitive and presumes no more knowledge of econometrics than a general familiarity with regressions. In a few places where it can be done naturally, the empirical material includes discussions of the ideas underlying more advanced econometric techniques.

Each chapter concludes with a set of problems. The problems range from relatively straightforward variations on the ideas in the text to extensions that tackle important new issues. The problems thus serve both as a way for readers to strengthen their understanding of the material and as a compact way of presenting significant extensions of the ideas in the text.[2]

The fact that the book is an *advanced* introduction to macroeconomics has two main consequences. The first is that the book uses a series of formal models to present and analyze the theories. Models identify particular features of reality and study their consequences in isolation. They thereby allow us to see clearly how different elements of the economy interact and what their implications are. As a result, they provide a rigorous way of investigating whether a proposed theory can answer a particular question and whether it generates additional predictions.

The book contains literally dozens of models. The main reason for this multiplicity is that we are interested in many issues. Features of the

---

[1] The chapters are largely independent. The growth and fluctuations sections are almost entirely self-contained (although Chapter 4 builds moderately on Part A of Chapter 2). There is also considerable independence among the chapters in each section. New growth theory (Chapter 3) can be covered either before or after the Ramsey and Diamond models (Chapter 2), and Keynesian models (Chapters 5 and 6) can be covered either before or after real-business-cycle theory (Chapter 4). Finally, the last five chapters are largely self-contained (although Chapter 7 relies moderately on Chapter 2, Chapter 9 relies moderately on Chapter 6, and Chapter 10 relies moderately on Chapter 5).

[2] A solutions manual prepared by Jeffrey Rohaly is available for use with the book.

economy that are crucial to one issue may be unimportant to others. Money, for example, is almost surely central to inflation and not to long-run growth. Incorporating money into models of growth would only obscure the analysis. Thus instead of trying to build a single model to analyze all the issues we are interested in, the book develops a series of models.

An additional reason for the multiplicity of models is that there is considerable disagreement about the answers to many of the questions we will be examining. When there is disagreement, the book presents the leading views and discusses their strengths and weaknesses. Because different theories emphasize different features of the economy, again it is more enlightening to investigate distinct models than to build one model incorporating all the features emphasized by the different views.

The second consequence of the book's advanced level is that it presumes some background in mathematics and economics. Mathematics provides compact ways of expressing ideas and powerful tools for analyzing them. The models are therefore mainly presented and analyzed mathematically. The key mathematical requirements are a thorough understanding of single-variable calculus and an introductory knowledge of multivariable calculus. Tools such as functions, logarithms, derivatives and partial derivatives, maximization subject to constraint, and Taylor-series approximations are used relatively freely. Knowledge of the basic ideas of probability—random variables, means, variances, covariances, and independence—is also assumed.

No mathematical background beyond this level is needed. More advanced tools (such as simple differential equations, the calculus of variations, and dynamic programming) are used sparingly, and they are explained as they are used. Indeed, since mathematical techniques are essential to further study and research in macroeconomics, models are sometimes analyzed in greater detail than is otherwise needed in order to illustrate the use of a particular method.

In terms of economics, the book assumes an understanding of microeconomics through the intermediate level. Familiarity with such ideas as profit maximization and utility maximization, supply and demand, equilibrium, efficiency, and the welfare properties of competitive equilibria is presumed. Little background in macroeconomics itself is absolutely necessary. Readers with no prior exposure to macroeconomics, however, are likely to find some of the concepts and terminology difficult, and to find that the pace is rapid (most notably in Chapter 5). These readers may wish to review an intermediate macroeconomics text before beginning the book, or to study such a book in conjunction with this one.

The book was designed for first-year graduate courses in macroeconomics. But it can be used in more advanced graduate courses and (either on its own or in conjunction with an intermediate text) for students with strong backgrounds in mathematics and economics in professional schools and advanced undergraduate programs. It can also provide a tour of the field for economists and others working in areas outside macroeconomics.

Chapter 1
THE SOLOW GROWTH MODEL

1.1 Some Basic Facts about Economic Growth

Over the past few centuries, standards of living in industrialized countries have reached levels almost unimaginable to our ancestors. Although comparisons are difficult, the best available evidence suggests that average real incomes today in the United States and Western Europe are between 10 and 30 times larger than a century ago, and between 50 and 300 times larger than two centuries ago.[1]

Moreover, worldwide growth is far from constant. Growth has been rising over most of modern history. Average growth rates in the industrialized countries were higher in the twentieth century than in the nineteenth, and higher in the nineteenth than in the eighteenth. Further, average incomes on the eve of the Industrial Revolution even in the wealthiest countries were not dramatically above subsistence levels; this tells us that average growth over the millennia before the Industrial Revolution must have been very, very low.

One important exception to this general pattern of increasing growth is the *productivity growth slowdown*. Average annual growth in output per person in the United States and other industrialized countries since the early 1970s has been about a percentage point below its earlier level. The data from the late 1990s suggest a rebound in productivity growth; whether this represents a temporary spurt or the end of the slowdown is not clear, however.

---

[1] Maddison (1995) reports and discusses basic data on average real incomes over modern history. Most of the uncertainty about the extent of long-term growth concerns the behavior not of nominal income, but of the price indexes needed to convert those figures into estimates of real income. Adjusting for quality changes and for the introduction of new goods is conceptually and practically difficult, and conventional price indexes do not make these adjustments well. See Nordhaus (1997) and Boskin, Dulberger, Gordon, Griliches, and Jorgenson (1998) for discussions of the issues involved and analyses of the biases in conventional price indexes.

There are also enormous differences in standards of living across parts of the world. Average real incomes in such countries as the United States, Germany, and Japan appear to exceed those in such countries as Bangladesh and Kenya by a factor of between 10 and 20.[2] As with worldwide growth, cross-country income differences are not immutable. Growth in individual countries often differs considerably from average worldwide growth; that is, there are often large changes in countries' relative incomes.

The most striking examples of large changes in relative incomes are *growth miracles* and *growth disasters*. Growth miracles are episodes where growth in a country far exceeds the world average over an extended period, with the result that the country moves rapidly up the world income distribution. Some prominent growth miracles are Japan and the newly industrializing countries (NICs) of East Asia—South Korea, Taiwan, Singapore, and Hong Kong. Average incomes in the NICs, for example, grew at an average annual rate of over 5 percent from the 1960s to the 1990s. As a result, their average incomes relative to that of the United States roughly tripled.

Growth disasters are episodes where a country's growth falls far short of the world average. Two very different examples of growth disasters are Argentina and many of the countries of sub-Saharan Africa. In 1900, Argentina's average income was only slightly behind those of the world's leaders, and it appeared poised to become a major industrialized country. But its growth performance over most of the twentieth century was dismal, and it is now near the middle of the world income distribution. Sub-Saharan African countries such as Chad, Ghana, and Mozambique have been extremely poor throughout their histories and have been unable to obtain any sustained growth in average incomes. As a result, their average incomes have remained close to subsistence levels while average world income has been rising steadily.

Other countries exhibit more complicated growth patterns. The Ivory Coast was held up as the growth model for Africa through the 1970s. From 1960 to 1978, real income per person grew at an average annual rate of almost 4 percent. But in the next decade, average income fell in half. To take another example, average growth in Mexico was extremely high in the 1960s and 1970s, negative in most of the 1980s, and again very high—with a brief but severe interruption in the mid-1990s—since then.

Over the whole of the modern era, cross-country income differences have widened on average. The fact that average incomes in the richest countries at the beginning of the Industrial Revolution were not far above subsistence means that the overall dispersion of average incomes across parts of the

---

[2] Comparisons of real incomes across countries are far from straightforward, but are much easier than comparisons over extended periods of time. The basic source for cross-country data on real income is the Penn World Tables. Summers and Heston (1991) describe these data and some of the major issues in comparisons of income across countries. The most recent version of these data is available at the National Bureau of Economic Research's web site, http://www.nber.org.

world must have been much smaller than it is today (Pritchett, 1997). Over the past few decades, however, there has been no strong tendency either toward continued divergence or toward convergence.

The implications of the vast differences in standards of living over time and across countries for human welfare are enormous. The differences are associated with large differences in nutrition, literacy, infant mortality, life expectancy, and other direct measures of well-being. And the welfare consequences of long-run growth swamp any possible effects of the short-run fluctuations that macroeconomics traditionally focuses on. During an average recession in the United States, for example, real income per person falls by a few percent relative to its usual path. In contrast, the productivity growth slowdown has reduced real income per person in the United States by about 25 percent relative to what it otherwise would have been. Other examples are even more startling. If real income per person in Bangladesh continues to grow at its postwar average rate of 1.4 percent, it will take close to 200 years for it to reach the current U.S. level. If Bangladesh achieves 3 percent growth, the process will take less than 100 years. And if it achieves 5 percent growth, as some countries have done, the time will be reduced to only 50 years. To quote Robert Lucas (1988), "Once one starts to think about [economic growth], it is hard to think about anything else."

The first three chapters of this book are therefore devoted to economic growth. We will investigate several models of growth. Although we will examine the models' mechanics in considerable detail, our goal is to learn what insights they offer concerning worldwide growth and income differences across countries. Indeed, the ultimate objective of research on economic growth is to determine whether there are possibilities for raising overall growth or bringing standards of living in poor countries closer to those in the world leaders.[3]

This chapter focuses on the model that economists have traditionally used to study these issues, the Solow growth model.[4] The Solow model is the starting point for almost all analyses of growth. Even models that depart fundamentally from Solow's are often best understood through comparison with the Solow model. Thus understanding the model is essential to understanding theories of growth.

The principal conclusion of the Solow model is that the accumulation of physical capital cannot account for either the vast growth over time in output per person or the vast geographic differences in output per person. Specifically, suppose that capital accumulation affects output through the conventional channel that capital makes a direct contribution to production, for which it is paid its marginal product. Then the Solow model implies that

---

[3] Jones (1998) provides a treatment of economic growth at a level slightly less advanced than this book's. Barro and Sala-i-Martin (1998) and Aghion and Howitt (1998) provide treatments at a slightly more advanced level.

[4] The Solow model (which is sometimes known as the Solow–Swan model) was developed by Robert Solow (Solow, 1956) and T. W. Swan (Swan, 1956).

the differences in real incomes that we are trying to understand are far too large to be accounted for by differences in capital inputs. The model treats other potential sources of differences in real incomes as either exogenous and thus not explained by the model (in the case of technological progress, for example) or absent altogether (in the case of positive externalities from capital, for example). Thus to address the central questions of growth theory, we must move beyond the Solow model.

Chapters 2 and 3 therefore extend and modify the Solow model. Chapter 2 investigates the determinants of saving and investment. The Solow model has no optimization in it; it simply takes the saving rate as exogenous and constant. Chapter 2 presents two models that make saving endogenous and potentially time-varying. In the first, saving and consumption decisions are made by a fixed set of infinitely lived households; in the second, the decisions are made by overlapping generations of households with finite horizons.

Relaxing the Solow model's assumption of a constant saving rate has three advantages. First, and most important for studying growth, it demonstrates that the Solow model's conclusions about the central questions of growth theory do not hinge on its assumption of a fixed saving rate. Second, it allows us to consider welfare issues. A model that directly specifies relations among aggregate variables does not provide a way to judge whether some outcomes are better or worse than others: without individuals in the model, we cannot say whether different outcomes make individuals better or worse off. The infinite-horizon and overlapping-generations models are built up from the behavior of individuals, and therefore can be used to discuss welfare issues. Third, infinite-horizon and overlapping-generations models are used to study many issues in economics other than economic growth; thus they are valuable tools.

Chapter 3 investigates more fundamental departures from the Solow model. Its models, in contrast to Chapter 2's, provide different answers than the Solow model to the central questions of growth theory. The first part of the chapter departs from the Solow model's treatment of technological progress as exogenous; it assumes instead that it is the result of the allocation of resources to the creation of new technologies. We will investigate the implications of such *endogenous technological progress* for economic growth and the determinants of the allocation of resources to innovative activities.

The main conclusion of this analysis is that endogenous technological progress is almost surely central to worldwide growth but probably has little to do with cross-country income differences. The second part of Chapter 3 therefore focuses specifically on those differences. We will find that understanding those differences requires considering two factors that are left out of the preceding analysis: differences in human as well as physical capital, and differences in productivity not stemming from differences in technology. This material explores both how those factors can help us understand the enormous differences in average incomes across countries and potential sources of differences in those factors.

We now turn to the Solow model.

1.2 Assumptions

Inputs and Output

The Solow model focuses on four variables: output (Y), capital (K), labor (L), and "knowledge" or the "effectiveness of labor" (A). At any time, the economy has some amounts of capital, labor, and knowledge, and these are combined to produce output. The production function takes the form

$$Y(t) = F(K(t), A(t)L(t)), \tag{1.1}$$

where t denotes time.

Two features of the production function should be noted. First, time does not enter the production function directly, but only through K, L, and A. That is, output changes over time only if the inputs to production change. In particular, the amount of output obtained from given quantities of capital and labor rises over time—there is technological progress—only if the amount of knowledge increases.

Second, A and L enter multiplicatively. AL is referred to as *effective labor*, and technological progress that enters in this fashion is known as *labor-augmenting* or *Harrod-neutral*.[5] This way of specifying how A enters, together with the other assumptions of the model, will imply that the ratio of capital to output, K/Y, eventually settles down. In practice, capital-output ratios do not show any clear upward or downward trend over extended periods. In addition, building the model so that the ratio is eventually constant makes the analysis much simpler. Assuming that A multiplies L is therefore very convenient.

The central assumptions of the Solow model concern the properties of the production function and the evolution of the three inputs into production (capital, labor, and knowledge) over time. We discuss each in turn.

Assumptions Concerning the Production Function

The model's critical assumption concerning the production function is that it has constant returns to scale in its two arguments, capital and effective labor. That is, doubling the quantities of capital and effective labor (for example, by doubling K and L with A held fixed) doubles the amount produced.

---

[5] If knowledge enters in the form $Y = F(AK, L)$, technological progress is *capital-augmenting*. If it enters in the form $Y = AF(K, L)$, technological progress is *Hicks-neutral*.

More generally, multiplying both arguments by any nonnegative constant c causes output to change by the same factor:

$$F(cK, cAL) = cF(K, AL) \qquad \text{for all } c \geq 0. \tag{1.2}$$

The assumption of constant returns can be thought of as combining two assumptions. The first is that the economy is big enough that the gains from specialization have been exhausted. In a very small economy, there are probably enough possibilities for further specialization that doubling the amounts of capital and labor more than doubles output. The Solow model assumes, however, that the economy is sufficiently large that, if capital and labor double, the new inputs are used in essentially the same way as the existing inputs, and thus that output doubles.

The second assumption is that inputs other than capital, labor, and knowledge are relatively unimportant. In particular, the model neglects land and other natural resources. If natural resources are important, doubling capital and labor could less than double output. In practice, however, as Section 1.8 describes, the availability of natural resources does not appear to be a major constraint on growth. Assuming constant returns to capital and labor alone therefore appears to be a reasonable approximation.

The assumption of constant returns allows us to work with the production function in *intensive form*. Setting $c = 1/AL$ in equation (1.2) yields

$$F\left(\frac{K}{AL}, 1\right) = \frac{1}{AL}F(K, AL). \tag{1.3}$$

Here K/AL is the amount of capital per unit of effective labor, and $F(K, AL)/AL$ is Y/AL, output per unit of effective labor. Define $k = K/AL$, $y = Y/AL$, and $f(k) = F(k, 1)$. Then we can rewrite (1.3) as

$$y = f(k). \tag{1.4}$$

That is, we can write output per unit of effective labor as a function of capital per unit of effective labor.

These new variables, k and y, are not of interest in their own right. Rather, they are tools for learning about the variables we are interested in. As we will see, the easiest way to analyze the model is to focus on the behavior of k, rather than to consider directly the behavior of the two arguments of the production function, K and AL. For example, we will determine the behavior of output per worker, Y/L, by writing it as $A(Y/AL)$, or $Af(k)$, and determining the behavior of A and k.

To see the intuition behind (1.4), think of dividing the economy into AL small economies, each with 1 unit of effective labor and K/AL units of capital. Since the production function has constant returns, each of these small economies produces $1/AL$ as much as is produced in the large, undivided economy. Thus the amount of output per unit of effective labor depends only on the quantity of capital per unit of effective labor, and not on the

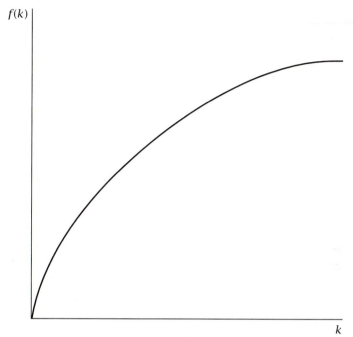

$f(k)$

k

FIGURE 1.1   An example of a production function

overall size of the economy. This is expressed mathematically in equation (1.4).

The intensive-form production function, $f(k)$, is assumed to satisfy $f(0) = 0, f'(k) > 0, f''(k) < 0.$[6] Since $F(K, AL)$ equals $ALf(K/AL)$, it follows that the marginal product of capital, $\partial F(K, AL)/\partial K$, equals $ALf'(K/AL)(1/AL)$, which is just $f'(k)$. Thus the assumptions that $f'(k)$ is positive and $f''(k)$ is negative imply that the marginal product of capital is positive, but that it declines as capital (per unit of effective labor) rises. In addition, $f(\bullet)$ is assumed to satisfy the *Inada conditions* (Inada, 1964): $\lim_{k \to 0} f'(k) = \infty, \lim_{k \to \infty} f'(k) = 0$. These conditions (which are stronger than needed for the model's central results) state that the marginal product of capital is very large when the capital stock is sufficiently small and that it becomes very small as the capital stock becomes large; their role is to ensure that the path of the economy does not diverge. A production function satisfying $f'(\bullet) > 0, f''(\bullet) < 0$, and the Inada conditions is shown in Figure 1.1.

Inada conditions

A specific example of a production function is the Cobb–Douglas function,

$$F(K, AL) = K^{\alpha}(AL)^{1-\alpha}, \qquad 0 < \alpha < 1. \tag{1.5}$$

---

[6] The notation $f'(\bullet)$ denotes the first derivative of $f(\bullet)$, and $f''(\bullet)$ the second derivative.

This production function is easy to analyze, and it appears to be a good first approximation to actual production functions. As a result, it is very useful.

It is easy to check that the Cobb–Douglas function has constant returns. Multiplying both inputs by c gives us

$$F(cK, cAL) = (cK)^\alpha (cAL)^{1-\alpha}$$
$$= c^\alpha c^{1-\alpha} K^\alpha (AL)^{1-\alpha} \tag{1.6}$$
$$= cF(K, AL).$$

To find the intensive form of the production function, divide both inputs by AL; this yields

$$f(k) \equiv F\left(\frac{K}{AL}, 1\right)$$
$$= \left(\frac{K}{AL}\right)^\alpha \tag{1.7}$$
$$= k^\alpha.$$

Equation (1.7) implies that $f'(k) = \alpha k^{\alpha-1}$. It is straightforward to check that this expression is positive, that it approaches infinity as k approaches zero, and that it approaches zero as k approaches infinity. Finally, $f''(k) = -(1 - \alpha)\alpha k^{\alpha-2}$, which is negative.[7]

The Evolution of the Inputs into Production

The remaining assumptions of the model concern how the stocks of labor, knowledge, and capital change over time. The model is set in continuous time; that is, the variables of the model are defined at every point in time.[8]

The initial levels of capital, labor, and knowledge are taken as given. Labor and knowledge grow at constant rates:

$$\dot{L}(t) = nL(t), \tag{1.8}$$
$$\dot{A}(t) = gA(t), \tag{1.9}$$

where n and g are exogenous parameters and where a dot over a variable denotes a derivative with respect to time (that is, $\dot{X}(t)$ is shorthand for $dX(t)/dt$).

---

[7] Note that with Cobb–Douglas production, labor-augmenting, capital-augmenting, and Hicks-neutral technological progress (see n. 5) are all essentially the same. For example, to rewrite (1.5) so that technological progress is Hicks-neutral, simply define $\tilde{A} = A^{1-\alpha}$; then $Y = \tilde{A}(K^\alpha L^{1-\alpha})$.

[8] The alternative is discrete time, where the variables are defined only at specific dates (usually $t = 0, 1, 2, \ldots$). The choice between continuous and discrete time is usually based on convenience. For example, the Solow model has essentially the same implications in discrete as in continuous time, but is easier to analyze in continuous time.

The *growth rate* of a variable refers to its proportional rate of change. That is, the phrase *the growth rate of X* refers to the quantity $\dot{X}(t)/X(t)$. Thus equation (1.8) implies that the growth rate of L is constant and equal to n, and (1.9) implies that A's growth rate is constant and equal to g.

A key fact about growth rates is that the growth rate of a variable equals the rate of change of its natural log. That is, $\dot{X}(t)/X(t)$ equals $d \ln X(t)/dt$. To see this, note that since $\ln X$ is a function of X and X is a function of t, we can use the chain rule to write

$$\frac{d \ln X(t)}{dt} = \frac{d \ln X(t)}{dX(t)} \frac{dX(t)}{dt}$$

$$= \frac{1}{X(t)} \dot{X}(t). \tag{1.10}$$

Applying the result that a variable's growth rate equals the rate of change of its log to (1.8) and (1.9) tells us that the rates of change of the logs of L and A are constant and that they equal n and g, respectively. Thus,

$$\ln L(t) = [\ln L(0)] + nt, \tag{1.11}$$

$$\ln A(t) = [\ln A(0)] + gt, \tag{1.12}$$

where $L(0)$ and $A(0)$ are the values of L and A at time 0. Exponentiating both sides of these equations gives us

$$L(t) = L(0)e^{nt}, \tag{1.13}$$

$$A(t) = A(0)e^{gt}. \tag{1.14}$$

Thus, our assumption is that L and A each grow exponentially.[9]

Output is divided between consumption and investment. The fraction of output devoted to investment, s, is exogenous and constant. One unit of output devoted to investment yields one unit of new capital. In addition, existing capital depreciates at rate δ. Thus

$$\dot{K}(t) = sY(t) - \delta K(t). \tag{1.15}$$

Although no restrictions are placed on n, g, and δ individually, their sum is assumed to be positive. This completes the description of the model.

Since this is the first model (of many!) we will encounter, a general comment about modeling is called for. The Solow model is grossly simplified in a host of ways. To give just a few examples, there is only a single good; government is absent; fluctuations in employment are ignored; production is described by an aggregate production function with just three inputs; and the rates of saving, depreciation, population growth, and technological progress are constant. It is natural to think of these features of the model as defects: the model omits many obvious features of the world, and surely some of those features are important to growth. But the purpose of

---

[9] See Problems 1.1 and 1.2 for more on basic properties of growth rates.

a model is not to be realistic. After all, we already possess a model that is completely realistic—the world itself. The problem with that "model" is that it is too complicated to understand. A model's purpose is to provide insights about particular features of the world. If a simplifying assumption causes a model to give incorrect answers *to the questions it is being used to address,* then that lack of realism may be a defect. (Even then, the simplification—by showing clearly the consequences of those features of the world in an idealized setting—may be a useful reference point.) If the simplification does not cause the model to provide incorrect answers to the questions it is being used to address, however, then the lack of realism is a virtue: by isolating the effect of interest more clearly, the simplification makes it easier to understand.

1.3   The Dynamics of the Model

We want to determine the behavior of the economy we have just described. The evolution of two of the three inputs into production, labor and knowledge, is exogenous. Thus to characterize the behavior of the economy, we must analyze the behavior of the third input, capital.

The Dynamics of k

Because the economy may be growing over time, it turns out to be much easier to focus on the capital stock per unit of effective labor, k, than on the unadjusted capital stock, K. Since $k = K/AL$, we can use the chain rule to find

$$\dot{k}(t) = \frac{\dot{K}(t)}{A(t)L(t)} - \frac{K(t)}{[A(t)L(t)]^2}[A(t)\dot{L}(t) + L(t)\dot{A}(t)]$$

$$= \frac{\dot{K}(t)}{A(t)L(t)} - \frac{K(t)}{A(t)L(t)}\frac{\dot{L}(t)}{L(t)} - \frac{K(t)}{A(t)L(t)}\frac{\dot{A}(t)}{A(t)}.$$

(1.16)

K/AL is simply k. From (1.8) and (1.9), $\dot{L}/L$ and $\dot{A}/A$ are n and g, respectively. $\dot{K}$ is given by (1.15). Substituting these facts into (1.16) yields

$$\dot{k}(t) = \frac{sY(t) - \delta K(t)}{A(t)L(t)} - k(t)n - k(t)g$$

$$= s\frac{Y(t)}{A(t)L(t)} - \delta k(t) - nk(t) - gk(t).$$

(1.17)

Finally, using the fact that Y/AL is given by $f(k)$, we have

$$\dot{k}(t) = sf(k(t)) - (n + g + \delta)k(t).$$

(1.18)

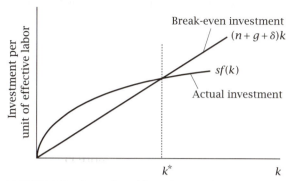

FIGURE 1.2   Actual and break-even investment

Equation (1.18) is the key equation of the Solow model. It states that the rate of change of the capital stock per unit of effective labor is the difference between two terms. The first, $sf(k)$, is actual investment per unit of effective labor: output per unit of effective labor is $f(k)$, and the fraction of that output that is invested is s. The second term, $(n + g + \delta)k$, is *break-even investment,* the amount of investment that must be done just to keep k at its existing level. There are two reasons that some investment is needed to prevent k from falling. First, existing capital is depreciating; this capital must be replaced to keep the capital stock from falling. This is the δk term in (1.18). Second, the quantity of effective labor is growing. Thus doing enough investment to keep the capital stock (K) constant is not enough to keep the capital stock per unit of effective labor (k) constant. Instead, since the quantity of effective labor is growing at rate $n + g$, the capital stock must grow at rate $n + g$ to hold k steady.[10] This is the $(n + g)k$ term in (1.18).

When actual investment per unit of effective labor exceeds the investment needed to break even, k is rising. When actual investment falls short of break-even investment, k is falling. And when the two are equal, k is constant.

Figure 1.2 plots the two terms of the expression for $\dot{k}$ as functions of k. Break-even investment, $(n + g + \delta)k$, is proportional to k. Actual investment, $sf(k)$, is a constant times output per unit of effective labor.

Since $f(0) = 0$, actual investment and break-even investment are equal at $k = 0$. The Inada conditions imply that at $k = 0$, $f'(k)$ is large, and thus that the $sf(k)$ line is steeper than the $(n + g + \delta)k$ line. Thus for small values of k, actual investment is larger than break-even investment. The Inada conditions also imply that $f'(k)$ falls toward zero as k becomes

---

[10] The fact that the growth rate of the quantity of effective labor, AL, equals $n + g$ is an instance of the fact that the growth rate of the product of two variables equals the sum of their growth rates. See Problem 1.1.

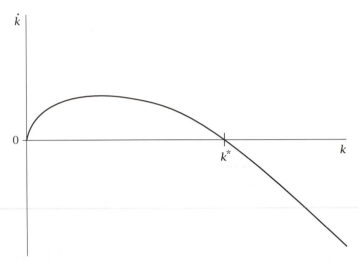

FIGURE 1.3   The phase diagram for k in the Solow model

large. At some point, the slope of the actual investment line falls below the slope of the break-even investment line. With the $sf(k)$ line flatter than the $(n + g + \delta)k$ line, the two must eventually cross. Finally, the fact that $f''(k) < 0$ implies that the two lines intersect only once for $k > 0$. We let k^* denote the value of k where actual investment and break-even investment are equal.

Figure 1.3 summarizes this information in the form of a *phase diagram,* which shows $\dot{k}$ as a function of k. If k is initially less than k^*, actual investment exceeds break-even investment, and so $\dot{k}$ is positive—that is, k is rising. If k exceeds k^*, $\dot{k}$ is negative. Finally, if k equals k^*, then $\dot{k}$ is zero. Thus, regardless of where k starts, it converges to k^*.[11]

The Balanced Growth Path

Since k converges to k^*, it is natural to ask how the variables of the model behave when k equals k^*. By assumption, labor and knowledge are growing at rates n and g, respectively. The capital stock, K, equals ALk; since k is constant at k^*, K is growing at rate $n + g$ (that is, $\dot{K}/K$ equals $n + g$). With both capital and effective labor growing at rate $n + g$, the assumption of constant returns implies that output, Y, is also growing at that rate. Finally, capital per worker, K/L, and output per worker, Y/L, are growing at rate g.

Thus the Solow model implies that, regardless of its starting point, the economy converges to a *balanced growth path*—a situation where each

convergence

---

[11] If k is initially zero, it remains there. We ignore this possibility in what follows.

variable of the model is growing at a constant rate. On the balanced growth path, the growth rate of output per worker is determined solely by the rate of technological progress.[12]

1.4   The Impact of a Change in the Saving Rate

The parameter of the Solow model that policy is most likely to affect is the saving rate. The division of the government's purchases between consumption and investment goods, the division of its revenues between taxes and borrowing, and its tax treatments of saving and investment are all likely to affect the fraction of output that is invested. Thus it is natural to investigate the effects of a change in the saving rate.

For concreteness, we will consider a Solow economy that is on a balanced growth path, and suppose that there is a permanent increase in s. In addition to demonstrating the model's implications concerning the role of saving, this experiment will illustrate the model's properties when the economy is not on a balanced growth path.

The Impact on Output

The increase in s shifts the actual investment line upward, and so k^* rises. This is shown in Figure 1.4. But k does not immediately jump to the new value of k^*. Initially, k is equal to the old value of k^*. At this level, actual investment now exceeds break-even investment—more resources are being devoted to investment than are needed to hold k constant—and so $\dot{k}$ is positive. Thus k begins to rise. It continues to rise until it reaches the new value of k^*, at which point it remains constant.

These results are summarized in the first three panels of Figure 1.5. t_0 denotes the time of the increase in the saving rate. By assumption, s jumps up at time t_0 and remains constant thereafter. Since the jump in s causes actual investment to exceed break-even investment by a strictly positive amount, $\dot{k}$ jumps from zero to a strictly positive amount. k rises gradually

---

[12] The broad behavior of the U.S. economy and many other major industrialized economies over the last century or more is described reasonably well by the balanced growth path of the Solow model. The growth rates of labor, capital, and output have each been roughly constant. The growth rates of output and capital have been about equal (so that the capital-output ratio has been approximately constant) and have been larger than the growth rate of labor (so that output per worker and capital per worker have been rising). This is often taken as evidence that it is reasonable to think of these economies as Solow-model economies on their balanced growth paths. Jones (1999a) argues, however, that the underlying determinants of the level of income on the balanced growth path have in fact been far from constant in these economies, and thus that the resemblance between these economies and the balanced growth path of the Solow model is misleading. We return to this issue in Section 3.3.

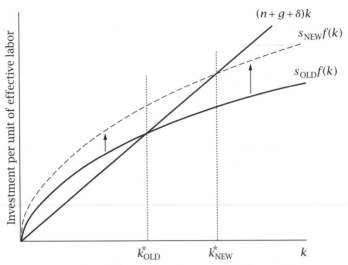

FIGURE 1.4   The effects of an increase in the saving rate on investment

from the old value of k^* to the new value, and $\dot{k}$ falls gradually back to zero.[13]

We are likely to be particularly interested in the behavior of output per worker, Y/L. Y/L equals $Af(k)$. When k is constant, Y/L grows at rate g, the growth rate of A. When k is increasing, Y/L grows both because A is increasing and because k is increasing. Thus its growth rate exceeds g. When k reaches the new value of k^*, however, again only the growth of A contributes to the growth of Y/L, and so the growth rate of Y/L returns to g. Thus a *permanent* increase in the saving rate produces a *temporary* increase in the growth rate of output per worker: k is rising for a time, but eventually it increases to the point where the additional saving is devoted entirely to maintaining the higher level of k.

The fourth and fifth panels of Figure 1.5 show how output per worker responds to the rise in the saving rate. The *growth rate* of output per worker, which is initially g, jumps upward at t_0 and then gradually returns to its initial level. Thus output per worker begins to rise above the path it was on and gradually settles into a higher path parallel to the first.[14]

In sum, a change in the saving rate has a *level effect* but not a *growth effect:* it changes the economy's balanced growth path, and thus the level

---

[13] For a sufficiently large rise in the saving rate, $\dot{k}$ rises for a while after t_0 before starting to fall back to zero.

[14] Because the growth rate of a variable equals the derivative with respect to time of its log, graphs in logs are often much easier to interpret than graphs in levels. For example, if a variable's growth rate is constant, the graph of its log as a function of time is a straight line. It is for this reason that Figure 1.5 shows the log of output per worker rather than its level.

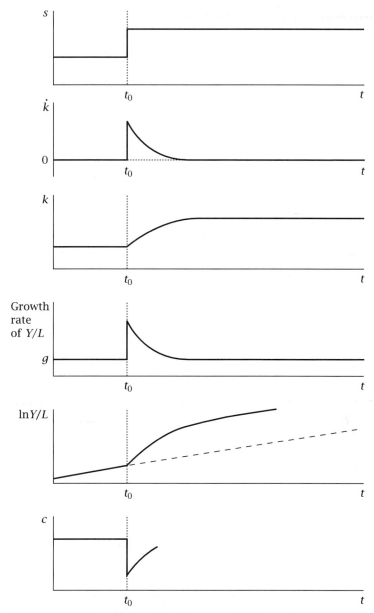

FIGURE 1.5   The effects of an increase in the saving rate

of output per worker at any point in time, but it does not affect the growth rate of output per worker on the balanced growth path. Indeed, in the Solow model only changes in the rate of technological progress have growth effects; all other changes have only level effects.

The Impact on Consumption

If we were to introduce households into the model, their welfare would depend not on output but on consumption: investment is simply an input into production in the future. Thus for many purposes we are likely to be more interested in the behavior of consumption than in the behavior of output.

Consumption per unit of effective labor equals output per unit of effective labor, $f(k)$, times the fraction of that output that is consumed, $1 - s$. Thus, since s changes discontinuously at t_0 and k does not, initially consumption per unit of effective labor jumps downward. Consumption then rises gradually as k rises and s remains at its higher level. This is shown in the last panel of Figure 1.5.

Whether consumption eventually exceeds its level before the rise in s is not immediately clear. Let c^* denote consumption per unit of effective labor on the balanced growth path. c^* equals output per unit of effective labor, $f(k^*)$, minus investment per unit of effective labor, $sf(k^*)$. On the balanced growth path, actual investment equals break-even investment, $(n + g + \delta)k^*$. Thus,

$$c^* = f(k^*) - (n + g + \delta)k^*. \tag{1.19}$$

k^* is determined by s and the other parameters of the model, n, g, and δ; we can therefore write $k^* = k^*(s, n, g, \delta)$. Thus (1.19) implies

$$\frac{\partial c^*}{\partial s} = [f'(k^*(s, n, g, \delta)) - (n + g + \delta)] \frac{\partial k^*(s, n, g, \delta)}{\partial s}. \tag{1.20}$$

We know that the increase in s raises k^*. Thus whether the increase raises or lowers consumption in the long run depends on whether $f'(k^*)$—the marginal product of capital—is more or less than $n + g + \delta$. Intuitively, when k rises, investment (per unit of effective labor) must rise by $n + g + \delta$ times the change in k for the increase to be sustained. If $f'(k^*)$ is less than $n+g+\delta$, then the additional output from the increased capital is not enough to maintain the capital stock at its higher level. In this case, consumption must fall to maintain the higher capital stock. If $f'(k^*)$ exceeds $n + g + \delta$, on the other hand, there is more than enough additional output to maintain k at its higher level, and so consumption rises.

$f'(k^*)$ can be either smaller or larger than $n + g + \delta$. This is shown in Figure 1.6. The figure shows not only $(n + g + \delta)k$ and $sf(k)$, but also $f(k)$. On the balanced growth path, consumption equals output less break-even investment; thus c is the distance between $f(k)$ and $(n+g+\delta)k$. In the top panel, $f'(k^*)$ is less than $n + g + \delta$, and so an increase in the saving rate lowers consumption even when the economy has reached the new balanced growth path. In the middle panel, the reverse holds, and so an increase in s raises consumption in the long run.

Finally, in the bottom panel, $f'(k^*)$ just equals $n + g + \delta$—that is, the $f(k)$ and $(n + g + \delta)k$ lines are parallel at $k = k^*$. In this case, a marginal change in s has no effect on consumption in the long run, and consumption

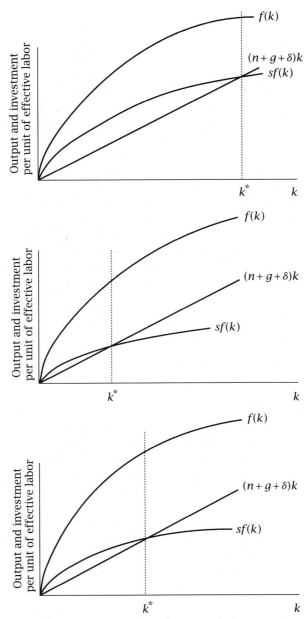

FIGURE 1.6   Output, investment, and consumption on the balanced growth path

is at its maximum possible level among balanced growth paths. This value of k^* is known as the *golden-rule* level of the capital stock. We will discuss the golden-rule capital stock further in Chapter 2. Among the questions we will address are whether the golden-rule capital stock is in fact desirable and whether there are situations in which a decentralized economy with endogenous saving converges to that capital stock. Of course, in the Solow model, where saving is exogenous, there is no more reason to expect the capital stock on the balanced growth path to equal the golden-rule level than there is to expect it to equal any other possible value.

1.5   Quantitative Implications

We are often interested not just in a model's qualitative implications, but in its quantitative predictions. If, for example, the impact of a moderate increase in saving on growth remains large after several centuries, the result that the impact is temporary is of limited interest.

For most models, including this one, obtaining exact quantitative results requires specifying functional forms and values of the parameters; it often also requires analyzing the model numerically. But in many cases, it is possible to learn a great deal by considering approximations around the long-run equilibrium. That is the approach we take here.

The Effect on Output in the Long Run

The long-run effect of a rise in saving on output is given by

$$\frac{\partial y^*}{\partial s} = f'(k^*) \, \frac{\partial k^*(s, n, g, \delta)}{\partial s}, \tag{1.21}$$

where $y^* = f(k^*)$ is the level of output per unit of effective labor on the balanced growth path. Thus to find $\partial y^*/\partial s$, we need to find $\partial k^*/\partial s$. To do this, note that k^* is defined by the condition that $\dot{k} = 0$; thus k^* satisfies

$$sf(k^*(s, n, g, \delta)) = (n + g + \delta)k^*(s, n, g, \delta). \tag{1.22}$$

Equation (1.22) holds for all values of s (and of n, g, and δ). Thus the derivatives of the two sides with respect to s are equal:[15]

$$sf'(k^*) \, \frac{\partial k^*}{\partial s} + f(k^*) = (n + g + \delta) \, \frac{\partial k^*}{\partial s}, \tag{1.23}$$

where the arguments of k^* are omitted for simplicity. This can be rear-

---

[15] This technique is known as *implicit differentiation*. Even though (1.22) does not explicitly give k^* as a function of s, n, g, and δ, it still determines how k^* depends on those variables. We can therefore differentiate the equation with respect to s and solve for $\partial k^*/\partial s$.

ranged to obtain[16]

$$\frac{\partial k^*}{\partial s} = \frac{f(k^*)}{(n + g + \delta) - sf'(k^*)}. \tag{1.24}$$

Substituting (1.24) into (1.21) yields

$$\frac{\partial y^*}{\partial s} = \frac{f'(k^*)f(k^*)}{(n + g + \delta) - sf'(k^*)}. \tag{1.25}$$

Two changes help in interpreting this expression. The first is to convert it to an elasticity by multiplying both sides by s/y^*. The second is to use the fact that $sf(k^*) = (n + g + \delta)k^*$ to substitute for s. Making these changes gives us

$$\frac{s}{y^*}\frac{\partial y^*}{\partial s} = \frac{s}{f(k^*)}\frac{f'(k^*)f(k^*)}{(n + g + \delta) - sf'(k^*)}$$

$$= \frac{(n + g + \delta)k^*f'(k^*)}{f(k^*)[(n + g + \delta) - (n + g + \delta)k^*f'(k^*)/f(k^*)]} \tag{1.26}$$

$$= \frac{k^*f'(k^*)/f(k^*)}{1 - [k^*f'(k^*)/f(k^*)]}.$$

$k^*f'(k^*)/f(k^*)$ is the elasticity of output with respect to capital at $k = k^*$. Denoting this by $\alpha_K(k^*)$, we have

$$\frac{s}{y^*}\frac{\partial y^*}{\partial s} = \frac{\alpha_K(k^*)}{1 - \alpha_K(k^*)}. \tag{1.27}$$

If markets are competitive and there are no externalities, capital earns its marginal product. In this case, the total amount received by capital (per unit of effective labor) on the balanced growth path is $k^*f'(k^*)$. Thus if capital earns its marginal product, the share of total income that goes to capital on the balanced growth path is $k^*f'(k^*)/f(k^*)$, or $\alpha_K(k^*)$.

In most countries, the share of income paid to capital is about one-third. If we use this as an estimate of $\alpha_K(k^*)$, it follows that the elasticity of output with respect to the saving rate in the long run is about one-half. Thus, for example, a 10 percent increase in the saving rate (from 20 percent of output to 22 percent, for instance) raises output per worker in the long run by about 5 percent relative to the path it would have followed. Even a 50 percent increase in s raises y^* only by about 22 percent. Thus significant changes in saving have only moderate effects on the level of output on the balanced growth path.

---

[16] We saw in the previous section that an increase in s raises k^*. To check that this is also implied by equation (1.24), note that $n + g + \delta$ is the slope of the break-even investment line and that $sf'(k^*)$ is the slope of the actual investment line at k^*. Since the break-even investment line is steeper than the actual investment line at k^* (see Figure 1.2), it follows that the denominator of (1.24) is positive and thus that $\partial k^*/\partial s > 0$.

Intuitively, a small value of $\alpha_K(k^*)$ makes the impact of saving on output low for two reasons. First, it implies that the actual investment curve, $sf(k)$, bends fairly sharply; as a result, an upward shift of the curve moves its intersection with the break-even investment line relatively little. Thus the impact of a change in s on k^* is small. Second, a low value of $\alpha_K(k^*)$ means that the impact of a change in k^* on y^* is small.

The Speed of Convergence

In practice, we are interested not only in the eventual effects of some change (such as a change in the saving rate), but also in how rapidly those effects occur. Again, we can use approximations around the long-run equilibrium to address this issue.

For simplicity, we focus on the behavior of k rather than y. Our goal is thus to determine how rapidly k approaches k^*. We know that $\dot{k}$ is determined by k: recall that the key equation of the model is $\dot{k} = sf(k) - (n + g + \delta)k$ (see [1.18]). Thus we can write $\dot{k} = \dot{k}(k)$. When k equals k^*, $\dot{k}$ is zero. A first-order Taylor-series approximation of $\dot{k}(k)$ around $k = k^*$ therefore yields

$$\dot{k} \simeq \left[\frac{\partial \dot{k}(k)}{\partial k} \bigg|_{k=k^*} \right] (k - k^*). \tag{1.28}$$

That is, $\dot{k}$ is approximately equal to the product of the difference between k and k^* and the derivative of $\dot{k}$ with respect to k at $k = k^*$.

Let λ denote $-\partial \dot{k}(k)/\partial k|_{k=k^*}$. With this definition, (1.28) becomes

$$\dot{k}(t) \simeq -\lambda[k(t) - k^*]. \tag{1.29}$$

Since $\dot{k}$ is positive when k is slightly below k^* and negative when it is slightly above, $\partial \dot{k}(k)/\partial k|_{k=k^*}$ is negative. Equivalently, λ is positive.

Equation (1.29) implies that in the vicinity of the balanced growth path, k moves toward k^* at a speed approximately proportional to its distance from k^*. That is, the growth rate of $k(t) - k^*$ is approximately constant and equal to $-\lambda$. This implies

$$k(t) \simeq k^* + e^{-\lambda t}[k(0) - k^*], \tag{1.30}$$

where $k(0)$ is the initial value of k. Note that (1.30) follows just from the facts that the system is stable (that is, that k converges to k^*) and that we are linearizing the equation for $\dot{k}$ around $k = k^*$.

It remains to find λ; this is where the specifics of the model enter the analysis. Differentiating expression (1.18) for $\dot{k}$ with respect to k and evaluating the resulting expression at $k = k^*$ yields

$$\lambda \equiv -\left.\frac{\partial \dot{k}(k)}{\partial k}\right|_{k=k^*} = -[sf'(k^*) - (n + g + \delta)]$$

$$= (n + g + \delta) - sf'(k^*)$$

$$= (n + g + \delta) - \frac{(n + g + \delta)k^*f'(k^*)}{f(k^*)} \qquad (1.31)$$

$$= [1 - \alpha_K(k^*)](n + g + \delta),$$

where the third line again uses the fact that $sf(k^*) = (n + g + \delta)k^*$ to substitute for s, and where the last line uses the definition of α_K. Thus, k converges to its balanced-growth-path value at rate $[1 - \alpha_K(k^*)](n+g+\delta)$. In addition, one can show that y approaches y^* at the same rate that k approaches k^*. That is, $y(t) - y^* \simeq e^{-\lambda t}[y(0) - y^*]$.

We can calibrate (1.31) to see how quickly actual economies are likely to approach their balanced growth paths. Typically, $n + g + \delta$ is about 6 percent per year (this would arise, for example, with 1 to 2 percent population growth, 1 to 2 percent growth in output per worker, and 3 to 4 percent depreciation). If capital's share is roughly one-third, $(1 - \alpha_K)(n + g + \delta)$ is thus roughly 4 percent. Therefore k and y move 4 percent of the remaining distance toward k^* and y^* each year, and take approximately 18 years to get halfway to their balanced-growth-path values.[17] Thus in our example of a 10 percent increase in the saving rate, output is $0.04(5\%) = 0.2\%$ above its previous path after 1 year; is $0.5(5\%) = 2.5\%$ above after 18 years; and asymptotically approaches 5 percent above the previous path. Thus not only is the overall impact of a substantial change in the saving rate modest, but it does not occur very quickly.[18]

---

[17] The time it takes for a variable (in this case, $y - y^*$) with a constant negative growth rate to fall in half is approximately equal to 70 divided by its growth rate in percent. (Similarly, the doubling time of a variable with positive growth is 70 divided by the growth rate.) Thus in this case the *half-life* is roughly $70/(4\%/\text{year})$, or about 18 years. More exactly, the half-life, t^*, is the solution to $e^{-\lambda t^*} = 0.5$, where λ is the rate of decrease. Taking logs of both sides, $t^* = -\ln(0.5)/\lambda \simeq 0.69/\lambda$.

[18] These results are derived from a Taylor-series approximation around the balanced growth path. Thus, formally, we can rely on them only in an arbitrarily small neighborhood around the balanced growth path. The question of whether Taylor-series approximations provide good guides for finite changes does not have a general answer. For the Solow model with conventional production functions, and for moderate changes in parameter values (such as those we have been considering), the Taylor-series approximations are generally quite reliable.

1.6   The Solow Model and the Central Questions of Growth Theory

The Solow model identifies two possible sources of variation—either over time or across parts of the world—in output per worker: differences in capital per worker (K/L) and differences in the effectiveness of labor (A). We have seen, however, that only growth in the effectiveness of labor can lead to permanent growth in output per worker, and that for reasonable cases the impact of changes in capital per worker on output per worker is modest. As a result, only differences in the effectiveness of labor have any reasonable hope of accounting for the vast differences in wealth across time and space. Specifically, the central conclusion of the Solow model is that if the returns that capital commands in the market are a rough guide to its contributions to output, then variations in the accumulation of physical capital do not account for a significant part of either worldwide economic growth or cross-country income differences.

There are two ways to see that the Solow model implies that differences in capital accumulation cannot account for large differences in incomes, one direct and the other indirect. The direct approach is to consider the required differences in capital per worker. Suppose we want to account for a difference of a factor of X in output per worker between two economies on the basis of differences in capital per worker. If output per worker differs by a factor of X, the difference in log output per worker between the two economies is $\ln X$. Since the elasticity of output per worker with respect to capital per worker is α_K, log capital per worker must differ by $(\ln X)/\alpha_K$. That is, capital per worker differs by a factor of $e^{(\ln X)/\alpha_K}$, or X^{1/α_K}.

Output per worker in the major industrialized countries today is on the order of 10 times larger than it was 100 years ago, and 10 times larger than it is in poor countries today. Thus we would like to account for values of X in the vicinity of 10. Our analysis implies that doing this on the basis of differences in capital requires a difference of a factor of $10^{1/\alpha_K}$ in capital per worker. For $\alpha_K = \frac{1}{3}$, this is a factor of 1000. Even if capital's share is one-half, which is well above what data on capital income suggest, one still needs a difference of a factor of 100.

There is no evidence of such differences in capital stocks. Capital-output ratios are roughly constant over time. Thus the capital stock per worker in industrialized countries is roughly 10 times larger than it was 100 years ago, not 100 or 1000 times larger. Similarly, although capital-output ratios vary somewhat across countries, the variation is not great. For example, the capital-output ratio appears to be 2 to 3 times larger in industrialized countries than in poor countries; thus capital per worker is "only" about 20 to 30 times larger. In sum, differences in capital per worker are far smaller than those needed to account for the differences in output per worker that we are trying to understand.[19]

---

[19] One can make the same point in terms of the rates of saving, population growth, and

The indirect way of seeing that the model cannot account for large variations in output per worker on the basis of differences in capital per worker is to notice that the required differences in capital imply enormous differences in the rate of return on capital (Lucas, 1990). If markets are competitive, the rate of return on capital equals its marginal product, $f'(k)$, minus depreciation, δ. Suppose that the production function is Cobb–Douglas (see equation [1.5]), which in intensive form is $f(k) = k^\alpha$. With this production function, the elasticity of output with respect to capital is simply α. The marginal product of capital is

$$f'(k) = \alpha k^{\alpha-1}$$
$$= \alpha y^{(\alpha-1)/\alpha}.$$

(1.32)

Equation (1.32) implies that the elasticity of the marginal product of capital with respect to output is $-(1-\alpha)/\alpha$. If $\alpha = \frac{1}{3}$, a tenfold difference in output per worker arising from differences in capital per worker thus implies a hundredfold difference in the marginal product of capital. And since the return to capital is $f'(k) - \delta$, the difference in rates of return is even larger.

Again, there is no evidence of such differences in rates of return. Direct measurement of returns on financial assets, for example, suggests only moderate variation over time and across countries. More tellingly, we can learn much about cross-country differences simply by examining where the holders of capital want to invest. If rates of return were larger by a factor of 10 or 100 in poor countries than in rich countries, there would be immense incentives to invest in poor countries. Such differences in rates of return would swamp such considerations as capital-market imperfections, government tax policies, fear of expropriation, and so on, and we would observe immense flows of capital from rich to poor countries. We do not see such flows.[20]

Thus differences in physical capital per worker cannot account for the differences in output per worker that we observe, at least if capital's contribution to output is roughly reflected by its private returns.

The other potential source of variation in output per worker in the Solow model is the effectiveness of labor. Attributing differences in standards of living to differences in the effectiveness of labor does not require huge differences in capital or in rates of return. Along a balanced growth path,

---

so on that determine capital per worker. For example, the elasticity of y^* with respect to s is $\alpha_K/(1 - \alpha_K)$ (see [1.27]). Thus accounting for a difference of a factor of 10 in output per worker on the basis of differences in s requires a difference of a factor of 100 in s if $\alpha_K = \frac{1}{3}$ and a difference of a factor of 10 if $\alpha_K = \frac{1}{2}$. Variations in actual saving rates are much smaller than this.

[20] One can try to avoid this conclusion by considering production functions where capital's marginal product falls less rapidly as k rises than it does in the Cobb–Douglas case. This approach encounters two major difficulties. First, since it implies that the marginal product of capital is similar in rich and poor countries, it implies that capital's share is much larger in rich countries. Second, and similarly, it implies that real wages are only slightly larger in rich than in poor countries. These implications appear grossly inconsistent with the facts.

for example, capital is growing at the same rate as output; and the marginal product of capital, $f'(k)$, is constant.

The Solow model's treatment of the effectiveness of labor is highly incomplete, however. Most obviously, the growth of the effectiveness of labor is exogenous: the model takes as given the behavior of the variable that it identifies as the driving force of growth. Thus it is only a small exaggeration to say that we have been modeling growth by assuming it.

More fundamentally, the model does not identify what the "effectiveness of labor" is; it is just a catchall for factors other than labor and capital that affect output. To proceed, we must take a stand concerning what we mean by the effectiveness of labor and what causes it to vary. One natural possibility is that the effectiveness of labor corresponds to abstract knowledge. To understand worldwide growth, it would then be necessary to analyze the determinants of the stock of knowledge over time. To understand cross-country differences in real incomes, one would have to explain why firms in some countries have access to more knowledge than firms in other countries, and why that greater knowledge is not rapidly transferred to poorer countries.

There are other possible interpretations of A; the education and skills of the labor force, the strength of property rights, the quality of infrastructure, cultural attitudes toward entrepreneurship and work, and so on. Or A may reflect a combination of forces. For any proposed view of what A represents, one would again have to address the questions of how it affects output, how it evolves over time, and why it differs across parts of the world.

The other possible way to proceed is to consider the possibility that capital is more important than the Solow model implies. If capital encompasses more than just physical capital, or if physical capital has positive externalities, then the private return on physical capital is not an accurate guide to capital's importance in production. In this case, the calculations we have done may be misleading, and it may be possible to resuscitate the view that differences in capital are central to differences in incomes.

These possibilities for addressing the fundamental questions of growth theory are the subject of Chapter 3.

1.7 Empirical Applications

Growth Accounting

In the Solow model, long-run growth of output per worker depends only on technological progress. But short-run growth can result from either technological progress or capital accumulation. Thus the model implies that determining the sources of short-run growth is an empirical issue. *Growth accounting,* which was pioneered by Abramovitz (1956) and Solow (1957), provides a way of tackling this subject.

To see how growth accounting works, consider again the production function $Y(t) = F(K(t), A(t)L(t))$. This implies

$$\dot{Y}(t) = \frac{\partial Y(t)}{\partial K(t)} \dot{K}(t) + \frac{\partial Y(t)}{\partial L(t)} \dot{L}(t) + \frac{\partial Y(t)}{\partial A(t)} \dot{A}(t). \qquad (1.33)$$

$\partial Y / \partial L$ and $\partial Y / \partial A$ denote $[\partial Y / \partial(AL)]A$ and $[\partial Y / \partial(AL)]L$, respectively. Dividing both sides by $Y(t)$ and rewriting the terms on the right-hand side yields

$$\frac{\dot{Y}(t)}{Y(t)} = \frac{K(t)}{Y(t)} \frac{\partial Y(t)}{\partial K(t)} \frac{\dot{K}(t)}{K(t)} + \frac{L(t)}{Y(t)} \frac{\partial Y(t)}{\partial L(t)} \frac{\dot{L}(t)}{L(t)} + \frac{A(t)}{Y(t)} \frac{\partial Y(t)}{\partial A(t)} \frac{\dot{A}(t)}{A(t)}$$

$$\equiv \alpha_K(t) \frac{\dot{K}(t)}{K(t)} + \alpha_L(t) \frac{\dot{L}(t)}{L(t)} + R(t). \qquad (1.34)$$

Here $\alpha_L(t)$ is the elasticity of output with respect to labor at time t, $\alpha_K(t)$ is again the elasticity of output with respect to capital, and $R(t) \equiv [A(t)/Y(t)][\partial Y(t)/\partial A(t)][\dot{A}(t)/A(t)]$. Subtracting $\dot{L}(t)/L(t)$ from both sides and using the fact that $\alpha_L(t) + \alpha_K(t) = 1$ (see Problem 1.9) gives an expression for the growth rate of output per worker:

$$\frac{\dot{Y}(t)}{Y(t)} - \frac{\dot{L}(t)}{L(t)} = \alpha_K(t) \left[\frac{\dot{K}(t)}{K(t)} - \frac{\dot{L}(t)}{L(t)} \right] + R(t). \qquad (1.35)$$

The growth rates of Y, K, and L are straightforward to measure. And we know that if capital earns its marginal product, α_K can be measured using data on the share of income that goes to capital. $R(t)$ can then be measured as the residual in (1.35). Thus (1.35) provides a way of decomposing the growth of output per worker into the contribution of growth of capital per worker and a remaining term, the *Solow residual.* The Solow residual is sometimes interpreted as a measure of the contribution of technological progress. As the derivation shows, however, it reflects all sources of growth other than the contribution of capital accumulation via its private return.

This basic framework can be extended in many ways (see, for example, Denison, 1967). The most common extensions are to consider different types of capital and labor and to adjust for changes in the quality of inputs. But more complicated adjustments are also possible. For example, if there is evidence of imperfect competition, one can try to adjust the data on income shares to obtain a better estimate of the elasticity of output with respect to the different inputs.

Growth accounting has been applied to many issues. For example, it has played a major role in a recent debate concerning the exceptionally rapid growth of the newly industrializing countries of East Asia. Young (1995) uses detailed growth accounting to argue that the higher growth in these countries than in the rest of the world is almost entirely due to rising investment, increasing labor force participation, and improving labor quality (in terms of education), and not to rapid technological progress and other forces affecting the Solow residual. Hsieh (1998a), however, observes that one can do growth accounting by examining the behavior of factor returns rather than quantities. If rapid growth comes solely from capital accumulation, for example, we will see either a large fall in the return to capital or a large rise in capital's share (or a combination). Doing the growth accounting this way, Hsieh finds a much larger role for the residual.

To give another example, growth accounting has been used extensively to study the productivity growth slowdown—the reduced growth rate of output per worker-hour in the United States and other industrialized countries that began in the early 1970s (see, for example, Denison, 1985; Baily and Gordon, 1988; Griliches, 1988; and Jorgenson, 1988). Some candidate explanations that have been proposed on the basis of this research include slower growth in workers' skills, the disruptions caused by the oil price increases of the 1970s, a slowdown in the rate of inventive activity, and the effects of government regulations.

In the mid-1990s, U.S. productivity growth returned to close to its level before the slowdown. Growth accounting has been used to study this rebound as well (Oliner and Sichel, 2000; Jorgenson and Stiroh, 2000; Whelan, 2000). This research suggests that computers and other types of information technology are the main source of the rebound. Until the mid-1990s, the rapid technological progress in computers and their broad adoption appear to have had little impact on aggregate productivity. Since then, however, their impact has been substantial.

Given that computer use is still spreading rapidly, this analysis suggests it is likely that the rapid productivity growth of the late 1990s will be sustained for at least a few more years. Even this is far from certain, however, and it is certainly far too soon to know whether the rebound will be long-lasting.

Convergence

An issue that has attracted considerable attention in empirical work on growth is whether poor countries tend to grow faster than rich countries. There are at least three reasons that one might expect such convergence. First, the Solow model predicts countries converge to their balanced growth paths. Thus to the extent that differences in output per worker arise from countries being at different points relative to their balanced growth paths, one would expect the poorer countries to catch up to the richer. Second, the Solow model implies that the rate of return on capital is lower in countries with more capital per worker. Thus there are incentives for capital to flow from rich to poor countries; this will also tend to cause convergence. And third, if there are lags in the diffusion of knowledge, income differences can arise because some countries are not yet employing the best available technologies. These differences might tend to shrink as poorer countries gain access to state-of-the-art methods.

Baumol

Baumol (1986) examines convergence from 1870 to 1979 among the 16 industrialized countries for which Maddison (1982) provides data. Baumol regresses output growth over this period on a constant and initial income; that is, he estimates

$$\ln\left[\left(\frac{Y}{N}\right)_{i,1979}\right] - \ln\left[\left(\frac{Y}{N}\right)_{i,1870}\right] = a + b\ln\left[\left(\frac{Y}{N}\right)_{i,1870}\right] + \varepsilon_i. \quad (1.36)$$

Here $\ln(Y/N)$ is log income per person, ε is an error term, and i indexes countries.[21] If there is convergence, b will be negative: countries with higher initial incomes have lower growth. A value for b of -1 corresponds to perfect convergence: higher initial income on average lowers subsequent growth one-for-one, and so output per person in 1979 is uncorrelated with its value in 1870. A value for b of 0, on the other hand, implies that growth is uncorrelated with initial income and thus that there is no convergence.

The results are

$$\ln\left[\left(\frac{Y}{N}\right)_{i,1979}\right] - \ln\left[\left(\frac{Y}{N}\right)_{i,1870}\right] = 8.457 - \underset{(0.094)}{0.995} \ln\left[\left(\frac{Y}{N}\right)_{i,1870}\right],$$

$$R^2 = 0.87, \qquad \text{s.e.e.} = 0.15, \quad (1.37)$$

where the number in parentheses, 0.094, is the standard error of the regression coefficient. Figure 1.7 shows the scatterplot corresponding to this regression.

The regression suggests almost perfect convergence. The estimate of b is almost exactly equal to -1, and it is estimated fairly precisely; the two-standard-error confidence interval is $(0.81, 1.18)$. In this sample, per capita income today is essentially unrelated to per capita income 100 years ago.

De Long (1988) demonstrates, however, that Baumol's finding is largely spurious. There are two problems. The first is *sample selection.* Since historical data are constructed retrospectively, the countries that have long data series are generally those that are the most industrialized today. Thus countries that were not rich 100 years ago are typically in the sample only if they grew rapidly over the next 100 years. Countries that were rich 100 years ago, in contrast, are generally included even if their subsequent growth was only moderate. Because of this, we are likely to see poorer countries growing faster than richer ones in the sample of countries we consider, even if there is no tendency for this to occur on average.

The natural way to eliminate this bias is to use a rule for choosing the sample that is not based on the variable we are trying to explain, which is growth over the period 1870–1979. Lack of data makes it impossible to include the entire world. De Long therefore considers the richest countries as of 1870; specifically, his sample consists of all countries at least

---

[21] Baumol considers output per worker rather than output per person. This choice has little effect on the results.

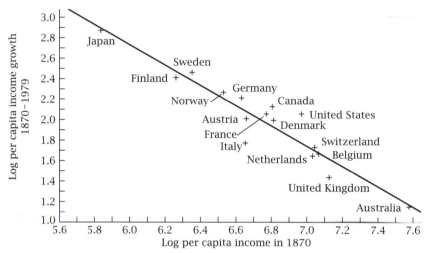

FIGURE 1.7   Initial income and subsequent growth in Baumol's sample (from De Long, 1988; used with permission)

as rich as the second poorest country in Baumol's sample in 1870, Finland. This causes him to add seven countries to Baumol's list (Argentina, Chile, East Germany, Ireland, New Zealand, Portugal, and Spain) and to drop one (Japan).[22]

Figure 1.8 shows the scatterplot for the unbiased sample. The inclusion of the new countries weakens the case for convergence considerably. The regression now produces an estimate of b of -0.566, with a standard error of 0.144. Thus accounting for the selection bias in Baumol's procedure eliminates about half of the convergence that he finds.

The second problem that De Long identifies is *measurement error*. Estimates of real income per capita in 1870 are imprecise. Measurement error again creates bias toward finding convergence. When 1870 income is overstated, growth over the period 1870–1979 is understated by an equal amount; when 1870 income is understated, the reverse occurs. Thus measured growth tends to be lower in countries with higher measured initial income even if there is no relation between actual growth and actual initial income.

---

[22] Since a large fraction of the world was richer than Japan in 1870, it is not possible to consider all countries at least as rich as Japan. In addition, one has to deal with the fact that countries' borders are not fixed. De Long chooses to use 1979 borders. Thus his 1870 income estimates are estimates of average incomes in 1870 in the geographic regions defined by 1979 borders.

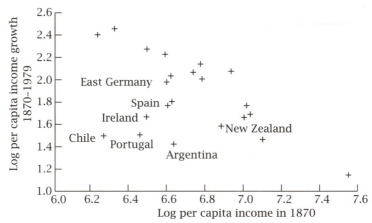

FIGURE 1.8 **Initial income and subsequent growth in the expanded sample (from De Long, 1988; used with permission)**

De Long therefore considers the following model:

$$\ln\left[\left(\frac{Y}{N}\right)_{i,1979}\right] - \ln\left[\left(\frac{Y}{N}\right)_{i,1870}\right]^* = a + b\ln\left[\left(\frac{Y}{N}\right)_{i,1870}\right]^* + \varepsilon_i, \quad (1.38)$$

$$\ln\left[\left(\frac{Y}{N}\right)_{i,1870}\right] = \ln\left[\left(\frac{Y}{N}\right)_{i,1870}\right]^* + u_i, \quad (1.39)$$

where $\ln[(Y/N)_{1870}]^*$ is the true value of log income per capita in 1870 and $\ln[(Y/N)_{1870}]$ is the measured value. ε and u are assumed to be uncorrelated with each other and with $\ln[(Y/N)_{1870}]^*$.

Unfortunately, it is not possible to estimate this model using only data on $\ln[(Y/N)_{1870}]$ and $\ln[(Y/N)_{1979}]$. The problem is that there are different hypotheses that make identical predictions about the data. For example, suppose we find that measured growth is negatively related to measured initial income. This is exactly what one would expect either if measurement error is unimportant and there is true convergence or if measurement error is important and there is no true convergence. Technically, the model is *not identified*.

De Long argues, however, that we have at least a rough idea of how good the 1870 data are, and thus have a sense of what is a reasonable value for the standard deviation of the measurement error. For example, $\sigma_u = 0.01$ implies that we have measured initial income to within an average of 1 percent; this is implausibly low. Similarly, $\sigma_u = 0.50$—an average error of 50 percent—seems implausibly high. De Long shows that if we fix a value of σ_u, we can estimate the remaining parameters.

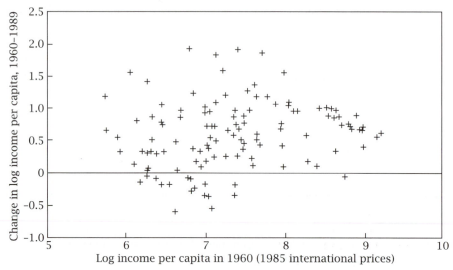

FIGURE 1.9   Initial income and subsequent growth in the postwar period

Even moderate measurement error has a substantial impact on the results. For the unbiased sample, the estimate of b reaches 0 (no tendency toward convergence) for $\sigma_u \simeq 0.15$, and is 1 (tremendous divergence) for $\sigma_u \simeq 0.20$. Thus plausible amounts of measurement error eliminate most or all of the remainder of Baumol's estimate of convergence.

It is also possible to investigate convergence for different samples of countries and different time periods. Figure 1.9 is a *convergence scatterplot* analogous to Figures 1.7 and 1.8 for virtually the entire non-Communist world for the period 1960–1989. As the figure shows, there is little evidence of convergence. We return to the issue of convergence in Section 3.12.

Saving and Investment

Consider a world where every country is described by the Solow model and where all countries have the same amount of capital per unit of effective labor. Now suppose that the saving rate in one country rises. If all the additional saving is invested domestically, the marginal product of capital in that country falls below that in other countries. The country's residents therefore have incentives to invest abroad. Thus if there are no impediments to capital flows, not all the additional saving is invested domestically. Instead, the investment resulting from the increased saving is spread uniformly over the whole world; the fact that the rise in saving occurred in one country has no special effect on investment there. Thus in the absence of barriers to capital movements, there is no reason to expect countries with high saving to also have high investment.

Feldstein and Horioka (1980) examine the association between saving and investment rates. They find that, contrary to this simple view, saving and investment rates are strongly correlated. Specifically, Feldstein and Horioka run a cross-country regression for 21 industrialized countries of the average share of investment in GDP during the period 1960–1974 on a constant and the average share of saving in GDP over the same period. The results are

$$\left(\frac{I}{Y}\right)_i = \underset{(0.018)}{0.035} + \underset{(0.074)}{0.887} \left(\frac{S}{Y}\right)_i, \qquad R^2 = 0.91, \qquad (1.40)$$

where again the numbers in parentheses are standard errors. Thus, rather than there being no relation between saving and investment, there is an almost one-to-one relation.

There are various possible explanations for Feldstein and Horioka's finding (see Obstfeld, 1986, for a discussion). One possibility, suggested by Feldstein and Horioka, is that significant barriers to capital mobility exist. In this case, differences in saving and investment across countries would be associated with rate-of-return differences.

Another possibility is that there are underlying variables that affect both saving and investment. For example, high tax rates can reduce both saving and investment (Barro, Mankiw, and Sala-i-Martin, 1995). Similarly, countries whose citizens have low discount rates, and thus high saving rates, may provide favorable investment climates in ways other than the high saving; for example, they may limit workers' ability to form strong unions.

Finally, the strong association between saving and investment can arise from government policies that offset forces that would otherwise make saving and investment differ. Governments may be averse to large gaps between saving and investment—after all, a large gap must be associated with a large trade deficit (if investment exceeds saving) or a large trade surplus (if saving exceeds investment). If economic forces would otherwise give rise to a large imbalance between saving and investment, the government may choose to adjust its own saving behavior or its tax treatment of saving or investment to bring them into rough balance.

In sum, the strong relationship between saving and investment differs dramatically from the predictions of a natural baseline model. Whether this difference reflects major departures from the baseline (such as large barriers to capital mobility) or something less fundamental (such as underlying forces affecting both saving and investment) is not known.

1.8   The Environment and Economic Growth

Natural resources, pollution, and other environmental considerations are absent from the Solow model. But at least since Malthus (1798) made his classic argument, many people have believed that these considerations are critical to the possibilities for long-run economic growth. For example, the amounts of oil and other natural resources on earth are fixed. This could mean that any attempt to embark on a path of perpetually rising output will eventually deplete those resources, and must therefore fail. Similarly, the fixed supply of land may become a binding constraint on our ability to produce. Or ever-increasing output may generate an ever-increasing stock of pollution that will bring growth to a halt.[23]

This section addresses the issue of how environmental limitations affect long-run growth. In thinking about this issue, it is important to distinguish between environmental factors for which there are well-defined property rights—notably natural resources and land—and those for which there are not—notably pollution-free air and water.

The existence of property rights for an environmental good has two important implications. The first is that markets provide valuable signals concerning how the good should be used. Suppose, for example, that the best available evidence indicates that the limited supply of oil will be an important limitation on our ability to produce at some point in the future. This means that oil will command a high price in the future. But this in turn implies that the owners of oil do not want to sell their oil cheaply today. Thus oil commands a high price today, and so current users have an incentive to conserve. In short, evidence that the fixed amount of oil is likely to limit our ability to produce in the future would not be grounds for government intervention. Such a situation, though unfortunate, would be addressed by the market.

The second implication of the existence of property rights for an environmental good is that we can use the good's price to obtain evidence about its importance in production. For example, since evidence that oil will be an important constraint on future production would lead to a high current price of oil, economists can use the current price to infer what the best available evidence suggests about oil's importance; they do not need to assess that evidence independently.

With environmental goods for which there are no property rights, the use of a good has externalities. For example, firms can pollute without compensating the people they harm. Thus the case for government intervention is much stronger. And there is no market price to provide a handy summary of the evidence concerning the good's importance. As a result, economists interested in environmental issues must attempt to assess that evidence themselves.

We will begin by considering environmental goods that are traded in markets. We will analyze both a simple baseline case and an important complication to the baseline. We will then turn to environmental goods for which there is no well-functioning market.

---

[23] An influential modern statement of these concerns is Meadows, Meadows, Randers, and Behrens (1972).

Natural Resources and Land: A Baseline Case

We want to extend our analysis to include natural resources and land. To keep the analysis manageable, we start with the case of Cobb–Douglas production. Thus the production function, (1.1), becomes

$$Y(t) = K(t)^{\alpha} R(t)^{\beta} T(t)^{\gamma} [A(t)L(t)]^{1-\alpha-\beta-\gamma},$$

$$\alpha > 0, \qquad \beta > 0, \qquad \gamma > 0, \qquad \alpha + \beta + \gamma < 1. \tag{1.41}$$

Here R denotes resources used in production, and T denotes the amount of land.

    The dynamics of capital, labor, and the effectiveness of labor are the same as before: $\dot{K}(t) = sY(t) - \delta K(t)$, $\dot{L}(t) = nL(t)$, and $\dot{A}(t) = gA(t)$. The new assumptions concern resources and land. Since the amount of land on earth is fixed, in the long run the quantity used in production cannot be growing. Thus we assume

$$\dot{T}(t) = 0. \tag{1.42}$$

Similarly, the facts that resource endowments are fixed and that resources are used in production imply that resource use must eventually decline. Thus, even though resource use has been rising historically, we assume

$$\dot{R}(t) = -bR(t), \qquad b > 0. \tag{1.43}$$

    The presence of resources and land in the production function means that K/AL no longer converges to some value. As a result, we cannot use our previous approach of focusing on K/AL to analyze the behavior of this economy. A useful strategy in such situations is to ask whether there can be a balanced growth path and, if so, what the growth rates of the economy's variables are on that path.

    By assumption, A, L, R, and T are each growing at a constant rate. Thus what is needed for a balanced growth path is that K and Y each grow at a constant rate. The equation of motion for capital, $\dot{K}(t) = sY(t) - \delta K(t)$, implies that the growth rate of K is

$$\frac{\dot{K}(t)}{K(t)} = s\frac{Y(t)}{K(t)} - \delta. \tag{1.44}$$

Thus for the growth rate of K to be constant, Y/K must be constant. That is, the growth rates of Y and K must be equal.

    We can use the production function, (1.41), to find when this can occur. Taking logs of both sides of (1.41) gives us

$$\ln Y(t) = \alpha \ln K(t) + \beta \ln R(t) + \gamma \ln T(t)$$

$$+ (1 - \alpha - \beta - \gamma)[\ln A(t) + \ln L(t)]. \tag{1.45}$$

We can now differentiate both sides of this expression with respect to time. Using the fact that the time derivative of the log of a variable equals the variable's growth rate, we obtain

$$g_Y(t) = \alpha g_K(t) + \beta g_R(t) + \gamma g_T(t) + (1 - \alpha - \beta - \gamma)[g_A(t) + g_L(t)], \quad (1.46)$$

where g_X denotes the growth rate of X. The growth rates of R, T, A, and L are $-b$, 0, g, and n, respectively. Thus (1.46) simplifies to

$$g_Y(t) = \alpha g_K(t) - \beta b + (1 - \alpha - \beta - \gamma)(n + g). \quad (1.47)$$

We can now use our finding above that g_Y and g_K must be equal if the economy is on a balanced growth path. Imposing $g_K = g_Y$ on (1.47) and solving for g_Y gives us

$$g_Y^{bgp} = \frac{(1 - \alpha - \beta - \gamma)(n + g) - \beta b}{1 - \alpha}, \quad (1.48)$$

where g_Y^{bgp} denotes the growth rate of Y on the balanced growth path.

This analysis leaves out a step: we have not determined whether the economy in fact converges to this balanced growth path. From (1.47), we know that if g_K exceeds its balanced-growth-path value, g_Y does as well, but by less than g_K does. Thus if g_K exceeds its balanced-growth-path value, Y/K is falling. Equation (1.44) tells us that g_K equals $s(Y/K) - \delta$. Thus if Y/K is falling, g_K is falling as well. That is, if g_K exceeds its balanced-growth-path value (which occurs when Y/K exceeds its balanced-growth-path value), it is falling. Similarly, if it is less than its balanced-growth-path value, it is rising. Thus g_K converges to its balanced-growth-path value, and so the economy converges to its balanced growth path.[24]

Equation (1.48) implies that the growth rate of output per worker on the balanced growth path is

$$g_{Y/L}^{bgp} = g_Y^{bgp} - g_L^{bgp}$$

$$= \frac{(1 - \alpha - \beta - \gamma)(n + g) - \beta b}{1 - \alpha} - n \quad (1.49)$$

$$= \frac{(1 - \alpha - \beta - \gamma)g - \beta b - (\beta + \gamma)n}{1 - \alpha}.$$

Equation (1.49) shows that growth in income per worker on the balanced growth path, $g_{Y/L}^{bgp}$, can be either positive or negative. That is, resource and land limitations can cause output per worker to eventually be falling, but they need not. The declining quantities of resources and land per worker

---

[24] This analysis overlooks one subtlety. If $(1 - \alpha - \beta - \gamma)(n + g) + (1 - \alpha)\delta - \beta b$ is negative, the condition $g_K = g_K^{bgp}$ holds only for a negative value of Y/K. And the statement that Y/K is falling when g_Y is less than g_K is not true if Y/K is zero or negative. As a result, if $(1 - \alpha - \beta - \gamma)(n + g) + (1 - \alpha)\delta - \beta b$ is negative, the economy does not converge to the balanced growth path described in the text, but to a situation where $Y/K = 0$ and $g_K = -\delta$. But for any reasonable parameter values, $(1 - \alpha - \beta - \gamma)(n + g) + (1 - \alpha)\delta - \beta b$ is positive. Thus this complication is not important.

are drags on growth. But technological progress is a spur to growth. If the spur created by technological progress is larger than the drags exerted by resources and land, then there is sustained growth in output per worker. This is precisely what has happened over the past few centuries.

An Illustrative Calculation

In recent history, the advantages of technological progress have outweighed the disadvantages of resource and land limitations. But this does not tell us how large those disadvantages are. For example, they might be large enough that only a moderate slowing of technological progress would make overall growth in income per worker negative.

Resource and land limitations reduce growth by causing resource use per worker and land per worker to be falling. Thus, as Nordhaus (1992) observes, to gauge how much these limitations are reducing growth, we need to ask how much greater growth would be if resources and land per worker were constant. Concretely, consider an economy identical to the one we have just considered except that the assumptions $\dot{T}(t) = 0$ and $\dot{R}(t) = -bR(t)$ are replaced with the assumptions $\dot{T}(t) = nT(t)$ and $\dot{R}(t) = nR(t)$. In this hypothetical economy, there are no resource and land limitations; both grow as population grows. Analysis parallel to that used to derive equation (1.49) shows that growth of output per worker on the balanced growth path of this economy is[25]

$$\tilde{g}_{Y/L}^{bgp} = \frac{1}{1 - \alpha}(1 - \alpha - \beta - \gamma)g. \tag{1.50}$$

The "growth drag" from resource and land limitations is the difference between growth in this hypothetical case and growth in the case of resource and land limitations:

$$\text{Drag} = \tilde{g}_{Y/L}^{bgp} - g_{Y/L}^{bgp}$$

$$= \frac{(1 - \alpha - \beta - \gamma)g - [(1 - \alpha - \beta - \gamma)g - \beta b - (\beta + \gamma)n]}{1 - \alpha} \tag{1.51}$$

$$= \frac{\beta b + (\beta + \gamma)n}{1 - \alpha}.$$

Thus, the growth drag is increasing in resources' share (β), land's share (γ), the rate that resource use is falling (b), the rate of population growth (n), and capital's share (α).

It is possible to quantify the size of this drag. Because resources and land are traded in markets, we can use income data to estimate their importance in production—that is, to estimate β and γ. As Nordhaus (1992)

---

[25] See Problem 1.14.

describes, these data suggest a combined value of $\beta + \gamma$ of about 0.2. Nordhaus goes on to use a somewhat more complicated version of the framework presented here to estimate the growth drag. His point estimate is a drag of 0.0024—that is, about a quarter of a percentage point per year. He finds that only about a quarter of the drag is due to the limited supply of land. Of the remainder, he estimates that the vast majority is due to limited energy resources.

Thus this evidence suggests that the reduction in growth caused by environmental limitations, while not trivial, is not large. In addition, since growth in income per worker has been far more than a quarter of a percentage point per year, the evidence suggests that there would have to be very large changes for resource and land limitations to cause income per worker to start falling.

A Complication

The stock of land is fixed, and resource use must eventually fall. Thus even though technology has been able to keep ahead of resource and land limitations over the past few centuries, it may still appear that those limitations must eventually become a binding constraint on our ability to produce.

The reason that this does not occur in our model is that production is Cobb-Douglas. With Cobb-Douglas production, a given percentage change in A always produces the same percentage change in output, regardless of how large A is relative to R and T. As a result, technological progress can always counterbalance declines in R/L and T/L.

This is not a general property of production functions, however. With Cobb-Douglas production, the elasticity of substitution between inputs is 1. If this elasticity is less than 1, the share of income going to the inputs that are becoming scarcer rises over time. Intuitively, as the production function becomes more like the Leontief case, the inputs that are becoming scarcer become increasingly important. Conversely, if the elasticity of substitution is greater than 1, the share of income going to the inputs that are becoming scarcer is falling. This, too, is intuitive: as the production function becomes closer to linear, the abundant factors benefit.

In terms of our earlier analysis, what this means is that if we do not restrict our attention to Cobb-Douglas production, the shares in expression (1.51) for the growth drag are no longer constant, but are functions of factor proportions. And if the elasticity of substitution is less than 1, the share of income going to resources and land is rising over time—and thus the growth drag is as well. Indeed, in this case the share of income going to the slowest-growing input—resources—approaches 1. Thus the growth drag approaches $b + n$. That is, asymptotically income per worker declines at rate $b + n$, the rate at which resource use per worker is falling. This case supports our apocalyptic intuition: in the long run, the fixed supply of resources leads to steadily declining incomes.

In fact, however, recognizing that production may not be Cobb–Douglas should not raise our estimate of the importance of resource and land limitations, but should reduce it. The reason is that the shares of income going to resources and land are falling rather than rising. We can write land's share as the real rental price of land multiplied by the ratio of land to output. The real rental price shows little trend, while the land-to-GDP ratio has been falling steadily. Thus land's share has been declining. Similarly, real resource prices have been falling moderately, and the ratio of resource use to GDP has also been falling. Thus resources' share has also been declining. And declining resource and land shares imply a falling growth drag.

The fact that land's and resources' shares have been declining despite the fact that these factors have been becoming relatively scarcer means that the elasticity of substitution between these inputs and the others must be greater than 1. At first glance, this may seem surprising. If we think in terms of narrowly defined goods—books, for example—possibilities for substitution among inputs may not seem particularly large. But if we recognize that what people value is not particular goods but the ultimate services they provide—information storage, for example—the idea that there are often large possibilities for substitution becomes more plausible. Information can be stored not only through books, but through oral tradition, stone tablets, microfilm, videotape, and disks. These different means of storage use capital, resources, land, and labor in very different proportions. As a result, the economy can respond to the increasing scarcity of resources and land by moving to means of information storage that use resources and land less intensively.

Pollution

Declining quantities of resources and land per worker are not the only ways that environmental problems can limit growth. Production creates pollution. This pollution reduces properly measured output. That is, if our data on real output accounted for all the outputs of production at prices that reflect their impacts on utility, pollution would enter with a negative price. In addition, pollution could rise to the point where it reduces conventionally measured output. For example, global warming could reduce output through its impact on sea levels and weather patterns.

Economic theory does not give us reason to be sanguine about pollution. Because those who pollute do not bear the costs of their pollution, an unregulated market leads to excessive pollution. Similarly, there is nothing to prevent an environmental catastrophe in an unregulated market. For example, suppose there is some critical level of pollution that would result in a sudden and drastic change in climate. Because pollution's effects are external, there is no market mechanism to prevent pollution from rising to such a level, or even a market price of a pollution-free environment to warn us that well-informed individuals believe a catastrophe is imminent.

Conceptually, the correct policy to deal with pollution is straightforward. We should estimate the dollar value of the negative externality and tax pollution by this amount. This would bring private and social costs in line, and thus would result in the socially optimal level of pollution.[26]

Although describing the optimal policy is easy, it is still useful to know how severe the problems posed by pollution are. In terms of understanding economic growth, we would like to know by how much pollution is likely to retard growth if no corrective measures are taken. In terms of policy, we would like to know how large a pollution tax is appropriate. We would also like to know whether, if pollution taxes are politically infeasible, the benefits of cruder regulatory approaches are likely to outweigh their costs. Finally, in terms of our own behavior, we would like to know how much effort an individual who cares about others' well-being should make to curtail his or her activities that cause pollution.

Since there are no market prices to use as guides, economists interested in pollution must begin by looking at the scientific evidence. In the case of global warming, for example, a reasonable point estimate is that in the absence of major intervention, the average temperature will rise by 3 degrees centigrade over the period 1990–2050, with various effects on climate (Nordhaus, 1992). Economists can help estimate the welfare consequences of these changes. To give just one example, experts on farming had estimated the likely impact of global warming on U.S. farmers' ability to continue growing their current crops. These studies concluded that global warming would have a significant negative impact. Mendelsohn, Nordhaus, and Shaw (1994), however, note that farmers can respond to changing weather patterns by moving into different crops, or even switching their land use out of crops altogether. They find that once these possibilities for substitution are taken into account, the overall effect of global warming on U.S. farmers is small and may be positive.

After considering the various channels through which global warming is likely to affect welfare, Nordhaus (1991) concludes that a reasonable estimate is that the overall welfare effect as of 2050 is likely to be slightly negative—the equivalent of a reduction in GDP of 1 to 2 percent. This corresponds to a reduction in average annual growth over the period 1990–2050 of only about 0.03 percentage points. Not surprisingly, Nordhaus finds that drastic measures to combat global warming, such as policies that would largely halt further warming by cutting emissions of greenhouse gases by 50 percent or more, would be much more harmful than simply doing nothing.

Using a similar approach, Nordhaus (1992) concludes that the welfare costs of other types of pollution are larger, but still limited. His point

---

[26] Alternatively, we could find the socially optimal level of pollution and auction off a quantity of tradable permits that allow that level of pollution. Weitzman (1974) provides the classic analysis of the choice between controlling prices or quantities.

estimate is that they will lower appropriately measured annual growth by roughly 0.04 percentage points.

Of course, it is possible that this reading of the scientific evidence or this effort to estimate welfare effects is far from the mark. It is also possible that considering horizons longer than the 50 to 100 years usually examined in such studies would change the conclusions substantially. But the fact remains that most economists who have studied environmental issues seriously, even ones whose initial positions were sympathetic to environmental concerns, have concluded that the likely impact of environmental problems on growth is at most moderate.[27]

Problems

1.1. Basic properties of growth rates. Use the fact that the growth rate of a variable equals the time derivative of its log to show:

(a) The growth rate of the product of two variables equals the sum of their growth rates. That is, if $Z(t) = X(t)Y(t)$, then $\dot{Z}(t)/Z(t) = [\dot{X}(t)/X(t)] + [\dot{Y}(t)/Y(t)]$.

(b) The growth rate of the ratio of two variables equals the difference of their growth rates. That is, if $Z(t) = X(t)/Y(t)$, then $\dot{Z}(t)/Z(t) = [\dot{X}(t)/X(t)] - [\dot{Y}(t)/Y(t)]$.

(c) If $Z(t) = X(t)^\alpha$, then $\dot{Z}(t)/Z(t) = \alpha \dot{X}(t)/X(t)$.

1.2. Suppose that the growth rate of some variable, X, is constant and equal to $a > 0$ from time 0 to time t_1; drops to 0 at time t_1; rises gradually from 0 to a from time t_1 to time t_2; and is constant and equal to a after time t_2.

(a) Sketch a graph of the growth rate of X as a function of time.

(b) Sketch a graph of $\ln X$ as a function of time.

1.3. Describe how, if at all, each of the following developments affects the break-even and actual investment lines in our basic diagram for the Solow model:

(a) The rate of depreciation falls.

(b) The rate of technological progress rises.

(c) The production function is Cobb–Douglas, $f(k) = k^\alpha$, and capital's share, α, rises.

(d) Workers exert more effort, so that output per unit of effective labor for a given value of capital per unit of effective labor is higher than before.

---

[27] This does not imply that environmental factors are always unimportant to long-run growth. Brander and Taylor (1998) make a strong case that Easter Island suffered an environmental disaster of the type envisioned by Malthusians sometime between its settlement around 400 and the arrival of Europeans in the 1700s. And they argue that other primitive societies may have also suffered such disasters.

1.4. Consider an economy with technological progress but without population growth that is on its balanced growth path. Now suppose there is a one-time jump in the number of workers.

(a) At the time of the jump, does output per unit of effective labor rise, fall, or stay the same? Why?

(b) After the initial change (if any) in output per unit of effective labor when the new workers appear, is there any further change in output per unit of effective labor? If so, does it rise or fall? Why?

(c) Once the economy has again reached a balanced growth path, is output per unit of effective labor higher, lower, or the same as it was before the new workers appeared? Why?

1.5. Suppose that the production function is Cobb–Douglas.

(a) Find expressions for k^*, y^*, and c^* as functions of the parameters of the model, s, n, δ, g, and α.

(b) What is the golden-rule value of k?

(c) What saving rate is needed to yield the golden-rule capital stock?

1.6. Consider a Solow economy that is on its balanced growth path. Assume for simplicity that there is no technological progress. Now suppose that the rate of population growth falls.

(a) What happens to the balanced-growth-path values of capital per worker, output per worker, and consumption per worker? Sketch the paths of these variables as the economy moves to its new balanced growth path.

(b) Describe the effect of the fall in population growth on the path of output (that is, total output, not output per worker).

1.7. Find the elasticity of output per unit of effective labor on the balanced growth path, y^*, with respect to the rate of population growth, n. If $\alpha_K(k^*) = \frac{1}{3}$, $g = 2\%$, and $\delta = 3\%$, by about how much does a fall in n from 2 percent to 1 percent raise y^*?

1.8. Suppose that investment as a fraction of output in the United States rises permanently from 0.15 to 0.18. Assume that capital's share is $\frac{1}{3}$.

(a) By about how much does output eventually rise relative to what it would have been without the rise in investment?

(b) By about how much does consumption rise relative to what it would have been without the rise in investment?

(c) What is the immediate effect of the rise in investment on consumption? About how long does it take for consumption to return to what it would have been without rise in investment?

1.9. Factor payments in the Solow model. Assume that both labor and capital are paid their marginal products. Let w denote $\partial F(K, AL)/\partial L$ and r denote $[\partial F(K, AL)/\partial K] - \delta$.

(a) Show that the marginal product of labor, w, is $A[f(k) - kf'(k)]$.

(b) Show that if both capital and labor are paid their marginal products, constant returns to scale imply that the total amount paid to the factors of production equals total net output. That is, show that under constant returns, $wL + rK = F(K, AL) - \delta K$.

(c) The return to capital (r) is roughly constant over time, as are the shares of output going to capital and to labor. Does a Solow economy on a balanced growth path exhibit these properties? What are the growth rates of w and r on a balanced growth path?

(d) Suppose the economy begins with a level of k less than k^*. As k moves toward k^*, is w growing at a rate greater than, less than, or equal to its growth rate on the balanced growth path? What about r?

1.10. Suppose that, as in Problem 1.9, capital and labor are paid their marginal products. In addition, suppose that all capital income is saved and all labor income is consumed. Thus $\dot{K} = [\partial F(K, AL)/\partial K]K - \delta K$.

(a) Show that this economy converges to a balanced growth path.

(b) Is k on the balanced growth path greater than, less than, or equal to the golden-rule level of k? What is the intuition for this result?

1.11. Embodied technological progress. (This follows Solow, 1960, and Sato, 1966.) One view of technological progress is that the productivity of capital goods built at t depends on the state of technology at t and is unaffected by subsequent technological progress. This is known as *embodied technological progress* (technological progress must be "embodied" in new capital before it can raise output). This problem asks you to investigate its effects.

(a) As a preliminary, let us modify the basic Solow model to make technological progress capital-augmenting rather than labor-augmenting. So that a balanced growth path exists, assume that the production function is Cobb–Douglas: $Y(t) = [A(t)K(t)]^{\alpha}L(t)^{1-\alpha}$. Assume that A grows at rate μ: $\dot{A}(t) = \mu A(t)$.

Show that the economy converges to a balanced growth path, and find the growth rates of Y and K on the balanced growth path. (Hint: Show that we can write $Y/(A^{\phi}L)$ as a function of $K/(A^{\phi}L)$, where $\phi = \alpha/(1-\alpha)$. Then analyze the dynamics of $K/(A^{\phi}L)$.)

(b) Now consider embodied technological progress. Specifically, let the production function be $Y(t) = J(t)^{\alpha}L(t)^{1-\alpha}$, where $J(t)$ is the effective capital stock. The dynamics of $J(t)$ are given by $\dot{J}(t) = sA(t)Y(t) - \delta J(t)$. The presence of the $A(t)$ term in this expression means that the productivity of investment at t depends on the technology at t.

Show that the economy converges to a balanced growth path. What are the growth rates of Y and J on the balanced growth path? (Hint: Let $\bar{J}(t) = J(t)/A(t)$. Then use the same approach as in (a), focusing on $\bar{J}/(A^{\phi}L)$ instead of $K/(A^{\phi}L)$.)

(c) What is the elasticity of output on the balanced growth path with respect to s?

(d) In the vicinity of the balanced growth path, how rapidly does the economy converge to the balanced growth path?

(e) Compare your results for (c) and (d) with the corresponding results in the text for the basic Solow model.

1.12. Consider a Solow economy on its balanced growth path. Suppose the growth-accounting techniques described in Section 1.7 are applied to this economy.

(a) What fraction of growth in output per worker does growth accounting attribute to growth in capital per worker? What fraction does it attribute to technological progress?

(b) How can you reconcile your results in (a) with the fact that the Solow model implies that the growth rate of output per worker on the balanced growth path is determined solely by the rate of technological progress?

1.13. (a) In the model of convergence and measurement error in equations (1.38) and (1.39), suppose the true value of b is -1. Does a regression of $\ln(Y/N)_{1979} - \ln(Y/N)_{1870}$ on a constant and $\ln(Y/N)_{1870}$ yield a biased estimate of b? Explain.

(b) Suppose there is measurement error in measured 1979 income per capita but not in 1870 income per capita. Does a regression of $\ln(Y/N)_{1979} - \ln(Y/N)_{1870}$ on a constant and $\ln(Y/N)_{1870}$ yield a biased estimate of b? Explain.

1.14. Derive equation (1.50). (Hint: Follow steps analogous to those in equations [1.47] and [1.48].)

Chapter 2
INFINITE-HORIZON AND OVERLAPPING-GENERATIONS MODELS

This chapter investigates two models that resemble the Solow model but in which the dynamics of economic aggregates are determined by decisions at the microeconomic level. Both models continue to treat the growth rates of labor and knowledge as exogenous. But the models derive the evolution of the capital stock from the interaction of maximizing households and firms in competitive markets. As a result, the saving rate is no longer exogenous, and it need not be constant.

The first model is conceptually the simplest. Competitive firms rent capital and hire labor to produce and sell output, and a fixed number of infinitely lived households supply labor, hold capital, consume, and save. This model, which was developed by Ramsey (1928), Cass (1965), and Koopmans (1965), avoids all market imperfections and all issues raised by heterogeneous households and links among generations. It therefore provides a natural benchmark case.

The second model is the overlapping-generations model developed by Diamond (1965). The key difference between the Diamond model and the Ramsey–Cass–Koopmans model is that the Diamond model assumes that there is continual entry of new households into the economy. As we will see, this seemingly small difference has important consequences.

Part A   The Ramsey–Cass–Koopmans Model

2.1   Assumptions

Firms

There are a large number of identical firms. Each has access to the production function $Y = F(K, AL)$, which satisfies the same assumptions as in

47

Chapter 1. The firms hire workers and rent capital in competitive factor markets, and sell their output in a competitive output market. Firms take A as given; as in the Solow model, A grows exogenously at rate g. The firms maximize profits. They are owned by the households, so any profits they earn accrue to the households.

Households

There are also a large number of identical households. The size of each household grows at rate n. Each member of the household supplies 1 unit of labor at every point in time. In addition, the household rents whatever capital it owns to firms. It has initial capital holdings of $K(0)/H$, where $K(0)$ is the initial amount of capital in the economy and H is the number of households. For simplicity, in this chapter we assume that there is no depreciation. The household divides its income (from the labor and capital it supplies and, potentially, from the profits it receives from firms) at each point in time between consumption and saving so as to maximize its lifetime utility.

The household's utility function takes the form

$$U = \int_{t=0}^{\infty} e^{-\rho t} u(C(t)) \frac{L(t)}{H} \, dt. \tag{2.1}$$

$C(t)$ is the consumption of each member of the household at time t. $u(\bullet)$ is the *instantaneous utility function,* which gives each member's utility at a given date. $L(t)$ is the total population of the economy; $L(t)/H$ is therefore the number of members of the household. Thus $u(C(t))L(t)/H$ is the household's total instantaneous utility at t. Finally, ρ is the discount rate; the greater is ρ, the less the household values future consumption relative to current consumption.[1]

The instantaneous utility function takes the form

$$u(C(t)) = \frac{C(t)^{1-\theta}}{1-\theta}, \qquad \theta > 0, \qquad \rho - n - (1-\theta)g > 0. \tag{2.2}$$

This functional form is needed for the economy to converge to a balanced growth path. It is known as *constant-relative-risk-aversion* (or *CRRA*) utility. The reason for the name is that the coefficient of relative risk aversion (which is defined as $-Cu''(C)/u'(C)$) for this utility function is θ, and thus is independent of C.

Since there is no uncertainty in this model, the household's attitude toward risk is not directly relevant. But θ also determines the household's willingness to shift consumption between different periods: the smaller is θ, the more slowly marginal utility falls as consumption rises, and so the

---

[1] One can also write utility as $\int_{t=0}^{\infty} e^{-\rho' t} u(C(t)) \, dt$, where $\rho' \equiv \rho - n$. Since $L(t) = L(0)e^{nt}$, this expression equals the expression in equation (2.1) divided by $L(0)/H$, and thus has the same implications for behavior.

more willing the household is to allow its consumption to vary over time. If θ is close to zero, for example, utility is almost linear in C, and so the household is willing to accept large swings in its consumption to take advantage of small differences between its discount rate and the rate of return it gets on its saving. Specifically, one can show that the elasticity of substitution between consumption at any two points in time is $1/\theta$.[2]

Three additional features of the instantaneous utility function are worth mentioning. First, $C^{1-\theta}$ is increasing in C if $\theta < 1$ but decreasing if $\theta > 1$; dividing $C^{1-\theta}$ by $1 - \theta$ thus ensures that the marginal utility of consumption is positive regardless of the value of θ. Second, in the special case of $\theta \to 1$, the instantaneous utility function simplifies to $\ln C$; this is often a useful case to consider.[3]   And third, the assumption that $\rho - n - (1 - \theta)g > 0$ ensures that lifetime utility does not diverge: if this condition does not hold, the household can attain infinite lifetime utility, and its maximization problem does not have a well-defined solution.[4]

2.2   The Behavior of Households and Firms

Firms

Firms' behavior is relatively simple. At each point in time they employ the stocks of labor and capital, pay them their marginal products, and sell the resulting output. Because the production function has constant returns and the economy is competitive, firms earn zero profits.

As described in Chapter 1, the marginal product of capital, $\partial F(K, AL)/\partial K$, is $f'(k)$, where $f(\bullet)$ is the intensive form of the production function. Because markets are competitive, capital earns its marginal product. And because there is no depreciation, the real rate of return on capital equals its earnings per unit time. Thus the real interest rate at time t is

$$r(t) = f'(k(t)). \tag{2.3}$$

Labor's marginal product of labor is $\partial F(K, AL)/\partial L$, which equals $A\partial F(K, AL)/\partial AL$. In terms of $f(\bullet)$, this is $A[f(k) - kf'(k)]$.[5] Thus the real wage at t is

$$W(t) = A(t)[f(k(t)) - k(t)f'(k(t))]. \tag{2.4}$$

---

[2] See Problem 2.2.

[3] To see this, first subtract $1/(1 - \theta)$ from the utility function; since this changes utility by a constant, it does not affect behavior. Then take the limit as θ approaches 1; this requires using l'Hôpital's rule. The result is $\ln C$.

[4] Phelps (1966a) discusses how growth models can be analyzed when households can obtain infinite utility.

[5] See Problem 1.9.

The wage per unit of *effective* labor is therefore

$$w(t) = f(k(t)) - k(t)f'(k(t)). \qquad (2.5)$$

Households' Budget Constraint

The representative household takes the paths of r and w as given. Its budget constraint is that the present value of its lifetime consumption cannot exceed its initial wealth plus the present value of its lifetime labor income. To write the budget constraint formally, we need to account for the fact that r may vary over time. To do this, define $R(t)$ as $\int_{\tau=0}^{t} r(\tau)\,d\tau$. One unit of the output good invested at time 0 yields $e^{R(t)}$ units of the good at t; equivalently, the value of 1 unit of output at time t in terms of output at time 0 is $e^{-R(t)}$. For example, if r is constant at some level $\bar{r}$, $R(t)$ is simply $\bar{r}t$ and the present value of 1 unit of output at t is $e^{-\bar{r}t}$. More generally, $e^{R(t)}$ shows the effects of continuously compounding interest over the period $[0,t]$.

Since the household has $L(t)/H$ members, its labor income at t is $W(t)L(t)/H$, and its consumption expenditures are $C(t)L(t)/H$. Its initial wealth is $1/H$ of total wealth at time 0, or $K(0)/H$. The household's budget constraint is therefore

$$\int_{t=0}^{\infty} e^{-R(t)} C(t) \frac{L(t)}{H}\,dt \le \frac{K(0)}{H} + \int_{t=0}^{\infty} e^{-R(t)} W(t) \frac{L(t)}{H}\,dt. \qquad (2.6)$$

In many cases, it is difficult to find the integrals in this expression. Fortunately, we can express the budget constraint in terms of the limiting behavior of the household's capital holdings; even when it is not possible to compute the integrals in (2.6), it is often possible to describe the limiting behavior of the economy. To see how the budget constraint can be rewritten in this way, first bring all the terms of (2.6) over to the same side and combine the two integrals; this gives us

$$\frac{K(0)}{H} + \int_{t=0}^{\infty} e^{-R(t)} [W(t) - C(t)] \frac{L(t)}{H}\,dt \ge 0. \qquad (2.7)$$

We can write the integral from $t = 0$ to $t = \infty$ as a limit. Thus (2.7) is equivalent to

$$\lim_{s \to \infty} \left[\frac{K(0)}{H} + \int_{t=0}^{s} e^{-R(t)} [W(t) - C(t)] \frac{L(t)}{H}\,dt \right] \ge 0. \qquad (2.8)$$

Now note that the household's capital holdings at time s are

$$\frac{K(s)}{H} = e^{R(s)} \frac{K(0)}{H} + \int_{t=0}^{s} e^{R(s)-R(t)} [W(t) - C(t)] \frac{L(t)}{H}\,dt. \qquad (2.9)$$

To understand (2.9), note that $e^{R(s)} K(0)/H$ is the contribution of the household's initial wealth to its wealth at s. The household's saving at t is

$[W(t) - C(t)]L(t)/H$ (which may be negative); $e^{R(s)-R(t)}$ shows how the value of that saving changes from t to s.

The expression in (2.9) is $e^{R(s)}$ times the expression in brackets in (2.8). Thus we can write the budget constraint simply as

$$\lim_{s \to \infty} e^{-R(s)} \frac{K(s)}{H} \geq 0. \tag{2.10}$$

Expressed in this form, the budget constraint states that the present value of the household's asset holdings cannot be negative in the limit.

Equation (2.10) is known as the *no-Ponzi-game condition*. A Ponzi game is a scheme in which someone issues debt and rolls it over forever. That is, the issuer always obtains the funds to pay off debt when it comes due by issuing new debt. Such a scheme allows the issuer to have a present value of lifetime consumption that exceeds the present value of his or her lifetime resources. By imposing the budget constraint (2.6) or (2.10), we are ruling out such schemes.[6]

Households' Maximization Problem

The representative household wants to maximize its lifetime utility subject to its budget constraint. As in the Solow model, it is easier to work with variables normalized by the quantity of effective labor. To do this, we need to express both the objective function and the budget constraint in terms of consumption and labor income per unit of effective labor.

We start with the objective function. Define $c(t)$ to be consumption per unit of effective labor. Thus $C(t)$, consumption per worker, equals $A(t)c(t)$. The household's instantaneous utility, (2.2), is therefore

$$\frac{C(t)^{1-\theta}}{1-\theta} = \frac{[A(t)c(t)]^{1-\theta}}{1-\theta}$$

$$= \frac{[A(0)e^{gt}]^{1-\theta}c(t)^{1-\theta}}{1-\theta} \tag{2.11}$$

$$= A(0)^{1-\theta}e^{(1-\theta)gt}\frac{c(t)^{1-\theta}}{1-\theta}.$$

---

[6] This analysis sweeps a subtlety under the rug: we have assumed rather than shown that households must satisfy the no-Ponzi-game condition. Because there are a finite number of households in the model, the assumption that Ponzi games are not feasible is correct. A household can run a Ponzi game only if at least one other household has a present value of lifetime consumption that is strictly less than the present value of its lifetime wealth. Since the marginal utility of consumption is always positive, no household will accept this. But in models with infinitely many households, such as the overlapping-generations model of Part B of this chapter, Ponzi games are possible in some situations. We return to this point in Section 11.1.

Substituting (2.11) and the fact that $L(t) = L(0)e^{nt}$ into the household's objective function, (2.1)–(2.2), yields

$$
\begin{aligned}
U &= \int_{t=0}^{\infty} e^{-\rho t}\frac{C(t)^{1-\theta}}{1-\theta}\frac{L(t)}{H}\,dt \\[2mm]
&= \int_{t=0}^{\infty} e^{-\rho t}\left[A(0)^{1-\theta}e^{(1-\theta)gt}\frac{c(t)^{1-\theta}}{1-\theta}\right]\frac{L(0)e^{nt}}{H}\,dt \\[2mm]
&= A(0)^{1-\theta}\frac{L(0)}{H}\int_{t=0}^{\infty} e^{-\rho t}e^{(1-\theta)gt}e^{nt}\frac{c(t)^{1-\theta}}{1-\theta}\,dt \\[2mm]
&\equiv B\int_{t=0}^{\infty} e^{-\beta t}\frac{c(t)^{1-\theta}}{1-\theta}\,dt,
\end{aligned}
\tag{2.12}
$$

where $B \equiv A(0)^{1-\theta}L(0)/H$ and $\beta \equiv \rho - n - (1-\theta)g$. From (2.2), β is assumed to be positive.

Now consider the budget constraint, (2.6). The household's total consumption at t, $C(t)L(t)/H$, equals consumption per unit of effective labor, $c(t)$, times the household's quantity of effective labor, $A(t)L(t)/H$. Similarly, its total labor income at t equals the wage per unit of effective labor, $w(t)$, times $A(t)L(t)/H$. And its initial capital holdings are capital per unit of effective labor at time 0, $k(0)$, times $A(0)L(0)/H$. Thus we can rewrite (2.6) as

$$
\int_{t=0}^{\infty} e^{-R(t)}c(t)\frac{A(t)L(t)}{H}\,dt \le k(0)\frac{A(0)L(0)}{H} + \int_{t=0}^{\infty} e^{-R(t)}w(t)\frac{A(t)L(t)}{H}\,dt.
\tag{2.13}
$$

$A(t)L(t)$ equals $A(0)L(0)e^{(n+g)t}$. Substituting this fact into (2.13) and dividing both sides by $A(0)L(0)/H$ yields

$$
\int_{t=0}^{\infty} e^{-R(t)}c(t)e^{(n+g)t}\,dt \le k(0) + \int_{t=0}^{\infty} e^{-R(t)}w(t)e^{(n+g)t}\,dt.
\tag{2.14}
$$

Finally, because $K(s)$ is proportional to $k(s)e^{(n+g)s}$, we can rewrite the no-Ponzi-game version of the budget constraint, (2.10), as

$$
\lim_{s \to \infty} e^{-R(s)}e^{(n+g)s}k(s) \ge 0.
\tag{2.15}
$$

Household Behavior

The household's problem is to choose the path of $c(t)$ to maximize lifetime utility, (2.12), subject to the budget constraint, (2.14). Although this involves choosing c at each instant of time (rather than choosing a finite set of variables, as in standard maximization problems), conventional maximization techniques can be used. Since the marginal utility of consumption is always positive, the household satisfies its budget constraint with equality. We can therefore use the objective function, (2.12), and the budget constraint, (2.14), to set up the Lagrangian:[7]

$$\mathcal{L} = B \int_{t=0}^{\infty} e^{-\beta t} \frac{c(t)^{1-\theta}}{1-\theta} \, dt$$

$$+ \lambda \left[k(0) + \int_{t=0}^{\infty} e^{-R(t)} e^{(n+g)t} w(t) \, dt - \int_{t=0}^{\infty} e^{-R(t)} e^{(n+g)t} c(t) \, dt \right].$$

$$(2.16)$$

The household chooses c at each point in time; that is, it chooses infinitely many $c(t)$'s. The first-order condition for an individual $c(t)$ is[8]

$$Be^{-\beta t} c(t)^{-\theta} = \lambda e^{-R(t)} e^{(n+g)t}. \tag{2.17}$$

The household's behavior is characterized by (2.17) and the budget constraint, (2.14).

To see what (2.17) implies for the behavior of consumption, first take logs of both sides:

$$\ln B - \beta t - \theta \ln c(t) = \ln \lambda - R(t) + (n+g)t$$

$$= \ln \lambda - \int_{\tau=0}^{t} r(\tau) \, d\tau + (n+g)t, \tag{2.18}$$

where the second line uses the definition of $R(t)$ as $\int_{\tau=0}^{t} r(\tau) \, d\tau$. Now note that since the two sides of (2.18) are equal for every t, the derivatives of the two sides with respect to t must be the same. This condition is

$$-\beta - \theta \frac{\dot{c}(t)}{c(t)} = -r(t) + (n+g), \tag{2.19}$$

where we have once again used the fact that the time derivative of the log of a variable equals its growth rate. Solving (2.19) for $\dot{c}(t)/c(t)$ yields

---

[7] For an introduction to maximization subject to equality constraints, see Dixit (1990, Chapter 2), Simon and Blume (1994, Chapters 18–19), or Chiang (1984, Chapter 12). For the case of inequality constraints, see Dixit (Chapter 3), Simon and Blume (Chapter 18), Chiang (Chapter 21), or Kreps (1990, Appendix 1).

[8] This step is slightly informal; the difficulty is that the terms in (2.17) are of order dt in (2.16); that is, they make an infinitesimal contribution to the Lagrangian. There are various ways of addressing this issue more formally than simply "canceling" the dt's (which is what we do in [2.17]). For example, we can model the household as choosing consumption over the finite intervals $[0, \Delta t], [\Delta t, 2\Delta t], [2\Delta t, 3\Delta t], \ldots$, with its consumption required to be constant within each interval, and then take the limit as Δt approaches zero. This also yields (2.17). Another possibility is to use the *calculus of variations* (see n. 14, below). In this particular application, however, the calculus-of-variations approach simplifies to the approach we have used here. That is, here the calculus of variations merely provides a formal justification for canceling the dt's in (2.17).

$$\frac{\dot{c}(t)}{c(t)} = \frac{r(t) - n - g - \beta}{\theta}$$

$$= \frac{r(t) - \rho - \theta g}{\theta},$$

(2.20)

where the second line uses the definition of β as $\rho - n - (1 - \theta)g$.

To interpret (2.20), note that since $C(t)$ (consumption per worker, rather than consumption per unit of effective labor) equals $c(t)A(t)$, the growth rate of C equals the growth rate of c plus the growth rate of A. That is, (2.20) implies that consumption per worker is growing at rate $[r(t) - \rho]/\theta$. Thus, (2.20) states that consumption per worker is rising if the real return exceeds the rate at which the household discounts future consumption, and is falling if the reverse holds. The smaller is θ—the less marginal utility changes as consumption changes—the larger are the changes in consumption in response to differences between the real interest rate and the discount rate.

Equation (2.20) is known as the *Euler equation* for this maximization problem. A more intuitive way of deriving (2.20) is to think of the household's consumption at two consecutive moments in time.[9]   Specifically, imagine the household reducing c at some date t by a small (formally, infinitesimal) amount Δc, investing this additional saving for a short (again, infinitesimal) period of time Δt, and then consuming the proceeds at time $t + \Delta t$; assume that when it does this, the household leaves consumption and capital holdings at all times other than t and $t + \Delta t$ unchanged. If the household is optimizing, the marginal impact of this change on lifetime utility must be zero. From (2.12), the marginal utility of $c(t)$ is $Be^{-\beta t}c(t)^{-\theta}$. Thus the change has a utility cost of $Be^{-\beta t}c(t)^{-\theta}\Delta c$. Since the instantaneous rate of return is $r(t)$, c at time $t + \Delta t$ can be increased by $e^{[r(t)-n-g]\Delta t}\Delta c$. Similarly, since c is growing at rate $\dot{c}(t)/c(t)$, we can write $c(t + \Delta t)$ as $c(t)e^{[\dot{c}(t)/c(t)]\Delta t}$; thus the marginal utility of $c(t+\Delta t)$ is $Be^{-\beta(t+\Delta t)}c(t+\Delta t)^{-\theta} = Be^{-\beta(t+\Delta t)}[c(t)e^{[\dot{c}(t)/c(t)]\Delta t}]^{-\theta}$. Thus for the path of consumption to be utility-maximizing, it must satisfy

$$Be^{-\beta t}c(t)^{-\theta}\Delta c = Be^{-\beta(t+\Delta t)}[c(t)e^{[\dot{c}(t)/c(t)]\Delta t}]^{-\theta}e^{[r(t)-n-g]\Delta t}\Delta c.$$ (2.21)

Dividing by $Be^{-\beta t}c(t)^{-\theta}\Delta c$ and taking logs yields

$$-\beta\Delta t - \theta\frac{\dot{c}(t)}{c(t)}\Delta t + [r(t) - n - g]\Delta t = 0.$$ (2.22)

Finally, dividing by Δt and rearranging yields the Euler equation in (2.20).

Intuitively, the Euler equation describes how c must behave over time given $c(0)$: if c does not evolve according to (2.20), the household can rearrange its consumption in a way that raises lifetime utility without changing the present value of its lifetime spending. The choice of $c(0)$ is then determined by the requirement that the present value of lifetime consumption

---

[9] The intuition for the Euler equation is considerably easier if time is discrete rather than continuous. See Section 2.9.

over the resulting path equals initial wealth plus the present value of future earnings. When $c(0)$ is chosen too low, consumption spending along the path satisfying (2.20) does not exhaust lifetime wealth, and so a higher path is possible; when $c(0)$ is set too high, consumption spending more than uses up lifetime wealth, and so the path is not feasible.[10]

2.3   The Dynamics of the Economy

The most convenient way to describe the behavior of the economy is in terms of the evolution of c and k.

The Dynamics of c

Since all households are the same, equation (2.20) describes the evolution of c not just for a single household but for the economy as a whole. Since $r(t) = f'(k(t))$, we can rewrite (2.20) as

$$\frac{\dot{c}(t)}{c(t)} = \frac{f'(k(t)) - \rho - \theta g}{\theta}. \qquad (2.23)$$

Thus $\dot{c}$ is zero when $f'(k)$ equals $\rho + \theta g$. Let k^* denote this level of k. When k exceeds k^*, $f'(k)$ is less than $\rho + \theta g$, and so $\dot{c}$ is negative; when k is less than k^*, $\dot{c}$ is positive.

This information is summarized in Figure 2.1. The arrows show the direction of motion of c. Thus c is rising if $k < k^*$ and falling if $k > k^*$. The $\dot{c} = 0$ line at $k = k^*$ indicates that c is constant for this value of k.[11]

The Dynamics of k

As in the Solow model, $\dot{k}$ equals actual investment minus break-even investment. Since we are assuming that there is no depreciation, break-even investment is $(n + g)k$. Actual investment is output minus consumption, $f(k) - c$. Thus,

$$\dot{k}(t) = f(k(t)) - c(t) - (n + g)k(t). \qquad (2.24)$$

For a given k, the level of c that implies $\dot{k} = 0$ is given by $f(k) - (n+g)k$; in terms of Figure 1.6 (Chapter 1), $\dot{k}$ is zero when consumption equals the difference between the actual output and break-even investment lines. This

---

[10] Formally, equation (2.20) implies $c(t) = c(0)e^{[R(t)-(\rho+\theta g)t]/\theta}$, which implies $e^{-R(t)}e^{(n+g)t}c(t) = c(0)e^{[(1-\theta)R(t)+(\theta n-\rho)t]/\theta}$. Thus $c(0)$ is determined by the fact that $c(0)\int_{t=0}^{\infty} e^{[(1-\theta)R(t)+(\theta n-\rho)t]/\theta}\,dt$ must equal the right-hand side of the budget constraint, (2.14).

[11] Note that (2.23) implies that $\dot{c}$ also equals zero when c is zero. That is, $\dot{c}$ is also zero along the horizontal axis of the diagram. But in equilibrium c is never zero, and so this is not relevant to the analysis of the model.

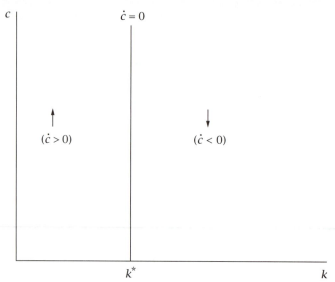

FIGURE 2.1   The dynamics of c

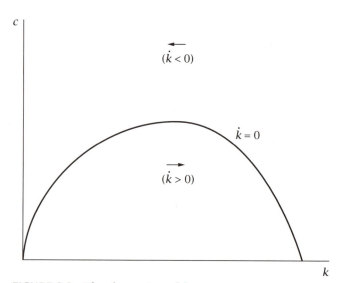

FIGURE 2.2   The dynamics of k

value of c is increasing in k until $f'(k) = n+g$ (the golden-rule level of k) and is then decreasing. When c exceeds the level that yields $\dot{k} = 0$, k is falling; when c is less than this level, k is rising. For k sufficiently large, break-even investment exceeds total output, and so $\dot{k}$ is negative for all positive values of c. This information is summarized in Figure 2.2; the arrows show the direction of motion of k.

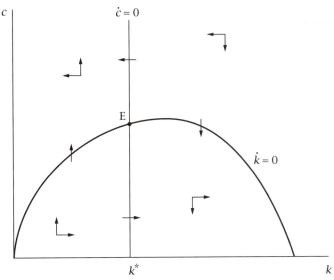

FIGURE 2.3 The dynamics of c and k

The Phase Diagram

Figure 2.3 combines the information in Figures 2.1 and 2.2. The arrows now show the directions of motion of both c and k. To the left of the $\dot{c} = 0$ locus and above the $\dot{k} = 0$ locus, for example, $\dot{c}$ is positive and $\dot{k}$ negative. Thus c is rising and k falling, and so the arrows point up and to the left. The arrows in the other sections of the diagram are based on similar reasoning. On the $\dot{c} = 0$ and $\dot{k} = 0$ curves, only one of c and k is changing. On the $\dot{c} = 0$ line above the $\dot{k} = 0$ locus, for example, c is constant and k is falling; thus the arrow points to the left. Finally, at Point E both $\dot{c}$ and $\dot{k}$ are zero; thus there is no movement from this point.[12]

Figure 2.3 is drawn with k^* (the level of k that implies $\dot{c} = 0$) less than the golden-rule level of k (the value of k associated with the peak of the $\dot{k} = 0$ locus). To see that this must be the case, recall that k^* is defined by $f'(k^*) = \rho + \theta g$, and that the golden-rule k is defined by $f'(k_{GR}) = n + g$. Since $f''(k)$ is negative, k^* is less than k_{GR} if and only if $\rho + \theta g$ is greater than $n + g$. This is equivalent to $\rho - n - (1 - \theta)g > 0$, which we have assumed

---

[12] There are two other points where c and k are constant. The first is the origin: if the economy starts with no capital and no consumption, it remains there. The second is the point where the $\dot{k} = 0$ curve crosses the horizontal axis. Here all of output is being used to hold k constant, so $c = 0$ and $f(k) = (n + g)k$. Since having consumption change from zero to any positive amount violates households' intertemporal optimization condition, (2.23), if the economy is at this point it must remain there to satisfy (2.23) and (2.24). As we will see shortly, however, the economy is never at this point.

to hold so that lifetime utility does not diverge (see [2.2]). Thus k^* is to the left of the peak of the $\dot{k} = 0$ curve.

The Initial Value of c

Figure 2.3 shows how c and k must evolve over time to satisfy households' intertemporal optimization condition (equation [2.23]) and the equation relating the change in k to output and consumption (equation [2.24]) *given initial values of c and k.* The initial value of k is given; but the initial value of c must be determined.

This issue is addressed in Figure 2.4. For concreteness, $k(0)$ is assumed to be less than k^*. The figure shows the trajectory of c and k for various assumptions concerning the initial level of c. If $c(0)$ is above the $\dot{k} = 0$ curve, at a point like A, then $\dot{c}$ is positive and $\dot{k}$ negative; thus the economy moves continually up and to the left in the diagram. If $c(0)$ is such that $\dot{k}$ is initially zero (Point B), the economy begins by moving directly up in (k, c) space; thereafter $\dot{c}$ is positive and $\dot{k}$ negative, and so the economy again moves up and to the left. If the economy begins slightly below the $\dot{k} = 0$ locus (Point C), $\dot{k}$ is initially positive but small (since $\dot{k}$ is a continuous function of c), and $\dot{c}$ is again positive. Thus in this case the economy initially

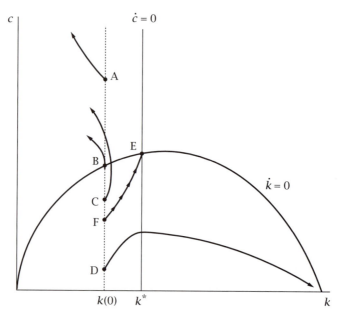

FIGURE 2.4   The behavior of c and k for various initial values of c

moves up and slightly to the right; after it crosses the $\dot{k} = 0$ locus, however, $\dot{k}$ becomes negative and once again the economy is on a path of rising c and falling k.

Point D shows a case of very low initial consumption. Here $\dot{c}$ and $\dot{k}$ are both initially positive. From (2.23), $\dot{c}$ is proportional to c; when c is small, $\dot{c}$ is therefore small. Thus c remains low, and so the economy eventually crosses the $\dot{c} = 0$ line. After this point, $\dot{c}$ becomes negative, and $\dot{k}$ remains positive. Thus the economy moves down and to the right.

$\dot{c}$ and $\dot{k}$ are continuous functions of c and k. Thus there is some critical point between Points C and D—Point F in the diagram—such that at that level of initial c, the economy converges to the stable point, Point E. For any level of consumption above this critical level, the $\dot{k} = 0$ curve is crossed before the $\dot{c} = 0$ line is reached, and so the economy ends up on a path of perpetually rising consumption and falling capital. And if consumption is less than the critical level, the $\dot{c} = 0$ locus is reached first, and so the economy embarks on a path of falling consumption and rising capital. But if consumption is just equal to the critical level, the economy converges to the point where both c and k are constant.

All these various trajectories satisfy equations (2.23) and (2.24). But we have not yet imposed the requirement that households satisfy their budget constraint, nor have we imposed the requirement that the economy's capital stock not be negative. These conditions determine which of the trajectories in fact describes the behavior of the economy.

If the economy starts at some point above F, c is high and rising. As a result, the equation of motion for k, (2.24), implies that k eventually reaches zero. For (2.23) and (2.24) to continue to be satisfied, c must continue to rise and k must become negative. But this cannot occur. Since output is zero when k is zero, c must drop to zero. This means that households are not satisfying their intertemporal optimization condition, (2.23). We can therefore rule out such paths.

To rule out paths starting below F, we use the budget constraint expressed in terms of the limiting behavior of capital holdings, equation (2.15): $\lim_{s \to \infty} e^{-R(s)} e^{(n+g)s} k(s) \geq 0$. If the economy starts at a point like D, eventually k exceeds the golden-rule capital stock. After that time, the real interest rate, $f'(k)$, is less than $n + g$, so $e^{-R(s)} e^{(n+g)s}$ is rising. Since k is also rising, $e^{-R(s)} e^{(n+g)s} k(s)$ diverges. Thus $\lim_{s \to \infty} e^{-R(s)} e^{(n+g)s} k(s)$ is infinity. From the derivation of (2.15), we know that this is equivalent to the statement that the present value of households' lifetime income is infinitely larger than the present value of their lifetime consumption. Thus households can attain higher utility, and so such a path cannot be an equilibrium.

Finally, if the economy begins at Point F, k converges to k^*, and so r converges to $f'(k^*) = \rho + \theta g$. Thus eventually $e^{-R(s)} e^{(n+g)s}$ is falling at rate $\rho - n - (1 - \theta)g = \beta > 0$, and so $\lim_{s \to \infty} e^{-R(s)} e^{(n+g)s} k(s)$ is zero. Thus the path beginning at F, and only this path, is possible.

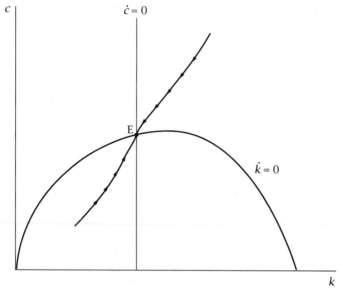

FIGURE 2.5   The saddle path

The Saddle Path

Although all of this discussion has been in terms of a single value of k, the idea is general. For any positive initial level of k, there is a unique initial level of c that is consistent with households' intertemporal optimization, the dynamics of the capital stock, households' budget constraint, and the requirement that k not be negative. The function giving this initial c as a function of k is known as the *saddle path;* it is shown in Figure 2.5. For any starting value for k, the initial c must be the value on the saddle path. The economy then moves along the saddle path to Point E.

2.4   Welfare

A natural question is whether the equilibrium of this economy represents a desirable outcome. The answer to this question is simple. The *first welfare theorem*, from microeconomics, tells us that if markets are competitive and complete and there are no externalities (and if the number of agents is finite), then the decentralized equilibrium is Pareto-efficient—that is, it is impossible to make anyone better off without making someone else worse off. Since the conditions of the first welfare theorem hold in our model, the equilibrium must be Pareto-efficient. And since all households have the same utility, this means that the decentralized equilibrium produces the highest possible utility among allocations that treat all households in the same way.

To see this more clearly, consider the problem facing a social planner who can dictate the division of output between consumption and investment at each date and who wants to maximize the lifetime utility of a representative household. This problem is identical to that of an individual household except that, rather than taking the paths of w and r as given, the planner takes into account the fact that these are determined by the path of k, which is in turn determined by (2.24).

The intuitive argument involving consumption at consecutive moments used to derive (2.20) or (2.23) applies to the social planner as well: reducing c by Δc at time t and investing the proceeds allows the planner to increase c at time $t + \Delta t$ by $e^{f'(k(t))\Delta t}e^{-(n+g)\Delta t}\Delta c$.[13] Thus $c(t)$ along the path chosen by the planner must satisfy (2.23). And since equation (2.24) giving the evolution of k reflects technology, not preferences, the social planner must obey it as well. Finally, as with the household's optimization problem, paths that require that the capital stock becomes negative can be ruled out on the grounds that they are not feasible, and paths that cause consumption to approach zero can be ruled out on the grounds that they do not maximize households' utility.

In short, the solution to the social planner's problem is for the initial value of c to be given by the value on the saddle path, and for c and k to then move along the saddle path. That is, the competitive equilibrium maximizes the welfare of the representative household.[14]

2.5 The Balanced Growth Path

Properties of the Balanced Growth Path

The behavior of the economy once it has converged to Point E is identical to that of the Solow economy on the balanced growth path. Capital, output, and consumption per unit of effective labor are constant. Since y and c are constant, the saving rate, $(y - c)/y$, is also constant. The total capital

---

[13] Note that this change does affect r and w over the (brief) interval from t to $t + \Delta t$. r falls by $f''(k)$ times the change in k, while w rises by $-f''(k)k$ times the change in k. But the effect of these changes on total income (per unit of effective labor), which is given by the change in w plus k times the change in r, is zero. That is, since capital is paid its marginal product, total payments to labor and to previously existing capital remain equal to the previous level of output (again per unit of effective labor). This is just a specific instance of the general result that the *pecuniary externalities*—externalities operating through prices—balance in the aggregate under competition.

[14] A formal solution to the planner's problem involves the use of the calculus of variations. For a formal statement and solution of the problem, see Blanchard and Fischer (1989, pp. 38–43). For an introduction to the calculus of variations, see Section 8.2; Kamien and Schwartz (1991); Dixit (1990, Chapter 10); or Obstfeld (1992).

stock, total output, and total consumption grow at rate $n + g$. And capital per worker, output per worker, and consumption per worker grow at rate g.

Thus the central implications of the Solow model concerning the driving forces of economic growth do not hinge on its assumption of a constant saving rate. Even when saving is endogenous, growth in the effectiveness of labor remains the only possible source of persistent growth in output per worker. And since the production function is the same as in the Solow model, one can repeat the calculations of Section 1.6 demonstrating that significant differences in output per worker can arise from differences in capital per worker only if the differences in capital per worker, and in rates of return to capital, are enormous.

The Balanced Growth Path and the Golden-Rule Level of Capital

The only notable difference between the balanced growth paths of the Solow and Ramsey–Cass–Koopmans models is that a balanced growth path with a capital stock above the golden-rule level is not possible in the Ramsey–Cass–Koopmans model. In the Solow model, a sufficiently high saving rate causes the economy to reach a balanced growth path with the property that there are feasible alternatives that involve higher consumption at every moment. In the Ramsey–Cass–Koopmans model, in contrast, saving is derived from the behavior of households whose utility depends on their consumption, and there are no externalities. As a result, it cannot be an equilibrium for the economy to follow a path where higher consumption can be attained in every period; if the economy were on such a path, households would reduce their saving and take advantage of this opportunity.

This can be seen in the phase diagram. Consider again Figure 2.5. If the initial capital stock exceeds the golden-rule level (that is, if $k(0)$ is greater than the k associated with the peak of the $\dot{k} = 0$ locus), initial consumption is above the level needed to keep k constant; thus $\dot{k}$ is negative. k gradually approaches k^*, which is below the golden-rule level.

Finally, the fact that k^* is less than the golden-rule capital stock implies that the economy does not converge to the balanced growth path that yields the maximum sustainable level of c. The intuition for this result is clearest in the case of g equal to zero, so that there is no long-run growth of consumption and output per worker. In this case, k^* is defined by $f'(k^*) = \rho$ (see [2.23]) and k_{GR} is defined by $f'(k_{GR}) = n$, and our assumption that $\rho - n - (1 - \theta)g > 0$ simplifies to $\rho > n$. Since k^* is less than k_{GR}, an increase in saving starting at $k = k^*$ would cause consumption per worker to eventually rise above its previous level and remain there (see Figure 1.5). But because households value present consumption more than future consumption, the benefit of the eventual permanent increase in consumption is bounded. At some point—specifically, when k exceeds k^*—the tradeoff between the temporary short-term sacrifice and the permanent long-term gain is sufficiently unfavorable that accepting it reduces rather than raises lifetime utility. Thus k converges to a value below the golden-rule level. Because k^* is the optimal level of k for the economy to converge to, it is known as the *modified golden-rule* capital stock.

2.6   The Effects of a Fall in the Discount Rate

Consider a Ramsey–Cass–Koopmans economy that is on its balanced growth path, and suppose that there is a fall in ρ, the discount rate. Since ρ is the parameter governing households' preferences between current and future consumption, this change is the closest analogue in this model to a rise in the saving rate in the Solow model.

Since the division of output between consumption and investment is determined by forward-looking households, we must specify whether the change is expected or unexpected. If a change is expected, households may alter their behavior before the change occurs. We therefore focus on the simple case where the change is unexpected. That is, households are optimizing given their belief that their discount rate will not change, and the economy is on the resulting balanced growth path. At some date households suddenly discover that their preferences have changed, and that they now discount future utility at a lower rate than before.[15]

Qualitative Effects

Since the evolution of k is determined by technology rather than preferences, ρ enters the equation for $\dot{c}$ but not the one for $\dot{k}$. Thus only the $\dot{c} = 0$ locus is affected. Recall equation (2.23): $\dot{c}(t)/c(t) = [f'(k(t)) - \rho - \theta g]/\theta$. Thus the value of k where $\dot{c}$ equals zero is defined by $f'(k^*) = \rho + \theta g$. Since $f''(\bullet)$ is negative, this means that the fall in ρ raises k^*. Thus the $\dot{c} = 0$ line shifts to the right. This is shown in Figure 2.6.

At the time of the change in ρ, the value of k—the *stock* of capital per unit of effective labor—is given by the history of the economy, and it cannot change discontinuously. In particular, k at the time of the change equals the value of k^* on the old balanced growth path. In contrast, c—the *rate* at which households are consuming—can jump at the time of the shock.

Given our analysis of the dynamics of the economy, it is clear what occurs: at the instant of the change, c jumps down so that the economy is

---

[15] See Section 2.7 and Problems 2.10 and 2.11 for examples of how to analyze anticipated changes.

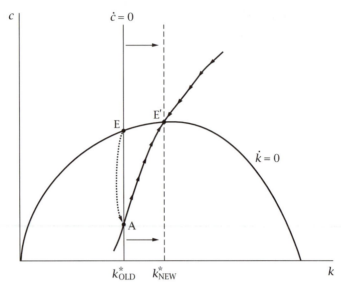

FIGURE 2.6   The effects of a fall in the discount rate

on the new saddle path (Point A in Figure 2.6).[16] Thereafter, c and k rise gradually to their new balanced-growth-path values; these are higher than their values on the original balanced growth path.

Thus the effects of a fall in the discount rate are similar to the effects of a rise in the saving rate in the Solow model with a capital stock below the golden-rule level. In both cases, k rises gradually to a new higher level, and in both c initially falls but then rises to a level above the one it started at. Thus, just as with a permanent rise in the saving rate in the Solow model, the permanent fall in the discount rate produces temporary increases in the growth rates of capital per worker and output per worker. The only difference between the two experiments is that, in the case of the fall in ρ, in general the fraction of output that is saved is not constant during the adjustment process.

The Rate of Adjustment and the Slope of the Saddle Path

Equations (2.23) and (2.24) describe $\dot{c}(t)$ and $\dot{k}(t)$ as functions of $k(t)$ and $c(t)$. A fruitful way to analyze their quantitative implications for the dynamics of the economy is to replace these nonlinear equations with linear

---

[16] Since we are assuming that the change is unexpected, the discontinuous change in c does not imply that households are not optimizing. Their original behavior is optimal given their beliefs; the fall in c is the optimal response to the new information that ρ is lower.

approximations around the balanced growth path. Thus we begin by taking first-order Taylor approximations to (2.23) and (2.24) around $k = k^*, c = c^*$. That is, we write

$$\dot{c} \simeq \frac{\partial \dot{c}}{\partial k}[k - k^*] + \frac{\partial \dot{c}}{\partial c}[c - c^*], \tag{2.25}$$

$$\dot{k} \simeq \frac{\partial \dot{k}}{\partial k}[k - k^*] + \frac{\partial \dot{k}}{\partial c}[c - c^*], \tag{2.26}$$

where $\partial \dot{c}/\partial k$, $\partial \dot{c}/\partial c$, $\partial \dot{k}/\partial k$, and $\partial \dot{k}/\partial c$ are all evaluated at $k = k^*, c = c^*$. Our strategy will be to treat (2.25) and (2.26) as exact and analyze the dynamics of the resulting system.[17]

It helps to define $\tilde{c} = c - c^*$ and $\tilde{k} = k - k^*$. Since c^* and k^* are both constant, $\dot{\tilde{c}}$ equals $\dot{c}$, and $\dot{\tilde{k}}$ equals $\dot{k}$. We can therefore rewrite (2.25) and (2.26) as

$$\dot{\tilde{c}} \simeq \frac{\partial \dot{c}}{\partial k}\tilde{k} + \frac{\partial \dot{c}}{\partial c}\tilde{c}, \tag{2.27}$$

$$\dot{\tilde{k}} \simeq \frac{\partial \dot{k}}{\partial k}\tilde{k} + \frac{\partial \dot{k}}{\partial c}\tilde{c}. \tag{2.28}$$

(Again, the derivatives are all evaluated at $k = k^*, c = c^*$.) Recall that $\dot{c} = \{[f'(k) - \rho - \theta g]/\theta\}c$ (equation [2.23]). Using this expression to compute the derivatives in (2.27) and evaluating them at $k = k^*, c = c^*$ gives us

$$\dot{\tilde{c}} \simeq \frac{f''(k^*)c^*}{\theta}\tilde{k}. \tag{2.29}$$

Similarly, (2.24) states that $\dot{k} = f(k) - c - (n + g)k$. We can use this to find the derivatives in (2.28); this yields

$$\dot{\tilde{k}} \simeq [f'(k^*) - (n + g)]\tilde{k} - \tilde{c}$$

$$= [(\rho + \theta g) - (n + g)]\tilde{k} - \tilde{c} \tag{2.30}$$

$$= \beta\tilde{k} - \tilde{c},$$

where the second line uses the fact that (2.23) implies that $f'(k^*) = \rho + \theta g$ and the third line uses the definition of β as $\rho - n - (1 - \theta)g$. Dividing both sides of (2.29) by $\tilde{c}$ and both sides of (2.30) by $\tilde{k}$ yields expressions for the growth rates of $\tilde{c}$ and $\tilde{k}$:

$$\frac{\dot{\tilde{c}}}{\tilde{c}} \simeq \frac{f''(k^*)c^*}{\theta}\frac{\tilde{k}}{\tilde{c}}, \tag{2.31}$$

---

[17] For a more formal introduction to the analysis of systems of differential equations (such as [2.25]-[2.26]), see Simon and Blume (1994, Chapter 25).

$$\frac{\dot{\tilde{k}}}{\tilde{k}} \simeq \beta - \frac{\tilde{c}}{\tilde{k}}. \tag{2.32}$$

Equations (2.31) and (2.32) imply that the growth rates of $\tilde{c}$ and $\tilde{k}$ depend only on the ratio of $\tilde{c}$ and $\tilde{k}$. Given this, consider what happens if the values of $\tilde{c}$ and $\tilde{k}$ are such that $\tilde{c}$ and $\tilde{k}$ are falling at the same rate (that is, if they imply $\dot{\tilde{c}}/\tilde{c} = \dot{\tilde{k}}/\tilde{k}$). This implies that the ratio of $\tilde{c}$ to $\tilde{k}$ is not changing, and thus that their growth rates are also not changing. Thus $\tilde{c}$ and $\tilde{k}$ continue to fall at equal rates. In terms of the diagram, from a point where $\tilde{c}$ and $\tilde{k}$ are falling at equal rates, the economy moves along a straight line to (k^*, c^*), with the distance from (k^*, c^*) falling at a constant rate.

Let μ denote $\dot{\tilde{c}}/\tilde{c}$. Equation (2.31) implies

$$\frac{\tilde{c}}{\tilde{k}} = \frac{f''(k^*)c^*}{\theta} \frac{1}{\mu}. \tag{2.33}$$

From (2.32), the condition that $\dot{\tilde{k}}/\tilde{k}$ equals $\dot{\tilde{c}}/\tilde{c}$ is thus

$$\mu = \beta - \frac{f''(k^*)c^*}{\theta} \frac{1}{\mu}, \tag{2.34}$$

or

$$\mu^2 - \beta\mu + \frac{f''(k^*)c^*}{\theta} = 0. \tag{2.35}$$

This is a quadratic equation in μ. The solutions are

$$\mu = \frac{\beta \pm [\beta^2 - 4f''(k^*)c^*/\theta]^{1/2}}{2}. \tag{2.36}$$

Let μ_1 and μ_2 denote these two values of μ.

If μ is positive, then $\tilde{c}$ and $\tilde{k}$ are growing; that is, instead of moving along a straight line toward (k^*, c^*), the economy is moving on a straight line away from (k^*, c^*). Thus if the economy is to converge to (k^*, c^*), then μ must be negative. Inspection of (2.36) shows that only one of the μ's, namely $\{\beta - [\beta^2 - 4f''(k^*)c^*/\theta]^{1/2}\}/2$, is negative. Let μ_1 denote this value of μ. Equation (2.33) (with $\mu = \mu_1$) then tells us how $\tilde{c}$ must be related to $\tilde{k}$ for both to be falling at rate μ_1.

Figure 2.7 shows the line along which the economy converges smoothly to (k^*, c^*); it is labeled AA. This is the saddle path of the linearized system. The figure also shows the line along which the economy moves directly away from (k^*, c^*); it is labeled BB. If the initial values of $c(0)$ and $k(0)$ lay along this line, (2.31) and (2.32) would imply that $\tilde{c}$ and $\tilde{k}$ would grow steadily at rate μ_2.[18] Since $f''(\bullet)$ is negative, (2.33) implies that the relation between $\tilde{c}$ and $\tilde{k}$ has the opposite sign from μ. Thus the saddle path AA is positively sloped, and the BB line is negatively sloped.

---

[18] Of course, it is not possible for the initial value of (k, c) to lie along the BB line. As we saw in Section 2.3, if it did, either k would eventually become negative or households would accumulate infinite wealth.

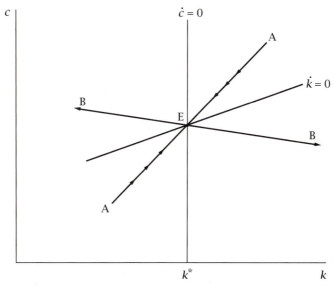

FIGURE 2.7   The linearized phase diagram

Thus if we linearize the equations for $\dot{c}$ and $\dot{k}$, we can characterize the dynamics of the economy in terms of the model's parameters. At time 0, c must jump to $c^* + [f''(k^*)c^*/(\theta\mu_1)](k-k^*)$. Thereafter, c and k converge to their balanced-growth-path values at rate μ_1; that is, $k(t) = k^* + e^{\mu_1 t}[k(0) - k^*]$ and $c(t) = c^* + e^{\mu_1 t}[c(0) - c^*].$[19]

---

[19] This analysis can be used to characterize the path of k and c implied by (2.29) and (2.30) if the initial value of (k, c) were on neither the AA nor BB line. (Again, this cannot occur in equilibrium; see n. 18.) Consider a point $(k - k^*, c - c^*)$ that can be written as a sum of a point on AA and a point on BB. That is, suppose we can find a $\tilde{k}_a$ and a $\tilde{k}_b$ such that

$$(\tilde{k}(0), \tilde{c}(0)) = \left(\tilde{k}_a, \frac{f''(k^*)c^*}{\theta\mu_1} \tilde{k}_a \right) + \left(\tilde{k}_b, \frac{f''(k^*)c^*}{\theta\mu_2} \tilde{k}_b \right)$$

$$\equiv (\tilde{k}_a, \tilde{c}_a) + (\tilde{k}_b, \tilde{c}_b).$$

The first point on the right-hand side is on AA, and the second is on BB (see [2.33]). Because $(\tilde{k}(0), \tilde{c}(0))$ is the sum of $(\tilde{k}_a, \tilde{c}_a)$ and $(\tilde{k}_b, \tilde{c}_b)$, and because (2.29) and (2.30) are linear, the economy's dynamics starting at $(\tilde{k}(0), \tilde{c}(0))$ are the sum of what they would be starting at $(\tilde{k}_a, \tilde{c}_a)$ and what they would be starting at $(\tilde{k}_b, \tilde{c}_b)$. Thus, $\tilde{k}(t) = e^{\mu_1}\tilde{k}_a + e^{\mu_2}\tilde{k}_b$, and similarly for $\tilde{c}(t)$. Because μ_1 is negative and μ_2 is positive, the first term goes to zero and the second term diverges. Thus asymptotically $\tilde{k}(t)$ and $\tilde{c}(t)$ grow at rate μ_2, and the economy approaches the BB line. The only way to avoid this outcome is for $\tilde{k}_b$ to be zero (which implies that $\tilde{c}_b$ is also zero)—that is, for the economy to begin on the saddle path AA.

Finally, note that we can write any point in $(\tilde{k}, \tilde{c})$ space as a sum of a point on AA and a point on BB: the equation above can be written as two linearly independent equations, one for $\tilde{k}(0)$ and one for $\tilde{c}(0)$, in two unknowns, $\tilde{k}_a$ and $\tilde{k}_b$. Thus this approach can be used to describe the dynamics implied by (2.29) and (2.30) for any assumed initial values of k and c.

The Speed of Adjustment

To understand the implications of (2.36) for the speed of convergence to the balanced growth path, consider our usual example of Cobb–Douglas production, $f(k) = k^\alpha$. This implies $f''(k^*) = \alpha(\alpha - 1)k^{*\alpha-2}$. Since consumption on the balanced growth path equals output minus break-even investment, consumption per unit of effective labor, c^*, equals $k^{*\alpha} - (n+g)k^*$. Thus in this case we can write the expression for μ_1 as

$$\mu_1 = \frac{1}{2}\left(\beta - \left\{\beta^2 - \frac{4}{\theta}\alpha(\alpha-1)k^{*\alpha-2}[k^{*\alpha} - (n+g)k^*]\right\}^{1/2}\right). \qquad (2.37)$$

Recall that on the balanced growth path, $f'(k)$ equals $\rho + \theta g$ (see [2.23]). For the Cobb–Douglas case, this is equivalent to $\alpha k^{*\alpha-1} = \rho + \theta g$, or $k^* = [(\rho + \theta g)/\alpha]^{1/(\alpha-1)}$. Substituting this into (2.37) and doing some uninteresting algebraic manipulations yields

$$\mu_1 = \frac{1}{2}\left(\beta - \left\{\beta^2 + \frac{4}{\theta}\frac{1-\alpha}{\alpha}(\rho+\theta g)[\rho+\theta g - \alpha(n+g)]\right\}^{1/2}\right). \qquad (2.38)$$

Equation (2.38) expresses the rate of adjustment in terms of the underlying parameters of the model.

To get a feel for the magnitudes involved, suppose $\alpha = \frac{1}{3}$, $\rho = 4\%$, $n = 2\%$, $g = 1\%$, and $\theta = 1$. One can show that these parameter values imply that on the balanced growth path, the real interest rate is 5 percent and the saving rate 20 percent. And since β is defined as $\rho - n - (1-\theta)g$, they imply $\beta = 2\%$. Equation (2.37) or (2.38) then implies $\mu_1 \simeq -5.4\%$. Thus adjustment is quite rapid in this case; for comparison, the Solow model with the same values of α, n, and g (and as here, no depreciation) implies an adjustment speed of 2 percent per year (see equation [1.31]). The reason for the difference is that in this example, the saving rate is greater than s^* when k is less than k^* and less than s^* when k is greater than k^*; in the Solow model, in contrast, s is constant by assumption.

2.7   The Effects of Government Purchases

Thus far, we have left government out of our model. Yet modern economies devote their resources not just to investment and private consumption but also to public uses. In the United States, for example, about 20 percent of total output is purchased by the government; in many other countries the figure is considerably higher. It is thus natural to extend our model to include a government sector.

Adding Government to the Model

Assume that the government buys output at rate $G(t)$ per unit of effective labor per unit time. Government purchases are assumed not to affect utility from private consumption; this can occur if the government devotes the goods to some activity that does not affect utility at all, or if utility equals the sum of utility from private consumption and utility from government-provided goods. Similarly, the purchases are assumed not to affect future output; that is, they are devoted to public consumption rather than public investment. The purchases are financed by lump-sum taxes of amount $G(t)$ per unit of effective labor per unit time; thus the government always runs a balanced budget. Consideration of deficit finance is postponed to Chapter 11. We will see there, however, that in this model the government's choice between tax and deficit finance has no impact on any important variables. Thus the assumption that the purchases are financed with current taxes only serves to simplify the presentation.

Investment is now the difference between output and the sum of private consumption and government purchases. Thus the equation of motion for k, (2.24), becomes

$$\dot{k}(t) = f(k(t)) - c(t) - G(t) - (n + g)k(t). \qquad (2.39)$$

A higher value of G shifts the $\dot{k} = 0$ locus down: the more goods that are purchased by the government, the fewer that can be purchased privately if k is to be held constant.

By assumption, households' preferences ([2.1]–[2.2] or [2.12]) are unchanged. Since the Euler equation ([2.20] or [2.23]) is derived from households' preferences without imposing their lifetime budget constraint, this condition continues to hold as before. The taxes that finance the government's purchases affect households' budget constraint, however. Specifically, (2.14) becomes

$$\int_{t=0}^{\infty} e^{-R(t)} c(t) e^{(n+g)t}\, dt \le k(0) + \int_{t=0}^{\infty} e^{-R(t)} [w(t) - G(t)] e^{(n+g)t}\, dt. \quad (2.40)$$

Reasoning parallel to that used before shows that this implies the same expression as before for the limiting behavior of k (equation [2.15]).

The Effects of Permanent and Temporary Changes in Government Purchases

To see the implications of the model, suppose that the economy is on a balanced growth path with $G(t)$ constant at some level G_L, and that there is an unexpected, permanent increase in G to G_H. From (2.39), the $\dot{k} = 0$ locus shifts down by the amount of the increase in G. Since government

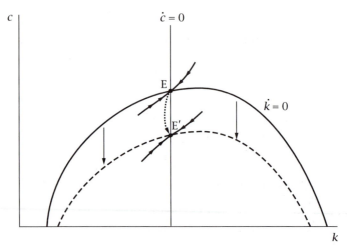

FIGURE 2.8   The effects of a permanent increase in government purchases

purchases do not affect the Euler equation, the $\dot{c} = 0$ locus is unaffected. This is shown in Figure 2.8.[20]

We know that in response to such a change, c must jump so that the economy is on its new saddle path. If not, then as before, either capital would become negative at some point or households would accumulate infinite wealth. In this case, the adjustment takes a simple form: c falls by the amount of the increase in G, and the economy is immediately on its new balanced growth path. Intuitively, the permanent increases in government purchases and taxes reduce households' lifetime wealth. Thus consumption falls immediately.

Because the increases in purchases and taxes are permanent, there is no scope for households to raise their utility by adjusting the time pattern of their consumption. Thus the size of the immediate fall in consumption is equal to the full amount of the increase in government purchases, and the capital stock and the real interest rate are unaffected. Note that this result differs from what we would get under the traditional approach of assuming that consumption depends only on current disposable income and that it moves less than one-for-one with that income. With that assumption, the rise in government purchases crowds out investment, and so the capital stock starts to fall and the real interest rate starts to rise. But this

---

[20] We assume that G_H is not so large that $\dot{k}$ is negative when $c = 0$. That is, the intersection of the new $\dot{k} = 0$ locus with the $\dot{c} = 0$ line is assumed to occur at a positive level of c. If it does not, the government's policy is not feasible. Even if c is always zero, $\dot{k}$ is negative, and eventually the economy's output per unit of effective labor is less than G_H.

approach assumes that households follow mechanical rules and do not do any intertemporal optimization.

A more complicated case is provided by an unanticipated increase in G that is expected to be temporary. For simplicity, assume that the terminal date is known with certainty. In this case, c does not fall by the full amount of the increase in G, $G_H - G_L$. To see this, note that if it did, consumption would jump up discontinuously at the time that government purchases returned to G_L; thus marginal utility would fall discontinuously. But since the return of G to G_L is anticipated, the discontinuity in marginal utility would also be anticipated, which cannot be optimal for households.

During the period of time that government purchases are high, $\dot{k}$ is determined by the capital-accumulation equation, (2.39), with $G = G_H$; after G returns to G_L, it is governed by (2.39) with $G = G_L$. The Euler equation, (2.23), determines the dynamics of c throughout, and c cannot change discontinuously at the time that G returns to G_L. These facts determine what happens at the time of the increase in G: c must jump to the value such that the dynamics implied by (2.39) with $G = G_H$ (and by [2.23]) bring the economy to the old saddle path at the time that G returns to its initial level. Thereafter, the economy moves along that saddle path to the old balanced growth path.[21]

This is depicted in Figure 2.9. Panel (a) shows a case where the increase in G is relatively long-lasting. In this case c falls by most of the amount of the increase in G. As the time of the return of G to G_L approaches, however, households increase their consumption and decrease their capital holdings in anticipation of the fall in G.

Since $r = f'(k)$, we can deduce the behavior of r from the behavior of k. Thus r rises gradually during the period that government spending is high and then slowly returns to its initial level. This is shown in Panel (b); t_0 denotes the time of the increase in G, and t_1 the time of its return to its initial value.

Finally, Panel (c) shows the case of a short-lived rise in G. Here households change their consumption relatively little, choosing instead to pay for most of the temporarily higher taxes out of their savings. Because government purchases are high for only a short period, the effects on the capital stock and the real interest rate are small.

Note that once again allowing for forward-looking behavior yields insights we would not get from the traditional approach of assuming that consumption depends only on current disposable income. With that approach, the duration of a change in government purchases is irrelevant.

---

[21] As in the previous example, because the initial change in G is unexpected, the discontinuities in consumption and marginal utility at that point do not mean that households are not behaving optimally. See n. 16.

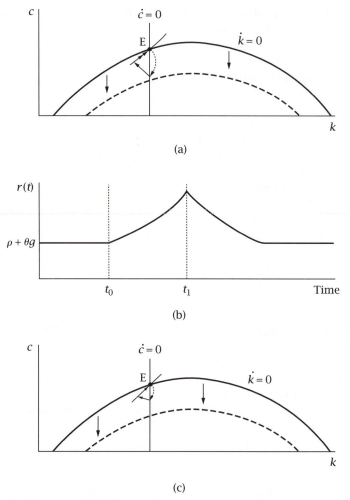

FIGURE 2.9   **The effects of a temporary increase in government purchases**

But the idea that households do not look ahead and put some weight on the likely future path of government purchases and taxes is implausible.

Empirical Application: Wars and Real Interest Rates

This analysis suggests that temporarily high government purchases cause real interest rates to rise, whereas permanently high purchases do not. Intuitively, when the government's purchases are high only temporarily, households expect their consumption to be greater in the future than it is in the present. To make them willing to accept this, the real interest rate must be high. When the government's purchases are permanently high, on the other hand, households' current consumption is low, and they expect it to remain low. Thus in this case, no movement in real interest rates is needed for households to accept their current low consumption.

A natural example of a period of temporarily high government purchases is a war. Thus our analysis predicts that real interest rates are high during wars. Barro (1987) tests this prediction by examining military spending and interest rates in the United Kingdom from 1729 to 1918. The most significant complication he faces is that, instead of having data on short-term real interest rates, he has data only on long-term nominal interest rates. Long-term interest rates should be, loosely speaking, a weighted average of expected short-term interest rates.[22] Thus, since our analysis implies that temporary increases in government purchases raise the short-term rate over an extended period, it also implies that they raise the long-term rate. Similarly, since the analysis implies that permanent increases never change the short-term rate, it predicts that they do not affect the long-term rate. In addition, the real interest rate equals the nominal rate minus expected inflation; thus the nominal rate should be corrected for changes in expected inflation. Barro does not find any evidence, however, of systematic changes in expected inflation in his sample period; thus the data are at least consistent with the view that movements in nominal rates represent changes in real rates.

Figure 2.10 plots British military spending as a share of GNP (relative to the mean of this series for the full sample) and the long-term interest rate. The spikes in the military spending series correspond to wars; for example, the spike around 1760 reflects the Seven Years' War, and the spike around 1780 corresponds to the American Revolution. The figure suggests that the interest rate is indeed higher during periods of temporarily high government purchases.

To test this formally, Barro estimates a process for the military purchases series and uses it to construct estimates of the temporary component of military spending. Not surprisingly in light of the figure, the estimated temporary component differs little from the raw series.[23] Barro then regresses the long-term interest rate on this estimate of temporary military spending. Because the residuals are serially correlated, he includes a first-order serial correlation correction. The results are

$$R_t = \ \underset{(0.27)}{3.54} \ + \ \underset{(0.7)}{2.6} \ \tilde{G}_t, \qquad \lambda = \ \underset{(0.03)}{0.91} \tag{2.41}$$

$$R^2 = 0.89, \qquad \text{s.e.e.} = 0.248, \qquad \text{D.W.} = 2.1.$$

---

[22] See Section 10.3.

[23] Since there is little permanent variation in military spending, the data cannot be used to investigate the effects of permanent changes in government purchases on interest rates.

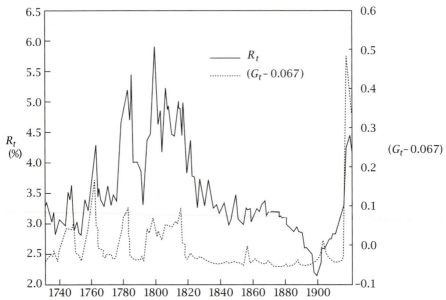

FIGURE 2.10   Temporary military spending and the long-term interest rate in the United Kingdom (from Barro, 1987; used with permission)

Here R_t is the long-term nominal interest rate, $\tilde{G}_t$ is the estimated value of temporary military spending as a fraction of GNP, λ is the first-order autoregressive parameter of the residual, and the numbers in parentheses are standard errors. Thus there is a statistically significant link between temporary military spending and interest rates. The results are even stronger when World War I is excluded: stopping the sample period in 1914 raises the coefficient on $\tilde{G}_t$ to 6.1 (and the standard error to 1.3). Barro argues that the comparatively small rise in the interest rate given the tremendous rise in military spending in World War I may have occurred because the government imposed price controls and used a variety of nonmarket means of allocating resources. If this is right, the results for the shorter sample may provide a better estimate of the impact of government purchases on interest rates in a market economy.

Thus the evidence from the United Kingdom supports the predictions of the theory. The success of the theory is not universal, however. In particular, for the United States real interest rates appear to have been, if anything, generally lower during wars than in other periods (Barro, 1993, pp. 321–322). The reasons for this anomalous behavior are not well understood. Thus the theory does not provide a full account of how real interest rates respond to changes in government purchases.

Part B   The Diamond Model

2.8   Assumptions

We now turn to the Diamond overlapping-generations model. The central difference between the Diamond model and the Ramsey–Cass–Koopmans model is that there is turnover in the population: rather than there being a fixed number of infinitely lived households, new individuals are continually being born, and old individuals are continually dying.

With turnover, it turns out to be simpler to assume that time is discrete rather than continuous; that is, the variables of the model are defined for $t = 0, 1, 2, \ldots$ rather than for all values of $t \geq 0$. To further simplify the analysis, the model assumes that each individual lives for only two periods. It is the general assumption of turnover in the population, however, and not the specific assumptions of discrete time and two-period lifetimes, that is crucial to the model's results.[24]

L_t individuals are born in period t. As before, population grows at rate n; thus $L_t = (1 + n)L_{t-1}$. Since individuals live for two periods, at time t there are L_t individuals in the first period of their lives and $L_{t-1} = L_t/(1+n)$ individuals in their second periods. Each individual supplies 1 unit of labor when he or she is young and divides the resulting labor income between first-period consumption and saving; in the second period, the individual simply consumes the saving and any interest he or she earns.

Let C_{1t} and C_{2t} denote the consumption in period t of young and old individuals. Thus the utility of an individual born at t, denoted U_t, depends on C_{1t} and C_{2t+1}. We again assume constant-relative-risk-aversion utility:

$$U_t = \frac{C_{1t}^{1-\theta}}{1-\theta} + \frac{1}{1+\rho}\frac{C_{2t+1}^{1-\theta}}{1-\theta}, \qquad \theta > 0, \qquad \rho > -1. \tag{2.42}$$

As before, this functional form is needed for balanced growth. Because lifetimes are finite, we no longer have to assume $\rho > n + (1 - \theta)g$ to ensure that lifetime utility does not diverge. If $\rho > 0$, individuals place greater weight on first-period than second-period consumption; if $\rho < 0$, the situation is reversed. The assumption $\rho > -1$ ensures that the weight on second-period consumption is positive.

Production is described by the same assumptions as before. There are many firms, each with the production function $Y_t = F(K_t, A_t L_t)$. $F(\bullet)$ again

---

[24] See Problem 2.14 for a discrete-time version of the Solow model. Blanchard (1985) develops a tractable continuous-time model in which the extent of the departure from the infinite-horizon benchmark is governed by a continuous parameter. Weil (1989a) considers a variant of Blanchard's model where new households enter the economy but existing households do not leave. He shows that the arrival of new households is sufficient to generate most of the main results of the Diamond and Blanchard models. Finally, Auerbach and Kotlikoff (1987) use simulations to investigate a much more realistic overlapping-generations model.

has constant returns to scale and satisfies the Inada conditions, and A again grows at exogenous rate g (so $A_t = [1 + g]A_{t-1}$). Markets are competitive; thus labor and capital earn their marginal products, and firms earn zero profits. As in the first part of the chapter, there is no depreciation. The real interest rate and the wage per unit of effective labor are therefore given as before by $r_t = f'(k_t)$ and $w_t = f(k_t) - k_t f'(k_t)$. Finally, there is some initial capital stock K_0 that is owned equally by all old individuals.

Thus, in period 0 the capital owned by the old and the labor supplied by the young are combined to produce output. Capital and labor are paid their marginal products. The old consume both their capital income and their existing wealth; they then die and exit the model. The young divide their labor income, $w_t A_t$, between consumption and saving. They carry their saving forward to the next period; thus the capital stock in period $t + 1$, K_{t+1}, equals the number of young individuals in period t, L_t, times each of these individuals' saving, $w_t A_t - C_{1t}$. This capital is combined with the labor supplied by the next generation of young individuals, and the process continues.

2.9   Household Behavior

The second-period consumption of an individual born at t is

$$C_{2t+1} = (1 + r_{t+1})(w_t A_t - C_{1t}). \tag{2.43}$$

Dividing both sides of this expression by $1 + r_{t+1}$ and bringing C_{1t} over to the left-hand side yields the budget constraint:

$$C_{1t} + \frac{1}{1 + r_{t+1}} C_{2t+1} = A_t w_t. \tag{2.44}$$

This condition states that the present value of lifetime consumption equals initial wealth (which is zero) plus the present value of lifetime labor income (which is $A_t w_t$).

The individual maximizes utility, (2.42), subject to the budget constraint, (2.44). We will consider two ways of solving this maximization problem. The first is to proceed along the lines of the intuitive derivation of the Euler equation for the Ramsey model in (2.21)–(2.22). Because the Diamond model is in discrete time, the intuitive derivation of the Euler equation is much easier here than in the Ramsey model. Specifically, imagine the individual decreasing C_{1t} by a small (formally, infinitesimal) amount ΔC and then using the additional saving and capital income to raise C_{2t+1} by $(1 + r_{t+1})\Delta C$. This change does not affect the present value of the individual's lifetime consumption stream. Thus if the individual is optimizing, the utility cost and benefit of the change must be equal. If the cost is less than the benefit, the individual can increase lifetime utility by making the change. And if the cost exceeds the benefit, the individual can increase utility by making the opposite change.

The marginal contributions of C_{1t} and C_{2t+1} to lifetime utility are $C_{1t}^{-\theta}$ and $[1/(1+\rho)]C_{2t+1}^{-\theta}$, respectively. Thus as we let ΔC approach 0, the utility cost of the change approaches $C_{1t}^{-\theta} \Delta C$ and the utility benefit approaches $[1/(1+\rho)]C_{2t+1}^{-\theta}(1+r_{t+1}) \Delta C$. As just described, these are equal when the individual is optimizing. Thus optimization requires

$$C_{1t}^{-\theta} \Delta C = \frac{1}{1+\rho}C_{2t+1}^{-\theta}(1+r_{t+1}) \Delta C. \tag{2.45}$$

Canceling the ΔC's and multiplying both sides by C_{2t+1}^{θ} gives us

$$\frac{C_{2t+1}^{\theta}}{C_{1t}^{\theta}} = \frac{1+r_{t+1}}{1+\rho}, \tag{2.46}$$

or

$$\frac{C_{2t+1}}{C_{1t}} = \left(\frac{1+r_{t+1}}{1+\rho}\right)^{1/\theta}. \tag{2.47}$$

This condition and the budget constraint describe the individual's behavior.

Expression (2.47) is analogous to the Euler equation, (2.20), in the Ramsey model. It implies that whether an individual's consumption is increasing or decreasing over time depends on whether the real rate of return is greater or less than the discount rate. θ again determines how much individuals' consumption varies in response to differences between r and ρ.

The second way to solve the individual's maximization problem is to set up the Lagrangian:

$$\mathcal{L} = \frac{C_{1t}^{1-\theta}}{1-\theta} + \frac{1}{1+\rho}\frac{C_{2t+1}^{1-\theta}}{1-\theta} + \lambda\left[A_t w_t - \left(C_{1t} + \frac{1}{1+r_{t+1}}C_{2t+1}\right)\right]. \tag{2.48}$$

The first-order conditions for C_{1t} and C_{2t+1} are

$$C_{1t}^{-\theta} = \lambda, \tag{2.49}$$

$$\frac{1}{1+\rho}C_{2t+1}^{-\theta} = \frac{1}{1+r_{t+1}}\lambda. \tag{2.50}$$

Substituting the first equation into the second yields

$$\frac{1}{1+\rho}C_{2t+1}^{-\theta} = \frac{1}{1+r_{t+1}}C_{1t}^{-\theta}. \tag{2.51}$$

This can be rearranged to obtain (2.47). As before, this condition and the budget constraint characterize utility-maximizing behavior.

We can use the Euler equation and the budget constraint to express C_{1t} in terms of labor income and the real interest rate. Specifically, multiplying both sides of (2.47) by C_{1t} and substituting into the budget constraint gives

$$C_{1t} + \frac{(1+r_{t+1})^{(1-\theta)/\theta}}{(1+\rho)^{1/\theta}}C_{1t} = A_t w_t. \tag{2.52}$$

This implies

$$C_{1t} = \frac{(1+\rho)^{1/\theta}}{(1+\rho)^{1/\theta} + (1+r_{t+1})^{(1-\theta)/\theta}} A_t w_t. \tag{2.53}$$

Equation (2.53) shows that the interest rate determines the fraction of income the individual consumes in the first period. Letting $s(r)$ denote the fraction of income saved, (2.53) implies

$$s(r) = \frac{(1+r)^{(1-\theta)/\theta}}{(1+\rho)^{1/\theta} + (1+r)^{(1-\theta)/\theta}}. \tag{2.54}$$

We can therefore rewrite (2.53) as

$$C_{1t} = [1 - s(r_{t+1})]A_t w_t. \tag{2.55}$$

Equation (2.54) implies that young individuals' saving is increasing in r if and only if $(1+r)^{(1-\theta)/\theta}$ is increasing in r. The derivative of $(1+r)^{(1-\theta)/\theta}$ with respect to r is $[(1-\theta)/\theta](1+r)^{(1-2\theta)/\theta}$. Thus s is increasing in r if θ is less than 1, and decreasing if θ is greater than 1. Intuitively, a rise in r has both an income and a substitution effect. The fact that the tradeoff between consumption in the two periods has become more favorable for second-period consumption tends to increase saving (the substitution effect), but the fact that a given amount of saving yields more second-period consumption tends to decrease saving (the income effect). When individuals are very willing to substitute consumption between the two periods to take advantage of rate-of-return incentives (that is, when θ is low), the substitution effect dominates. When individuals have strong preferences for similar levels of consumption in the two periods (that is, when θ is high), the income effect dominates. And in the special case of $\theta = 1$ (logarithmic utility), the two effects balance, and young individuals' saving rate is independent of r.

2.10   The Dynamics of the Economy

The Equation of Motion of k

As in the infinite-horizon model, we can aggregate individuals' behavior to characterize the dynamics of the economy. As described above, the capital stock in period $t + 1$ is the amount saved by young individuals in period t. Thus,

$$K_{t+1} = s(r_{t+1})L_t A_t w_t. \tag{2.56}$$

Note that because saving in period t depends on labor income in that period and on the return on capital that savers expect in the next period, it is w in period t and r in period $t + 1$ that enter the expression for the capital stock in period $t + 1$.

Dividing both sides of (2.56) by $L_{t+1}A_{t+1}$ gives us an expression for $K_{t+1}/(A_{t+1}L_{t+1})$, capital per unit of effective labor:

$$k_{t+1} = \frac{1}{(1+n)(1+g)} s(r_{t+1})w_t. \tag{2.57}$$

We can then substitute for r_{t+1} and w_t to obtain

$$k_{t+1} = \frac{1}{(1+n)(1+g)} s(f'(k_{t+1}))[f(k_t) - k_t f'(k_t)]. \tag{2.58}$$

The Evolution of k

Equation (2.58) implicitly defines k_{t+1} as a function of k_t. (It defines k_{t+1} only implicitly because k_{t+1} appears on the right-hand side as well as the left-hand side.) It therefore determines how k evolves over time given its initial value. A value of k_t such that $k_{t+1} = k_t$ satisfies (2.58) is an equilibrium value of k: once k reaches that value, it remains there. We therefore want to know whether there is an equilibrium value (or values) of k, and whether k converges to such a value if it does not begin at one.

To answer these questions, we need to describe how k_{t+1} depends on k_t. Unfortunately, we can say relatively little about this for the general case. We therefore begin by considering the case of logarithmic utility and Cobb–Douglas production. With these assumptions, (2.58) takes a particularly simple form. We then briefly discuss what occurs when these assumptions are relaxed.

Logarithmic Utility and Cobb–Douglas Production

When θ is 1, the fraction of labor income saved is $1/(2+\rho)$ (see equation [2.54]). And when production is Cobb–Douglas, $f(k)$ is k^α and w is $(1-\alpha)k^\alpha$. Equation (2.58) therefore becomes

$$k_{t+1} = \frac{1}{(1+n)(1+g)} \frac{1}{2+\rho} (1-\alpha)k_t^\alpha. \tag{2.59}$$

Figure 2.11 shows k_{t+1} as a function of k_t. A point where the k_{t+1} function intersects the 45-degree line is a point where k_{t+1} equals k_t. In the special case we are considering, k_{t+1} equals k_t at $k_t = 0$; it rises above k_t when k_t is small; and it then crosses the 45-degree line and remains below. There is thus a unique equilibrium level of k (aside from $k = 0$), which is denoted k^*.

k^* is globally stable: wherever k starts (other than at 0), it converges to k^*. Suppose, for example, that the initial value of k, k_0, is greater than k^*. Because k_{t+1} is less than k_t when k_t exceeds k^*, k_1 is less than k_0. And because k_0 exceeds k^* and k_{t+1} is increasing in k_t, k_1 is larger than k^*. Thus k_1 is between k^* and k_0: k moves partway toward k^*. This process is

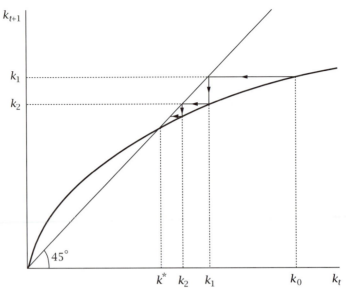

FIGURE 2.11   The dynamics of k

repeated each period, and so k converges smoothly to k^*. A similar analysis applies when k_0 is less than k^*.

These dynamics are shown by the arrows in Figure 2.11. Given k_0, the height of the k_{t+1} function shows k_1 on the vertical axis. To find k_2, we first need to find k_1 on the horizontal axis; to do this, we move across to the 45-degree line. The height of the k_{t+1} function at this point then shows k_2, and so on.

The properties of the economy once it has converged to its balanced growth path are the same as those of the Solow and Ramsey economies on their balanced growth paths: the saving rate is constant, output per worker is growing at rate g, the capital-output ratio is constant, and so on.

To see how the economy responds to shocks, consider our usual example of a fall in the discount rate, ρ, when the economy is initially on its balanced growth path. The fall in the discount rate causes the young to save a greater fraction of their labor income. Thus the k_{t+1} function shifts up. This is depicted in Figure 2.12. The upward shift of the k_{t+1} function increases k^*, the value of k on the balanced growth path. As the figure shows, k rises monotonically from the old value of k^* to the new one.

Thus the effects of a fall in the discount rate in the Diamond model in the case we are considering are similar to its effects in the Ramsey-Cass-Koopmans model, and to the effects of a rise in the saving rate in the Solow model. The change shifts the paths over time of output and capital per worker permanently up, but it leads only to temporary increases in the growth rates of these variables.

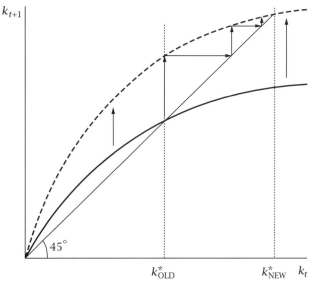

FIGURE 2.12 The effects of a fall in the discount rate

The Speed of Convergence

Once again, we may be interested in the model's quantitative as well as qualitative implications. In the special case we are considering, we can solve for the balanced-growth-path values of k and y. Equation (2.59) gives k_{t+1} as a function of k_t. The economy is on its balanced growth path when these two are equal. That is, k^* is defined by

$$k^* = \frac{1}{(1+n)(1+g)} \frac{1}{2+\rho}(1-\alpha)k^{*\alpha}. \tag{2.60}$$

Solving this expression for k^* yields

$$k^* = \left[\frac{1-\alpha}{(1+n)(1+g)(2+\rho)}\right]^{1/(1-\alpha)}. \tag{2.61}$$

Since y equals k^α, this implies

$$y^* = \left[\frac{1-\alpha}{(1+n)(1+g)(2+\rho)}\right]^{\alpha/(1-\alpha)}. \tag{2.62}$$

This expression shows how the model's parameters affect output per unit of effective labor on the balanced growth path. If we want to, we can choose values for the parameters and obtain quantitative predictions about the long-run effects of various developments.[25]

We can also find how quickly the economy converges to the balanced growth path. To do this, we again linearize around the balanced growth path. That is, we replace the equation of motion for k, (2.59), with a first-order approximation around $k = k^*$. We know that when k_t equals k^*, k_{t+1} also equals k^*. Thus,

$$k_{t+1} \simeq k^* + \left(\frac{dk_{t+1}}{dk_t} \bigg|_{k_t=k^*} \right) (k_t - k^*). \tag{2.63}$$

Let λ denote dk_{t+1}/dk_t evaluated at $k_t = k^*$. We can thus rewrite (2.63) as $k_{t+1} - k^* \simeq \lambda(k_t - k^*)$. This implies

$$k_t - k^* \simeq \lambda^t (k_0 - k^*), \tag{2.64}$$

where k_0 is the initial value of k.

The convergence to the balanced growth path is determined by λ. If λ is between 0 and 1, the system converges smoothly. If λ is between -1 and 0, there are damped oscillations toward k^*: k alternates between being greater and less than k^*, but each period it gets closer. If λ is greater than 1, the system explodes. Finally, if λ is less than -1, there are explosive oscillations.

To find λ, we return to (2.59): $k_{t+1} = (1 - \alpha)k_t^\alpha/[(1 + n)(1 + g)(2 + \rho)]$. Thus,

$$\lambda \equiv \frac{dk_{t+1}}{dk_t} \bigg|_{k_t=k^*} = \alpha \frac{1 - \alpha}{(1 + n)(1 + g)(2 + \rho)} k^{*\alpha-1}$$

$$= \alpha \frac{1 - \alpha}{(1 + n)(1 + g)(2 + \rho)} \left[\frac{1 - \alpha}{(1 + n)(1 + g)(2 + \rho)} \right]^{(\alpha-1)/(1-\alpha)} \tag{2.65}$$

$$= \alpha,$$

where the second line uses equation (2.61) to substitute for k^*. That is, λ is simply α, capital's share.

Since α is between 0 and 1, this analysis implies that k converges smoothly to k^*. If α is one-third, for example, k moves two-thirds of the way toward k^* each period.[26]

The rate of convergence in the Diamond model differs from that in the Solow model (and in a discrete-time version of the Solow model—see Problem 2.14). The reason is that although the saving of the young is a constant

---

[25] In choosing parameter values, it is important to keep in mind that individuals are assumed to live for only two periods. Thus, for example, n should be thought of as population growth not over a year, but over half a lifetime.

[26] Recall, however, that each period in the model corresponds to half of a person's lifetime.

fraction of their income and their income is a constant fraction of total income, the dissaving of the old is not a constant fraction of total income. The dissaving of the old as a fraction of output is $K_t/F(K_t, A_tL_t)$, or $k_t/f(k_t)$. The fact that there are diminishing returns to capital implies that this ratio is increasing in k. Since this term enters negatively into saving, it follows that total saving as a fraction of output is a decreasing function of k. Thus total saving as a fraction of output is above its balanced-growth-path value when $k < k^*$, and is below when $k > k^*$. As a result, convergence is more rapid than in the Solow model.

The General Case

Let us now relax the assumptions of logarithmic utility and Cobb–Douglas production. It turns out that, despite the simplicity of the model, a wide range of behaviors of the economy are possible. Rather than attempting a comprehensive analysis, we simply discuss some of the more interesting cases.[27]

To understand the possibilities intuitively, it is helpful to rewrite the equation of motion, (2.58), as

$$k_{t+1} = \frac{1}{(1+n)(1+g)}s(f'(k_{t+1}))\frac{f(k_t) - k_tf'(k_t)}{f(k_t)}f(k_t). \tag{2.66}$$

Equation (2.66) expresses capital per unit of effective labor in period $t + 1$ as the product of four terms. From right to left, those four terms are the following: output per unit of effective labor at t, the fraction of that output that is paid to labor, the fraction of that labor income that is saved, and the ratio of the amount of effective labor in period t to the amount in period $t + 1$.

Figure 2.13 shows some possible forms for the relation between k_{t+1} and k_t other than the well-behaved case shown in Figure 2.11. Panel (a) shows a case with multiple values of k^*. In the case shown, k_1^* and k_3^* are stable: if k starts slightly away from one of these points, it converges to that level. k_2^* is unstable (as is $k = 0$). If k starts slightly below k_2^*, then k_{t+1} is less than k_t each period, and so k converges to k_1^*. If k begins slightly above k_2^*, it converges to k_3^*.

To understand the possibility of multiple values of k^*, note that since output per unit of capital is lower when k is higher (capital has a diminishing marginal product), for there to be two k^*'s the saving of the young as a fraction of total output must be higher at the higher k^*. When the fraction of output going to labor and the fraction of labor income saved are constant, the saving of the young is a constant fraction of total output, and so multiple k^*'s are not possible. This is what occurs with Cobb–Douglas production

---

[27] Galor and Ryder (1989) analyze some of these issues in greater detail.

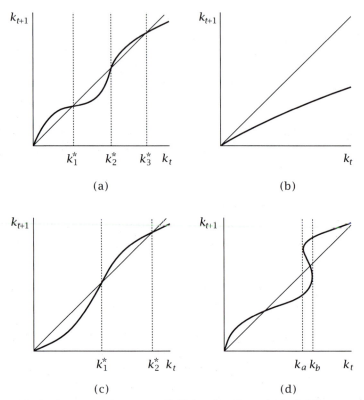

FIGURE 2.13   Various possibilities for the relationship between k_t and k_{t+1}

and logarithmic utility. But if labor's share is greater at higher levels of k (which occurs if $f(\bullet)$ is more sharply curved than in the Cobb–Douglas case) or if workers save a greater fraction of their income when the rate of return is lower (which occurs if $\theta > 1$), or both, there may be more than one level of k at which saving reproduces the existing capital stock.

Panel (b) shows a case in which k_{t+1} is always less than k_t, and in which k therefore converges to zero regardless of its initial value. What is needed for this to occur is for either labor's share or the fraction of labor income saved (or both) to approach zero as k approaches zero.

Panel (c) shows a case in which k converges to zero if its initial value is sufficiently low, but to a strictly positive level if its initial value is sufficiently high. Specifically, if $k_0 < k_1^*$, then k approaches zero; if $k_0 > k_1^*$, then k converges to k_2^*.

Finally, Panel (d) shows a case in which k_{t+1} is not uniquely determined by k_t: when k_t is between k_a and k_b, there are three possible values of k_{t+1}. This can happen if saving is a decreasing function of the interest rate. When saving is decreasing in r, saving is high if individuals expect a high value of k_{t+1} and therefore expect r to be low, and is low when individuals expect a low value of k_{t+1}. If saving is sufficiently responsive to r, and if r is sufficiently responsive to k, there can be more than one value of k_{t+1} that is consistent with a given k_t. Thus the path of the economy is indeterminate: equation (2.58) (or [2.66]) does not fully determine how k evolves over time given its initial value. This raises the possibility that *self-fulfilling prophecies* and *sunspots* can affect the behavior of the economy and that the economy can exhibit fluctuations even though there are no exogenous disturbances. Depending on precisely what is assumed, various dynamics are possible.[28]

Thus assuming that there are overlapping generations rather than infinitely lived households has potentially important implications for the dynamics of the economy: for example, sustained growth may not be possible, or it may depend on initial conditions.

At the same time, the model does no better than the Solow and Ramsey models at answering our basic questions about growth. Because of the Inada conditions, k_{t+1} must be less than k_t for k_t sufficiently large. Specifically, since the saving of the young cannot exceed the economy's total output, k_{t+1} must be less than or equal to $f(k_t)/[(1 + n)(1 + g)]$. And because the marginal product of capital approaches zero as k becomes large, this must eventually be less than k_t. The fact that k_{t+1} is eventually less than k_t implies that unbounded growth of k is not possible. Thus, once again, growth in the effectiveness of labor is the only potential source of long-run growth in output per worker. Because of the possibility of multiple k^*'s, the model does imply that otherwise identical economies can converge to different balanced growth paths simply because of differences in their initial conditions. But, as in the Solow and Ramsey models, we can account for quantitatively large differences in output per worker in this way only by positing immense differences in capital per worker and in rates of return.

2.11 The Possibility of Dynamic Inefficiency

The one major difference between the balanced growth paths of the Diamond and Ramsey-Cass-Koopmans models involves welfare. We saw that the equilibrium of the Ramsey-Cass-Koopmans model maximizes the welfare of the representative household. In the Diamond model, individuals born at different times attain different levels of utility, and so the appropriate way to evaluate social welfare is not clear. If we specify welfare as some weighted sum of the utilities of different generations, there is no reason to expect the decentralized equilibrium to maximize welfare, since the weights we assign to the different generations are arbitrary.

---

[28] These issues are briefly discussed further in Section 6.11.

A minimal criterion for efficiency, however, is that the equilibrium be Pareto-efficient. It turns out that the equilibrium of the Diamond model need not satisfy even this standard. In particular, the capital stock on the balanced growth path of the Diamond model may exceed the golden-rule level, so that a permanent increase in consumption is possible.

To see this possibility as simply as possible, assume that utility is logarithmic, production is Cobb–Douglas, and g is zero. With $g = 0$, equation (2.61) for the value of k on the balanced growth path simplifies to

$$k^* = \left[\frac{1}{1+n} \frac{1}{2+\rho} (1-\alpha) \right]^{1/(1-\alpha)}. \tag{2.67}$$

Thus the marginal product of capital on the balanced growth path, $\alpha k^{*\alpha-1}$, is

$$f'(k^*) = \frac{\alpha}{1-\alpha}(1+n)(2+\rho). \tag{2.68}$$

The golden-rule capital stock is defined by $f'(k_{GR}) = n$. $f'(k^*)$ can be either more or less than $f'(k_{GR})$. In particular, for α sufficiently small, $f'(k^*)$ is less than $f'(k_{GR})$—the capital stock on the balanced growth path exceeds the golden-rule level.

To see why it is inefficient for k^* to exceed k_{GR}, imagine introducing a social planner into a Diamond economy that is on its balanced growth path with $k^* > k_{GR}$. If the planner does nothing to alter k, the amount of output per worker available each period for consumption is output, $f(k^*)$, minus the new investment needed to maintain k at k^*, nk^*. This is shown by the crosses in Figure 2.14. Suppose instead, however, that in some period, period t_0, the planner allocates more resources to consumption and fewer to saving than usual, so that capital per worker the next period is k_{GR}, and that thereafter he or she maintains k at k_{GR}. Under this plan, the resources per worker available for consumption in period t_0 are $f(k^*) + (k^* - k_{GR}) - nk_{GR}$. In each subsequent period, the output per worker available for consumption is $f(k_{GR}) - nk_{GR}$. Since k_{GR} maximizes $f(k) - nk$, $f(k_{GR}) - nk_{GR}$ exceeds $f(k^*) - nk^*$. And since k^* is greater than k_{GR}, $f(k^*) + (k^* - k_{GR}) - nk_{GR}$ is even larger than $f(k_{GR}) - nk_{GR}$. The path of total consumption under this policy is shown by the circles in Figure 2.14. As the figure shows, this policy makes more resources available for consumption in every period than the policy of maintaining k at k^*. Given this, it must be possible for the planner to allocate consumption between the young and the old each period to make every generation better off.

Thus the equilibrium of the Diamond model can be Pareto-inefficient. This may seem puzzling: given that markets are competitive and there are no externalities, how can the usual result that equilibria are Pareto-efficient fail? The reason is that the standard result assumes not only competition and an absence of externalities, but also a finite number of agents. Specifically, the possibility of inefficiency in the Diamond model stems from the

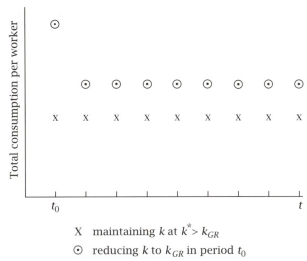

X   maintaining k at $k^* > k_{GR}$

⊙   reducing k to k_{GR} in period t_0

FIGURE 2.14   How reducing k to the golden-rule level affects the path of consumption per worker

fact that the infinity of generations gives the planner a means of providing for the consumption of the old that is not available to the market. If individuals in the market economy want to consume in old age, their only choice is to hold capital, even if its rate of return is low. The planner, however, need not have the consumption of the old determined by the capital stock and its rate of return. Instead, he or she can divide the resources available for consumption between the young and old in any manner. The planner can take, for example, 1 unit of labor income from each young person and transfer it to the old; since there are $1 + n$ young people for each old person, this increases the consumption of each old person by $1 + n$ units. The planner can prevent this change from making anyone worse off by requiring the next generation of young to do the same thing in the following period, and then continuing this process every period. If the marginal product of capital is less than n—that is, if the capital stock exceeds the golden-rule level—this way of transferring resources between youth and old age is more efficient than saving, and so the planner can improve on the decentralized allocation.

Because this type of inefficiency differs from conventional sources of inefficiency, and because it stems from the intertemporal structure of the economy, it is known as *dynamic inefficiency*.[29]

---

[29] Problem 2.19 investigates the sources of dynamic inefficiency further.

Empirical Application: Are Modern Economies Dynamically Efficient?

The Diamond model shows that it is possible for a decentralized economy to accumulate capital beyond the golden-rule level, and thus to produce an allocation that is Pareto-inefficient. Given that capital accumulation in actual economies is not dictated by social planners, this raises the issue of whether actual economies might be dynamically inefficient. If they were, there would be important implications for public policy: the great concern about low rates of saving would be entirely misplaced, and there would be an easy way of increasing both present and future consumption.

At first glance, dynamic inefficiency appears to be a possibility for the United States and other major economies. A balanced growth path is dynamically inefficient if the real rate of return, $f'(k^*) - \delta$, is less than the growth rate of the economy. A straightforward measure of the real rate of return is the real interest rate on short-term government debt. In the United States over the past 50 years, this interest rate has averaged only a few tenths of a percent; this is much less than the average growth rate of the economy, which is about 3 percent. Similar findings hold for other major industrialized countries. Thus the real interest rate is less than the golden-rule level, which suggests that these economies have overaccumulated capital.

There is a problem with this argument, however. In a world of certainty, all interest rates must be equal; thus there is no ambiguity in what is meant by "the" rate of return. But if there is uncertainty, different assets can have different expected returns. Suppose, for example, we assess dynamic efficiency by examining the marginal product of capital net of depreciation instead of the return on a fairly safe asset. If capital earns its marginal product, the net marginal product can be estimated as the ratio of overall capital income minus total depreciation to the value of the capital stock. For the United States, this ratio is about 10 percent, which is much greater than the economy's growth rate. Thus, using this approach, we would conclude that the U.S. economy is dynamically efficient. Our simple theoretical model, in which the marginal product of capital and the safe interest rate are the same, provides no guidance concerning which of these contradictory conclusions is correct.

Abel, Mankiw, Summers, and Zeckhauser (1989) tackle the issue of how to assess dynamic efficiency in a world of uncertainty. Their principal theoretical result is that under uncertainty, the condition for dynamic efficiency is that net capital income exceed investment. For the balanced growth path of an economy with certainty, this condition is the same as the usual comparison of the real interest rate with the economy's growth rate. In this case, net capital income is the real interest rate times the stock of capital, and investment is the growth rate of the economy times the stock of capital. Thus capital income exceeds investment if and only if the real interest rate exceeds the economy's growth rate. But Abel et al. show that under uncertainty these two conditions are not equivalent, and that it is the comparison of capital income and investment that provides the correct way of judging whether there is dynamic efficiency. Intuitively, a capital sector that is on net making resources available by producing more output than it is using for new investment is contributing to consumption, whereas one that is using more in resources than it is producing is not.

Abel et al.'s principal empirical result is that the condition for dynamic efficiency seems to be satisfied in practice. They measure capital income as national income minus employees' compensation and the part of the income of the self-employed that appears to represent labor income;[30] investment is taken directly from the national income accounts. They find that capital income consistently exceeds investment in the United States and in the six other major industrialized countries they consider. Even in Japan, where investment is remarkably high, the profit rate is so great that the returns to capital comfortably exceed investment. Thus, although decentralized economies can produce dynamically inefficient outcomes in principle, they do not appear to in practice.

2.12   Government in the Diamond Model

As in the infinite-horizon model, a natural question to ask of the Diamond model is what occurs if we introduce a government that makes purchases and levies taxes. For simplicity, we focus on the case of logarithmic utility and Cobb–Douglas production.

Let G_t denote the government's purchases of goods per unit of effective labor in period t. We again assume that it finances those purchases by lump-sum taxes on the young.

When the government finances its purchases entirely with taxes, workers' after-tax income in period t is $(1 - \alpha)k_t^\alpha - G_t$ rather than $(1 - \alpha)k_t^\alpha$. The equation of motion for k, equation (2.59), therefore becomes

$$k_{t+1} = \frac{1}{(1 + n)(1 + g)} \frac{1}{2 + \rho} [(1 - \alpha)k_t^\alpha - G_t]. \qquad (2.69)$$

A higher G_t therefore reduces k_{t+1} for a given k_t.

To see the effects of government purchases, suppose that the economy is on a balanced growth path with G constant, and that G increases permanently. From (2.69), this shifts the k_{t+1} function down; this is shown in Figure 2.15. The downward shift of the k_{t+1} function reduces k^*. Thus— in contrast to what occurs in the infinite-horizon model—higher government purchases lead to a lower capital stock and a higher equilibrium real

---

[30] They argue that adjusting these figures to account for land income and monopoly rents does not change the basic results.

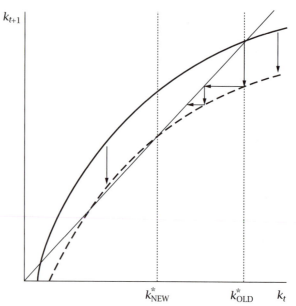

FIGURE 2.15   The effects of a permanent increase in government purchases

interest rate. Intuitively, since individuals live for two periods, they reduce their first-period consumption less than one-for-one with the increase in G. But since taxes are levied only in the first period of life, this means that their saving falls. As usual, the economy moves smoothly from the initial balanced growth path to the new one.

As a second example, consider a temporary increase in government purchases from G_L to G_H, again with the economy initially on its balanced growth path. The dynamics of k are thus described by (2.69) with $G = G_H$ during the period that government purchases are high and by (2.69) with $G = G_L$ before and after. That is, the fact that individuals know that government purchases will return to G_L does not affect the behavior of the economy during the time that purchases are high. The saving of the young—and hence next period's capital stock—is determined by their after-tax labor income, which is determined by the current capital stock and by the government's current purchases. Thus during the time that government purchases are high, k gradually falls and r gradually increases. Once G returns to G_L, k rises gradually back to its initial level.[31]

---

[31] The result that future values of G do not affect the current behavior of the economy does not depend on the assumption of logarithmic utility. Without logarithmic utility, the saving of the current period's young depends on the rate of return as well as on after-tax labor income. But the rate of return is determined by the next period's capital-labor ratio, which is not affected by government purchases in that period.

Problems

2.1. Consider N firms each with the constant-returns-to-scale production function $Y = F(K, AL)$, or (using the intensive form) $Y = ALf(k)$. Assume $f'(\bullet) > 0, f''(\bullet) < 0$. Assume that all firms can hire labor at wage wA and rent capital at cost r, and that all firms have the same value of A.

    (a) Consider the problem of a firm trying to produce Y units of output at minimum cost. Show that the cost-minimizing level of k is uniquely defined and is independent of Y, and that all firms therefore choose the same value of k.

    (b) Show that the total output of the N cost-minimizing firms equals the output that a single firm with the same production function has if it uses all the labor and capital used by the N firms.

2.2. The elasticity of substitution with constant-relative-risk-aversion utility. Consider an individual who lives for two periods and whose utility is given by equation (2.42). Let P_1 and P_2 denote the prices of consumption in the two periods, and let W denote the value of the individual's lifetime income; thus the budget constraint is $P_1 C_1 + P_2 C_2 = W$.

    (a) What are the individual's utility-maximizing choices of C_1 and C_2, given P_1, P_2, and W?

    (b) The elasticity of substitution between consumption in the two periods is $-[(P_1/P_2)/(C_1/C_2)][\partial(C_1/C_2)/\partial(P_1/P_2)]$, or $-\partial\ln(C_1/C_2)/\partial\ln(P_1/P_2)$. Show that with the utility function (2.42), the elasticity of substitution between C_1 and C_2 is $1/\theta$.

2.3. (a) Suppose it is known in advance that at some time t_0 the government will confiscate half of whatever wealth each household holds at that time. Does consumption change discontinuously at time t_0? If so, why (and what is the condition relating consumption immediately before t_0 to consumption immediately after)? If not, why not?

    (b) Suppose it is known in advance that at t_0 the government will confiscate from each household an amount of wealth equal to half of the wealth of the average household at that time. Does consumption change discontinuously at time t_0? If so, why (and what is the condition relating consumption immediately before t_0 to consumption immediately after)? If not, why not?

2.4. Assume that the instantaneous utility function $u(C)$ in equation (2.1) is $\ln C$. Consider the problem of a household maximizing (2.1) subject to (2.6). Find an expression for C at each time as a function of initial wealth plus the present value of labor income, the path of $r(t)$, and the parameters of the utility function.

2.5. Consider a household with utility given by (2.1)–(2.2). Assume that the real interest rate is constant, and let W denote the household's initial wealth plus the present value of its lifetime labor income (the right-hand side of [2.6]). Find the utility-maximizing path of C, given r, W, and the parameters of the utility function.

2.6. The productivity slowdown and saving. Consider a Ramsey–Cass–Koopmans economy that is on its balanced growth path, and suppose there is a permanent fall in g.

(a) How, if at all, does this affect the $\dot{k} = 0$ curve?

(b) How, if at all, does this affect the $\dot{c} = 0$ curve?

(c) What happens to c at the time of the change?

(d) Find an expression for the impact of a marginal change in g on the fraction of output that is saved on the balanced growth path. Can one tell whether this expression is positive or negative?

(e) For the case where the production function is Cobb–Douglas, $f(k) = k^{\alpha}$, rewrite your answer to part (d) in terms of ρ, n, g, θ, and α. (Hint: Use the fact that $f'(k^*) = \rho + \theta g$.)

2.7. Describe how each of the following affects the $\dot{c} = 0$ and $\dot{k} = 0$ curves in Figure 2.5, and thus how they affect the balanced-growth-path values of c and k:

(a) A rise in θ.

(b) A downward shift of the production function.

(c) A change in the rate of depreciation from the value of zero assumed in the text to some positive level.

2.8. Derive an expression analogous to (2.38) for the case of a positive depreciation rate.

2.9. Capital taxation in the Ramsey–Cass–Koopmans model. Consider a Ramsey–Cass–Koopmans economy that is on its balanced growth path. Suppose that at some time, which we will call time 0, the government switches to a policy of taxing investment income at rate τ. Thus the real interest rate that households face is now given by $r(t) = (1 - \tau)f'(k(t))$. Assume that the government returns the revenue it collects from this tax through lump-sum transfers. Finally, assume that this change in tax policy is unanticipated.

(a) How does the tax affect the $\dot{c} = 0$ locus? The $\dot{k} = 0$ locus?

(b) How does the economy respond to the adoption of the tax at time 0? What are the dynamics after time 0?

(c) How do the values of c and k on the new balanced growth path compare with their values on the old balanced growth path?

(d) (This is based on Barro, Mankiw, and Sala-i-Martin, 1995.) Suppose there are many economies like this one. Workers' preferences are the same in each country, but the tax rates on investment income may vary across countries. Assume that each country is on its balanced growth path.

    (i) Show that the saving rate on the balanced growth path, $(y^* - c^*)/y^*$, is decreasing in τ.

    (ii) Do citizens in low-τ, high-k^*, high-saving countries have any incentive to invest in low-saving countries? Why or why not?

(e) Does your answer to part (c) imply that a policy of *subsidizing* investment (that is, making $\tau < 0$), and raising the revenue for this subsidy through lump-sum taxes, increases welfare? Why or why not?

(f) How, if at all, do the answers to parts (a) and (b) change if the government does not rebate the revenue from the tax but instead uses it to make government purchases?

2.10. Using the phase diagram to analyze the impact of an anticipated change. Consider the policy described in Problem 2.9, but suppose that instead of announcing and implementing the tax at time 0, the government announces at time 0 that at some later time, time t_1, investment income will begin to be taxed at rate τ.

(a) Draw the phase diagram showing the dynamics of c and k after time t_1.

(b) Can c change discontinuously at time t_1? Why or why not?

(c) Draw the phase diagram showing the dynamics of c and k before t_1.

(d) In light of your answers to parts (a), (b), and (c), what must c do at time 0?

(e) Summarize your results by sketching the paths of c and k as functions of time.

2.11. Using the phase diagram to analyze the impact of unanticipated and anticipated temporary changes. Analyze the following two variations on Problem 2.10:

(a) At time 0, the government announces that it will tax investment income at rate τ from time 0 until some later date t_1; thereafter investment income will again be untaxed.

(b) At time 0, the government announces that from time t_1 to some later time t_2, it will tax investment income at rate τ; before t_1 and after t_2, investment income will not be taxed.

2.12. The analysis of government policies in the Ramsey–Cass–Koopmans model in the text assumes that government purchases do not affect utility from private consumption. The opposite extreme is that government purchases and private consumption are perfect substitutes. Specifically, suppose that the utility function (2.12) is modified to be

$$U = B \int_{t=0}^{\infty} e^{-\beta t} \frac{[c(t) + G(t)]^{1-\theta}}{1 - \theta} \, dt.$$

If the economy is initially on its balanced growth path and if households' preferences are given by U, what are the effects of a temporary increase in government purchases on the paths of consumption, capital, and the interest rate?

2.13. Consider the Diamond model with logarithmic utility and Cobb–Douglas production. Describe how each of the following affects k_{t+1} as a function of k_t:

(a) A rise in n.

(b) A downward shift of the production function (that is, $f(k)$ takes the form Bk^α, and B falls).

(c) A rise in α.

2.14. **A discrete-time version of the Solow model.** Suppose $Y_t = F(K_t, A_t L_t)$, with $F(\bullet)$ having constant returns to scale and the intensive form of the production function satisfying the Inada conditions. Suppose also that $A_{t+1} = (1+g)A_t$, $L_{t+1} = (1+n)L_t$, and $K_{t+1} = K_t + sY_t - \delta K_t$.

(a) Find an expression for k_{t+1} as a function of k_t.

(b) Sketch k_{t+1} as a function of k_t. Does the economy have a balanced growth path? If the initial level of k differs from the value on the balanced growth path, does the economy converge to the balanced growth path?

(c) Find an expression for consumption per unit of effective labor on the balanced growth path as a function of the balanced-growth-path value of k. What is the marginal product of capital, $f'(k)$, when k maximizes consumption per unit of effective labor on the balanced growth path?

(d) Assume that the production function is Cobb–Douglas.

   (i) What is k_{t+1} as a function of k_t?

   (ii) What is k^*, the value of k on the balanced growth path?

   (iii) Along the lines of equations (2.63)–(2.65), in the text, linearize the expression in subpart (i) around $k_t = k^*$, and find the rate of convergence of k to k^*.

2.15. **Depreciation in the Diamond model and microeconomic foundations for the Solow model.** Suppose that in the Diamond model capital depreciates at rate δ, so that $r_t = f'(k_t) - \delta$.

(a) How, if at all, does this change in the model affect equation (2.58) giving k_{t+1} as a function of k_t?

(b) In the special case of logarithmic utility, Cobb–Douglas production, and $\delta = 1$, what is the equation for k_{t+1} as a function of k_t? Compare this with the analogous expression for the discrete-time version of the Solow model with $\delta = 1$ from part (a) of Problem 2.14.

2.16. **Social security in the Diamond model.** Consider a Diamond economy where g is zero, production is Cobb–Douglas, and utility is logarithmic.

(a) **Pay-as-you-go social security.** Suppose the government taxes each young individual an amount T and uses the proceeds to pay benefits to old individuals; thus each old person receives $(1+n)T$.

   (i) How, if at all, does this change affect equation (2.59) giving k_{t+1} as a function of k_t?

   (ii) How, if at all, does this change affect the balanced-growth-path value of k?

   (iii) If the economy is initially on a balanced growth path that is dynamically efficient, how does a marginal increase in T affect the welfare of current and future generations? What happens if the initial balanced growth path is dynamically inefficient?

(b) **Fully funded social security.** Suppose the government taxes each young person an amount T and uses the proceeds to purchase capital. Individuals born at t therefore receive $(1 + r_{t+1})T$ when they are old.

    (i) How, if at all, does this change affect equation (2.59) giving k_{t+1} as a function of k_t?

    (ii) How, if at all, does this change affect the balanced-growth-path value of k?

2.17. The basic overlapping-generations model. (This follows Samuelson, 1958, and Allais, 1947.) Suppose, as in the Diamond model, that L_t two-period-lived individuals are born in period t and that $L_t = (1 + n)L_{t-1}$. For simplicity, let utility be logarithmic with no discounting: $U_t = \ln(C_{1t}) + \ln(C_{2t+1})$.

The production side of the economy is simpler than in the Diamond model. Each individual born at time t is endowed with A units of the economy's single good. The good can be either consumed or stored. Each unit stored yields $x > 0$ units of the good in the following period.[32]

Finally, assume that in the initial period, period 0, in addition to the L_0 young individuals each endowed with A units of the good, there are $[1/(1 + n)]L_0$ individuals who are alive only in period 0. Each of these "old" individuals is endowed with some amount Z of the good; their utility is simply their consumption in the initial period, C_{20}.

(a) Describe the decentralized equilibrium of this economy. (Hint: Given the overlapping-generations structure, will the members of any generation engage in transactions with members of another generation?)

(b) Consider paths where the fraction of agents' endowments that is stored, f_t, is constant over time. What is total consumption (that is, consumption of all the young plus consumption of all the old) per person on such a path as a function of f? If $x < 1 + n$, what value of f satisfying $0 \le f \le 1$ maximizes consumption per person? Is the decentralized equilibrium Pareto-efficient in this case? If not, how can a social planner raise welfare?

2.18. Stationary monetary equilibria in the Samuelson overlapping-generations model. (Again this follows Samuelson, 1958.) Consider the setup described in Problem 2.17. Assume that $x < 1 + n$. Suppose that the old individuals in period 0, in addition to being endowed with Z units of the good, are each endowed with M units of a storable, divisible commodity, which we will call money. Money is not a source of utility.

(a) Consider an individual born at t. Suppose the price of the good in units of money is P_t in t and P_{t+1} in $t + 1$. Thus the individual can sell units of endowment for P_t units of money and then use that money to buy P_t/P_{t+1} units of the next generation's endowment the following period. What is the individual's behavior as a function of P_t/P_{t+1}?

---

[32] Note that this is the same as the Diamond economy with $g = 0$, $F(K_t, AL_t) = AL_t + xK_t$, and $\delta = 1$. With this production function, since individuals supply 1 unit of labor when they are young, an individual born in t obtains A units of the good. And each unit saved yields $1 + r = 1 + \partial F(K, AL)/\partial K - \delta = 1 + x - 1 = x$ units of second-period consumption.

(b) Show that there is an equilibrium with $P_{t+1} = P_t/(1 + n)$ for all $t \geq 0$ and no storage, and thus that the presence of "money" allows the economy to reach the golden-rule level of storage.

(c) Show that there are also equilibria with $P_{t+1} = P_t/x$ for all $t \geq 0$.

(d) Finally, explain why $P_t = \infty$ for all t (that is, money is worthless) is also an equilibrium. Explain why this is the *only* equilibrium if the economy ends at some date, as in Problem 2.19(b) below. (Hint: Reason backward from the last period.)

2.19. The source of dynamic inefficiency. There are two ways in which the Diamond and Samuelson models differ from textbook models. First, markets are incomplete: because individuals cannot trade with individuals who have not been born, some possible transactions are ruled out. Second, because time goes on forever, there are an infinite number of agents. This problem asks you to investigate which of these is the source of the possibility of dynamic inefficiency. For simplicity, it focuses on the Samuelson overlapping-generations model (see the previous two problems), again with log utility and no discounting. To simplify further, it assumes $n = 0$ and $0 < x < 1$. The basic issues, however, are general.

(a) **Incomplete markets.** Suppose we eliminate incomplete markets from the model by allowing all agents to trade in a competitive market "before" the beginning of time. That is, a Walrasian auctioneer calls out prices $Q_0, Q_1, Q_2, \ldots$ for the good at each date. Individuals can then make sales and purchases at these prices given their endowments and their ability to store. The budget constraint of an individual born at t is thus $Q_t C_{1t} + Q_{t+1} C_{2t+1} = Q_t(A - S_t) + Q_{t+1}x S_t$, where S_t (which must satisfy $0 \leq S_t \leq A$) is the amount the individual stores.

  (i) Suppose the auctioneer announces $Q_{t+1} = Q_t/x$ for all $t > 0$. Show that in this case individuals are indifferent concerning how much to store, that there is a set of storage decisions such that markets clear at every date, and that this equilibrium is the same as the equilibrium described in part (a) of Problem 2.17.

  (ii) Suppose the auctioneer announces prices that fail to satisfy $Q_{t+1} = Q_t/x$ at some date. Show that at the first date that does not satisfy this condition the market for the good cannot clear, and thus that the proposed price path cannot be an equilibrium.

(b) **Infinite duration.** Suppose that the economy ends at some date T. That is, suppose the individuals born at T live only one period (and hence seek to maximize C_{1T}), and that thereafter no individuals are born. Show that the decentralized equilibrium is Pareto-efficient.

(c) In light of these answers, is it incomplete markets or infinite duration that is the source of dynamic inefficiency?

2.20. Explosive paths in the Samuelson overlapping-generations model. (Black, 1974; Brock, 1975; Calvo, 1978a.) Consider the setup described in Problem 2.18. Assume that x is zero, and assume that utility is constant-relative-risk-aversion with $\theta < 1$ rather than logarithmic. Finally, assume for simplicity that $n = 0$.

(*a*) What is the behavior of an individual born at t as a function of P_t/P_{t+1}? Show that the amount of his or her endowment that the individual sells for money is an increasing function of P_t/P_{t+1} and approaches zero as this ratio approaches zero.

(*b*) Suppose $P_0/P_1 < 1$. How much of the good are the individuals born in period 0 planning to buy in period 1 from the individuals born then? What must P_1/P_2 be for the individuals born in period 1 to want to supply this amount?

(*c*) Iterating this reasoning forward, what is the qualitative behavior of P_t/P_{t+1} over time? Does this represent an equilibrium path for the economy?

(*d*) Can there be an equilibrium path with $P_0/P_1 > 1$?

Chapter 3
NEW GROWTH THEORY

The models we have seen so far do not provide satisfying answers to our central questions about economic growth. The models' principal result is a negative one: if capital's earnings reflect its contribution to output and if its share in total income is modest, then capital accumulation cannot account for a large part of either long-run growth or cross-country income differences. And the only determinant of income in the models other than capital is a mystery variable, the "effectiveness of labor" (A), whose exact meaning is not specified and whose behavior is taken as exogenous.

This chapter therefore investigates the fundamental questions of growth theory more deeply. The first part of the chapter examines the accumulation of knowledge. One can think of the models we will consider there as elaborations of the Solow model and the models of Chapter 2. They treat capital accumulation and its role in production in ways that are similar to those earlier models. But they differ from the earlier models in explicitly interpreting the effectiveness of labor as knowledge and in formally modeling its evolution over time. We will analyze the dynamics of the economy when knowledge accumulation is endogenous and consider various views concerning how knowledge is produced and what determines the allocation of resources to knowledge production.

The conclusions of the first part of the chapter are mixed: we will see that knowledge accumulation is probably central to worldwide growth, but probably not central to cross-country income differences. The second part of the chapter therefore focuses on these differences. It begins by considering human as well as physical capital. But we will see that the evidence suggests that much of the variation in income across countries comes from differences in output for given amounts of physical and human capital. We will therefore go on to investigate how variations in institutions can cause such differences and discuss some hypotheses about the reasons for such institutional variations. The chapter concludes by applying the analysis to cross-country differences in income growth rather than income levels.

Part A Research and Development Models

3.1 Framework and Assumptions

Overview

The view of growth that is most in keeping with the models we have seen is that the effectiveness of labor represents knowledge or technology. Certainly it is plausible that technological progress is the reason that more output can be produced today from a given quantity of capital and labor than could be produced a century or two ago. The natural extension of Chapters 1 and 2 is thus to model the growth of A rather than to take it as given.

To do this, we need to introduce an explicit *research and development* (or *R&D*) sector and then model the production of new technologies. We also need to model the allocation of resources between conventional goods production and R&D.

In our formal modeling, we will take a fairly mechanical view of the production of new technologies. Specifically, we will assume a largely conventional production function in which labor, capital, and technology are combined to produce improvements in technology in a deterministic way. Of course, this is not a complete description of technological progress. But it is reasonable to think that, all else equal, devoting more resources to research yields more discoveries; this is what the production function captures. Since we are interested in growth over extended periods, modeling the randomness in technological progress would give little additional insight. And if we want to analyze the consequences of changes in other determinants of the success of R&D, we can introduce a shift parameter in the knowledge production function and examine the effects of changes in that parameter. The model provides no insight, however, concerning what those other determinants of the success of research activity are.

We make two other major simplifications. First, both the R&D and goods production functions are assumed to be generalized Cobb–Douglas functions; that is, they are power functions, but the sum of the exponents on the inputs is not necessarily restricted to 1. Second, in the spirit of the Solow model, the model takes the fraction of output saved and the fractions of the labor force and the capital stock used in the R&D sector as exogenous and constant. These assumptions do not change the model's main implications.

Specifics

The specific model we consider is a simplified version of the models of R&D and growth developed by P. Romer (1990), Grossman and Helpman (1991a), and Aghion and Howitt (1992).[1] The model, like the others we have studied, involves four variables: labor (L), capital (K), technology (A), and output (Y). The model is set in continuous time. There are two sectors, a goods-producing sector where output is produced and an R&D sector where additions to the stock of knowledge are made. Fraction a_L of the labor force is used in the R&D sector and fraction $1 - a_L$ in the goods-producing sector. Similarly, fraction a_K of the capital stock is used in R&D and the rest in goods production. Both a_L and a_K are exogenous and constant. Because the use of an idea or a piece of knowledge in one place does not prevent it from being used elsewhere, both sectors use the full stock of knowledge, A.

The quantity of output produced at time t is thus

$$Y(t) = [(1 - a_K)K(t)]^\alpha [A(t)(1 - a_L)L(t)]^{1-\alpha}, \qquad 0 < \alpha < 1. \qquad (3.1)$$

Aside from the $1 - a_K$ and $1 - a_L$ terms and the restriction to the Cobb–Douglas functional form, this production function is identical to those of our earlier models. Note that equation (3.1) implies constant returns to capital and labor: with a given technology, doubling the inputs doubles the amount that can be produced.

The production of new ideas depends on the quantities of capital and labor engaged in research and on the level of technology. Given our assumption of generalized Cobb–Douglas production, we therefore write

$$\dot{A}(t) = B[a_K K(t)]^\beta [a_L L(t)]^\gamma A(t)^\theta, \qquad B > 0, \qquad \beta \geq 0, \qquad \gamma \geq 0, \qquad (3.2)$$

where B is a shift parameter.

Notice that the production function for knowledge is not assumed to have constant returns to scale to capital and labor. The standard argument that there must be at least constant returns is a replication one: if the inputs double, the new inputs can do exactly what the old ones were doing, thereby doubling the amount produced. But in the case of knowledge production, exactly replicating what the existing inputs were doing would cause the same set of discoveries to be made twice, thereby leaving $\dot{A}$ unchanged. Thus it is possible that there are diminishing returns in R&D. At the same time, interactions among researchers, fixed setup costs, and so on may be important enough in R&D that doubling capital and labor more than doubles output. We therefore also allow for the possibility of increasing returns.

The parameter θ reflects the effect of the existing stock of knowledge on the success of R&D. This effect can operate in either direction. On the one hand, past discoveries may provide ideas and tools that make future discoveries easier. In this case, θ is positive. On the other hand, the easiest

---

[1] See also Uzawa (1965); Shell (1966, 1967); and Phelps (1966b).

discoveries may be made first. In this case, it is harder to make new discoveries when the stock of knowledge is greater; thus θ is negative. Because of these conflicting effects, no restriction is placed on θ in (3.2).

As in the Solow model, the saving rate is exogenous and constant. In addition, depreciation is set to zero for simplicity. Thus,

$$\dot{K}(t) = sY(t). \tag{3.3}$$

Finally, we continue to treat population growth as exogenous. For simplicity, we do not consider the possibility that it is negative. Thus,

$$\dot{L}(t) = nL(t), \qquad n \ge 0. \tag{3.4}$$

This completes the description of the model.[2]

Because the model has two stock variables whose behavior is endogenous, K and A, it is more complicated to analyze than the Solow model. We therefore begin by considering the model without capital; that is, we set α and β to zero. This case shows most of the model's central messages. We then turn to the general case.

3.2   The Model without Capital

The Dynamics of Knowledge Accumulation

When there is no capital in the model, the production function for output (equation [3.1]) becomes

$$Y(t) = A(t)(1 - a_L)L(t). \tag{3.5}$$

Similarly, the production function for new knowledge (equation [3.2]) is now

$$\dot{A}(t) = B[a_L L(t)]^\gamma A(t)^\theta. \tag{3.6}$$

Population growth continues to be described by equation (3.4).

Equation (3.5) implies that output per worker is proportional to A, and thus that the growth rate of output per worker equals the growth rate of A. We therefore focus on the dynamics of A, which are given by (3.6). This equation implies that the growth rate of A, denoted g_A, is

$$g_A(t) \equiv \frac{\dot{A}(t)}{A(t)} \tag{3.7}$$

$$= B a_L^\gamma L(t)^\gamma A(t)^{\theta-1}.$$

---

[2] The model contains the Solow model with Cobb-Douglas production as a special case: if β, γ, a_K, and a_L are all 0 and θ is 1, the production function for knowledge becomes $\dot{A} = BA$ (which implies that A grows at a constant rate), and the other equations of the model simplify to the corresponding equations of the Solow model.

Taking logs of both sides of (3.7) and differentiating the two sides with respect to time gives us an expression for the *growth rate* of g_A (that is, for the growth rate of the growth rate of A)

growth rate of the growth rate

$$\frac{\dot{g}_A(t)}{g_A(t)} = \gamma n + (\theta - 1)g_A(t). \tag{3.8}$$

Multiplying both sides of this expression by $g_A(t)$ yields

$$\dot{g}_A(t) = \gamma n g_A(t) + (\theta - 1)[g_A(t)]^2. \tag{3.9}$$ *see notes*

The initial values of L and A and the parameters of the model determine the initial value of g_A (by [3.7]). Equation (3.9) then determines the subsequent behavior of g_A.

To describe further how the growth rate of A behaves (and thus to characterize the behavior of output per worker), we must distinguish among the cases $\theta < 1$, $\theta > 1$, and $\theta = 1$. We discuss each in turn.

Case 1: $\theta < 1$

Figure 3.1 shows the phase diagram for g_A when θ is less than 1. That is, it plots $\dot{g}_A$ as a function of A for this case. Because the production function for knowledge, (3.6), implies that g_A is always positive, the diagram considers only positive values of g_A. As the diagram shows, equation (3.9) implies that for the case of θ less than 1, $\dot{g}_A$ is positive for small positive values of g_A and negative for large values. We will use g_A^* to denote the unique positive value of g_A that implies that $\dot{g}_A$ is zero. From (3.9), g_A^* is defined

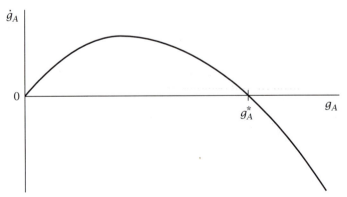

FIGURE 3.1   The dynamics of the growth rate of knowledge when $\theta < 1$

by $yn + (\theta - 1)g_A^* = 0$. Solving this for g_A^* yields

$$g_A^* = \frac{y}{1 - \theta}n. \tag{3.10}$$

This analysis implies that regardless of the economy's initial conditions, g_A converges to g_A^*. If the parameter values and the initial values of L and A imply $g_A(0) < g_A^*$, for example, $\dot{g}_A$ is positive; that is, g_A is rising. It continues to rise until it reaches g_A^*. Similarly, if $g_A(0) > 0$, then g_A falls until it reaches g_A^*. Once g_A reaches g_A^*, both A and Y/L grow steadily at rate g_A^*. Thus the economy is on a balanced growth path.

This model is our first example of a model of *endogenous growth*. In this model, in contrast to the Solow, Ramsey, and Diamond models, the long-run growth rate of output per worker is determined within the model rather than by an exogenous rate of technological progress.

The model implies that the long-run growth rate of output per worker, g_A^*, is an increasing function of the rate of population growth, n. Indeed, positive population growth is necessary for sustained growth of output per worker. This may seem troubling; for example, the growth rate of output per worker is not on average higher in countries with faster population growth.

If we think of the model as one of *worldwide* economic growth, however, this result is reasonable. A natural interpretation of the model is that A represents knowledge that can be used anywhere in the world. With this interpretation, the model does not imply that countries with greater population growth enjoy greater income growth, only that higher worldwide population growth raises worldwide income growth. And it is plausible that, at least up to the point where resource limitations (which are omitted from the model) become important, higher population is beneficial to the growth of worldwide knowledge: the larger the population is, the more people there are to make new discoveries. Recall from the equation for knowledge production, (3.6), that $\theta < 1$ corresponds to the case where knowledge may be helpful in generating new knowledge, but where it is not so helpful that the generation of new knowledge rises more than proportionally with the existing stock. What the result about the necessity of positive population growth to sustained growth of output per worker is telling us is that in this case, growth would taper off in the absence of population growth.

Equation (3.10) also implies that although the rate of population growth affects long-run growth, the fraction of the labor force engaged in R&D (a_L) does not. This too may seem surprising: since growth is driven by technological progress and technological progress is endogenous, it is natural to expect an increase in the fraction of the economy's resources devoted to technological progress to increase long-run growth. The reason that this does not occur is that, because θ is less than 1, the increase in a_L has a level effect but not a growth effect on the path of A. Equation (3.7) implies that the increase in a_L causes an immediate increase in g_A. But as the phase diagram shows, because of the limited contribution of the additional

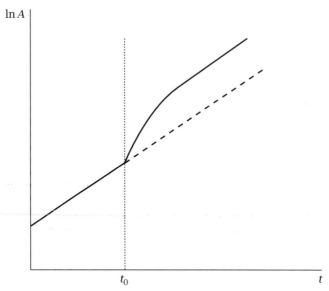

FIGURE 3.2   The impact of a rise in the fraction of the labor force engaged in R&D when $\theta < 1$

knowledge to the production of new knowledge, this increase in the growth rate of knowledge is not sustained. Thus, paralleling the impact of a rise in the saving rate on the path of output in the Solow model, the increase in a_L results in a rise in g_A followed by a gradual return to its initial level; the level of A therefore moves gradually to a parallel path higher than its initial one. This is shown in Figure 3.2.[3]

Case 2: $\theta > 1$

The second case to consider is θ greater than 1. This corresponds to the case where the production of new knowledge rises more than proportionally with the existing stock. Recall from equation (3.9) that $\dot{g}_A = \gamma n g_A + (\theta - 1)g_A^2$. When θ exceeds 1, this equation implies that $\dot{g}_A$ is positive for all possible values of g_A. Further, it implies that $\dot{g}_A$ is increasing in g_A (since g_A must be positive). The phase diagram is shown in Figure 3.3.

The implications of this case for long-run growth are very different from those of the previous case. As the phase diagram shows, the economy exhibits ever-increasing growth rather than convergence to a balanced growth path. Intuitively, here knowledge is so useful in the production of new knowledge that each marginal increase in its level results in so much more new knowledge that the growth rate of knowledge rises rather than falls. Thus once the accumulation of knowledge begins—which it necessarily does in the model—the economy embarks on a path of ever-increasing growth.

---

[3] See Problem 3.1 for an analysis of how the change in a_L affects the path of output.

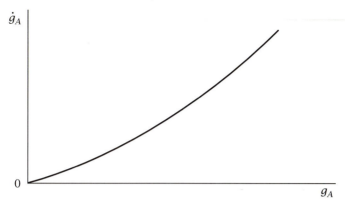

FIGURE 3.3 **The dynamics of the growth rate of knowledge when** $\theta > 1$

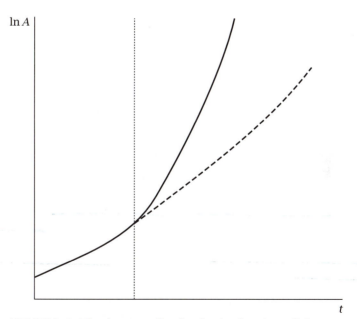

FIGURE 3.4 **The impact of a rise in the fraction of the labor force engaged in R&D when** $\theta > 1$

The impact of an increase in the fraction of the labor force engaged in R&D is now dramatic. From Equation (3.7), an increase in a_L causes an immediate increase in g_A, as before. But $\dot{g}_A$ is an increasing function of g_A; thus $\dot{g}_A$ rises as well. And the more rapidly g_A rises, the more rapidly its growth rate rises. Thus the increase in a_L leads to an ever-widening gap between the new path of A and the path it would have followed otherwise. This is depicted in Figure 3.4.

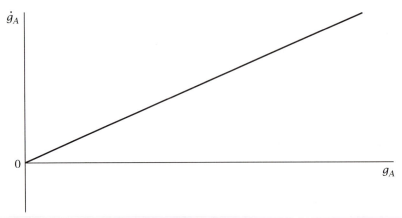

FIGURE 3.5   The dynamics of the growth rate of knowledge when $\theta = 1$ and $n > 0$

Case 3: $\theta = 1$

When θ is exactly equal to 1, existing knowledge is just productive enough in generating new knowledge that the production of new knowledge is proportional to the stock. In this case, expressions (3.7) and (3.9) for g_A and $\dot{g}_A$ simplify to

$$g_A(t) = Ba_L^{\gamma}L(t)^{\gamma},\tag{3.11}$$

$$\dot{g}_A(t) = \gamma n g_A(t).\tag{3.12}$$

If population growth is positive, g_A is growing over time; in this case the dynamics of the model are similar to those when $\theta > 1$. Figure 3.5 shows the phase diagram for this case.[4]

If population growth is zero (or if γ is zero), g_A is constant regardless of its initial situation. Thus there is no adjustment toward a balanced growth path: no matter where it begins, the economy immediately exhibits steady growth. As equations (3.5) and (3.11) show, the growth rates of knowledge, output, and output per worker are all equal to $Ba_L^{\gamma}L^{\gamma}$ in this case. Thus in this case a_L affects the long-run growth rate of the economy.

Since the output good in this economy has no use other than in consumption, it is natural to think of it as being entirely consumed. Thus $1 - a_L$ is

---

[4] In the cases of $\theta > 1$ and of $\theta = 1$ and $n > 0$, the model implies not merely that growth is increasing, but that it rises so fast that output reaches infinity in a finite amount of time. Consider, for example, the case of $\theta > 1$ with $n = 0$. One can check that $A(t) = c_1/(c_2 - t)^{1/(\theta-1)}$, with $c_1 = 1/[(\theta - 1)Ba_L^{\gamma}L^{\gamma}]^{1/(\theta-1)}$ and c_2 chosen so that $A(0)$ equals the initial value of A, satisfies (3.6). Thus A explodes at time c_2. Since output cannot reach infinity in a finite time, this implies that the model must break down at some point. But it does not mean that it cannot provide a good description over the relevant range. Indeed, Section 3.7 presents evidence that a model similar to this one provides a good approximation to historical data over many thousands of years.

the fraction of society's resources devoted to producing goods for current consumption, and a_L is the fraction devoted to producing a good (namely, knowledge) that is useful for producing output in the future. Thus one can think of a_L as a measure of the saving rate in this economy.

With this interpretation, this case of the model provides a simple example of a model where the saving rate affects long-run growth. Models of this form are known as *linear growth models;* for reasons that will become clear in Section 3.4, they are also known as *Y = AK models.* Because of their simplicity, linear growth models have received a great deal of attention in work on endogenous growth.

The Importance of Returns to Scale to Produced Factors

The reason that these three cases have such different implications is that whether θ is less than, greater than, or equal to 1 determines whether there are decreasing, increasing, or constant returns to scale to *produced* factors of production. The growth of labor is exogenous, and we have eliminated capital from the model; thus knowledge is the only produced factor. There are constant returns to knowledge in goods production. Thus whether there are on the whole increasing, decreasing, or constant returns to knowledge in this economy is determined by the returns to scale to knowledge in knowledge production—that is, by θ.

To see why the returns to the produced input are critical to the behavior of the economy, suppose that the economy is on some path, and suppose there is an exogenous increase in A of 1 percent. If θ is exactly equal to 1, $\dot{A}$ grows by 1 percent as well: knowledge is just productive enough in the production of new knowledge that the increase in A is self-sustaining. Thus the jump in A has no effect on its growth rate. If θ exceeds 1, the 1 percent increase in A causes more than a 1 percent increase in $\dot{A}$. Thus in this case the increase in A raises the growth rate of A. Finally, if θ is less than 1, the 1 percent increase in A results in an increase of less than 1 percent in $\dot{A}$, and so the growth rate of knowledge falls.

3.3 The General Case

We now want to reintroduce capital into the model and determine how this modifies the earlier analysis. Thus the model is now described by equations (3.1)–(3.4) rather than by (3.4)–(3.6).

The Dynamics of Knowledge and Capital

As mentioned above, when the model includes capital, there are two endogenous stock variables, A and K. Paralleling our analysis of the simple model, we focus on the dynamics of the growth rates of A and K. Substituting the production function, (3.1), into the expression for capital accumulation, (3.3), yields

$$\dot{K}(t) = s(1 - a_K)^\alpha (1 - a_L)^{1-\alpha} K(t)^\alpha A(t)^{1-\alpha} L(t)^{1-\alpha}. \qquad (3.13)$$

Dividing both sides by $K(t)$ and defining $c_K = s(1 - a_K)^\alpha (1 - a_L)^{1-\alpha}$ gives us

$$g_K(t) \equiv \frac{\dot{K}(t)}{K(t)}$$

$$= c_K \left[\frac{A(t)L(t)}{K(t)} \right]^{1-\alpha}. \qquad (3.14)$$

Taking logs of both sides and differentiating with respect to time yields

$$\frac{\dot{g}_K(t)}{g_K(t)} = (1 - \alpha)[g_A(t) + n - g_K(t)]. \qquad (3.15)$$

From (3.13), g_K is always positive. Thus g_K is rising if $g_A + n - g_K$ is positive, falling if this expression is negative, and constant if it is zero. This information is summarized in Figure 3.6. In (g_A, g_K) space, the locus of points where g_K is constant has an intercept of n and a slope of 1. Above the locus, g_K is falling; below the locus, it is rising.

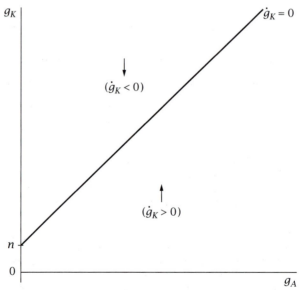

FIGURE 3.6   **The dynamics of the growth rate of capital in the general version of the model**

Similarly, dividing both sides of equation (3.2), $\dot{A} = B(a_K K)^\beta (a_L L)^\gamma A^\theta$, by A yields an expression for the growth rate of A:

$$g_A(t) = c_A K(t)^\beta L(t)^\gamma A(t)^{\theta-1}, \tag{3.16}$$

where $c_A \equiv B a_K^\beta a_L^\gamma$. Aside from the presence of the K^β term, this is essentially the same as equation (3.7) in the simple version of the model. Taking logs and differentiating with respect to time gives

$$\frac{\dot{g}_A(t)}{g_A(t)} = \beta g_K(t) + \gamma n + (\theta - 1) g_A(t). \tag{3.17}$$

Thus g_A is rising if $\beta g_K + \gamma n + (\theta - 1) g_A$ is positive, falling if it is negative, and constant if it is zero. This is shown in Figure 3.7. The set of points where g_A is constant has an intercept of $-\gamma n/\beta$ and a slope of $(1 - \theta)/\beta$ (the figure is drawn for the case of $\theta < 1$, so this slope is shown as positive). Above this locus, g_A is rising; and below the locus, it is falling.

The production function for output (equation [3.1]) exhibits constant returns to scale in the two produced factors of production, capital and knowledge. Thus whether there are on net increasing, decreasing, or constant returns to scale to the produced factors depends on their returns to scale in the production function for knowledge, equation (3.2). As that equation shows, the degree of returns to scale to K and A in knowledge production is $\beta + \theta$: increasing both K and A by a factor of X increases $\dot{A}$ by a factor of

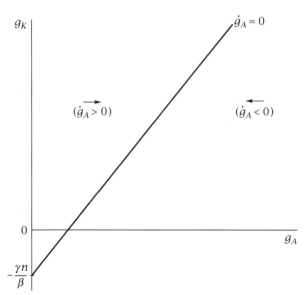

FIGURE 3.7   The dynamics of the growth rate of knowledge in the general version of the model

$X^{\beta+\theta}$. Thus the key determinant of the economy's behavior is now not how θ compares with 1, but how $\beta + \theta$ compares with 1. As before, we discuss each of the three possibilities.

Case 1: $\beta + \theta < 1$

If $\beta + \theta$ is less than 1, $(1 - \theta)/\beta$ is greater than 1. Thus the locus of points where $\dot{g}_A = 0$ is steeper than the locus where $\dot{g}_K = 0$. This case is shown in Figure 3.8. The initial values of g_A and g_K are determined by the parameters of the model and by the initial values of A, K, and L. Their dynamics are then as shown in the figure.

The figure shows that regardless of where g_A and g_K begin, they converge to Point E in the diagram. Both $\dot{g}_A$ and $\dot{g}_K$ are zero at this point. Thus the values of g_A and g_K at Point E, which we denote g_A^* and g_K^*, must satisfy

$$g_A^* + n - g_K^* = 0 \tag{3.18}$$

and

$$\beta g_K^* + \gamma n + (\theta - 1)g_A^* = 0. \tag{3.19}$$

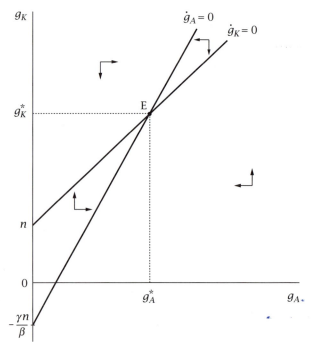

FIGURE 3.8   The dynamics of the growth rates of capital and knowledge when $\beta + \theta < 1$

Rewriting (3.18) as $g_K^* = g_A^* + n$ and substituting into (3.19) yields

$$\beta g_A^* + (\beta + \gamma)n + (\theta - 1)g_A^* = 0, \tag{3.20}$$

or

$$g_A^* = \frac{\beta + \gamma}{1 - (\theta + \beta)}n. \tag{3.21}$$

From above, g_K^* is simply $g_A^* + n$. Equation (3.1) then implies that when A and K are growing at these rates, output is growing at rate g_K^*. Output per worker is therefore growing at rate g_A^*.

This case is similar to the case when θ is less than 1 in the version of the model without capital. Here, as in that case, the long-run growth rate of the economy is endogenous, and again long-run growth is an increasing function of population growth and is zero if population growth is zero. The fractions of the labor force and the capital stock engaged in R&D, a_L and a_K, do not affect long-run growth; nor does the saving rate, s. The reason that these parameters do not affect long-run growth is essentially the same as the reason that a_L does not affect long-run growth in the simple version of the model.[5]

Case 2: $\beta + \theta > 1$

In this case, the loci where g_A and g_K are constant diverge, as shown in Figure 3.9. As the phase diagram shows, regardless of where the economy starts, it eventually enters the region between the two loci. Once this occurs, the growth rates of both A and K, and hence the growth rate of output, increase continually. One can show that increases in s and n cause output per worker to rise above its previous trajectory by an ever-increasing amount. The effects of changes in a_L and a_K are more complicated, however, since they involve shifts of resources between the two sectors. Thus this case is analogous to the case when θ exceeds 1 in the simple model.

Case 3: $\beta + \theta = 1$

The final possibility is that $\beta + \theta$ equals 1. In this case, $(1 - \theta)/\beta$ equals 1, and thus the $\dot{g}_A = 0$ and $\dot{g}_K = 0$ loci have the same slope. If n is positive, the $\dot{g}_K = 0$ line lies above the $\dot{g}_A = 0$ line, and the dynamics of the economy are similar to those when $\beta + \theta > 1$; this case is shown in Panel (a) of Figure 3.10.

If n is 0, on the other hand, the two loci lie directly on top of each other, as shown in Panel (b) of the figure. The figure shows that, regardless of where the economy begins, it converges to a balanced growth path. As in the case

---

[5] See Problem 3.4 for a more detailed analysis of the impact of a change in the saving rate in this model.

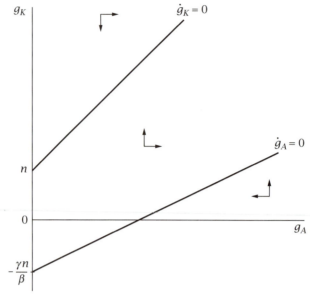

FIGURE 3.9   **The dynamics of the growth rates of capital and knowledge when $\beta + \theta > 1$**

of $\theta = 1$ and $n = 0$ in the model without capital, the phase diagram does not tell us what balanced growth path the economy converges to. One can show, however, that the economy has a unique balanced growth path, and that the economy's growth rate on that path is a complicated function of the parameters. Increases in the saving rate and in the size of the population increase this long-run growth rate; the intuition is essentially the same as the intuition for why increases in a_L and L increase long-run growth when there is no capital. And, as in Case 2, increases in a_L and a_K have ambiguous effects on long-run growth. Unfortunately, the derivation of the long-run growth rate is tedious and not particularly insightful. Thus we will not work through the details.[6]

A specific example of a model of knowledge accumulation and growth whose macroeconomic side fits into this framework is P. Romer's model of "endogenous technological change" (Romer, 1990; the microeconomic side of Romer's model, which may be of greater importance, is considered in Section 3.4 and in Problems 3.6–3.8). As here, population growth is zero, and there are constant returns to scale to the produced inputs in both sectors. In addition, R&D uses labor and the existing stock of knowledge, but not physical capital. Thus in our notation, the production function for new knowledge is

$$\dot{A}(t) = B a_L L A(t). \tag{3.22}$$

---

[6] See Problem 3.5.

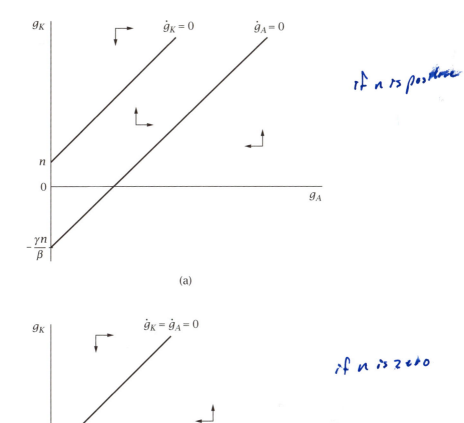

(a)

(b)

if n is positive

if n is zero

FIGURE 3.10 **The dynamics of the growth rates of capital and knowledge when $\beta + \theta = 1$**

Since all physical capital is used to produce goods, goods production is

$$Y(t) = K(t)^{\alpha}[(1 - a_L)LA(t)]^{1-\alpha}. \tag{3.23}$$

Our usual assumption of a constant saving rate ($\dot{K}(t) = sY(t)$) completes the model.[7] This is the case we have been considering with $\beta = 0$, $\theta = 1$, and $\gamma = 1$. To see the implications of this version of the model, note that (3.22) implies that A grows steadily at rate $Ba_L L$. This means the model is

---

[7] At the aggregate level, Romer's model differs in two minor respects from this. First, a_L and s are built up from microeconomic relationships, and are thus endogenous and potentially time-varying; in equilibrium they are constant, however. Second, his model distinguishes between skilled and unskilled labor; unskilled labor is used only in goods production. The stocks of both types of labor are exogenous and constant, however.

identical to the Solow model with $n = \delta = 0$ and with the rate of technological progress equal to $Ba_L L$. Thus (since there is no population growth), the growth rates of output and capital on the balanced growth path are $Ba_L L$. This model provides an example of a situation where long-run growth is endogenous (and depends on parameters other than population growth), but is not affected by the saving rate.

Scale Effects and Growth

One important motivation for work on new growth theory is a desire to understand variations in long-run growth. As a result, early new growth models focused on constant or increasing returns to produced factors, where changes in saving rates and resources devoted to R&D permanently change growth. Jones (1995) points out an important problem with these models, however. Over the postwar period, the forces that the models suggest affect long-run growth have all been trending upward. Population has been rising steadily, saving rates have increased, the fraction of resources devoted to human-capital accumulation has risen considerably, and the fraction of resources devoted to R&D appears to have increased sharply. Thus new growth models with constant or increasing returns imply that growth should have increased considerably. But in fact, growth shows no discernible trend.

The simplest interpretation of Jones's results is that there are decreasing returns to produced factors; this is the interpretation proposed by Jones. Several recent papers suggest another possibility, however. They continue to assume constant or increasing returns to produced factors, but add a channel through which the overall expansion of the economy does not lead to faster growth. Specifically, they assume that it is the amount of R&D activity per sector that determines growth, and that the number of sectors grows with the economy. As a result, growth is steady despite the fact that population is rising. But because of the returns to produced factors, increases in the fraction of resources devoted to R&D permanently raise growth. Thus the models maintain the ability of early new growth models to potentially explain variations in long-run growth, but do not imply that worldwide population growth leads to ever-increasing growth (see, for example, Peretto, 1998; Dinopoulos and Thompson, 1998; and Howitt, 1999).

There are two difficulties with this line of argument. First, it is not just population that has been trending up. The basic fact emphasized by Jones is that R&D's share and rates of investment in physical and human capital have been rising as well. Thus the failure of growth to rise is puzzling for these second-generation new growth models as well. Second, as Jones (1999b) points out, the parameter restrictions needed in these models to eliminate scale effects on growth are strong and appear arbitrary.

With decreasing returns, the lack of a trend in growth is not puzzling. In this case, a rise in, say, the saving rate or R&D's share leads to a temporary period of above-normal growth. As a result, repeated rises in these variables lead not to increasing growth, but to an extended period of above-normal growth. This suggests that despite the relative steadiness of growth, one should not think of the United States and other major economies as being on conventional balanced growth paths (Jones, 1999a).

Saving rates and R&D's share cannot continue rising indefinitely (though in the case of the R&D share, the current share is sufficiently low that it can continue to rise at a rapid rate for a substantial period). Thus one corollary of this analysis is that in the absence of countervailing forces, growth must slow at some point. Moreover, the calculations in Jones (1999a) suggest that the slowdown would be considerable.

3.4   The Nature of Knowledge and the Determinants of the Allocation of Resources to R&D

Overview

The previous analysis takes the saving rate, s, and the fractions of inputs devoted to R&D, a_L and a_K, as given. The models of Chapter 2 (and of Chapter 7 as well) show the ingredients needed to make s endogenous. This leaves the question of what determines a_L and a_K. This section is devoted to that issue.

So far we have simply described the "A" variable produced by R&D as knowledge. But knowledge comes in many forms. It is useful to think of there being a continuum of types of knowledge, ranging from the highly abstract to the highly applied. At one extreme is basic scientific knowledge with broad applicability, such as the Pythagorean theorem, the germ theory of disease, and the theory of quantum mechanics. At the other extreme is knowledge about specific goods, such as how to start a particular lawn mower on a cold morning. There are a wide range of ideas in between, from the design of the transistor or the invention of the record player to an improved layout for the kitchen of a fast-food restaurant or a recipe for a better-tasting soft drink.

Many of these different types of knowledge play important roles in economic growth. Imagine, for example, that 100 years ago there had been a halt to basic scientific progress, or to the invention of applied technologies useful in broad classes of goods, or to the invention of new products, or to improvements in the design and use of products after their invention. These changes would have had different effects on growth, and those effects would have occurred with different lags, but it seems likely that all of them would have led to substantial reductions in growth.

There is no reason to expect the determinants of the accumulation of these different types of knowledge to be the same: the forces underlying, for example, the advancement of basic mathematics are different from those behind improvements in the design of fast-food restaurants. There is thus no reason to expect a unified theory of the growth of knowledge. Rather, we should expect to find various factors underlying the accumulation of knowledge.

At the same time, as Romer (1990) emphasizes, all types of knowledge share one essential feature: they are *nonrival.* That is, the use of an item of knowledge, whether it is the Pythagorean theorem or a soft-drink recipe, in one application makes its use by someone else no more difficult. Conventional private economic goods, in contrast, are *rival:* the use of, say, an item of clothing by one individual precludes its simultaneous use by someone else.

An immediate implication of this fundamental property of knowledge is that the production and allocation of knowledge cannot be completely governed by competitive market forces. The marginal cost of supplying an item of knowledge to an additional user, once the knowledge has been discovered, is zero. Thus the rental price of knowledge in a competitive market is zero. But then the creation of knowledge could not be motivated by the desire for private economic gain. It follows that either knowledge is sold at above its marginal cost or its development is not motivated by market forces. Thus some departure from a competitive model is needed.

Romer emphasizes that, although all knowledge is nonrival, it is heterogeneous along a second dimension: *excludability.* A good is excludable if it is possible to prevent others from using it. Thus conventional private goods are excludable: the owner of a piece of clothing can prevent others from using it.

In the case of knowledge, excludability depends both on the nature of the knowledge itself and on economic institutions governing property rights. Patent laws, for example, give inventors rights over the use of their designs and discoveries. Under a different set of laws, inventors' ability to prevent the use of their discoveries by others might be smaller. To give another example, copyright laws give an author who finds a better organization for a textbook little ability to prevent other authors from adopting that organization. Thus the excludability of the superior organization is limited. (Because, however, the copyright laws prevent other authors from simply copying the entire textbook, adoption of the improved organization requires some effort; as a result there is some degree of excludability, and thus some potential to earn a return from the superior organization.) But it would be possible to alter the law to give authors stronger rights concerning the use of similar organizations by others.

In some cases, excludability is more dependent on the nature of the knowledge and less dependent on the legal system. The recipe for Coca-Cola is sufficiently complex that it can be kept secret without copyright or patent protection. The technology for recording television programs onto videocassette is sufficiently simple that the makers of the programs were unable to prevent viewers from recording the programs (and the "knowledge" they contained) even before courts ruled that such recording for personal use is legal.

The degree of excludability is likely to have a strong influence on how the development and allocation of knowledge depart from perfect competition. If a type of knowledge is entirely nonexcludable, there can be no private gain in its development; thus R&D in these areas must come from elsewhere. But when knowledge is excludable, the producers of new knowledge can license the right to use the knowledge at positive prices, and hence hope to earn positive returns on their R&D efforts.

With these broad remarks, we can now turn to a discussion of some of the major forces governing the allocation of resources to the development of knowledge. Four forces have received the most attention: support for basic scientific research, private incentives for R&D and innovation, alternative opportunities for talented individuals, and learning-by-doing.

Support for Basic Scientific Research

Basic scientific knowledge has traditionally been made available relatively freely; the same is true of the results of research undertaken in such institutions as modern universities and medieval monasteries. Thus this research is not motivated by the desire to earn private returns in the market. Instead it is supported by governments, charities, and wealthy individuals and is pursued by individuals motivated by this support, by desire for fame, and perhaps even by love of knowledge.

The economics of this type of knowledge are relatively straightforward. Since it is given away at zero cost and since it is useful in production, it has a positive externality. Thus its production should be subsidized.[8] If one added, for example, the infinitely lived households of the Ramsey model to a model of growth based on this view of knowledge accumulation, one could compute the optimal research subsidy. Phelps (1966b), Nordhaus (1967), and Shell (1966, 1967) provide examples of this type of analysis.

Private Incentives for R&D and Innovation

Many innovations, ranging from the introductions of entirely new products to small improvements in existing goods, receive little or no external support and are motivated almost entirely by the desire for private gain. The modeling of these private R&D activities and of their implications for economic growth has been the subject of considerable research; important examples include Romer (1990), Grossman and Helpman (1991a), and Aghion and Howitt (1992).

---

[8] This implication makes academics sympathetic to this view of knowledge.

As described above, for R&D to result from economic incentives, the knowledge created by this R&D must be at least somewhat excludable. Thus the developer of a new idea has some degree of market power. Typically, the developer is modeled as having exclusive control over the use of the idea and as licensing its use to the producers of final goods. The fee that the innovator can charge for the use of the idea is limited by the usefulness of the idea in production, or by the possibility that others, motivated by the prospect of high returns, will devote resources to learning the idea. The quantities of the factors of production engaged in R&D are modeled in turn as resulting from factor movements that equate the private factor payments in R&D with the factor payments in the production of final goods.

The Romer, Grossman–Helpman, and Aghion–Howitt models provide examples of complete models that formalize these notions. At the macroeconomic level, the models are similar to the third case in the previous section ($\theta + \beta = 1$ and $n = 0$), since that model is tractable and since it implies that the quantity of resources engaged in R&D may affect long-run growth. The models' microeconomic structures, however, are much richer.[9]

Since economies like these are not perfectly competitive, their equilibria are not in general optimal. In particular, the decentralized equilibria may have inefficient divisions of resources between R&D and conventional goods production. Three externalities from R&D have been identified: the *consumer-surplus* effect, the *business-stealing* effect, and the *R&D* effect.

The consumer-surplus effect is that the individuals or firms licensing ideas from innovators obtain some surplus, since innovators cannot engage in perfect price discrimination. Thus this is a positive externality from R&D.

The business-stealing effect is that the introduction of a superior technology typically makes existing technologies less attractive, and therefore harms the owners of those technologies. This externality is negative.[10]

Finally, the R&D effect is that innovators are generally assumed not to control the use of their knowledge in the production of additional knowledge. In terms of the model of the previous section, innovators are assumed to earn returns on the use of their knowledge in goods production (equation [3.1]) but not in knowledge production (equation [3.2]). This assumption matches the institutional fact that a description of a new technology must be made available after a patent is granted, so that the knowledge can be used by other inventors. Thus the development of new knowledge has a positive externality on others engaged in R&D.

The net effect of these three externalities is ambiguous. It is possible to construct examples where the business-stealing externality outweighs both

---

[9] See Problems 3.6–3.8.

[10] Both the consumer-surplus and business-stealing effects are pecuniary externalities: they operate through markets rather than outside them. As described in Section 2.4, such externalities do not cause inefficiency in a competitive market. For example, the fact that an individual's love of carrots drives up the price of carrots harms other carrot buyers, but benefits carrot producers. In the competitive case, these harms and benefits balance, and so the competitive equilibrium is Pareto-efficient. But when there are departures from perfect competition, pecuniary externalities can cause inefficiency.

the consumer-surplus and R&D externalities. In this case the incentives to capture the profits being earned by other innovators cause too many resources to be devoted to R&D. The result is that the economy's equilibrium growth rate may be inefficiently high (Aghion and Howitt, 1992). It is generally believed, however, that the normal situation is for the overall externality from R&D to be positive. In the model developed by Romer (1990), for example, the consumer-surplus and business-stealing effects just balance, so on net only the positive R&D effect remains. In this case the equilibrium level of R&D is inefficiently low, and R&D subsidies can increase welfare.

There can be additional externalities as well. For example, if innovators have only incomplete control over the use of their ideas in goods production (that is, if there is only partial excludability), there is an additional reason that the private return to R&D is below the social return. On the other hand, the fact that the first individual to create an invention is awarded exclusive rights to the invention can create excessive incentives for some kinds of R&D; for example, the private returns to activities that cause one inventor to complete an invention just ahead of a competitor can exceed the social returns.[11]

Alternative Opportunities for Talented Individuals

Baumol (1990) and Murphy, Shleifer, and Vishny (1991) observe that major innovations and advances in knowledge are often the result of the work of extremely talented individuals. They also observe that highly talented individuals typically have choices other than just pursuing innovations and producing goods. These observations suggest that the economic incentives and social forces influencing the activities of highly talented individuals may be important to the accumulation of knowledge.

Baumol takes a historical view of this issue. He argues that, in various places and times, military conquest, political and religious leadership, tax collection, criminal activity, philosophical contemplation, financial dealings, and manipulation of the legal system have been attractive to the most talented members of society. He also argues that these activities often have negligible (or even negative) social returns. That is, his argument is that these activities are often forms of *rent-seeking*—attempts to capture existing wealth rather than to create new wealth. Finally, he argues that there has been a strong link between how societies direct the energies of their most able members and whether the societies flourish over the long term.

Murphy, Shleifer, and Vishny provide a general discussion of the forces that influence talented individuals' decisions whether to pursue activities that are socially productive. They emphasize three factors in particular. The first is the size of the relevant market: the larger is the market from which a talented individual can reap returns, the greater are the incentives

---

[11] See Reinganum (1989) for an introduction to some of the issues raised by such *patent races*.

to enter a given activity. Thus, for example, low transportation costs and an absence of barriers to trade encourage entrepreneurship; poorly defined property rights that make much of an economy's wealth vulnerable to expropriation encourage rent-seeking. The second factor is the degree of diminishing returns. Activities whose scale is limited by the entrepreneur's time (performing surgeries, for example) do not offer the same potential returns as activities whose returns are limited only by the scale of the market (creating inventions, for instance). Thus, for example, well-functioning capital markets that permit firms to expand rapidly tend to promote entrepreneurship over rent-seeking. The final factor is the ability to keep the returns from one's activities. Thus, clear property rights tend to encourage entrepreneurship, whereas legally sanctioned rent-seeking (through government or religion, for example) tends to encourage socially unproductive activities.

Learning-by-Doing

The final determinant of knowledge accumulation is somewhat different in character. The central idea is that, as individuals produce goods, they inevitably think of ways of improving the production process. For example, Arrow (1962) cites the empirical regularity that after a new airplane design is introduced, the time required to build the frame of the marginal aircraft is inversely proportional to the cube root of the number of aircraft of that model that have already been produced; this improvement in productivity occurs without any evident innovations in the production process. Thus the accumulation of knowledge occurs in part not as a result of deliberate efforts, but as a side effect of conventional economic activity. This type of knowledge accumulation is known as *learning-by-doing*.

When learning-by-doing is the source of technological progress, the rate of knowledge accumulation depends not on the fraction of the economy's resources engaged in R&D, but on how much new knowledge is generated by conventional economic activity. Analyzing learning-by-doing therefore requires some changes to our model. All inputs are now engaged in goods production; thus the production function becomes

$$Y(t) = K(t)^{\alpha}[A(t)L(t)]^{1-\alpha}. \tag{3.24}$$

The simplest case of learning-by-doing is when learning occurs as a side effect of the production of new capital. With this formulation, since the increase in knowledge is a function of the increase in capital, the stock of knowledge is a function of the stock of capital. Thus there is only one stock variable whose behavior is endogenous.[12] Making our usual choice of a

---

[12] See Problem 3.9 for the case in which knowledge accumulation occurs as a side effect of goods production rather than of capital accumulation.

power function, we have

$$A(t) = BK(t)^\phi, \qquad B > 0, \qquad \phi > 0. \tag{3.25}$$

Equations (3.24)–(3.25), together with (3.3)–(3.4) describing the accumulation of capital and labor, characterize the economy.

To analyze the properties of this economy, begin by substituting (3.25) into (3.24); this yields

$$Y(t) = K(t)^\alpha B^{1-\alpha} K(t)^{\phi(1-\alpha)} L(t)^{1-\alpha}. \tag{3.26}$$

Since $\dot{K}(t) = sY(t)$, the dynamics of K are given by

$$\dot{K}(t) = sB^{1-\alpha} K(t)^\alpha K(t)^{\phi(1-\alpha)} L(t)^{1-\alpha}. \tag{3.27}$$

In our model of knowledge accumulation without capital in Section 3.2, the dynamics of A are given by $\dot{A}(t) = B[a_L L(t)]^\gamma A(t)^\theta$ (equation [3.6]). Comparing equation (3.27) of the learning-by-doing model with this equation shows that the structures of the two models are similar. In the model of Section 3.2, there is a single productive input, knowledge. Here, we can think of there also being only one productive input, capital. As equations (3.6) and (3.27) show, the dynamics of the two models are essentially the same. Thus we can use the results of our analysis of the earlier model to analyze this one. There, the key determinant of the economy's dynamics is how θ compares with 1. Here, by analogy, it is how $\alpha + \phi(1 - \alpha)$ compares with 1, which is equivalent to how ϕ compares with 1.

If ϕ is less than 1, the long-run growth rate of the economy is a function of the rate of population growth, n. If ϕ is greater than 1, there is explosive growth. And if ϕ equals 1, there is explosive growth if n is positive and steady growth if n equals 0.

Once again, a case that has received particular attention is $\phi = 1$ and $n = 0$. In this case, the production function (equation [3.26]) becomes

$$Y(t) = bK(t), \qquad b \equiv B^{1-\alpha} L^{1-\alpha}. \tag{3.28}$$

Capital accumulation is therefore given by

$$\dot{K}(t) = sbK(t). \tag{3.29}$$

As in the similar cases we have already considered, the dynamics of this economy are straightforward. Equation (3.29) immediately implies that K grows steadily at rate sb. And since output is proportional to K, it also grows at this rate. Thus we have another example of a model in which long-run growth is endogenous and depends on the saving rate. Here it occurs because the contribution of capital is larger than its conventional contribution: increased capital raises output not only through its direct contribution to production (the K^α term in [3.26]), but also by indirectly contributing to the development of new ideas and thereby making all other capital more productive (the $K^{\phi(1-\alpha)}$ term in [3.26]). Because the production function in these models is often written using the symbol "A" rather than the "b" used in (3.28), these models are often referred to as "$Y = AK$" models.[13]

3.5 Endogenous Saving in Models of Knowledge Accumulation: An Example[14]

The analysis in the previous sections, following the spirit of the Solow model, takes the saving rate as given. But again we sometimes want to model saving behavior as arising from the choices of optimizing individuals or households, particularly if we are interested in welfare issues.

Making saving endogenous in models like the ones we have been considering is often difficult. Here we consider only the simplest case: a single produced input, constant returns to that input, and no population growth. That is, we consider the case of $\theta = 1$ and $n = 0$ in the model with knowledge but without physical capital, or the case of $\phi = 1$ and $n = 0$ in the learning-by-doing model. For concreteness, the discussion is phrased in terms of the learning-by-doing model. We continue to assume no depreciation for simplicity.[15]

Assume that the division of output between consumption and saving is determined by the choices of infinitely lived households like those of the Ramsey model of Chapter 2. Since there is no population growth, we can assume that each household has exactly one member. Thus the representative household's utility function is

$$U = \int_{t=0}^{\infty} e^{-\rho t} \frac{C(t)^{1-\sigma}}{1-\sigma} \, dt, \qquad \rho > 0, \qquad \sigma > 0, \qquad (3.30)$$

where C is the household's consumption, ρ is its discount rate, and σ is its coefficient of relative risk aversion. (Except for the use of σ rather than

---

[13] The model in P. Romer (1986) that launched new growth theory fits fairly well into this category. There are two main differences. First, the role played by physical capital here is played by knowledge in Romer's model: privately controlled knowledge both contributes directly to production at a particular firm and adds to aggregate knowledge, which contributes to production at all firms. Second, knowledge accumulation occurs through a separate production function rather than through forgone output; there are increasing returns to knowledge in goods production and (asymptotically) constant returns in knowledge accumulation. As a result, the economy converges to a constant growth rate.

[14] Readers who have not read Chapter 2 may wish to skip this section.

[15] Making saving endogenous in the cases either of multiple produced inputs or nonconstant returns is considerably more complex. Mulligan and Sala-i-Martin (1993) analyze the case of two produced inputs and no population growth, with constant returns to the two inputs. Romer (1986) is an example of a model with a single produced input, nonconstant returns, and endogenous saving. See also Barro and Sala-i-Martin (1998, Chapter 5).

θ and the fact that the size of the household is normalized to 1, this is identical to equations [2.1]–[2.2].) Capital and labor are paid their private marginal products. Households take their initial wealth and the paths of interest rates and wages as given, and choose the path of consumption to maximize U.

Recall that with learning-by-doing, capital affects output at a given firm both through its direct contribution and through its impact on knowledge. The production function for a single firm, firm i, is

$$Y_i(t) = K_i(t)^{\alpha}[A(t)L_i(t)]^{1-\alpha}, \tag{3.31}$$

where K_i and L_i are the amounts of capital and labor employed by the firm. Although each firm takes A as given, it is in fact determined by the aggregate capital stock. Specifically, given our assumption that ϕ equals 1, $A(t)$ equals $BK(t)$ (see [3.25]). Thus firm i's output is

$$Y_i(t) = B^{1-\alpha}K(t)^{1-\alpha}K_i(t)^{\alpha}L_i(t)^{1-\alpha}. \tag{3.32}$$

Factor markets are competitive. Thus capital and labor earn their private marginal products. The marginal product of capital at firm i is

$$\frac{\partial Y_i(t)}{\partial K_i(t)} = \alpha B^{1-\alpha}K(t)^{1-\alpha}K_i(t)^{\alpha-1}L_i(t)^{1-\alpha}$$

$$= \alpha B^{1-\alpha}K(t)^{1-\alpha}[K_i(t)/L_i(t)]^{-(1-\alpha)}. \tag{3.33}$$

Since the marginal product of capital cannot differ across firms in equilibrium, (3.33) implies that the capital-labor ratio must be the same at each firm. Thus K_i/L_i must equal the aggregate capital-labor ratio, K/L. In addition, with no depreciation the marginal product of capital must equal the real interest rate. Substituting these facts into (3.33) gives us

$$r(t) = \alpha B^{1-\alpha}K(t)^{1-\alpha}[K(t)/L]^{-(1-\alpha)}$$

$$= \alpha B^{1-\alpha}L^{1-\alpha}$$

$$= \alpha b \tag{3.34}$$

$$\equiv \bar{r},$$

where the third line uses the definition of b as $B^{1-\alpha}L^{1-\alpha}$ (see [3.28]). Thus with constant returns to capital and no population growth, the real interest rate is constant.

Similarly, the wage is given by the private marginal product of labor:

$$w(t) = (1-\alpha)B^{1-\alpha}K(t)^{1-\alpha}[K_i(t)/L_i(t)]^{\alpha}$$

$$= (1-\alpha)B^{1-\alpha}K(t)L^{-\alpha}, \tag{3.35}$$

$$= (1-\alpha)b\frac{K(t)}{L},$$

where the second line again uses the fact that, in equilibrium, each firm's capital-labor ratio equals the aggregate ratio, K/L. Thus the real wage is proportional to the capital stock.

From Chapter 2, we know that the consumption path of a household whose utility is given by (3.30) satisfies

$$\frac{\dot{C}(t)}{C(t)} = \frac{r(t) - \rho}{\sigma} \tag{3.36}$$

(see equation [2.20]). Since r is constant and equal to $\bar{r}$, consumption grows steadily at rate $(\bar{r} - \rho)/\sigma$. Let $\bar{g}$ denote this growth rate, and assume that it is less than $\bar{r}$.

The fact that consumption grows at rate $\bar{g}$ suggests that the capital stock and output also grow at this rate: if they did not, the saving rate would be continually rising or continually falling. To see if this is indeed the case, we need to consider households' budget contraint. From Section 2.2, we know that households are satisfying their budget constraint if and only if the limit of the present value of their capital holdings is zero (see equation [2.10]). In this model, since the real interest rate is constant at $\bar{r}$, this condition is

$$\lim_{t \to \infty} e^{-\bar{r}t} K(t) = 0. \tag{3.37}$$

Since $\bar{g}$ is less than $\bar{r}$ by assumption, this condition is satisfied if K grows at rate $\bar{g}$. That is, if households choose the level of consumption that causes the capital stock to grow at rate $\bar{g}$, they satisfy their budget constraint. Thus this is an equilibrium.[16]

Further, one can use households' budget constraint to show that this is the only equilibrium. Suppose, for example, that $C(0)$ exceeds the level that causes the growth rate of the capital stock at $t = 0$ to equal $\bar{g}$. Then consumption must be higher at every point in time than when the capital stock grows at rate $\bar{g}$ (since C must grow at rate $\bar{g}$ in any equilibrium), and capital must therefore be lower. This implies that the present value of lifetime consumption is strictly higher than when capital grows at rate $\bar{g}$ and that the present value of lifetime labor income is strictly lower. But since households are satisfying their budget constraint with equality when capital grows at rate $\bar{g}$, this means that here they are violating the budget constraint, and thus this path is not possible. A similar argument shows that if $C(0)$ is less than the level that causes capital to grow at rate $\bar{g}$, the present value of lifetime consumption is strictly less than lifetime wealth.

This analysis implies that if the economy is subjected to some kind of shock (a change in ρ, for example), the ratio of consumption to the capital stock jumps immediately to its new balanced-growth-path value, and consumption, capital, and output all immediately begin growing at a constant rate. Thus there are no transitional dynamics to reach the balanced growth path. Intuitively, the fact that production is linear means that there is nothing special about any particular level of the capital stock or of the

---

[16] If $\bar{g}$ exceeds $\bar{r}$, households can attain infinite lifetime utility. Thus we would need a different set of tools in this case.

capital-labor ratio. For example, if a war suddenly halves the capital stock, households respond simply by halving their consumption at every date.

We found in Section 3.4 that with learning-by-doing and exogenous saving, the economy's growth rate equals sb, where s is the saving rate. Here, with endogenous saving, it is straightforward to check that our analysis implies that the saving rate is constant and equal to $\bar{g}/b$. Since $\bar{g}$ equals $(\alpha b - \rho)/\sigma$, this implies that the saving rate is $(\alpha b - \rho)/(\sigma b)$. Thus, for example, a lower value of households' discount rate, ρ, raises the saving rate and thereby increases long-run growth. A higher value of α also increases saving and growth: when the private marginal product of capital (αb) is closer to the social marginal product (b), households save more, and thus growth is higher. One implication is that unless α equals 1, the growth rate produced by the decentralized equilibrium is less than the socially optimal growth rate: a social planner would account for the full marginal product of capital rather than just the private marginal product, and would thus choose a saving rate of $(b - \rho)/(\sigma b)$, and hence a growth rate of $(b - \rho)/\sigma$.

3.6 Models of Knowledge Accumulation and the Central Questions of Growth Theory

Our analysis of economic growth is motivated by two issues: the growth over time in standards of living, and their disparities across different parts of the world. It is therefore natural to ask what the models of R&D and knowledge accumulation have to say about these issues.

With regard to worldwide growth, it seems plausible that the forces that the models focus on are important. At an informal level, the growth of knowledge appears to be the central reason that output and standards of living are so much higher today than in previous centuries. And as described in Chapter 1, formal growth-accounting studies attribute large portions of the increases in output per worker over extended periods to the unexplained residual component, which may reflect technological progress.

It would of course be desirable to refine the ideas we have been considering by improving our understanding of what types of knowledge are most important for growth, their quantitative importance, and the forces determining how knowledge is accumulated. But it seems likely that the kinds of forces we have been considering are important. Thus, the general directions of research suggested by these models seem promising for understanding worldwide growth.

With regard to cross-country differences in real incomes, the relevance of the models is less clear. There are two difficulties. The first is quantitative. As Problem 3.13 asks you to demonstrate, if one believes that economies are described by something like the Solow model but do not all have access to the same technology, the lags in the diffusion of knowledge from rich to poor countries that are needed to account for observed differences in incomes are extremely long—on the order of a century or more. It is hard to believe that the reason that some countries are so poor is that they do not have access to the improvements in technology that have occurred over the past century.

The second difficulty is conceptual. As emphasized in Section 3.5, technology is nonrival: its use by one firm does not prevent its use by others. This naturally raises the question of why poor countries do not have access to the same technology as rich countries. If the relevant knowledge is publicly available, poor countries can become rich by having their workers or managers read the appropriate literature. And if the relevant knowledge is proprietary knowledge produced by private R&D, poor countries can become rich by instituting a credible program for respecting foreign firms' property rights. With such a program, the firms in developed countries with proprietary knowledge would open factories in poor countries, hire their inexpensive labor, and produce output using the proprietary technology. The result would be that the marginal product of labor in poor countries, and hence wages, would rapidly rise to the level of developed countries.

Although lack of confidence on the part of foreign firms in the security of their property rights is surely an important problem in many poor countries, it is difficult to believe that this alone is the cause of the countries' poverty. There are numerous examples of poor regions or countries, ranging from European colonies over the past few centuries to many countries today, where foreign investors can establish plants and use their know-how with a high degree of confidence that the political environment will be relatively stable, their plants will not be nationalized, and their profits will not be taxed at exorbitant rates. Yet we do not see incomes in those areas jumping to the levels of industrialized countries.

One may reasonably object to this argument on the grounds that the difficulty that such countries face is not lack of access to advanced technology, but lack of ability to use that technology. But this objection implies that the main source of differences in standards of living is not different levels of knowledge or technology, but differences in whatever factors allow richer countries to take better advantage of advanced technology. Understanding differences in incomes therefore requires understanding the reasons for the differences in these factors. This task is taken up in Part B of the chapter.

3.7 Empirical Application: Population Growth and Technological Change since 1 Million B.C.

Kremer (1993) demonstrates that models of endogenous knowledge accumulation have important implications for human history over the very long run. He first notes that essentially all models of the endogenous growth of knowledge predict that technological progress is an increasing function of population size. The reasoning is simple: the larger the population, the more people there are to make discoveries, and thus the more rapidly knowledge accumulates.[17]

Kremer then argues that over almost all of human history, technological progress has led mainly to increases in population rather than increases in output per person. Population grew by several orders of magnitude between prehistoric times and the Industrial Revolution. But since incomes at the beginning of the Industrial Revolution were not far above subsistence levels, it is not possible that output per person rose by anything close to the same amount as population. Only in the past few centuries, Kremer argues, has the impact of technological progress fallen to any substantial degree on output per person. Putting these observations together, Kremer concludes that models of endogenous technological progress predict that over most of human history, the rate of population growth should have been rising.

A Simple Model

Kremer's formal model is a straightforward variation on the models we have been considering. The simplest version consists of three equations. First, output depends on technology, labor, and land:

$$Y(t) = T^{\alpha}[A(t)L(t)]^{1-\alpha}, \tag{3.38}$$

where T denotes the fixed stock of land. (Capital is neglected for simplicity, and land is included to keep population finite.) Second, additions to knowledge are proportional to population, and also depend on the stock of knowledge:

$$\dot{A}(t) = BL(t)A(t)^{\theta}. \tag{3.39}$$

And third, population adjusts so that output per person equals the subsistence level, denoted $\overline{y}$:

$$\frac{Y(t)}{L(t)} = \overline{y}. \tag{3.40}$$

Aside from this Malthusian assumption about the determination of population, this model is similar to the model of Section 3.2 with $y = 1$.[18]

We solve the model in two steps. The first step is to find the size of the population that can be supported on the fixed stock of land at a given time.

---

[17] This effect can be seen clearly in the models we have been considering in the case of constant returns to produced inputs and no population growth.

[18] For other growth models that treat population growth as endogenous, see Barro and Becker (1988, 1989); Becker, Murphy, and Tamura (1990); and Galor and Weil (1996).

Substituting expression (3.38) for output into the Malthusian population condition, (3.40), yields

$$\frac{T^{\alpha}[A(t)L(t)]^{1-\alpha}}{L(t)} = \overline{y}. \tag{3.41}$$

Solving this condition for $L(t)$ gives us

$$L(t) = \left(\frac{1}{\overline{y}}\right)^{1/\alpha} A(t)^{(1-\alpha)/\alpha}T. \tag{3.42}$$

This equation states that the population that can be supported is decreasing in the subsistence level of output, increasing in technology, and proportional to the amount of land.

The second step is to find the dynamics of technology and population. Since both $\overline{y}$ and T are constant, (3.42) implies that the growth rate of L is $(1 - \alpha)/\alpha$ times the growth rate of A:

$$\frac{\dot{L}(t)}{L(t)} = \frac{1 - \alpha}{\alpha} \frac{\dot{A}(t)}{A(t)}. \tag{3.43}$$

In the special case of $\theta = 1$, equation (3.39) for knowledge accumulation implies that $\dot{A}(t)/A(t)$ is simply $BL(t)$. Thus in this case, (3.43) implies that the growth rate of population is proportional to the level of population. In the general case, one can show that the model implies that the rate of population growth is proportional to $L(t)^{\psi}$, where $\psi = 1 - [(1 - \theta)\alpha/(1 - \alpha)]$.[19] Thus population growth is increasing in the size of the population unless α is large or θ is much less than 1 (or a combination of the two). Intuitively, Kremer's model implies increasing growth even with diminishing returns to knowledge in the production of new knowledge (that is, even with $\theta < 1$) because labor is now a produced factor: improvements in technology lead to higher population, which in turn leads to further improvements in technology. Further, the effect is likely to be substantial. For example, even if α is $\frac{1}{3}$ and θ is $\frac{1}{2}$ rather than 1, then $1 - [(1 - \theta)\alpha/(1 - \alpha)]$ is 0.75.

Results

Kremer tests the model's predictions using population estimates extending back to 1 million B.C. that have been constructed by archaeologists and anthropologists. Figure 3.11 shows the resulting scatterplot of population growth against population. Each observation shows the level of population at the beginning of some period and the average annual growth rate of population over that period. The length of the periods considered falls

---

[19] To see this, divide both sides of (3.39) by A to obtain an expression for $\dot{A}/A$. Then use (3.41) to express A in terms of L, and substitute the result into the expression for $\dot{A}/A$. Expression (3.43) then implies that $\dot{L}/L$ equals a constant times $L(t)^{\psi}$.

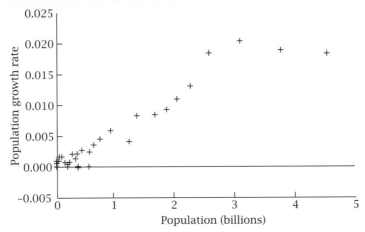

FIGURE 3.11 **The level and growth rate of population, 1 million B.C. to 1990 (from Kremer, 1993; used with permission)**

gradually from many thousand years early in the sample to 10 years at the end. Because the periods considered for the early part of the sample are so long, even substantial errors in the early population estimates would have little impact on the estimated growth rates.

The figure shows a strongly positive, and approximately linear, relationship between population growth and the level of population. A regression of growth on a constant and population (in billions) yields

$$n_t = -0.0023 + 0.524\ L_t, \qquad R^2 = 0.92, \qquad D.W. = 1.10, \qquad (3.44)$$
$$(0.0355) \quad (0.026)$$

where n is population growth and L is population, and where the numbers in parentheses are standard errors. Thus there is an overwhelmingly statistically significant association between the level of population and its growth rate.

The argument that technological progress is a worldwide phenomenon fails if there are regions that are completely cut off from one another. Kremer uses this observation to propose a second test of theories of endogenous knowledge accumulation. From the disappearance of the intercontinental land bridges at the end of the last ice age to the voyages of the European explorers, Eurasia-Africa, the Americas, Australia, and Tasmania were almost completely isolated from one another. The model implies that at the time of the separation, the populations of each region had the same technology; thus the initial populations should have been approximately proportional to the land areas of the regions (see equation [3.42]). The model predicts that during the period that the regions were separate, technological progress was faster in the regions with larger populations. The theory thus predicts that, when contact between the regions was reestablished around 1500, population density was highest in the largest regions. Intuitively, inventions that would allow a given area to support more people, such as the domestication of animals and the development of agriculture, were much more likely in Eurasia-Africa, with its population of millions, than in Tasmania, with its population of a few thousand.

The data confirm this prediction. The land areas of the four regions are 84 million square kilometers for Eurasia-Africa, 38 million for the Americas, 8 million for Australia, and 0.1 million for Tasmania. Population estimates for the four regions in 1500 imply densities of approximately 4.9 people per square kilometer for Eurasia-Africa, 0.4 for the Americas, and 0.03 for both Australia and Tasmania.[20]

Discussion

What do we learn from the confirmation of the model's time-series and cross-section predictions? The basic source of Kremer's predictions is the idea that the rate of increase in the stock of knowledge is increasing in population: innovations do not arrive exogenously, but are made by people. Although this idea is assumed away in the Solow, Ramsey, and Diamond models, it is hardly controversial. Thus Kremer's main qualitative findings for the most part confirm predictions that are quite unsurprising.

Any tractable model of technological progress and population growth over many millennia must inevitably be so simplified that it would closely match the quantitative features of the data only by luck. For example, it would be foolish to attach much importance to the finding that population growth appears to be roughly proportional to the level of population rather than to $L^{0.75}$ or $L^{0.9}$. Thus, Kremer's evidence tells us little about, say, the exact value of θ in equation (3.39).

The value of Kremer's evidence, then, lies not in discriminating among alternative theories of growth, but in using growth theory to help understand major features of human history. The dynamics of human population over the very long run and the relative technological performance of different regions in the era before 1500 are important issues. Kremer's evidence shows that the ideas of new growth theory shed significant light on them.

---

[20] Kremer argues that, since Australia is largely desert, these figures understate Australia's effective population density. He also argues that direct evidence suggests that Australia was more technologically advanced than Tasmania. Finally, he notes that there was in fact a fifth separate region, Flinders Island, a 680-square-kilometer island between Tasmania and Australia. Humans died out entirely on Flinders Island around 3000 B.C.

Population Growth versus Growth in Income per Person over the Very Long Run

As described above, over nearly all of history technological progress has led almost entirely to higher population rather than to higher average income. But this has not been true over the past few centuries: the enormous technological progress of the modern era has led not only to vast population growth, but also to vast increases in average income.

It may appear that explaining this change requires appealing to some demographic change, such as the development of contraceptive techniques or preferences for fewer children when technological progress is rapid. In fact, however, Kremer shows that the explanation is much simpler. Malthusian population dynamics are not instantaneous. Rather, at low levels of income, population growth is an increasing function of income. That is, Kremer argues that instead of assuming that Y/L always equals $\overline{y}$ (equation [3.40]), it is more realistic to assume $n = n(y)$, with $n(\overline{y}) = 0$ and $n'(\bullet) > 0$ in the vicinity of $\overline{y}$.

This formulation implies that when income rises, population growth rises, tending to push income back down. When technological progress is slow, the fact that the adjustment is not immediate is of little importance. With slow technological progress, population adjusts rapidly enough to keep income per person very close to $\overline{y}$. Income and population growth rise very slowly, but almost all of technological progress is reflected in higher population rather than higher average income. But when population becomes large enough that technological progress is relatively rapid, this no longer occurs; instead, a large fraction of the effect of technological progress falls on average income rather than on population. Thus, a small and natural variation on Kremer's basic model explains another important feature of human history.[21]

A further extension of the demographic assumptions leads to additional interesting implications. The evidence suggests that preferences are such that once average income is sufficiently high, population growth is decreasing in income. That is, $n(y)$ appears to be decreasing in y when y exceeds some y^*. With this modification, the model predicts that population growth peaks at some point and then declines.[22] This reinforces the tendency for an increasing fraction of the effect of technological progress to fall on average income rather than on population. And if $n(y)$ is negative for y sufficiently large, population itself peaks at some point. In this case, assuming that θ is less than or equal to 1, the economy converges to a path where

---

[21] See Section III of Kremer's paper for a formal analysis of these points.

[22] The facts that the population does not adjust immediately and that beyond some point population growth is decreasing in income can explain why the relationship between the level of population and its growth rate shown in Figure 3.11 breaks down somewhat for the last two observations in the figure, which correspond to the period after 1970.

both the growth rate of average income and the level of the population are converging to 0.[23]

Part B   Cross-Country Income Differences

A fundamental goal of research on economic growth is to understand the vast variation in average income per person around the world. So far, however, our main conclusions about this variation have been negative. A principal conclusion of the Solow model is that if physical capital's share in income is a reasonable measure of capital's importance in production, differences in capital do not account for the enormous income differences across countries. The Ramsey–Cass–Koopmans and Diamond models have the same implication. And a principal conclusion of Part A of this chapter is that since technology is nonrival, differences in technology are unlikely to be important to cross-country income differences.

The remainder of this chapter attempts to move beyond these negative conclusions. The first step is to recognize that physical capital is not the only type of capital: to determine whether differences in capital are important to differences in income, we need to consider human capital as well. Section 3.8 therefore extends our analysis of growth to include human capital. Section 3.9 turns to the evidence. Specifically, it decomposes income differences across countries into the contributions of physical capital, of human capital, and of output for given amounts of capital. We will see that variations in both physical and human capital are of nonnegligible importance, but that variations in output for given capital stocks are the most important source of income differences among countries. We will also see that countries that perform well along one of these three dimensions generally perform well along the others. This suggests that there may be underlying forces that are important to all three of these immediate determinants of income per person.

We will therefore need to go deeper and investigate the sources of differences in these determinants of average incomes. Section 3.10 introduces the idea that the allocation of resources between activities that raise overall output and ones that redistribute it may be crucial. Section 3.11 analyzes a simple model of this division of resources between production and rent-seeking. Finally, Section 3.12 asks what insights our analysis provides about cross-country differences in income growth rather than in income levels.

---

[23] Of course, we should not expect any single model to capture the major features of all of history. For example, it seems likely that sometime over the next several centuries, genetic engineering will progress to the point where the concept of a "person" is no longer well defined. When that occurs, a different type of model will be needed.

3.8   Extending the Solow Model to Include Human Capital

This section develops a model of growth that includes human as well as physical capital.[24] Because the model is not intended to explain growth in overall world income, it follows the Solow model and takes worldwide technological progress as exogenous. Further, our eventual goal is to make quantitative statements about cross-country income differences. The model therefore assumes Cobb–Douglas production; this makes the model tractable and leads easily to quantitative analysis. A further advantage of the Cobb–Douglas assumption is that it appears to be a reasonably accurate approximation to actual production functions. Our desire to do quantitative analysis also means that it is easiest to consider a model that, in the spirit of the Solow model, takes the saving rate and the allocation of resources to human-capital accumulation as exogenous. This will allow us to relate the model to observable quantities rather than to unobservable preference parameters.

Before we proceed, it is important to be clear about the difference between human capital and abstract knowledge. Although the acquisition of human capital by a worker involves learning, there is a clear conceptual distinction between human capital and abstract knowledge. Human capital consists of the acquired abilities, skills, and knowledge of individual workers. Thus, like conventional economic goods, it is rival and excludable. For example, the fact that an engineer's full effort is being devoted to one activity precludes the simultaneous use of his or her skills in another activity. In contrast, if an algorithm is being used in one activity, that in no way makes its use in another activity more difficult or less productive.

Assumptions

The model is set in continuous time. Output at time t is

$$Y(t) = K(t)^{\alpha}[A(t)H(t)]^{1-\alpha}. \tag{3.45}$$

Y, K, and A are the same as in the Solow model: Y is output, K is capital, and A is the effectiveness of labor. H is the total amount of productive services supplied by workers. That is, it is the total contribution of workers of different skill levels to production. It therefore includes the contributions of both raw labor (that is, skills that individuals are endowed with) and human capital (that is, acquired skills).

The dynamics of K and A are the same as in the Solow model. An exogenous fraction s of output is saved, and capital depreciates at an exogenous

---

[24] Jones (1998, Chapter 3) presents a similar model.

rate δ. Thus,

$$\dot{K}(t) = sY(t) - \delta K(t). \tag{3.46}$$

Technological progress occurs at an exogenous rate g:

$$\dot{A}(t) = gA(t). \tag{3.47}$$

The model revolves around its assumptions about how the quantity of human capital, H, is determined. Paralleling the treatment of physical capital, the model takes the allocation of resources to human-capital accumulation as exogenous. Nonetheless, we must take a stand about the amount of human capital created by a given amount of resources devoted to human-capital accumulation; that is, we must take a stand about the production function for human capital. The model assumes that the amount of human capital each worker has depends only on the number of years of education he or she obtains. This is equivalent to assuming that the only input into the production function for human capital is students' time. The next section briefly discusses what happens if physical capital and existing workers' human capital are also inputs to human-capital production.

For tractability, the model also assumes that each worker obtains the same amount of education, denoted E. We focus on the case where E is constant over time. Thus, our assumption is

$$H(t) = L(t)G(E), \tag{3.48}$$

where L is the number of workers and $G(\bullet)$ is a function giving human capital per worker as a function of years of education per worker.[25] As in the Solow model, the number of workers grows at an exogenous rate n (at least when E is constant):

$$\dot{L}(t) = nL(t). \tag{3.49}$$

It is reasonable to assume that the more education a worker has, the more human capital he or she has. That is, we assume $G'(\bullet) > 0$. But there is no reason to impose $G''(\bullet) < 0$. As individuals acquire human capital, their ability to acquire additional human capital may improve. To put it differently, the first few years of education may provide individuals mainly with basic tools, such as the ability to read, count, and follow directions, that by themselves do not allow the individuals to contribute much to output but that are essential for acquiring additional human capital.

The microeconomic evidence suggests that a reasonable approximation is that each additional year of education increases an individual's wage by the same *percentage* amount. If wages reflect the labor services that individuals supply, this implies that $G'(\bullet)$ is indeed increasing. Specifically, it implies that $G(\bullet)$ takes the form

---

[25] Expression (3.48) implies that of total labor services, $LG(0)$ is raw labor and the remainder, $L[G(E) - G(0)]$, is human capital. If $G(0)$ is much smaller than $G(E)$, almost all of labor services are human capital.

$$G(E) = e^{\phi E}, \qquad \phi > 0, \tag{3.50}$$

where we have normalized $G(0)$ to 1. For the most part, however, we will not impose this functional form in our analysis.

Analyzing the Model

The dynamics of the model are exactly like those of the Solow model. The easiest way to see this is to define k as physical capital per unit of effective labor services. That is, define $k = K/[AG(E)L]$. Analysis like that in Section 1.3 shows that the dynamics of k are identical to those in the Solow model. That is,

$$\begin{aligned}
\dot{k}(t) &= sf(k(t)) - (n + g + \delta)k(t) \\
&= sk(t)^{\alpha} - (n + g + \delta)k(t).
\end{aligned} \tag{3.51}$$

In the first line, $f(\bullet)$ is the intensive form of the production function; that is, it gives output per unit of effective labor services, y, as a function of physical capital per unit of effective labor services, k (see Section 1.2). The second line uses the fact that the production function is Cobb–Douglas.

As in the Solow model, k converges to the point where $\dot{k} = 0$. From (3.51), this value of k is $[s/(n + g + \delta)]^{1/(1-\alpha)}$, which we will denote k^*. We also know that once k reaches k^*, the economy is on a balanced growth path with output per worker growing at rate g.

In addition, this analysis implies that the qualitative and quantitative effects of a change in the saving rate are the same as in the Solow model. To see this, note that since the equation of motion for k is identical to that in the Solow model, the effects of a change in s on the path of k are identical to those in the Solow model. And since output per unit of effective labor services, y, is determined by k, it follows that the impact on the path of y is identical. Finally, output per worker equals output per unit of effective labor services, y, times effective labor services per worker, $AG(E)$: $Y/L = AG(E)y$. The path of $AG(E)$ is not affected by the change in the saving rate: A grows at exogenous rate g, and $G(E)$ is constant. Thus the impact of the change on the path of output per worker is determined entirely by its impact on the path of y.

We can also describe the long-run effects of a rise in the number of years of schooling per worker, E. Since E does not enter the equation for $\dot{k}$, the balanced-growth-path value of k is unchanged, and so the balanced-growth-path value of y is unchanged. And since Y/L equals $AG(E)y$, it follows that the rise in E increases output per worker on the balanced growth path by the same proportion that it increases $G(E)$.

This model has two implications for cross-country income differences. First, it identifies an additional potential source of these differences: they can stem from differences in human capital as well as physical capital.

Second, given the model's assumptions about how human capital is accumulated, it implies that recognizing the existence of human capital does not change the Solow model's implications about the effects of physical-capital accumulation. That is, the effects of a change in the saving rate are no different in this model than they are in the Solow model.

Students and Workers

Thus far, our analysis focuses on output per *worker*. In the case of a change in the saving rate, the behavior of output per person is the same as that of output per worker. But a change in the amount of time individuals spend in school changes the proportion of the population that is working. Thus in this case, the effects on output per person differ from the effects on output per worker.

To address this issue, we need some additional demographic assumptions. The easiest and most natural ones are that each individual has some fixed lifespan, T, and that individuals spend the first E years of life in school and the remaining $T - E$ years working. Further, for the overall population to be growing at rate n and the age distribution to be well behaved, the number of people born per unit time must grow at rate n.

With these assumptions, the total population at t equals the number of people born from $t - T$ to t. Thus if we use $N(t)$ to denote the population at t and $B(t)$ to denote the number of people born at t,

$$N(t) = \int_{\tau=0}^{T} B(t - \tau) \, d\tau$$

$$= \int_{\tau=0}^{T} B(t)e^{-n\tau} d\tau \tag{3.52}$$

$$= \frac{1 - e^{-nT}}{n} B(t),$$

where the second line uses the fact that the number of people born per unit time grows at rate n.

Similarly, the number of workers at time t equals the number of individuals who are alive and no longer in school. Thus it equals the number of people born from $t - T$ to $t - E$:

$$L(t) = \int_{\tau=E}^{T} B(t - \tau) \, d\tau$$

$$= \int_{\tau=E}^{T} B(t)e^{-n\tau} \, d\tau \tag{3.53}$$

$$= \frac{e^{-nE} - e^{-nT}}{n} B(t).$$

Combining expressions (3.52) and (3.53) shows that the ratio of the number of workers to the total population is

$$\frac{L(t)}{N(t)} = \frac{e^{-nE} - e^{-nT}}{1 - e^{-nT}}. \tag{3.54}$$

This analysis allows us to find output per person (as opposed to output per worker) on the balanced growth path. Output per person equals output per unit of effective labor services, y, times the amount of effective labor services supplied by the average person. And the amount of effective labor services supplied by the average person equals the amount supplied by the average worker, $A(t)G(E)$, times the fraction of the population that is working, $(e^{-nE} - e^{-nT})/(1 - e^{-nT})$. Thus,

$$\left(\frac{Y}{N}\right)^* = y^* A(t) G(E) \frac{e^{-nE} - e^{-nT}}{1 - e^{-nT}}, \tag{3.55}$$

where y^* equals $f(k^*)$, output per unit of effective labor services on the balanced growth path.

We saw above that a change in E does not affect y^*. In addition, the path of A is exogenous. Thus our analysis implies that a change in the amount of education each person receives, E, alters output per person on the balanced growth path by the same proportion that it changes $G(E)[(e^{-nE} - e^{-nT})/(1 - e^{-nT})]$. A rise in education therefore has a positive and a negative effect on output per person. Each worker has more human capital; that is, the $G(E)$ term rises. But a smaller fraction of the population is working; that is, the $(e^{-nE} - e^{-nT})/(1 - e^{-nT})$ term falls. Thus a rise in E can either raise or lower output per person in the long run.[26]

The specifics of how the economy converges to its new balanced growth path in response to a rise in E are somewhat complicated. In the short run, the rise reduces output relative to what it otherwise would have been. In addition, the adjustment to the new balanced growth path is very gradual. To see these points, suppose the economy is on a balanced growth path with $E = E_0$. Now suppose that everyone born after some time, t_0, obtains $E_1 > E_0$ years of education. This change first affects the economy at date $t_0 + E_0$. From this date until $t_0 + E_1$, everyone who is working still has E_0 years of education, and some individuals who would have been working if E had not risen are still in school. The highly educated individuals start to enter the labor force at date $t_0 + E_1$. The average level of education in the labor force does not reach its new balanced-growth-path value until date $t_0 + T$, however. And even then, the stock of physical capital is still adjusting to the changed path of effective labor services, and so the adjustment to the new balanced growth path is not complete.

These results about the effects of an increase in education on the path of output per person are similar to the Solow model's implications about the effects of an increase in the saving rate on the path of consumption

---

[26] See Problem 3.16 for an analysis of the "golden-rule" level of E in this model.

per person. In both cases, the shift in resources leads to a short-run fall in the variable of interest (output per person in this model, consumption per person in the Solow model). And in both cases, the long-run effect on the variable of interest is ambiguous.

3.9   Empirical Application: Accounting for Cross-Country Income Differences

An essential step in understanding income differences among countries is to determine to what extent they are due to differences in physical-capital accumulation, differences in human-capital accumulation, and other factors. This question is tackled empirically by Hall and Jones (1999) and Klenow and Rodríguez-Clare (1997). Loosely speaking, their idea is to do growth accounting (see Section 1.7), but to do it across countries rather than over time. These authors measure differences in the accumulation of physical and human capital, and then use a framework like the model of the previous section to estimate the quantitative importance of those differences to income differences. They then estimate the importance of other forces as a residual.

Procedure

Hall and Jones and Klenow and Rodríguez-Clare begin by assuming, as we did in the previous section, that output in a given country is a Cobb–Douglas combination of physical capital and effective labor services:

$$Y_i = K_i^\alpha (A_i H_i)^{1-\alpha}, \tag{3.56}$$

where i indexes countries. A's contribution will be measured as a residual; thus it reflects not just technology or knowledge, but all forces that determine output for given amounts of physical capital and labor services.

Dividing both sides of (3.56) by the number of workers, L_i, and taking logs yields

$$\ln \frac{Y_i}{L_i} = \alpha \ln \frac{K_i}{L_i} + (1 - \alpha) \ln \frac{H_i}{L_i} + (1 - \alpha) \ln A_i. \tag{3.57}$$

The basic idea in these papers, as in growth accounting over time, is to measure directly all the ingredients of this equation other than A_i and then compute A_i as a residual. Thus (3.57) can be used to decompose differences in output per worker into the contributions of physical capital per worker, labor services per worker, and a residual.

Klenow and Rodríguez-Clare and Hall and Jones observe, however, that this decomposition is not the most interesting one. Suppose, for example, that the level of A rises with no change in the saving rate or in education per worker. The resulting higher output increases the amount of physical capital (since the premise of the example is that the saving *rate* is unchanged). When the country reaches its new balanced growth path, physical capital and output are both higher by the same proportion as the increase in A. The decomposition in (3.57) therefore attributes fraction α of the long-run increase in output per worker in response to the increase in A to physical capital per worker. It would be more useful to have a decomposition that attributes all the increase to the residual, since the rise in A was the underlying source of the increase in output per worker.

To address this issue, Klenow and Rodríguez-Clare and Hall and Jones subtract $\alpha \ln(Y_i/L_i)$ from both sides of (3.57). This yields

$$(1-\alpha)\ln\frac{Y_i}{L_i} = \left(\alpha\ln\frac{K_i}{L_i} - \alpha\ln\frac{Y_i}{L_i}\right) + (1-\alpha)\ln\frac{H_i}{L_i} + (1-\alpha)\ln A_i$$

$$= \alpha\ln\frac{K_i}{Y_i} + (1-\alpha)\ln\frac{H_i}{L_i} + (1-\alpha)\ln A_i. \tag{3.58}$$

Dividing both sides by $1-\alpha$ gives us

$$\ln\frac{Y_i}{L_i} = \frac{\alpha}{1-\alpha}\ln\frac{K_i}{Y_i} + \ln\frac{H_i}{L_i} + \ln A_i. \tag{3.59}$$

Equation (3.59) expresses output per worker in terms of physical-capital intensity (that is, the capital-output ratio, K/Y), labor services per worker, and a residual. It is no more correct than equation (3.57): both result from manipulating the production function, (3.56). But (3.59) is more insightful for our purposes: it assigns the long-run effects of changes in labor services per worker and the residual entirely to those variables.

Data and Basic Results

Data on output and the number of workers are available from the Penn World Tables.[27] Hall and Jones and Klenow and Rodríguez-Clare construct estimates of physical-capital stocks from the Penn World Tables and reasonable assumptions about the initial stocks and depreciation. Data on income shares suggest that α, physical capital's share in the production function, is around $\frac{1}{3}$.

The hardest part of the analysis is to estimate the stock of labor services, H. Hall and Jones take the simplest approach. They consider only years of schooling. Specifically, they assume that H_i takes the form $e^{\phi(E_i)}L_i$, where E_i is the average number of years of education of workers in country i and $\phi(\bullet)$ is an increasing function. In the previous section, we considered the possibility of a linear $\phi(\bullet)$ function: $\phi(E) = \phi E$. Hall and Jones argue,

---

[27] These data are described by Summers and Heston (1991) and are available online from the National Bureau of Economic Research.

however, that the microeconomic evidence suggests that the percentage increase in earnings from an additional year of schooling falls as the amount of schooling rises. On the basis of this evidence, they assume that $\phi(E)$ is a piecewise linear function with a slope of 0.134 for E below 4 years, 0.101 for E between 4 and 8 years, and 0.068 for E above 8 years.

Armed with these data and assumptions, Hall and Jones use expression (3.59) to estimate the contributions of physical-capital intensity, schooling, and the residual to output per worker in each country. They summarize their results by comparing the five richest countries in their sample with the five poorest. Average output per worker in the rich group exceeds the average in the poor group by a stunning factor of 31.7. On a log scale, this is a difference of 3.5. The difference in the average $[\alpha/(1-\alpha)]\ln(K/Y)$ between the two groups is 0.6; in $\ln(H/L)$, 0.8; and in $\ln A$, 2.1. That is, only about a sixth of the gap between the richest and poorest countries is due proximately to differences in physical-capital intensity, and less than a quarter is due proximately to differences in schooling. Klenow and Rodríguez-Clare, using slightly different assumptions, reach similar conclusions.

The other important finding from Hall and Jones's and Klenow and Rodríguez-Clare's decompositions is that the contributions of physical capital, schooling, and the residual are not independent. Hall and Jones, for example, find a substantial correlation across countries between their estimates of $\ln(H_i/L_i)$ and $\ln A_i$ ($\rho = 0.52$), and a modest one between their estimates of $[\alpha/(1-\alpha)]\ln(K_i/L_i)$ and $\ln A_i$ ($\rho = 0.25$); they also find a substantial correlation between the two capital terms ($\rho = 0.60$). This suggests that there may be underlying forces that affect all the proximate determinants of output per worker.

Differences in Human-Capital Quality

There are two potential problems with Hall and Jones's and Klenow and Rodríguez-Clare's accounting exercises. First, like all growth-accounting calculations, they measure physical and human capital's contributions to output by their market earnings. If there are externalities from physical or human capital, their marginal products differ from their earnings. As a result, the cross-country accounting procedure misestimates their contribution to cross-country income differences. We will return to this issue at the end of Section 3.10.

The second potential problem is specific to the calculations just described. Those calculations ignore all differences in human capital other than differences in years of education. But there are many other sources of variation in human capital. School quality, on-the-job training, informal human-capital acquisition, child-rearing, and even prenatal care vary significantly across countries. The resulting differences in human capital may be large.

One way to incorporate differences in human-capital quality into the analysis is to continue to use the decomposition in equation (3.59), but to obtain a more comprehensive measure of human capital. A natural approach to comparing the overall human capital of workers in different countries is to compare the wages they would earn in the same labor market. Since the United States has immigrants from many countries, this can be done by examining the wages of immigrants from different countries in the United States. Of course, there are complications. For example, immigrants are not chosen randomly from the workers in their home countries, and they may have characteristics that affect their earnings in the United States that would not affect their earnings in their home countries. Nonetheless, looking at immigrants' wages provides important information about whether there are large differences in human-capital quality.

Klenow and Rodríguez-Clare use the work of Borjas (1987) to carry out this exercise. They find that Borjas's estimates imply that, on average, the wage that a worker with a given amount of education earns in the United States is 0.12 percent higher when income per person in the immigrant's home country is 1 percent higher. This suggests that when we look at countries whose log incomes differ by 3.5, the logs of their human-capital qualities for given levels of education differ by about 0.12 times 3.5, or 0.4. And indeed, Borjas finds a difference of roughly 40 percent in wages for a given level of education between immigrants from the richest and poorest countries he considers. Recall that the decomposition in (3.59) attributed roughly 0.8 of the overall gap in log income between the richest and poorest countries to differences in their workers' years of education. Borjas's results imply that a decomposition like (3.59) with a comprehensive measure of human capital assigns an additional 0.4 of the gap to differences in human capital, and thus 0.4 less to the residual. This leaves an overall decomposition of 0.6, or about a sixth, to physical capital; 1.2, or about a third, to human capital; and 1.7, or about a half, to the residual. In short, broadening the measure of human capital does not change the main conclusions from Hall and Jones's and Klenow and Rodríguez-Clare's analysis.[28]

---

[28] The approach of using the decomposition in equation (3.59) with a broader measure of human capital has a disadvantage like that of our preliminary decomposition, (3.57). Physical capital is likely to affect human-capital quality. For example, differences in the amount of physical capital in schools are likely to be one source of differences in school quality. When physical capital affects human-capital quality, a rise in the saving rate or in the residual raises income per worker partly by raising human-capital quality via a higher stock of physical capital. With a comprehensive measure of human capital, the decomposition in (3.59) assigns that portion of the rise in income to human-capital quality; ideally, however, we would rather assign it to the underlying change in the saving rate or in the residual. Thus, we would prefer to assign some of the additional 0.4 that our approach assigns to human capital to physical capital and the residual. That is, the overall figure of 1.2 is a generous estimate of the importance of human capital.

The alternative is to specify a production function for human capital and then use this to create a decomposition that is more informative. Klenow and Rodríguez-Clare consider

Factor Returns and Factor Flows

In Section 1.6, we encountered an overwhelming argument against the hypothesis that cross-country income differences are due solely to differences in physical capital: this hypothesis implies that the marginal product of capital is enormously larger in poor countries than in rich ones, and thus that there are vast incentives for capital to flow from rich to poor countries. It is therefore important to check what Hall and Jones's and Klenow and Rodríguez-Clare's estimates of the sources of income differences suggest about factors' marginal products.

Recall that we found a difference of about 0.6 in $[\alpha/(1-\alpha)]\ln(Y/K)$ between the richest and poorest countries. This stems from a difference in $\ln(Y/K)$ of about 1.2 and an assumed value of $\alpha/(1-\alpha)$ of 0.5. With Cobb–Douglas production, the marginal product of physical capital is $\alpha Y/K$. Thus a difference in $\ln(Y/K)$ of 1.2 translates into a difference in the marginal product of physical capital of about a factor of $e^{1.2}$, or 3.3. That is, if the Cobb–Douglas assumption and the data on capital and output are roughly correct, there are large differences in the marginal product of capital between rich and poor countries.

We saw in Section 1.6 that explaining the entire income gap between rich and poor countries on the basis of physical capital with α roughly equal to $\frac{1}{3}$ requires a difference of a factor of about 1000 in the marginal product of capital. Such differences surely do not exist. Differences of a factor of 3 or so, on the other hand, are not implausible. Most obviously, different countries tax capital at very different rates. Probably more important, there is substantial variation across countries in the risk of partial loss of capital or its return to government expropriation, litigation, theft and extortion, bribe-taking officials, and collective action by workers. Finally, there are significant barriers to international capital mobility, especially in poor countries. Thus even returns that have been adjusted for taxes and expropriation risk may differ substantially across countries.

Workers generally want to move to richer countries. We want to determine whether Hall and Jones's and Klenow and Rodríguez-Clare's results are consistent with this fact. To do this, note that the marginal product of labor services, which we will denote MPH, is $(1-\alpha)Y/H$. Equation (3.59) implies $Y = (K/Y)^{\alpha/(1-\alpha)}HA$. Thus,

$$\text{MPH} = (1-\alpha)\left(\frac{K}{Y}\right)^{\alpha/(1-\alpha)} A. \tag{3.60}$$

The results of the cross-country growth accounting described above suggest

---

this approach. It turns out, however, that the results are quite sensitive to the details of how the production function for human capital is specified.

that both $(K/Y)^{\alpha/(1-\alpha)}$ and A are generally higher in richer countries, and that the differences in A are large. Thus, the results imply that the marginal product of a worker supplying a given amount of labor services is substantially higher in richer countries. That is, Hall and Jones's and Klenow and Rodríguez-Clare's findings are quite consistent with the fact that workers generally want to move to richer countries.

3.10   Social Infrastructure

Overview

The analysis in the previous section tells us about the roles of physical-capital accumulation, human-capital accumulation, and output for given quantities of capital in cross-country income differences. But we would like to go deeper and investigate the determinants of these proximate sources of income differences.

A leading candidate hypothesis is that differences in these determinants of income stem largely from differences in what Hall and Jones call *social infrastructure*. By social infrastructure, Hall and Jones mean institutions and policies that encourage investment and production over consumption and diversion. Note that two distinctions are being made here. The first is between consumption and investment. The use of resources to create physical and human capital increases future output, while their use to create goods and services for current consumption does not. The second distinction is between production and diversion. Production refers to activities that increase the economy's total output at a point in time. Diversion, which we encountered in Section 3.4 under the name *rent-seeking*, refers to activities that merely reallocate that output.

Discussions of diversion or rent-seeking often focus on its most obvious forms, such as crime, lobbying for tax benefits, and frivolous lawsuits. Since these activities use only small fractions of resources in advanced economies, it is natural to think that rent-seeking is not of great importance in those countries. But rent-seeking consists of much more than these pure forms. Much of economic activity has elements of rent-seeking. Such commonplace activities as firms engaging in price discrimination, workers providing documentation for performance evaluations, and consumers clipping coupons have large elements of rent-seeking. Indeed, such everyday actions as locking one's car or going to a concert early to try to get a ticket involve rent-seeking. Thus even in advanced countries, substantial fractions of resources are probably devoted to rent-seeking. And it seems plausible that the fraction is considerably higher in less developed countries. If this is correct, differences in rent-seeking may be an important source of cross-country income differences. Likewise, as described in Section 3.4, the extent of rent-seeking in the world as a whole may be an important determinant of worldwide growth.[29]

There are many different aspects of social infrastructure. It is useful to divide them into three groups. The first group consists of features of the government's fiscal policy. For example, the tax treatment of investment and the allocation of government spending between investment projects and other spending directly affect allocations between investment and consumption. Only slightly more subtly, high tax rates induce such forms of rent-seeking as devoting resources to tax evasion and working in the underground economy despite its relative inefficiency.

The second group of institutions and policies that make up social infrastructure consists of factors that determine the environment that private decisions are made in. If crime is unchecked or there is civil war or foreign invasion, private rewards to investment and to activities that raise overall output are low. At a more mundane level, if contracts are not enforced or the courts' interpretation of them is unpredictable, long-term investment projects are less attractive. Similarly, competition, with its rewards for activities that increase overall output, is more likely when the government allows free trade and limits monopoly power.

The final group of policies that constitute social infrastructure consists of rent-seeking activities by the government itself. As Hall and Jones stress, although well-designed government policies can be an important source of beneficial social infrastructure, the government can be a major rent-seeker. Government expropriation, the solicitation of bribes, and the doling out of benefits in response to lobbying or to actions that benefit government officials can be important forms of rent-seeking.

Because social infrastructure has many dimensions, poor social infrastructure takes many forms. There can be Stalinist central planning where property rights and economic incentives are minimal. There can be "kleptocracy"—an economy run by an oligarchy or a dictatorship whose main interest is personal enrichment and preservation of power, and which relies on expropriation and corruption. There can be near anarchy, where property and lives are extremely insecure. And so on.

Evidence

The idea that institutions and policies that affect choices between consumption and investment and between production and diversion are crucial to

---

[29] The seminal paper on rent-seeking is Tullock (1967). Laband and Sophocleus (1992) attempt to estimate the overall extent of diversion in the U.S. economy. Rent-seeking is important to many phenomena other than cross-country income differences. For example, Krueger (1974) shows its importance for understanding the effects of tariffs and other government interventions, and Posner (1975) argues that it is essential to understanding the welfare effects of monopoly.

economic performance dates back at least to Adam Smith. But it has recently received renewed attention. Important papers include Baumol (1990); Murphy, Shleifer, and Vishny (1991); Olson (1996); Sachs and Warner (1995); Knack and Keefer (1995); Mauro (1995); and Hall and Jones (1999). One distinguishing feature of this recent work is that it attempts to provide empirical evidence about the importance of social infrastructure.

Several pieces of evidence suggest that social infrastructure is important to differences in income among countries. The first, and maybe most compelling, is the evidence provided by the experience of divided countries (Olson, 1996). For most of the post-World War II period, both Germany and Korea were divided into two countries. Similarly, Hong Kong and Taiwan were separated from China. Many variables that might affect income, such as climate, natural resources, initial levels of physical and human capital, and cultural attitudes toward work, thrift, and entrepreneurship, were similar in the different parts of these divided areas. Their social infrastructures, however, were very different: East Germany, North Korea, and China were communist, while West Germany, South Korea, Hong Kong, and Taiwan had relatively free-market economies.

The market-oriented regimes were dramatically more successful economically than the communist ones. In 1990, when Germany was reunited, output per worker was about $2\frac{1}{2}$ times larger in the West than in the East. When China reacquired Hong Kong in 1997, output per worker was about 10 times larger in Hong Kong than in the mainland. Similarly, output per worker is between 5 and 10 times higher in Taiwan than in mainland China. We have no reliable data on output per worker in North Korea; but South Korea's output per worker is only slightly lower than Taiwan's, while all the evidence suggests that North Korea's is much lower than China's. In sum, in the cases of these very large cross-country income differences, differences in social infrastructure appear to have been crucial. More generally, the evidence provided by these historical accidents strongly suggests that social infrastructure has a large effect on income.

A second type of evidence is provided by cross-country differences in the capital-output ratio. If the production function is roughly Cobb–Douglas, differences in the capital-output ratio imply differences in the marginal product of capital. The analysis in the previous section suggests that there are substantial differences in the capital-output ratio, and hence in the marginal product of capital. And the discussion there suggested that these differences may be to a large extent the result of differences in the gap between the marginal product of capital and private incentives to invest. Some candidate explanations of differences in this gap included differences in tax rates, corruption, risk of expropriation, and so on—that is, differences in various types of social infrastructure. In other words, the capital-output ratio is a rough measure of social infrastructure.

The accounting analysis in the previous section implies that there is a large correlation between the capital-output ratio and overall output per

worker. Using Hall and Jones's estimates, for example, the correlation between $\ln(K_i/Y_i)$ and $\ln(Y_i/L_i)$ is 0.6. That is, there is a substantial correlation between this simple measure of social infrastructure and overall
income per worker.

The final piece of evidence comes from attempts to estimate the relationship between social infrastructure and economic performance statistically. Such studies are carried out by Sachs and Warner (1995); Knack and
Keefer (1995); Mauro (1995); Murphy, Shleifer, and Vishny (1991); Temple
and Johnson (1998); Acemoglu, Johnson, and Robinson (2000); and Hall and
Jones. These papers derive measures of social infrastructure and examine
how the measures are related to the level or growth rate of average income.[30]
One of the most thorough attempts is Hall and Jones's. They attempt to account for the facts that measures of social infrastructure are imperfect and
that there are almost surely unmeasured forces that are correlated with social infrastructure and that affect economic performance. Hall and Jones
argue that the data suggest that social infrastructure has a quantitatively
large and statistically significant impact on output per worker, and that
variations in social infrastructure account for a large part of cross-country
income differences. But because their corrections for measurement error
and correlation of social infrastructure with omitted variables are surely
imperfect, this evidence is far from decisive.[31]

The Determinants of Social Infrastructure

If we could, we would like to go even deeper and examine what determines
social infrastructure. Unfortunately, there has been little work on this issue. Our knowledge consists of little more than speculation and scraps of
evidence.

One set of speculations focuses on incentives, particularly those of individuals with power under the existing system. The clearest example of the
importance of incentives to social infrastructure is provided by absolute
dictators. An absolute dictator can expropriate any wealth that individuals
accumulate; but the knowledge that dictators can do this discourages individuals from accumulating wealth in the first place. Thus for the dictator
to encourage saving and entrepreneurship, he or she may need to give up
some power. Doing so might make it possible to make everyone, including
the dictator, much better off. But in practice, for reasons that are not well
understood, it is difficult for a dictator to do this in a way that does not
involve some risk of losing power (and perhaps much more) entirely. Fur-

---

[30] See also the historical evidence in Baumol (1990); Olson (1982); North (1981); and De
Long and Shleifer (1993).

[31] Rodríguez and Rodrik (1999) provide an important critique of the measure of social
infrastructure developed by Sachs and Warner (1995). Since Hall and Jones employ Sachs
and Warner's measure, Rodríguez and Rodrik's critique is relevant to their analysis as well.

ther, the dictator is likely to have little difficulty in amassing large amounts of wealth even in a poor economy. Thus he or she is unlikely to accept even a small chance of being overthrown in return for a large increase in expected wealth. The result may be that an absolute dictator prefers a social infrastructure that leads to low average income (De Long and Shleifer, 1993; North, 1981; Jones, 1998, pp. 138–140).

Similar considerations may be relevant for other individuals who benefit from an existing system, such as bribe-taking government officials and workers earning above-market wages in industries where production occurs using labor-intensive, inefficient technologies. If the existing system is highly inefficient, it should be possible to compensate these individuals generously for agreeing to move to a more efficient system. But again, in practice we rarely observe such arrangements, and as a result these individuals have a large stake in the continuation of the existing system (Shleifer and Vishny, 1993; Parente and Prescott, 1999; Acemoglu and Robinson, 2000a, 2000b).

A second set of speculations focuses on factors that fall under the heading of culture. Societies have fairly persistent characteristics arising from religion, family structure, and so on that can have important effects on social infrastructure. For example, different religions suggest different views about the relative importance of tradition, authority, and individual initiative. The implicit or explicit messages of the prevailing religion about these factors may influence individuals' views, and may in turn affect the society's choice of social infrastructure. To give another example, there seems to be considerable variation across countries in norms of civic responsibility and in the extent to which people generally view one another as trustworthy (Knack and Keefer, 1997; La Porta, Lopez-de-Silanes, Shleifer, and Vishny, 1997). Again, these difference are likely to affect social infrastructure. As a final example, countries differ greatly in their ethnic diversity, and countries with greater ethnic diversity appear to have less favorable social infrastructure (Easterly and Levine, 1997).

The final main set of speculations focuses on individuals' beliefs about what types of policies and institutions are best for economic development. For example, Sachs and Warner (1995) emphasize that in the early postwar period, the relative merits of state planning and markets were not at all clear. The major market economies had just been through the Great Depression, while the Soviet Union had gone from a backward economy to one of the world's leading industrial countries in just a few decades. Reasonable people disagreed about the merits of alternative forms of social infrastructure. As a result, one important source of differences in social infrastructure was differences in leaders' judgments.

The combination of beliefs and incentives in the determination of social infrastructure creates the possibility of "vicious circles" in social infrastructure. A country may initially adopt a relatively centralized, interventionist system because its leaders sincerely believe that this system is best for the majority of the population. But the adoption of such a system creates groups with interests in its continuation. Thus even as the evidence accumulates that other types of social infrastructure are preferable, the system is very difficult to change. This may capture important elements of the determination of social infrastructure in many sub-Saharan African countries after they became independent (Krueger, 1993).

Limitations and Extensions

The definition of social infrastructure as institutions and policies that promote production and investment over diversion and consumption is very broad. Indeed, it is hard to think of any aspect of institutions and policies that affect a country's income that would not arguably constitute part of social infrastructure. As a result, the statement that differences in social infrastructure are crucial for cross-country income differences does not deliver anything approaching precise predictions about what country characteristics are associated with higher incomes. Similarly, it does not suggest specific advice for a policymaker seeking to raise standards of living.

There are two ways that one could make the hypothesis that social infrastructure is critical to economic performance more precise. First, one could identify particular aspects of social infrastructure that are especially important. For example, many informal arguments emphasize some specific element of social infrastructure, such as secure property rights, political stability, or market orientation. Second, one could identify variables affected by social infrastructure that are especially important. For example, suppose there is a specific type of capital that has large positive externalities. Then institutions and policies that affect investment in that type of capital are especially important to economic performance.

Empirical work on cross-country income differences has identified a host of variables that are associated with better economic performance. Examples include financial development (King and Levine, 1993a, 1993b; Jappelli and Pagano, 1994; Jayaratne and Strahan, 1996; Levine and Zervos, 1998); low microeconomic distortions (Easterly, 1993); political stability (Barro, 1991); and low inflation (Fischer, 1993; Cukierman, Kalaitzidakis, Summers, and Webb, 1993; Bruno and Easterly, 1998). In all these cases, it is reasonable to be concerned that the variable being examined may be correlated with omitted forces that affect economic performance, and thus that the statistical association may not reflect a true impact of the variable. But suppose that for some of these variables, the empirical findings survive scrutiny and imply that the variable has a quantitatively important effect. Then the findings would imply that aspects of social infrastructure that affect those variables are especially important to economic performance, as are other determinants of those variables.

One potential determinant of economic performance that has received considerable attention is externalities from capital. In this view, capital earns less than its marginal product. High-skill workers create innovations, which benefit all workers, and increase other workers' human capital in ways for which they are not compensated. The accumulation of physical capital causes workers to acquire human capital and promotes the development of new techniques of production; again, the owners of the capital are not fully compensated for these contributions. We encountered such possibilities in the learning-by-doing models of Sections 3.4 and 3.5 in Part A of this chapter.[32]

If this view is correct, Klenow and Rodríguez-Clare's and Hall and Jones's accounting exercises are uninformative. If capital has positive externalities, a decomposition that uses its private returns to measure its marginal product understates its importance. Further, this view is consistent with the finding of the accounting exercises that the estimated contributions of capital and the residual are positively correlated: in this view, some of what these exercises attribute to the residual in fact reflects capital's contribution.

This view implies that the key determinants of cross-country income differences are factors that give rise to differences in capital accumulation. This implies that only some aspects of social infrastructure are critical, and that factors other than social infrastructure that affect capital accumulation, such as cultural attitudes toward thrift and education, are important as well.

Two types of evidence, however, argue against the view that externalities from capital are crucial to cross-country income differences. First, there is no compelling microeconomic evidence of local externalities from capital large enough to account for the enormous income differences we observe. Second, direct observation of how poor economies function strongly suggests that differences in the allocation of resources between productive and unproductive activities are important to income differences: in many countries, crime, corruption, and heavy-handed government intervention are pervasive and appear to harm economic performance severely. The experiences of divided countries are a glaring example of this. Highly statist economies such as East Germany and North Korea are often very successful at the accumulation of physical and human capital, and often achieve higher capital-output ratios than their market-oriented counterparts. But these countries' economic performance is generally dismal.[33]

---

[32] For such externalities to contribute to cross-country income differences, they must be somewhat localized. If the externalities are global (as would be the case if capital accumulation produces additional knowledge, as in the learning-by-doing models), they raise world income but do not produce differences among countries.

[33] Early theoretical models of externalities from capital include P. Romer (1986), Lucas (1988), and Rebelo (1991). When applied naively to the issue of cross-country income differences, these models tend to have the counterfactual implication that countries with higher saving rates have permanently higher growth rates. More recent models of capital externalities that focus explicitly on the issue of income differences among countries generally avoid this implication. See, for example, Basu and Weil (1999). De Long and Summers (1991, 1992) provide empirical evidence of a strong association between investment in a particular kind

3.11   A Model of Production, Protection, and Predation

The previous section considers the possibility that the allocation of re-sources between production and rent-seeking is a crucial determinant of average income. This section presents and analyzes a simple model of this allocation. Acemoglu (1995); Murphy, Shleifer, and Vishny (1993); and Grossman and Kim (1995, 1996) present more elaborate models.

Assumptions

Individuals can be either producers or predators. Predators attempt to ob-tain others' output; producers devote resources both to producing output and to protecting it from others. Thus there are three uses of resources: production, protection, and predation.

Individuals maximize the amount of output they obtain. Thus (as long as solutions are interior), producers allocate their resources between produc-tion and protection so that their marginal returns from the two activities are equal. Likewise, individuals move between being producers and predators until the private rewards to the two are the same.

Each individual is endowed with 1 unit of time. Let f denote the frac-tion of his or her time that a representative producer devotes to protection. The production function for output is one-for-one; thus the representative producer's output is $1 - f$. The producer loses some fraction, L, of that output to rent-seekers. L depends on f and on the fraction of the popula-tion who are rent-seekers, R: $L = L(f, R)$. $L(\bullet)$ satisfies a set of plausible assumptions: $L(f, 0) = 0$ (nothing is lost when there are no rent-seekers); $L_f \leq 0$ and $L_R \geq 0$ (the fraction lost is decreasing in resources devoted to protection and increasing in the number of rent-seekers); $L_{ff} \geq 0$ (there are diminishing marginal benefits to protection); and $L_{fR} \leq 0$ (the marginal benefits of protection are greater when there are more rent-seekers).

The total amount of output lost by producers (per person in the econ-omy) is the product of three terms: $1 - R$ (the fraction of individuals who are producers), $1 - f$ (output per producer), and L (the fraction of output that is lost). Thus each rent-seeker obtains $(1-R)(1-f)L(f, R)/R$. Our final assumption about $L(\bullet)$ is that this quantity is nonincreasing in R for a given f. That is, total resources lost per rent-seeker are falling in the number of rent-seekers.

---

of capital—machinery—and economic performance. An important open question is whether this association arises because of large externalities from equipment investment or because high equipment investment is correlated with favorable social infrastructure. On the other side, Bils and Klenow (2000) provide evidence that the correlation between schooling and growth is too large to reflect an impact of schooling on growth even if there are externalities from human capital.

Analyzing the Model

The first step in analyzing the model is to consider how producers allocate their time between producing output and protecting it from rent-seekers. The representative producer's problem is

$$\text{Max}_{f}[1 - L(f, R)](1 - f). \tag{3.61}$$

The first-order condition is

$$-[1 - L(f, R)] - (1 - f)L_f(f, R) = 0. \tag{3.62}$$

We can rearrange this to obtain

$$\frac{1}{1 - f} = \frac{-L_f(f, R)}{1 - L(f, R)}. \tag{3.63}$$

The producer's goal is to maximize the product of $1 - L(f, R)$ and $1 - f$. An increase in f raises the first term and lowers the second. The producer is indifferent about changing f when the percentage increase in the $1 - L(f, R)$ term just equals the percentage decrease in the $1 - f$ term; that is, the elasticities of the two terms with respect to f must be equal and opposite. This is the condition expressed in (3.63). The assumptions that $L_f \leq 0$ and $L_{ff} \geq 0$ ensure that the second-order condition is satisfied. We assume interior solutions throughout.

A key question concerns how changes in the fraction of rent-seekers, R, affect the fraction of resources that producers devote to production. Implicitly differentiating expression (3.62) with respect to R gives

$$L_f \frac{df}{dR} + L_R - (1 - f)\left(L_{ff}\frac{df}{dR} + L_{fR}\right) + L_f \frac{df}{dR} = 0, \tag{3.64}$$

or

$$\frac{df}{dR} = \frac{L_R - (1 - f)L_{fR}}{(1 - f)L_{ff} - 2L_f}. \tag{3.65}$$

Our assumptions about $L(\bullet)$ imply that this expression is positive: a rise in the number of rent-seekers causes producers to devote more of their resources to protection. We therefore write $f = f(R)$, with $f'(R) > 0$.

The second step is to analyze the division of the population between producers and predators. Equilibrium requires that income per producer and income per predator be equal. Each producer's income is $[1 - L(f(R), R)][1 - f(R)]$. Each rent-seeker's income is $(1 - R)[1 - f(R)]L(f(R), R)/R$. Thus equilibrium requires

$$[1 - L(f(R), R)][1 - f(R)] = \frac{1 - R}{R}[1 - f(R)]L(f(R), R). \tag{3.66}$$

Figure 3.12 plots the two sides of equation (3.66) as functions of R. Both sides are decreasing in R. The left-hand side, producers' income, is decreasing in the number of rent-seekers because a rise in the number of

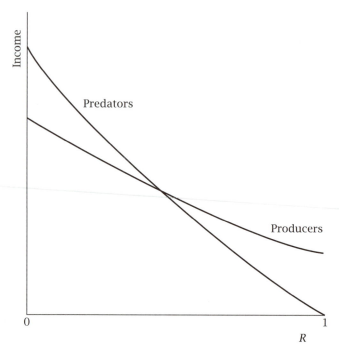

FIGURE 3.12   Producers' and predators' incomes as functions of the fraction of the population engaged in predation

rent-seekers causes producers to lose more of their output.[34] The right-hand side, rent-seekers' income, falls as R rises for two reasons. First, $(1-R)L(f,R)/R$ is decreasing in R by assumption. That is, the total amount of resources that rent-seekers obtain, given the resources producers devote to protection, is assumed to rise less than proportionally with the number of rent-seekers. Second, when R rises, f rises. This increase in the resources that producers devote to protection reduces rent-seekers' income both because producers' output falls and because rent-seekers obtain a smaller fraction of it. In addition, we know that when $R = 1$, rent-seekers' income is zero: when there are no producers, there is nothing for predators to prey on.

---

[34] In addition, a change in the number of rent-seekers causes producers to change the fraction of resources they devote to protection, f. But because producers choose f so that its marginal impact on their income is zero, the fact that f changes when R changes is irrelevant to how the change in R changes their income. Formally, we can write producers' income as $Y^{\text{PROD}}(f(R),R)$. Thus, $dY^{\text{PROD}}/dR = (\partial Y^{\text{PROD}}/\partial f)f'(R) + \partial Y^{\text{PROD}}/\partial R$. But producers choose f so that $\partial Y^{\text{PROD}}/\partial f = 0$. Thus dY^{PROD}/dR simplifies to $\partial Y^{\text{PROD}}/\partial R$. This is a specific example of the *envelope theorem*.

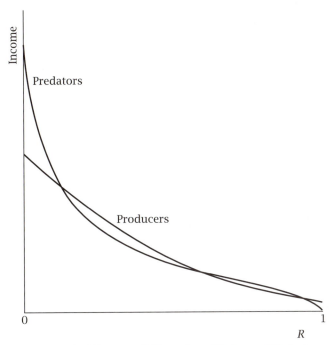

FIGURE 3.13 The possibility of multiple equilibria in the prevalence of predation

Figure 3.12 shows a case where producers' and predators' incomes are equal for only one level of R, so there is a unique equilibrium. It is plausible that when $R = 0$, the income of a person entering rent-seeking would be high: everyone else is producing, and no resources are being devoted to protection. And we know that rent-seekers' income is zero when $R = 1$. Thus the case shown in the figure is reasonable. But it is possible that there is more than one equilibrium. Figure 3.13 shows such a case.

Discussion

In this simple model, output is below potential for two reasons. Some individuals choose rent-seeking rather than production, and those who produce devote some of their resources to protecting their output from rent-seekers. If no resources were devoted to predation or prevention, each person's income would rise from $(1 - f)(1 - R)$ to 1.

To see how the model works, consider a simple example. Suppose rent-seekers face a chance of detection. If a rent-seeker is detected, the output that he or she has taken from producers is confiscated. To keep matters

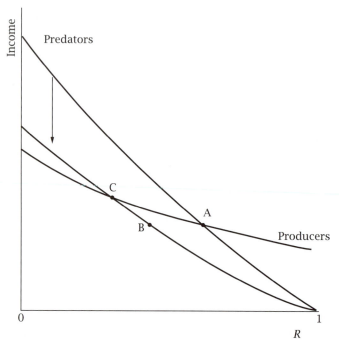

FIGURE 3.14   The effects of predators facing a probability of detection

simple, assume it is not possible to determine who the resources were taken from; thus they are distributed equally to every member of the population.

The chance of detection does not affect producers' losses for a given f and R, and so it does not affect their choice of f given R. That is, the $f(R)$ function is unchanged. But the possibility of detection causes rent-seekers' expected income for a given R to be lower. In terms of our diagram, the line showing predators' income shifts down. This is shown in Figure 3.14. The result is that R, the fraction of rent-seekers, falls. And note that R falls by even more than the amount needed to restore rent-seekers' income to its initial level. As R falls, the attractiveness of producing rises, inducing a further fall in R. In terms of the diagram, the economy moves from its initial situation at Point A not to B, where rent-seekers' income is unchanged, but to C, where producers' and rent-seekers' incomes are again equal. That is, loosely speaking, there is a multiplier effect of the fall in the attractiveness of rent-seeking.[35]

Furthermore, since $f(R)$ is increasing, the fall in R causes a fall in f, the fraction of resources that producers devote to protection. That is, f falls

[35] See Section 6.11 for more on the general idea of multipliers.

not because the $f(R)$ function shifts, but because the change in R causes a movement along the function. Both the fall in R and the fall in f raise income per person, $(1 - R)(1 - f)$.[36]

The basic model illustrates one channel through which rent-seeking can be self-reinforcing: if something happens to increase the number of rent-seekers, the attractiveness of producing falls, causing a further increase in the number of rent-seekers. This is the multiplier effect described above. But there are other channels through which rent-seeking can be self-reinforcing. For example, there is a "safety in numbers" effect. When there are more rent-seekers, each one is less likely to be caught, and so the attractiveness of rent-seeking is greater (Acemoglu, 1995). Similarly, the availability of resources to detect and punish rent-seekers and social sanctions against rent-seeking are likely to be smaller when there is more rent-seeking.

One useful extension of the model is to include capital. Suppose final output is produced using a Cobb–Douglas combination of capital and labor, and capital's share is α. As always with Cobb–Douglas production, the marginal product of capital is $\alpha Y/K$. But since producers keep only fraction $1 - L$ of their output, the private marginal product of capital is $1 - L$ times this amount. Thus high values of L discourage capital accumulation.

To see this concretely, suppose there is no depreciation, and suppose capital moves freely among countries to equate capital's private marginal product with the world rate of return, r^*. Then equilibrium requires

$$(1 - L)\alpha\frac{Y}{K} = r^*, \tag{3.67}$$

or

$$\frac{K}{Y} = \frac{(1 - L)\alpha}{r*}. \tag{3.68}$$

Thus, a rise in predation (L) lowers the capital-output ratio. Equivalently, the rise in predation lowers the capital-labor ratio. Thus higher predation reduces output by reducing not only the fraction of the economy's inputs that are devoted to production, but also by reducing the quantity of inputs available.

Similar comments apply to human capital: when rent-seeking is more prevalent, the incentives to accumulate human capital are smaller. Thus again greater rent-seeking reduces the economy's capacity to produce.

These effects are even stronger if capital itself is at risk. Suppose there is a probability p of each unit of capital being lost to rent-seekers. Then the expected private rate of return on 1 unit of capital is $[(1 - L)\alpha Y/K] - p$. If this must equal the world rate of return, r^*, the equilibrium capital-

---

[36] Note that the income measure in Figure 3.14 does not include the resources taken from rent-seekers and distributed equally to everyone. Thus the rise in overall income from the fact that rent-seekers face a chance of detection is larger than the rise in income shown in the figure.

output ratio is

$$\frac{K}{Y} = \frac{(1-L)\alpha}{r^* + p}.\qquad(3.69)$$

This quantity is falling in p.

3.12 Differences in Growth Rates

Our discussion so far has focused on differences in countries' average levels of income per person. But recall from Section 1.1 that relative incomes are not fixed; they often change by large amounts, sometimes in just a few decades. It is therefore natural to ask what insights our discussion of cross-country differences in income levels provides about differences in income growth.

Convergence to Balanced Growth Paths

We begin with the case where the underlying determinants of long-run relative income per person across countries are constant over time. That is, we begin by ignoring changes in relative saving rates, years of education, and long-run determinants of output for a given set of inputs.

Countries' incomes do not jump immediately to their long-run paths. For example, if part of a country's capital stock is destroyed in a war, capital returns to its long-run path only gradually. During the return, capital per worker is growing at a rate faster than it will in the long run, and so the economy is undergoing a period of above-normal growth. More generally, one source of differences in growth rates across countries is differences in the countries' initial positions relative to their long-run paths. Countries that begin below their long-run paths grow more rapidly than countries that begin above.

To see this more formally, assume for simplicity that differences in output per worker across countries stem only from differences in physical capital per worker. That is, human capital per worker and output for given inputs are the same in all countries. Assume that output is determined by a standard production function, $Y_i(t) = F(K_i(t), A(t)L_i(t))$, with constant returns. Because of the constant-returns assumption, we can write output per worker in country i as

$$\frac{Y_i(t)}{L_i(t)} = A(t)f(k_i(t)).\qquad(3.70)$$

(As in earlier models, $k \equiv K/(AL)$ and $f(k) \equiv F(k, 1)$.) By assumption, the path of A is the same in all countries. Thus (3.70) implies that differences in growth come only from differences in the behavior of k.

In the Solow and Ramsey models, each economy has a balanced-growth-path value of k, and the rate of change of k is approximately proportional to its departure from its balanced-growth-path value (see Sections 1.5 and 2.6). If we assume that the same is true here, we have

$$\dot{k}_i(t) = \lambda[k_i^* - k_i(t)], \tag{3.71}$$

where k_i^* is the balanced-growth-path value of k in country i and $\lambda > 0$ is the rate of convergence. Equation (3.71) implies that when a country is farther below its balanced growth path, its capital per unit of effective labor rises more rapidly, and so its growth in income per worker is greater.

There are two possibilities concerning the values of k_i^*. The first is that they are the same in all countries. In this case, all countries have the same income per worker on their balanced growth paths. Differences in average income stem only from differences in where countries stand relative to the common balanced growth path. Thus in this case, the model predicts that the lower a country's income per person, the faster its growth. This is known as *unconditional convergence.*

The other possibility is that the k_i^*'s vary across countries. In this case, there is a persistent component of cross-country income differences. Countries that are poor because their saving rates are low, for example, show no tendency to grow faster than other countries. But differences that stem from countries being at different points relative to their balanced growth paths gradually disappear as the countries converge to those balanced growth paths. That is, the model predicts *conditional convergence*: countries that are poorer after controlling for the determinants of income on the balanced growth path grow faster (Barro and Sala-i-Martin, 1991, 1992; Mankiw, D. Romer, and Weil, 1992).

These ideas extend to situations where initial income differences do not arise just from differences in physical capital. With human capital, as with physical capital, capital per worker does not move immediately to its long-run level. For example, if the young spend more years in school than previous generations, average human capital per worker rises gradually as new workers enter the labor force and old workers leave. Similarly, workers and capital cannot switch immediately and costlessly between rent-seeking and productive activities. Thus the allocation of resources between these activities does not jump immediately to its long-run level. Again, countries that begin with incomes below their long-run paths experience periods of temporarily high growth as they move to their long-run paths.

This framework provides valuable insights into differences in growth among the industrialized countries in the postwar period. Long-run fundamentals—saving rates, levels of education, and incentives for production rather than diversion—are broadly similar in these countries. Yet, because World War II affected the countries very differently, they had very different average incomes at the beginning of the postwar period. For example, average incomes in Japan and Germany were far below those in the

United States and Canada. Thus the bulk of the variation in initial income came from differences in where countries stood relative to their long-run paths rather than from differences in those paths. As a result, the industrialized countries that were the poorest at the start of the postwar period have grown the fastest. That is, these countries are described reasonably well by unconditional convergence (Dowrick and Nguyen, 1989; Mankiw, Romer, and Weil, 1992).

Changes in Fundamentals

So far we have assumed that the underlying determinants of countries' relative long-run levels of income per worker are fixed. The fact that those underlying determinants can change creates another source of differences in growth among countries.

To see this, begin again with the case where incomes per worker differ only because of differences in physical capital per worker. As before, assume that economies have balanced growth paths they would converge to in the absence of shocks. Recall equation (3.71): $\dot{k}_i(t) = \lambda[k_i^* - k_i(t)]$. We want to consider growth over some interval of time where k_i^* need not be constant. To see the issues involved, it turns out to be easiest to assume that time is discrete and to consider growth over just two periods. Assume that the change in k_i from period t to period $t+1$, denoted, Δk_{it+1}, depends on the period-t values of k_i^* and k_i. The equation analogous to (3.71) is thus

$$\Delta k_{it+1} = \lambda(k_{it}^* - k_{it}), \qquad (3.72)$$

with λ assumed to be between 0 and 1. The change in k_i from t to $t+2$ is therefore

$$\Delta k_{it+1} + \Delta k_{it+2} = \lambda(k_{it}^* - k_{it}) + \lambda(k_{it+1}^* - k_{it+1}). \qquad (3.73)$$

To interpret this expression, rewrite k_{it+1}^* as $k_{it}^* + \Delta k_{it+1}^*$. Likewise, rewrite k_{it+1} as $k_{it} + \Delta k_{it+1}$. Thus (3.73) becomes

$$
\begin{aligned}
\Delta k_{it+1} + \Delta k_{it+2} &= \lambda(k_{it}^* - k_{it}) + \lambda(k_{it}^* + \Delta k_{it+1}^* - k_{it} - \Delta k_{it+1}) \\
&= \lambda(k_{it}^* - k_{it}) + \lambda[k_{it}^* + \Delta k_{it+1}^* - k_{it} - \lambda(k_{it}^* - k_{it})] \quad (3.74) \\
&= [\lambda + \lambda(1 - \lambda)](k_{it}^* - k_{it}) + \lambda \Delta k_{it+1}^*,
\end{aligned}
$$

where the second line uses (3.72) to substitute for Δk_{it+1}.

It is also useful to consider the continuous-time case. One can show that if k_i^* does not change discretely, then (3.71) implies that the change in k over some interval, say from 0 to T, is

$$k_i(T) - k_i(0) = (1 - e^{-\lambda T})[k_i^*(0) - k_i(0)] + \int_{\tau=0}^{T} (1 - e^{-\lambda(T-\tau)})\dot{k}_i^*(\tau)\, d\tau. \quad (3.75)$$

Expressions (3.74) and (3.75) show that we can decompose that change in k over an interval into two terms. The first depends on the country's initial position relative to its balanced growth path. This is the conditional-convergence effect we discussed above. The second term depends on changes in the balanced growth path during the interval. A rise in the balanced-growth-path value of k, for example, raises growth. Further, as the expression for the continuous-time case shows (and as one would expect), such a rise has a larger effect if it occurs earlier in the interval.

For simplicity, this analysis focuses on physical capital. But analogous results apply to human capital and efficiency: growth depends on countries' starting points relative to their balanced growth paths and on changes in their balanced growth paths.

This analysis shows that the issue of convergence is more complicated than our earlier discussion suggests. Overall convergence depends not only on the distribution of countries' initial positions relative to their long-run paths and on the dispersion of those long-run paths, but also on the distribution of changes in the underlying determinants of countries' long-run paths. For example, there can be overall convergence as a result of convergence of fundamentals.

It is tempting to infer from this that there are strong forces promoting convergence. A country's average income can be far below the world average either because it is far below its long-run path or because its long-run path has unusually low income. In the first case, the country is likely to grow rapidly as it converges to its long-run path. In the second case, the country can grow rapidly by improving its fundamentals. For example, it can adopt policies and institutions that have proved successful in wealthier countries.

Unfortunately, the evidence does not support this conclusion. Over the postwar period, poorer countries have shown no tendency to grow faster than rich ones. This appears to reflect two factors. First, little of the initial gap between poor and rich countries was due to poor countries being below their long-run paths and rich countries being above. In fact, there is some evidence that it was rich countries that tended to begin farther below their long-run paths (Cho and Graham, 1996). This could reflect the fact that World War II disproportionately affected those countries. Second, although there are many cases where fundamentals improved in poor countries, there are also many cases where they worsened.

Further, recall from Section 1.1 that if we look over the past several centuries, the overall pattern has been one of strong divergence. Countries that were slightly industrialized in 1800—mainly the countries of Western Europe plus the United States and Canada—are now overwhelmingly richer than the poorer countries of the world. What appears to have happened is that these countries improved their fundamentals dramatically while many poor countries did not.

Growth Miracles and Disasters

This analysis provides us with a framework for understanding the most extreme cases of changes in countries' relative incomes: growth miracles and disasters. A period of very rapid or very slow growth relative to the rest of the world can occur as a result of either a shock that pushes an economy very far from its long-run path or a large change in fundamentals. Shocks large enough to move an economy very far from its long-run path are rare, however. The best example might be the impact of World War II on West Germany. On the eve of the war, average income per person in the region that became West Germany was about three-quarters of that of the United States. In 1946, after the end of the war, it was about one-quarter the level in the United States. West German output grew rapidly over the next several decades as the country returned toward its long-run trajectory. In the 20 years after 1946, growth of income per person in West Germany averaged more than 7 percent per year. As a result, its average income in 1966 was again about three-quarters of that of the United States (Maddison, 1995).[37]

Such large disturbances are rare, however. As a result, growth miracles and disasters are usually the result of large changes in fundamentals. Further, since social infrastructure is central to fundamentals, most growth miracles and disasters are the result of large, rapid changes in social infrastructure.

Not surprisingly, growth miracles and disasters appear to be more common under strong dictators; large, rapid changes in institutions are difficult in democracies. More surprisingly, there is not a clear correlation between the dictators' motives and the nature of the changes in social infrastructure. Large favorable shifts in social infrastructure can occur under dictators who are far from benevolent (to put it mildly), and large unfavorable shifts can occur under dictators whose main objective is to improve the well-being of the average citizen of their countries. Some apparent examples of major shifts toward favorable social infrastructure, followed by periods of miraculous growth, are Singapore and South Korea around 1960, Chile in the early 1970s, and China around 1990. Some examples of the opposite pattern include Argentina after World War II, many newly independent African countries in the early 1960s, China's "cultural revolution" of the mid-1960s, and Uganda in the early 1970s.

It is possible that the evidence about what types of social infrastructure are most conducive to high levels of average income is becoming increasingly clear, and that as a result many of the world's poorer countries are beginning, or are about to begin, growth miracles. Unfortunately, it is too soon to know whether this optimistic view is correct.

Problems

3.1. Consider the model of Section 3.2 with $\theta < 1$.

(a) On the balanced growth path, $\dot{A} = g_A^* A(t)$, where g_A^* is the balanced-growth-path value of g_A. Use this fact and equation (3.6) to derive an

---

[37] East Germany, in contrast, suffered an unfavorable change in fundamentals in the form of the imposition of communism. Thus its recovery was much weaker.

expression for $A(t)$ on the balanced growth path in terms of B, a_L, γ, θ, and $L(t)$.

(b) Use your answer to part (a) and the production function, (3.5), to obtain an expression for $Y(t)$ on the balanced growth path. Find the value of a_L that maximizes output on the balanced growth path.

3.2. Consider two economies (indexed by $i = 1, 2$) described by $Y_i(t) = K_i(t)^\theta$ and $\dot{K}_i(t) = s_i Y_i(t)$, where $\theta > 1$. Suppose that the two economies have the same initial value of K, but that $s_1 > s_2$. Show that Y_1/Y_2 is continually rising.

3.3. Consider the economy analyzed in Section 3.3. Assume that $\theta + \beta < 1$ and $n > 0$, and that the economy is on its balanced growth path. Describe how each of the following changes affects the $\dot{g}_A = 0$ and $\dot{g}_K = 0$ lines and the position of the economy in (g_A, g_K) space at the moment of the change:

(a) An increase in n.

(b) An increase in a_K.

(c) An increase in θ.

3.4. Consider the economy described in Section 3.3, and assume $\beta + \theta < 1$ and $n > 0$. Suppose the economy is initially on its balanced growth path, and that there is a permanent increase in s.

(a) How, if at all, does the change affect the $\dot{g}_A = 0$ and $\dot{g}_K = 0$ loci? How, if at all, does it affect the location of the economy in (g_A, g_K) space at the time of the change?

(b) What are the dynamics of g_A and g_K after the increase in s? Sketch the path of log output per worker.

(c) Intuitively, how does the effect of the increase in s compare with its effect in the Solow model?

3.5. Consider the model of Section 3.3 with $\beta + \theta = 1$ and $n = 0$.

(a) Using (3.14) and (3.16), find the value that A/K must have for g_K and g_A to be equal.

(b) Using your result in part (a), find the growth rate of A and K when $g_K = g_A$.

(c) How does an increase in s affect the long-run growth rate of the economy?

(d) What value of a_K maximizes the long-run growth rate of the economy? Intuitively, why is this value not increasing in β, the importance of capital in the R&D sector?

3.6. The Ethier production function. (Ethier, 1982.) Suppose the production function is $Y = [(1 - a_L)L]^{1-\alpha} \int_{i=0}^{A} x(i)^\alpha di$, $0 < \alpha < 1$, where $x(i)$ is the amount of capital good i that is used and A measures the range of potential capital goods.

(a) Suppose $x(i)$ equals K/A for $0 \le i \le A$, and equals 0 otherwise. What is Y as a function of a_L, L, K, and A?

(b) Suppose that the rental price of capital good i is $p(i)$ and that the wage is w. Consider the problem of a firm wanting to produce 1 unit of output at minimum cost.

(*i*) Set up the Lagrangian for the firm's minimization problem.

(*ii*) Find the first-order condition for $x(i)$.

(*iii*) Show that this first-order condition implies that the elasticity of demand for capital good i is $-1/(1 - \alpha) \equiv -\eta$. (Note that this implies that, since the profit-maximizing price of a monopolist is $\eta/(\eta - 1)$ times cost, the profits of a monopolistic supplier of capital good i at the profit-maximizing price are $(1/\eta)p(i)x(i)$, or $(1 - \alpha)p(i)x(i)$, where $p(i)$ is the profit-maximizing rental price of the capital good and $x(i)$ is the quantity demanded at that price.)

3.7. The Romer model. (P. Romer, 1990.) Consider the same setup as in Problem 3.6. In addition, suppose that $\dot{K}(t) = Y(t) - C(t)$, $\dot{A}(t) = Ba_L L(t)A(t)$, and $\dot{L}(t) = 0$. Suppose also that the economy is populated by infinitely lived households with constant-relative-risk-aversion preferences; thus $\dot{C}(t)/C(t) = [r(t) - \rho]/\theta$. Finally, assume that both goods-producing and knowledge-producing firms take the wage as given, that labor is mobile between the two sectors, and that goods-producing firms take the rental prices of the capital goods as given.

Let us look for a balanced growth path where K, A, Y, and C are all growing at the same rate; where r and a_L are both constant; and where $x(i)$ and $p(i)$ are independent of i and constant over time. Let $\bar{p}$ and $\bar{x} = K/A$ denote the level of the $p(i)$'s and the $x(i)$'s on the balanced growth path.

(*a*) Use the result in part (*b*)(iii) of Problem 3.6 to express the present discounted value of the profits from renting out a capital good as a function of $\bar{p}$, $\bar{x}$, r, and α.

(*b*) Given the result in part (*a*) and the expression for $\dot{A}$, what will be the wage of a worker in the knowledge-producing sector?

(*c*) Use the production function to find an expression for the marginal product of labor in the goods-producing sector.

(*d*) Use the production function to find an expression for the marginal product of capital good i in goods production.

(*e*) Combine your results in parts (*b*)-(*d*) to find an expression for $(1 - a_L)L$ in terms of r and the parameters of the model.

(*f*) Use the expression for $\dot{A}$ to express the growth rate of the economy on the balanced growth path in terms of B, a_L, and L.

(*g*) Use the fact that $\dot{C}/C = (r - \rho)/\theta$ and the results in parts (*e*) and (*f*) to solve for a_L, r, and the growth rate of the economy on the balanced growth path.

(*h*) Is it possible for the value of a_L you found in part (*g*) to be negative? If so, since the amount of labor in knowledge production cannot actually be negative, what do you think the balanced growth path would be in this case? Is it possible for the value of a_L you found in part (*g*) to be greater than 1?

3.8. The model in Sections 3.1–3.2 takes the fraction of workers engaged in R&D, a_L, as given. In the model analyzed in Problems 3.6–3.7, describe how each of the following affects the balanced-growth-path value of a_L, and provide a sentence of intuition in each case:

(a) A fall in ρ.

(b) A rise in B.

(c) A rise in L.

3.9. Learning-by-doing. Suppose that output is given by equation (3.24), $Y(t) = K(t)^\alpha [A(t)L(t)]^{1-\alpha}$; that L is constant and equal to 1; that $\dot{K}(t) = sY(t)$; and that knowledge accumulation occurs as a side effect of goods production: $\dot{A}(t) = BY(t)$.

(a) Find expressions for $g_A(t)$ and $g_K(t)$ in terms of $A(t)$, $K(t)$, and the parameters.

(b) Sketch the $\dot{g}_A = 0$ and $\dot{g}_K = 0$ lines in (g_A, g_K) space.

(c) Does the economy converge to a balanced growth path? If so, what are the growth rates of K, A, and Y on the balanced growth path?

(d) How does an increase in s affect long-run growth?

3.10. Suppose that output at firm i is given by $Y_i = K_i^\alpha L_i^{1-\alpha}(K^\phi L^{-\phi})$. Here K_i and L_i are the amounts of capital and labor used by the firm; K and L are the aggregate amounts of capital and labor; and $\alpha > 0$, $\phi > 0$, and $0 < \alpha + \phi < 1$. Assume that factors are paid their private marginal products; thus $r = \partial Y_i / \partial K_i$. Assume that the dynamics of K and L are given by $\dot{K} = sY$ and $\dot{L} = nL$, and that K_i / L_i is the same for all firms.

(a) What is r as a function of K/L?

(b) What is K/L on the balanced growth path? What is r on the balanced growth path?

(c) "If an increase in domestic saving raises domestic investment, positive externalities from capital would mitigate the decline in the private marginal product of capital. Thus the combination of positive externalities from capital and moderate barriers to capital mobility may be the source of Feldstein and Horioka's findings about saving and investment described in Chapter 1." Does your analysis in parts (a) and (b) support this claim? Explain intuitively.

3.11. (This follows Rebelo, 1991.) Assume that there are two factors of production: capital and land. Capital is used in both sectors, whereas land is used only in producing consumption goods. Specifically, the production functions are $C(t) = K_C(t)^\alpha T^{1-\alpha}$ and $\dot{K}(t) = BK_K(t)$, where K_C and K_K are the amounts of capital used in the two sectors (so $K_C(t) + K_K(t) = K(t)$) and T is the amount of land, and $0 < \alpha < 1$ and $B > 0$. Factors are paid their marginal products, and capital can move freely between the two sectors. T is normalized to 1 for simplicity.

(a) Let $P_K(t)$ denote the price of capital goods relative to consumption goods at time t. Use the fact that the earnings of capital in units of consumption goods in the two sectors must be equal to derive a condition relating $P_K(t)$, $K_C(t)$, and the parameters α and B. If K_C is growing at rate $g_K(t)$, at what rate must P_K be growing (or falling)? Let $g_P(t)$ denote this growth rate.

(b) The real interest rate in terms of consumption is $B + g_P(t)$.[38] Thus, assuming that households have our standard utility function, (3.30), the growth rate of consumption must be $(B + g_P - \rho)/\sigma \equiv g_C$. Assume $\rho < B$.

   (i) Use your results in part (a) to express $g_C(t)$ in terms of $g_K(t)$ rather than $g_P(t)$.

   (ii) Given the production function for consumption goods, at what rate must K_C be growing for C to be growing at rate $g_C(t)$?

   (iii) Combine your answers to (i) and (ii) to solve for $g_K(t)$ and $g_C(t)$ in terms of the underlying parameters.

(c) Suppose that investment income is taxed at rate τ, so that the real interest rate households face is $(1 - \tau)(B + g_P)$. How, if at all, does τ affect the equilibrium growth rate of consumption?

3.12. (This follows Krugman, 1979; see also Grossman and Helpman, 1991b.) Suppose the world consists of two regions, the "North" and the "South." Output and capital accumulation in region i ($i = N, S$) are given by $Y_i(t) = K_i(t)^{\alpha}[A_i(t)(1 - a_{Li})L_i]^{1-\alpha}$ and $\dot{K}_i(t) = s_i Y_i(t)$. New technologies are developed in the North. Specifically, $\dot{A}_N(t) = B a_{LN} L_N A_N(t)$. Improvements in Southern technology, on the other hand, are made by learning from Northern technology: $\dot{A}_S(t) = \mu a_{LS} L_S [A_N(t) - A_S(t)]$ if $A_N(t) > A_S(t)$; otherwise $\dot{A}_S(t) = 0$. Here a_{LN} is the fraction of the Northern labor force engaged in R&D, and a_{LS} is the fraction of the Southern labor force engaged in learning Northern technology; the rest of the notation is standard. Note that L_N and L_S are assumed constant.

(a) What is the long-run growth rate of Northern output per worker?

(b) Define $Z(t) = A_S(t)/A_N(t)$. Find an expression for $\dot{Z}$ as a function of Z and the parameters of the model. Is Z stable? If so, what value does it converge to? What is the long-run growth rate of Southern output per worker?

(c) Assume $a_{LN} = a_{LS}$ and $s_N = s_S$. What is the ratio of output per worker in the South to output per worker in the North when both economies have converged to their balanced growth paths?

3.13. Delays in the transmission of knowledge to poor countries.

(a) Assume that the world consists of two regions, the North and the South. The North is described by $Y_N(t) = A_N(t)(1 - a_L)L_N$ and $\dot{A}_N(t) = a_L L_N A_N(t)$. The South does not do R&D but simply uses the technology developed in the North; however, the technology used in the South lags the North's by τ years. Thus $Y_S(t) = A_S(t)L_S$ and $A_S(t) = A_N(t - \tau)$. If the growth rate of output per worker in the North is 3 percent per year,

---

[38] To see this, note that capital in the investment sector produces new capital at rate B and changes in value relative to the consumption good at rate g_P. (Because the return to capital is the same in the two sectors, the same must be true of capital in the consumption sector.)

and if a_L is close to 0, what must τ be for output per worker in the North to exceed that in the South by a factor of 10?

(b) Suppose instead that both the North and the South are described by the Solow model: $y_i(t) = f(k_i(t))$, where $y_i(t) \equiv Y_i(t)/[A_i(t)L_i(t)]$ and $k_i(t) \equiv K_i(t)/[A_i(t)L_i(t)]$ ($i = N,S$). As in the Solow model, assume $\dot{K}_i(t) = sY_i(t) - \delta K_i(t)$ and $\dot{L}_i(t) = nL_i(t)$; the two countries are assumed to have the same saving rates and rates of population growth. Finally, $\dot{A}_N(t) = gA_N(t)$ and $A_S(t) = A_N(t - \tau)$.

   (i) Show that the value of k on the balanced growth path, k^*, is the same for the two countries.

   (ii) Does introducing capital change the answer to part (a)? Explain. (Continue to assume $g = 3\%$.)

3.14. Consider the following model with physical and human capital:

$$Y(t) = [(1 - a_K)K(t)]^\alpha [(1 - a_H)H(t)]^{1-\alpha}, \quad 0 < \alpha < 1, \quad 0 < a_K < 1, \quad 0 < a_H < 1,$$

$$\dot{K}(t) = sY(t) - \delta_K K(t),$$

$$\dot{H}(t) = B[a_K K(t)]^\gamma [a_H H(t)]^\phi [A(t)L(t)]^{1-\gamma-\phi} - \delta_H H(t), \quad \gamma > 0, \phi > 0, \gamma + \phi < 1,$$

$$\dot{L}(t) = nL(t),$$

$$\dot{A}(t) = gA(t),$$

where a_K and a_H are the fractions of the stocks of physical and human capital used in the education sector.

This model assumes that human capital is produced in its own sector with its own production function. Bodies (L) are useful only as something to be educated, not as an input into the production of final goods. Similarly, knowledge (A) is useful only as something that can be conveyed to students, not as a direct input to goods production.

(a) Define $k = K/(AL)$ and $h = H/(AL)$. Derive equations for $\dot{k}$ and $\dot{h}$.

(b) Find an equation describing the set of combinations of h and k such that $\dot{k} = 0$. Sketch in (h, k) space. Do the same for $\dot{h} = 0$.

(c) Does this economy have a balanced growth path? If so, is it unique? Is it stable? What are the growth rates of output per person, physical capital per person, and human capital per person on the balanced growth path?

(d) Suppose the economy is initially on a balanced growth path, and that there is a permanent increase in s. How does this change affect the path of output per person over time?

3.15. Increasing returns in a model with human capital. (This follows Lucas, 1988.) Suppose that $Y(t) = K(t)^\alpha [(1 - a_H)H(t)]^\beta$, $\dot{H}(t) = Ba_H H(t)$, and $\dot{K}(t) = sY(t)$. Assume $0 < \alpha < 1$, $0 < \beta < 1$, and $\alpha + \beta > 1$.[39]

---

[39] Lucas's model differs from this formulation by letting a_H and s be endogenous and potentially time-varying, and by assuming that the social and private returns to human capital differ.

(a) What is the growth rate of H?

(b) Does the economy converge to a balanced growth path? If so, what are the growth rates of K and Y on the balanced growth path?

3.16. The golden-rule level of education. Consider the model of Section 3.8 with the assumption that $G(E)$ takes the form $G(E) = e^{\phi E}$.

(a) Find an expression that characterizes the value of E that maximizes the level of output per person on the balanced growth path.

(b) Describe how, if at all, the golden-rule level of E (that is, the level of E you characterized in part (a)) is affected by each of the following changes:

(i) A rise in T.

(ii) A fall in n.

3.17. Endogenizing the choice of E. (This follows Bils and Klenow, 1998.) Suppose that the wage of a worker with education E at time t is $be^{gt}e^{\phi E}$. Consider a worker born at time 0 who will be in school for the first E years of life and will work for the remaining $T - E$ years. Assume that the interest rate is constant and equal to $\bar{r}$.

(a) What is the present discounted value of the worker's lifetime earnings as a function of E, T, b, $\bar{r}$, ϕ, and g?

(b) Find the first-order condition for the value of E that maximizes the expression you found in part (a). Let E^* denote this value of E.

(c) Describe how each of the following developments affects E^*:

(i) A rise in T.

(ii) A rise in $\bar{r}$.

(iii) A rise in g.

3.18. Consider the model of producers and predators in Section 3.11. Suppose, however, that production is given by $(1 - f)B$ (rather than by $1 - f$), with $B > 0$. Now suppose there is a rise in B. Describe, how, if at all, this change affects:

(a) Producers' choice of f for a given R.

(b) The curves in Figue 3.12 showing producers' and predators' incomes as functions of R.

(c) The equilibrium level (or levels) of R.

3.19. Convergence regressions.

(a) **Convergence.** Let y_i denote log output per worker in country i. Suppose all countries have the same balanced-growth-path level of log income per worker, y^*. Suppose also that y_i evolves according to $dy_i(t)/dt = -\lambda[y_i(t) - y^*]$.

(i) What is $y_i(t)$ as a function of $y_i(0)$, y^*, λ, and t?

(*ii*) Suppose that $y_i(t)$ in fact equals the expression you derived in part (*i*) plus a mean-zero random disturbance that is uncorrelated with $y_i(0)$. Consider a cross-country growth regression of the form $y_i(t) - y_i(0) = \alpha + \beta y_i(0) + \varepsilon_i$. What is the relation between β, the coefficient on $y_i(0)$ in the regression, and λ, the speed of convergence? (Hint: For a univariate OLS regression, the coefficient on the right-hand-side variable equals the covariance between the right-hand-side and left-hand-side variables divided by the variance of the right-hand-side variable.) Given this, how could you estimate λ from an estimate of β?

(*iii*) If β in part (*ii*) is negative (so that rich countries on average grow less than poor countries), is $\text{Var}(y_i(t))$ necessarily less than $\text{Var}(y_i(0))$, so that the cross-country variance of income is falling? Explain. If β is positive, is $\text{Var}(y_i(t))$ necessarily more than $\text{Var}(y_i(0))$? Explain.

(*b*) **Conditional convergence.** Suppose $y_i^* = a + bX_i$, and that $dy_i(t)/dt = -\lambda[y_i(t) - y_i^*]$.

(*i*) What is $y_i(t)$ as a function of $y_i(0)$, y_i^*, λ, and t?

(*ii*) Suppose that $y_i(0) = y_i^* + u_i$ and that $y_i(t)$ equals the expression you derived in part (i) plus a mean-zero random disturbance, e_i, where X_i, u_i, and e_i are uncorrelated with one another. Consider a cross-country growth regression of the form $y_i(t) - y_i(0) = \alpha + \beta y_i(0) + \varepsilon_i$. Suppose one attempts to infer λ from the estimate of β using the formula in part (*a*)(ii). Will this lead to a correct estimate of λ, an overestimate, or an underestimate?

(*iii*) Consider a cross-country growth regression of the form $y_i(t) - y_i(0) = \alpha + \beta y_i(0) + \gamma X_i + \varepsilon_i$. Under the same assumptions as in part (ii), how could one estimate b, the effect of X on the balanced-growth-path value of y, from estimates of β and γ?

Chapter 4
REAL-BUSINESS-CYCLE THEORY

4.1 Introduction: Some Facts about Economic Fluctuations

Modern economies undergo significant short-run variations in aggregate output and employment. At some times, output and employment are falling and unemployment is rising; at others, output and employment are rising rapidly and unemployment is falling. Consider, for example, the United States in the early 1980s. Between the third quarter of 1981 and the third quarter of 1982, real GDP fell by 2.9 percent, the fraction of the adult population employed fell by 1.3 percentage points, and the unemployment rate rose from 7.4 to 9.9 percent. Then over the next 2 years, real GDP grew by 12.8 percent, the fraction of the adult population employed rose by 2 percentage points, and the unemployment rate fell back to 7.4 percent.

Understanding the causes of aggregate fluctuations is a central goal of macroeconomics. This chapter and the two that follow present the leading theories concerning the sources and nature of macroeconomic fluctuations. Before we turn to the theories, this section presents a brief overview of some major facts about short-run fluctuations. For concreteness, and because of the central role of the U.S. experience in shaping macroeconomic thought, the focus is on the United States.

A first important fact about fluctuations is that they do not exhibit any simple regular or cyclical pattern. Figure 4.1 plots seasonally adjusted real GDP quarterly since 1947, and Table 4.1 summarizes the behavior of real GDP in the nine postwar recessions.[1] The figure and table show that output declines vary considerably in size and spacing. The falls in real GDP range from 1.1 percent in 1970 to 3.7 percent in 1957–1958. The times between the end of one recession and the beginning of the next range from 4 quarters in 1980–1981 to 10 years in 1960–1970. The patterns of the output

---

[1] The formal dating of recessions for the United States is not based solely on the behavior of real GDP. Instead, recessions are identified judgmentally by the National Bureau of Economic Research (NBER) on the basis of various indicators. For that reason, the dates of the official NBER peaks and troughs differ somewhat from the dates shown in Table 4.1. Moore and Zarnowitz (1986) describe the modern NBER methodology.

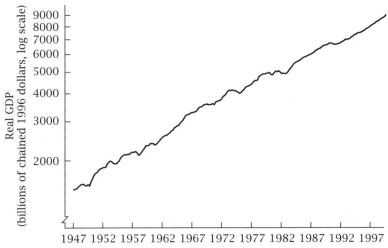

FIGURE 4.1   U.S. real GDP, 1947–1999

TABLE 4.1   Recessions in the United States since World War II

Year and quarter of peak in real GDP	Number of quarters until trough in real GDP	Change in real GDP, peak to trough
1948:4	2	−1.7%
1953:2	3	−2.7
1957:3	2	−3.7
1960:1	3	−1.6
1970:3	1	−1.1
1973:4	5	−3.4
1980:1	2	−2.2
1981:3	4	−2.9
1990:2	3	−1.5

declines also vary greatly. In the 1980 recession, over 90 percent of the overall decline of 2.2 percent took place in a single quarter; in the 1990–1991 recession, the decline of 1.5 percent took place gradually over three quarters; and in the 1981–1982 recession, output fell by 2.8 percent over two quarters, then rose by 0.4 percent, and then fell by another 0.5 percent.

Because output movements are not regular, modern macroeconomics has generally turned away from attempts to interpret fluctuations as combinations of deterministic cycles of different lengths; efforts to discern regular Kitchin (3-year), Juglar (10-year), Kuznets (20-year), and Kondratiev (50-year) cycles have been largely abandoned as unproductive.[2]   Instead, the

---

[2] There is an important exception to the claim that fluctuations are irregular: there are large seasonal fluctuations that are similar in many ways to conventional business-cycle fluctuations. See Barsky and Miron (1989) and Miron (1996).

TABLE 4.2   Behavior of the components of output in
            recessions

Component of GDP	Average share in GDP	Average share in fall in GDP in recessions relative to normal growth
Consumption		
Durables	8.4%	15.6%
Nondurables	25.8	11.2
Services	29.5	9.1
Investment		
Residential	4.7	20.9
Fixed nonresidential	10.7	11.7
Inventories	0.7	40.6
Net exports	−0.4	−12.3
Government purchases	20.6	3.3

prevailing view is that the economy is perturbed by disturbances of various types and sizes at more or less random intervals, and that those disturbances then propagate through the economy. Where the major macroeconomic schools of thought differ is in their hypotheses concerning these shocks and propagation mechanisms.

A second important fact is that fluctuations are distributed very unevenly over the components of output. Table 4.2 shows both the average shares of each of the components in total output and their average shares in the declines in output (relative to its normal growth) in recessions. As the table shows, even though inventory investment on average accounts for only a trivial fraction of GDP, its fluctuations account for close to half of the shortfall in growth relative to normal in recessions: inventory accumulation is on average large and positive at peaks, and large and negative at troughs. Residential investment (that is, housing) and consumer purchases of durable goods also account for disproportionate shares of output fluctuations. Consumer purchases of nondurables and services, government purchases, and net exports are relatively stable.[3] Although there is some variation across recessions, the general pattern shown in Table 4.2 holds in most. And the same components that decline disproportionately when aggregate output is falling also rise disproportionately when output is growing at above-normal rates.

A third set of facts involves asymmetries in output movements. There are no large asymmetries between rises and falls in output; that is, output growth is distributed roughly symmetrically around its mean. There does,

---

[3] The entries for net exports indicate that they are on average negative over the postwar period, and that they typically grow—that is, become less negative—during recessions.

however, appear to be asymmetry of a second type: output seems to be characterized by relatively long periods when it is slightly above its usual path, interrupted by brief periods when it is relatively far below.[4]

A fourth set of facts concerns output fluctuations before the postwar era. In a series of papers, C. Romer (1986a, 1986b, 1989, 1994) demonstrates that there are important biases in traditional estimates of major macroeconomic time series for the period before World War II. She shows that once those biases are accounted for, aggregate fluctuations do not appear dramatically different before the Great Depression than in the first four decades or so after World War II. Output movements in the era before the Depression appear slightly larger, and slightly less persistent; but there was no sharp change in the character of fluctuations. Since such features of the economy as the sectoral composition of output and role of government were very different in the two eras, this suggests either that the character of fluctuations is determined by forces that changed much less over time, or that there was a set of changes to the economy that had roughly offsetting effects on overall fluctuations.[5]

Interestingly, the U.S. economy became much more stable around the time Romer began this research. In the nearly two decades following the 1981–1982 recession, the United States underwent only a single, quite mild recession, and the expansion following that recession is the longest period without a recession on record. We will return to the issue of this recent stability in Section 10.5.

A corollary of the findings about output movements before the Great Depression is that the collapse in the Depression and the rebound of the 1930s and World War II dwarf any fluctuations before or since. Real GDP in the United States fell by 27 percent between 1929 and 1933, with estimated unemployment reaching 25 percent in 1933. Over the next 11 years, real GDP rose at an average annual rate of 10 percent; as a result, unemployment in 1944 was 1.2 percent. Finally, real GDP declined by 13 percent between 1944 and 1947, and unemployment rose to 3.9 percent.[6]

Finally, Table 4.3 summarizes the behavior of some important macroeconomic variables during recessions. Not surprisingly, employment falls and unemployment rises during recessions. The table shows that, in addition, the length of the average workweek falls. The declines in employment and hours are generally small relative to the falls in output. Thus productivity— output per worker-hour—almost always declines during recessions. The

---

[4] More precisely, periods of extremely low growth quickly followed by extremely high growth are much more common than periods exhibiting the reverse pattern. See, for example, De Long and Summers (1986a); Sichel (1993); Beaudry and Koop (1993); McQueen and Thorley (1993); Acemoglu and Scott (1997); and Hess and Iwata (1997).

[5] See Balke and Gordon (1989) and Sheffrin (1988) for further discussion of pre-Depression versus post-World War II fluctuations.

[6] For two recent discussions of the status of our understanding of the Great Depression, see C. Romer (1993) and Bernanke (1995).

TABLE 4.3   Behavior of some important macroeconomic variables in recessions

Variable	Average change in recessions	Number of recessions in which variable falls
Real GDP*	−4.7%	9/9
Employment*	−3.6%	9/9
Unemployment rate (percentage points)	+1.9	0/9
Average weekly hours, production workers, manufacturing	−2.3%	9/9
Output per hour, nonfarm business*	−1.9%	8/9
Inflation (GDP deflator; percentage points)	−0.3	4/9
Real compensation per hour, nonfarm business*	−0.7%	7/9
Nominal interest rate on 3-month Treasury bills (percentage points)	−2.0	8/9
Ex post real interest rate on 3-month Treasury bills (percentage points)	−1.7	9/9
Real money stock (M-2/GDP deflator)*†	−1.1%	3/6

*Change in recessions is computed relative to the variable's average growth over the full postwar period, 1947–1999.

†Available only beginning in 1959.

conjunction of the declines in productivity and hours implies that movements in the unemployment rate are generally smaller than the movements in output. The relationship between movements in output and the unemployment rate is known as *Okun's law*. As originally formulated by Okun (1962), the "law" stated that a shortfall in GDP of 3 percent relative to normal growth produces a 1 percentage-point rise in the unemployment rate; a more accurate description of the current relationship is 2 to 1.

The remaining lines of Table 4.3 summarize the behavior of various price and financial variables. Inflation shows no clear pattern.[7] The real wage, at least as measured in aggregate data, tends to fall slightly in recessions. Nominal and real interest rates decline, while the real money stock shows no clear pattern.

4.2 Theories of Fluctuations

It is natural to begin by asking whether aggregate fluctuations can be understood using a *Walrasian* model—that is, a competitive model without any externalities, asymmetric information, missing markets, or other imperfec-

---

[7] Different ways of summarizing the cyclical behavior of inflation and the price level give different results. Because of this, the cyclical behavior of inflation and of the price level, and the implications of that behavior, are controversial. See Kydland and Prescott (1990); Cooley and Ohanian (1991); Backus and Kehoe (1992); Ball and Mankiw (1994); Raon and Sola (1995); and Rotemberg (1996).

tions. If they can, then the analysis of fluctuations may not require any fundamental departure from conventional microeconomic analysis.

As emphasized in Chapter 2, the Ramsey model is the natural Walrasian baseline model of the aggregate economy: the model excludes not only market imperfections, but also all issues raised by heterogeneity among households. This chapter is therefore devoted to extending a variant of the Ramsey model to incorporate aggregate fluctuations. This requires modifying the model in two ways. First, there must be a source of disturbances: without shocks, the Ramsey model converges to a balanced growth path and then grows smoothly. The initial extensions of the Ramsey model to include fluctuations emphasized shocks to the economy's technology—that is, changes in the production function from period to period.[8] More recently, work in this area has also emphasized changes in government purchases.[9] Both types of shocks represent real—as opposed to monetary, or nominal— disturbances: technology shocks change the amount that is produced from a given quantity of inputs, and government-purchases shocks change the quantity of goods available to the private economy for a given level of production. For this reason, the models are known as *real-business-cycle* (or *RBC*) models.

The second change that is needed to the Ramsey model is to allow for variations in employment. In all the models we have seen, labor supply is exogenous and either constant or growing smoothly. Real-business-cycle theory focuses on the question of whether a Walrasian model provides a good description of the main features of observed fluctuations. Models in this literature therefore allow for changes in employment by making households' utility depend not just on their consumption but also on the amount they work; employment is then determined by the intersection of labor supply and labor demand.

As discussed in the final section of this chapter, purely Walrasian models appear to have, at best, limited success in capturing the central features of fluctuations. As a result, some departure from basic real-business-cycle models seems needed. One approach is to keep many features of the real-business-cycle approach but to add non-Walrasian ingredients. Such *real-business-cycle-style* models are discussed briefly in the final section of this chapter.

Many macroeconomists believe, however, that the technology shocks and the propagation mechanisms of real-business-cycle models are of little relevance to actual fluctuations, and that nominal disturbances and a failure of nominal prices and wages to adjust fully to those disturbances are central to fluctuations. Chapters 5 and 6 are therefore devoted to *Keynesian* theories of fluctuations. To focus on the consequences and causes of

---

[8] The seminal papers include Kydland and Prescott (1982); Long and Plosser (1983); Prescott (1986); and Black (1982).

[9] See Aiyagari, Christiano, and Eichenbaum (1992); Baxter and King (1993); and Christiano and Eichenbaum (1992).

incomplete nominal adjustment, these chapters investigate price stickiness in models that are dramatically simplified on the real side. Chapter 5 takes nominal stickiness as given and investigates its effects. Chapter 6 tackles the question of why nominal prices might not respond fully to disturbances.

One conclusion of Chapter 6 is that significant nominal stickiness is much more likely to arise if there are departures from a Walrasian model in addition to some type of direct impediment to instantaneous nominal adjustment: imperfections in the goods, credit, and labor markets may greatly magnify the consequences of barriers to nominal flexibility. Thus modern Keynesian theories differ from baseline real-business-cycle models not only by including barriers to complete nominal adjustment, but also in their analysis of how the economy would operate in the absence of those barriers.

This division of theories of fluctuations into ones focusing on real shocks impinging on a Walrasian economy and ones focusing on nominal disturbances affecting an economy with significant imperfections oversimplifies matters in two important ways. First, it omits the possibility of *real non-Walrasian* theories. That is, it may be that nominal shocks and nominal stickiness are not important to fluctuations, but that there are other departures from the Walrasian baseline that are central to fluctuations. There are a host of possible non-Walrasian features of the economy—such as imperfect competition, externalities, asymmetric information, departures from rationality, and failures of markets to clear—and thus a host of possible real non-Walrasian theories of fluctuations. Thus we will not attempt to discuss them comprehensively. Instead, we will consider them briefly at the end of Chapter 6.

Second, this simple division suggests a much sharper split of macroeconomics into different approaches than actually exists. Modern real-business-cycle-style models often include nominal stickiness and real imperfections in the markets for goods, credit, and labor. In fact, because of the modelers' desire to build complete general equilibrium models, these models' assumptions about, say, price stickiness are sometimes more extreme than the corresponding assumptions in modern Keynesian models. And recent models stemming from the Keynesian tradition are rarely as simplified on the real side as those presented in Chapters 5 and 6. It is an exaggeration to say that there are no major disagreements about the best approach to modeling fluctuations or about the causes of fluctuations. But it is an equal exaggeration to describe macroeconomists as sharply divided into real-business-cycle theorists and Keynesians.

4.3 A Baseline Real-Business-Cycle Model

We now turn to a specific real-business-cycle model. The assumptions and functional forms are similar to those used in most such models (see, for example, Prescott, 1986; Christiano and Eichenbaum, 1992; Baxter and King,

1993; and Campbell, 1994). The model is a discrete-time variation of the Ramsey model of Chapter 2. Because our goal is to describe the quantitative behavior of the economy, we will assume specific functional forms for the production and utility functions.

The economy consists of a large number of identical, price-taking firms and a large number of identical, price-taking households. As in the Ramsey model, households are infinitely lived. The inputs to production are again capital (K), labor (L), and "technology" (A). The production function is Cobb–Douglas; thus output in period t is

$$Y_t = K_t^\alpha (A_t L_t)^{1-\alpha}, \qquad 0 < \alpha < 1. \tag{4.1}$$

Output is divided among consumption (C), investment (I), and government purchases (G). Fraction δ of capital depreciates each period. Thus the capital stock in period $t + 1$ is

$$
\begin{aligned}
K_{t+1} &= K_t + I_t - \delta K_t \\
&= K_t + Y_t - C_t - G_t - \delta K_t.
\end{aligned} \tag{4.2}
$$

The government's purchases are financed by lump-sum taxes that are assumed to equal the purchases each period.[10]

Labor and capital are paid their marginal products. Thus the real wage and the real interest rate in period t are

$$
\begin{aligned}
w_t &= (1 - \alpha) K_t^\alpha (A_t L_t)^{-\alpha} A_t \\
&= (1 - \alpha) \left(\frac{K_t}{A_t L_t} \right)^\alpha A_t,
\end{aligned} \tag{4.3}
$$

$$r_t = \alpha \left(\frac{A_t L_t}{K_t} \right)^{1-\alpha} - \delta. \tag{4.4}$$

The representative household maximizes the expected value of

$$U = \sum_{t=0}^{\infty} e^{-\rho t} u(c_t, 1 - \ell_t) \frac{N_t}{H}. \tag{4.5}$$

$u(\bullet)$ is the instantaneous utility function of the representative member of the household, and ρ is the discount rate.[11] N_t is population and H is

---

[10] As in the Ramsey model, the choice between debt and tax finance in fact has no impact on outcomes in this model. Thus the assumption of tax finance is made just for expositional convenience. Section 11.2 describes why the form of finance is irrelevant in models like this one.

[11] The usual way to express discounting in a discrete-time model is as $1/(1+\rho)^t$ rather than as $e^{-\rho t}$. But because of the log-linear structure of this model, the exponential formulation is more natural here. There is no important difference between the two approaches, however; specifically, if we define $\rho' = e^\rho - 1$, then $e^{-\rho t} = 1/(1 + \rho')^t$. The log-linear structure of the model is also the reason behind the exponential formulations for population growth and for trend growth of technology and government purchases (see equations [4.6], [4.8], and [4.10] below).

the number of households; thus N_t/H is the number of members of the household. Population grows exogenously at rate n:

$$\ln N_t = \overline{N} + nt, \qquad n < \rho. \tag{4.6}$$

Thus the level of N_t is given by $N_t = e^{\overline{N}+nt}$.

The instantaneous utility function, $u(\bullet)$, has two arguments. The first is consumption per member of the household, c. The second is leisure per member, which is the difference between the time endowment per member (normalized to 1 for simplicity) and the amount each member works, ℓ. Since all households are the same, $c = C/N$ and $\ell = L/N$. For simplicity, $u(\bullet)$ is log-linear in the two arguments:

$$u_t = \ln c_t + b \ln(1 - \ell_t), \qquad b > 0. \tag{4.7}$$

The final assumptions of the model concern the behavior of the two driving variables, technology and government purchases. Consider technology first. To capture trend growth, the model assumes that in the absence of any shocks, $\ln A_t$ would be $\overline{A} + gt$, where g is the rate of technological progress. But technology is also subject to random disturbances. Thus,

$$\ln A_t = \overline{A} + gt + \tilde{A}_t, \tag{4.8}$$

where $\tilde{A}$ reflects the effects of the shocks; $\tilde{A}$ is assumed to follow a *first-order autoregressive process*. That is,

$$\tilde{A}_t = \rho_A \tilde{A}_{t-1} + \varepsilon_{A,t}, \qquad -1 < \rho_A < 1, \tag{4.9}$$

where the $\varepsilon_{A,t}$'s are *white-noise* disturbances—a series of mean-zero shocks that are uncorrelated with one another. Equation (4.9) states that the random component of $\ln A_t$, $\tilde{A}_t$, equals fraction ρ_A of the previous period's value plus a random term. If ρ_A is positive, this means that the effects of a shock to technology disappear gradually over time.

We make similar assumptions about government purchases. The trend growth rate of per capita government purchases equals the trend growth rate of technology; if this were not the case, over time government purchases would become arbitrarily large or arbitrarily small relative to the economy. Thus,

$$\ln G_t = \overline{G} + (n + g)t + \tilde{G}_t, \tag{4.10}$$

$$\tilde{G}_t = \rho_G \tilde{G}_{t-1} + \varepsilon_{G,t}, \qquad -1 < \rho_G < 1, \tag{4.11}$$

where the ε_G's are white-noise disturbances that are uncorrelated with the ε_A's. This completes the description of the model.

4.4   Household Behavior

The two most important differences between this model and the Ramsey model are the inclusion of leisure in the utility function and the introduction of randomness in technology and government purchases. Before we analyze the model's general properties, this section discusses these features' implications for households' behavior.

Intertemporal Substitution in Labor Supply

To see what the utility function implies for labor supply, consider first the case where the household lives only for one period and has no initial wealth. In addition, assume for simplicity that the household has only one member. In this case, the household's objective function is just $\ln c + b \ln(1 - \ell)$, and its budget constraint is $c = w\ell$.

The Lagrangian for the household's maximization problem is

$$\mathcal{L} = \ln c + b \ln(1 - \ell) + \lambda(w\ell - c). \tag{4.12}$$

The first-order conditions for c and ℓ, respectively, are

$$\frac{1}{c} - \lambda = 0, \tag{4.13}$$

$$-\frac{b}{1 - \ell} + \lambda w = 0. \tag{4.14}$$

Since the budget constraint requires $c = w\ell$, (4.13) implies $\lambda = 1/(w\ell)$. Substituting this into (4.14) yields

$$-\frac{b}{1 - \ell} + \frac{1}{\ell} = 0. \tag{4.15}$$

The wage does not enter (4.15). Thus labor supply (the value of ℓ that satisfies [4.15]) is independent of the wage. Intuitively, because utility is logarithmic in consumption and the household has no initial wealth, the income and substitution effects of a change in the wage offset each other.

The fact that the level of the wage does not affect labor supply in the static case does not mean that variations in the wage do not affect labor supply when the household's horizon is more than one period. This can be seen most easily when the household lives for two periods. Continue to assume that it has no initial wealth and that it has only one member; in addition, assume that there is no uncertainty about the interest rate or the second-period wage.

The household's lifetime budget constraint is now

$$c_1 + \frac{1}{1 + r} c_2 = w_1 \ell_1 + \frac{1}{1 + r} w_2 \ell_2, \tag{4.16}$$

where r is the real interest rate. The Lagrangian is

$$\mathcal{L} = \ln c_1 + b \ln(1 - \ell_1) + e^{-\rho} [\ln c_2 + b \ln(1 - \ell_2)]$$

$$+ \lambda \left[w_1 \ell_1 + \frac{1}{1 + r} w_2 \ell_2 - c_1 - \frac{1}{1 + r} c_2 \right]. \tag{4.17}$$

The household's choice variables are c_1, c_2, ℓ_1, and ℓ_2. Only the first-order conditions for ℓ_1 and ℓ_2 are needed, however, to show the effect of the relative wage in the two periods on relative labor supply. These first-order conditions are

$$\frac{b}{1 - \ell_1} = \lambda w_1, \tag{4.18}$$

$$\frac{e^{-\rho} b}{1 - \ell_2} = \frac{1}{1 + r} \lambda w_2. \tag{4.19}$$

To see the implications of (4.18)–(4.19), divide both sides of (4.18) by w_1 and both sides of (4.19) by $w_2/(1 + r)$, and equate the two resulting expressions for λ. This yields

$$\frac{e^{-\rho} b}{1 - \ell_2} \frac{1 + r}{w_2} = \frac{b}{1 - \ell_1} \frac{1}{w_1}, \tag{4.20}$$

or

$$\frac{1 - \ell_1}{1 - \ell_2} = \frac{1}{e^{-\rho}(1 + r)} \frac{w_2}{w_1}. \tag{4.21}$$

Equation (4.21) implies that relative labor supply in the two periods responds to the relative wage. If, for example, w_1 rises relative to w_2, the household decreases first-period leisure relative to second-period leisure; that is, it increases first-period labor supply relative to second-period supply. Because of the logarithmic functional form, the elasticity of substitution between leisure in the two periods is 1.

Equation (4.21) also implies that a rise in r raises first-period labor supply relative to second-period supply. Intuitively, a rise in r increases the attractiveness of working today and saving relative to working tomorrow. As we will see, this effect of the interest rate on labor supply is crucial to employment fluctuations in real-business-cycle models. These responses of labor supply to the relative wage and the interest rate are known as *intertemporal substitution* in labor supply (Lucas and Rapping, 1969).

Household Optimization under Uncertainty

The second way that the household's optimization problem differs from its problem in the Ramsey model is that it faces uncertainty about rates of return and future wages. Because of this uncertainty, the household does not choose deterministic paths for consumption and labor supply. Instead, its choices of c and ℓ at any date potentially depend on all the shocks to technology and government purchases up to that date. This makes a complete description of the household's behavior quite complicated. Fortunately, we can describe key features of its behavior without fully solving its optimization problem. Recall that in the Ramsey model, we were able to derive an equation relating present consumption to the interest rate and consumption a short time later (the Euler equation) before imposing the budget constraint and determining the level of consumption. With uncertainty, the analogous equation relates consumption in the current period to *expectations* concerning interest rates and consumption in the next period. We will derive this equation using the informal approach we used in equations (2.21)–(2.22) to derive the Euler equation.[12]

Consider the household in period t. Suppose it reduces current consumption per member by a small amount Δc and then uses the resulting greater wealth to increase consumption per member in the next period above what it otherwise would have been. If the household is behaving optimally, a marginal change of this type must leave expected utility unchanged.

Equations (4.5) and (4.7) imply that the marginal utility of consumption per member in period t is $e^{-\rho t}(N_t/H)(1/c_t)$. Thus the utility cost of this change is $e^{-\rho t}(N_t/H)(\Delta c/c_t)$. Since the household has e^n times as many members in period $t+1$ as in period t, the increase in consumption per member in period $t+1$ is $e^{-n}(1+r_{t+1})\Delta c$. The marginal utility of period-$t+1$ consumption per member is $e^{-\rho(t+1)}(N_{t+1}/H)(1/c_{t+1})$. Thus the expected utility benefit as of period t is $E_t[e^{-\rho(t+1)}(N_{t+1}/H)e^{-n}(1+r_{t+1})/c_{t+1}]\Delta c$, where E_t denotes expectations conditional on what the household knows in period t (that is, given the history of the economy up through period t). Equating the costs and expected benefits implies

$$e^{-\rho t}\frac{N_t}{H}\frac{\Delta c}{c_t} = E_t\left[e^{-\rho(t+1)}\frac{N_{t+1}}{H}e^{-n}\frac{1}{c_{t+1}}(1+r_{t+1})\right]\Delta c. \qquad (4.22)$$

Since $e^{-\rho(t+1)}(N_{t+1}/H)e^{-n}$ is not uncertain and since $N_{t+1}=N_t e^n$, this simplifies to

$$\frac{1}{c_t} = e^{-\rho}E_t\left[\frac{1}{c_{t+1}}(1+r_{t+1})\right]. \qquad (4.23)$$

This is the analogue of equation (2.20) in the Ramsey model.

Note that the expression on the right-hand side of (4.23) is *not* the same as $e^{-\rho}E_t[1/c_{t+1}]E_t[1+r_{t+1}]$. That is, the tradeoff between present and future consumption depends not just on the expectations of future marginal utility and of the rate of return, but also on their interaction. Specifically, the expectation of the product of two variables equals the product of their expectations plus their covariance. Thus (4.23) implies

$$\frac{1}{c_t} = e^{-\rho}\left\{E_t\left[\frac{1}{c_{t+1}}\right]E_t[1+r_{t+1}] + \mathrm{Cov}\left(\frac{1}{c_{t+1}},1+r_{t+1}\right)\right\}, \qquad (4.24)$$

where $\mathrm{Cov}(1/c_{t+1},1+r_{t+1})$ denotes the covariance of $1/c_{t+1}$ and $1+r_{t+1}$. Suppose, for example, that when r_{t+1} is high, c_{t+1} is also high. In this case,

---

[12] The household's problem can be analyzed more formally using *dynamic programming* (see Section 9.4, below; Dixit, 1990, Chapter 11; or Kreps, 1990, Appendix 2). This also yields (4.23) below.

$\text{Cov}(1/c_{t+1}, 1 + r_{t+1})$ is negative; that is, the return to saving is high in the times when the marginal utility of consumption is low. This makes saving less attractive than it is if $1/c_{t+1}$ and r_{t+1} are uncorrelated, and thus tends to raise current consumption.

Chapter 7 discusses the impact of uncertainty on optimal consumption further.

The Tradeoff between Consumption and Labor Supply

The household chooses not only consumption at each date, but also labor supply. Thus a second first-order condition for the household's optimization problem relates its current consumption and labor supply. Specifically, imagine the household increasing its labor supply per member in period t by a small amount $\Delta\ell$ and using the resulting income to increase its consumption in that period. Again if the household is behaving optimally, a marginal change of this type must leave expected utility unchanged.

From equations (4.5) and (4.7), the marginal disutility of working in period t is $e^{-\rho t}(N_t/H)[b/(1-\ell_t)]$. Thus the change has a utility cost of $e^{-\rho t}(N_t/H)[b/(1-\ell_t)]\Delta\ell$. And since the change raises consumption per member by $w_t\Delta\ell$, it has a utility benefit of $e^{-\rho t}(N_t/H)(1/c_t)w_t\Delta\ell$. Equating the cost and benefit gives us

$$e^{-\rho t}\frac{N_t}{H}\frac{b}{1-\ell_t}\Delta\ell = e^{-\rho t}\frac{N_t}{H}\frac{1}{c_t}w_t\Delta\ell, \tag{4.25}$$

or

$$\frac{c_t}{1-\ell_t} = \frac{w_t}{b}. \tag{4.26}$$

Equation (4.26) relates current leisure and consumption, given the wage. Because it involves current variables, which are known, uncertainty does not enter. Equations (4.23) and (4.26) are the key equations describing households' behavior.

4.5   A Special Case of the Model

Simplifying Assumptions

The model of Section 4.3 cannot be solved analytically. The basic problem, as Campbell (1994) emphasizes, is that it contains a mixture of ingredients that are linear—such as depreciation and the division of output into consumption, investment, and government purchases—and ones that are log-linear—such as the production function and preferences. In this section, we therefore investigate a simplified version of the model.

Specifically, we make two changes to the model: we eliminate government, and we assume 100 percent depreciation each period.[13] Thus equations (4.10) and (4.11), which describe the behavior of government purchases, are dropped from the model. And equations (4.2) and (4.4), which describe the evolution of the capital stock and the determination of the real interest rate, become

$$K_{t+1} = Y_t - C_t, \tag{4.27}$$

$$1 + r_t = \alpha \left(\frac{A_t L_t}{K_t} \right)^{1-\alpha}. \tag{4.28}$$

The elimination of government can be justified on the grounds that doing so allows us to isolate the effects of technology shocks. The grounds for the assumption of complete depreciation, on the other hand, are only that it allows us to solve the model analytically.

Solving the Model

Because markets are competitive, externalities are absent, and there are a finite number of individuals, the model's equilibrium must correspond to the Pareto optimum. Because of this, we can find the equilibrium either by ignoring markets and finding the social optimum directly, or by solving for the competitive equilibrium. We will take the second approach, on the grounds that it is easier to apply to variations of the model where Pareto efficiency fails. Finding the social optimum is sometimes easier, however; as a result, many real-business-cycle models are solved that way.[14]

The solution to the model focuses on two variables, labor supply per person, ℓ, and the fraction of output that is saved, s. The basic strategy is to rewrite the equations of the model in log-linear form, substituting $(1 - s)Y$ for C whenever it appears. We will then determine how ℓ and s must depend on the current technology and on the capital stock inherited from the previous period to satisfy the equilibrium conditions. We will focus on the two conditions for household optimization, (4.23) and (4.26); the remaining equations follow mechanically from accounting and from competition.

We will find that s is independent of technology and the capital stock. Intuitively, the combination of logarithmic utility, Cobb–Douglas production, and 100 percent depreciation causes movements in both technology

---

[13] With these changes, the model corresponds to a one-sector version of Long and Plosser's (1983) real-business-cycle model. McCallum (1989) investigates this model. In addition, except for the assumption of $\delta = 1$, the model corresponds to the basic case considered by Prescott (1986). It is straightforward to assume that a constant fraction of output is purchased by the government instead of eliminating government altogether.

[14] See Problem 4.11 for the solution using the social-optimum approach.

and capital to have offsetting income and substitution effects on saving. It is the fact that s is constant that allows the model to be solved analytically.

Consider (4.23) first; this condition is $1/c_t = e^{-\rho}E_t[(1+r_{t+1})/c_{t+1}]$. Since $c_t = (1 - s_t)Y_t/N_t$, rewriting (4.23) along the lines just suggested gives us

$$-\ln\left[(1 - s_t)\frac{Y_t}{N_t}\right] = -\rho + \ln E_t\left[\frac{1 + r_{t+1}}{(1 - s_{t+1})Y_{t+1}/N_{t+1}}\right]. \tag{4.29}$$

Since the production function is Cobb–Douglas and depreciation is 100 percent, $1 + r_{t+1} = \alpha Y_{t+1}/K_{t+1}$. In addition, 100 percent depreciation implies that $K_{t+1} = Y_t - C_t = s_t Y_t$. Substituting these facts into (4.29) yields

$$-\ln(1 - s_t) - \ln Y_t + \ln N_t$$

$$= -\rho + \ln E_t\left[\frac{\alpha Y_{t+1}}{K_{t+1}(1 - s_{t+1})Y_{t+1}/N_{t+1}}\right]$$

$$= -\rho + \ln E_t\left[\frac{\alpha N_{t+1}}{s_t(1 - s_{t+1})Y_t}\right] \tag{4.30}$$

$$= -\rho + \ln \alpha + \ln N_t + n - \ln s_t - \ln Y_t + \ln E_t\left[\frac{1}{1 - s_{t+1}}\right],$$

where the final line uses the facts that α, N_{t+1}, s_t, and Y_t are known at date t and that N is growing at rate n. Equation (4.30) simplifies to

$$\ln s_t - \ln(1 - s_t) = -\rho + n + \ln \alpha + \ln E_t\left[\frac{1}{1 - s_{t+1}}\right]. \tag{4.31}$$

Technology (A) and capital (K) do not enter (4.31). Thus there is a constant value of s that satisfies this condition. To see this, note that if s is constant at some value $\hat{s}$, then s_{t+1} is not uncertain, and so $E_t[1/(1 - s_{t+1})]$ is simply $1/(1 - \hat{s})$. Thus (4.31) becomes

$$\ln \hat{s} = \ln \alpha + n - \rho, \tag{4.32}$$

or

$$\hat{s} = \alpha e^{n-\rho}. \tag{4.33}$$

Thus the saving rate is constant.

Now consider (4.26), which states $c_t/(1 - \ell_t) = w_t/b$. Since $c_t = C_t/N_t = (1 - \hat{s})Y_t/N_t$, we can rewrite this condition as

$$\ln\left[(1 - \hat{s})\frac{Y_t}{N_t}\right] - \ln(1 - \ell_t) = \ln w_t - \ln b. \tag{4.34}$$

Since the production function is Cobb–Douglas, $w_t = (1-\alpha)Y_t/(\ell_t N_t)$. Substituting this fact into (4.34) yields

$$\ln(1 - \hat{s}) + \ln Y_t - \ln N_t - \ln(1 - \ell_t)$$

$$= \ln(1 - \alpha) + \ln Y_t - \ln \ell_t - \ln N_t - \ln b. \tag{4.35}$$

Canceling terms and rearranging gives us

$$\ln \ell_t - \ln(1 - \ell_t) = \ln(1 - \alpha) - \ln(1 - \hat{s}) - \ln b. \qquad (4.36)$$

Finally, straightforward algebra yields

$$\ell_t = \frac{1 - \alpha}{(1 - \alpha) + b(1 - \hat{s})}$$

$$\equiv \hat{\ell}. \qquad (4.37)$$

Thus labor supply is also constant. The reason this occurs despite households' willingness to substitute their labor supply intertemporally is that movements in either technology or capital have offsetting impacts on the relative-wage and interest-rate effects on labor supply. An improvement in technology, for example, raises current wages relative to expected future wages, and thus acts to raise labor supply. But, by raising the amount saved, it also lowers the expected interest rate, which acts to reduce labor supply. In the specific case we are considering, these two effects exactly balance.

The remaining equations of the model do not involve optimization; they follow from technology, accounting, and competition. Thus we have found a solution to the model with s and ℓ constant.

As described above, any competitive equilibrium of this model is also a solution to the problem of maximizing the expected utility of the representative household. Standard results about optimization imply that this problem has a unique solution (see Stokey, Lucas, and Prescott, 1989, for example). Thus the equilibrium we have found must be the only one.

Discussion

This model provides an example of an economy where real shocks drive output movements. Because the economy is Walrasian, the movements are the optimal responses to the shocks. Thus, contrary to the conventional wisdom about macroeconomic fluctuations, here fluctuations do not reflect any market failures, and government interventions to mitigate them can only reduce welfare. In short, the implication of real-business-cycle models, in their strongest form, is that observed aggregate output movements represent the time-varying Pareto optimum.

The specific form of the output fluctuations implied by the model is determined by the dynamics of technology and the behavior of the capital stock.[15] In particular, the production function, $Y_t = K_t^\alpha (A_t L_t)^{1-\alpha}$, implies

$$\ln Y_t = \alpha \ln K_t + (1 - \alpha)(\ln A_t + \ln L_t). \qquad (4.38)$$

---

[15] The discussion that follows is based on McCallum (1989).

We know that $K_t = \hat{s} Y_{t-1}$ and $L_t = \hat{\ell} N_t$; thus

$$\ln Y_t = \alpha \ln \hat{s} + \alpha \ln Y_{t-1} + (1 - \alpha)(\ln A_t + \ln \hat{\ell} + \ln N_t)$$

$$= \alpha \ln \hat{s} + \alpha \ln Y_{t-1} + (1 - \alpha)(\overline{A} + gt) \tag{4.39}$$

$$+ (1 - \alpha)\tilde{A}_t + (1 - \alpha)(\ln \hat{\ell} + \overline{N} + nt),$$

where the last line uses the facts that $\ln A_t = \overline{A} + gt + \tilde{A}_t$ and $\ln N_t = \overline{N} + nt$ (see [4.6] and [4.8]).

The two components of the right-hand side of (4.39) that do not follow deterministic paths are $\alpha \ln Y_{t-1}$ and $(1-\alpha)\tilde{A}_t$. It must therefore be possible to rewrite (4.39) in the form

$$\tilde{Y}_t = \alpha \tilde{Y}_{t-1} + (1 - \alpha)\tilde{A}_t, \tag{4.40}$$

where $\tilde{Y}_t$ is the difference between $\ln Y_t$ and the value it would take if $\ln A_t$ equaled $\overline{A} + gt$ each period (see Problem 4.14 for the details).

To see what (4.40) implies concerning the dynamics of output, note that since it holds each period, it implies $\tilde{Y}_{t-1} = \alpha \tilde{Y}_{t-2} + (1 - \alpha)\tilde{A}_{t-1}$, or

$$\tilde{A}_{t-1} = \frac{1}{1 - \alpha}\left(\tilde{Y}_{t-1} - \alpha \tilde{Y}_{t-2}\right). \tag{4.41}$$

Recall that (4.9) states that $\tilde{A}_t = \rho_A \tilde{A}_{t-1} + \varepsilon_{A,t}$. Substituting this fact and (4.41) into (4.40), we obtain

$$\tilde{Y}_t = \alpha \tilde{Y}_{t-1} + (1 - \alpha)(\rho_A \tilde{A}_{t-1} + \varepsilon_{A,t})$$

$$= \alpha \tilde{Y}_{t-1} + \rho_A(\tilde{Y}_{t-1} - \alpha \tilde{Y}_{t-2}) + (1 - \alpha)\varepsilon_{A,t} \tag{4.42}$$

$$= (\alpha + \rho_A)\tilde{Y}_{t-1} - \alpha \rho_A \tilde{Y}_{t-2} + (1 - \alpha)\varepsilon_{A,t}.$$

Thus, departures of log output from its normal path follow a *second-order autoregressive process*; that is, $\tilde{Y}$ can be written as a linear combination of its two previous values plus a white-noise disturbance.[16]

The combination of a positive coefficient on the first lag of $\tilde{Y}_t$ and a negative coefficient on the second lag can cause output to have a "hump-shaped" response to disturbances. Suppose, for example, that $\alpha = \frac{1}{3}$ and $\rho_A = 0.9$. Consider a one-time shock of $1/(1 - \alpha)$ to ε_A. Using (4.42) iteratively shows that the shock raises log output relative to the path it would have otherwise

---

[16] Readers who are familiar with the use of *lag operators* can derive (4.42) using that approach. In lag operator notation, $\tilde{Y}_{t-1}$ is $L\tilde{Y}_t$, where L maps variables to their previous period's value. Thus (4.40) can be written as $\tilde{Y}_t = \alpha L\tilde{Y}_t + (1 - \alpha)\tilde{A}_t$, or $(1 - \alpha L)\tilde{Y}_t = (1 - \alpha)\tilde{A}_t$. Similarly, we can rewrite (4.9) as $(1 - \rho_A L)\tilde{A}_t = \varepsilon_{A,t}$, or $\tilde{A}_t = (1 - \rho_A L)^{-1}\varepsilon_{A,t}$. Thus we have $(1 - \alpha L)\tilde{Y}_t = (1 - \alpha)(1 - \rho_A L)^{-1}\varepsilon_{A,t}$. "Multiplying" through by $1 - \rho_A L$ yields $(1 - \alpha L)(1 - \rho_A L)\tilde{Y}_t = (1 - \alpha)\varepsilon_{A,t}$, or $[1 - (\alpha + \rho_A)L + \alpha\rho_A L^2]\tilde{Y}_t = (1 - \alpha)\varepsilon_{A,t}$. This is equivalent to $\tilde{Y}_t = (\alpha + \rho_A)L\tilde{Y}_t - \alpha\rho_A L^2\tilde{Y}_t + (1 - \alpha)\varepsilon_{A,t}$, which corresponds to (4.42). (See Section 6.6 for a discussion of lag operators and of the legitimacy of manipulating them in these kinds of ways.)

followed by 1 in the period of the shock ($1 - \alpha$ times the shock), 1.23 in the next period ($\alpha + \rho_A$ times 1), 1.22 in the following period ($\alpha + \rho_A$ times 1.23, minus α times ρ_A times 1), then 1.14, 1.03, 0.94, 0.84, 0.76, 0.68,... in subsequent periods.

Because α is not large, the dynamics of output are determined largely by the persistence of the technology shocks, ρ_A. If $\rho_A = 0$, for example, (4.42) simplifies to $\tilde{Y}_t = \alpha \tilde{Y}_{t-1} + (1 - \alpha)\varepsilon_{A,t}$. If $\alpha = \frac{1}{3}$, this implies that almost nine-tenths of the initial effect of a shock disappears after only two periods. Even if $\rho_A = \frac{1}{2}$, two-thirds of the initial effect is gone after three periods. Thus the model does not have any mechanism that translates transitory technology disturbances into significant long-lasting output movements. We will see that the same is true of the more general version of the model.

Nonetheless, these results show that this model yields interesting output dynamics. Indeed, if actual U.S. log output is detrended linearly, it follows a process similar to the hump-shaped one described above (Blanchard, 1981; this result is sensitive to the detrending, however).

In other ways, however, this special case of the model does not do a good job of matching major features of fluctuations. Most obviously, the saving rate is constant—so that consumption and investment are equally volatile—and labor input does not vary. In practice, as we saw in Section 4.1, investment varies much more than consumption, and employment and hours are strongly procyclical—that is, they move in the same direction as aggregate output. In addition, the model predicts that the real wage is highly procyclical. Because of the Cobb–Douglas production function, the real wage is $(1 - \alpha)Y/L$; since L does not respond to technology shocks, this means that the real wage rises one-for-one with Y. In actual fluctuations, in contrast, the real wage appears to be only moderately procyclical.

Thus the model must be modified if it is to capture many of the major features of observed output movements. The next section shows that introducing depreciation of less than 100 percent and shocks to government purchases improves the model's predictions concerning movements in employment, saving, and the real wage.

To see intuitively how lower depreciation improves the fit of the model, consider the extreme case of no depreciation and no growth, so that investment is zero in the absence of shocks. In this situation, a positive technology shock, by raising the marginal product of capital in the next period, makes it optimal for households to undertake some investment. Thus the saving rate rises. The fact that saving is temporarily high means that expected consumption growth is higher than it would be with a constant saving rate; from consumers' intertemporal optimization condition, (4.23), this requires the expected interest rate to be higher. But we know that a higher interest rate increases current labor supply. Thus introducing incomplete depreciation causes investment and employment to respond more to shocks.

The reason that introducing shocks to government purchases improves the fit of the model is straightforward: it breaks the tight link between output and the real wage. Since an increase in government purchases increases households' lifetime tax liability, it reduces their lifetime wealth. This causes them to consume less leisure—that is, to work more. When labor supply rises without any change in technology, the real wage falls; thus output and the real wage move in opposite directions. It follows that with shocks to both government purchases and technology, the model can generate an overall pattern of real wage movements that is not strongly procyclical.

4.6   Solving the Model in the General Case

Overview

As discussed above, the full model of Section 4.3 cannot be solved analytically. This is true of almost all real-business-cycle models. Papers in this area generally address this difficulty by solving the models numerically. That is, once a model is presented, parameter values are chosen, and the model's quantitative implications for the variances and correlations of various macroeconomic variables are discussed.

As Campbell (1994) emphasizes, this procedure provides little guidance concerning the sources of the models' implications. He argues that one should instead take first-order Taylor approximations of the equations of the models in the logs of the relevant variables around the models' balanced growth paths in the absence of shocks, and then investigate the properties of these approximate models.[17] He also argues that one should focus on how the variables of a model respond to shocks instead of merely describing the model's implications for variances and correlations.

This section applies Campbell's method to the model of Section 4.3. Unfortunately, even though taking a log-linear approximation to the model allows it to be solved analytically, the analysis remains cumbersome. For that reason, we will only describe the broad features of the derivation and results without going through the specifics in detail.

Log-Linearizing the Model around the Balanced Growth Path[18]

In any period, the state of the economy is described by the capital stock inherited from the previous period and by the current values of technology and government purchases. The two variables that are endogenous each period are consumption and employment.

---

[17] Kimball (1991) employs a similar approach.

[18] See Problem 4.10 for the balanced growth path of the model in the absence of shocks.

If we log-linearize the model around the nonstochastic balanced growth path, the rules for consumption and employment must take the form

$$\tilde{C}_t \simeq a_{CK}\tilde{K}_t + a_{CA}\tilde{A}_t + a_{CG}\tilde{G}_t, \tag{4.43}$$

$$\tilde{L}_t \simeq a_{LK}\tilde{K}_t + a_{LA}\tilde{A}_t + a_{LG}\tilde{G}_t, \tag{4.44}$$

where the a's will be functions of the underlying parameters of the model. As before, a tilde ($\tilde{}$) over a variable denotes the difference between the log of that variable and the log of its balanced-growth-path value. Thus, for example, $\tilde{A}_t$ denotes $\ln A_t - (\overline{A} + gt)$. Equations (4.43) and (4.44) state that log consumption and log employment are linear functions of the logs of K, A, and G, and that consumption and employment are equal to their balanced-growth-path values when K, A, and G are all equal to theirs. Since we are building a version of the model that is log-linear around the balanced growth path by construction, we know that these conditions must hold. To solve the model, we must determine the values of the a's.

As with the simple version of the model, we will focus on the two conditions for household optimization, (4.23) and (4.26). For a set of a's to be a solution to the model, they must imply that households are satisfying these conditions. It turns out that the restrictions that this requirement puts on the a's fully determine them, and thus tell us the solution to the model.

This solution method is known as the *method of undetermined coefficients*. The idea is to use theory (or, in some cases, educated guesswork) to find the general functional form of the solution, and then to determine what values the coefficients in the functional form must take to satisfy the equations of the model. This method is useful in many situations.

The Intratemporal First-Order Condition

Begin by considering households' first-order condition for the tradeoff between current consumption and labor supply, $c_t/(1 - \ell_t) = w_t/b$ (equation [4.26]). Using equation (4.3), $w_t = (1 - \alpha)[K_t/A_tL_t]^\alpha A_t$, to substitute for the wage and taking logs, we can write this condition as

$$\ln c_t - \ln(1 - \ell_t) = \ln\left(\frac{1 - \alpha}{b}\right) + (1 - \alpha)\ln A_t + \alpha \ln K_t - \alpha \ln L_t. \tag{4.45}$$

We want to find a first-order Taylor-series approximation to this expression in the logs of the variables of the model around the balanced growth path the economy would follow if there were no shocks. Approximating the right-hand side is straightforward: the difference between the actual value of the right-hand side and its balanced-growth-path value is $(1 - \alpha)\tilde{A}_t + \alpha\tilde{K}_t - \alpha\tilde{L}_t$. To approximate the left-hand side, note that since population growth is not affected by the shocks, $\tilde{C}_t = \tilde{c}_t$: log total consumption differs from its balanced-growth-path value only to the extent that log consumption per worker differs from its balanced-growth-path value.

Similarly, $\tilde{\ell}_t = \tilde{L}_t$. The derivative of the left-hand side of (4.45) with respect to $\ln c_t$ is simply 1. The derivative with respect to $\ln \ell_t$ at $\ell_t = \ell^*$ is $\ell^*/(1 - \ell^*)$, where ℓ^* is the value of ℓ on the balanced growth path. Thus, log-linearizing (4.45) around the balanced growth path yields

$$\tilde{C}_t + \frac{\ell^*}{1 - \ell^*}\tilde{L}_t = (1 - \alpha)\tilde{A}_t + \alpha\tilde{K}_t - \alpha\tilde{L}_t. \tag{4.46}$$

We can now use the fact that $\tilde{C}_t$ and $\tilde{L}_t$ are linear functions of $\tilde{K}_t, \tilde{A}_t$, and $\tilde{G}_t$. Substituting (4.43) and (4.44) into (4.46) yields

$$a_{CK}\tilde{K}_t + a_{CA}\tilde{A}_t + a_{CG}\tilde{G}_t + \left(\frac{\ell^*}{1 - \ell^*} + \alpha\right)(a_{LK}\tilde{K}_t + a_{LA}\tilde{A}_t + a_{LG}\tilde{G}_t)$$

$$= \alpha\tilde{K}_t + (1 - \alpha)\tilde{A}_t. \tag{4.47}$$

Equation (4.47) must hold for all values of $\tilde{K}$, $\tilde{A}$, and $\tilde{G}$. If it does not, then for some combinations of $\tilde{K}$, $\tilde{A}$, and $\tilde{G}$, households can raise their utility by changing their current consumption and labor supply. Thus the coefficients on $\tilde{K}$ on the two sides of (4.47) must be equal, and similarly for the coefficients on $\tilde{A}$ and on $\tilde{G}$. Thus the a's must satisfy

$$a_{CK} + \left(\frac{\ell^*}{1 - \ell^*} + \alpha\right)a_{LK} = \alpha, \tag{4.48}$$

$$a_{CA} + \left(\frac{\ell^*}{1 - \ell^*} + \alpha\right)a_{LA} = 1 - \alpha, \tag{4.49}$$

$$a_{CG} + \left(\frac{\ell^*}{1 - \ell^*} + \alpha\right)a_{LG} = 0. \tag{4.50}$$

To understand these conditions, consider first (4.50), which relates the responses of consumption and employment to movements in government purchases. Government purchases do not directly enter (4.45); that is, they do not affect the wage for a given level of labor supply. If households increase their labor supply in response to an increase in government purchases, the wage falls and the marginal disutility of working rises. Thus, they will do this only if the marginal utility of consumption is higher—that is, if consumption is lower. Thus if labor supply and consumption respond to changes in government purchases, they must move in opposite directions. Equation (4.50) tells us not only this qualitative result, but also how the movements in labor supply and consumption must be related.

Now consider an increase in A (equation [4.49]). An improvement in technology raises the wage for a given level of labor supply. Thus if neither labor supply nor consumption responds, households can raise their utility by working more and increasing their current consumption. Thus households must increase either labor supply or consumption (or both); this is what is captured in (4.49).

Finally, the restrictions that (4.45) puts on the responses of labor supply and consumption to movements in capital are similar to the restrictions it puts on their responses to movements in technology. The only difference is that the elasticity of the wage with respect to capital, given L, is α rather than $1 - \alpha$. This is what is shown in (4.48).

The Intertemporal First-Order Condition

The analysis of the first-order condition relating current consumption and next period's consumption, $1/c_t = e^{-\rho}E_t[(1 + r_{t+1})/c_{t+1}]$ (equation [4.23]), is more complicated. The basic idea is the following. Begin by defining $\tilde{Z}_{t+1}$ as the difference between the log of $(1 + r_{t+1})/c_{t+1}$ and the log of its balanced-growth-path value. Now note that since (4.43) holds at each date, it implies

$$\tilde{C}_{t+1} \simeq a_{CK}\tilde{K}_{t+1} + a_{CA}\tilde{A}_{t+1} + a_{CG}\tilde{G}_{t+1}. \tag{4.51}$$

We can then use this expression for $\tilde{C}_{t+1}$ and equation (4.4) for r_{t+1} to express $\tilde{Z}_{t+1}$ in terms of $\tilde{K}_{t+1}$, $\tilde{A}_{t+1}$, and $\tilde{G}_{t+1}$.[19] Since $\tilde{K}_{t+1}$ is an endogenous variable, we need to eliminate it from this expression. Specifically, we can log-linearize the equation of motion for capital, (4.2), to write $\tilde{K}_{t+1}$ in terms of $\tilde{K}_t$, $\tilde{A}_t$, $\tilde{G}_t$, $\tilde{L}_t$, and $\tilde{C}_t$; we can then use (4.43) and (4.44) to substitute for $\tilde{L}_t$ and $\tilde{C}_t$. This yields an expression of the form

$$\tilde{K}_{t+1} \simeq b_{KK}\tilde{K}_t + b_{KA}\tilde{A}_t + b_{KG}\tilde{G}_t, \tag{4.52}$$

where the b's are complicated functions of the parameters of the model and of the a's.[20]

Substituting (4.52) into the expression for $\tilde{Z}_{t+1}$ in terms of $\tilde{K}_{t+1}, \tilde{A}_{t+1}$, and $\tilde{G}_{t+1}$ then gives us an expression for $\tilde{Z}_{t+1}$ in terms of $\tilde{A}_{t+1}$, $\tilde{G}_{t+1}$, $\tilde{K}_t$, $\tilde{A}_t$, and $\tilde{G}_t$. The final step is to use this to find $E_t[\tilde{Z}_{t+1}]$ in terms of $\tilde{K}_t, \tilde{A}_t$, and $\tilde{G}_t$.[21] Substituting this into (4.23) gives us three additional restrictions on the a's; this is enough to determine the a's in terms of the underlying parameters.

---

[19] Equation (4.44) for $\tilde{L}$ is used to substitute for $\tilde{L}_{t+1}$ in the expression for r_{t+1}.

[20] See Problem 4.15.

[21] There is one complication here. As emphasized in Section 4.4, (4.23) involves not just the expectations of next-period values, but their entire distribution. That is, what is appropriate in the log-linearized version of (4.23) is not $E_t[\tilde{Z}_{t+1}]$, but $\ln E_t[e^{\tilde{Z}_{t+1}}]$. Campbell (1994) addresses this difficulty by assuming that $\tilde{Z}$ is normally distributed with constant variance; that is, $e^{\tilde{Z}}$ has a *lognormal* distribution. Standard results about this distribution then imply that $\ln E_t[e^{\tilde{Z}_{t+1}}]$ equals $E_t[\tilde{Z}_{t+1}]$ plus a constant. Thus we can express the log of the right-hand side of (4.23) in terms of $E_t[\tilde{Z}_{t+1}]$ and constants. Finally, Campbell notes that given the log-linear structure of the model, if the underlying shocks—the ε_A's and ε_G's in (4.9) and (4.11)—are normally distributed with constant variance, his assumption about the distribution of $\tilde{Z}_{t+1}$ is correct.

Unfortunately, the model is sufficiently complicated that solving for the a's is tedious, and the resulting expressions for the a's in terms of the underlying parameters of the model are complicated. Even if we wrote down those expressions, the effects of the parameters of the model on the a's, and hence on the economy's response to shocks, would not be transparent.

Thus, despite the comparative simplicity of the model and our use of approximations, we must still resort to numerical methods to describe the model's properties. What we will do is choose a set of baseline parameter values and discuss their implications for the a's in (4.43)–(4.44) and the b's in (4.52). Once we have determined the values of the a's and b's, equations (4.43), (4.44), and (4.52) specify (approximately) how consumption, employment, and capital respond to shocks to technology and government purchases. The remaining equations of the model can then be used to describe the responses of the model's other variables—output, investment, the wage, and the interest rate. For example, we can substitute equation (4.44) for $\tilde{L}$ into the log-linearized version of the production function to find the model's implications for output:

$$
\begin{aligned}
\tilde{Y}_t &= \alpha\tilde{K}_t + (1 - \alpha)(\tilde{L}_t + \tilde{A}_t) \\
&= \alpha\tilde{K}_t + (1 - \alpha)(a_{LK}\tilde{K}_t + a_{LA}\tilde{A}_t + a_{LG}\tilde{G}_t + \tilde{A}_t) \qquad (4.53) \\
&= [\alpha + (1 - \alpha)a_{LK}]\tilde{K}_t + (1 - \alpha)(1 + a_{LA})\tilde{A}_t + (1 - \alpha)a_{LG}\tilde{G}_t.
\end{aligned}
$$

4.7 Implications

Following Campbell, assume that each period corresponds to a quarter, and take for baseline parameter values $\alpha = \frac{1}{3}$, $g = 0.5\%$, $n = 0.25\%$, $\delta = 2.5\%$, $\rho_A = 0.95$, $\rho_G = 0.95$, and $\overline{G}$, ρ, and b such that $(G/Y)^* = 0.2$, $r^* = 1.5\%$, and $\ell^* = \frac{1}{3}$.[22]

The Effects of Technology Shocks

One can show that these parameter values imply $a_{LA} \simeq 0.35$, $a_{LK} \simeq -0.31$, $a_{CA} \simeq 0.38$, $a_{CK} \simeq 0.59$, $b_{KA} \simeq 0.08$, and $b_{KK} \simeq 0.95$. These values can be used to trace out the effects of a change in technology. Consider, for example, a positive 1 percent technology shock. In the period of the shock, capital (which is inherited from the previous period) is unchanged, labor supply rises by 0.35 percent, and consumption rises by 0.38 percent. Since the production function is $K^{1/3}(AL)^{2/3}$, output increases by 0.90 percent. In the next period, technology is 0.95 percent above normal (since $\rho_A = 0.95$),

---

[22] See Problem 4.10 for the implications of these parameter values for the balanced growth path.

capital is higher by 0.08 percent (since $b_{KA} \simeq 0.08$), labor supply is higher by 0.31 percent (0.35 times 0.95, minus 0.31 times 0.08), and consumption is higher by 0.41 percent (0.38 times 0.95, plus 0.59 times 0.08); the effects on A, K, and L imply that output is 0.86 percent above normal. And so on.

Figures 4.2 and 4.3 show the shock's effects on the major quantity variables of the model. By assumption, the effects on the level of technology die away slowly. Capital accumulates gradually and then slowly returns to normal; the peak effect is an increase of 0.60 percent after 20 quarters. Labor supply jumps by 0.35 percent in the period of the shock and then declines relatively rapidly, falling below normal after 15 quarters. It reaches a low of −0.09 percent after 33 quarters and then slowly comes back to normal. The net result of the movements in A, K, and L is that output increases in the period of the shock and then gradually returns to normal. Consumption responds less, and more slowly, than output; thus investment is more volatile than consumption.

Figure 4.4 shows the percentage movement in the wage and the change in percentage points in the interest rate at an annual rate. The wage rises and then returns very slowly to normal. Because the changes in the wage (after the unexpected jump at the time of the shock) are small, wage movements contribute little to the variations in labor supply. The annual interest rate

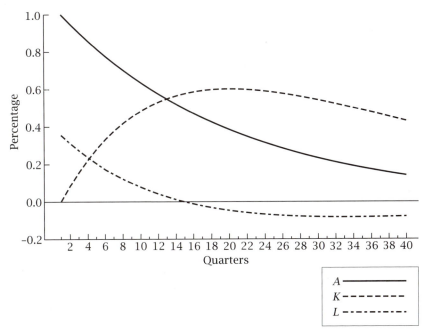

FIGURE 4.2 **The effects of a 1 percent technology shock on the paths of technology, capital, and labor**

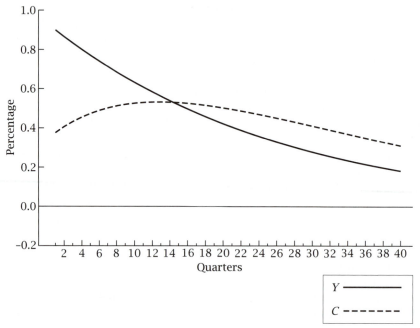

FIGURE 4.3   The effects of a 1 percent technology shock on the paths of output and consumption

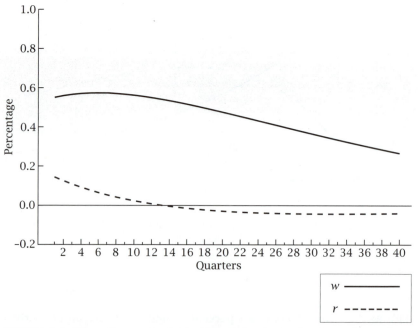

FIGURE 4.4   The effects of a 1 percent technology shock on the paths of the wage and the interest rate

increases by about one-seventh of a percentage point in the period of the shock and then returns to normal fairly quickly. Because the capital stock moves more slowly than labor supply, the interest rate dips below normal after 14 quarters. These movements in the interest rate are the main source of the movements in labor supply.

To understand the movements in the interest rate and consumption, start by considering the case where labor supply is inelastic, and recall that $r = \alpha(AL/K)^{1-\alpha} - \delta$. The immediate effect of the increase in A is to raise r. Since the increase in A dies out only slowly, r must remain high unless K increases rapidly. And since depreciation is low, a rapid rise in K would require a large increase in the fraction of output that is invested. But if the saving rate were to rise by so much that r returned immediately to its usual level, this would mean that consumption was expected to grow rapidly even though r equaled its normal value; this would violate households' intertemporal first-order condition, (4.23). Thus, instead, households raise the fraction of their income that they save, but not by enough to return r immediately to its usual level. And since the increase in A is persistent, the increase in the saving rate is also persistent. As technology returns to normal, the slow adjustment of the capital stock eventually causes A/K to fall below its initial value, and thus causes r to fall below its usual value. When this occurs, the saving rate falls below its balanced-growth-path level.

When we allow for variations in labor supply, some of the adjustments of the capital stock occur through changes in labor supply rather than the saving rate: households build up the capital stock during the early phase partly by increasing labor supply, and bring it back to normal in the later phase partly by decreasing labor supply.

The parameter that the results are most sensitive to is ρ_A. When technology shocks are less persistent, the wealth effect of a shock is smaller (because its impact is shorter-lived), and its intertemporal-substitution effect is larger. As a result, a_{CA} is increasing in ρ_A, and a_{LA} and b_{KA} are decreasing; a_{CK}, a_{LK}, and b_{KK} are unaffected. If ρ_A declines from the baseline value of 0.95 to 0.5, for example, a_{CA} falls from 0.38 to 0.11, a_{LA} rises from 0.35 to 0.66, and b_{KA} rises from 0.08 to 0.12. The result is sharper, shorter output fluctuations. In this case, a 1 percent technology shock raises output by 1.11 percent in the period of the shock, but only by 0.30 percent two periods later. If $\rho_A = 1$, then a_{CA} rises to 0.63, a_{LA} falls to 0.05, and b_{KA} falls to 0.04. The result is that employment fluctuations are small and output fluctuations are much more gradual. For example, a 1 percent shock causes output to increase by 0.70 percent immediately (only slightly larger than the direct effect of 0.67 percent), and then to rise very gradually to 1 percent above its initial level.

In addition, suppose we generalize the way that leisure enters the instantaneous utility function, (4.7), to allow the intertemporal elasticity of substitution in labor supply to take on values other than 1.[23] With this change, this elasticity also has important effects on the economy's response

---

[23] See Campbell (1994) and Problem 4.4.

to shocks: the larger the elasticity, the more responsive labor supply is to technology and capital. If the elasticity rises from 1 to 2, for example, a_{LA} increases from 0.35 to 0.48 and a_{LK} increases from -0.31 to -0.41 (in addition, a_{CA}, a_{CK}, b_{KA}, and b_{KK} all change moderately). As a result, fluctuations are larger when the intertemporal elasticity of substitution is higher.[24]

The Effects of Changes in Government Purchases

Our baseline parameter values imply $a_{CG} \simeq -0.13$, $a_{LG} \simeq 0.15$, and $b_{KG} \simeq -0.004$; a_{CK}, a_{LK}, and b_{KK} are as before. Intuitively, an increase in government purchases causes consumption to fall and labor supply to rise because of its negative wealth effects. And because the rise in government purchases is not permanent, agents also respond by decreasing their capital holdings.

Since the elasticity of output with respect to L is $\frac{2}{3}$, the value of a_{LG} of 0.15 means that output rises by about 0.1 percent in response to a 1 percent government-purchases shock. Since output on the balanced growth path is 5 times government purchases, this means that Y rises by about one-half as much as G. And since one can show that consumption on the balanced growth path is about $2\frac{1}{2}$ times government purchases, the value of a_{CG} of -0.13 means that C falls by about one-third as much as G increases. The remaining one-sixth of the adjustment takes the form of lower investment.

Figures 4.5–4.7 trace out the effects of a positive 1 percent government-purchases shock. The capital stock is only slightly affected; the maximum impact is a decline of 0.03 percent after 20 quarters. Employment increases and then gradually returns to normal; in contrast to what occurs with technology shocks, there is no overshooting. Because technology is unchanged and the capital stock moves little, the movements in output are small and track the changes in employment fairly closely. Consumption declines at the time of the shock and then gradually returns to normal. The increase in employment and the fall in the capital stock cause the wage to fall and the interest rate to rise. The anticipated wage movements after the period of the shock are small and positive; thus, as before, the source of the increases in labor supply is the increases in the interest rate.

As with technology, the persistence of movements in government purchases has important effects on how the economy responds to shocks. If ρ_G falls to 0.5, for example, a_{CG} falls from -0.13 to -0.03, a_{LG} falls from 0.15 to 0.03, and b_{KG} increases from -0.004 to -0.020: because movements in purchases are much shorter-lived, much more of the response takes the form of reductions in capital holdings. These values imply that output rises

---

[24] In addition, Kimball (1991) shows that if we relax the assumption of a Cobb–Douglas production function, the elasticity of substitution between capital and labor has important effects on the economy's response to shocks.

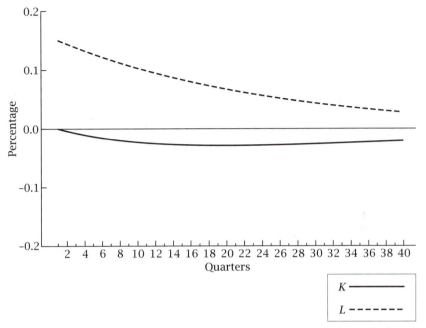

FIGURE 4.5 The effects of a 1 percent government-purchases shock on the paths of capital and labor

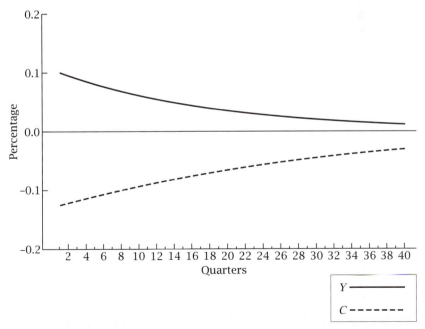

FIGURE 4.6 The effects of a 1 percent government-purchases shock on the paths of output and consumption

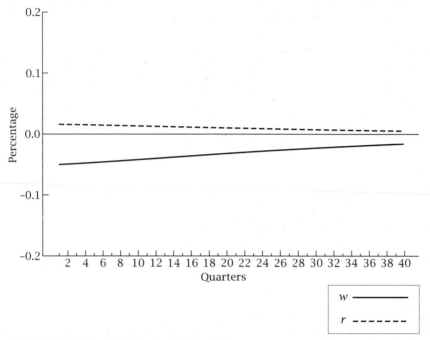

FIGURE 4.7   **The effects of a 1 percent government-purchases shock on the paths of the wage and the interest rate**

by about one-tenth of the increase in government purchases, that consumption falls by about one-tenth of the increase, and that investment falls by about four-fifths of the increase. In response to a 1 percent shock, for example, output increases by just 0.02 percent in the period of the shock and then falls below normal, with a low of −0.004 percent after 7 quarters.

4.8   Empirical Application: The Persistence of Output Fluctuations

Introduction

Real-business-cycle models emphasize shifts in technology as a central source of output fluctuations. The specific model analyzed in this chapter assumes that technology fluctuates around a deterministic trend; as a result, the effects of a given technological shock eventually approach zero. But this assumption is made purely for convenience. It seems plausible that changes in technology have a significant permanent component. For example, an innovation today may have little impact on the likelihood of additional innovations in the future, and thus on the expected behavior of the *growth* of technology in the future. In this case, the innovation raises the expected path of the *level* of technology permanently. Thus real-business-cycle models are quite consistent with a large permanent component of output fluctuations. In traditional Keynesian models, in contrast, output movements are largely the result of monetary and other aggregate demand disturbances coupled with sluggish adjustment of nominal prices or wages. Since the models assume that prices and wages adjust eventually, under natural assumptions they imply that changes in aggregate demand have no long-run effects. For this reason, natural baseline versions of these models predict that output fluctuates around a deterministic trend path. These considerations have sparked a considerable literature on the persistence of output movements.

Nelson and Plosser's Test

The persistence of fluctuations was first addressed by Nelson and Plosser (1982), who consider the question of whether fluctuations have a permanent component (see also McCulloch, 1975). The idea behind their test is conceptually simple, though it turns out to involve some econometric complications. If output movements are fluctuations around a deterministic trend, then output growth will tend to be less than normal when output is above its trend and more than normal when it is below its trend. That is, consider a regression of the form

$$\Delta \ln y_t = a + b\{\ln y_{t-1} - [\alpha + \beta(t-1)]\} + \varepsilon_t, \tag{4.54}$$

where $\ln y$ is log real GDP, $\alpha + \beta t$ is its trend path, and ε_t is a mean-zero disturbance uncorrelated with $\ln y_{t-1} - [\alpha + \beta(t-1)]$. (The regression can also include other variables that may affect output growth.) The term $\ln y_{t-1} - [\alpha + \beta(t-1)]$ is the difference between log output and the trend in period $t-1$. Thus if output tends to revert toward the trend, b is negative; if it does not, b is zero.

We can rewrite (4.54) as

$$\Delta \ln y_t = \alpha' + \beta't + b\ln y_{t-1} + \varepsilon_t, \tag{4.55}$$

where $\alpha' \equiv a - b\alpha + b\beta$ and $\beta' \equiv -b\beta$. Thus to test for trend reversion versus permanent shocks, we need only estimate (4.55) and test whether $b = 0$. Note that with this formulation, the null hypothesis is that output does not revert toward a trend. Formally, the null hypothesis is that output is *non-stationary* or has a *unit root*; the alternative is that it is *trend-stationary*.[25]

---

[25] The term *trend-stationary* means that the difference between actual output and a deterministic trend is not explosive. The term *unit root* arises from the lag operator methodology (see n. 16 above and Section 6.6). If output has a permanent component, it must be

There is, however, an important econometric complication in carrying out this test: under the null hypothesis, ordinary least squares (OLS) estimates of b are biased toward negative values. To see why, consider the case of $\beta = 0$; thus (4.55) becomes

$$\Delta \ln y_t = \alpha' + b \ln y_{t-1} + \varepsilon_t. \tag{4.56}$$

Assume for simplicity that the ε's are independent, identically distributed, mean-zero disturbances. The $\ln y_{t-1}$'s are combinations of the ε's. Specifically, under the null hypothesis of $b = 0$, $\ln y_{t-1}$ is $\ln y_0 + (t - 1)\alpha' + \varepsilon_1 + \varepsilon_2 + \cdots + \varepsilon_{t-1}$. Since the ε's are not correlated with one another, ε_t is uncorrelated with $\ln y_{t-1}$. It might therefore appear that OLS is unbiased. But the requirement for OLS to be unbiased is not just that the disturbance term is uncorrelated with the contemporaneous value of the right-hand-side variable, but that it is uncorrelated with the right-hand-side variable at all leads and lags. The fact that the past ε's enter positively into $\ln y_{t-1}$ means that $\ln y_{t-1}$ is positively correlated with past values of the error term. One can show that this causes the estimates of b from OLS to be biased toward negative values.[26] That is, even when the null hypothesis that output has no tendency to revert toward a trend is true, OLS tends to suggest that output is trend-reverting.

This econometric complication is an example of a more general difficulty: the behavior of statistical estimators when variables are highly persistent is often complex and unintuitive. Care needs to be taken in such situations, and conventional econometric tests often cannot be used.

Because of the negative bias in estimates of b under the null hypothesis, one cannot use conventional t-tests of the significance of the OLS estimates of b from (4.55) or (4.56) to test whether output is trend-stationary. Nelson and Plosser therefore employ a *Dickey–Fuller unit-root test* (Dickey and Fuller, 1979). Dickey and Fuller use a Monte Carlo experiment to determine the distribution of the t-statistic on b from OLS estimates of equations like (4.55) and (4.56) when the true value of b is 0. That is, they use a random number generator to choose ε's; they then generate a time series for $\ln y$ using (4.55) or (4.56) with b set to 0; and then they estimate (4.55) or (4.56) by OLS and find the t-statistic on b. They repeat this procedure many times. The resulting distribution of the t-statistic, instead of being symmetric around 0, is considerably skewed toward negative values. For example, Nelson and Plosser report that for the case of 100 observations with true parameter values of $\alpha' = 1$ and $b = 0$, the average value of the t-statistic

---

differenced to produce a stationary series. In lag-operator notation, $\ln y_{t-1}$ is written as $L \ln y_t$, and thus $\Delta \ln y_t$ is written as $(1 - L) \ln y_t$. The polynomial $1 - L$ is equal to 0 for $L = 1$; that is, it has a "unit root." For comparison, consider, for example, the stationary process $\ln y_t = \rho \ln y_{t-1} + \varepsilon_t$, $|\rho| < 1$. In lag operator notation, this is $(1 - \rho L) \ln y_t = \varepsilon_t$. The polynomial $1 - \rho L$ is equal to 0 for $L = 1/\rho$, which is greater than 1 in absolute value. More generally, stationary processes have roots *outside the unit circle*.

[26] For a simple case, see Problem 4.16.

on b is -2.22. The t-statistic is greater in absolute value than the standard 5 percent critical value of -1.96 65 percent of the time, and it is greater than -3.45 5 percent of the time. Thus an investigator who is unaware of the econometric complications and therefore uses standard critical values is more likely than not to reject the hypothesis of nonstationarity at the 5 percent level even if it is true. In a Dickey–Fuller test, however, one compares the t-statistic on b not with the standard t-distribution, but with the distribution produced by the Monte Carlo experiment. Thus, for example, a t-statistic greater than -3.45 in absolute value is needed to reject the null hypothesis of $b = 0$ at the 5 percent level.

With this lengthy econometric preface, we can now describe Nelson and Plosser's results. They estimate equations slightly more complex than (4.55) for U.S. real GNP, real GNP per capita, industrial production, and employment. They find that the OLS estimates of b are between -0.1 and -0.2, with t-statistics ranging from -2.5 to -3.0. These are comfortably less than the correct 5 percent critical value of -3.45. Based on this and other evidence, Nelson and Plosser conclude that one cannot reject the null hypothesis that fluctuations have a permanent component.

Campbell and Mankiw's Test

An obvious limitation of simply testing for the existence of a permanent component of fluctuations is that it cannot tell us anything about how big such a permanent component might be. The literature since Nelson and Plosser has therefore focused on determining the extent of persistence in output movements. Campbell and Mankiw (1987) propose a natural measure of persistence. They consider several specific processes for the change in log output. To take one example, they consider the third-order autoregressive (or AR-3) case:

$$\Delta \ln y_t = a + b_1 \Delta \ln y_{t-1} + b_2 \Delta \ln y_{t-2} + b_3 \Delta \ln y_{t-3} + \varepsilon_t. \tag{4.57}$$

Campbell and Mankiw estimate (4.57) and compute the implied response of the level of $\ln y$ to a 1-unit shock to ε.[27] Their measure of persistence is the value that this forecast converges to. Intuitively, this measure is the answer to the question: If output is 1 percent higher this period than expected, by what percent should I change my forecast of output in the distant future? If output is trend-stationary, the answer to this question is 0. If output is a random walk (so $\Delta \ln y_t$ is simply $a + \varepsilon_t$), the answer is 1 percent.

Campbell and Mankiw's results are surprising: this measure of persistence generally *exceeds* 1. That is, shocks to output are generally followed

---

[27] If ε is perturbed by 1 in a single period, (4.57) implies that $\Delta \ln y$ is changed by 1 in that period, b_1 in the next period, $b_1^2 + b_2$ in the following period, and so on. Thus $\ln y$ is changed by 1 in the period of the shock, $1 + b_1$ in the next period, $1 + b_1 + b_1^2 + b_2$ in the following period, and so on.

by further output movements in the same direction. For the AR-3 case considered in (4.57), the estimated persistence measure is 1.57. Campbell and Mankiw consider various other processes for the change in log output; for most of them (though not all), the persistence measure takes on similar values.

Discussion

There are two major problems with the general idea of investigating the persistence of fluctuations, one statistical and one theoretical. The statistical problem is that it is difficult to learn about long-term characteristics of output movements from data covering limited time spans. The existence of a permanent component to fluctuations and the asymptotic response of output to an innovation concern characteristics of the data at infinite horizons. As a result, no finite amount of data can shed *any* light on these issues. Suppose, for example, output movements are highly persistent in some sample. Although this is consistent with the presence of a permanent component to fluctuations, it is equally consistent with the view that output reverts extremely slowly to a deterministic trend. Alternatively, suppose we observe that output returns rapidly to some trend over a sample. Such a finding is completely consistent not only with trend stationarity, but also with the view that a small portion of output movements is not just permanent, but explosive—so that the correct reaction to an output innovation is to drastically revise one's forecast of output in the distant future.[28]

Thus at the very least, the appropriate questions are whether output fluctuations have a large, highly persistent component, and how output forecasts at moderately long horizons should be affected by output innovations, and not questions about characteristics of the data at infinite horizons. Clearly, similar modifications are needed in any other situation where researchers claim to be providing evidence about the properties of series at infinite horizons.

Even if we shift the focus from infinite to moderately long horizons, the data are unlikely to be highly informative. Consider, for example, Campbell and Mankiw's procedure for the AR-3 case described above. Campbell and Mankiw are using the relationship between current output growth and its three most recent lagged values to make inferences about output's long-run behavior. This is risky. Suppose, for example, that output growth is actually AR-20 instead of AR-3, and that the coefficients on the 17 additional lagged values of $\Delta \ln y$ are all small, but all negative. In a sample of plausible size, it is difficult to distinguish this case from the AR-3 case. But the long-run effects of an output shock may be much smaller.

This difficulty arises from the brevity of the sample, not from the specifics of Campbell and Mankiw's procedure. The basic problem is that sam-

---

[28] See Blough (1992) and Campbell and Perron (1991).

ples of plausible length contain few independent, long subsamples. As a result, no procedure is likely to provide decisive evidence about the long-term effects of shocks. Various approaches to studying persistence have been employed. The point estimates generally suggest considerable persistence (though probably somewhat less than Campbell and Mankiw found). At horizons of more than about 5 years, however, the estimates are not very precise. Thus the data are also consistent with the view that the effects of output shocks die out gradually at moderate horizons.[29]

The theoretical difficulty with this literature is that there is only a weak case that the persistence of output movements, even if it could be measured precisely, provides much information about the driving forces of economic fluctuations. Since technology may have an important trend-reverting component, and since real-business-cycle models allow for shocks coming from sources other than technology, these models are consistent with low as well as high persistence. And Keynesian models do not require that persistence be low. To begin with, although they attribute the bulk of short-run fluctuations to aggregate demand disturbances, they do not assume that the processes that drive long-run growth follow a deterministic trend; thus they allow at least one part of output movements to be highly persistent. More importantly, the part of fluctuations that is due to aggregate demand movements may also be quite persistent. A shift by the Federal Reserve to a policy of extended gradual disinflation, for example, may reduce output over a long period if nominal prices and wages adjust only gradually. And if technological progress results in part from learning-by-doing (see Section 3.4), output changes caused by aggregate demand movements affect technology.

Thus in the end, the main contribution of the literature on persistence is to sound some warnings about time-series econometrics: mechanically removing trends or otherwise ignoring the potential complications caused by persistent movements can cause statistical procedures to yield highly misleading results.

4.9   Additional Empirical Applications

Calibrating a Real-Business-Cycle Model

How should we judge how well a real-business-cycle model fits the data? The standard approach is *calibration* (Kydland and Prescott, 1982). The basic idea of calibration is to choose parameter values on the basis of microeconomic evidence and then to compare the model's predictions concerning the variances and covariances of various series with those in the data.

---

[29] See, for example, Cochrane (1988, 1994); Christiano and Eichenbaum (1990); Perron (1989); Watson (1986); Beaudry and Koop (1993); and Rudebusch (1993). Campbell and Mankiw (1989b); Cogley (1990); and Fatás (2000) present evidence for countries other than the United States.

Calibration has two potential advantages over estimating models econometrically. First, because parameter values are selected on the basis of microeconomic evidence, a large body of information beyond that usually employed can be brought to bear, and the models can therefore be held to a higher standard. Second, the economic importance of a statistical rejection, or lack of rejection, of a model is often hard to interpret. A model that fits the data well along every dimension except one unimportant one may be overwhelmingly rejected statistically. Or a model may fail to be rejected simply because the data are consistent with a wide range of possibilities.[30]

To see how calibration works in practice, consider the baseline real-business-cycle model of Prescott (1986) and Hansen (1985). This model differs from the model we have been considering in two ways. First, government is absent. Second, the trend component of technology is not assumed to follow a simple linear path; instead, a smooth but nonlinear trend is removed from the data before the model's predictions and actual fluctuations are compared.[31]

We consider the parameter values proposed by Hansen and Wright (1992), which are similar to those suggested by Prescott and by Hansen. Based on data on factor shares, the capital-output ratio, and the investment-output ratio, Hansen and Wright set $\alpha = 0.36$, $\delta = 2.5\%$ per quarter, and $\rho = 1\%$ per quarter. Based on the average division of discretionary time between work and nonwork activities, they set b to 2. They choose the parameters of the process for technology on the basis of the empirical behavior of the Solow residual, $\ln R_t \equiv \ln Y_t - [\alpha \ln K_t + (1 - \alpha) \ln L_t]$. As described in Chapter 1, the Solow residual is a measure of all influences on output growth other than the contributions of capital and labor through their private marginal products. Under the assumptions of real-business-cycle theory, the only such other influence on output is technology, and so the Solow residual is a measure of technological change. Based on the behavior of the Solow residual, Hansen and Wright set $\rho_A = 0.95$ and the standard deviation of the quarterly ε_A's to 1.1 percent.[32]

The model's implications for some key features of fluctuations are shown in Table 4.4. The figures in the first column are from actual U.S. data; those in the second column are from the model. All of the numbers are based

---

[30] See Altug (1989) and Christiano and Eichenbaum (1992) for examples of traditional econometric estimation of real-business-cycle models.

[31] The detrending procedure that is used is known as the *Hodrick–Prescott filter* (Hodrick and Prescott, 1997). As the discussion of permanent shocks and detrending in the previous section suggests, this procedure may not be innocuous (Cogley and Nason, 1995a).

[32] In addition, Prescott argues that, under the assumption that technology multiplies an expression of form $F(K, L)$, the absence of a strong trend in capital's share suggests that $F(\bullet)$ is approximately Cobb–Douglas. Similarly, he argues on the basis of the lack of a trend in leisure per person and of studies of substitution between consumption in different periods that (4.7) provides a good approximation to the instantaneous utility function. Thus the choices of functional forms are not arbitrary.

TABLE 4.4   A calibrated real-business-cycle model
versus actual data

	U.S. data	Baseline real-business-cycle model
σ_Y	1.92	1.30
σ_C/σ_Y	0.45	0.31
σ_I/σ_Y	2.78	3.15
σ_L/σ_Y	0.96	0.49
$\text{Corr}(L, Y/L)$	−0.14	0.93

Source: Hansen and Wright (1992).

on the deviation-from-trend components of the variables, with the trends found using the nonlinear procedure employed by Prescott and Hansen.

The first line of the table reports the standard deviation of output. The model produces output fluctuations that are only moderately smaller than those observed in practice. This finding is the basis for Prescott's (1986) famous conclusion that aggregate fluctuations are not just consistent with a competitive, neoclassical model, but are in fact predicted by such a model. The second and third lines of the table show that both in the United States and in the model, consumption is considerably less volatile than output, and investment is considerably more volatile.

The final two lines of the table show that the baseline model is less successful in its predictions about the contributions of variations in labor input and in output per unit of labor input to aggregate fluctuations. In the U.S. economy, labor input is nearly as volatile as output; in the model it is much less so. And in the United States, labor input and productivity are essentially uncorrelated; in the model they move together closely.

Thus a simple calibration exercise can be used to identify a model's major successes and failures. In doing so, it suggests ways in which the model might be modified to improve its fit with the data. For example, additional sources of shocks would be likely to increase output fluctuations and to reduce the correlation between movements in labor input and in productivity. Indeed, Hansen and Wright show that, for their suggested parameter values, adding government-purchases shocks along the lines of the model of this chapter lowers the correlation of L and Y/L from 0.93 to 0.49; the change has little effect on the magnitude of output fluctuations, however.

Productivity Movements in the Great Depression

Technological shocks are one of the key ingredients of real-business-cycle models. The main piece of macroeconomic evidence for the presence of substantial technological shocks is the considerable short-term variation in the Solow residual. For example, as described above, Prescott and Hansen and Wright estimate the magnitude of technology shocks from the behavior of the Solow residual.

The alternative to the view that variations in the Solow residual largely reflect shifts in technology is that output fluctuations arising from other sources affect the measured Solow residual. For example, if firms use their capital and labor more intensively in response to a disturbance other than a technology shock that increases output, then a Solow residual calculated assuming constant utilization will rise when output increases.

If we can identify a source of output movements other than changes in technology, we can test between these two views of the source of short-run variation in the Solow residual. The real-business-cycle view predicts that the Solow residual will not move systematically in the face of output fluctuations that do not result from technology shocks. The alternative view—that the variation is caused by output movements and that technology shocks have little to do with short-run output fluctuations—predicts that the Solow residual will move just as much with aggregate output when the output movements are known not to be due to technology shocks as it does at other times.

Bernanke and Parkinson (1991) carry out a simple test along these lines. Given that output per person fell sharply in the Great Depression, and given that substantial technological regress is unlikely, the output movements in the Depression were probably not due to technology shocks. Bernanke and Parkinson therefore propose to compare how the measured Solow residual moves with output in the Depression with how it moves with output in the postwar period. If technology shocks are a central source of fluctuations in the postwar period but not in the Depression, the Solow residual and output will move together only in the postwar period.

Because of a lack of reliable data on capital, Bernanke and Parkinson do not follow precisely this procedure. Instead of looking at the relation between movements in the Solow residual and in output, they look at the relation between movements in output and in labor input. Their basic regression is

$$\Delta \ln y_{it} = a + b_i \Delta \ln L_{it} + \varepsilon_{it}, \tag{4.58}$$

where $\Delta \ln y$ is the change in log output, $\Delta \ln L$ is the change in the log of the number of person-hours, and i indexes industries and t indexes time.

If the capital stock exhibits little short-run variation (which is true in the postwar period), then the Solow residual is approximately equal to the percentage change in output minus the product of labor's share and the percentage change in person-hours (see equation [1.34]). Since the real-business-cycle view is that output movements not arising from technology shocks do not affect the Solow residual, it therefore predicts that the estimated b_i's for the Depression sample will roughly equal labor's share (which averages about 0.5 for the industries considered by Bernanke and Parkinson). For a period like the postwar sample, where the real-business-cycle view is that the fluctuations in labor input arise largely from technology shocks, the estimated b_i's should be higher. The alternative view

TABLE 4.5   Bernanke and Parkinson's results

Industry	Estimate of b 1929–1939	Estimate of b 1955–1988
Steel	1.51 (0.17)	1.66 (0.10)
Lumber	1.07 (0.05)	0.86 (0.05)
Automobiles	1.21 (0.15)	1.05 (0.06)
Petroleum	0.42 (0.07)	−0.04 (0.03)
Textiles	1.09 (0.17)	1.03 (0.13)
Leather	0.58 (0.08)	0.83 (0.03)
Rubber	1.21 (0.07)	0.98 (0.06)
Pulp	1.11 (0.10)	1.04 (0.38)
Stone, clay, and glass	1.11 (0.07)	0.94 (0.10)
Nonferrous metals	1.38 (0.03)	1.23 (0.07)

Standard errors are in parentheses.

Source: Bernanke and Parkinson (1991).

predicts that the estimated b_i's will be roughly the same in the two periods.

Bernanke and Parkinson estimate (4.58) using quarterly data for each of 10 industries for two sample periods, 1929–1939 and 1955–1988. Table 4.5 summarizes their results. In the Depression sample, the estimated b_i's exceed 1 for 8 of the 10 industries, with an average value of 1.07. The average for the postwar sample is 0.96. Eight of the ten b_i's are actually larger in the Depression than in the postwar period. Thus it appears that supporters of real-business-cycle theory must argue either that the Depression was caused by large negative technological shocks, or that for some reason the Solow residual is a poor measure of technological change in the Depression but not in other periods.

4.10   Extensions and Limitations

Extensions

This chapter focuses on a specific real-business-cycle model. Research in this area, however, has considered many variations and extensions of this basic model. Here we discuss a few of the most important.

One variation of the model that has attracted considerable attention is the *indivisible-labor* version. Changes in labor input come not just from continuous changes in hours, but also from movements into and out of employment. To investigate the implications of this fact, Rogerson (1988) and Hansen (1985) consider the extreme case where ℓ for each individual has only two possible values, 0 (which corresponds to not being employed) and some positive value, ℓ_0 (which corresponds to being employed). Rogerson and Hansen justify this assumption by arguing that there are fixed costs of working.

This change in the model greatly increases the responsiveness of labor input to shocks; this in turn increases both the size of output fluctuations and the share of changes in labor input in those fluctuations. From the results of the calibration exercise described in the previous section, we know that these changes improve the fit of the model.

To see why assuming all-or-nothing employment increases fluctuations in labor input, assume that once the number of workers employed is determined, individuals are divided between employment and unemployment randomly. The number of workers employed in period t, denoted by E_t, must satisfy $E_t \ell_0 = L_t$; thus the probability that any given individual is employed in period t is $(L_t / \ell_0) / N_t$. Each individual's expected utility from leisure in period t is therefore

$$\frac{L_t / \ell_0}{N_t} b \ln(1 - \ell_0) + \frac{N_t - (L_t / \ell_0)}{N_t} b \ln 1. \tag{4.59}$$

This expression is linear in L_t: individuals are not averse to employment fluctuations. In contrast, when all individuals work the same amount, utility from leisure in period t is $b \ln[1 - (L_t / N_t)]$. This expression has a negative second derivative with respect to L_t: there is increasing marginal disutility of working. As a result, L_t varies less in response to a given amount of variation in wages in the conventional version of the model than in the indivisible-labor version. Hansen and Wright (1992) report that introducing indivisible labor into the Prescott model discussed in the previous section raises the standard deviation of output from 1.30 to 1.73 percent (versus 1.92 percent in the data), and the ratio of the standard deviation of total hours to the standard deviation of output from 0.49 to 0.76 (versus 0.96 in the data).[33]

A second major extension is to include distortionary taxes (see Greenwood and Huffman, 1991; Baxter and King, 1993; Campbell, 1994; Braun, 1994; and McGrattan, 1994). A particularly appealing case is proportional output taxation, so $T_t = \tau_t Y_t$, where τ_t is the tax rate in period t. Output taxation corresponds to equal tax rates on capital and labor, which is a reasonable first approximation for many countries. With output taxation,

---

[33] Because the instantaneous utility function, (4.7), is separable between consumption and leisure, expected utility is maximized when employed and unemployed workers have the same consumption. Thus the indivisible-labor model implies that the unemployed are better off than the employed. See Problem 9.6 and Rogerson and Wright (1988).

a change in $1 - \tau$ is, from the point of view of private agents, just like a change in technology, $A^{1-\alpha}$: it changes the amount of output they obtain from a given amount of capital and labor. Thus for a given process for $1 - \tau$, after-tax output behaves just as total output does in a model without taxation in which $A^{1-\alpha}$ follows that same process. This makes the analysis of distortionary taxation straightforward (Campbell, 1994).

Since tax revenues are used to finance government purchases, it is natural to analyze the effects of distortionary taxation and government purchases together. Doing this can change our earlier analysis of the effects of government purchases significantly. Baxter and King (1993) show, for example, that in response to a temporary increase in government purchases financed by a temporary increase in distortionary taxation, the tax-induced incentives for intertemporal substitution typically outweigh the interest-rate effects, so that aggregate output falls rather than rises.

Another important extension of real models of fluctuations is the inclusion of multiple sectors and sector-specific shocks. Long and Plosser (1983) develop a multisector model similar to the model of Section 4.5 and investigate its implications for the transmission of shocks among sectors. Lilien (1982), building on the theoretical work of Lucas and Prescott (1974), proposes a distinct mechanism through which sectoral technology or relative-demand shocks can cause employment fluctuations. The basic idea is that if the reallocation of labor across sectors is time-consuming, employment falls more rapidly in the sectors suffering negative shocks than it rises in the sectors facing favorable shocks. As a result, sector-specific shocks cause temporary increases in unemployment. Lilien found that a simple measure of the size of sector-specific disturbances appeared to account for a large fraction of the variation in aggregate employment. Subsequent research, however, has shown that Lilien's original measure is flawed and that his results are almost surely too strong. This work has not reached any firm conclusions concerning the contribution of sectoral shocks to fluctuations or to average unemployment, however.[34]

These are only a few of a large number of extensions of real-business-cycle models. At this point, these models are an active and rapidly evolving subject of research.[35]

---

[34] See Abraham and Katz (1986); Murphy and Topel (1987a); Lougani, Rush, and Tave (1990); Davis and Haltiwanger (1990, 1999); and Brainard and Cutler (1993).

[35] Some of the other factors that have been incorporated into the models include lags in the investment process, or *time-to-build* (Kydland and Prescott, 1992); non-time-separable utility (so that instantaneous utility at t does not depend just on c_t and ℓ_t) (Kydland and Prescott, 1982); home production (Benhabib, Rogerson, and Wright, 1991, and Greenwood and Hercowitz, 1991); roles for government-provided goods and capital in utility and production (for example, Christiano and Eichenbaum, 1992, and Baxter and King, 1993); multiple countries (for example, Baxter and Crucini, 1993); embodied technological change (Greenwood, Hercowitz, and Huffman, 1988, and Hornstein and Krusell, 1996); and variable capital utilization and labor hoarding (Greenwood, Hercowitz, and Huffman, 1988; Burnside, Eichenbaum, and Rebelo, 1993; Burnside and Eichenbaum, 1996).

Objections

Four objections to the basic real-business-cycle model have received particular attention.[36] The first concerns the technology shocks. The model posits technology shocks with a standard deviation of about 1 percent each quarter. It seems likely that such large technological innovations would often be readily apparent. Yet it is usually difficult to identify specific innovations associated with the large quarter-to-quarter swings in the Solow residual.

More importantly, there is significant evidence that short-run variations in the Solow residual reflect more than changes in the pace of technological innovation. As described above, Bernanke and Parkinson find that the Solow residual moves just as much with output in the Great Depression as it does in the postwar period, even though it seems unlikely that the Depression was caused by technological regress. This is just one example of a broader pattern. Mankiw (1989) shows that the Solow residual behaves similarly in the World War II boom—which was also probably not due to technology shocks—as it does during other periods. Hall (1988a) demonstrates that movements in the Solow residual are correlated with the political party of the President, changes in military purchases, and oil price movements; yet none of these variables seem likely to affect technology significantly in the short run.[37]

These findings suggest that variations in the Solow residual may be a poor measure of technology shocks. There are several reasons that a rise in output stemming from a source other than a positive technology shock can cause the measured Solow residual to rise. The leading possibilities are increasing returns, increases in the intensity of capital and labor utilization, and the reallocation of inputs toward more productive firms. The evidence suggests that the variation in utilization is important and provides less support for increasing returns. Less work has been done on reallocation.[38]

Technology shocks are central to the basic real-business-cycle model. Thus if true technology shocks are considerably smaller than the variation in the Solow residual suggests, the model's ability to account for fluctuations is much smaller than the calibration exercise of the previous section implies.

The second criticism of the model concerns not its shocks but one of its central propagation mechanisms, intertemporal substitution in labor supply. Variations in the incentives to work in different periods drive employment fluctuations in the model. Thus a significant willingness to substitute labor supply between periods is needed for important employment fluctua-

---

[36] Most of these objections are raised by Summers (1986a) and Mankiw (1989).

[37] As Hall explains, oil price movements should not affect productivity once oil's role in production is accounted for.

[38] Some recent papers in this area are Basu (1995, 1996); Burnside, Eichenbaum, and Rebelo (1995); Caballero and Lyons (1992) and the critique by Basu and Fernald (1995); Basu and Fernald (1997); and Bils and Klenow (1998).

tions. Microeconomic studies, however, have had little success in detecting significant intertemporal elasticities of substitution in labor supply. The results of Ball (1990) are typical (see also Altonji, 1986, and Card, 1991). Ball divides the workers in a panel data set into those who say that their labor-supply decisions are constrained by the availability of jobs or hours and those who say they are unconstrained. He then investigates the predictions of a model where fluctuations in work are driven by intertemporal optimization for each of the two groups. The results are consistent with what the workers report: the model is rejected for the ones who say they are constrained, and not rejected for the ones who say they are unconstrained. More tellingly, for the workers who say they are unconstrained, the estimated labor-supply elasticities in response to transitory wage changes are small. Thus Ball's results suggest that fluctuations in overall labor supply are driven primarily by forces other than intertemporal substitution.

The third criticism concerns the basic real-business-cycle model's omission of monetary disturbances. A central feature of the model is that fluctuations are due to real rather than monetary shocks. Yet, as described in Section 5.5, there is considerable evidence that monetary shocks have important real effects. If this is correct, it means more than just that baseline real-business-cycle models omit one source of output movements. As described in the next two chapters, the leading candidate explanations of real effects of monetary changes rest on incomplete adjustment of nominal prices or wages. But, as we will see there, incomplete nominal adjustment implies a new channel through which other disturbances, such as changes in government purchases, have real effects. We will also see that incomplete nominal adjustment is most likely to arise when labor, credit, and goods markets depart significantly from the competitive assumptions of pure real-business-cycle theory. Thus if there is substantial monetary nonneutrality, many of the central features of the basic real-business-cycle model might need to be abandoned or greatly modified.

Finally, Cogley and Nason (1995b) and Rotemberg and Woodford (1996) show that the dynamics of the basic real-business-cycle model do not look at all like what one would think of as a business cycle. Cogley and Nason's point is that the model has no significant propagation mechanisms: the dynamics of output follow the dynamics of the shocks quite closely. That is, the model produces realistic output dynamics only to the extent that it assumes them in the driving processes. Rotemberg and Woodford's point is that there are important predictable movements in output, consumption, and hours in actual economies, but not in the baseline real-business-cycle model. In the data, for example, times when hours are unusually low or the ratio of consumption to income is unusually high are typically followed by above-normal output growth. Rotemberg and Woodford show that predictable output movements in the basic real-business-cycle model are much smaller than what we observe in the data, and have very different characteristics.

Real-Business-Cycle-Style Models

Because of these and other difficulties, the proposition that macroeconomic fluctuations are well described by a model where aggregate technology shocks and other real disturbances impinge on a Walrasian economy now has relatively little support among macroeconomists.[39] Nonetheless, real-business-cycle theory has led to an active research program. The program is no longer characterized by strong views about shocks and propagation mechanisms. Papers in the real-business-cycle tradition have considered a wide range of non-Walrasian ingredients, including rigid nominal prices or wages and monetary disturbances (for example, Cho and Cooley, 1995; King, 1991; Cho, Cooley, and Phaneuf, 1997); externalities from capital (for example, Christiano and Harrison, 1999); efficiency wages (for example, Danthine and Donaldson, 1990); job search (for example, Merz, 1995, and Andolfatto, 1996); and uninsurable idiosyncratic risk (for example, Krusell and Smith, 1998). Instead, what distinguishes the real-business-cycle research program is its approach to modeling. That is, current divisions in work on fluctuations are more about modeling strategy than about the nature of fluctuations.

Models growing out of the real-business-cycle tradition have three distinguishing characteristics. First, the "default" modeling choices are Walrasian. That is, the models often begin with a pure real-business-cycle model like those of this chapter and make changes to it. For example, if a modeler in the real-business-cycle tradition is interested in the impact of efficiency wages, he or she is likely to let consumption decisions be made by infinitely lived households that face no borrowing constraints. A modeler working in the Keynesian tradition interested in the same question is much more likely to take a shortcut that implies that consumption equals current income (such as considering a static model or excluding capital).

The use of a Walrasian baseline imposes discipline: the modeler is not free to make a long list of non-Walrasian assumptions that generate the results he or she desires. It also makes clear what non-Walrasian features are essential to the results. But it makes the models more complicated, and thereby makes the sources of the results more difficult to discern. And it may cause modelers to adopt assumptions that are not good approximations for analyzing the questions at hand.

The second key characteristic of real-business-cycle-style modeling is that it focuses on general equilibrium. Consider, for example, the issue we will discuss in Part C of Chapter 6 of whether small costs of price adjustment can cause substantial nominal rigidity. A Keynesian macroeconomist interested in this question might focus on a single firm's response to a one-time monetary disturbance. A real-business-cycle macroeconomist is much

---

[39] The fact that King and Rebelo (1999) titled their recent defense of real-business-cycle theory "Resuscitating Real Business Cycles" gives a sense of current opinion.

more likely to build a dynamic model where the money supply follows a stochastic process and examine the resulting general equilibrium. Because modern models in the real-business-cycle tradition focus on general equilibrium and fully specify the behavior of the driving variables, they are often referred to as *dynamic stochastic general equilibrium* (or *DSGE*) models.

The focus on general equilibrium guards against the possibility that the effect being considered has implausible implications along some dimension the modeler would not otherwise consider. But again this comes at the cost of making the analysis more complicated. As a result, the analysis must often take a simpler approach to modeling the central issue of interest. For example, as described in Section 4.2, real-business-cycle-style models of price stickiness often make simpler and stronger assumptions about the stickiness than Keynesian models do. In addition, the greater complexity again makes it harder to see the intuition for the results.

The third central characteristic of the real-business-cycle research program is that models are evaluated by calibration. That is, as described in Section 4.9, the models are judged to a large extent by their success in matching major variances and covariances in the data. It would be a mistake to think that the leading alternative is formal estimation and testing. Rather, the central difference here between real-business-cycle-style and Keynesian-style macroeconomics is again that between a broad and a narrow focus. Modelers in the Keynesian tradition are likely to assess their models by considering the microeconomic evidence about the models' central ingredients and by the models' consistency with a handful of "stylized facts" that the modelers view as crucial.

Like the other key features of real-business-cycle-style models, calibration imposes discipline and can uncover unexpected implications. But real-business-cycle analysis has moved away from the original idea of using microeconomic evidence to tie down essentially all the relevant parameters and functional forms: given the models' wide variety of forms, they have some flexibility in matching the data. As a result, we do not know how informative it is when they match important moments of the data relatively well. Nor, because the models are generally not tested against alternatives, do we know whether there are other, perhaps completely different, models that can match the moments just as well.

Further, given the state of economic knowledge, it is not clear that matching the major moments of the data should be viewed as a desirable feature of a model.[40] Even the most complicated models of fluctuations are grossly simplified descriptions of reality. It would be remarkable if none of the simplifications had quantitatively important effects on the models' implications. But given this, it is hard to see how the fact that a model does or does not match aggregate data is informative about its overall usefulness.

These simple pictures of real-business-cycle-style and Keynesian modeling are two ends of a continuum rather than the only approaches to

---

[40] The argument that follows is due to Matthew Shapiro.

analyzing short-run fluctuations. Different models employ Walrasian base-line assumptions, a complete general-equilibrium specification, and calibration to varying degrees.

It is tempting to say that both the Keynesian and real-business-cycle approaches are valuable, and that macroeconomists should therefore pursue both. There is clearly much truth in this statement. For example, the proposition that both partial-equilibrium and general-equilibrium models are valuable is unassailable. But there are tradeoffs: simultaneously pursuing general-equilibrium and partial-equilibrium analysis, calibration and other means of model evaluation, and fully specified dynamic models and simple static models means that less attention can be paid to any one avenue. Thus saying that both approaches have merit avoids the harder question of when each approach is more valuable and what mix is appropriate for analyzing a particular issue. Unfortunately, we have little systematic evidence on this question. As a result, macroeconomists have little choice but to make tentative judgments, based on the currently available models and evidence, about what types of inquiry are most promising. And they must remain open to the possibility that those judgments will need to be revised.

Problems

4.1. Redo the calculations reported in Table 4.1, 4.2, or 4.3 for any country other than the United States.

4.2. Redo the calculations reported in Table 4.3 for the following:[41]

(a) Employees' compensation as a share of national income.

(b) The labor force participation rate.

(c) The federal government budget deficit as a share of GDP.

(d) The Standard and Poor's 500 composite stock price index.

(e) The difference in yields between Moody's Baa and Aaa bonds.

(f) The difference in yields between 10-year and 3-month U.S. Treasury securities.

(g) The weighted average exchange rate of the U.S. dollar against major currencies.

4.3. Let A_0 denote the value of A in period 0, and let the behavior of $\ln A$ be given by equations (4.8)–(4.9).

(a) Express $\ln A_1$, $\ln A_2$, and $\ln A_3$ in terms of $\ln A_0$, ε_{A1}, ε_{A2}, ε_{A3}, $\overline{A}$, and g.

(b) In light of the fact that the expectations of the ε_A's are zero, what are the expectations of $\ln A_1$, $\ln A_2$, and $\ln A_3$ given $\ln A_0$, $\overline{A}$, and g?

---

[41] Annual values for all these series are published in the *Economic Report of the President*. Quarterly values are available from the Citibase data bank.

4.4. Suppose the period-t utility function, u_t, is $u_t = \ln c_t + b(1 - \ell_t)^{1-\gamma}/(1 - \gamma)$, $b > 0$, $\gamma > 0$, rather than (4.7).

(a) Consider the one-period problem analogous to that investigated in (4.12)–(4.15). How, if at all, does labor supply depend on the wage?

(b) Consider the two-period problem analogous to that investigated in (4.16)–(4.21). How does the relative demand for leisure in the two periods depend on the relative wage? How does it depend on the interest rate? Explain intuitively why γ affects the responsiveness of labor supply to wages and the interest rate.

4.5. Consider the problem investigated in (4.16)–(4.21).

(a) Show that an increase in both w_1 and w_2 that leaves w_1/w_2 unchanged does not affect ℓ_1 or ℓ_2.

(b) Now assume that the household has initial wealth of amount $Z > 0$.

  (i) Does (4.23) continue to hold? Why or why not?

  (ii) Does the result in (a) continue to hold? Why or why not?

4.6. Suppose an individual lives for two periods and has utility $\ln C_1 + \ln C_2$.

(a) Suppose the individual has labor income of Y_1 in the first period of life and 0 in the second period. Second-period consumption is thus $(1 + r)(Y_1 - C_1)$; r, the rate of return, is potentially random.

  (i) Find the first-order condition for the individual's choice of C_1.

  (ii) Suppose r changes from being certain to being uncertain, without any change in $E[r]$. How, if at all, does C_1 respond to this change?

(b) Suppose the individual has labor income of 0 in the first period and Y_2 in the second. Second-period consumption is thus $Y_2 - (1 + r)C_1.Y_2$ is certain; again, r may be random.

  (i) Find the first-order condition for the individual's choice of C_1.

  (ii) Suppose r changes from being certain to being uncertain, without any change in $E[r]$. How, if at all, does C_1 respond to this change?

4.7. (a) Use an argument analogous to that used to derive equation (4.23) to show that household optimization requires $b/(1 - \ell_t) = e^{-\rho}E_t[w_t(1 + r_{t+1})b/[w_{t+1}(1 - \ell_{t+1})]]$.

(b) Show that this condition is implied by (4.23) and (4.26). (Note that [4.26] must hold in every period.)

4.8. **A simplified real-business-cycle model with additive technology shocks.** (This follows Blanchard and Fischer, 1989, pp. 329–331.) Consider an economy consisting of a constant population of infinitely lived individuals. The representative individual maximizes the expected value of $\sum_{t=0}^{\infty} u(C_t)/(1 + \rho)^t$, $\rho > 0$. The instantaneous utility function, $u(C_t)$, is $u(C_t) = C_t - \theta C_t^2$, $\theta > 0$. Assume that C is always in the range where $u'(C)$ is positive.

Output is linear in capital, plus an additive disturbance: $Y_t = AK_t + e_t$. There is no depreciation; thus $K_{t+1} = K_t + Y_t - C_t$, and the interest rate is A. Assume $A = \rho$. Finally, the disturbance follows a first-order autoregressive process: $e_t = \phi e_{t-1} + \varepsilon_t$, where $-1 < \phi < 1$ and where the ε_t's are mean-zero, i.i.d. shocks.

(a) Find the first-order condition (Euler equation) relating C_t and expectations of C_{t+1}.

(b) Guess that consumption takes the form $C_t = \alpha + \beta K_t + \gamma e_t$. Given this guess, what is K_{t+1} as a function of K_t and e_t?

(c) What values must the parameters α, β, and γ have for the first-order condition in part (a) to be satisfied for all values of K_t and e_t?

(d) What are the effects of a one-time shock to ε on the paths of Y, K, and C?

4.9. **A simplified real-business-cycle model with taste shocks.** (This follows Blanchard and Fischer, 1989, p. 361.) Consider the setup in Problem 4.8. Assume, however, that the technological disturbances (the e's) are absent and that the instantaneous utility function is $u(C_t) = C_t - \theta(C_t + v_t)^2$. The v's are mean-zero, i.i.d. shocks.

(a) Find the first-order condition (Euler equation) relating C_t and expectations of C_{t+1}.

(b) Guess that consumption takes the form $C_t = \alpha + \beta K_t + \gamma v_t$. Given this guess, what is K_{t+1} as a function of K_t and v_t?

(c) What values must the parameters α, β, and γ have for the first-order condition in (a) to be satisfied for all values of K_t and v_t?

(d) What are the effects of a one-time shock to v on the paths of Y, K, and C?

4.10. **The balanced growth path of the model of Section 4.3.** Consider the model of Section 4.3 without any shocks. Let y^*, k^*, c^*, and G^* denote the values of $Y/(AL), K/(AL), C/(AL)$, and $G/(AL)$ on the balanced growth path; w^* the value of w/A; ℓ^* the value of L/N; and r^* the value of r.

(a) Use equations (4.1)–(4.4), (4.23), and (4.26) and the fact that y^*, k^*, c^*, w^*, ℓ^*, and r^* are constant on the balanced growth path to find six equations in these six variables. (Hint: The fact that c in (4.23) is consumption per person, C/N, and c^* is the balanced-growth-path value of consumption per unit of effective labor, $C/(AL)$, implies that $c = c^*\ell^*A$ on the balanced growth path.)

(b) Consider the parameter values assumed in Section 4.7. What are the implied shares of consumption and investment in output on the balanced growth path? What is the implied ratio of capital to annual output on the balanced growth path?

4.11. **Solving a real-business-cycle model by finding the social optimum.**[42] Consider the model of Section 4.5. Assume for simplicity that $n = g = \overline{A} = \overline{N} = 0$. Let $V(K_t, A_t)$, the *value function,* be the expected present value from the cur-

---

[42] This problem uses dynamic programming and the method of undetermined coefficients. These two methods are explained in Section 9.4 and Section 4.6, respectively.

rent period forward of lifetime utility of the representative individual as a function of the capital stock and technology.

(*a*) Explain intuitively why $V(\bullet)$ must satisfy

$$V(K_t, A_t) = \max_{C_t, \ell_t}\{[\ln C_t + b\ln(1 - \ell_t)] + e^{-\rho}E_t[V(K_{t+1}, A_{t+1})]\}.$$

This condition is known as the *Bellman equation*.

Given the log-linear structure of the model, let us guess that $V(\bullet)$ takes the form $V(K_t, A_t) = \beta_0 + \beta_K \ln K_t + \beta_A \ln A_t$, where the values of the β's are to be determined. Substituting this conjectured form and the facts that $K_{t+1} = Y_t - C_t$ and $E_t[\ln A_{t+1}] = \rho_A \ln A_t$ into the Bellman equation yields

$$V(K_t, A_t) = \max_{C_t, \ell_t}\{\ln C_t + b\ln(1 - \ell_t) + e^{-\rho}[\beta_0 + \beta_K \ln(Y_t - C_t) + \beta_A\rho_A \ln A_t]\}.$$

(*b*) Find the first-order condition for C_t. Show that it implies that C_t/Y_t does not depend on K_t or A_t.

(*c*) Find the first-order condition for ℓ_t. Use this condition and the result in part (*b*) to show that ℓ_t does not depend on K_t or A_t.

(*d*) Substitute the production function and the results in parts (*b*) and (*c*) for the optimal C_t and ℓ_t into the equation above for $V(\bullet)$, and show that the resulting expression has the form $V(K_t, A_t) = \beta'_0 + \beta'_K \ln K_t + \beta'_A \ln A_t$.

(*e*) What must β_K and β_A be so that $\beta'_K = \beta_K$ and $\beta'_A = \beta_A$?[43]

(*f*) What are the implied values of C/Y and ℓ? Are they the same as those found in Section 4.5 for the case of $n = g = 0$?

4.12. Suppose technology follows some process other than (4.8)–(4.9). Do $s_t = \hat{s}$ and $\ell_t = \hat{\ell}$ for all t continue to solve the model of Section 4.5? Why or why not?

4.13. Consider the model of Section 4.5. Suppose, however, that the instantaneous utility function, u_t, is given by $u_t = \ln c_t + b(1 - \ell_t)^{1-\gamma}/(1 - \gamma), b > 0, \gamma > 0$, rather than by (4.7) (see Problem 4.4).

(*a*) Find the first-order condition analogous to equation (4.26) that relates current leisure and consumption, given the wage.

(*b*) With this change in the model, is the saving rate (s) still constant?

(*c*) Is leisure per person $(1 - \ell)$ still constant?

4.14. (*a*) If the $\tilde{A}_t$'s are uniformly 0 and if $\ln Y_t$ evolves according to (4.39), what path does $\ln Y_t$ settle down to? (Hint: Note that we can rewrite (4.39) as $\ln Y_t - (n + g)t = Q + \alpha[\ln Y_{t-1} - (n + g)(t - 1)] + (1 - \alpha)\tilde{A}_t$, where $Q \equiv \alpha \ln \hat{s} + (1 - \alpha)(\bar{A} + \ln \hat{\ell} + \bar{N}) - \alpha(n + g)$.)

(*b*) Defining $\tilde{Y}_t$ as the difference between $\ln Y_t$ and the path found in (*a*), derive (4.40).

---

[43] The calculation of β_0 is tedious and is therefore omitted.

4.15. The derivation of the log-linearized equation of motion for capital. Consider the equation of motion for capital, $K_{t+1} = K_t + K_t^\alpha (A_t L_t)^{1-\alpha} - C_t - G_t - \delta K_t$.

(a) (i) Show that $\partial \ln K_{t+1} / \partial \ln K_t$ (holding A_t, L_t, C_t, and G_t fixed) is $(1 + r_{t+1})(K_t / K_{t+1})$.

  (ii) Show that this implies that $\partial \ln K_{t+1} / \partial \ln K_t$ evaluated at the balanced growth path is $(1 + r^*)/e^{n+g}$.[44]

(b) Show that

$$\tilde{K}_{t+1} \simeq \lambda_1 \tilde{K}_t + \lambda_2 (\tilde{A}_t + \tilde{L}_t) + \lambda_3 \tilde{G}_t + (1 - \lambda_1 - \lambda_2 - \lambda_3)\tilde{C}_t,$$

where $\lambda_1 = (1 + r^*)/e^{n+g}, \lambda_2 \equiv (1 - \alpha)(r^* + \delta)/(\alpha e^{n+g})$, and $\lambda_3 = -(r^* + \delta)(G/Y)^*/(\alpha e^{n+g})$; and where $(G/Y)^*$ denotes the ratio of G to Y on the balanced growth path without shocks. (Hints: Since the production function is Cobb–Douglas, $Y^* = (r^* + \delta)K^*/\alpha$. On the balanced growth path, $K_{t+1} = e^{n+g}K_t$, which implies that $C^* = Y^* - G^* - \delta K^* - (e^{n+g} - 1)K^*$.)

(c) Use the result in (b) and equations (4.43)–(4.44) to derive (4.52), where $b_{KK} = \lambda_1 + \lambda_2 a_{LK} + (1 - \lambda_1 - \lambda_2 - \lambda_3)a_{CK}, b_{KA} = \lambda_2(1 + a_{LA}) + (1 - \lambda_1 - \lambda_2 - \lambda_3)a_{CA}$, and $b_{KG} = \lambda_2 a_{LG} + \lambda_3 + (1 - \lambda_1 - \lambda_2 - \lambda_3)a_{CG}$.

4.16. A Monte Carlo experiment and the source of bias in OLS estimates of trend reversion. Suppose output growth is described simply by $\Delta \ln y_t = \varepsilon_t$, where the ε's are independent, mean-zero disturbances. Normalize the initial value of $\ln y$, denoted by $\ln y_0$, to 0. This problem asks you to consider what occurs in this situation if one estimates equation (4.56), $\Delta \ln y_t = \alpha' + b \ln y_{t-1} + \varepsilon_t$, by ordinary least squares.

(a) Suppose the sample size is 3, and suppose each ε is equal to 1 with probability $\frac{1}{2}$ and -1 with probability $\frac{1}{2}$. For each of the eight possible realizations of $(\varepsilon_1, \varepsilon_2, \varepsilon_3)$ $((1, 1, 1), (1, 1, -1)$, and so on), what is the OLS estimate of b? What is the average of the estimates? Explain intuitively why the estimates differ systematically from the true value of $b = 0$.

(b) Suppose the sample size is 200, and suppose each ε is normally distributed with a mean of 0 and a variance of 1. Using a random-number generator on a computer, generate 200 such ε's; then generate $\ln y$'s using $\Delta \ln y_t = \varepsilon_t$ and $\ln y_0 = 0$; then estimate (4.56) by OLS; finally, record the estimate of b. Repeat this process 500 times. What is the average estimate of b? What fraction of the estimated b's is negative?

---

[44] One could express r^* in terms of the discount rate ρ. Campbell (1994) argues, however, that it is easier to discuss the model's implications in terms of r^* than ρ.

Chapter 5
TRADITIONAL KEYNESIAN THEORIES OF FLUCTUATIONS

This chapter and the next develop models of fluctuations based on the assumption that there are barriers to the instantaneous adjustment of nominal prices and wages. As we will see, sluggish nominal adjustment causes changes in the aggregate demand for goods at a given level of prices to affect the amount that firms produce. As a result, it causes purely monetary disturbances (which affect only demand) to change employment and output. In addition, many real shocks, including changes in government purchases, investment demand, and technology, affect aggregate demand at a given price level; thus sluggish price adjustment creates a channel other than the intertemporal-substitution and capital-accumulation mechanisms of basic real-business-cycle models through which these shocks affect employment and output.

This chapter takes nominal stickiness as given. It has two main goals. The first is to investigate aggregate demand. We will examine the determinants of aggregate demand at a given price level and the effects of changes in the price level. The second is to consider alternative assumptions about the form of nominal rigidity. We will investigate different assumptions' implications for firms' willingness to change output in response to changes in aggregate demand and for the behavior of real wages, markups, and inflation. Chapter 6 then turns to the questions of why nominal prices and wages might not adjust immediately to disturbances.

The models of this chapter are based on traditional Keynesian models. Thus both their substance and their modeling strategy are at the other extreme from the pure real-business-cycle models of Chapter 4. The models in this chapter often directly specify relationships among aggregate variables. The relationships are often static, and the models' implications for the behavior of some variables (such as the capital stock) are sometimes omitted from the analysis. In addition, rather than specifying stochastic processes for the exogenous variables, the analysis focuses on the effects of one-time changes. And the models are so stylized that any effort to see how well they match overall features of the economy is of little value.

217

The remainder of the chapter consists of six sections. Sections 5.1 and 5.2 develop the aggregate demand side of the standard Keynesian model. These sections take as given that nominal prices and wages are not completely flexible, and that firms change their output in response to changes in demand. Section 5.1 assumes a closed economy, and Section 5.2 considers the open-economy case.

Sections 5.3 and 5.4 consider aggregate supply. Section 5.3 shows how different combinations of wage rigidity, price rigidity, and non-Walrasian features of the labor and goods markets yield different implications about the effect of shifts in aggregate demand on output, unemployment, the real wage, and the markup. Section 5.4 discusses short-run and long-run output-inflation tradeoffs.

Finally, Sections 5.5 and 5.6 discuss some empirical evidence about the real effects of monetary changes and the cyclical behavior of the real wage.

5.1 Review of the Textbook Keynesian Model of Aggregate Demand

The textbook Keynesian model is traditionally summarized by two curves in output-price or output-inflation space, an aggregate demand (*AD*) curve and an aggregate supply (*AS*) curve. The *AD* curve slopes down and the *AS* curve slopes up. These curves are shown in Figure 5.1.

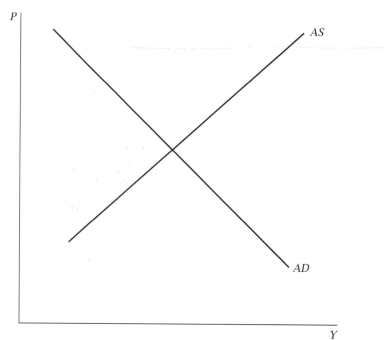

FIGURE 5.1   The *AS-AD* diagram

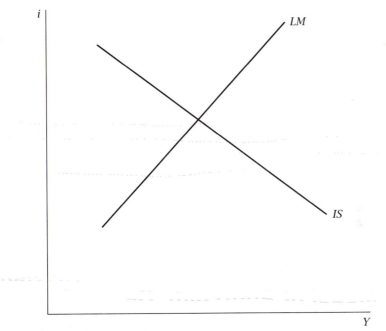

FIGURE 5.2 The *IS-LM* diagram

The fact that the aggregate supply curve is upward-sloping rather than vertical is the critical feature of the model. If the *AS* curve is vertical, changes on the demand side of the economy affect only prices. But if it is merely upward-sloping, changes in aggregate demand affect both prices and output.

The *AD* curve summarizes the demand side of the economy. It is derived from two familiar curves in output-interest rate space, the *IS* and *LM* curves. These are shown in Figure 5.2. The curves are drawn for a given price level; as we will see shortly, considering different values of the price level allows us to use the *IS* and *LM* curves to derive the *AD* curve. Although there are innumerable variations and extensions of the *IS-LM* model, here we consider a standard version.

The *IS* Curve

The *IS* curve shows the combinations of output and the interest rate such that planned and actual expenditures on output are equal.[1] Planned real expenditure depends positively on real income, negatively on the real interest rate, positively on government purchases of goods and services, and

---

[1] The *IS* curve is often described as showing equilibrium in the goods market. But since supply is ignored, this is not an accurate description.

negatively on taxes:

$$E = E(Y, i - \pi^e, G, T), \quad 0 < E_Y < 1, \ E_{i-\pi^e} < 0, \ E_G > 0, \ E_T < 0. \quad (5.1)$$

Here E is planned real expenditure, Y is real output, i is the nominal interest rate, π^e is expected inflation, G is real government purchases, and T is real taxes. E_Y, $E_{i-\pi^e}$, and so on denote the partial derivatives of $E(\bullet)$. G, T, and π^e are all taken as given.[2] The negative effect of the real interest rate on planned expenditure operates through firms' investment decisions and through consumers' purchases, particularly of durable goods. Planned expenditure is assumed to increase less than one-for-one with income; that is, $0 < E_Y < 1$.

In textbook treatments, E is often expressed in terms of its component parts, and strong assumptions are made about how the determinants of planned expenditure enter. A standard formulation is

$$E = C(Y - T) + I(i - \pi^e) + G, \quad (5.2)$$

where $C(\bullet)$ is consumption and $I(\bullet)$ is investment. The restrictions imposed in this specification may be highly unrealistic. For example, there is considerable evidence that the real interest rate affects consumption, and almost overwhelming evidence that income influences investment. To give another example, there is little basis for assuming that income and taxes have equal and opposite effects on spending. Since the general formulation in (5.1) is only slightly more difficult, we will use it in what follows.

If one treats goods that a firm produces and then holds as inventories as purchased by the firm, then all output is purchased by someone. Thus actual expenditure equals the economy's output, Y. In equilibrium, planned and actual expenditures must be equal. If planned expenditure falls short of actual expenditure, for example, firms are accumulating unwanted inventories; they will respond by cutting their production. Thus equilibrium requires

$$E = Y. \quad (5.3)$$

Substituting (5.3) into (5.1) yields

$$Y = E(Y, i - \pi^e, G, T). \quad (5.4)$$

Figure 5.3, the *Keynesian cross*, depicts equations (5.1) and (5.3) in (Y, E) space for a given level of the interest rate. Equation (5.3) is just the 45-degree line. Since planned expenditure increases less than one-for-one with Y, the set of points satisfying (5.1) is less steep than the 45-degree line. The point where the planned expenditure curve crosses the 45-degree line (Point A)

---

[2] Properly speaking, expected inflation should be determined within the model rather than taken as given, since the path of the price level will be determined within the model. Taking π^e as given here simplifies the discussion without altering the model's main implications, however.

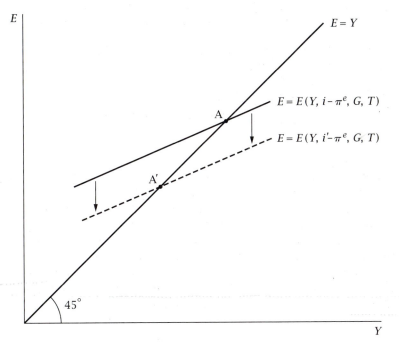

FIGURE 5.3   The Keynesian cross

shows the unique level of income where actual and planned expenditures are equal for the given interest rate.[3]

An increase in the interest rate shifts the planned expenditure line down (since $E(\bullet)$ is decreasing in $i - \pi^e$), and thus reduces the level of income at which actual and planned expenditures are equal; in terms of the diagram, an increase in the interest rate from i to i' shifts the intersection of the two lines from Point A to Point A'. Thus the IS curve slopes down.

Differentiating both sides of (5.4) with respect to i yields

$$\left.\frac{dY}{di}\right|_{IS} = E_Y \left(\left.\frac{dY}{di}\right|_{IS}\right) + E_{i-\pi^e}, \tag{5.5}$$

or

$$\left.\frac{dY}{di}\right|_{IS} = \frac{E_{i-\pi^e}}{1 - E_Y}, \tag{5.6}$$

where $\left.\frac{dY}{di}\right|_{IS}$ denotes dY/di along the IS curve. Since this is an expression for dY/di (rather than di/dY), it implies that the IS curve is flatter when either $E_{i-\pi^e}$ or E_Y is larger. Intuitively, the larger the effect of the interest

---

[3] The Keynesian cross is sometimes described as a theory of income determination. But this is correct only if the interest rate can be treated as fixed, which is often inappropriate.

rate on planned expenditure, the larger the downward shift of the planned expenditure line, and thus the larger the fall in output. Similarly, the steeper the planned expenditure line, the more output must fall in response to a given downward shift of the planned expenditure line to reach a point where planned and actual expenditures are again in balance, and thus the larger the fall in output. This last effect is the famous *multiplier:* because E depends on Y, the fall in Y needed to restore the equality of E and Y is larger than the amount that E falls at a given Y.

The *LM* Curve

The *LM* curve shows the combinations of output and the interest rate that lead to equilibrium in the money market for a given price level. It is simplest to think of money as high-powered money—currency and reserves—issued by the government. Since high-powered money pays no nominal interest, the opportunity cost of holding it is the nominal interest rate. The demand for real money balances is therefore a decreasing function of the nominal interest rate. In addition, since the volume of transactions is greater when output is higher, the demand for real balances is increasing in output. The nominal money supply is set by the government. Putting all this together, the condition for the supply and demand of real balances to be equal at a given price level is

$$\frac{M}{P} = L(i, Y), \qquad L_i < 0, \qquad L_Y > 0, \tag{5.7}$$

where M is the quantity of money and P is the price level.

Since $L(\bullet)$ is decreasing in i and increasing in Y, the set of combinations of i and Y that satisfy (5.7) is upward-sloping. Formally, differentiating both sides of (5.7) with respect to Y and rearranging yields

$$\left.\frac{di}{dY}\right|_{LM} = -\frac{L_Y}{L_i} > 0. \tag{5.8}$$

Thus increases in the income elasticity of money demand and decreases in the interest elasticity (in absolute value) make the *LM* curve steeper.[4]

Implicitly, the *IS-LM* model treats all assets other than money as perfect substitutes. The market for these other assets is then suppressed by Walras's law. Specifically, total wealth in the economy equals the total value of all assets, and the total value of any individual's asset holdings must equal his or her total wealth. Thus if the market for every asset but one clears,

---

[4] This presentation makes the standard assumption that M is exogenous. Taylor (1998) and D. Romer (2000) have recently proposed replacing this assumption with an assumption that the central bank adjusts M to make the real interest rate an increasing function of inflation, and perhaps of output as well. They argue that this alternative better describes what central banks do and leads to a model that is easier to analyze. It is too soon to know whether this approach will become the standard textbook formulation. Since this approach and the usual one have similar implications for our purposes, we maintain the usual assumption of an exogenous money supply.

the market for the remaining asset must clear as well. In the *IS-LM* model there are only two assets (money and everything else), and so only one asset-market equilibrium condition is needed. Many important extensions of the *IS-LM* model investigate the consequences of relaxing the assumption that all assets other than money are perfect substitutes.[5]

The *AD* Curve

The intersection of the *IS* and *LM* curves shows the values of i and Y such that the money market clears and actual and planned expenditures are equal for given levels of M, P, π^e, G, and T. To see how the *IS* and *LM* curves imply the existence of a downward-sloping relationship between P and Y, consider the effects of assuming a higher value of P. Since the price level does not enter the planned expenditure function, $E(\bullet)$, the *IS* curve is unaffected. The rise in the price level reduces the supply of real money balances, however. Thus a higher interest rate is needed to clear the money market for a given level of income, and so the *LM* curve shifts up. As a result, i rises and Y falls. This is shown in Figure 5.4. Thus the level of output at the

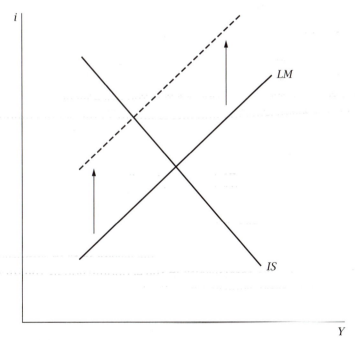

FIGURE 5.4   The effects of an increase in the price level

---

[5] Two classic references are Tobin and Brainard (1963) and Tobin (1969). A large recent literature relaxes the assumption that assets held by banks, particularly their loans, are perfect substitutes for other interest-bearing assets. See Bernanke and Blinder (1988) and Kashyap and Stein (1994).

intersection of the IS and LM curves is a decreasing function of the price level. This is what is shown by the aggregate demand curve.

To find the slope of the AD curve, differentiate (5.4) and (5.7) with respect to P. This yields two equations in two unknowns:

$$\frac{dY}{dP}\bigg|_{AD} = E_Y \frac{dY}{dP}\bigg|_{AD} + E_{i-\pi^e} \frac{di}{dP}\bigg|_{AD}, \tag{5.9}$$

$$-\frac{M}{P^2} = L_i \frac{di}{dP}\bigg|_{AD} + L_Y \frac{dY}{dP}\bigg|_{AD}. \tag{5.10}$$

These can be solved to obtain

$$\frac{dY}{dP}\bigg|_{AD} = \frac{-M/P^2}{[(1 - E_Y)L_i/E_{i-\pi^e}] + L_Y}. \tag{5.11}$$

This expression is unambiguously negative, and it shows the determinants of the slope of the aggregate demand curve.

Example: The Effects of an Increase in Government Purchases

The IS and LM curves provide a simple model of aggregate demand that can be used to analyze many issues. Suppose, for example, that government purchases rise. The increase in G raises planned expenditure for a given level of output and the interest rate. The planned expenditure line in Figure 5.3 therefore shifts up, and so the level of Y such that actual and planned expenditures are equal is higher for a given level of the interest rate. Thus the IS curve shifts to the right; this is shown in Panel (a) of Figure 5.5. The shift in the IS curve raises Y (and i) for a given price level, and thus moves the AD curve outward; this is shown in Panel (b) of the figure.[6]

The impact of this change in aggregate demand on output and the price level depends on the aggregate supply curve. If it is vertical, only the price level increases. If it is horizontal, only output increases. And if it is upward-sloping but not vertical, both output and the price level increase.

Thus, incomplete adjustment of nominal prices introduces a new channel through which shocks affect output. For some reason, which we have not yet specified, nominal prices do not adjust fully in the short run. As a result, any change in the demand for goods at a given price level affects output. In contrast, the intertemporal-substitution and wealth effects that drive employment fluctuations in real-business-cycle models would correspond to effects of government purchases on the aggregate supply curve—that is, they would affect not the quantity of output that households and firms want to buy at a given price level, but the quantity that firms want to produce at a given price level.

---

[6] The IS-LM diagram is drawn for a given value of P. Thus the amount that output increases in the IS-LM diagram is the same as the amount that the aggregate demand curve shifts to the right at the value of P assumed in the IS-LM diagram.

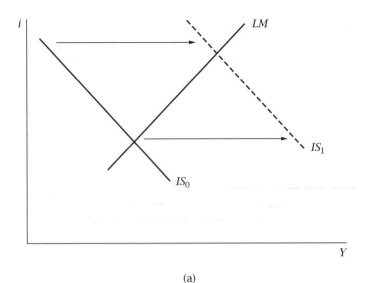

(a)

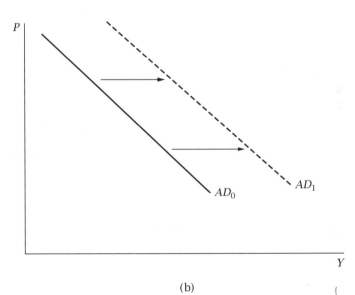

(b)

FIGURE 5.5   The effects of an increase in government purchases

5.2   The Open Economy

In most practical applications, the exchange rate and international trade are important to short-run fluctuations. This section therefore extends the *IS-LM* model to the case of an open economy.[7]

---

[7] See Obstfeld and Rogoff (1996) for the state-of-the-art treatment of open-economy macroeconomics.

The Real Exchange Rate and Planned Expenditure

It is simplest to think of the rest of the world as consisting of a single country. Let ε denote the nominal exchange rate—specifically, the price of a unit of foreign currency in terms of domestic currency. With this definition, a rise in the exchange rate means that foreign currency has become more expensive, and therefore corresponds to a weakening, or depreciation, of the domestic currency. Similarly, a fall in ε corresponds to an appreciation of the domestic currency. Let P^* denote the price level abroad (that is, the price of foreign goods in units of foreign currency). These definitions imply that the real exchange rate—the price of foreign goods in units of domestic goods—is $\varepsilon P^*/P$.

A higher real exchange rate implies that foreign goods have become more expensive relative to domestic goods. Both domestic residents and foreigners are therefore likely to increase their purchases of domestic goods relative to foreign ones. Thus planned expenditure rises. Mathematically, equation (5.4) becomes

$$Y = E\left(Y, i - \pi^e, G, T, \frac{\varepsilon P^*}{P}\right), \tag{5.12}$$

with $E(\bullet)$ increasing in $\varepsilon P^*/P$.[8] Money demand is likely to be largely unaffected by the exchange rate; thus the LM curve is the same as before.

Since any individual country is small relative to the entire rest of the world, it is reasonable to take the foreign price level as given. But it is not reasonable to take the exchange rate as given. Equations (5.7) and (5.12), together with the AS curve, are thus not a complete model.

At this point one can make different assumptions about the exchange-rate regime (floating or fixed), capital mobility (perfect or imperfect), and exchange-rate expectations (static or rational). What set of assumptions is appropriate depends on the economy being studied and the questions being asked. Here we discuss some of the most important possibilities.

The Mundell–Fleming Model

The simplest assumptions about capital movements are that there are no barriers to capital mobility and that investors are risk-neutral; we will refer to this case as *perfect capital mobility.* Barriers to foreign investment in most industrialized countries are small, and many investors appear willing to make large changes in their portfolios in response to small rate-of-return differences. As a result, perfect capital mobility is likely to be a good approximation for many purposes.

For exchange-rate expectations, the simplest assumption is that investors do not expect the exchange rate to change. This assumption can be

---

[8] The function is often assumed to take the specific form $C(Y - T) + I(i - \pi^e) + G + NX(\varepsilon P^*/P)$, where NX denotes net exports.

justified both on the grounds of ease and on the grounds that it is difficult to find evidence of predictable exchange-rate movements (Meese and Rogoff, 1983). These assumptions about capital mobility and exchange-rate expectations lead to the famous Mundell–Fleming model (Mundell, 1968; Fleming, 1962).

Perfect capital mobility implies that if there were any difference in the expected rate of return between domestic and foreign assets, investors would put all their wealth into the asset with the higher yield. Since both types of assets must be held by someone, it follows that the expected rates of return on the two assets must be equal. The expected rate of return on foreign assets in terms of domestic currency is the foreign interest rate plus any expected increase in the price of foreign currency. With static exchange-rate expectations, the expected change in the price of foreign currency is zero. Thus the requirement that the expected rates of return are equal is simply

$$i = i^*, \tag{5.13}$$

where i^* is the foreign interest rate; i^* is taken as given.

At this point it is necessary to distinguish between floating and fixed exchange rates. With a floating exchange rate, aggregate demand is described by the three equations (5.7), (5.12), and (5.13) in the three unknowns i, Y, and ε. Since i is determined trivially by the requirement that it equals i^*, the system immediately reduces to two equations in Y and ε:

$$\frac{M}{P} = L(i^*, Y), \tag{5.14}$$

$$Y = E\left(Y, i^* - \pi^e, G, T, \frac{\varepsilon P^*}{P}\right). \tag{5.15}$$

Figure 5.6 plots the sets of points satisfying (5.14) and (5.15) in output-exchange rate space. Since an increase in $\varepsilon P^*/P$ raises planned expenditure, the set of solutions to (5.15) is upward-sloping; this is shown as the IS^* curve in the figure. And since the exchange rate does not affect money demand, the set of solutions to (5.14) is vertical; this is shown as the LM^* curve.

The fact that the LM^* curve is vertical means that output for a given price level—that is, the position of the AD curve—is determined entirely in the money market. To take the same example as in the previous section, suppose that government purchases rise. This change shifts the IS^* curve to the right. As shown in Figure 5.7, however, at a given price level this leads only to appreciation of the exchange rate and has no effect on output. Thus the aggregate demand curve is unaffected.

Assuming a fixed rather than a floating exchange rate requires two changes to the model. First, the exchange rate is now pegged at some level $\overline{\varepsilon}$:

$$\varepsilon = \overline{\varepsilon}. \tag{5.16}$$

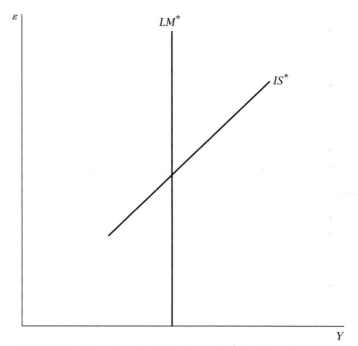

FIGURE 5.6 The Mundell–Fleming model with a floating exchange rate

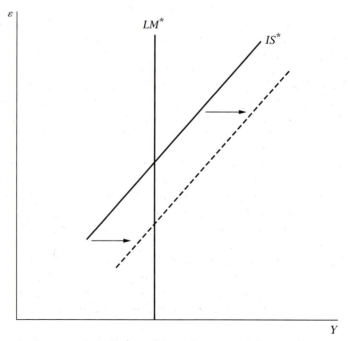

FIGURE 5.7 The effects of an increase in government purchases with a floating exchange rate

Second, the money supply becomes endogenous rather than exogenous. For the government to fix the exchange rate, it must stand ready to buy or sell domestic currency in exchange for foreign currency at the rate $\bar{\varepsilon}$. The government therefore cannot independently set M, but must let it adjust to ensure that the exchange rate remains at $\bar{\varepsilon}$.

The aggregate demand side of the model with a fixed exchange rate therefore consists of the LM equation, (5.7); the IS equation, (5.12); the interest-rate equation, (5.13); and the exchange-rate equation, (5.16). Once again, we can substitute the $i = i^*$ condition into the IS and LM equations to simplify the system. This gives us the LM^* equation, (5.14); the IS^* equation, (5.15); and the exchange-rate equation, (5.16). In addition, the LM^* equation, $M/P = L(i^*, Y)$, serves only to determine M and can therefore be neglected. Thus we are left with the IS^* equation and the exchange-rate equation. The IS^* curve is upward-sloping as before, and the exchange-rate equation is simply a horizontal line at $\bar{\varepsilon}$. Figure 5.8 depicts the solutions to these equations in output-exchange rate space.

The results for this case are the opposite of those for a floating exchange rate. Changes in planned expenditure now affect aggregate demand. A rise in government purchases, for example, shifts the IS^* curve to the right and thus raises output for a given price level. Disturbances in the money market, in contrast, have no effect on Y for a given P. A rise in the demand for money, for example, leads only to an increase in the money supply.

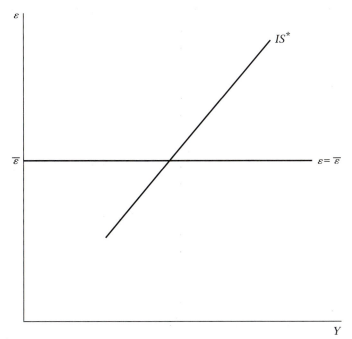

FIGURE 5.8   The Mundell–Fleming model with a fixed exchange rate

Finally, with a fixed exchange rate, the exchange rate itself is a policy instrument. For example, a devaluation—an increase in the fixed exchange rate, $\bar{\varepsilon}$—stimulates net exports and thus increases aggregate demand.

Rational Exchange-Rate Expectations and Overshooting

The Mundell–Fleming model assumes that exchange-rate expectations are static. But with a floating exchange rate, it turns out that when plausible assumptions about the dynamics of prices and output are added to the model, there are predictable changes in exchange rates. Thus static expectations are not rational: an investor with static expectations is making systematic errors in his or her exchange-rate forecasts. Such an investor can therefore earn a higher average rate of return by using information that helps to forecast exchange-rate movements. Thus it is natural to ask what happens if investors form their expectations concerning movements in the exchange rate using all the available information—that is, if they have rational expectations. Since static expectations *are* rational when the exchange rate is fixed and likely to remain so, we focus on a floating exchange rate.[9]

When expectations are not static, perfect capital mobility no longer necessarily implies that domestic and foreign interest rates are equal. Consider an investor at some time t deciding where to hold his or her wealth. If the investor puts a dollar into a domestic asset that earns a continuously compounded rate of return of i, at time $t + \Delta t$ he or she will have $e^{i\Delta t}$ dollars. Suppose the investor instead invests in foreign assets. At t, the investor's dollar can be used to purchase foreign assets that are worth $1/\varepsilon(t)$ units of foreign currency; after Δt these assets are worth $e^{i^*\Delta t}/\varepsilon(t)$ units of foreign currency; and this foreign currency can be used to buy $\varepsilon(t + \Delta t)e^{i^*\Delta t}/\varepsilon(t)$ dollars.

Under perfect capital mobility, these two ways of investing the dollar must have the same expected payoff. $\varepsilon(t)$, i, and i^* are known, but $\varepsilon(t + \Delta t)$ may be uncertain. Thus we have

$$e^{i\Delta t} = \frac{E[\varepsilon(t + \Delta t)]}{\varepsilon(t)} e^{i^*\Delta t}. \tag{5.17}$$

Equation (5.17) holds for all values of Δt. The derivatives of both sides with respect to Δt are therefore equal:

$$e^{i\Delta t}i = \frac{E[\varepsilon(t + \Delta t)]}{\varepsilon(t)} e^{i^*\Delta t}i^* + e^{i^*\Delta t}\frac{E[\dot{\varepsilon}(t + \Delta t)]}{\varepsilon(t)}. \tag{5.18}$$

---

[9] Rational expectations may differ from static expectations under a fixed exchange rate if there is some probability of a change in the exchange rate. In addition, there are cases that fall between floating and fixed exchange rates. One that has attracted considerable attention is the *target band,* such as those used in the European Monetary System in the 1980s and 1990s. See Krugman (1991), for example.

When this expression is evaluated at $\Delta t = 0$, it simplifies to

$$i = i^* + \frac{E[\dot{\varepsilon}(t)]}{\varepsilon(t)}. \tag{5.19}$$

Equation (5.19) states that under perfect capital mobility, interest-rate differences must be offset by expectations of exchange-rate movements. The domestic interest rate can exceed the foreign interest rate, for example, only if the domestic currency is expected to depreciate at a rate equal to the interest-rate differential. Equation (5.19) is known as *uncovered interest-rate parity*.[10]

The possibility of expected exchange-rate movements associated with interest-rate differences gives rise to the possibility of *exchange-rate over-shooting* (Dornbusch, 1976). "Overshooting" refers to a situation where the initial reaction of a variable to a shock is greater than its long-run response. To see how the exchange rate can overshoot, suppose that initially $i = i^*$ and the exchange rate is not expected to change, and that there is then an increase in the money supply. As stressed later in the chapter, Keynesian models generally imply that monetary disturbances have no real effects in the long run. Thus the long-run effect of the shock will be to cause both the price level and the exchange rate to rise proportionally with the increase in money.

Now consider the short-run effect of the shock. If the monetary expansion reduces the interest rate, then (5.19) implies that $E[\dot{\varepsilon}]$ must be negative: if i is less than i^*, investors will hold domestic assets only if they expect the domestic currency to appreciate. But this means that the domestic currency is worth less now than it will be in the long run; that is, it must have depreciated by so much at the time of the shock that it has overshot its expected long-run value.

This leaves the question of whether the monetary expansion reduces the domestic interest rate. A particularly simple case occurs in a variant of the model where producers cannot change output in the very short run, so that the *IS* equation, (5.12), need not be satisfied at every moment. With both prices and output fixed, the only variable that can adjust to ensure that the *LM* equation, (5.7), is satisfied is the interest rate. Thus i must fall in response to an increase in M, and so there must be exchange-rate overshooting.

The intuition for this result is straightforward. If at the time of the shock the exchange rate merely depreciates to its new long-run equilibrium level, the interest-rate differential causes all investors to want to purchase

---

[10] The parity is "uncovered" because although positive expected profits can be made by purchasing one country's assets and selling the other's when (5.19) fails, these profits are not riskless. The alternative is *covered interest-rate parity*, which refers to the relationship in (5.18) with the expected future exchange rate replaced by the price in futures markets of commitments to buy or sell foreign currency at a later date. Failure of covered interest-rate parity would imply a riskless profit opportunity.

foreign currency to obtain the higher-yielding foreign assets. This cannot be an equilibrium. Instead, the price of domestic currency is bid down until it is sufficiently below its expected long-run level that the expected appreciation just balances the lower interest rate on domestic assets.

When the *IS* equation is assumed to hold continuously, an increase in M no longer necessarily reduces i. Thus in this case there can be either undershooting or overshooting. Which occurs turns out to be a complicated function of the parameters of the model (see Dornbusch, 1976, and Problem 5.10).

Imperfect Capital Mobility

The assumptions that there are no barriers to capital movements between countries and that investors are risk-neutral are surely too strong. Trans-action costs and the desire to diversify, for example, cause investors not to put all their wealth into a single country's assets in response to a small difference in expected returns. It is therefore natural to consider the effects of imperfect capital mobility. We focus on the case of a floating exchange rate, and for simplicity we revert to the assumption of static exchange-rate expectations.

A simple way to model imperfect capital mobility is to assume that cap-ital flows depend on the difference between domestic and foreign interest rates. Specifically, define the capital flow, CF, as foreigners' purchases of domestic assets minus domestic residents' purchases of foreign assets. Our assumption is

$$CF = CF(i - i^*), \qquad CF'(\bullet) > 0. \tag{5.20}$$

The capital flow, CF, and net exports, NX, must sum to 0. If net exports are negative, for example, this means that the country's sales of goods and services to foreigners are not sufficient to pay for its imports. The country must therefore be paying for the excess by selling assets to foreigners—that is, CF must be equal and opposite to NX. Thus equilibrium requires[11]

$$CF(i - i^*) + NX\left(Y, i - \pi^e, G, T, \frac{\varepsilon P^*}{P}\right) = 0. \tag{5.21}$$

The aggregate demand side of the model now consists of the *IS* equa-tion, (5.12); the *LM* equation, (5.7); and the balance-of-payments equation, (5.21). If net exports are the only component of planned expenditure that is affected by the exchange rate, the model can be analyzed graphically. With this assumption, we can write planned expenditure as the sum of domestic

---

[11] With perfect capital mobility, CF is minus infinity if i is less than i^*, is plus infinity if i is greater than i^*, and can take on any value—since investors are indifferent about which country's assets to hold—if i equals i^*. Thus (5.21) can hold in this case only if $i = i^*$.

residents' planned expenditure (on both domestic and foreign goods) and net exports:

$$Y = E^D(Y, i - \pi^e, G, T) + NX\left(Y, i - \pi^e, G, T, \frac{\varepsilon P^*}{P}\right),$$ (5.22)

where $E^D(\bullet)$ is domestic residents' planned expenditure. $E^D(\bullet)$ is assumed to satisfy $0 < E^D_Y < 1$, $E^D_{i-\pi^e} < 0$, $E^D_G > 0$, and $E^D_T < 0$. We can then use (5.21) to substitute for net exports, and thereby eliminate the exchange rate from the model:

$$Y = E^D(Y, i - \pi^e, G, T) - CF(i - i^*).$$ (5.23)

Since $CF(i - i^*)$ is increasing in i, the set of points satisfying (5.23) is downward-sloping in (Y, i) space. This locus is shown in Figure 5.9 as the IS^{**} curve. Note that the exchange rate is implicitly changing as we move along the curve. Since the interest rate affects Y in (5.23) both through its direct effect on domestic demand and through its effect on the exchange rate and net exports, the IS^{**} curve is flatter than a conventional IS curve. In the extreme case of perfect capital mobility, the IS^{**} curve is flat at i^*. The LM curve is the same as before.

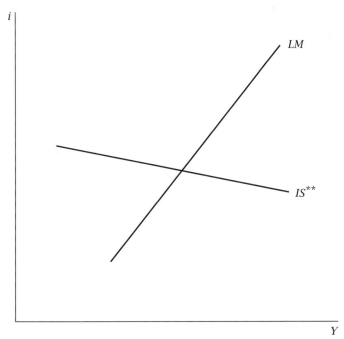

FIGURE 5.9 **The case of imperfect capital mobility and a floating exchange rate**

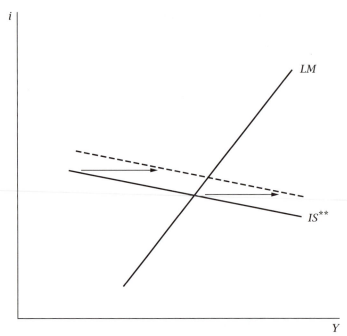

FIGURE 5.10   The effects of an increase in government purchases with imperfect capital mobility and a floating exchange rate

The results for this case typically fall between those for a closed economy and those for perfect capital mobility. Consider again the effects of an increase in government purchases. Since this increase raises expenditure for a given interest rate, the IS^{**} curve shifts to the right, as shown in Figure 5.10. Thus, in contrast to what happens with perfect capital mobility, i and Y rise for a given price level. Since the IS^{**} curve is flatter than the closed-economy IS curve, however, the effects are weaker than they are in a closed economy. The effects of other shocks can be analyzed in similar ways.

5.3   Alternative Assumptions about Wage and Price Rigidity

We now turn to the aggregate supply side of the model. This section describes various ways that a nonvertical AS curve might arise. In all of them, incomplete nominal adjustment is assumed rather than derived. Thus this section's purpose is not to discuss possible microeconomic foundations of nominal stickiness; that is the job of Chapter 6. Instead, the goal is to explore some combinations of nominal wage and price rigidity and characteristics of the labor and goods markets that give rise to a nonvertical *AS* curve. The different sets of assumptions have different implications for unemployment, for the behavior of the real wage and the markup in response to aggregate demand fluctuations, and for firms' pricing behavior.

We consider four sets of assumptions. The first two are valuable baselines. Both, however, appear to fail as even remotely approximate descriptions of actual economies. The other two are more complicated and potentially more accurate. Together, the four cases illustrate the wide range of possibilities.

Case 1: Keynes's Model

The aggregate supply portion of the model in Keynes's *General Theory* (1936) begins with the assumption that the nominal wage is rigid (at least over some range):

$$W = \overline{W}. \tag{5.24}$$

Output is produced by competitive firms. Labor, L, is the only factor of production that is variable in the short run, and is subject to decreasing returns:

$$Y = F(L), \qquad F'(\bullet) > 0, \qquad F''(\bullet) < 0. \tag{5.25}$$

Since firms are competitive, they hire labor up to the point where the marginal product of labor equals the real wage:

$$F'(L) = \frac{W}{P}. \tag{5.26}$$

Equations (5.24)–(5.26) imply an upward-sloping *AS* curve. Since the wage is fixed, a higher price level implies a lower real wage. Firms respond by raising employment, which increases output. Thus there is a positive relationship between P and Y.

The reason that incomplete nominal adjustment causes shifts in aggregate demand to change output in this case is straightforward. With rigid nominal wages, increases in the price level reduce the real wage and therefore increase the amount that firms want to sell. As a result, increases in aggregate demand lead not just to increases in prices, but to increases in both prices and output.

Figure 5.11 shows the situation in the labor market for a given price level. Employment and the real wage are determined by labor demand at the real wage that is implied by the fixed nominal wage and the price level (Point E in the diagram). Thus there is involuntary unemployment: some workers would like to work at the prevailing wage but cannot. The amount of unemployment is the difference between supply and demand at the prevailing real wage (distance EA in the diagram).

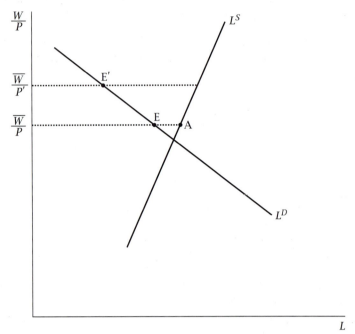

FIGURE 5.11   The labor market with sticky wages, flexible prices, and a competitive goods market

Fluctuations in aggregate demand lead to movements of employment and the real wage along the downward-sloping labor demand curve. A decline in demand, for example, leads to a fall in the price level, a rise in the real wage, and a fall in employment. This is shown as Point E′ in the diagram. This view of aggregate supply therefore implies a countercyclical real wage in response to aggregate demand shocks. This prediction has been subject to extensive testing beginning shortly after the publication of the *General Theory*. It has consistently failed to find support. As described in Section 5.6, our current understanding suggests that real wages are moderately procyclical.[12]

Case 2: Sticky Prices, Flexible Wages, and a Competitive Labor Market

The view of aggregate supply in the *General Theory* assumes that the goods market is competitive and goods prices are completely flexible, and that

---

[12] In his important paper responding to early studies of the cyclical behavior of wages, Keynes (1939) largely disavowed the specific formulation of aggregate supply in the *General Theory*, saying that he had chosen it to keep the model as classical as possible and to simplify the presentation. His 1939 view of aggregate supply is closer to Case 4, below.

the source of nominal stickiness is entirely in the labor market. This raises the question of what occurs in the reverse case where the labor market is competitive and wages are completely flexible, and where the source of incomplete nominal adjustment is entirely in the goods market.

The assumption that goods prices are not completely flexible is almost always coupled with the assumption that there is imperfect competition in the goods market. This is done for two reasons. First, with perfect competition, at the flexible-price equilibrium firms are selling the amount they want. A rise in demand from its initial level with prices unchanged therefore causes them to ration buyers. With imperfect competition, in contrast, price exceeds marginal cost and firms are better off if they can sell more at the prevailing price. It is therefore reasonable to assume that if prices do not adjust, then over some range firms are willing to produce to satisfy demand.

Second, the eventual goal of the theory is to derive rather than assume incomplete price adjustment. To do this, it is better to have price-setters (such as the firms in a model with imperfect competition) than an outside actor who sets prices (such as the Walrasian auctioneer of competitive models).[13]

With this view, prices rather than wages are assumed rigid:

$$P = \overline{P}. \tag{5.27}$$

Wages are flexible; thus workers are on their labor supply curve, which is assumed to be upward-sloping:[14]

$$L = L^s \left(\frac{W}{P} \right), \qquad L^{s\prime}(\bullet) > 0. \tag{5.28}$$

As before, employment and output are related by the production function, $Y = F(L)$ (equation [5.25]). Finally, firms meet demand at the prevailing price as long as it does not exceed the level where marginal cost equals price; we let Y^{MAX} denote this level of output.

With these strong assumptions about price rigidity, the aggregate supply curve is not just nonvertical, but horizontal. Specifically, it is a horizontal line at $\overline{P}$ out to Y^{MAX}; this is shown in Figure 5.12. Fluctuations in aggregate demand cause firms to change employment and output at the fixed price

---

[13] An important exception to the usual pairing of incomplete price adjustment with imperfect competition is found in the *disequilibrium* literature. These models typically assume a competitive goods market, and they consider the possibility of rationing by firms. In addition, the models typically have wage rigidity as well as price rigidity and allow for rationing (of either workers or firms) in the labor market. See, for example, Barro and Grossman (1971); Solow and Stiglitz (1968); and Malinvaud (1977). Benassy (1976) extends disequilibrium models to imperfect competition.

[14] Note that by writing labor supply as a function only of the real wage, we are ignoring the intertemporal-substitution and interest-rate effects that are central to employment fluctuations in basic real-business-cycle models. In principle, these effects can be incorporated into the model. But since they are not critical to the issues we are analyzing here, they are omitted for simplicity.

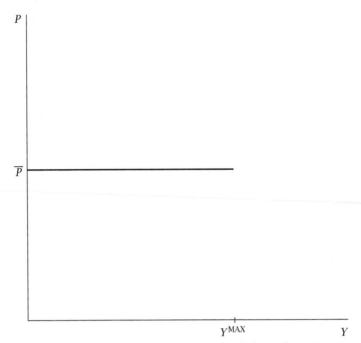

FIGURE 5.12   Aggregate supply with rigid goods prices

level, $\overline{P}$. And if aggregate demand ever becomes so large that demand at $\overline{P}$ exceeds Y^{MAX}, output equals Y^{MAX} and firms ration sales of their goods.

Figure 5.13 shows this model's implications for the labor market. Firms' demand for labor is determined by their desire to meet the demand for their goods. Thus, as long as the real wage is not so high that it is un-profitable to meet the full demand, the labor demand curve is a vertical line in employment-wage space. The term *effective labor demand* is used to describe a situation, such as this, where the quantity of labor demanded de-pends on the amount of goods that firms are able to sell.[15] The real wage is determined by the intersection of the effective labor demand curve and the labor supply curve (Point E). Thus workers are on their labor supply curve, and there is no unemployment.

This model implies a procyclical real wage in the face of demand fluctu-ations. A fall in aggregate demand, for example, leads to a fall in effective labor demand, and thus to a fall in the real wage as workers move down their labor supply curve (to Point E′ in the diagram). If labor supply is relatively

---

[15] If the real wage is so high that it is not profitable for firms to meet the demand for their goods, the quantity of labor demanded is determined by the condition that the marginal product equals the real wage. Thus this portion of the labor demand curve is downward-sloping.

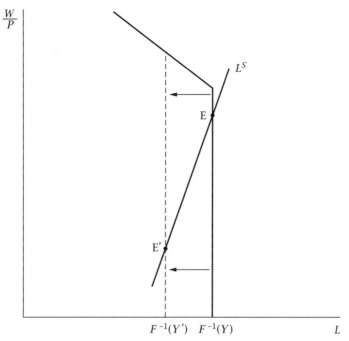

FIGURE 5.13 A competitive labor market when prices are sticky and wages are flexible

unresponsive to the real wage, the real wage varies greatly when aggregate demand changes.

Finally, this model implies a countercyclical markup (ratio of price to marginal cost) in response to demand fluctuations. A rise in demand, for example, leads to a rise in costs, both because the wage rises and because the marginal product of labor declines as output rises. Prices, however, stay fixed, and so the ratio of price to marginal cost falls.

Because markups are harder to measure than real wages, it is harder to determine their cyclical behavior. Nonetheless, work in this area has largely reached a consensus that markups are significantly countercyclical. See, for example, Bils (1987); Warner and Barsky (1995); Chevalier and Scharfstein (1996); and Sbordone (1998). Rotemberg and Woodford (1999) synthesize much of the evidence and discuss its implications.

The reason that incomplete nominal adjustment causes changes in aggregate demand to affect output is quite different in this case than in the previous one. A fall in aggregate demand, for example, lowers the amount that firms are able to sell at the prevailing price level; thus they reduce their production. In the previous model, in contrast, a fall in aggregate demand, by raising the real wage, reduces the amount that firms want to sell.

This model of aggregate supply is important for three reasons. First, it is the natural starting point for models in which nominal stickiness

involves prices rather than wages. Second, it shows that there is no necessary connection between nominal rigidity and unemployment. And third,
it is easy to use; because of this, models like it often appear in the theoretical
literature.

Case 3: Sticky Prices, Flexible Wages, and Real Labor Market Imperfections

Since output fluctuations appear to be associated with unemployment fluctuations, it is natural to ask whether movements in aggregate demand can
lead to changes in unemployment when it is nominal prices that adjust
sluggishly. To see how this can occur, suppose that nominal wages are still
flexible, but that there is some non-Walrasian feature of the labor market
that causes the real wage to remain above the level that equates demand
and supply. Chapter 9 investigates characteristics of the labor market that
can cause this to occur and how the real wage may vary with the level of aggregate economic activity in such situations. For now, let us simply assume
that firms have some "real-wage function." Thus we write

$$\frac{W}{P} = w(L), \qquad w'(\bullet) \geq 0. \tag{5.29}$$

For concreteness, one can think of firms paying more than market-clearing
wages for *efficiency-wage* reasons (see Sections 9.2–9.4). As before, prices
are fixed at $\overline{P}$, and output and employment are related by the production
function, $Y = F(L)$.

These assumptions, like the previous ones, imply a flat aggregate supply
curve up to the point where marginal cost equals $\overline{P}$; thus again changes in
aggregate demand have real effects. This case's implications for the labor
market are different than the previous one's, however. This is shown in
Figure 5.14. Employment and the real wage are now determined by the
intersection of the effective labor demand curve and the real-wage function.
In contrast to the previous case, there is unemployment; the amount is
given by distance EA in the diagram. Fluctuations in labor demand lead to
movements along the real-wage function rather than along the labor supply
curve. Thus the elasticity of labor supply no longer determines how the
real wage responds to aggregate demand movements. And if the real-wage
function is flatter than the labor supply curve, unemployment rises when
demand falls.

Case 4: Sticky Wages, Flexible Prices, and Imperfect Competition

Just as Case 3 extends Case 2 by introducing real imperfections in the labor market, the final case extends Case 1 by introducing real imperfections
in the goods market. Specifically, assume (as in Case 1) that the nominal

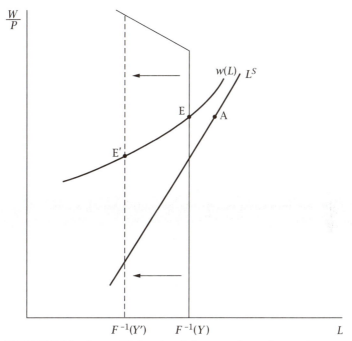

FIGURE 5.14   A non-Walrasian labor market when prices are sticky and nominal wages are flexible

wage is rigid at $\overline{W}$ and that nominal prices are flexible, and continue to assume that output and employment are related by the production function. Now, however, assume that the goods market is imperfectly competitive. With imperfect competition, price is a markup over marginal cost. Paralleling our assumptions about the real wage in Case 3, we do not model the determinants of the markup, but simply assume that there is a "markup function." With these assumptions, price is given by

$$P = \mu(L)\frac{W}{F'(L)}; \tag{5.30}$$

$W/F'(L)$ is marginal cost and μ is the markup.

Equation (5.30) implies that the real wage, W/P, is given by $F'(L)/\mu(L)$. Without any restriction on $\mu(L)$, one cannot say how W/P varies with L. If μ is constant, the real wage is countercyclical because of the diminishing marginal product of labor, just as in Case 1. Since the nominal wage is fixed, the price level must rise when output rises; thus the AS curve slopes up. Again as in Case 1, there is unemployment as long as labor supply is less than the level of employment determined by the intersection of AS and AD.

If $\mu(L)$ is sufficiently countercyclical—that is, if the markup is sufficiently lower in booms than in recoveries—the real wage can be acyclical or procyclical even though the nominal rigidity is entirely in the labor market. A particularly simple case occurs when $\mu(L)$ is precisely as countercyclical as $F'(L)$. In this situation, the real wage must be constant. Since the nominal wage is constant by assumption, the price level is constant as well. Thus the AS curve is horizontal.[16] If $\mu(L)$ is more countercyclical than $F'(L)$, then P must fall when L rises, and so the aggregate supply curve is actually downward-sloping. In all these cases, employment continues to be determined by the level of output at the intersection of the AS and AD curves.

Figure 5.15 shows this case's implications for the labor market. The real wage equals $F'(L)/\mu(L)$, which can be decreasing in L (Panel (a)), constant (Panel (b)), or increasing (Panel (c)). The intersection of the AS and AD curves determines Y (and hence L) and P, and thus where on the $F'(L)/\mu(L)$ locus the economy is. Unemployment again equals the difference between labor supply and employment at the prevailing real wage.

In short, different views about the sources of incomplete nominal adjustment and the characteristics of labor and goods markets have different implications for unemployment, the real wage, and the markup. As a result, Keynesian theories do not make strong predictions about the behavior of these variables. For example, the fact that the real wage does not appear to be countercyclical is perfectly consistent with the view that the aggregate supply curve is nonvertical. The behavior of these variables can be used, however, to test specific Keynesian models. The absence of a countercyclical real wage, for example, appears to be strong evidence against the view that fluctuations are driven by changes in aggregate demand and that Keynes's original model provides a good description of aggregate supply.

5.4 Output-Inflation Tradeoffs

A Permanent Output-Inflation Tradeoff?

The models of the previous section are based on simple forms of nominal stickiness. In all of them, nominal wages or nominal prices are completely fixed in the short run. In addition, if the level at which wages or prices are fixed is determined by the previous period's wages and prices, the models imply a permanent tradeoff between output and inflation.

To see this, consider our first model of aggregate supply; this is the model with fixed wages, flexible prices, and a competitive goods market. Suppose that $\overline{W}$ is proportional to the previous period's price level; that is, suppose that wages are adjusted to make up for the previous period's inflation. Thus the aggregate supply side of the economy is described by

$$W_t = AP_{t-1}, \qquad A > 0, \tag{5.31}$$

$$Y_t = F(L_t), \qquad F'(\bullet) > 0, \qquad F''(\bullet) < 0, \tag{5.32}$$

---

[16] Since $\mu(L)$ cannot be less than 1, it cannot be everywhere decreasing in L. Thus eventually the AS curve must turn up.

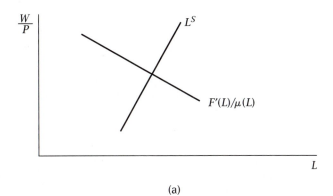

(a)

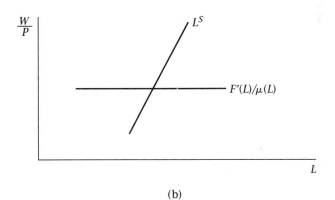

(b)

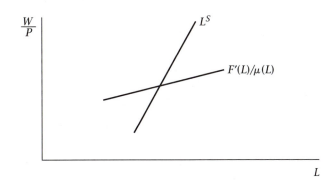

(c)

FIGURE 5.15 The labor market with sticky wages, flexible prices, and an imperfectly competitive goods market

$$F'(L_t) = \frac{W_t}{P_t}. \tag{5.33}$$

Assume that initially the AD and AS curves are steady, and that the price level and output are therefore constant. This situation is shown by curves AD_0 and AS_0 in Figure 5.16. Now suppose that in some period—period 1, for convenience—policymakers use fiscal or monetary policy to shift the AD curve out to AD_1; the price level therefore rises from P_0 to P_1 and output rises from Y_0 to Y_1. Because P_1 is higher than P_0, the wage set for period 2 is higher than the one that was set for period 1. Specifically, the wage is adjusted for the previous period's inflation, and so the period-2 wage exceeds the period-1 wage by a factor of P_1/P_0:

$$\frac{W_2}{W_1} = \frac{AP_1}{AP_0}$$

$$= \frac{P_1}{P_0}. \tag{5.34}$$

This implies that if the price level in period 2 is the same as in period 1, the real wage is $AP_1/P_1 = A$, which is the same as the real wage in period 0. Thus employment and output would be the same as they were in period

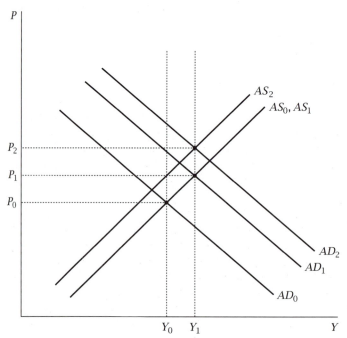

FIGURE 5.16   Using aggregate demand policy to permanently raise output under a simple model of aggregate supply

0. That is, AS_2 goes through the point (Y_0, P_1); this is shown in the figure. Thus if policymakers shift the aggregate demand curve out further to AD_2, output remains at Y_1 and the price level rises further to P_2.

This process can continue indefinitely, with the price level continually rising and Y equal to Y_1 every period. And if policymakers pursue even more expansionary policies, they can keep output at an even higher level, at the cost of higher inflation. Thus the model implies a permanent output-inflation tradeoff. Since higher output is associated with lower unemployment, it also implies a permanent unemployment-inflation tradeoff.

In a famous paper, Phillips (1958) showed that there was in fact a strong and relatively stable negative relationship between unemployment and wage inflation in the United Kingdom over the previous century.[17] Subsequent researchers found a similar relationship between unemployment and price inflation—a relationship that became known as the *Phillips curve*. Thus there appeared to be both theoretical and empirical support for a stable unemployment-inflation tradeoff.

The Natural Rate

The case for this stable tradeoff was shattered in the late 1960s and early 1970s. On the theoretical side, the attack took the form of the *natural-rate hypothesis* of Friedman (1968) and Phelps (1968). Friedman and Phelps argued that the idea that nominal variables, such as the money supply or inflation, could permanently affect real variables, such as output or unemployment, was unreasonable; in the long run, they argued, the behavior of real variables is determined by real forces.

In the specific case of the output-inflation or unemployment-inflation tradeoff, Friedman's and Phelps's argument was that a shift by policymakers to permanently expansionary policy would, sooner or later, change the way that prices or wages are set. Consider again the example analyzed in Figure 5.16. When policymakers adopt permanently more expansionary policies, they permanently increase output and employment, and (with this version of the aggregate supply curve) they permanently reduce the real wage. Yet there is no reason for workers and firms to settle on different levels of employment and the real wage just because inflation is higher: if there are forces causing the employment and real wage that prevail in the absence of inflation to be an equilibrium, those same forces are present when there is inflation. Thus wages will not always be adjusted mechanically for the previous period's inflation. Sooner or later, they will be set to account for the expansionary policies that workers and firms know are going to be undertaken. Once this occurs, employment, output, and the real wage will return to the levels that prevailed in the absence of inflation.

---

[17] See also Lipsey (1960) and Samuelson and Solow (1960).

In short, the natural-rate hypothesis states that there is some "normal" or "natural" rate of unemployment, and that monetary policy cannot keep unemployment below this level indefinitely. The precise determinants of the natural rate are unimportant. Friedman's and Phelps's argument was simply that it was determined by real rather than nominal forces. In Friedman's famous definition (1968, p. 8):

> "The natural rate of unemployment" ... is the level that would be ground out by the Walrasian system of general equilibrium equations, provided there is embedded in them the actual structural characteristics of the labor and commodity markets, including market imperfections, stochastic variability in demands and supplies, the cost of gathering information about job vacancies and labor availabilities, the costs of mobility, and so on.

The empirical downfall of the stable unemployment-inflation tradeoff is illustrated by Figure 5.17, which shows the combinations of unemployment and inflation in the United States from 1961 to 1999. The points for the 1960s fall along a fairly stable, downward-sloping curve. The points since then do not.

One source of the empirical failure of the Phillips curve is mundane: if there are disturbances to aggregate supply rather than aggregate demand, then even the models of the previous section imply that high inflation and

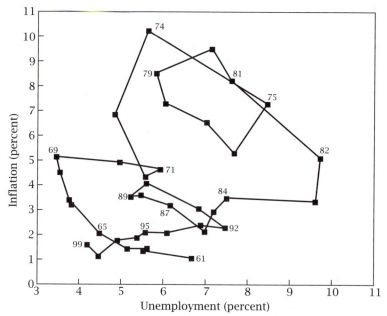

FIGURE 5.17   Unemployment and inflation in the United States, 1961–1999

high unemployment can occur together. And there certainly are plausible candidates for significant supply shocks in the 1970s. For example, there were tremendous increases in oil prices in 1973–74 and 1978–79; such increases are likely to cause firms to charge higher prices for a given level of wages. To give another example, there were large influxes of new workers into the labor force during this period; such influxes may increase unemployment for a given level of wages.

Yet these supply shocks cannot explain all the failings of the Phillips curve in the 1970s and 1980s. In 1981 and 1982, for example, there were no identifiable large supply shocks, yet both inflation and unemployment were much higher than they were at any time in the 1960s. The reason, if Friedman and Phelps are right, is that the high inflation of the 1970s changed how prices and wages were set.[18]

Thus, the models of price and wage behavior that imply a stable relationship between inflation and unemployment do not provide even a moderately accurate description of the dynamics of inflation and the choices facing policymakers. They must therefore be modified if they are to be used to address these issues.

The Expectations-Augmented Phillips Curve

In analyzing the long run, it is easiest to state directly that prices and wages are fully flexible, so that changes in aggregate demand have no real effects. Thus the *long-run aggregate supply* (or *LRAS*) curve is vertical, and disturbances on the demand side of the economy do not affect output in the long run. The level of output at which the long-run aggregate supply curve is vertical is known as the *natural rate of output,* or *potential* or *full-employment output,* and is denoted $\overline{Y}$. This is shown in Figure 5.18.

The conclusion that the long-run aggregate supply curve is vertical does not answer the question of how to model aggregate supply in the short run. Modern Keynesian formulations of short-run aggregate supply differ from the simple models in equations (5.31)–(5.33) and in Section 5.3 in three ways. First, neither wages nor prices are assumed to be completely unresponsive to the current state of the economy. Instead, higher output is assumed to be associated with higher wages and prices. One implication is that the short-run aggregate supply curve is upward-sloping even if it is prices rather than wages that do not adjust immediately to disturbances. Second, the possibility of supply shocks is allowed for. Third, and most important, adjustment to past and expected future inflation is assumed to be more complicated than the simple formulation in (5.31).

---

[18] In addition, the importance of supply shocks to the behavior of inflation in the 1970s is controversial. See Barsky and Kilian (2000).

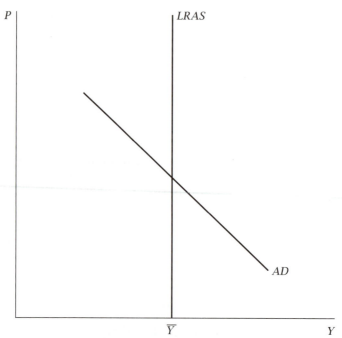

FIGURE 5.18   The long-run aggregate supply curve and the aggregate demand curve

A typical modern Keynesian formulation of aggregate supply is

$$\ln P_t = \ln P_{t-1} + \pi_t^* + \lambda(\ln Y_t - \ln \overline{Y}_t) + \varepsilon_t^S, \qquad \lambda > 0, \tag{5.35}$$

or

$$\pi_t = \pi_t^* + \lambda(\ln Y_t - \ln \overline{Y}_t) + \varepsilon_t^S, \tag{5.36}$$

where $\pi_t \equiv \ln P_t - \ln P_{t-1}$ is inflation. The $\lambda(\ln Y - \ln \overline{Y})$ term implies that at any time there is an upward-sloping relationship between inflation and output; the relationship is log-linear for simplicity. Equation (5.36) takes no stand concerning whether it is nominal prices or wages, or some combination of the two, that are the source of the incomplete adjustment.[19] The ε^S term captures supply shocks.

The key difference between (5.36) and the earlier models of aggregate supply is the π^* term. Tautologically, π^* is what inflation would be if output is equal to its natural rate and there are no supply shocks. π^* is

---

[19] Equation (5.36) can be combined with Case 2 or 3 of Section 5.3 by assuming that the nominal wage is completely flexible and using the assumption in (5.36) in place of the assumption that P equals $\overline{P}$. Similarly, one can assume that wage inflation is given by an expression analogous to (5.36) and use that assumption in place of the assumption that W equals $\overline{W}$ in Case 1 or 4; this implies somewhat more complicated behavior of price inflation, however.

known as *core* or *underlying* inflation. Equation (5.36) is referred to as the *expectations-augmented Phillips curve*—although, as we will see shortly, modern Keynesian theories do not necessarily interpret π^* as expected inflation.

A simple model of π^* that is useful for fixing ideas is that it equals the previous period's actual inflation:

$$\pi_t^* = \pi_{t-1}. \tag{5.37}$$

With this formulation, there is a tradeoff between output and the *change* in inflation, but no permanent tradeoff between output and inflation. For inflation to be held steady at any level, output must equal the natural rate. And any level of inflation is sustainable. But for inflation to fall, there must be a period when output is below the natural rate.[20]

This model is much more successful than models with a permanent output-inflation tradeoff at fitting the macroeconomic history of the United States over the past quarter-century. Consider, for example, the behavior of unemployment and inflation from 1980 to 1995. The model attributes the combination of high inflation and high unemployment in the early 1980s to contractionary shifts in aggregate demand with inflation starting from a high level. The high unemployment was associated with falls in inflation (and with larger falls when unemployment was higher), just as the model predicts. Once unemployment fell below the 6 to 7 percent range in the mid-1980s, inflation began to creep up. When unemployment returned to this range at the end of the decade, inflation held steady. Inflation again declined when unemployment rose above 7 percent in 1992, and it again held steady when unemployment fell below 7 percent in 1993 and 1994. All these movements are consistent with the model.

Even the modified model is not a complete success, however. Staiger, Stock, and Watson (1997) show that although on average inflation falls when unemployment is high, the relationship is not particularly close, and that this is true even when one controls for observable supply shocks. The behavior of inflation and unemployment in the second half of the 1990s is an important example of this lack of a tight relationship: inflation failed to rise even though unemployment was well below previous estimates of the natural rate.[21]

Once core inflation is added to the model, it is more convenient to describe the behavior of the economy in output-inflation space than in output-price level space. The aggregate supply curve, (5.36), implies an

---

[20] The standard rule of thumb is that for each percentage point that the unemployment rate exceeds the natural rate, inflation falls by one-half percentage point per year. And, as we saw in Section 4.1, for each percentage point that u exceeds $\bar{u}$, Y is roughly 2 percent less than $\overline{Y}$. Thus if each period corresponds to a year, λ in equation (5.36) is about $\frac{1}{4}$.

[21] Ex post, economists have proposed explanations of this behavior based on supply shocks and declines in the natural rate. But this does not change the fact that the model's ex ante predictive success in this episode was minimal.

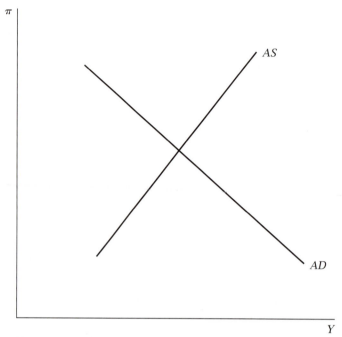

FIGURE 5.19   The AS and AD curves in output-inflation space

upward-sloping relationship between output and inflation. And the aggregate demand side of the model implies a downward-sloping relationship between the two variables. To see this, note that for a given value of the previous period's price level, the price level in the current period is an increasing function of the inflation rate. Thus a higher value of inflation implies a lower level of M/P and hence a lower level of output. These AS and AD curves are shown in Figure 5.19.

Although the model of core inflation in (5.37) is often useful, it has important limitations. For example, if we interpret a period as being fairly short (such as a quarter), core inflation is likely to take more than one period to respond fully to changes in actual inflation. In this case, it is reasonable to replace the right-hand side of (5.37) with a weighted average of inflation over the previous several periods.

Perhaps the most important drawback of the model of aggregate supply in (5.36)–(5.37) is that it assumes that the behavior of core inflation is independent of the economic environment. For example, if the formulation in (5.37) always held, there would be a permanent tradeoff between output and the change in inflation. That is, equations (5.36) and (5.37) imply that if policymakers are willing to accept ever-increasing inflation, they can push output permanently above its natural rate. But the same arguments that Friedman and Phelps make against a permanent output-inflation trade-off imply that if policymakers attempt to pursue this strategy, workers and firms will eventually stop following (5.36)–(5.37) and will adjust their behavior to account for the increases in inflation they know are going to occur; as a result, output will return to its natural rate.

In his original presentation of the natural-rate hypothesis, Friedman discussed another, more realistic, example of how the behavior of core inflation may depend on the environment: how rapidly core inflation adjusts to changes in inflation is likely to depend on how long-lasting actual movements in inflation typically are. If this is right, then in a situation like the one that Phillips studied, where there are many transitory movements in inflation, core inflation will vary little; the data will therefore suggest a stable relationship between output and inflation. But in a setting like the modern United States, where there are sustained periods of high and of low inflation, core inflation will vary more, and thus there will be no consistent link between output and the level of inflation.

Carrying these criticisms of (5.36)–(5.37) to their logical extreme would suggest that we replace core inflation in (5.36) with expected inflation:

$$\pi_t = \pi_t^e + \lambda(\ln Y_t - \ln \overline{Y}_t) + \varepsilon_t^S, \tag{5.38}$$

where π_t^e is expected inflation. This formulation captures the ideas in the previous examples. For example, (5.38) implies that unless expectations are grossly irrational, no policy can permanently raise output above its natural rate, since that requires that workers' and firms' forecasts of inflation are always too low. Similarly, since expectations of future inflation respond less to current inflation when movements in inflation tend to be shorter-lived, (5.38) is consistent with Friedman's example of how the output-inflation relationship is likely to vary with the behavior of actual inflation.

Nonetheless, modern Keynesian analyses generally do not use the model of aggregate supply in (5.38). The central reason is that, as we will see in Part A of Chapter 6, if one assumes that price- and wage-setters are rational in forming their expectations, then (5.38) has strong implications—implications that do not appear to be supported by the data. Alternatively, if one assumes that workers and firms do not form their expectations rationally, one is resting the theory on irrationality.

A natural compromise between the models of core inflation in (5.37) and in (5.38) is to assume that core inflation is a weighted average of past inflation and expected inflation. With this assumption, the short-run aggregate supply curve is given by

$$\pi_t = \phi\pi_t^e + (1 - \phi)\pi_{t-1} + \lambda(\ln Y_t - \ln \overline{Y}_t) + \varepsilon_t^S, \qquad 0 \le \phi \le 1. \tag{5.39}$$

Modern Keynesian theories typically allow for the possibility that ϕ is positive; that is, they let core inflation not just be a mechanical function of past inflation. But they typically also assume that ϕ is strictly less than 1. Thus the theories assume that there is some *inertia* in wage and price inflation. That is, they assume that there is some link between past and future inflation beyond effects operating through expectations.

The theories usually stop short, however, of specifying models of aggregate supply that are intended to hold generally. Instead, the models largely fall into two groups. The first group consists of models where some type of aggregate supply curve or nominal stickiness is built up from specific assumptions about the microeconomic environment. These models (such as those of Section 5.3) typically have strong forms of nominal rigidity; they are intended to illustrate particular issues but not to provide good approximations to actual behavior. We will encounter many of these models in the next chapter. The second group of models consists of specific formulations, such as the one in (5.36)–(5.37), that are intended to be useful summaries of aggregate supply behavior in specific situations but that are not intended to be universal.

The failure of modern Keynesian theory to develop a general model of aggregate supply makes the theory harder to apply in novel situations. It also, by making the models less precise, makes them harder to confront with the data—a point we will return to at the end of the next chapter.

5.5 Empirical Application: Money and Output

Perhaps the most important difference between real and Keynesian theories of fluctuations involves their predictions concerning the effects of monetary changes. In basic real-business-cycle models, purely monetary disturbances have no real effects. In Keynesian models, they have important effects on employment and output.

The St. Louis Equation

This observation suggests a natural test of real versus Keynesian theories: why not just regress output on money? Such regressions have a long history. One of the earliest and most straightforward money-output regressions was carried out by Leonall Andersen and Jerry Jordan of the Federal Reserve Bank of St. Louis (Andersen and Jordan, 1968). For that reason, the regression of output on money is known as the *St. Louis equation.*

Here we consider an example of the St. Louis equation. The left-hand-side variable is the change in the log of real GDP. The main right-hand-side variable is the change in the log of the money stock, as measured by $M2$; since any effect of money on output may occur with a lag, the contemporaneous and four lagged values are included. The regression also includes a constant and a time trend (to account for trends in output and money growth). The data are quarterly, and the sample period is 1959–1999.

The results are

$$\Delta \ln Y_t = \begin{array}{c} 0.0016 \\ (0.0034) \end{array} - \begin{array}{c} 0.03 \ \Delta \ln m_t + \\ (0.12) \end{array} \begin{array}{c} 0.17 \ \Delta \ln m_{t-1} + \\ (0.14) \end{array} \begin{array}{c} 0.17 \ \Delta \ln m_{t-2} \\ (0.14) \end{array}$$

$$+ \begin{array}{c} 0.02 \ \Delta \ln m_{t-3} - \\ (0.14) \end{array} \begin{array}{c} 0.02 \ \Delta \ln m_{t-4} + \\ (0.12) \end{array} \begin{array}{c} 0.0008 \ t, \\ (0.0016) \end{array} \qquad (5.40)$$

$$\overline{R}^2 = 0.050, \qquad \text{D.W.} = 1.55, \qquad \text{s.e.e.} = 0.009,$$

where the numbers in parentheses are standard errors. The sum of the coefficients on the current and four lagged values of the money-growth variable is 0.33, with a standard error of 0.11. Thus the estimates suggest that a 1 percent increase in the money stock is associated with an increase of $\frac{1}{3}$ percent in output over the next year, and the null hypothesis of no association is rejected at high levels of significance.

Does this regression, then, provide powerful evidence in support of monetary over real theories of fluctuations? The answer is no. There are several basic problems with a regression like this one. First, causation may run from output to money rather than from money to output. A simple story, formalized by King and Plosser (1984), is that when firms plan to increase production, they may increase their money holdings because they will need to purchase more intermediate inputs. Similarly, households may increase their money holdings when they plan to increase their purchases. Aggregate measures of the money stock, such as $M2$, are not set directly by the Federal Reserve but are determined by the interaction of the supply of high-powered money with the behavior of the banking system and the public. Thus shifts in money demand stemming from changes in firms' and households' production plans can lead to changes in the money stock. As a result, we may see changes in the money stock in advance of output movements even if the changes in money are not causing the output movements.

The second major problem with the St. Louis equation involves the determinants of monetary policy. Suppose the Federal Reserve adjusts the money stock to try to offset other factors that influence aggregate output. Then if monetary changes have real effects and the Federal Reserve's efforts to stabilize the economy are successful, we will observe fluctuations in money without movements in output (Kareken and Solow, 1963). Thus, just as we cannot conclude from the positive correlation between money and output that money causes output, if we fail to observe such a correlation we cannot conclude that money does not cause output.[22]

---

[22] Similarly, suppose that monetary and fiscal policy are coordinated, so that the two usually move in the same direction. Then if fiscal policy affects real output, there will be a relationship between monetary policy and output movements even if monetary changes do not have real effects.

The third difficulty with the St. Louis equation is that there have been a series of large shifts in the demand for money over the past two decades. At least some of the shifts are probably due to financial innovation and deregulation, but their causes are not entirely understood.[23] If the Federal Reserve does not adjust the money supply fully in response to these disturbances, the *IS-LM-AS* model predicts that they will lead to a negative relationship between money and output; a positive money demand shock, for example, will increase the money stock but increase the interest rate and reduce output. And even if the Federal Reserve accommodates the shifts, the fact that they are so large may cause a few observations to have a disproportionate effect on the results.

As a result of the money demand shifts, the estimated relationship between money and output is sensitive to such matters as the sample period and the measure of money. For example, if equation (5.40) is estimated using $M1$ in place of $M2$, or if it is estimated over a slightly different sample period, the results change considerably.

Because of these difficulties, regressions like (5.40) cannot be used to provide strong evidence concerning the relative merits of monetary and real theories of fluctuations.

Other Types of Evidence

A very different approach to testing whether monetary shocks have real effects stems from the work of Friedman and Schwartz (1963). Friedman and Schwartz undertake a careful historical analysis of the sources of movements in the money stock in the United States from the end of the Civil War to 1960. On the basis of this analysis, they argue that many of the movements in money, especially the largest ones, were mainly the result of developments in the monetary sector of the economy rather than the response of the money stock to real developments. Friedman and Schwartz demonstrate that these monetary movements were followed by output movements in the same direction. Thus, Friedman and Schwartz conclude, unless the money-output relationship in these episodes is an extraordinary fluke, it must reflect causation running from money to output rather than in the opposite direction.[24]

C. Romer and D. Romer (1989) provide more recent evidence along the same lines. They search the records of the Federal Reserve for the postwar period for evidence of policy shifts designed to lower inflation that were not motivated by developments on the real side of the economy. They identify six such shifts, and find that all of them were followed by recessions. For

---

[23] The classic reference is Goldfeld (1976).

[24] See especially Chapter 13 of their book—an item that every macroeconomist should read.

example, in October 1979, shortly after Paul Volcker became chairman of the Federal Reserve Board, the Federal Reserve tightened monetary policy dramatically. The change appears to have been motivated by a desire to reduce inflation, and not by the presence of other forces that would have caused output to decline in any event. Yet it was followed by one of the largest recessions in postwar U.S. history.[25]

What Friedman and Schwartz and Romer and Romer are doing is searching for *natural experiments* to determine the effects of monetary shocks. If economies were laboratories, economists could randomly perturb the money supply and examine the subsequent output movements. Since the monetary disturbances would be chosen at random, the possibility that they were caused by output movements, or that there were other factors systematically causing the changes in both money and output, could be ruled out.

Unfortunately for economic science (though fortunately for other reasons), economies are not laboratories. The closest we can come to a laboratory experiment is to look for times when historical developments bring about monetary changes that are not caused by the behavior of output. For example, Friedman and Schwartz argue that the death in 1928 of Benjamin Strong, the president of the Federal Reserve Bank of New York, provides an example of such an independent monetary disturbance. Strong's death, Friedman and Schwartz argue, left a power vacuum in the Federal Reserve System and therefore caused monetary policy to be conducted very differently over the next several years than it otherwise would have been.[26]

---

[25] It is possible that similar studies of open economies could provide stronger evidence concerning the importance of monetary forces. For example, shifts in monetary policy to combat high rates of inflation in small, highly open economies appear to be associated with large changes in real exchange rates, real interest rates, and real output. What we observe is more complicated than anti-inflationary monetary policy being consistently followed by low output, however. In particular, when the policy attempts to reduce inflation by targeting the exchange rate, there is typically an output boom in the short run. Why this occurs is not known. Likewise, the more general question of whether the evidence from inflation stabilizations in open economies provides strong evidence of monetary nonneutrality is unresolved. Analyzing stabilizations is complicated by the fact that the policy shifts are often accompanied by fiscal reforms and by large changes in uncertainty. See, for example, Sargent (1982), Rebelo and Végh (1995), and Calvo and Végh (1999).

[26] In effect, natural experiments provide potential instrumental variables for the St. Louis equation. The way to address the problem that there may be correlation between money growth and other factors that affect real output is to find variables that are correlated with money growth but uncorrelated with the other factors. One can then estimate the money-output regression by *instrumental variables* (or *two-stage least squares*). That is, one can examine how output growth is related to the component of money growth that is correlated with the instruments, and that is therefore uncorrelated with the omitted factors. Or, if one is interested simply in whether monetary movements affect real output but not in the precise values of the coefficients, one can estimate the *reduced form* of the model— that is, one can regress output growth directly on the instruments. In effect, Friedman and Schwartz and Romer and Romer are using historical evidence about the source of monetary developments to try to find such instruments, and then examining the reduced-form relationship between output movements and their proposed instruments.

Natural experiments such as Strong's death are unlikely to be as ideal as genuine randomized experiments for determining the effects of monetary changes. There is room for disagreement concerning whether any episodes are sufficiently clear-cut to be viewed as independent monetary disturbances, and if so, what set of episodes should be considered. But since randomized experiments are not possible, the evidence provided by natural experiments may be the best we can obtain.

A related approach is to use the evidence provided by specific monetary interventions to investigate the impact of monetary changes on relative prices. For example, as described in Section 10.3, Cook and Hahn (1989) confirm formally the common observation that Federal Reserve open-market operations are associated with changes in nominal interest rates. Given the discrete nature of the open-market operations and the specifics of how their timing is determined, it is not plausible that they occur endogenously at times when interest rates would have moved in any event. And although the issue has not been investigated formally, the fact that monetary expansions lower nominal rates strongly suggests that the changes in nominal rates represent changes in real rates as well. For example, monetary expansions lower nominal interest rates for terms as short as a day; it seems unlikely that they reduce expected inflation over such horizons.[27] Since real and Keynesian theories agree that changes in real rates affect real behavior, this evidence suggests that monetary changes have real effects.

Similarly, the nominal exchange-rate regime appears to affect the behavior of real exchange rates. Under a fixed exchange rate, the central bank adjusts the money supply to keep the nominal exchange rate constant; under a floating exchange rate, it does not. There is strong evidence that not just nominal but also real exchange rates are much less volatile under fixed than floating exchange rates. In addition, when a central bank switches from pegging the nominal exchange rate against one currency to pegging the nominal exchange rate against another, the volatility of the two associated real exchange rates seems to change sharply as well. (See, for example, Genberg, 1978; Stockman, 1983; Mussa, 1986; and Baxter and Stockman, 1989.) Since shifts between exchange-rate regimes are usually discrete, explaining this behavior of real exchange rates without appealing to real effects of monetary forces appears to require positing sudden large changes in the real shocks affecting economies. And again, both real and Keynesian theories predict that the behavior of real exchange rates has real effects.

The most significant limitation of this evidence is that the importance of these apparent effects of monetary changes on real interest rates and real exchange rates for quantities has not been determined. Baxter and Stockman (1989), for example, do not find any clear difference in the behavior of economic aggregates under floating and fixed exchange rates. Since real-business-cycle theories attribute fairly large changes in quantities to rela-

---

[27] Barro (1989) presents a model where monetary expansions lower expected inflation. The model requires that prices jump instantaneously in response to the expansions, however.

tively modest movements in relative prices, however, a finding that the price changes were not important would be puzzling from the perspective of both real and Keynesian theories.

More Sophisticated Statistical Evidence

Because of these kinds of evidence, the proposition that monetary disturbances have real effects has substantial support among macroeconomists. But these kinds of evidence are of little use in determining the details of policy's effects. For example, Friedman and Schwartz and Romer and Romer identify sufficiently few episodes that their evidence cannot be used to obtain quantitative estimates of any precision of policy's impact on output or to shed much light on the merits of different hypotheses about the timing of different variables' responses to monetary changes.

The desire to obtain a more detailed picture of monetary policy's effects has motivated a large amount of recent work reexamining the statistical relationship between monetary policy and the economy. Most of the work has been done in the context of *vector autoregressions*, or VARs. In its simplest form, a VAR is a system of equations where each variable in the system is regressed on a set of its own lagged values and lagged values of each of the other variables (for example, Sims, 1980; Hamilton, 1994, Chapter 11, provides a general introduction to VARs). Early VARs put little or no structure on the system. As a result, most attempts to make inferences from them about the effects of monetary policy suffered from the same problems of omitted variables, reverse causation, and money-demand shifts that doom the St. Louis equation (Cooley and LeRoy, 1985).

More recent VARs improve on the early attempts in two ways. First, since the Federal Reserve has generally let the money stock fluctuate in response to money-demand shifts, the more recent VARs choose measures of monetary policy other than the money stock. The most common choice is the Federal funds rate (Bernanke and Blinder, 1992). Second, and more important, they recognize that drawing inferences about the economy from the data requires a model. They therefore make assumptions about the conduct of policy and its effects that allow the estimates of the VAR parameters to be mapped into estimates of policy's impact on macroeconomic variables. These *structural VARs* were pioneered by Sims (1986), Bernanke (1986), and Blanchard and Watson (1986). Important recent contributions in the context of monetary policy include Sims (1992); Bernanke and Mihov (1998); Christiano, Eichenbaum, and Evans (1996); Leeper, Sims, and Zha (1996); Cochrane (1998); and Barth and Ramey (2000). The results of these studies are broadly consistent with the evidence discussed above. More importantly, these studies provide a variety of evidence about lags in policy's effects, its impact on financial markets, and other issues.

Unfortunately, it is not clear that modern VARs have in fact solved the difficulties with simpler money-output regressions (Rudebusch, 1998). Perhaps most importantly, this research has yet to find a compelling way of addressing the difficulty that the Federal Reserve may be adjusting policy in response to information it has about future economic developments that the VARs do not control for. Consider, for example, the Federal Reserve's interest-rate cuts in the autumn of 1998. Since the economy was in a boom (which is not a situation where the Federal Reserve normally cuts interest rates), the typical VAR identifies the cuts as expansionary monetary-policy shocks, and as therefore appropriate to use to investigate policy's effects. In fact, however, the Federal Reserve made the cuts because it believed the East Asian financial crisis was likely to lead to slower growth of aggregate demand in the United States; it lowered interest rates only to offset this contractionary shock. Thus looking at the behavior of the macroeconomy after the interest-rate cuts is not a good way of determining the impact of monetary policy. This example suggests that monetary policymaking is sufficiently complicated that it is extremely difficult to control for the full set of factors that influence policy and that may also directly influence the economy.

5.6   The Cyclical Behavior of the Real Wage

Economists have been interested in the cyclical behavior of the real wage ever since the appearance of Keynes's *General Theory*. Early studies of this issue examined aggregate data. The general conclusion of this literature is that the real wage in the United States and other countries is approximately acyclical or moderately procyclical (see, for example, Geary and Kennan, 1982).

Focusing on aggregate wage data is risky, however: the set of workers that make up the aggregate is not constant over the business cycle. Employment is more cyclical for lower-skill, lower-wage workers. Thus, lower-skill workers constitute a larger fraction of employed individuals in booms than in recessions. As a result, examining aggregate data is likely to understate the extent of procyclical movements in the typical individual's real wage. To put it differently, the skill-adjusted aggregate real wage is likely to be more procyclical than the unadjusted aggregate real wage.

Because of this possibility, various authors, beginning with Bils (1985), have examined the cyclical behavior of real wages using panel data. One of the most thorough and careful attempts is that of Solon, Barsky, and Parker (1994). They employ U.S. data from the Panel Study of Income Dynamics (commonly referred to as the PSID) for the period 1967–1987. As Solon, Barsky, and Parker describe, the aggregate real wage is unusually procyclical in this period. Specifically, they report that in this period a rise in the unemployment rate of 1 percentage point is associated with a fall in the aggregate real wage of 0.6 percent (with a standard error of 0.17 percent).

Solon, Barsky, and Parker consider two approaches to addressing composition bias. The first is to consider only individuals who are employed throughout their sample period and to examine the cyclical behavior of the aggregate real wage for this group. The second approach uses more observations. Loosely speaking, Solon, Barsky, and Parker estimate a regression of the form

$$\Delta \ln w_{it} = a' X_{it} + b \Delta u_t + e_{it}. \tag{5.41}$$

Here i indexes individuals and t years, w is the real wage, u is the unemployment rate, and X is a vector of control variables. They use all available observations; that is, observation it is included if individual i is employed in both year $t - 1$ and year t. The fact that the individual must be employed in both years to be included is what addresses the possibility of composition bias.[28]

The results of the two approaches are quite similar: the real wage is roughly twice as procyclical at the individual level as in the aggregate. A fall in the unemployment rate of 1 percentage point is associated with a rise in a typical worker's real wage of about 1.2 percent. That is, the real wage is quite procyclical at the individual level. And with both approaches, the estimates are highly statistically significant.

One concern is that these results might reflect not composition bias, but differences between the workers in the PSID and the population as a whole. To address this possibility, Solon, Barsky, and Parker perform the following exercise. They construct an aggregate real wage series for the PSID in the conventional way; that is, they compute the real wage in a given year as the average real wage paid to individuals in the PSID who are employed in that year. Since the set of workers used in computing this wage varies from year to year, these estimates are subject to composition bias. Thus, comparing the estimates of wage cyclicality for this measure with those for a conventional aggregate wage measure shows the importance of the PSID sample. And comparing the estimates from this measure with the panel data estimates shows the importance of composition bias.

When they perform this exercise, Solon, Barsky, and Parker find that the cyclicality of the aggregate PSID real wage is virtually identical to that of the conventional aggregate real wage. Thus, the difference between the panel data estimates and the aggregate estimates reflects composition bias.

Solon, Barsky, and Parker are not the first authors to examine the cyclical behavior of the real wage using panel data. Yet they find much greater composition bias than earlier researchers. If we are to put much weight on their results, we need to understand why this is.

Solon, Barsky, and Parker discuss this issue in the context of three earlier studies: Blank (1990), Coleman (1984), and Bils (1985). Blank's results in fact indicate considerable composition bias. She was interested in other

---

[28] Because of the need to avoid composition bias, Solon, Barsky, and Parker do not use all PSID workers with either approach. Thus it is possible that their procedures suffer from a different type of composition bias. Suppose, for example, that wages conditional on being employed are highly countercyclical for individuals who work only sporadically. Then by excluding these workers, Solon, Barsky, and Parker are overstating the procyclicality of wages for the typical individual. This possibility seems farfetched, however.

issues, however, and so did not call attention to this finding. Coleman focused on the fact that movements in an aggregate real wage series and in a series purged of composition bias show essentially the same *correlation* with movements in the unemployment rate. He failed to note that the *magnitude* of the movements in the corrected series is much larger. This is an illustration of the general principle that in doing empirical work, it is important to consider not just statistical measures such as correlations and t-statistics, but also the economic magnitudes of the estimates. Finally, Bils found that real wages at the individual level are substantially procyclical. But he found that an aggregate real wage series for his sample was nearly as procyclical, and thus he concluded that composition bias is not large. His sample, however, consisted only of young men. Thus a finding that there is some composition bias within this fairly homogeneous group does not rule out the possibility that there is substantial bias in the population as a whole.

Can we conclude from Solon, Barsky, and Parker's findings that short-run fluctuations in the quantity of labor represent movements along an upward-sloping short-run labor supply curve? Solon, Barsky, and Parker argue that we cannot, for two reasons. First, they find that explaining their results in this way requires a labor supply elasticity in response to cyclical wage variation of 1.0 to 1.4. They argue that microeconomic studies suggest that this elasticity is implausibly high even in response to purely temporary changes. More importantly, they point out that short-run wage movements are far from purely temporary; this makes an explanation based on movements along the labor supply function even more problematic. Second, as described above, the aggregate real wage is unusually procyclical in Solon, Barsky, and Parker's sample period. If the same is true of individuals' wages, explaining employment movements on the basis of shifts along the labor supply function in other periods is even more difficult.

Thus, Solon, Barsky, and Parker's evidence does not eliminate the likelihood that non-Walrasian features of the labor market (or, possibly, shifts in labor supply) are important to the comovement of the quantity of labor and real wages. Nonetheless, it significantly changes our understanding of a basic fact about short-run fluctuations, and therefore about what we should demand of our models of macroeconomic fluctuations.

Problems

5.1. Consider the *IS-LM* model presented in Section 5.1. In this model, what are di/dM and dY/dM for a given value of P?

5.2. The derivation of the *LM* curve assumes that M is exogenous. But suppose instead that the Federal Reserve has some target interest rate $\bar{i}$ and that it adjusts M to keep i always equal to $\bar{i}$.

    (*a*) With this policy, what is the slope of the "*LM* curve" (that is, the set of combinations of i and Y that cause money demand and supply to be equal)?

(b) With this policy, what is the slope of the AD curve?

5.3. The government budget in the standard Keynesian model.

(a) **The balanced budget multiplier.** (See Haavelmo, 1945.) Suppose that planned expenditure is given by (5.2), $E = C(Y - T) + I(i - \pi^e) + G$.

(i) How do equal increases in G and T affect the position of the IS curve? Specifically, what is the effect on Y for a given level of i?

(ii) How do equal increases in G and T affect the position of the AD curve? Specifically, what is the effect on Y for a given level of P?

(b) **Automatic stabilizers.** Suppose that tax revenues, T, instead of being exogenous, are a function of income: $T = T(Y)$, $T'(Y) > 0$. With this change, find how an increase in $T'(Y)$ affects the following:

(i) The slope of the IS curve.

(ii) The effects of changes in G and M on Y for a given P.

5.4. The liquidity trap and the Pigou effect. Assume that the nominal interest rate is so low that the opportunity cost of holding money is negligible. Suppose that as a result people are indifferent concerning the division of their wealth between money and other assets, and that they are therefore willing to change their money holdings without any change in the interest rate.

(a) **The liquidity trap.** (Keynes, 1936.) In this situation, what is the slope of the AD curve? If prices are completely flexible (so the AS curve is vertical), is aggregate demand irrelevant to output?

(b) **The Pigou effect.** (Pigou, 1943.) Suppose that, in addition, planned expenditure depends on real wealth as well as the variables in (5.1). Since the public's holdings of high-powered money are one component of wealth, a fall in the price level increases real wealth. If prices are completely flexible (so the AS curve is vertical), is aggregate demand irrelevant to output?

5.5. The Mundell effect. (Mundell, 1963.) In the IS-LM model, how does a fall in expected inflation π^e affect i, Y, and $i - \pi^e$?

5.6. The multiplier-accelerator. (Samuelson, 1939.) Consider the following model of income determination. (1) Consumption depends on the previous period's income: $C_t = a + bY_{t-1}$. (2) The desired capital stock (or inventory stock) is proportional to the previous period's output: $K_t^* = cY_{t-1}$. (3) Investment equals the difference between the desired capital stock and the stock inherited from the previous period: $I_t = K_t^* - K_{t-1} = K_t^* - cY_{t-2}$. (4) Government purchases are constant: $G_t = \overline{G}$. (5) $Y_t = C_t + I_t + G_t$.

(a) Express Y_t in terms of Y_{t-1}, Y_{t-2}, and the parameters of the model.

(b) Suppose $b = 0.9$ and $c = 0.5$. Suppose there is a one-time disturbance to government purchases; specifically, suppose that G is equal to $\overline{G} + 1$ in period t and is equal to $\overline{G}$ in all other periods. How does this shock affect output over time?

5.7. (This follows Mankiw and Summers, 1986.) Suppose that the demand for real money balances depends on the interest rate, i, and on *disposable* income

$Y - T$; in other words, suppose that the correct way to write the *LM* equation is $M/P = L(i, Y - T)$.

(a) With this change to the *IS-LM-AS* model, can one tell whether a tax cut (that is, a fall in *T*) increases or decreases output? Assume a closed economy.

(b) Redo part (a) assuming an open economy under the assumptions that the exchange rate is floating, exchange-rate expectations are static, and capital is perfectly mobile.

(c) Redo part (b) assuming a fixed exchange rate.

5.8. Describe how each of the following changes affects income, the exchange rate, and net exports at a given price level under (1) a floating exchange rate and perfect capital mobility; (2) a fixed exchange rate and perfect capital mobility; and (3) a floating exchange rate and imperfect capital mobility. Assume static exchange-rate expectations, and assume that planned expenditure is given by the expression in n. 8.

(a) The demand for money at a given *i* and *Y* falls.

(b) The foreign interest rate rises.

(c) The country adopts protectionist policies, so that net exports at a given real exchange rate are higher than before.

5.9. Exchange-market intervention. Suppose that the central bank intervenes in the foreign exchange market by purchasing foreign currency for dollars, and that it *sterilizes* this intervention by selling bonds for dollars to keep the money stock unchanged. With this intervention, *NX* and *CF* must sum to a positive amount rather than to 0 (see equation [5.21]).

(a) What are the effects of this intervention on output, the exchange rate, and the price level under a floating exchange rate, static exchange-rate expectations, and imperfect capital mobility?

(b) How, if at all, do the results in part (a) change if capital is perfectly mobile?

5.10. The algebra of exchange-rate overshooting. Consider a simplified open-economy model: $m - p = hy - ki$, $y = b(\varepsilon - p) - a(i - \dot{p})$, $i = \dot{\varepsilon}$, $\dot{p} = \theta y$. The variables *y*, *m*, *p*, and *ε* are the logs of output, money, the price level, and the exchange rate, respectively; *i* is the nominal interest rate; and $\dot{p}$ is inflation. All variables are expressed as deviations from their usual values; p^* and i^* are normalized to 0, and are therefore omitted. The main changes from our usual model are that price adjustment takes a particularly simple form and that the equations are linear. *h*, *k*, *b*, *a*, and θ are all positive.

Assume that initially $y = i = \dot{p} = m = p = 0$. Now suppose that there is a permanent increase in *m*.

(a) Show that once prices have adjusted fully (so $\dot{p} = 0$), $y = i = 0$ and $p = \varepsilon = m$.

(b) Show that there are parameter values such that at the time of the increase in *m*, *ε* jumps immediately to exactly *m* and then remains constant, so that there is neither overshooting nor undershooting.[29]

---

[29] The result that there are parameter values such that the exchange rate neither

5.11. Consider the model of aggregate demand in an open economy with imperfect capital mobility in Section 5.2, without the simplification assumed in equation (5.22). In addition to our usual assumptions, assume $NX_{\varepsilon P*/P} \geq E_{\varepsilon P*/P}$, $NX_{i-\pi^e} \geq 0$, $NX_Y \leq 0$, and $E_Y - NX_Y < 1$.

(a) Derive an expression for the slope of the IS^{**} curve (that is, the combinations of i and Y associated with the (i, Y, ε) combinations that solve [5.12] and [5.21]).

(b) Does ε rise, fall, or remain constant as we move down the IS^{**} curve?

(c) Is it still true that greater capital mobility (that is, a larger value of $CF'(\bullet)$) makes the IS^{**} curve flatter?

5.12. The analysis of Case 1 in Section 5.3 assumes that employment is determined by labor demand. A more realistic assumption may be that employment at a given real wage equals the minimum of demand and supply; this is known as the *short-side rule*.

(a) Draw diagrams showing the situation in the labor market under this assumption when

   (i) P is at the level that generates the maximum possible output.

   (ii) P is above the level that generates the maximum possible output.

(b) With this assumption, what does the aggregate supply curve look like?

5.13. Consider the model of aggregate supply in Case 2 of Section 5.3. Suppose that aggregate demand at $\overline{P}$ equals Y^{MAX}. Show the resulting situation in the labor market.

5.14. Suppose that the production function is $Y = AF(L)$ (where $F'(\bullet) > 0$, $F''(\bullet) < 0$, and $A > 0$), and that A falls. How does this negative technology shock affect the AS curve under each of the models of aggregate supply in Section 5.3?

5.15. **Destabilizing price flexibility.** (De Long and Summers, 1986b.) Consider the following closed-economy variant of the model in Problem 5.10: $y = -a(i - \dot{p})$, $m - p = -ki$, $\dot{p} = \theta y$. Assume $a > 0$, $k > 0$, $\theta > 0$, and $a\theta < 1$.

(a) Assume that initially $y = i = \dot{p} = m = p = 0$. Now suppose that at some time, time 0 for convenience, there is a permanent drop in m to some lower level, m'.

   (i) What are the values of y and i at time 0? (Note that p cannot jump at the time of the change.) How does an increase in θ, the speed of price adjustment, affect $y(0)$? Explain intuitively.

   (ii) What is the path of y after time 0?

(b) Suppose we measure the total amount of output volatility caused by the change in m as $V = \int_{t=0}^{\infty} y(t)^2\, dt$. How is V affected by an increase in the speed of price adjustment, θ?

---

overshoots nor undershoots in response to a monetary disturbance implies that, except in unusual cases, there are perturbations of these parameter values that lead to each result. Showing this is complicated, however, and is therefore omitted.

5.16. Redo the regression reported in equation (5.40):

   (*a*) Incorporating more recent data.

   (*b*) Incorporating more recent data, and using $M1$ rather than $M2$.

   (*c*) Including eight lags of the change in log money rather than four.

Chapter **6**
MICROECONOMIC FOUNDATIONS OF INCOMPLETE NOMINAL ADJUSTMENT

The sluggish adjustment of nominal wages and prices is central to Keynesian models. Investigating the microeconomic foundations of that sluggish adjustment is necessary for making the models fully specified, for doing welfare analysis, and for considering alternative policies. To give one example, some critics of traditional Keynesian models argue that the models' assumptions about price stickiness are inconsistent with any reasonable model of microeconomic behavior; they therefore conclude that microeconomic theory provides a strong case against the models' relevance. More generally, if the conditions needed for nominal stickiness appear implausible or inconsistent with microeconomic evidence, this would suggest that gradual nominal adjustment is unlikely to be important. If the needed conditions appear realistic, on the other hand, this would support the importance of nominal stickiness.

A more important example of the relevance of the microeconomic foundations of incomplete nominal adjustment is that the nature of that incomplete adjustment matters for policy. We will see that if monetary shocks have real effects for the reasons described by the Lucas imperfect-information model (which is presented in Part A of the chapter), systematic feedback rules from economic developments to monetary policy have no effect on the real economy. Similarly, if nominal prices and wages are fully flexible, monetary policy is irrelevant to real variables. At the other extreme, if there is a stable relationship between output and inflation, then (as we saw in Chapter 5) monetary policy can raise output permanently. And as we will see, the nature of incomplete nominal adjustment also has implications for such issues as the output costs of alternative approaches to reducing inflation, the output-inflation relationship under different conditions, and the impact of stabilization policy on average output.

It is important to emphasize that the issue we are interested in is incomplete adjustment of *nominal* prices and wages. There are many reasons—involving uncertainty, information and renegotiation costs, incentives, and so on—why prices and wages may not adjust freely to equate supply and demand, or that firms may not change their prices and wages completely and immediately in response to shocks. But simply introducing some departure from perfect markets is not enough to imply that nominal disturbances matter. All the models of unemployment in Chapter 9, for example, are real models. If one appends a monetary sector to those models without any further complications, the classical dichotomy continues to hold: monetary disturbances cause all nominal prices and wages to change, leaving the real equilibrium (with whatever non-Walrasian features it involves) unchanged. Any microeconomic basis for failure of the classical dichotomy requires some kind of *nominal* imperfection.

The models that follow examine three candidate nominal imperfections. In the model of Part A, which is based on the work of Lucas (1972) and Phelps (1970), the nominal imperfection is that producers do not observe the aggregate price level; as a result, they make their production decisions without full knowledge of the relative prices they will receive for their goods. In the models of staggered adjustment in Part B, monetary shocks have real effects because not all prices or wages are adjusted simultaneously. Finally, in Part C, the real effects of monetary changes stem from small costs of changing nominal prices or wages or from some other small friction in nominal adjustment.

Part A   The Lucas Imperfect-Information Model

The central idea of the Lucas–Phelps model is that when a producer observes a change in the price of his or her product, he or she does not know whether it reflects a change in the good's relative price or a change in the aggregate price level. A change in the relative price alters the optimal amount to produce. A change in the aggregate price level, on the other hand, leaves optimal production unchanged.

When the price of the producer's good increases, there is some chance that the increase reflects a rise in the price level, and some chance that it reflects a rise in the good's relative price. The rational response for the producer is to attribute part of the change to an increase in the price level and part to an increase in the relative price, and therefore to increase output somewhat. This implies that the aggregate supply curve slopes up: when the aggregate price level rises, all producers see increases in the prices of their goods, and (not knowing that the increases reflect a rise in the price level) thus raise their output.

The next two sections develop this idea in a model where individuals produce goods using their own labor, sell their output in competitive markets, and use the proceeds to buy other producers' output. The model has two types of shocks. First, there are random shifts in preferences that change the relative demands for different goods. These shocks lead to changes in relative prices and in the relative production of different goods. Second, there are disturbances to the money supply, or more generally, to aggregate demand. When these shocks are observed, they change only the aggregate price level and have no real effects. But when they are unobserved, they change both the price level and aggregate output.

As a preliminary, Section 6.1 considers the case where the money stock is publicly observed; in this situation, money is neutral. Section 6.2 then turns to the case where the money stock is not observed.

6.1   The Case of Perfect Information

Producer Behavior

There are many different goods in the economy. Consider a representative producer of a typical good, good i. The individual's production function is simply

$$Q_i = L_i, \tag{6.1}$$

where L_i is the amount that the individual works and Q_i the amount he or she produces. The individual's consumption, C_i, equals his or her real income; this equals revenue, $P_i Q_i$, divided by the price of the market basket of goods, P. P is an index of the prices of all goods (see equation [6.9], below).

Utility depends positively on consumption and negatively on the amount worked. For simplicity, it takes the form

$$U_i = C_i - \frac{1}{\gamma} L_i^\gamma, \qquad \gamma > 1. \tag{6.2}$$

Thus there is constant marginal utility of consumption and increasing marginal disutility of work.

When the aggregate price level P is known, the individual's maximization problem is simple. Substituting $C_i = P_i Q_i / P$ and $Q_i = L_i$ into (6.2), we can rewrite utility as

$$U_i = \frac{P_i L_i}{P} - \frac{1}{\gamma} L_i^\gamma. \tag{6.3}$$

Since markets are assumed to be competitive, the individual chooses L_i to maximize utility taking P_i and P as given. The first-order condition is

$$\frac{P_i}{P} - L_i^{\gamma-1} = 0, \tag{6.4}$$

or

$$L_i = \left(\frac{P_i}{P}\right)^{1/(\gamma-1)}. \tag{6.5}$$

Letting lowercase letters denote the logarithms of the corresponding upper-case variables, we can rewrite this condition as

$$\ell_i = \frac{1}{\gamma-1}(p_i - p). \tag{6.6}$$

Thus the individual's labor supply and production are increasing in the relative price of his or her product.

Demand

Producers' behavior determines the supply curves of the various goods. Determining the equilibrium in each market requires specifying the demand curves as well. The demand for a given good is assumed to depend on three factors: real income, the good's relative price, and a random disturbance to preferences. For tractability, demand is log-linear. Specifically, the demand for good i is

$$q_i = y + z_i - \eta(p_i - p), \qquad \eta > 0, \tag{6.7}$$

where y is log aggregate real income, z_i is the shock to the demand for good i, and η is the elasticity of demand for each good. q_i is the demand per producer of good i.[1] The z_i's have a mean of 0 across goods; thus they are purely relative demand shocks. y is assumed to equal the average across goods of the q_i's, and p is the average of the p_i's:

$$y = \overline{q}_i, \tag{6.8}$$

$$p = \overline{p}_i. \tag{6.9}$$

Intuitively, (6.7)–(6.9) state that the demand for a good is higher when total production (and thus total income) is higher, when its price is low relative to other prices, and when individuals have stronger preferences for it.[2]

---

[1] That is, the total (log) demand for good i is $\ln N + y + z_i - \eta(p_i - p)$, where N is the number of producers of each good.

[2] Although (6.7)–(6.9) are intuitive, deriving these exact functional forms from individuals' preferences over the various goods requires some approximations. The difficulty is that if preferences are such that demand for each good takes the constant-elasticity form in (6.7), the corresponding (log) price index is exactly equal to the average of the individual p_i's only in the special case of $\eta = 1$. See Problem 6.2. This issue has no effect on the basic messages of the model.

Finally, the aggregate demand side of the model is

$$y = m - p. \tag{6.10}$$

There are various interpretations of (6.10). The simplest, and most appropriate for our purposes, is that it is just a shortcut approach to modeling aggregate demand. Equation (6.10) implies an inverse relationship between the price level and output, which is the essential feature of aggregate demand. Since our focus is on aggregate supply, there is little point in modeling aggregate demand more fully. Under this interpretation, M should be thought of as a generic variable affecting aggregate demand rather than as money.

It is also possible to derive (6.10) from models with more complete monetary specifications. Blanchard and Kiyotaki (1987), for example, replace C_i in the utility function, (6.2), with a Cobb–Douglas combination of C_i and the individual's real money balances, M_i/P. With an appropriate specification of how money enters the budget constraint, this gives rise to (6.10). Rotemberg (1987) derives (6.10) from a *cash-in-advance constraint.* Under Blanchard and Kiyotaki's and Rotemberg's interpretations of (6.10), it is natural to think of m as literally money; in this case the right-hand side should be modified to be $m + v - p$, where v captures aggregate demand disturbances other than shifts in money supply.

Equilibrium

Equilibrium in the market for good i requires that demand per producer equal supply. From (6.6) and (6.7), this requires

$$\frac{1}{y-1}(p_i - p) = y + z_i - \eta(p_i - p). \tag{6.11}$$

Solving this expression for p_i yields

$$p_i = \frac{y-1}{1+\eta y - \eta}(y + z_i) + p. \tag{6.12}$$

This expression implies that p, the average of the p_i's, is given by

$$p = \frac{y-1}{1+\eta y - \eta}y + p, \tag{6.13}$$

where we have used the fact that the average of the z_i's is 0. Equation (6.13) implies that the equilibrium value of y is simply[3]

$$y = 0. \tag{6.14}$$

---

[3] The result that equilibrium log output is 0 implies that the equilibrium *level* of output is 1. This results from the $1/\gamma$ term multiplying L_i^γ in the utility function, (6.2).

Finally, (6.14) and (6.10) imply

$$p = m. \tag{6.15}$$

Not surprisingly, money is neutral in this version of the model: an increase in m leads to an equal increase in all p_i's, and hence in the overall price index, p. No real variables are affected.

6.2   The Case of Imperfect Information

We now consider the more interesting case where producers observe the prices of their own goods but not the aggregate price level.

Producer Behavior

Defining the relative price of good i by $r_i = p_i - p$, we can write

$$\begin{aligned} p_i &= p + (p_i - p) \\ &= p + r_i. \end{aligned} \tag{6.16}$$

Thus, in logs, the variable that the individual observes—the price of his or her good—equals the sum of the aggregate price level and the good's relative price.

The individual would like to base his or her production decision on r_i alone (see [6.6]). The individual does not observe r_i, but must estimate it given the observation of p_i.[4] At this point, Lucas makes two simplifying assumptions. First, he assumes that the individual finds the expectation of r_i given p_i, and then produces as much as he or she would if this estimate were certain. Thus (6.6) becomes

$$\ell_i = \frac{1}{\gamma - 1} E[r_i \mid p_i]. \tag{6.17}$$

As Problem 6.1 shows, this *certainty-equivalence* behavior is not identical to maximizing expected utility: in general, the utility-maximizing choice of ℓ_i depends not just on the individual's estimate of r_i, but also on his or her uncertainty about r_i. The assumption that individuals use certainty equivalence, however, simplifies the analysis and has no effect on the central messages of the model.

Second, and very importantly, Lucas assumes that the producer finds the expectation of r_i given p_i rationally. That is, $E[r_i \mid p_i]$ is assumed to

---

[4] If the individual knew others' prices as a result of making purchases, he or she could deduce p, and hence r_i. This can be ruled out in several ways. One approach is to assume that the household consists of two individuals, a "producer" and a "shopper," and that communication between them is limited. In Lucas's original model, the problem is avoided by assuming an overlapping-generations structure where individuals produce in the first period of their lives and make purchases in the second.

be the true expectation of r_i given p_i and given the actual joint distribution of the two variables. Today, this assumption of *rational expectations* seems no more peculiar than the assumption that individuals maximize utility. When Lucas introduced Muth's (1960, 1961) idea of rational expectations into macroeconomics, however, it was highly controversial. As we will see, it is one source—but by no means the only one—of the strong implications of Lucas's model.

To make the computation of $E[r_i \mid p_i]$ tractable, the monetary shock (m) and the shocks to the demands for the individual goods (the z_i's) are assumed to be normally distributed. m has a mean of $E[m]$ and a variance of V_m. The z_i's have a mean of 0 and a variance of V_z, and are independent of m. We will see that these assumptions imply that p and r_i are normal and independent. Since p_i equals $p + r_i$, this means that it is also normal; its mean is the sum of the means of p and r_i, and its variance is the sum of their variances. As we will see, the means of p and $r_i, E[p]$ and $E[r]$, are equal to $E[m]$ and 0, respectively; and their variances, V_p and V_r, are complicated functions of V_m and V_z and of the other parameters of the model.

The individual's problem is to find the expectation of r_i given p_i. An important result in statistics is that when two variables are jointly normally distributed (as with r_i and p_i here), the expectation of one is a linear function of the observation of the other. Thus $E[r_i \mid p_i]$ takes the form

$$E[r_i \mid p_i] = \alpha + \beta p_i. \tag{6.18}$$

In this particular case, where p_i equals r_i plus an independent variable, (6.18) takes the specific form

$$
\begin{aligned}
E[r_i \mid p_i] &= -\frac{V_r}{V_r + V_p} E[p] + \frac{V_r}{V_r + V_p} p_i \\
&= \frac{V_r}{V_r + V_p} (p_i - E[p]).
\end{aligned}
\tag{6.19}
$$

Equation (6.19) is intuitive. First, it implies that if p_i equals its mean, then the expectation of r_i equals its mean (which is 0). Second, it states that the expectation of r_i exceeds its mean if p_i exceeds its mean, and is less than its mean if p_i is less than its mean. Third, it tells us that the fraction of the departure of p_i from its mean that is estimated to be due to the departure of r_i from its mean is $V_r/(V_r + V_p)$; this is the fraction of the overall variance of p_i ($V_r + V_p$) that is due to the variance of r_i (V_r). If, for example, V_p is 0, all the variation in p_i is due to r_i, and so $E[r_i \mid p_i]$ is $p_i - E[p]$. If V_r and V_p are equal, half of the variance in p_i is due to r_i, and so $E[r_i \mid p_i] = (p_i - E[p])/2$. And so on.[5]

---

[5] This conditional-expectations problem is referred to as *signal extraction*. The variable that the individual observes, p_i, equals the *signal*, r_i, plus *noise*, p. Equation (6.19) shows how the individual can best extract an estimate of the signal from the observation of p_i. The ratio of V_r to V_p is referred to as the *signal-to-noise ratio*.

Substituting (6.19) into (6.17) yields the individual's labor supply:

$$\ell_i = \frac{1}{y-1}\frac{V_r}{V_r + V_p}(p_i - E[p])$$

$$\equiv b(p_i - E[p]).$$

(6.20)

Averaging (6.20) across producers (and using the definitions of y and p) gives us an expression for overall output:

$$y = b(p - E[p]).$$

(6.21)

Equation (6.21) is the *Lucas supply curve.* It states that the departure of output from its normal level (which is zero in the model) is an increasing function of the surprise in the price level.

The Lucas supply curve is essentially the same as the expectations-augmented Phillips curve of Chapter 5 with core inflation replaced by expected inflation (see equation [5.38]). Both state that if we neglect disturbances to supply, output is above normal only to the extent that inflation (and hence the price level) is greater than expected. Thus the Lucas model provides microeconomic foundations for this view of aggregate supply.

Equilibrium

Combining the Lucas supply curve, (6.21), with the aggregate demand equation, $y = m - p$ (equation [6.10]), and solving for p and y yields

$$p = \frac{1}{1+b}m + \frac{b}{1+b}E[p],$$

(6.22)

$$y = \frac{b}{1+b}m - \frac{b}{1+b}E[p].$$

(6.23)

We can use (6.22) to find $E[p]$. Ex post, after m is determined, the two sides of (6.22) are equal. Thus it must be that ex ante, before m is determined, the *expectations* of the two sides are equal. Taking the expectations of both sides of (6.22), we obtain

$$E[p] = \frac{1}{1+b}E[m] + \frac{b}{1+b}E[p],$$

(6.24)

or

$$E[p] = E[m].$$

(6.25)

Using (6.25) and the fact that $m = E[m] + (m - E[m])$, we can rewrite (6.22) and (6.23) as

$$p = E[m] + \frac{1}{1+b}(m - E[m]),$$

(6.26)

$$y = \frac{b}{1+b}(m - E[m]).$$

(6.27)

Equations (6.26) and (6.27) show the key implications of the model: the component of aggregate demand that is observed, $E[m]$, affects only prices, but the component that is not observed, $m - E[m]$, has real effects. Consider, for concreteness, an unobserved increase in m—that is, a higher realization of m given its distribution. This increase in the money supply raises aggregate demand, and thus produces an outward shift in the demand curve for each good. Since the increase is not observed, each supplier's best guess is that some portion of the rise in the demand for his or her product reflects a relative price shock. Thus producers increase their output.

The effects of an observed increase in m are very different. Specifically, consider the effects of an upward shift in the entire distribution of m, with the realization of $m - E[m]$ held fixed. In this case, each supplier attributes the rise in the demand for his or her product to money, and thus does not change his or her output. Of course, the taste shocks cause variations in relative prices and in output across goods (just as they do in the case of an unobserved shock), but on average real output does not rise. Thus observed changes in aggregate demand affect only prices.

To complete the model, we must express b in terms of underlying parameters rather than in terms of the variances of p and r_i. Recall that $b = [1/(y - 1)][V_r/(V_r + V_p)]$ (see [6.20]). Equation (6.26) implies $V_p = V_m/(1 + b)^2$. The demand curve, (6.7), and the supply curve, (6.21), can be used to find V_r, the variance of $p_i - p$. Specifically, we can substitute $y = b(p - E[p])$ into (6.7) to obtain $q_i = b(p - E[p]) + z_i - \eta(p_i - p)$, and we can rewrite (6.20) as $\ell_i = b(p_i - p) + b(p - E[p])$. Solving these two equations for $p_i - p$ then yields $p_i - p = z_i/(\eta + b)$. Thus $V_r = V_z/(\eta + b)^2$.

Substituting the expressions for V_p and V_r into the definition of b (see [6.20]) yields

$$b = \frac{1}{y - 1}\left[\frac{V_z}{V_z + \dfrac{(\eta + b)^2}{(1 + b)^2}V_m}\right]. \tag{6.28}$$

Equation (6.28) implicitly defines b in terms of V_z, V_m, and y, and thus completes the model. It is straightforward to show that b is increasing in V_z and decreasing in V_m. In the special case of $\eta = 1$, we can obtain a closed-form expression for b:

$$b = \frac{1}{y - 1}\frac{V_z}{V_z + V_m}. \tag{6.29}$$

Finally, note that the results that $p = E[m] + [1/(1 + b)](m - E[m])$ and $r_i = z_i/(\eta + b)$ imply that p and r_i are linear functions of m and z_i. Since m and z_i are independent, p and r_i are independent; and since linear functions of normal variables are normal, p and r_i are normal. This confirms the assumptions made above about these variables.

6.3   Implications and Limitations

The Phillips Curve and the Lucas Critique

Lucas's model implies that unexpectedly high realizations of aggregate demand lead to both higher output and higher-than-expected prices. As a result, for reasonable specifications of the behavior of aggregate demand, the model implies a positive association between output and inflation. Suppose, for example, that m is a random walk with drift:

$$m_t = m_{t-1} + c + u_t, \tag{6.30}$$

where u is white noise. This specification implies that the expectation of m_t is $m_{t-1} + c$ and that the unobserved component of m_t is u_t. Thus, from (6.26) and (6.27),

$$p_t = m_{t-1} + c + \frac{1}{1+b}u_t, \tag{6.31}$$

$$y_t = \frac{b}{1+b}u_t. \tag{6.32}$$

Equation (6.31) implies that $p_{t-1} = m_{t-2} + c + [u_{t-1}/(1+b)]$. The rate of inflation (measured as the change in the log price level) is thus

$$\pi_t = (m_{t-1} - m_{t-2}) + \frac{1}{1+b}u_t - \frac{1}{1+b}u_{t-1}$$

$$= c + \frac{b}{1+b}u_{t-1} + \frac{1}{1+b}u_t. \tag{6.33}$$

Note that u_t appears in both (6.32) and (6.33) with a positive sign, and that u_t and u_{t-1} are uncorrelated. These facts imply that output and inflation are positively correlated. Intuitively, high unexpected money growth leads, through the Lucas supply curve, to increases in both prices and output. The model therefore implies a positive relationship between output and inflation—a Phillips curve.

But although there is a statistical output-inflation relationship, there is no exploitable tradeoff between high output and low inflation. Suppose that policymakers decide to raise average money growth (for example, by raising c in equation [6.30]). If the change is not publicly known, there is an interval when unobserved money growth is typically positive, and output is therefore usually above normal. Once individuals determine that the change has occurred, however, unobserved money growth is again on average zero, and so average real output is unchanged. And if the increase in average money growth is known, expected money growth jumps immediately and there is not even a brief interval of high output. The idea that the statistical relationship between output and inflation may change if policymakers attempt to take advantage of it is not just a theoretical curiosity: as we saw in Chapter 5, when average inflation rose in the late 1960s and early 1970s, the traditional output-inflation relationship collapsed.

The central idea underlying this analysis is of wider relevance. Expectations are likely to be important to many relationships among aggregate variables, and changes in policy are likely to affect those expectations. As a result, shifts in policy can change aggregate relationships. In short, if policymakers attempt to take advantage of statistical relationships, effects operating through expectations may cause the relationships to break down. This is the famous *Lucas critique* (Lucas, 1976).

The Phillips curve is the most famous application of the Lucas critique. Another example is temporary changes in taxes. There is a close relationship between disposable income and consumption spending. Yet to some extent this relationship arises not because current disposable income determines current spending, but because current income is strongly correlated with *permanent* income (see Chapter 7)—that is, it is highly correlated with households' expectations of their disposable incomes in the future. If policymakers attempt to reduce consumption through a tax increase that is known to be temporary, the relationship between current income and expected future income, and hence the relationship between current income and spending, will change. Again this is not just a theoretical possibility. The United States enacted a temporary tax surcharge in 1968, and the impact on consumption was considerably smaller than was expected on the basis of the statistical relationship between disposable income and spending (see, for example, Dolde, 1979).

Anticipated and Unanticipated Money

The result that only unobserved aggregate demand shocks have real effects has a strong implication: monetary policy can stabilize output only if policymakers have information that is not available to private agents. Any portion of policy that is a response to publicly available information—such as interest rates, the unemployment rate, or the index of leading indicators—is irrelevant to the real economy (Sargent and Wallace, 1975; Barro, 1976).

To see this, let aggregate demand, m, equal $m^* + v$, where m^* is a policy variable and v a disturbance outside the government's control. If the government does not pursue activist policy but simply keeps m^* constant (or growing at a steady rate), the unobserved shock to aggregate demand in some period is the realization of v less the expectation of v given the information available to private agents. If m^* is instead a function of public information, individuals can deduce m^*, and so the situation is unchanged. Thus systematic policy rules cannot stabilize output.

If the government observes variables correlated with v that are not known to the public, it can use this information to stabilize output: it can change m^* to offset the movements in v that it expects on the basis of its

private information. But this is not an appealing defense of Keynesian stabilization policy, for two reasons. First, a central element of conventional
stabilization policy involves reactions to general, publicly available information that the economy is in a boom or a recession. Second, if superior
information is the basis for potential stabilization, there is a much easier
way for the government to accomplish that stabilization than following a
complex policy rule: it can simply announce the information that the public
does not have.[6]

Ball (1991), building on the work of Sargent (1983), argues that the Lucas
model's predictions concerning observed policy can be tested by looking at
times of announced shifts to tighter monetary policy to combat inflation.
The Lucas model predicts that there should be no systematic relationship
between real variables and any publicly known information about monetary policy. Thus it implies that output growth should not be on average
different from normal following such announcements. But Ball argues that
when policymakers do not carry through with the announced policy, inflation typically changes little and output growth generally remains about
normal, and that when they do carry through, inflation typically declines
and output growth usually falls below normal. Thus, he concludes, output
growth is on average below normal following the announcements, which is
not consistent with Lucas's model.

Empirical Application: International Evidence on Output-Inflation Tradeoffs

In the Lucas model, suppliers' responses to changes in prices are determined
by the relative importance of aggregate and idiosyncratic shocks. If aggregate shocks are large, for example, suppliers attribute most of the changes
in the prices of their goods to changes in the price level, and so they alter their production relatively little in response to variations in prices (see
[6.20]). The Lucas model therefore predicts that the real effect of a given
aggregate demand shock is smaller in an economy where the variance of
those shocks is larger.

---

[6] A large literature, pioneered by Barro (1977a, 1978) and significantly extended by
Mishkin (1982, 1983), tests Lucas's predictions concerning the impacts of observed and
unobserved monetary policy using the money stock as the measure of policy. In Barro's formulation, the basic idea is to regress output on measures of forecastable and unforecastable
money growth and a set of control variables. Unfortunately, these tests suffer from the same
difficulties as regressions of money on output (see Section 5.5). For example, a positive correlation between unexpected changes in the money stock and output movements can reflect
an impact of output on money demand rather than an impact of money on output. Similarly, the absence of an association between predictable movements in money and changes
in output can arise not because observed monetary changes have no real effects, but because
the Federal Reserve is adjusting the money supply to offset the impact of other factors on
output. See also Problem 6.3.

To test this prediction, one must find a measure of aggregate demand shocks. Lucas (1973) uses the change in the log of nominal GDP. For this to be precisely correct, two conditions must be satisfied. First, the aggregate demand curve must be unit-elastic; in this case, changes in aggregate supply affect P and Y but not their product, and so nominal GDP is determined entirely by aggregate demand. Second, the change in log nominal GDP must not be predictable or observable; that is, letting x denote log nominal GDP, Δx must take the form $a + u_t$, where u_t is white noise. With this process, the change in log nominal GDP (relative to its average change) is also the unobserved change. Although these conditions are surely not satisfied exactly, they may be accurate enough to be reasonable approximations.

Under these assumptions, the real effects of an aggregate demand shock in a given country can be estimated by regressing log real GDP (or the change in log real GDP) on the change in log nominal GDP and control variables. The specification Lucas employs is

$$y_t = c + yt + \tau \, \Delta x_t + \lambda y_{t-1}, \tag{6.34}$$

where y is log real GDP, t is time, and Δx is the change in log nominal GDP.

Lucas estimates (6.34) separately for various countries. He then asks whether the estimated τ's—the estimates of the responsiveness of output to aggregate demand movements—are related to the average size of countries' aggregate demand shocks. A simple way to do this is to estimate

$$\tau_i = \alpha + \beta \sigma_{\Delta x, i}, \tag{6.35}$$

where τ_i is the estimate of the real impact of an aggregate demand shift obtained by estimating (6.34) for country i and $\sigma_{\Delta x, i}$ is the standard deviation of the change in log nominal GDP in country i. Lucas's theory predicts that nominal shocks have smaller real effects in settings where aggregate demand is more volatile, and thus that β is negative.

Lucas employs a relatively small sample. His test has been extended to much larger samples, with various modifications in specification, in several studies. Figure 6.1, from Ball, Mankiw, and D. Romer (1988), is typical of the results. It shows a scatterplot of τ versus $\sigma_{\Delta x}$ for 43 countries. The corresponding regression is

$$\tau_i = \begin{array}{cc} 0.388 & - \quad 1.639 \; \sigma_{\Delta x, i}, \\ (0.057) & (0.482) \end{array} \tag{6.36}$$

$$\overline{R}^2 = 0.201, \quad \text{s.e.e.} = 0.245,$$

where the numbers in parentheses are standard errors. Thus there is a highly statistically significant negative relationship between the variability of nominal GDP growth and the estimated effect of a given change in aggregate demand, just as the model predicts.

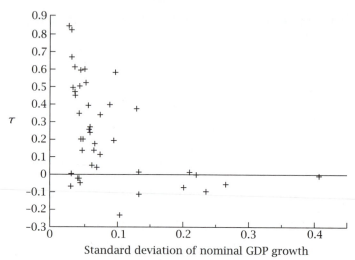

FIGURE 6.1   **The output-inflation tradeoff and the variability of aggregate demand (from Ball, Mankiw, and Romer, 1988)**

Difficulties

If, as suggested above, announced shifts toward disinflationary policies are on average followed by below-normal output growth, then the Lucas model does not provide a complete account of the effects of aggregate demand shifts. The more important question, however, is whether the Lucas model accounts for an important element of the effects of aggregate demand. Two major objections have been raised in this regard.

The first difficulty is that the employment fluctuations in the Lucas model, like those in real-business-cycle models, arise from changes in labor supply in response to changes in the perceived benefits of working. Thus to generate substantial employment fluctuations, the model requires a significant short-run elasticity of labor supply. But, as described in Section 4.10, there is no strong evidence of such a high elasticity.

The second difficulty concerns the assumption of imperfect information. In modern economies, high-quality information about changes in prices is released with only brief lags. Thus, other than in times of hyperinflation, individuals can estimate aggregate price movements with considerable accuracy at little cost. In light of this, it is difficult to see how they can be significantly confused between relative and aggregate price level movements.

These difficulties suggest that the specific mechanisms emphasized in the model may be relatively unimportant to fluctuations, at least in most settings.[7] But we will see in Section 6.9 that there are reasons other than intertemporal substitution that small changes in real wages or relative prices may be associated with large changes in employment and output, and that there are reasons individuals may choose not to take advantage of low-cost opportunities to acquire information relevant to their pricing decisions. Thus, as we will discuss there, it may be possible to resuscitate Lucas's central idea that unexpected monetary shocks may create confusion between relative and aggregate price changes, and thereby have important effects on aggregate output.

Part B   Staggered Price Adjustment

The next source of nominal imperfections we consider is staggered adjustment of wages or prices. In one important respect, models of staggered adjustment are a reversion to traditional Keynesian models: sluggish nominal adjustment is assumed rather than derived. But the models are nonetheless important to the microeconomic foundations of nominal price and wage rigidity. There are three reasons.

First (and least important for our purposes), the Lucas model was initially perceived as showing that rational expectations alone are enough to undo many of the central results of traditional Keynesian theory, most notably the stabilizing powers of aggregate demand policy. If this were right, defending the traditional Keynesian position would require demonstrating that expectations are systematically irrational. Models of staggered adjustment show that this is unnecessary: if not all prices or wages are free to change every period, aggregate demand policy can be stabilizing even under rational expectations.

Second, the models make assumptions about imperfect adjustment at the level of individual price- or wage-setters and then aggregate individual behavior to find the implications for the macroeconomy. In that regard,

---

[7] In addition, the model implies that departures of output from the flexible-price level are not at all persistent. y depends only on $m - E[m]$. And by definition, $m - E[m]$ cannot have any predictable component. Thus the model implies that y is white noise—that is, that it displays no pattern of either positive or negative correlation over time. This does not appear to be a good description of actual economies. A monetary contraction, such as the Federal Reserve's decision in 1979 to disinflate, leads to abnormally low output over an extended time, not to a single period of low output followed by an immediate return to normal.

This difficulty can be addressed by introducing some reason that the economy's initial response to an unobserved monetary shock triggers dynamics that cause output to remain away from normal even after the shock has become known. Examples of such mechanisms include inventory dynamics (Blinder and Fischer, 1981), capital accumulation (Lucas, 1975), and one-time costs of recruiting and training new workers. Thus the prediction of white-noise output movements is an artifact of the simple form of the model we have been considering, and not a robust implication.

the models lay the groundwork for the models of the next section, where nominal rigidity is derived from optimizing behavior at the microeconomic level.

Finally, the models show that interactions among price-setters can either magnify or dampen the effects of barriers to price adjustment. A consistent theme of the results in this section is that macroeconomic nominal rigidity is not related in any simple way to microeconomic price rigidity. We will see cases where a small amount of microeconomic rigidity leads to a large amount of rigidity in the aggregate, and others where a large amount of microeconomic rigidity yields little or no rigidity in the aggregate.

We consider three models of staggered price adjustment: the Fischer, or Fischer–Phelps–Taylor, model (Fischer, 1977a; Phelps and Taylor, 1977); the Taylor model (Taylor, 1979, 1980); and the Caplin–Spulber model (Caplin and Spulber, 1987).[8] The first two, the Fischer and Taylor models, posit that wages or prices are set by multiperiod contracts or commitments. In each period, the contracts governing some fraction of wages or prices expire and must be renewed. The central result of the models is that multiperiod contracts lead to gradual adjustment of the price level to nominal disturbances. As a result, aggregate demand disturbances have real effects, and policy rules can be stabilizing even under rational expectations.

The Fischer and Taylor models differ in one important respect. The Fischer model assumes that prices (or wages) are *predetermined* but not *fixed.* That is, when a multiperiod contract sets prices for several periods, it can specify a *different* price for each period. In the Taylor model, in contrast, prices are fixed: a contract must specify the *same* price each period it is in effect. This distinction proves to be important.

In both the Fischer and Taylor models, the length of time that a price is in effect is determined when the price is set. Thus price adjustment is *time-dependent.* The Caplin–Spulber model provides a simple example of a model of *state-dependent* pricing. Under state-dependent pricing, price changes are triggered not by the passage of time, but by developments within the economy. As a result, the fraction of prices that change in a given time interval is endogenous. Once again, this seemingly modest change in assumptions has important consequences.[9]

---

[8] An important earlier paper is Akerlof (1969). See also Phelps (1978) and Blanchard (1983).

[9] All three models take the staggering of price changes as given. But at least for the Fischer and Taylor models, if the timing of price changes is made endogenous, the result is synchronized rather than staggered adjustment (see Problem 6.8). Staggering can arise endogenously from firms' desire to acquire information by observing other firms' prices before setting their own (Ball and Cecchetti, 1988), from firm-specific shocks (Ball and D. Romer, 1989; Caballero and Engel, 1991), and from strategic interactions among firms (Maskin and Tirole, 1988).

6.4 A Model of Imperfect Competition and Price-Setting

Before turning to staggered adjustment, we first examine an economy of imperfectly competitive price-setters with complete price flexibility. There are two reasons for analyzing this model. First, as we will see, imperfect competition alone has interesting macroeconomic consequences. Second, the models in the rest of the chapter are concerned with the causes and effects of barriers to price adjustment. To address these issues, we will need a model that shows us what prices firms would choose in the absence of barriers to adjustment and what happens when prices depart from those levels.

Assumptions

The model is a variant on the model described in Part A of this chapter. The economy consists of a large number of individuals. Each one sets the price of some good and is the sole producer of that good. As in Part A, labor is the only input into production. But individuals do not produce their own goods directly; instead there is a competitive labor market where they can both sell their labor and hire workers.[10]

As before, the demand for each good is log-linear; for simplicity, the shocks to the demands for the individual goods (the z_i's) are absent. Thus, $q_i = y - \eta(p_i - p)$ (see [6.7]). p is the (log) price level; as in Part A, it is the average of the p_i's. To ensure that a profit-maximizing price exists, η is assumed to be greater than 1. Sellers with market power set price above marginal cost; thus if they cannot adjust their prices, they are willing to produce to satisfy demand in the face of small fluctuations in demand. In the remainder of the chapter, sellers are therefore assumed not to ration customers.

As in the Lucas model, the utility of a typical individual is $U_i = C_i - L_i^\gamma/\gamma$ (see [6.2]); again C_i is the individual's income divided by the price index, and L_i is the amount that he or she works. The production function is the same as before: the output of good i equals the amount of labor used in its production. Individual i's income is the sum of profit income, $(P_i - W)Q_i$, and labor income, WL_i, where Q_i is the output of good i and W is the nominal wage. Thus,

$$U_i = \frac{(P_i - W)Q_i + WL_i}{P} - \frac{1}{\gamma}L_i^\gamma. \tag{6.37}$$

---

[10] The absence of an economy-wide labor market is critical to the Lucas model: with such a market, individuals' observation of the nominal wage would allow them to deduce the money supply, and would thus make nominal shocks neutral. In contrast, assuming a competitive labor market in the current model is not crucial to the results.

Finally, the aggregate demand side of the model is again given by $y = m - p$ (equation [6.10]); y is again the average of the q_i's. In contrast to the Lucas model, the money supply is publicly observed.[11]

Individual Behavior

Converting the demand equation, $q_i = y - \eta(p_i - p)$, from logs to levels yields $Q_i = Y(P_i/P)^{-\eta}$. Substituting this into expression (6.37) gives us

$$U_i = \frac{(P_i - W)Y(P_i/P)^{-\eta} + WL_i}{P} - \frac{1}{\gamma}L_i^\gamma. \tag{6.38}$$

The individual has two choice variables, the price of his or her good (P_i) and the amount he or she works (L_i). The first-order condition for P_i is

$$\frac{Y(P_i/P)^{-\eta} - (P_i - W)\eta Y(P_i/P)^{-\eta-1}(1/P)}{P} = 0. \tag{6.39}$$

Multiplying this expression by $(P_i/P)^{\eta+1}P$, dividing by Y, and rearranging yields

$$\frac{P_i}{P} = \frac{\eta}{\eta - 1}\frac{W}{P}. \tag{6.40}$$

That is, we get the standard result that a producer with market power sets price as a markup over marginal cost, with the size of the markup determined by the elasticity of demand.

Now consider labor supply. From (6.38), the first-order condition for L_i is

$$\frac{W}{P} - L_i^{\gamma-1} = 0, \tag{6.41}$$

or

$$L_i = \left(\frac{W}{P}\right)^{1/(\gamma-1)}. \tag{6.42}$$

Thus labor supply is an increasing function of the real wage; the elasticity is $1/(\gamma - 1)$.

Equilibrium

Because of the symmetry of the model, in equilibrium each individual works the same amount and produces the same amount. Equilibrium output is

---

[11] As described in n. 2 and Problem 6.2, when individuals' preferences over the different goods give rise to the assumed constant-elasticity demand curves for each product, the appropriate (log) price and output indexes are not exactly equal to the averages of the p_i's and the q_i's. Problem 6.4 shows, however, that the results of this section are unchanged when the exact indexes are used.

thus equal to the common level of labor supply. We can therefore use (6.41) or (6.42) to express the real wage as a function of output:

$$\frac{W}{P} = Y^{\gamma-1}.$$ (6.43)

Substituting this expression into the price equation, (6.40), yields an expression for each producer's desired relative price as a function of aggregate output:

$$\frac{P_i^*}{P} = \frac{\eta}{\eta-1} Y^{\gamma-1}.$$ (6.44)

For future reference, it is useful to write this expression in logarithms:

$$p_i^* - p = \ln\frac{\eta}{\eta-1} + (\gamma-1)y$$

$$\equiv c + \phi y.$$ (6.45)

Since producers are symmetric, each charges the same price. The price index, P, therefore equals this common price. Equilibrium therefore requires that each producer, taking P as given, sets his or her own price equal to P; that is, each producer's desired relative price must equal 1. From (6.44), this condition is $[\eta/(\eta-1)]Y^{\gamma-1} = 1$, or

$$Y = \left(\frac{\eta-1}{\eta}\right)^{1/(\gamma-1)}.$$ (6.46)

This is the equilibrium level of output.

Finally, we can use the aggregate demand equation, $Y = M/P$, to find the equilibrium price level:

$$P = \frac{M}{Y}$$

$$= \frac{M}{\left(\dfrac{\eta-1}{\eta}\right)^{1/(\gamma-1)}}.$$ (6.47)

Implications

When producers have market power, they produce less than the socially optimal amount. To see this, note that in a symmetric allocation each individual supplies some amount $\bar{L}$ of labor, and production of each good and each individual's consumption are equal to that $\bar{L}$. Thus the problem of finding the best symmetric allocation reduces to choosing $\bar{L}$ to maximize $\bar{L} - (1/\gamma)\bar{L}^{\gamma}$. The solution is simply $\bar{L} = 1$. As (6.46) shows, equilibrium output is less than this. Intuitively, the fact that producers face downward-sloping demand curves means that the marginal revenue product of labor is less than its marginal product. As a result, the real wage is less than the marginal product of labor: from (6.40) (and the fact that each P_i equals P in equilibrium), the real wage is $(\eta - 1)/\eta$; the marginal product of labor, in contrast, is 1. This reduces the quantity of labor supplied, and thus causes equilibrium output to be less than optimal. From (6.46), equilibrium output is $[(\eta - 1)/\eta]^{1/(\gamma-1)}$; thus the gap between the equilibrium and optimal levels of output is greater when producers have more market power (that is, when η is lower) and when labor supply is more responsive to the real wage (that is, when γ is lower).

The fact that equilibrium output is inefficiently low under imperfect competition has important implications for fluctuations. To begin with, it implies that recessions and booms have asymmetric effects on welfare (Mankiw, 1985). In practice, periods when output is unusually high are viewed as good times, and periods when output is unusually low are viewed as bad times. Now consider a model where fluctuations arise from incomplete nominal adjustment in the face of monetary shocks. If the equilibrium in the absence of shocks is optimal, both times of high output and times of low output are departures from the optimum, and thus both are undesirable. But if equilibrium output is less than optimal, a boom brings output closer to the social optimum, whereas a recession pushes it farther away.

In addition, the gap between equilibrium and optimal output implies that pricing decisions have externalities. Suppose that the economy is initially in equilibrium, and consider the effects of a marginal reduction in all prices. M/P rises, and so aggregate output rises. This affects the representative individual through two channels. First, the prevailing real wage rises (see [6.43]). But since initially the individual is neither a net purchaser nor a net supplier of labor, at the margin the increase does not affect his or her welfare. Second, because aggregate output increases, the demand curve for the individual's good, $Y(P_i/P)^{-\eta}$, shifts out. Since the individual is selling at a price that exceeds marginal cost, this change raises his or her welfare. Thus under imperfect competition, pricing decisions have externalities, and those externalities operate through the overall demand for goods. This externality is often referred to as an *aggregate demand externality* (Blanchard and Kiyotaki, 1987).

The final implication of this analysis is that imperfect competition alone does not imply monetary nonneutrality. A change in the money stock leads to proportional changes in the nominal wage and all nominal prices; output and the real wage are unchanged (see [6.46] and [6.47]).

Finally, since a pricing equation of the form (6.45) is important in later sections, it is worth noting that the basic idea captured by the equation is much more general than the specific model of price-setters' desired prices we are considering here. Equation (6.45) states that $p_i^* - p$ takes the form $c + \phi y$; that is, it states that a price-setter's optimal relative price is increasing in aggregate output. In the particular model we are considering, this arises from increases in the prevailing real wage when output rises. But in a more general setting, it can also arise from increases in the costs of other inputs, from diminishing returns, or from costs of adjusting output.

The fact that price-setters' desired real prices are increasing in aggregate output is necessary for the flexible-price equilibrium to be stable. To see this, note that we can use the fact that $y = m - p$ to rewrite (6.45) as

$$p_i^* = c + (1 - \phi)p + \phi m. \tag{6.48}$$

If ϕ is negative, an increase in the price level raises each price-setter's desired price more than one-for-one. This means that if p is above the level that causes individuals to charge a relative price of 1, each individual wants to charge more than the prevailing price level; and if p is below its equilibrium value, each individual wants to charge less than the prevailing price level. Thus ϕ must be positive for the flexible-price equilibrium to be stable.

6.5 Predetermined Prices

Framework and Assumptions

We now turn to the Fischer model of staggered price adjustment. In particular, we consider a variant on the model of the previous section where price-setters cannot set their prices freely each period. Instead, each price-setter sets prices every other period for the next two periods. As emphasized above, the model assumes that the price-setter can set different prices for the two periods. In any given period, half of the individuals are setting their prices for the next two periods. Thus at any point, half of the prices in effect are those set the previous period, and half are those set two periods ago.[12]

For simplicity, we normalize the constant in the equation for price-setters' desired prices, (6.45) (or [6.48]), to 0; thus the desired price of individual i in period t is $p_{it}^* = \phi m_t + (1 - \phi)p_t$. Otherwise the model is the same as that of the previous section. The behavior of m is treated as exogenous; no specific assumptions are made about the process that it follows. Thus, for example, information about m_t may be revealed gradually in the periods leading up to t; the expectation of m_t as of period $t - 1$, $E_{t-1}m_t$, may therefore differ from the expectation of m_t the period before, $E_{t-2}m_t$.

Paralleling our assumption of certainty equivalence in the Lucas model, we assume that an individual choosing his or her prices in period t for the next two periods sets the log prices equal to the expectations, given the

---

[12] The original versions of these models focused on staggered adjustment of wages; prices were in principle flexible but were determined as markups over wages. For simplicity, we assume instead that staggered adjustment applies directly to prices. Staggered wage adjustment has essentially the same implications.

information available through t, of the profit-maximizing log prices in the two periods. As in the Lucas model, price-setters form their expectations rationally.

Solving the Model

In any period, half of prices are ones set in the previous period, and half are ones set two periods ago. Thus the average price is

$$p_t = \tfrac{1}{2}(p_t^1 + p_t^2), \tag{6.49}$$

where p_t^1 denotes the price set for t by individuals who set their prices in $t-1$, and p_t^2 the price set for t by individuals setting prices in $t-2$. Since we have assumed certainty-equivalence pricing behavior (and since all price-setters in a given period face the same problem), p_t^1 equals the expectation as of period $t-1$ of p_{it}^*, and p_t^2 equals the expectation as of $t-2$ of p_{it}^*. Thus,

$$p_t^1 = E_{t-1}p_{it}^*$$
$$= E_{t-1}[\phi m_t + (1-\phi)p_t] \tag{6.50}$$
$$= \phi E_{t-1}m_t + (1-\phi)\tfrac{1}{2}(p_t^1 + p_t^2),$$

$$p_t^2 = E_{t-2}p_{it}^*$$
$$\tag{6.51}$$
$$= \phi E_{t-2}m_t + (1-\phi)\tfrac{1}{2}(E_{t-2}p_t^1 + p_t^2),$$

where $E_{t-\tau}$ denotes expectations conditional on information available through period $t-\tau$. Equation (6.50) uses the fact that p_t^2 is already determined when p_t^1 is set, and thus is not uncertain.

Our goal is to find how the price level and output evolve over time, given the behavior of m. To do this, we begin by solving (6.50) for p_t^1; this yields

$$p_t^1 = \frac{2\phi}{1+\phi}E_{t-1}m_t + \frac{1-\phi}{1+\phi}p_t^2. \tag{6.52}$$

We can now use the fact that expectations are rational to find the behavior of the individuals setting their prices in period $t-2$. Since the left- and right-hand sides of (6.52) are equal, and since expectations are rational, the expectation as of $t-2$ of the two sides must be equal. Thus,

$$E_{t-2}p_t^1 = \frac{2\phi}{1+\phi}E_{t-2}m_t + \frac{1-\phi}{1+\phi}p_t^2. \tag{6.53}$$

Equation (6.53) uses the fact that $E_{t-2}E_{t-1}m_t$ is simply $E_{t-2}m_t$; otherwise price-setters would be expecting to revise their estimate of m_t either up or down, which would imply that their original estimate was not rational. The fact that the current expectation of a future expectation of a variable equals the current expectation of the variable is known as the *law of iterated projections.*

We can substitute (6.53) into (6.51) to obtain

$$p_t^2 = \phi E_{t-2} m_t + (1 - \phi) \frac{1}{2} \left(\frac{2\phi}{1 + \phi} E_{t-2} m_t + \frac{1 - \phi}{1 + \phi} p_t^2 + p_t^2 \right). \tag{6.54}$$

Solving this expression for p_t^2 yields simply

$$p_t^2 = E_{t-2} m_t. \tag{6.55}$$

We can now combine the results and describe the equilibrium. Substituting (6.55) into (6.52) and simplifying gives

$$p_t^1 = E_{t-2} m_t + \frac{2\phi}{1 + \phi} (E_{t-1} m_t - E_{t-2} m_t). \tag{6.56}$$

Finally, substituting (6.55) and (6.56) into the expressions for the price level and output, $p_t = (p_t^1 + p_t^2)/2$ and $y_t = m_t - p_t$, implies

$$p_t = E_{t-2} m_t + \frac{\phi}{1 + \phi} (E_{t-1} m_t - E_{t-2} m_t), \tag{6.57}$$

$$y_t = \frac{1}{1 + \phi} (E_{t-1} m_t - E_{t-2} m_t) + (m_t - E_{t-1} m_t). \tag{6.58}$$

Implications

Equation (6.58) shows the model's main implications. First, as in the Lucas model, unanticipated aggregate demand shifts have real effects; this is shown by the $m_t - E_{t-1} m_t$ term. Because price-setters are assumed not to know m_t when they set their prices, these shocks are passed one-for-one into output.

Second, and crucially, aggregate demand shifts that become anticipated after the first prices are set affect output. Consider information about aggregate demand in t that becomes available between period $t - 2$ and period $t - 1$. In practice, this might correspond to the release of survey results or other leading indicators of future economic activity, or to indications of likely shifts in monetary policy. As (6.57) and (6.58) show, proportion $1/(1 + \phi)$ of a change in m that becomes expected between $t - 2$ and $t - 1$ is passed into output, and the remainder goes into prices. The reason that the change is not neutral is straightforward: not all prices are completely flexible in the short run.

An immediate corollary is that policy rules can stabilize the economy. As in Section 6.3, suppose that m_t equals $m_t^* + v_t$, where m_t^* is controlled by policy and v_t represents other aggregate demand movements. Assume that the policymaker is subject to the same informational constraints as price-setters, and must therefore choose m_t^* before the exact value of v_t is known. Nonetheless, as long as the policymaker can adjust m_t in response to information learned between $t - 2$ and $t - 1$, there is a role for stabilization policy. From (6.58), when $m_t = m_t^* + v_t$, y_t depends on $(m_t^* + v_t) - E_{t-1}(m_t^* + v_t)$ and on $E_{t-1}(m_t^* + v_t) - E_{t-2}(m_t^* + v_t)$. By adjusting m_t^* to offset $E_{t-1}v_t - E_{t-2}v_t$, the policymaker can offset the effects of these changes in v on output, even if this information about v is publicly known.

An additional implication of these results is that interactions among price-setters can either increase or decrease the effects of microeconomic price stickiness. Consider an aggregate demand shift that becomes known after the first prices are set. One might expect that since half of prices are already set and the other half are free to adjust, half of the shift is passed into prices and half into output. Equations (6.57) and (6.58) show that in general this is not correct. The key parameter is ϕ: the proportion of the shift that is passed into output is not $\frac{1}{2}$ but $1/(1 + \phi)$ (see [6.58]).

Recall from equation (6.45) that ϕ is the responsiveness of price-setters' desired real prices to aggregate real output: $p_{it}^* - p_t = c + \phi y_t$. A lower value of ϕ therefore corresponds to greater *real rigidity* (Ball and D. Romer, 1990). Real rigidity alone does not cause monetary disturbances to have real effects: if prices can adjust freely, money is neutral regardless of the value of ϕ. But real rigidity magnifies the effect of nominal rigidity: given that price-setters do not adjust their prices freely, a higher degree of real rigidity (that is, a lower value of ϕ) increases the real effects of a given monetary change. The reason for this is that a low value of ϕ implies that price-setters are reluctant to allow variations in their relative prices. As a result, the price-setters that are free to adjust their prices do not allow their prices to differ greatly from the ones already set, and so the real effects of a monetary shock are large. If ϕ exceeds 1, in contrast, the later price-setters make large price changes, and the aggregate real effects of changes in m are small.[13]

Finally, the model implies that output does not depend on $E_{t-2}m_t$ (given the values of $E_{t-1}m_t - E_{t-2}m_t$ and $m_t - E_{t-1}m_t$). That is, any information about aggregate demand that all price-setters have had a chance to respond to has no effect on output.

6.6   Fixed Prices

The Model

We now change the model of the previous section by assuming that when an individual sets prices for two periods, he or she must set the same price for both periods; in the terminology introduced earlier, prices are not just predetermined, but fixed.

---

[13] Haltiwanger and Waldman (1989) show more generally how a small fraction of agents who do not respond to shocks can have a disproportionate effect on the economy.

We make two other, less significant changes to the model. First, an individual setting a price in period t now does so for periods t and $t + 1$ rather than for periods $t + 1$ and $t + 2$. This change simplifies the model without affecting the main results. Second, the model is much easier to solve if we posit a specific process for m. A simple assumption is that m is a random walk:

$$m_t = m_{t-1} + u_t, \tag{6.59}$$

where u is white noise. The key feature of this process is that an innovation to m (the u term) has a long-lasting effect on its level.

Let x_t denote the price chosen by individuals who set their prices in period t. We make the usual certainty-equivalence assumption that price-setters try to get their prices as close as possible to the optimal prices. Here this implies

$$x_t = \tfrac{1}{2}(p_{it}^* + E_t p_{it+1}^*)$$
$$= \tfrac{1}{2}\{[\phi m_t + (1 - \phi)p_t] + [\phi E_t m_{t+1} + (1 - \phi)E_t p_{t+1}]\}, \tag{6.60}$$

where the second line uses the fact that $p^* = \phi m + (1 - \phi)p$.

Since half of prices are set each period, p_t is the average of x_t and x_{t-1}. In addition, since m is a random walk, $E_t m_{t+1}$ equals m_t. Substituting these facts into (6.60) gives us

$$x_t = \phi m_t + \tfrac{1}{4}(1 - \phi)(x_{t-1} + 2x_t + E_t x_{t+1}). \tag{6.61}$$

Solving for x_t yields

$$x_t = A(x_{t-1} + E_t x_{t+1}) + (1 - 2A)m_t,$$
$$A \equiv \frac{1}{2}\frac{1 - \phi}{1 + \phi}. \tag{6.62}$$

Equation (6.62) is the key equation of the model.

Equation (6.62) expresses x_t in terms of m_t, x_{t-1}, and the expectation of x_{t+1}. To solve the model, we need to eliminate the expectation of x_{t+1} from this expression. We will solve the model in two different ways, first using the method of undetermined coefficients and then using *lag operators*. The method of undetermined coefficients is simpler. But there are cases where it is cumbersome or intractable; in those cases the use of lag operators is often fruitful.

The Method of Undetermined Coefficients

As described in Section 4.6, the idea of the method of undetermined coefficients is to guess the general functional form of the solution and then to use the model to determine the precise coefficients. In the model we are considering, in period t two variables are given: the money stock, m_t, and the prices set the previous period, x_{t-1}. In addition, the model is linear. It is therefore reasonable to guess that x_t is a linear function of x_{t-1} and m_t:

$$x_t = \mu + \lambda x_{t-1} + \nu m_t. \tag{6.63}$$

Our goal is to determine whether there are values of μ, λ, and ν that yield a solution of the model.

Although we could now proceed to find μ, λ, and ν, it simplifies the algebra if we first use our knowledge of the model to restrict (6.63). We have normalized the constant in the expression for individuals' desired prices to 0, so that $p_{it}^* - p_t = \phi y_t$. As a result, the equilibrium with flexible prices is for y to equal 0 and for each price to equal m. In light of this, consider a situation where x_{t-1} and m_t are equal. If period-t price-setters also set their prices to m_t, the economy is at its flexible-price equilibrium. In addition, since m follows a random walk, the period-t price-setters have no reason to expect m_{t+1} to be on average either more or less than m_t, and hence no reason to expect x_{t+1} to depart on average from m_t. Thus in this situation p_{it}^* and $E_t p_{it+1}^*$ are both equal to m_t, and so price-setters will choose $x_t = m_t$. In sum, it is reasonable to guess that if $x_{t-1} = m_t$, then $x_t = m_t$. In terms of (6.63), this condition is

$$\mu + \lambda m_t + \nu m_t = m_t \tag{6.64}$$

for all m_t.

Two conditions are needed for (6.64) to hold. The first is $\lambda + \nu = 1$; otherwise (6.64) cannot be satisfied for all values of m_t. Second, when we impose $\lambda + \nu = 1$, (6.64) implies $\mu = 0$. Substituting these conditions into (6.63) yields

$$x_t = \lambda x_{t-1} + (1 - \lambda)m_t. \tag{6.65}$$

Our goal is now to find a value of λ that solves the model.

Since (6.65) holds each period, it implies $x_{t+1} = \lambda x_t + (1 - \lambda)m_{t+1}$. Thus the expectation as of period t of x_{t+1} is $\lambda x_t + (1 - \lambda)E_t m_{t+1}$, which equals $\lambda x_t + (1 - \lambda)m_t$. Using (6.65) to substitute for x_t then gives us

$$E_t x_{t+1} = \lambda[\lambda x_{t-1} + (1 - \lambda)m_t] + (1 - \lambda)m_t$$
$$= \lambda^2 x_{t-1} + (1 - \lambda^2)m_t. \tag{6.66}$$

Substituting this expression into (6.62) yields

$$x_t = A[x_{t-1} + \lambda^2 x_{t-1} + (1 - \lambda^2)m_t] + (1 - 2A)m_t$$
$$= (A + A\lambda^2)x_{t-1} + [A(1 - \lambda^2) + (1 - 2A)]m_t. \tag{6.67}$$

Thus, if price-setters believe that x_t is a linear function of x_{t-1} and m_t of the form assumed in (6.65), then, acting to maximize their profits, they will indeed set their prices as a linear function of these variables. If we have found a solution of the model, these two linear equations must be the same. Comparison of (6.65) and (6.67) shows that this requires

$$A + A\lambda^2 = \lambda \tag{6.68}$$

and

$$A(1 - \lambda^2) + (1 - 2A) = 1 - \lambda. \tag{6.69}$$

Consider (6.68). This is a quadratic equation in λ. The solution is

$$\lambda = \frac{1 \pm \sqrt{1 - 4A^2}}{2A}. \tag{6.70}$$

One can show that these two values of λ also satisfy (6.69). Using the definition of A in equation (6.62), one can show that the two values of λ are

$$\lambda_1 = \frac{1 - \sqrt{\phi}}{1 + \sqrt{\phi}}, \tag{6.71}$$

$$\lambda_2 = \frac{1 + \sqrt{\phi}}{1 - \sqrt{\phi}}. \tag{6.72}$$

Of the two values of λ, only $\lambda = \lambda_1$ gives reasonable results. When $\lambda = \lambda_1$, $|\lambda| < 1$, and so the economy is stable. When $\lambda = \lambda_2$, in contrast, $|\lambda| > 1$, and thus the economy is unstable: the slightest disturbance sends output off toward plus or minus infinity. As a result, the assumptions underlying the model—for example, that sellers do not ration buyers—break down. For that reason, we focus on $\lambda = \lambda_1$.

Thus equation (6.65) with $\lambda = \lambda_1$ solves the model: if price-setters believe that others are using that rule to set their prices, they find it in their own interests to use that same rule.

We can now describe the behavior of output. y_t equals $m_t - p_t$, which in turn equals $m_t - (x_{t-1} + x_t)/2$. With the behavior of x given by (6.65), this implies

$$y_t = m_t - \tfrac{1}{2}\{[\lambda x_{t-2} + (1 - \lambda)m_{t-1}] + [\lambda x_{t-1} + (1 - \lambda)m_t]\} \tag{6.73}$$

$$= m_t - [\lambda \tfrac{1}{2}(x_{t-2} + x_{t-1}) + (1 - \lambda)\tfrac{1}{2}(m_{t-1} + m_t)].$$

Using the facts that $m_t = m_{t-1} + u_t$ and $(x_{t-1} + x_{t-2})/2 = p_{t-1}$, we can simplify this to

$$y_t = m_{t-1} + u_t - [\lambda p_{t-1} + (1 - \lambda)m_{t-1} + (1 - \lambda)\tfrac{1}{2}u_t]$$

$$= \lambda(m_{t-1} - p_{t-1}) + \frac{1 + \lambda}{2}u_t \tag{6.74}$$

$$= \lambda y_{t-1} + \frac{1 + \lambda}{2}u_t.$$

Implications

Equation (6.74) is the key result of the model. As long as λ_1 is positive (which is true if $\phi < 1$), (6.74) implies that shocks to aggregate demand have long-lasting effects on output—effects that persist *even after all price-setters have changed their prices.* Suppose the economy is initially at the equilibrium with flexible prices (so y is steady at 0), and consider the effects of a positive shock of size u^0 in some period. In the period of the shock, not all price-setters adjust their prices, and so not surprisingly, y rises; from (6.74), $y = [(1+\lambda)/2]u^0$. In the following period, even though the remaining price-setters are able to adjust their prices, y does not return to normal even in the absence of a further shock: from (6.74), y is $\lambda[(1+\lambda)/2]u^0$. Thereafter output returns slowly to normal, with $y_t = \lambda y_{t-1}$ each period.

The response of the price level to the shock is the flip side of the response of output. The price level rises by $[1-(1+\lambda)/2]u^0$ in the initial period, and then fraction $1-\lambda$ of the remaining distance from u^0 in each subsequent period. Thus the economy exhibits price-level inertia.

The source of the long-lasting real effects of monetary shocks is again price-setters' reluctance to allow variations in their relative prices. Recall that $p_{it}^* = \phi m_t + (1-\phi)p_t$, and that $\lambda_1 > 0$ only if $\phi < 1$. Thus there is gradual adjustment only if desired prices are an increasing function of the price level. Suppose each price-setter adjusted fully to the shock at the first opportunity. In this case, the price-setters who adjusted their prices in the period of the shock would adjust by the full amount of the shock, and the remainder would do the same in the next period. Thus y would rise by $u^0/2$ in the initial period and return to normal in the next.

To see why this rapid adjustment cannot be the equilibrium if ϕ is less than 1, consider the individuals who adjust their prices immediately. By assumption, all prices have been adjusted by the second period, and so in that period everyone is charging his or her optimal price. But since $\phi < 1$, the optimal price is lower when the price level is lower, and so the price that is optimal in the period of the shock, when not all prices have been adjusted, is less than the optimal price in the next period. Thus these individuals should not adjust their prices fully in the period of the shock. This in turn implies that it is not optimal for the remaining individuals to adjust their prices fully in the subsequent period. And the knowledge that they will not do this further dampens the initial response of the individuals who adjust their prices in the period of the shock. The end result of these forward- and backward-looking interactions is the gradual adjustment shown in equation (6.65).

Thus, as in the model with prices that are predetermined but not fixed, the extent of incomplete price adjustment in the aggregate can be larger than one might expect simply from the knowledge that not all prices are adjusted every period. Indeed, the extent of aggregate price sluggishness is even larger in this case, since it persists even after every price has changed. And again a low value of ϕ—that is, a high degree of real rigidity—is critical to this result. If ϕ is 1, then λ is 0, and so each price-setter adjusts his or her price fully to changes in m at the earliest opportunity. If ϕ exceeds 1, λ is negative, and so p moves by more than m in the period after the shock, and thereafter the adjustment toward the long-run equilibrium is oscillatory.

Lag Operators

A different, more general approach to solving the model is to use lag operators. The lag operator, which we denote by L, is a function that lags variables. That is, the lag operator applied to any variable gives the previous period's value of the variable: $Lz_t = z_{t-1}$.

To see the usefulness of lag operators, consider our model without the restriction that m follows a random walk. Equation (6.60) continues to hold. If we proceed analogously to the derivation of (6.62), but without imposing $E_t m_{t+1} = m_t$, straightforward algebra yields

$$x_t = A(x_{t-1} + E_t x_{t+1}) + \frac{1-2A}{2} m_t + \frac{1-2A}{2} E_t m_{t+1}, \qquad (6.75)$$

where A is as before. Note that (6.75) simplifies to (6.62) if $E_t m_{t+1} = m_t$.

The first step is to rewrite this expression using lag operators. x_{t-1} is the lag of x_t: $x_{t-1} = Lx_t$. In addition, if we adopt the rule that when L is applied to an expression involving expectations, it lags the date of the variables but not the date of the expectations, then x_t is the lag of $E_t x_{t+1}$: $LE_t x_{t+1} = E_t x_t = x_t$.[14] Equivalently, using L^{-1} to denote the inverse lag function, $E_t x_{t+1} = L^{-1} x_t$. Similarly, $E_t m_{t+1} = L^{-1} m_t$. Thus we can rewrite (6.75) as

$$x_t = A(Lx_t + L^{-1} x_t) + \frac{1-2A}{2} m_t + \frac{1-2A}{2} L^{-1} m_t, \qquad (6.76)$$

or

$$(I - AL - AL^{-1})x_t = \frac{1-2A}{2}(I + L^{-1})m_t. \qquad (6.77)$$

Here I is the identity operator (so $Iz_t = z_t$ for any z). Thus $(I + L^{-1})m_t$ is shorthand for $m_t + L^{-1} m_t$, and $(I - AL - AL^{-1})x_t$ is shorthand for $x_t - Ax_{t-1} - AE_t x_{t+1}$.

Now observe that we can "factor" $I - AL - AL^{-1}$ as $(I - \lambda L^{-1})(I - \lambda L)(A/\lambda)$, where λ is again given by (6.70). Thus we have

$$(I - \lambda L^{-1})(I - \lambda L)x_t = \frac{\lambda}{A}\frac{1-2A}{2}(I + L^{-1})m_t. \qquad (6.78)$$

This formulation of "multiplying" expressions involving the lag operator should be interpreted in the natural way: $(I - \lambda L^{-1})(I - \lambda L)x_t$ is shorthand for $(I - \lambda L)x_t$ minus λ times the inverse lag operator applied to $(I - \lambda L)x_t$, and thus equals $(x_t - \lambda Lx_t) - (\lambda L^{-1} x_t - \lambda^2 x_t)$. Simple algebra and the definition of λ can be used to verify that (6.78) and (6.77) are equivalent.

---

[14] Since $E_t x_{t-1} = x_{t-1}$ and $E_t m_t = m_t$, we can think of all the variables in (6.75) as being expectations as of t. Thus in the analysis that follows, the lag operator should always be interpreted as keeping all variables as expectations as of t. The *backshift operator*, B, is used to denote the function that lags both the date of the variable and the date of the expectations. Thus, for example, $BE_t x_{t+1} = E_{t-1} x_t$. Whether the lag operator or the backshift operator is more useful depends on the application; in the present case it is the lag operator.

As before, to solve the model we need to eliminate the term involving the expectation of the future value of an endogenous variable. In (6.78), $E_t x_{t+1}$ appears (implicitly) on the left-hand side because of the $I - \lambda L^{-1}$ term. It is thus natural to "divide" both sides by $I - \lambda L^{-1}$. That is, consider applying the operator $I + \lambda L^{-1} + \lambda^2 L^{-2} + \lambda^3 L^{-3} + \cdots$ to both sides of (6.78). $I + \lambda L^{-1} + \lambda^2 L^{-2} + \cdots$ times $I - \lambda L^{-1}$ is simply I; thus the left-hand side is $(I - \lambda L)x_t$. And $I + \lambda L^{-1} + \lambda^2 L^{-2} + \cdots$ times $I + L^{-1}$ is $I + (1+\lambda)L^{-1} + (1+\lambda)\lambda L^{-2} + (1+\lambda)\lambda^2 L^{-3} + \cdots$.[15] Thus (6.78) becomes

$$(I - \lambda L)x_t = \frac{\lambda}{A}\frac{1-2A}{2}[I + (1+\lambda)L^{-1} + (1+\lambda)\lambda L^{-2} + (1+\lambda)\lambda^2 L^{-3} + \cdots]m_t.$$
(6.79)

Rewriting this expression without lag operators yields

$$x_t = \lambda x_{t-1} + \frac{\lambda}{A}\frac{1-2A}{2}[m_t + (1+\lambda)(E_t m_{t+1} + \lambda E_t m_{t+2} + \lambda^2 E_t m_{t+3} + \cdots)].$$
(6.80)

Expression (6.80) characterizes the behavior of newly set prices in terms of the exogenous money supply process. To find the behavior of the aggregate price level and output, we only have to substitute this expression into the expressions for p ($p_t = (x_t + x_{t-1})/2$) and y ($y_t = m_t - p_t$).

In the special case when m is a random walk, all the $E_t m_{t+i}$'s are equal to m_t. In this case, (6.80) simplifies to

$$x_t = \lambda x_{t-1} + \frac{\lambda}{A}\frac{1-2A}{2}\left(1 + \frac{1+\lambda}{1-\lambda}\right)m_t.$$
(6.81)

It is straightforward to show that expression (6.68), $A + A\lambda^2 = \lambda$, implies that equation (6.81) reduces to equation (6.65), $x_t = \lambda x_{t-1} + (1-\lambda)m_t$. Thus when m is a random walk, we obtain the same result as before. But we have also solved the model for a general process for m.

Although this use of lag operators may seem mysterious, in fact it is no more than a compact way of carrying out perfectly standard manipulations. We could have first derived (6.77) (expressed without using lag operators) by simple algebra. We could then have noted that since (6.77) holds at each date, it must be the case that

$$E_t x_{t+k} - AE_t x_{t+k-1} - AE_t x_{t+k+1} = \frac{1-2A}{2}(E_t m_{t+k} + E_t m_{t+k+1})$$
(6.82)

for all $k \geq 0$.[16] Since the left- and right-hand sides of (6.82) are equal, it must be the case that the left-hand side for $k = 0$ plus λ times the left-hand

---

[15] Since the operator $I + \lambda L^{-1} + \lambda^2 L^{-2} + \cdots$ is an infinite sum, this requires that $\lim_{n\to\infty}(I + \lambda L^{-1} + \lambda^2 L^{-2} + \cdots + \lambda^n L^{-n})(I + L^{-1})m_t$ exists. This requires that $\lambda^n L^{-(n+1)}m_t$ (which equals $\lambda^n E_t m_{t+n+1}$) converges to 0. For the case where $\lambda = \lambda_1$ (so $|\lambda| < 1$) and where m is a random walk, this condition is satisfied.

[16] The reason that we cannot assume that (6.82) holds for $k < 0$ is that the law of iterated projections does not apply backward: the expectation today of the expectation at some date *in the past* of a variable need not equal the expectation today of the variable.

side for $k = 1$ plus λ^2 times the left-hand side for $k = 2$ and so on equals the right-hand side for $k = 0$ plus λ times the right-hand side for $k = 1$ plus λ^2 times the right-hand side for $k = 2$ and so on. Computing these two expressions yields (6.80). Thus lag operators are not essential; they serve merely to simplify the notation and to suggest ways of proceeding that might otherwise be missed.[17]

The Taylor Model and Inflation Inertia

As described in Chapter 5, modern Keynesian specifications of the output-inflation tradeoff assume that inflation exhibits inertia—that is, that aggregate demand policies can reduce inflation only at the cost of a period of low output and high unemployment. Such inflation inertia is central to Keynesian accounts of output behavior during many periods of disinflation, such as in the United States in the early 1980s. As discussed above, the Taylor model exhibits price-level inertia: the price level adjusts fully to a monetary shock only after a sustained departure of output from its normal level. As a result, it is often claimed that the Taylor model accounts for inflation inertia.

Fuhrer and Moore (1995) demonstrate, however, that this claim is incorrect (see also Ball, 1994a). To see why, return to the basic equation describing price-setting, $x_t = (p_{it}^* + E_t p_{it+1}^*)/2$ (equation [6.60]). Since $p^* = p + \phi y$, this implies

$$x_t = \tfrac{1}{2}\left(p_t + \phi y_t + E_t p_{t+1} + \phi E_t y_{t+1}\right)$$

$$= \tfrac{1}{2}\left[\tfrac{1}{2}(x_{t-1} + x_t) + \phi y_t + \tfrac{1}{2}(x_t + E_t x_{t+1}) + \phi E_t y_{t+1}\right]. \tag{6.83}$$

Solving this equation for x_t yields

$$x_t = \tfrac{1}{2}(x_{t-1} + E_t x_{t+1}) + \phi(y_t + E_t y_{t+1}). \tag{6.84}$$

To see this expression's implications for inflation, define $\pi_t^x = x_t - x_{t-1}$. Now multiply both sides of (6.84) by 2 and subtract $x_{t-1} + x_t$ from both sides. This yields

$$\pi_t^x = E_t \pi_{t+1}^x + 2\phi(y_t + E_t y_{t+1}). \tag{6.85}$$

If we define $u_{t+1} = \pi_{t+1}^x - E_t \pi_{t+1}^x$, then (6.85) implies

$$\pi_{t+1}^x = \pi_t^x - 2\phi(y_t + E_t y_{t+1}) + u_{t+1}. \tag{6.86}$$

The key feature of (6.86) is that the terms in y enter negatively: high levels of output are associated with *falls* in inflation. That is, the fact that

---

[17] For a more thorough introduction to lag operators and their uses, see Sargent (1987a, Chapter 9).

price (and wage) changes are staggered does not account for the difficulty of reducing inflation.[18]

To see the intuition for why falling inflation is not associated with below-normal output in the model, note that the statement that π^x_{t+1} is less than π^x_t is equivalent to the statement that x_t exceeds the average of x_{t-1} and x_{t+1}. Now note that price-setters in period t would not choose to have x_t exceed the average of x_{t-1} and x_{t+1} when output is below normal. On the contrary, below-normal output leads them to choose a value of x_t that is less than the average of x_{t-1} and x_{t+1}. That is, below-normal output is associated with rising inflation in the model.[19]

6.7 The Caplin–Spulber Model

The Fischer and Taylor models assume that the timing of price changes is determined solely by the passage of time. This is a good approximation for some prices, such as wages set by union contracts, wages that are adjusted annually, and prices in some catalogues. But it is not a good description of others. Many retail stores, for example, can adjust the timing of their price changes fairly freely in response to economic developments. It is therefore natural to analyze the consequences of such state-dependent pricing. Our final model of staggered price changes, the Caplin–Spulber model, provides an example of such an analysis.

The model is set in continuous time. Each individual's optimal price at time t, $p^*_i(t)$, is again $\phi m(t) + (1-\phi)p(t)$. Money growth is always positive; as we will see, this causes p^*_i to always be increasing. The key assumption of the model is that price-setters follow an Ss pricing policy. Specifically, whenever a price-setter adjusts his or her price, he or she sets it so that the difference between the actual price and the optimal price at that time, $p_i - p^*_i$, equals some target level, S. The individual then keeps the nominal price fixed until money growth has raised p^*_i sufficiently that $p_i - p^*_i$ has fallen to some trigger level, s. He or she then resets $p_i - p^*_i$ to S, and the process begins anew.

---

[18] Using (6.84) and the fact that $p_t = (x_t + x_{t-1})/2$, one can derive an expression for price inflation similar to (6.86): $\pi_{t+1} = \pi_t - \phi(y_{t-1} + E_{t-1}y_t + y_t + E_t y_{t+1}) + (\pi_{t+1} - E_t \pi_{t+1}) + (\pi_t - E_{t-1}\pi_t)$. Again, the terms in y enter negatively.

[19] Another way to see why the Taylor model exhibits price-level inertia but not inflation inertia is to consider the solution of the model when aggregate demand is not a random walk, equation (6.80). Consider a Taylor economy with steady inflation and output equal to its flexible-price value, and consider two possible changes in policy. In the first, there is a one-time downward adjustment in the path of money; that is, money growth is low for one period but then returns to its usual value. In the second, the shift to lower money growth is permanent. Equation (6.80) shows that the prices that individuals set depend on the entire expected future path of money. The permanent fall in money growth leads to much larger reductions in the expected future values of the money stock than does the one-time shift. As a result, the permanent change in money growth has a much larger effect on newly set prices than does the one-time reduction.

Such an Ss policy is optimal when inflation is steady, aggregate output is constant, and there is a fixed cost of each nominal price change (Barro, 1972; Sheshinski and Weiss, 1977). In addition, as Caplin and Spulber describe, it is also optimal in some cases where inflation or output is not constant. And even when it is not fully optimal, it provides a simple and tractable example of state-dependent pricing.

Two technical assumptions complete the model. First, to keep prices from overshooting s and to prevent bunching of the distribution of prices across price-setters, m changes continuously. Second, the initial distribution of $p_i - p_i^*$ across price-setters is uniform between s and S. The remaining assumptions are the same as in the Fischer and Taylor models.

Under these assumptions, money is completely neutral in the aggregate despite the price stickiness at the level of the individual price-setters. To see this, consider an increase in m of amount $\Delta m < S - s$ over some period of time. We want to find the resulting changes in the price level and output, Δp and Δy. Since $p_i^* = (1 - \phi)p + \phi m$, the rise in each price-setter's optimal price is $(1 - \phi)\Delta p + \phi \Delta m$. Price-setters change their prices if $p_i - p_i^*$ falls below s; thus price-setters with initial values of $p_i - p_i^*$ that are less than $s + [(1 - \phi)\Delta p + \phi \Delta m]$ change their prices. Since the initial values of $p_i - p_i^*$ are distributed uniformly between s and S, this means that the fraction of price-setters who change their prices is $[(1 - \phi)\Delta p + \phi \Delta m]/(S - s)$. Each price-setter who changes his or her price does so at the moment when his or her value of $p_i - p_i^*$ reaches s; thus each price increase is of amount $S - s$. Putting all this together gives us

$$\Delta p = \frac{(1 - \phi)\Delta p + \phi \Delta m}{S - s}(S - s)$$

$$= (1 - \phi)\Delta p + \phi \Delta m.$$

(6.87)

Equation (6.87) implies that $\Delta p = \Delta m$, and thus that $\Delta y = 0$. Thus the change in money has no impact on aggregate output.[20]

To understand the intuition for this result, consider the case where $\phi = 1$, so that $p_i - p_i^*$ is just $p_i - m$. Now think of arranging the points in the interval $(s, S]$ around the circumference of a circle; this is shown in Figure 6.2. Initially, price-setters are distributed uniformly around the circle. Now notice that an increase in m of Δm moves every price-setter around the circle counterclockwise by a distance Δm. To see this, consider first a price-setter, such as the one at Point A, with an initial value of $p_i - p_i^*$ that is greater than $s + \Delta m$. Such a price-setter does not raise his or her price when m rises by Δm. Since p_i^* rises by Δm, for this price-setter $p_i - p_i^*$ therefore falls

---

[20] In addition, this result helps to justify the assumption that the initial distribution of $p_i - p_i^*$ is uniform between s and S. For each price-setter, $p_i - p_i^*$ equals each value between s and S once during the interval between any two price changes; thus there is no reason to expect a concentration anywhere within the interval. Indeed, Caplin and Spulber show that under simple assumptions, a given price-setter's $p_i - p_i^*$ is equally likely to take on any value between s and S.

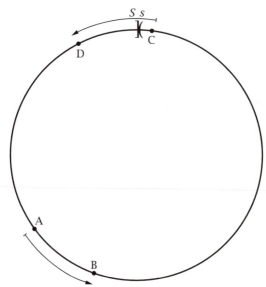

**FIGURE 6.2   The effects of an increase in
the money stock in the
Caplin–Spulber model**

by Δm. Thus the price-setter moves counterclockwise by amount Δm. Now consider a price-setter, such as the one at Point C, with an initial value of $p_i - p_i^*$ that is of the form $s + k$, where k is less than Δm. For this price-setter, $p_i - p_i^*$ falls until m has risen by k; thus he or she is moving counterclockwise around the circle. At the instant that the increase in m reaches k, p_i jumps by $S - s$, and so $p_i - p_i^*$ jumps from s to S. In terms of the diagram, however, this is just an infinitesimal move around the circle. As m continues to rise, the price-setter does not change his or her price further, and thus continues to travel around the circle. Thus the total distance the price-setter travels is also Δm.

Since the price-setters are initially distributed uniformly around the circle, and since each one moves the same distance, they end up still uniformly distributed. Thus the distribution of $p_i - m$ is unchanged. Since p is the average of the p_i's, this implies that $p - m$ is also unchanged.

The reason for the sharp difference between the results of this model and those of the Taylor model is the nature of the price adjustment policies. In the Caplin–Spulber model, the number of price-setters changing their prices at any time is larger when the money supply is increasing more rapidly; given the specific assumptions that Caplin and Spulber make, this has the effect that the aggregate price level responds fully to changes in m. In the Taylor model, in contrast, the number of price-setters changing their prices at any time is fixed; as a result, the price level does not respond fully to changes in m.

The neutrality of money in the Caplin–Spulber model is not a robust result about settings where fixed costs of changing nominal prices cause the number of price-setters changing prices at any time to be endogenous. If, for example, inflation can be negative as well as positive, or if there are idiosyncratic shocks that sometimes cause price-setters to lower their nominal prices, then the resulting extensions of Ss rules generally cause monetary shocks to have real effects (see, for example, Iwai, 1981; Caplin and Leahy, 1991; and Problem 6.12). In addition, the values of S and s may change in response to changes in aggregate demand. If, for example, high money growth today signals high money growth in the future, price-setters widen their Ss bands when there is a positive monetary shock; as a result, no price-setters adjust their prices in the short run (since no price-setters are now at the new, lower trigger point s), and so the positive shock raises output (Tsiddon, 1991).[21]

Thus Caplin and Spulber's model is not important for its specific results about the effects of aggregate demand shocks. Rather, the model is important for two reasons. First, it introduces the idea of state-dependent price changes. Second, it demonstrates another reason that the relation between microeconomic and macroeconomic rigidity is complex. The Fischer and Taylor models show that temporary fixity of some prices can have a disproportionate effect on the response of the aggregate price level to aggregate demand disturbances. The Caplin–Spulber model, in contrast, shows that the adjustment of some prices can have a disproportionate effect: a small fraction of price-setters making large price changes can be enough to generate neutrality in the aggregate. Thus together, the Fischer, Taylor, and Caplin–Spulber models show that any complete treatment of price rigidity requires careful attention both to the nature of price adjustment policies and to how those policies interact to determine the behavior of the aggregate price level.

Part C   New Keynesian Economics[22]

The Lucas, Fischer, and Taylor models are not fully satisfactory accounts of real effects of aggregate demand disturbances. The models assume the existence of imperfections that agents could overcome easily—imperfect knowledge of the price level in the Lucas model, and infrequent adjustment of prices or wages in the Fischer and Taylor models. Quite accurate information about movements in the price level is easily available, and the cost of much more frequent price or wage adjustments (through indexation or

---

[21] See Caballero and Engel (1991, 1993) for more detailed analyses of these issues.

[22] In places, the material through Section 6.9 draws on D. Romer (1993).

other means) is small. This raises the question of why agents would permit nominal disturbances to lead to substantial fluctuations in output rather than take the small measures needed to largely eliminate the nominal imperfections.

The central idea of a great deal of research on the real effects of nominal shocks is that this question applies not just to these particular models, but to all candidate sources of nominal imperfections. Individuals are mainly concerned with real prices and quantities: real wages, hours of work, real consumption levels, and the like. Nominal magnitudes matter to them only in ways that are minor and easily overcome. Prices and wages are quoted in nominal terms, but it costs little to change (or index) them. Individuals are not fully informed about the aggregate price level, but they can obtain accurate information at little cost. Debt contracts are usually specified in nominal terms, but they too could be indexed with little difficulty. And individuals hold modest amounts of currency, which is denominated in nominal terms, but they can change their holdings easily. There is no way in which nominal magnitudes are of great direct importance to individuals.

Thus, according to this *new Keynesian* view, if nominal imperfections are important to fluctuations in aggregate activity, it must be that nominal frictions that are small at the microeconomic level somehow have a large effect on the macroeconomy. Much of the research on the microeconomic foundations of nominal rigidity is devoted to addressing the question of whether this can plausibly be the case.[23]

For concreteness, most of this section addresses this question for a specific view about the nominal imperfection. In particular, we focus on a static model where firms face a *menu cost* of price adjustment—a small fixed cost of changing a nominal price. (The standard example is the cost incurred by a restaurant in printing new menus—hence the name.) But, as described at the end of Section 6.9, essentially the same issues arise with other views about the barriers to nominal adjustment. In addition, the analysis focuses on the question of whether menu costs can lead to significant nominal stickiness in response to a one-time monetary shock. As a result, the analysis is more successful in characterizing the microeconomic conditions that yield sluggish adjustment than in finding the implications of those conditions for the specifics of price adjustment.

Section 6.8 shows that introducing price-setting and menu costs into an economy that is otherwise Walrasian is probably not enough to generate substantial nominal rigidity. Section 6.9 is therefore devoted to the issue of what else is needed for menu costs to have important effects. Section 6.10 considers some relevant empirical work. Finally, Sections 6.11 and 6.12 discuss some extensions and limitations of the theory.

---

[23] The seminal papers are Mankiw (1985) and Akerlof and Yellen (1985). See also Parkin (1986); Rotemberg (1982); and Blanchard and Kiyotaki (1987).

6.8 Are Small Frictions Enough?

General Considerations

Consider an economy of many price-setting firms. Assume that it is initially at its flexible-price equilibrium. That is, each firm's price is such that if aggregate demand is at its expected level, marginal revenue equals marginal cost. After prices are set, aggregate demand is determined; at this point each firm can change its price by paying a menu cost. For simplicity, prices are assumed to be set afresh at the start of each period. This means that the dynamic pricing issues that are the subject of Part B of this chapter are irrelevant; it also means that if a firm pays the menu cost, it sets its price to the new profit-maximizing level.

Our focus is on the question of when firms change their prices in response to a departure of aggregate demand from its expected level. For concreteness, suppose that demand is less than expected. Since the economy is large, each firm takes the actions of other firms as given. Constant nominal prices are thus an equilibrium if, when all other firms hold their prices fixed, the maximum gain to a representative firm from changing its price is less than the menu cost of price adjustment.[24]

We can analyze this issue using the marginal revenue–marginal cost diagram in Figure 6.3. The economy begins in equilibrium; thus the representative firm is producing at the point where marginal cost equals marginal revenue (Point A in the diagram). A fall in aggregate demand with other prices unchanged reduces aggregate output, and thus shifts inward the demand curve that the firm faces—at a given price, demand for the firm's product is lower. Thus the marginal revenue curve shifts in. If the firm does not change its price, its output is determined by demand at the existing price (Point B). At this level of output, marginal revenue exceeds marginal cost, and so the firm has some incentive to lower its price and raise output.[25] If the firm changes its price, it produces at the point where marginal cost and marginal revenue are equal (Point C). The area of the shaded triangle in the diagram shows the additional profits to be gained from reducing price and increasing quantity produced. For the firm to be willing to hold its price fixed, the area of the triangle must be small.

The diagram reveals a crucial point: the firm's incentive to reduce its price may be small even if it is harmed greatly by the fall in demand. The firm would prefer to face the original, higher demand curve, but of course it can only choose a point on the new demand curve. This is an example of the aggregate demand externality described in Section 6.4: the representative

---

[24] The condition for price adjustment by all firms to be an equilibrium is not simply the reverse of this. As a result, there can be cases when both price adjustment and unchanged prices are equilibria. See Problem 6.15.

[25] The fall in aggregate output is likely to reduce the prevailing wage, and therefore to shift the marginal cost curve down. For simplicity, this effect is not shown in the figure.

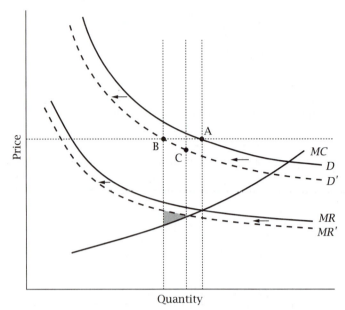

FIGURE 6.3   A representative firm's incentive to change its price in response to a fall in aggregate output (from D. Romer, 1993)

firm is harmed by the failure of other firms to cut their prices in the face of the fall in the money supply, just as it is harmed in Section 6.4 by a decision by all firms to raise their prices. As a result, the firm may find that the gain from reducing its price is small even if the shift in its demand curve is large. Thus there is no contradiction between the view that recessions have large costs and the hypothesis that they are caused by falls in aggregate demand and small barriers to price adjustment.

It is not possible, however, to proceed further using a purely diagrammatic analysis. To answer the question of whether the firm's incentive to change its price is likely to be more or less than the menu cost for plausible cases, we must turn to a specific model and find the incentive for price adjustment for reasonable parameter values.

A Quantitative Example

As a baseline case, we use the model of imperfect competition of Section 6.4. Recall that in that model, firm i's real profit income equals the quantity sold, $Y(P_i/P)^{-\eta}$, times price minus cost, $(P_i/P) - (W/P)$ (see [6.38]). In addition, labor-market equilibrium requires that the real wage equals $Y^{1/\nu}$, where $\nu \equiv 1/(\gamma - 1)$ is the elasticity of labor supply (see [6.43]). Thus,

$$\pi_i = Y \left(\frac{P_i}{P}\right)^{-\eta} \left(\frac{P_i}{P} - Y^{1/\nu}\right)$$

$$= \frac{M}{P} \left(\frac{P_i}{P}\right)^{1-\eta} - \left(\frac{M}{P}\right)^{(1+\nu)/\nu} \left(\frac{P_i}{P}\right)^{-\eta},$$

(6.88)

where the second line uses the fact that $Y = M/P$. We know from our earlier analysis of this model that the profit-maximizing real price in the absence of the menu cost is $\eta/(\eta - 1)$ times marginal cost, or $[\eta/(\eta - 1)](M/P)^{1/\nu}$ (see [6.44]). It follows that the equilibrium when prices are flexible occurs when $[\eta/(\eta - 1)](M/P)^{1/\nu} = 1$, or $M/P = [(\eta - 1)/\eta]^\nu$ (see [6.46]).

We want to find the condition for unchanged nominal prices to be a Nash equilibrium in the face of a departure of M from its expected value. That is, we want to find the condition under which, if all other firms do not adjust their prices, a representative firm will not want to pay the menu cost and adjust its own price. This condition is $\pi_{\text{ADJ}} - \pi_{\text{FIXED}} < Z$, where π_{ADJ} is the representative firm's profits if it adjusts its price to the new profit-maximizing level and other firms do not, π_{FIXED} is its profits if no prices change, and Z is the menu cost. Thus we need to find these two profit levels.

Initially all firms are charging the same price, and by assumption, other firms do not change their prices. Thus if firm i does not adjust its price, we have $P_i = P$. Substituting this into (6.88) yields

$$\pi_{\text{FIXED}} = \frac{M}{P} - \left(\frac{M}{P}\right)^{(1+\nu)/\nu}.$$

(6.89)

If the firm does adjust its price, it sets it to the profit-maximizing value, $[\eta/(\eta - 1)](M/P)^{1/\nu}$. Substituting this into (6.88) yields

$$\pi_{\text{ADJ}} = \frac{M}{P} \left(\frac{\eta}{\eta - 1}\right)^{1-\eta} \left(\frac{M}{P}\right)^{(1-\eta)/\nu} - \left(\frac{M}{P}\right)^{(1+\nu)/\nu} \left(\frac{\eta}{\eta - 1}\right)^{-\eta} \left(\frac{M}{P}\right)^{-\eta/\nu}$$

$$= \frac{1}{\eta - 1} \left(\frac{\eta}{\eta - 1}\right)^{-\eta} \left(\frac{M}{P}\right)^{(1+\nu-\eta)/\nu}.$$

(6.90)

It is straightforward to check that π_{ADJ} and π_{FIXED} are equal when M/P equals its flexible-price equilibrium value, and that otherwise π_{ADJ} is greater than π_{FIXED}.

To find the firm's incentive to change its price, we need values for η and ν. Since labor supply appears relatively inelastic, consider $\nu = 0.1$. Suppose also that $\eta = 5$, which implies that price is 1.25 times marginal cost. These parameter values imply that the flexible-price level of output is $Y^* = [(\eta - 1)/\eta]^\nu \simeq 0.978$. Now consider a firm's incentive to adjust its price in response to a 3 percent fall in M with other prices unchanged. Substituting $\nu = 0.1, \eta = 5$, and $Y = 0.97Y^*$ into (6.89) and (6.90) yields $\pi_{\text{ADJ}} - \pi_{\text{FIXED}} \simeq 0.253$.

Since Y^* is about 1, this calculation implies that the representative firm's incentive to pay the menu cost in response to a 3 percent change in output is about a quarter of revenue. No plausible cost of price adjustment can prevent firms from changing their prices in the face of this incentive. Thus, in this setting firms adjust their prices in the face of all but the smallest shocks, and money is virtually neutral.[26]

The source of the difficulty lies in the labor market. The labor market clears, and labor supply is relatively inelastic. Thus, as in Case 2 of Section 5.3, the real wage falls considerably when aggregate output falls. Producers' costs are therefore very low, and thus they have a strong incentive to cut their prices and raise output. But this means that unchanged nominal prices cannot be an equilibrium.[27]

6.9   The Need for Real Rigidity

General Considerations

Consider again a firm that is deciding whether to change its price in the face of a fall in aggregate demand with other prices held fixed. Figure 6.4 shows the firm's profits as a function of its price. The fall in aggregate output affects this function in two ways. First, it shifts the profit function vertically. The fact that the demand for the firm's good falls tends to shift the function down. The fact that the real wage falls, on the other hand, tends to shift the function up. In the case shown in the figure, the net effect is a downward shift. As described above, the firm cannot undo this change. Second, the firm's profit-maximizing price is less than before.[28] This the firm can do something about. If the firm does not pay the menu cost, its price remains the same, and so it is not charging the new profit-maximizing price. If the firm pays the menu cost, on the other hand, it can go to the peak of the profit function.

---

[26] Although $\pi_{ADJ} - \pi_{FIXED}$ is sensitive to the values of v and η, there are no remotely reasonable values that imply that the incentive for price adjustment is small. Consider, for example, $\eta = 3$ (implying a markup of 50 percent) and $v = \frac{1}{3}$. Even with these extreme values, the incentive to pay the menu cost is 0.8 percent of the flexible-price level of revenue for a 3 percent fall in output, and 2.4 percent for a 5 percent fall. Even though these incentives are much smaller than those in the baseline calculation, they are still surely larger than the barriers to price adjustment for most firms.

[27] It is not possible to avoid the problem by assuming that the cost of adjustment applies to wages rather than prices. In this case, the incentive to cut prices would indeed be low. But the incentive to cut wages would be high: firms (which could greatly reduce their labor costs) and workers (who could greatly increase their hours of work) would bid wages down.

[28] This corresponds to the assumption that the profit-maximizing relative price is increasing in aggregate output; that is, it corresponds to the assumption that $\phi > 0$ in the pricing equation, (6.45). As described in Section 6.4, this condition is needed for the equilibrium with flexible prices to be stable.

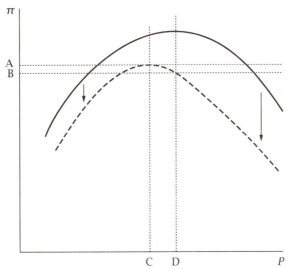

FIGURE 6.4 The impact of a fall in aggregate output on the representative firm's profits as a function of its price

The firm's incentive to adjust its price is thus given by the distance AB in the diagram. This distance depends on two factors: the difference between the old and new profit-maximizing prices, and the curvature of the profit function. We consider each in turn.

Since other firms' prices are unchanged, a change in the firm's nominal price is also a change in its real price. In addition, the fact that others' prices are unchanged means that the shift in aggregate demand changes aggregate output. Thus the difference between the firm's new and old profit-maximizing prices (distance CD in the figure) is determined by how the profit-maximizing real price depends on aggregate output—that is, by the degree of real rigidity. Greater real rigidity, holding the curvature of the profit function fixed, reduces the firm's incentive to adjust its price in response to an aggregate demand movement if other firms do not change their prices. The intuition is the same as the intuition for why greater real rigidity increases the real effects of nominal shocks in the Fischer and Taylor models: greater real rigidity means that firms do not want their prices to depart greatly from others' prices.

The curvature of the profit function determines the cost of a given departure of price from the profit-maximizing level. When profits are less sensitive to departures from the optimum, the incentive for price adjustment is smaller (for a given degree of real rigidity), and so the range of shocks for which nonadjustment of prices is an equilibrium is larger. Thus, in general terms, what is needed for small costs of price adjustment to generate substantial nominal rigidity is some combination of real rigidity and of insensitivity of the profit function.

Seen in terms of real rigidity and insensitivity of the profit function, it is easy to see why the incentive for price adjustment in our baseline calculation is so large: there is immense "real flexibility" rather than real rigidity. Since the profit-maximizing real price is $[\eta/(\eta-1)]Y^{1/\nu}$, its elasticity with respect to output is $1/\nu$. If the elasticity of labor supply, ν, is small, the elasticity of $(P_i/P)^*$ with respect to Y is therefore large. A value of ν of 0.1, for example, implies an elasticity of $(P_i/P)^*$ with respect to Y of 10.

A well-known analogy may help to make clear how the combination of menu costs with either real rigidity or insensitivity of the profit function (or both) can lead to considerable nominal stickiness: monetary disturbances may have real effects for the same reasons that the switch to daylight saving time does.[29] The resetting of clocks is a purely nominal change—it simply alters the labels assigned to different times of day. But the change is associated with changes in real schedules—that is, the times of various activities relative to the sun. And in contrast to the case of monetary disturbances, there can be no doubt that the switch to daylight saving time is the cause of the changes in real schedules.

If there were literally no cost to changing nominal schedules and communicating this information to others, daylight saving time would just cause everyone to do this and would have no effect on real schedules. Thus for daylight saving time to change real schedules, there must be some cost to changing nominal schedules. These costs are analogous to the menu costs of changing prices; and like the menu costs, they do not appear to be large. The reason that these small costs cause the switch to have real effects appears to be that individuals and businesses are generally much more concerned about their schedules relative to one another's than about their schedules relative to the sun. Thus, given that others do not change their scheduled hours, each individual does not wish to incur the cost of changing his or hers. This is analogous to the effects of real rigidity in the price-setting case. Finally, the less concerned that individuals are about precisely what their schedules are, the less willing they are to incur the cost of changing them; this is analogous to the insensitivity of the profit function in the price-setting case.

Specific Sources of Real Rigidity

A great deal of research on macroeconomic fluctuations is concerned with specific factors that can give rise to real rigidity or to insensitivity of the profit function. This work is done in various ways. For example, one can focus on the partial-equilibrium question of how some feature of financial, goods, or labor markets affects either a firm's incentive to adjust its real

---

[29] This analogy is originally due to Friedman (1953, p. 173), in the context of exchange rates.

price in response to a change in aggregate output or the sensitivity of its profits to departures from the optimum. Or one can add the candidate feature to a calibrated dynamic stochastic general equilibrium model that includes barriers to nominal adjustment, and ask how the addition affects such properties of the model as the variance of output, the covariance of money growth and output growth, and the real effects of a monetary disturbance. Or one need not focus on monetary disturbances and nominal imperfections at all. As we will see in Section 6.11, most forces that make the real economy more responsive to monetary shocks when there are nominal frictions make it more responsive to other types of shocks. As a result, many analyses of specific sources of real rigidity and insensitivity focus on their general implications for the effects of shocks, or on their implications for some type of shock other than monetary shocks.

Here we will take the approach of considering a single firm's incentive to adjust its price in response to a change in aggregate output when other firms do not change their prices. To do this, consider again the marginal revenue–marginal cost framework of Figure 6.3. On the cost side, when the fall in marginal cost as a result of the fall in aggregate output is smaller, the firm's incentive to cut its price and increase its output is smaller; thus nominal rigidity is more likely to be an equilibrium. This can occur in two ways. First, a smaller downward shift of the profit function in response to a fall in aggregate output implies a smaller decline in the firm's profit-maximizing price—that is, it corresponds to greater real rigidity.[30] Second, a flatter marginal cost curve implies both greater insensitivity of the profit function and greater real rigidity.

On the revenue side, when the fall in marginal revenue in response to a decline in aggregate output is larger, the gap between marginal revenue and marginal cost at the representative firm's initial price is smaller, and so the incentive for price adjustment is smaller. Specifically, a larger leftward shift of the marginal revenue curve corresponds to increased real rigidity, and so reduces the incentive for price adjustment. In addition, a steeper marginal revenue curve (for a given leftward shift) also increases the degree of real rigidity, and so again acts to reduce the incentive for adjustment.

Since there are many potential determinants of the cyclical behavior of marginal cost and marginal revenue, the hypothesis that small frictions in price adjustment result in considerable nominal rigidity is not tied to any specific view of the structure of the economy. On the cost side, researchers have identified various factors that may make costs less procyclical than in our baseline case. One factor that may be quantitatively important is input-output linkages that cause firms to face constant costs for their inputs when prices are sticky (Basu, 1995). A factor that has been the subject of considerable recent research is capital-market imperfections that raise

---

[30] Recall that for simplicity the marginal cost curve was not shown as shifting in Figure 6.3 (see n. 25). There is no reason to expect it to stay fixed in general, however.

the cost of finance in recessions. This can occur through reductions in cash flow (Bernanke and Gertler, 1989) or declines in asset values (Kiyotaki and Moore, 1997). Another factor that has received a great deal of attention is thick-market externalities and other external economies of scale. These externalities have the potential to make purchasing inputs and selling products easier in times of high economic activity. Although this is an appealing idea, its empirical importance is unknown.[31]

On the revenue side, any factor that makes firms' desired markups countercyclical increases real rigidity. Typically, when the desired markup is more countercyclical, the marginal revenue curve shifts down more in a recession. One specific factor that might make this occur is thick-market effects that make it easier for firms to disseminate information and for consumers to acquire it when aggregate output is high, and thus make demand more elastic (Warner and Barsky, 1995). Another is the combination of long-term relationships between customers and firms and capital-market imperfections. With long-term relationships, some of the increased revenues from cutting prices and thereby attracting new customers come in the future. And with capital-market imperfections, firms may face short-term financing difficulties in recessions that lower the present value to them of these future revenues (see, for example, Greenwald, Stiglitz, and Weiss, 1984, and Chevalier and Scharfstein, 1996). Three other factors that tend to make desired markups lower when output is higher are shifts in the composition of demand toward goods with more elastic demand, increased competition as a result of entry, and the fact that higher sales increase the incentive for firms to deviate from patterns of implicit collusion by cutting their prices (Rotemberg and Woodford, 1999, Section 4.2). Finally, an example of a factor on the revenue side that affects real rigidity by making the marginal revenue curve steeper (rather than by causing it to shift more in response to movements in aggregate output) is imperfect information that makes existing customers more responsive to price increases than prospective new customers are to price decreases (for example, Stiglitz, 1979; Woglom, 1982; and Ball and D. Romer, 1990).[32]

Although the new Keynesian view of fluctuations does not depend on any specific source of real rigidity and insensitivity of the profit function, it almost surely requires that the cost of labor not fall nearly as dramatically as it would if labor supply is relatively inelastic and workers are on their labor supply curves. If these conditions hold, the incentive for price adjustment

---

[31] The classic reference is Diamond (1982). See also Caballero and Lyons (1992); Cooper and Haltiwanger (1996); and Basu and Fernald (1995).

[32] As described in Section 5.3, markups appear to be at least moderately countercyclical. If this occurs because firms' *desired* markups are countercyclical, then there are real rigidities on the revenue side. But this is not the case if, as argued by Sbordone (1998), markups are countercyclical only because barriers to nominal price adjustment cause firms not to adjust their prices in the face of procyclical fluctuations in marginal cost.

created by the huge swings in the cost of labor almost surely swamps the effects of other factors.

At a general level, real wages might not be highly procyclical for two reasons. First, short-run aggregate labor supply could be relatively elastic (as a result of intertemporal substitution, for example). But as described in Section 4.10, this view of the labor market has had limited empirical success.

Second, imperfections in the labor market, such as those that are the subject of Chapter 9, can cause workers to be off their labor supply curves over at least part of the business cycle. In the efficiency-wage, contracting, and search and matching models presented there, the cost of labor to firms may differ from the opportunity cost of time to workers. The models thus break the link between the elasticity of labor supply and the response of the cost of labor to demand disturbances. Indeed, Chapter 9 presents several models that imply relatively acyclical wages (or relatively acyclical costs of labor to firms) despite inelastic labor supply. If imperfections like these cause real wages to respond little to demand disturbances, they greatly reduce firms' incentive to vary their prices in response to these demand shifts.[33]

A Second Quantitative Example

To see the potential importance of labor-market imperfections, consider the following variation (from Ball and Romer, 1990) on our example of firms' incentives to change prices in response to a monetary disturbance. Suppose that for some reason firms pay wages above the market-clearing level, and that the elasticity of the real wage with respect to aggregate output is β:

$$\frac{W}{P} = AY^{\beta}. \tag{6.91}$$

Thus, as in Case 3 of Section 5.3, the cyclical behavior of the real wage is determined by a "real-wage function" rather than by the elasticity of labor supply.

With the remainder of the model as before, firm i's profits are given by (6.37) with the real wage equal to AY^{β} rather than $Y^{1/\nu}$. It follows that

$$\pi_i = \frac{M}{P} \left(\frac{P_i}{P} \right)^{1-\eta} - A \left(\frac{M}{P} \right)^{1+\beta} \left(\frac{P_i}{P} \right)^{-\eta} \tag{6.92}$$

---

[33] In addition, the possibility of substantial real rigidities in the labor market suggests that small barriers to nominal adjustment may cause nominal disturbances to have substantial real effects through stickiness of nominal wages rather than of nominal prices. If wages display substantial real rigidity, a demand-driven expansion leads only to small increases in optimal real wages. As a result, just as small frictions in nominal price adjustment can lead to substantial nominal price rigidity, small frictions in nominal wage adjustment can lead to substantial nominal wage rigidity.

(compare [6.88]). The profit-maximizing real price is again $\eta/(\eta - 1)$ times the real wage; thus it is $[\eta/(\eta - 1)]AY^\beta$. It follows that equilibrium output under flexible prices is $[(\eta - 1)/(\eta A)]^{1/\beta}$. Assume that A and β are such that labor supply at the flexible-price equilibrium exceeds the amount of labor employed by firms.[34]

Now consider the representative firm's incentive to change its price in the face of a decline in aggregate demand, again assuming that other firms do not change their prices. If the firm does not change its price, then $P_i/P = 1$, and so (6.92) implies

$$\pi_{\text{FIXED}} = \frac{M}{P} - A\left(\frac{M}{P}\right)^{1+\beta}. \tag{6.93}$$

If the firm changes its price, it charges a real price of $[\eta/(\eta - 1)]AY^\beta$. Substituting this expression into (6.92) yields

$$\pi_{\text{ADJ}} = \frac{M}{P}\left(\frac{\eta}{\eta - 1}\right)^{1-\eta} A^{1-\eta}\left(\frac{M}{P}\right)^{\beta(1-\eta)}$$

$$- A\left(\frac{M}{P}\right)^{1+\beta}\left(\frac{\eta}{\eta - 1}\right)^{-\eta} A^{-\eta}\left(\frac{M}{P}\right)^{-\beta\eta} \tag{6.94}$$

$$= A^{1-\eta}\frac{1}{\eta - 1}\left(\frac{\eta}{\eta - 1}\right)^{-\eta}\left(\frac{M}{P}\right)^{1+\beta-\beta\eta}.$$

If β, the parameter that governs the cyclical behavior of the real wage, is small, the effect of this change in the model on the incentive for price adjustment is dramatic. Suppose, for example, that $\beta = 0.1$, that $\eta = 5$ as before, and that $A = 0.806$ (so that the flexible-price level of Y is 0.928, or about 95 percent of its level with $v = 0.1$ and a clearing labor market). Substituting these parameter values into (6.93) and (6.94) implies that if the money stock falls by 3 percent and firms do not adjust their prices, the representative firm's gain from changing its price is approximately 0.0000168, or about 0.0018 percent of the revenue it gets at the flexible-price equilibrium. Even if M falls by 5 percent and $\beta = 0.25$ (and A is changed to 0.815, so that the flexible-price level of Y continues to be 0.928), the incentive for price adjustment is only 0.03 percent of the firm's flexible-price revenue.

This example shows how real rigidity and small barriers to nominal price adjustment can produce a large amount of nominal rigidity. But the example almost surely involves an unrealistic degree of real rigidity in the labor market: the example assumes that the elasticity of the real wage with respect to output is only 0.1, while the evidence discussed in Section 5.6 suggests that

---

[34] When prices are flexible, each firm sets its relative price to $[\eta/(\eta - 1)](W/P)$. Thus the real wage at the flexible-price equilibrium must be $(\eta - 1)/\eta$, and so labor supply is $[(\eta - 1)/\eta]^v$. Thus the condition that labor supply exceeds demand at the flexible-price equilibrium is $[(\eta - 1)/\eta]^v > [(\eta - 1)/(\eta A)]^{1/\beta}$.

the true elasticity is considerably higher. A more realistic account would probably involve less real rigidity in the labor market, but would include the presence of other forces dampening fluctuations in costs and making desired markups countercyclical.

Other Frictions

The barriers to complete adjustment to nominal disturbances need not be in price and wage adjustment. For example, one line of research examines the consequences of the fact that debt contracts are often not indexed; that is, loan agreements and bonds generally specify streams of nominal payments the borrower must make to the lender. Nominal disturbances therefore cause redistributions. A negative nominal shock, for example, increases borrowers' real debt burdens. If capital markets are perfect, such redistributions do not have any important real effects; investments continue to be made if the risk-adjusted expected payoffs exceed the costs, regardless of whether the funds for the projects can be supplied by the entrepreneurs or have to be raised in capital markets.

But actual capital markets are not perfect. Asymmetric information between lenders and borrowers, coupled with risk aversion or limited liability, generally makes the first-best outcome unattainable. The presence of risk aversion or limited liability means that the borrowers usually do not bear the full cost of very bad outcomes of their investment projects. But if borrowers are partially insured against bad outcomes, they have an incentive to take advantage of the asymmetric information between themselves and lenders by borrowing only if they know their projects are risky (adverse selection) or by taking risks on the projects they undertake (moral hazard). These difficulties cause lenders to charge a premium on their loans. As a result, there is generally less investment, and less efficient investment, when it is financed externally than when it is funded by the entrepreneurs' own funds.

In such settings, redistributions matter: transferring wealth from entrepreneurs to lenders makes the entrepreneurs more dependent on external finance, and thus reduces investment. Thus if debt contracts are not indexed, nominal disturbances are likely to have real effects. Indeed, price and wage flexibility can increase the distributional effects of nominal shocks, and thus potentially increase their real effects. This channel for real effects of nominal shocks is known as *debt deflation*.[35]

This view of the nature of nominal imperfections must confront the same issues that face theories based on frictions in nominal price adjustment. For example, when a decline in the money stock redistributes wealth from firms

---

[35] The term is due to Irving Fisher (1933). For a modern treatment, see Bernanke and Gertler (1989). Section 8.7 develops a model of investment and the effects of changes in entrepreneurs' wealth when financial markets are imperfect.

to lenders because of nonindexation of debt contracts, firms' marginal cost curves shift up. For reasonable cases, this upward shift is not large. If marginal cost falls greatly when aggregate output falls (because real wages decline sharply, for example) and marginal revenue does not, the modest increase in costs caused by the fall in the money stock leads to only a small decline in aggregate output.[36] If marginal cost changes little and marginal revenue is very responsive to aggregate output, on the other hand, the small change in costs leads to large changes in output. Thus the same kinds of forces needed to cause small barriers to price adjustment to lead to large fluctuations in aggregate output are also needed for small costs to indexing debt contracts to have this effect.

This discussion suggests an alternative interpretation of the Lucas model. Recall that Lucas's model is based on the assumptions of imperfect information about the aggregate price level and considerable intertemporal substitution in labor supply, and that neither of these assumptions appears to be a good first approximation. The discussion here, however, suggests that Lucas's central results do not rest on these assumptions. Suppose that price-setters choose not to acquire current information about the price level, and that the behavior of the economy is therefore described by the Lucas model. In such a situation, price-setters' incentive to obtain information about the price level, and to adjust their pricing and output decisions accordingly, is determined by the same considerations that determine their incentive to adjust their nominal prices in menu-cost models. As we have seen, there are many possible mechanisms other than intertemporal substitution that can cause this incentive to be small. Thus neither unavailability of information about the price level nor intertemporal substitution is essential to the mechanism identified by Lucas. The friction in nominal adjustment may therefore be a small inconvenience or cost of obtaining information about the price level (or of adjusting one's pricing decisions in light of that information). Whether this friction is important in practice remains an open question.[37]

---

[36] If a small decline in borrowers' wealth causes a discontinuous drop in their ability to borrow, the increase in costs is no longer small (see, for example, Mankiw, 1986a, and Bernanke and Gertler, 1990). But it is not clear why a small fall in borrowers' wealth would induce lenders to stop lending if, at the same time, labor costs (for example) had dropped sharply. In addition, it is not clear why small redistributions would have large effects on the number of entrepreneurs who can borrow.

[37] Another line of work investigates the consequences of the fact that at any given time, not all agents are adjusting their holdings of high-powered money. Thus when the monetary authority changes the quantity of high-powered money, it cannot achieve a proportionate change in everyone's holdings. As a result, a change in the money stock generally affects real money balances even if all prices and wages are perfectly flexible. Under appropriate conditions (such as an impact of real balances on consumption), this change in real balances affects the real interest rate. And if the real interest rate affects aggregate supply, the result is that aggregate output changes. The seminal papers here are Grossman and Weiss (1983) and Rotemberg (1984). For a recent treatment, see Christiano, Eichenbaum, and Evans (1997).

6.10 Empirical Applications

The Average Inflation Rate and the Output-Inflation Tradeoff

Ball, Mankiw, and D. Romer (1988) point out that if the real effects of aggregate demand movements arise from frictions in price adjustment, then the average rate of inflation is likely to influence the size of those effects. Their argument is straightforward. When average inflation is higher, firms must adjust their prices more often to keep up with the price level. This implies that when there is an aggregate demand disturbance, firms can pass it into prices more quickly. Thus its real effects are smaller.

Ball, Mankiw, and Romer's basic test of this prediction is analogous to Lucas's test of his prediction that the variance of aggregate demand should influence the real effects of demand shocks. Following Lucas, they first estimate the real impact of aggregate demand shifts (denoted τ_i) in a large number of countries using the specification in equation (6.34). They then ask how those estimated impacts are related to average inflation.

Figure 6.5 shows a scatterplot of the estimated τ_i's versus average inflation for the 43 countries considered by Ball, Mankiw, and Romer. The figure suggests a negative relationship. The corresponding regression (with a quadratic term included to account for the nonlinearity apparent in the figure) is

$$\tau_i = \begin{array}{ccc} 0.600 & - & 4.835\ \overline{\pi}_i + & 7.118\ \overline{\pi}_i^2, \\ (0.079) & (1.074) & (2.088) \end{array} \tag{6.95}$$

$$\overline{R}^2 = 0.388, \qquad \text{s.e.e.} = 0.215,$$

where $\overline{\pi}_i$ is average inflation in country i and the numbers in parentheses are standard errors. The point estimates imply that $\partial \tau / \partial \overline{\pi} = -4.835 + 2(7.118)\overline{\pi}$, which is negative for $\overline{\pi} < 4.835/[2(7.118)] \simeq 34\%$. Thus there is a statistically significant negative relationship between average inflation and the estimated real impact of aggregate demand movements.

Recall that the Lucas model predicts that the variance of aggregate demand shocks affects τ, and that the data appear consistent with this prediction. Moreover, countries with higher average inflation generally have more variable aggregate demand. Thus it is possible that the results in (6.95) arise not because $\overline{\pi}$ directly affects τ, but because it is correlated with the standard deviation of nominal GNP growth (σ_x), which does directly affect τ. Alternatively, it is possible that the earlier results, which appeared supportive of the Lucas model, in fact arise from the fact that σ_x and $\overline{\pi}$ are correlated.

The appropriate way to test between these two views is to include both variables in the regression. Again quadratic terms are included to allow for

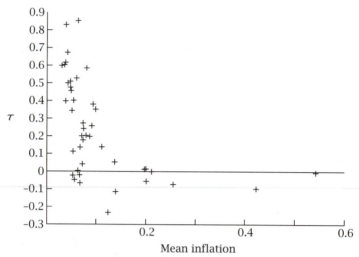

FIGURE 6.5   The output-inflation tradeoff and average inflation (from Ball, Mankiw, and Romer, 1988)

nonlinearities. The results are

$$\tau_i = \underset{(0.086)}{0.589} - \underset{(1.973)}{5.729}\,\overline{\pi}_i + \underset{(3.849)}{8.406}\,\overline{\pi}_i^2 + \underset{(2.467)}{1.241}\,\sigma_x - \underset{(7.062)}{2.380}\,\sigma_x^2,$$

$$\overline{R}^2 = 0.359, \qquad \text{s.e.e.} = 0.219.$$

(6.96)

The coefficients on the average inflation variables are essentially the same as in the previous regression, and they remain statistically significant. The variability terms, in contrast, play little role. The null hypothesis that the coefficients on both σ_x and σ_x^2 are 0 cannot be rejected at any reasonable confidence level, and the point estimates imply that reasonable changes in σ_x have quantitatively small effects on τ; for example, a change in σ_x from 0.05 to 0.10 changes τ by only 0.04. Thus the results appear to favor the new Keynesian view over the Lucas model.[38]

Kiley (2000) extends this analysis to the persistence of output movements. He first notes that new Keynesian models imply that departures of output from normal are less persistent when average inflation is higher. The intuition is again that higher average inflation increases the frequency of price adjustment, and therefore causes the economy to return to its flexible-price equilibrium more rapidly after a shock. He finds that the data support this implication as well.

---

[38] The lack of a discernible link between σ_x and τ, however, is a puzzle not only for the Lucas model but also for models based on small frictions: an increase in the variability of shocks should make firms change their prices more often, and should therefore reduce the real impact of a change in aggregate demand.

Microeconomic Evidence on Price Adjustment

The central assumption of the analysis of this part of the chapter is that there is some kind of barrier to complete price adjustment at the level of individual firms. It is therefore natural to investigate pricing policies at the microeconomic level. By doing so, one can hope to learn both whether there are barriers to price adjustment and, if so, what form they take.

Prominent examples of such studies include Carlton (1986); Cecchetti (1986); Lach and Tsiddon (1992); Kashyap (1995); and Blinder (1998). There are two general themes to the results. First, infrequent price adjustment is common. For example, Carlton and Blinder, who examine the broadest ranges of goods, find that intervals between price changes are typically about a year. And price changes for some goods are much less frequent. Cecchetti, for example, finds that the newsstand prices of magazines are changed on average only every 3 years.

The second theme of these studies is that the price adjustments do not follow any simple pattern. The behavior of L.L. Bean catalog prices, documented by Kashyap, is representative. As in the other studies, the frequency of price changes is low: on average, the price of a good is changed only after inflation has eroded its real price by about 10 percent. Only an extremely large cost of price adjustment, or an extremely small cost of failing to charge the price that is optimal in the absence of adjustment costs, can reconcile this finding with a menu-cost view. In addition, although Bean issues more than 20 catalogs a year, prices are changed in only two of the catalogs (fall and spring). Even in these catalogs, most prices are usually not changed. Neither fact supports the view that the barrier to price adjustment is the cost of printing and posting a new price. In addition, the spacing of the changes is highly irregular; thus the results are not at all consistent with the assumption of the Fischer and Taylor models that there is a fixed interval between changes. Finally, the size of changes varies tremendously, and small changes are as likely as large changes to be followed quickly by an additional change; if the barrier to price adjustment is some kind of fixed cost, then under reasonable assumptions the changes would be fairly uniform in size, and the firm would make a relatively small change only if it expected the new price to be in effect for a relatively long time. Thus, the microeconomic evidence on price adjustment is puzzling.

Levy, Bergen, Dutta, and Venable (1997) look at a different aspect of the microeconomics of price adjustment: they attempt to assess the costs of changing nominal prices. Specifically, they report data on each step of the process of changing prices at supermarkets, such as the costs of putting on new price tags or signs on the shelves, of entering the new prices into the computer system, and of checking the prices and correcting errors.

This approach does not address the possibility that there may be more sophisticated, less expensive ways of adjusting prices to aggregate disturbances. For example, a store could have a prominently displayed discount factor that it used at checkout to subtract some proportion from the amount due; it could then change the discount factor rather than the shelf prices in response to aggregate shocks. The costs of changing the discount factor would be dramatically less than the cost of changing the posted price on every item in the store.

Despite this limitation, it is still interesting to know how large the costs of changing prices are. Levy, Bergen, Dutta, and Venable's basic finding is that the costs are surprisingly high. For the average store in their sample, expenditures on changing prices amount to between 0.5 and 1 percent of revenues. To put it differently, the average cost of a price change in their stores in 1991–1992 was about 50 cents. Thus the common statement that the physical costs of nominal price changes are extremely small is not always correct: for the stores that Levy, Bergen, Dutta, and Venable consider, these costs, while not large, are far from trivial.

6.11 Coordination-Failure Models and Real Non-Walrasian Theories

Coordination-Failure Models

All the models of fluctuations we have examined imply that when prices are flexible, the economy has a unique equilibrium. Thus fluctuations arise only from changes in the flexible-price equilibrium (as in real-business-cycle models) or from departures of the economy from that equilibrium (as in models with nominal stickiness). If more than one level of output is a flexible-price equilibrium, however, fluctuations can also arise from movements of the economy among different equilibria.

Cooper and John (1988) present a simple framework for analyzing multiple equilibria in aggregate activity. The economy consists of many identical agents. Each agent chooses the value of some variable, which we call output for concreteness, taking others' choices as given. Let $U_i = V(y_i, y)$ be agent i's payoff when he or she chooses output y_i and all others choose y. (We will consider only symmetric equilibria; thus we do not need to specify what happens when others' choices are heterogeneous.) Let $y_i^*(y)$ denote the representative agent's optimal choice of y_i given y. Assume that $V(\bullet)$ is sufficiently well behaved that $y_i^*(y)$ is uniquely defined for any y, continuous, and always between 0 and some upper bound $\overline{y}$. $y_i^*(y)$ is referred to as the *reaction function*.

Equilibrium occurs when $y_i^*(y) = y$. In such a situation, if each agent believes that other agents will produce y, each agent in fact chooses to produce y.

Figure 6.6 shows an economy without multiple equilibria. The figure plots the reaction function, $y_i^*(y)$. Equilibrium occurs when the reaction function crosses the 45-degree line. Since there is only one crossing, the equilibrium is unique.

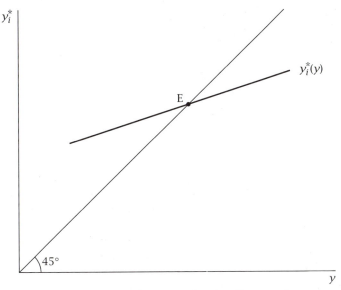

FIGURE 6.6 **A reaction function that implies a unique equilibrium**

Figure 6.7 shows a case with multiple equilibria. Since $y_i^*(y)$ is bounded between 0 and $\overline{y}$, it must begin above the 45-degree line and end up below. And since it is continuous, it must cross the 45-degree line an odd number of times (if we ignore the possibility of tangencies). The figure shows a case with three crossings and thus three equilibrium levels of output. Under plausible assumptions, the equilibrium at Point A is unstable. If, for example, agents expect output to be slightly above the level at A, they produce slightly more than they expect others to produce. With natural assumptions about dynamics, this causes the economy to move away from A. The equilibria at B and C, however, are stable.

With multiple equilibria, fundamentals do not fully determine outcomes. If agents expect the economy to be at C, it ends up there; if they expect it to be at B, it ends up there instead. Thus *animal spirits, self-fulfilling prophecies,* and *sunspots* can affect aggregate outcomes.[39]

It is plausible that $V(y_i, y)$ is increasing in y—that is, that a typical individual is better off when aggregate output is higher. In the model of Section 6.4, for example, higher aggregate output shifts the demand curve that the representative firm faces outward, and thus increases the real price the firm

---

[39] A sunspot equilibrium occurs when some variable that has no inherent effect on the economy matters because agents believe that it does. Any model with multiple equilibria has the potential for sunspots: if agents believe that the economy will be at one equilibrium when the extraneous variable takes on a high value and at another when it takes on a low value, they behave in ways that validate this belief. For more on these issues, see Cass and Shell (1983); Woodford (1990, 1991); and Benhabib and Farmer (1999).

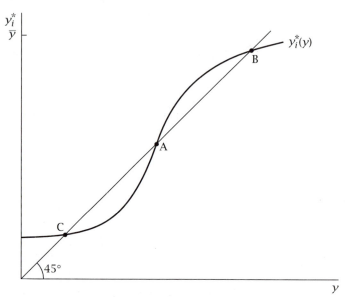

FIGURE 6.7   A reaction function that implies multiple equilibria

obtains for a given level of its output. If $V(y_i, y)$ is increasing in y, equilibria with higher output involve higher welfare. To see this, consider two equilibrium levels of output, y_1 and y_2, with $y_2 > y_1$. Since $V(y_i, y)$ is increasing in y, $V(y_1, y_2)$ is greater than $V(y_1, y_1)$. And since y_2 is an equilibrium, $y_i = y_2$ maximizes $V(y_i, y)$ given $y = y_2$, and so $V(y_2, y_2)$ exceeds $V(y_1, y_2)$. Thus the representative agent is better off at the higher-output equilibrium.[40]

Models with multiple, Pareto-ranked equilibria are known as *coordination-failure* models. The possibility of coordination failure implies that the economy can get stuck in an underemployment equilibrium. That is, output can be inefficiently low just because everyone believes that it will be. In such a situation, there is no force tending to restore output to normal. As a result, there may be scope for government policies that coordinate expectations on a high-output equilibrium; for example, a temporary stimulus might permanently move the economy to a better equilibrium.

There is an important link between multiple equilibria and our earlier discussion of real rigidity. Recall that there is a high degree of real rigidity when, in response to an increase in the price level and the consequent

---

[40] There is no necessary connection between the slope of the reaction function and the welfare properties of equilibria. If agents' maximization problem has an interior solution, $y_i^*(y)$ is defined by $V_1(y_i^*(y), y) = 0$, where subscripts denote partial derivatives. Differentiating this condition with respect to y yields $y_i^{*\prime}(y) = V_{12}/(-V_{11})$. Since V_{11} must be negative for $y_i^*(y)$ to be an interior maximum, the sign of $y_i^{*\prime}(y)$ is given by the sign of V_{12}. Relative welfare in different equilibria, on the other hand, is determined by V_2. Thus the issues of whether there are multiple equilibria and whether a high-output equilibrium is preferable to a low-output one are distinct.

decline in aggregate output, the representative firm wants to reduce its relative price only slightly. In terms of output, this corresponds to a reaction function with a slope slightly less than 1: when aggregate output falls, the representative firm wants its sales to decline almost as much as others'. The existence of multiple equilibria requires that over some range, declines in aggregate output cause the representative firm to want to *raise* its price and thus *reduce* its sales relative to others'; that is, what is needed is that the reaction function have a slope greater than 1 over some range. In short, coordination failure requires that real rigidity be very strong over some range.

One implication of this observation is that, since there are many potential sources of real rigidity, there are many potential sources of coordination failure. Thus there are many possible models that fit Cooper and John's general framework. Examples include Diamond (1982); Bryant (1983); Shleifer (1986); Kiyotaki (1988); Howitt and McAfee (1988); Murphy, Shleifer, and Vishny (1989); Pagano (1989); Matsuyama (1991); Durlauf (1993); Galí (1994); and Lamont (1995).

Empirical Application: Experimental Evidence on Coordination-Failure Games

Coordination-failure models have more than one Nash equilibrium. Traditional game theory predicts that such economies will arrive at one of their equilibria, but does not predict which one. Various theories of equilibrium refinements make predictions about which equilibrium will be reached. For example, a common view is that Pareto-superior equilibria are focal, and that economies where there is the potential for coordination failure therefore attain the best possible equilibrium. There are other possibilities as well. For example, it may be that each agent is unsure about what rule others are using to choose among the possible outcomes, and that as a result such economies do not reach any of their equilibria.

One approach to testing theories that has been pursued extensively in recent years, especially in game theory, is the use of experiments. Experiments have the advantage that they allow researchers to control the economic environment precisely. They have the disadvantages, however, that they are often not feasible and that behavior may be different in the laboratory than in similar situations in practice.

Van Huyck, Battalio, and Beil (1990, 1991) and Cooper, DeJong, Forsythe, and Ross (1990, 1992) test coordination-failure theories experimentally. Van Huyck, Battalio, and Beil (1990) consider the coordination-failure game proposed by Bryant (1983). In Bryant's game, each of N agents chooses an effort level over the range $[0, \bar{e}]$. The payoff to agent i is

$$U_i = \alpha \min[e_1, e_2, \ldots, e_N] - \beta e_i, \qquad \alpha > \beta > 0. \qquad (6.97)$$

The best equilibrium is for every agent to choose the maximum effort level, $\bar{e}$; this gives each agent a payoff of $(\alpha - \beta)\bar{e}$. But any common effort level in $[0, \bar{e}]$ is also a Nash equilibrium: if every agent other than agent i sets his or her effort to some level $\hat{e}$, i also wants to choose effort of $\hat{e}$. Since each agent's payoff is increasing in the common effort level, Bryant's game is a coordination-failure model with a continuum of equilibria.

Van Huyck, Battalio, and Beil consider a version of Bryant's game with effort restricted to the integers 1 through 7, α = $0.20, β = $0.10, and N between 14 and 16.[41] They report several main results. The first concerns the first time a group plays the game; since Bryant's model is not one of repeated play, this situation may correspond most closely to the model. Van Huyck, Battalio, and Beil find that in the first play, the players do not reach any of the equilibria. The most common levels of effort are 5 and 7, but there is a great deal of dispersion. Thus, no deterministic theory of equilibrium selection successfully describes behavior.

Second, repeated play of the game results in rapid movement toward low effort. Among five of the seven experimental groups, the minimum effort in the first period is more than 1. But in all seven groups, by the fourth play the minimum level of effort reaches 1 and remains there in every subsequent round. Thus there is strong coordination failure.

Third, the game fails to converge to any equilibrium. Each group played the game 10 times, for a total of 70 trials. Yet in none of the 70 trials do all the players choose the same effort. Even in the last several trials, which are preceded in every group by a string of trials where the minimum effort is 1, more than a quarter of players choose effort greater than 1.

Finally, even modifying the payoff function to induce "coordination successes" does not prevent reversion to inefficient outcomes. After the initial 10 trials, each group played 5 trials with the parameter β in (6.97) set to 0. With β = 0, there is no cost to higher effort; as a result, most of (though not all) the groups converge to the Pareto-efficient outcome of e_i = 7 for all players. But when β is changed back to $0.10, there is rapid reversion to the situation where most players choose the minimum effort.

Van Huyck, Battalio, and Beil's results suggest that predictions from deductive theories of behavior should be treated with caution: even though Bryant's game is fairly simple, actual behavior does not correspond well with the predictions of any standard theory. The results also suggest that coordination-failure models can give rise to complicated behavior and dynamics.

Real Non-Walrasian Theories

Substantial real rigidity, even if it is not strong enough to cause multiple equilibria, can make the equilibrium highly sensitive to disturbances. Consider the case where the reaction function is upward-sloping with a slope slightly less than 1. As shown in Figure 6.8, this leads to a unique equilib-

---

[41] In addition, they add a constant of $0.60 to the payoff function so that no one can lose money.

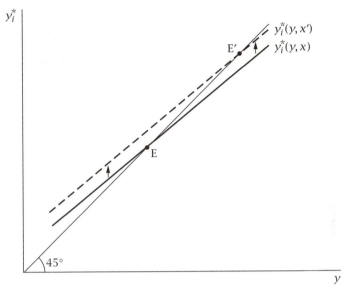

FIGURE 6.8   A reaction function that implies a unique but fragile equilibrium

rium. Now let x be some variable that shifts the reaction function; thus we now write the reaction function as $y_i = y_i^*(y, x)$. The equilibrium level of y for a given x, denoted $\hat{y}(x)$, is defined by the condition $y_i^*(\hat{y}(x), x) = \hat{y}(x)$. Differentiating this condition with respect to x yields

$$\frac{\partial y_i^*}{\partial y} \hat{y}'(x) + \frac{\partial y_i^*}{\partial x} = \hat{y}'(x), \tag{6.98}$$

or

$$\hat{y}'(x) = \frac{1}{1 - (\partial y_i^*/\partial y)} \frac{\partial y_i^*}{\partial x}. \tag{6.99}$$

Equation (6.99) shows that when the reaction function slopes up, there is a "multiplier" that magnifies the effect of the shift of the reaction function at a given level of y, $\partial y_i^*/\partial x$. In terms of the diagram, the impact on the equilibrium level of y is larger than the upward shift of the reaction function. The closer the slope is to 1, the larger the multiplier is.

In a situation like this, any factor that affects the reaction function has a large impact on overall economic activity. In the terminology of Summers (1988), the equilibrium is *fragile.* Thus it is possible that there is substantial real rigidity but that fluctuations are driven by real rather than nominal shocks. When there is substantial real rigidity, technology shocks, credit-market disruptions, changes in government spending and tax rates, shifts in uncertainty about future policies, and other real disturbances can all be important sources of output movements. Since, as we have seen, there is unlikely to be substantial real rigidity in a Walrasian model, we refer to theories of fluctuations based on real rigidities and real disturbances as *real non-Walrasian theories.* Just as there are many candidate real rigidities, there are many possible theories of this type.[42]

This discussion suggests that whether there are multiple flexible-price equilibria or merely a unique but fragile equilibrium is not crucial to fluctuations. Suppose first that (as we have been assuming throughout this section) there are no barriers to nominal adjustment. If there are multiple equilibria, fluctuations can occur without any disturbances at all as the economy moves among the different equilibria. With a unique but fragile equilibrium, on the other hand, fluctuations can occur in response to small disturbances as the equilibrium is greatly affected by the shocks.

The situation is similar with small barriers to price adjustment. Strong real rigidity (plus appropriate insensitivity of the profit function) causes firms' incentives to adjust their prices in response to a nominal disturbance to be small; whether the real rigidity is strong enough to create multiple equilibria when prices are flexible is not important.

6.12   Limitations

Keynesian theory encompasses a wide range of models, most of which are intended to address specific issues rather than to approximate the behavior of the economy as a whole. In addition, Keynesian accounts of fluctuations usually ascribe important roles to many different kinds of shocks and many different types of market imperfections.

These features of the Keynesian approach form the basis for the major criticism that can be made against it: Keynesian models are so vague and so flexible that they are almost impossible to refute. Like Ptolemaic astronomers with their epicycles to explain every new observation, Keynesian macroeconomists can modify their theories and postulate unobserved shocks to fit the data in almost any situation.

It is easy to find examples of the flexibility of Keynesian analysis, involving issues ranging from the basic assumptions of the models to the specifics of individual episodes. Shortly after the publication of the *General Theory,* Dunlop (1938) provided strong evidence against its prediction of a countercyclical real wage. Rather than abandoning his theory, Keynes (1939) merely argued that its description of price-setting behavior should

---

[42] Accepting that there is substantial real rigidity does not require adopting the view that many types of shocks are important to fluctuations. In the daylight saving time example, for instance, although there appears to be considerable real rigidity in individuals' preferences about their schedules, we do not observe sharp short-run variations in economy-wide real schedules arising from sources other than changes in the time standard. Finally, an intermediate possibility is that when there are large real rigidities, many kinds of shocks, both real and nominal, are important to fluctuations (see, for example, Greenwald and Stiglitz, 1988).

be changed. To give another example, the Keynesian response to the breakdown of the output-inflation relationship in the late 1960s and early 1970s was simply to modify the models to include supply shocks and core inflation. Similarly, confronted with clear evidence that the microeconomics of nominal adjustment differ greatly from what one would expect if the only barriers to adjustment are small fixed costs of changing prices, new Keynesians did not discard their theories; instead they argued that the actual barriers to nominal flexibility are a complicated combination of adjustment costs and other factors (D. Romer, 1993), or that menu costs are just a metaphor that is no more intended to describe reality than is the Walrasian auctioneer of competitive models (Ball and Mankiw, 1994). And so on.

The same flexibility characterizes not just Keynesian models, but Keynesian accounts of specific episodes. The models allow for disturbances in essentially every sector of the economy—money supply, money demand, fiscal policy, consumption, investment, price-setting, wage-setting, and international trade—and thus are consistent with almost any combination of movements in the different variables. For example, conventional Keynesian accounts attribute the 1981–1982 U.S. recession to tight monetary policy. The fact that most measures of money growth did not decline sharply is not viewed as an important problem for this view, but is accounted for by postulating a shift in money demand that was only partly accommodated by the Federal Reserve. Similarly, conventional Keynesian accounts attribute a large part of the 1990–1991 U.S. recession to an unexplained fall in "consumer confidence." And the conjunction of rapid output growth, very low unemployment, and steady or falling inflation in the United States in the second half of the 1990s is attributed to a large extent to favorable supply shocks and declines in the natural rate of unemployment—developments that are deduced largely from the behavior of these macroeconomic variables.

It is possible that the economy is complicated, that there are many types of shocks, and that the modifications of Keynesian models reflect gradual progress in our understanding of the economy. But a theory that is so flexible that it cannot be contradicted by any set of observations is devoid of content. Thus if Keynesian theory is to be useful, there must be some questions about which it delivers clear predictions.

One issue on which Keynesian theory appears to provide such predictions is the real effects of nominal disturbances. A central element of all Keynesian models is that nominal prices or wages do not adjust immediately. As a result, the models predict that independent monetary disturbances affect real activity. If this prediction is contradicted by the data, it appears that the models will have to be abandoned rather than modified, and that the study of fluctuations will have to pursue the real-business-cycle models of Chapter 4 or the real non-Walrasian theories of the previous section. Conversely, if the conclusion of Section 5.5 that monetary shocks have important real effects survives, theories of fluctuations are likely to require an important Keynesian element. Even in this case, however, it would be very desirable to improve and narrow Keynesian theory to a point where it gives richer and more precise predictions.

Problems

6.1. Consider the problem facing an individual in the Lucas model when P_i/P is unknown. The individual chooses L_i to maximize the expectation of U_i; U_i continues to be given by equation (6.3).

(a) Find the first-order condition for L_i, and rearrange it to obtain an expression for L_i in terms of $E[P_i/P]$. Take logs of this expression to obtain an expression for ℓ_i.

(b) How does the amount of labor the individual supplies if he or she follows the certainty-equivalence rule in (6.17) compare with the optimal amount derived in part (a)? (Hint: How does $E[\ln(P_i/P)]$ compare with $\ln(E[P_i/P])$?)

(c) Suppose that (as in the Lucas model) $\ln(P_i/P) = E[\ln(P_i/P) \mid P_i] + u_i$, where u_i is normal with a mean of 0 and a variance that is independent of P_i. Show that this implies that $\ln\{E[(P_i/P) \mid P_i]\} = E[\ln(P_i/P) \mid P_i] + C$, where C is a constant whose value is independent of P_i. (Hint: Note that $P_i/P = \exp\{E[\ln(P_i/P) \mid P_i]\} \exp(u_i)$, and show that this implies that the ℓ_i that maximizes expected utility differs from the certainty-equivalence rule in (6.17) only by a constant.)

6.2. (This follows Dixit and Stiglitz, 1977.) Suppose that the consumption index C_i in equation (6.2) is $C_i = [\int_{j=0}^{1} Z_j^{1/\eta} C_{ij}^{(\eta-1)/\eta} \, dj]^{\eta/(\eta-1)}$, where C_{ij} is the individual's consumption of good j and Z_j is the taste shock for good j. Suppose the individual has amount Y_i to spend on goods. Thus the budget constraint is $\int_{j=0}^{1} P_j C_{ij} \, dj = Y_i$.

(a) Find the first-order condition for the problem of maximizing C_i subject to the budget constraint. Solve for C_{ij} in terms of Z_j, P_j, and the Lagrange multiplier on the budget constraint.

(b) Use the budget constraint to find C_{ij} in terms of Z_j, P_j, Y_i, and the Z's and P's.

(c) Substitute your result in part (b) into the expression for C_i and show that $C_i = Y_i/P$, where $P \equiv (\int_{j=0}^{1} Z_j P_j^{1-\eta} \, dj)^{1/(1-\eta)}$.

(d) Use the results in part (b) and part (c) to show that $C_{ij} = Z_j (P_j/P)^{-\eta} (Y_i/P)$.

(e) Compare your results with (6.7) and (6.9) in the text.

6.3. **Observational equivalence.** (Sargent, 1976.) Suppose that the money supply is determined by $m_t = c'z_{t-1} + e_t$, where c and z are vectors and e_t is an i.i.d. disturbance uncorrelated with z_{t-1}. e_t is unpredictable and unobservable. Thus the expected component of m_t is $c'z_{t-1}$, and the unexpected component is e_t. In setting the money supply, the Federal Reserve responds only to variables that matter for real activity; that is, the variables in z directly affect y.

Now consider the following two models: (*i*) Only unexpected money matters, so $y_t = a'z_{t-1} + be_t + v_t$; (*ii*) all money matters, so $y_t = \alpha'z_{t-1} + \beta m_t + v_t$. In each specification, the disturbance is i.i.d. and uncorrelated with z_{t-1} and e_t.

(*a*) Is it possible to distinguish between these two theories? That is, given a candidate set of parameter values under, say, model (*i*), are there parameter values under model (*ii*) that have the same predictions? Explain.

(*b*) Suppose that the Federal Reserve also responds to some variables that do not directly affect output; that is, suppose $m_t = c'z_{t-1} + y'w_{t-1} + e_t$ and that models (*i*) and (*ii*) are as before (with their distubances now uncorrelated with w_{t-1} as well as with z_{t-1} and e_t). In this case, is it possible to distinguish between the two theories? Explain.

6.4. Suppose the economy is described by the model of Section 6.4. Assume, however, that P is the price index described in part (*c*) of Problem 6.2 (with all the Z_j's equal to 1 for simplicity). In addition, assume that money-market equilibrium requires that total spending in the economy equal M. With these changes, is it still the case that in equilibrium, output of each good is given by (6.46) and that the price of each good is given by (6.47)?

6.5. Indexation. (See Gray, 1976, 1978, and Fischer, 1977b. This problem follows Ball, 1988.) Suppose production at firm i is given by $Y_i = SL_i^\alpha$, where S is a supply shock and $0 < \alpha \le 1$. Thus in logs, $y_i = s + \alpha\ell_i$. Prices are flexible; thus (setting the constant term to 0 for simplicity), $p_i = w_i + (1 - \alpha)\ell_i - s$. Aggregating the output and price equations yields $y = s + \alpha\ell$ and $p = w + (1 - \alpha)\ell - s$. Wages are partially indexed to prices: $w = \theta p$, where $0 \le \theta \le 1$. Finally, aggregate demand is given by $y = m - p$. s and m are independent, mean-zero random variables with variances V_s and V_m.

(*a*) What are p, y, ℓ, and w as functions of m and s and the parameters α and θ? How does indexation affect the response of employment to monetary shocks? How does it affect the response to supply shocks?

(*b*) What value of θ minimizes the variance of employment?

(*c*) Suppose the demand for a single firm's output is $y_i = y - \eta(p_i - p)$. Suppose all firms other than firm i index their wages to the price level by $w = \theta p$ as before, but that firm i indexes its wage to the price level by $w_i = \theta_i p$. Firm i continues to set its price as $p_i = w_i + (1 - \alpha)\ell_i - s$. The production function and the pricing equation then imply that $y_i = y - \phi(w_i - w)$, where $\phi \equiv \alpha\eta/[\alpha + (1 - \alpha)\eta]$.

   (*i*) What is employment at firm i, ℓ_i, as a function of $m, s, \alpha, \eta, \theta$, and θ_i?

   (*ii*) What value of θ_i minimizes the variance of ℓ_i?

   (*iii*) Find the Nash equilibrium value of θ. That is, find the value of θ such that if aggregate indexation is given by θ, the representative firm minimizes the variance of ℓ_i by setting $\theta_i = \theta$. Compare this value with the value found in part (*b*).

6.6. Synchronized price-setting. Consider the Taylor model. Suppose, however, that every other period all the individuals set their prices for that period and the next. That is, in period t prices are set for t and $t + 1$; in $t + 1$, no prices are set; in $t + 2$, prices are set for $t + 2$ and $t + 3$; and so on. As in the Taylor model, prices are both predetermined and fixed, and individuals set their prices according to (6.60). Finally, assume that m follows a random walk.

(a) What is the representative individual's price in period t, x_t, as a function of m_t, $E_t m_{t+1}$, p_t, and $E_t p_{t+1}$?

(b) Use the fact that synchronization implies that p_t and p_{t+1} are both equal to x_t to solve for x_t in terms of m_t and $E_t m_{t+1}$.

(c) What are y_t and y_{t+1}? Does the central result of the Taylor model—that nominal disturbances continue to have real effects after all prices have been changed—still hold? Explain intuitively.

6.7. The Fischer model with unbalanced price-setting. Suppose the economy is as described by the model of Section 6.5, except that instead of half of the individuals setting their prices each period, fraction f set their prices in odd periods and fraction $1 - f$ set their prices in even periods. Thus the price level is $fp_t^1 + (1 - f)p_t^2$ if t is even and $(1 - f)p_t^1 + fp_t^2$ if t is odd. Derive expressions analogous to (6.57) and (6.58) for p_t and y_t for even and odd periods.

6.8. The instability of staggered price-setting. (See Fethke and Policano, 1986; Ball and Cecchetti, 1988; and Ball and D. Romer, 1989.) Suppose the economy is described as in Problem 6.7, and assume for simplicity that m is a random walk (so $m_t = m_{t-1} + u_t$, where u is white noise and has a constant variance). Assume that the amount of profits an individual loses over two periods relative to always having $p_i = p^*$ is proportional to $(p_{it} - p_{it}^*)^2 + (p_{it+1} - p_{it+1}^*)^2$. If $f < \frac{1}{2}$ and $\phi < 1$, is the expected value of this loss larger for the individuals who set their prices in odd periods or for the individuals who set their prices in even periods? In light of this, would you expect to see staggered price-setting if $\phi < 1$?

6.9. Consider the Taylor model with the money stock white noise rather than a random walk; that is, $m_t = \varepsilon_t$, where ε_t is serially uncorrelated. Solve the model using the method of undetermined coefficients. (Hint: In the equation analogous to (6.63), is it still reasonable to impose $\lambda + v = 1$?)

6.10. Repeat Problem 6.9 using lag operators.

6.11. (This follows Ball, 1994a.) Consider a continuous-time version of the Taylor model, so that $p(t) = (1/T) \int_{\tau=0}^{T} x(t - \tau)d\tau$, where T is the interval between each individual's price changes and $x(t - \tau)$ is the price set by individuals who set their prices at time $t - \tau$. Assume that $\phi = 1$, so that $p_i^*(t) = m(t)$; thus $x(t) = (1/T) \int_{\tau=0}^{T} E_t m(t + \tau)d\tau$.

(a) Suppose that initially $m(t) = gt$ $(g > 0)$, and that $E_t m(t + \tau)$ is therefore $(t + \tau)g$. What are $x(t)$, $p(t)$, and $y(t) = m(t) - p(t)$?

(b) Suppose that at time 0 the government announces that it is steadily reducing money growth to 0 over the next interval T of time. Thus $m(t) = t[1 - (t/2T)]g$ for $0 < t < T$, and $m(t) = gT/2$ for $t \geq T$. The change is unexpected, so that prices set before $t = 0$ are as in part (a).

(*i*) Show that if $x(t) = gT/2$ for all $t > 0$, then $p(t) = m(t)$ for all $t > 0$, and thus that output is the same as it would be without the change in policy.

(*ii*) For $0 < t < T$, are the prices that firms set more than, less than, or equal to $gT/2$? What about for $T \leq t \leq 2T$? Given this, how does output during the period $(0, 2T)$ compare with what it would be without the change in policy?

6.12. **State-dependent pricing with both positive and negative inflation.** (This follows Caplin and Leahy, 1991.) Consider an economy like that of the Caplin–Spulber model. Suppose, however, that m can either rise or fall, and that firms therefore follow a two-sided Ss policy: if $p_i - p_i^*(t)$ reaches either S or $-S$, firm i changes p_i so that $p_i - p_i^*(t)$ equals 0. As in the Caplin–Spulber model, changes in m are continuous.

Assume for simplicity that $p_i^*(t) = m(t)$. In addition, assume that $p_i - p_i^*(t)$ is initially distributed uniformly over some interval of width S; that is, $p_i - p_i^*(t)$ is distributed uniformly on $[X, X + S]$ for some X between $-S$ and 0. This is shown in Figure 6.9: the distribution of $p_i - p_i^*(t)$ is an "elevator" of height S in a "shaft" of height $2S$.

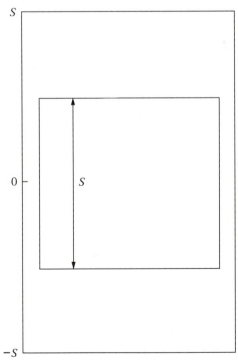

FIGURE 6.9 **The distribution of**
$p_i - p_i^*(t)$ **in the**
Caplin–Leahy model

(a) Explain why, given these assumptions, $p_i - p_i^*(t)$ continues to be distributed uniformly over some interval of width S. (In terms of the diagram, this means that although the elevator may move in the shaft, it remains of height S.)

(b) Are there any positions of the elevator (that is, any values of X) where an infinitesimal increase in m of dm raises average prices by less than dm? by more than dm? by exactly dm? Thus, what does this model imply about the real effects of monetary shocks?

6.13. Consider an economy consisting of some firms with flexible prices and some with rigid prices. Let p^f denote the price set by a representative flexible-price firm and p^r the price set by a representative rigid-price firm. Flexible-price firms set their prices after m is known; rigid-price firms set their prices before m is known. Thus flexible-price firms set $p^f = p_i^* = (1-\phi)p + \phi m$, and rigid-price firms set $p^r = Ep_i^* = (1-\phi)Ep + \phi Em$, where E denotes the expectation of a variable as of when the rigid-price firms set their prices.

Assume that fraction q of firms have rigid prices, so that $p = qp^r + (1 - q)p^f$.

(a) Find p^f in terms of p^r, m, and the parameters of the model (ϕ and q).

(b) Find p^r in terms of Em and the parameters of the model.

(c) (i) Do anticipated changes in m (that is, changes that are expected as of when rigid-price firms set their prices) affect y? Why or why not?

   (ii) Do unanticipated changes in m affect y? Why or why not?

6.14. Consider an economy consisting of many imperfectly competitive, price-setting firms. The profits of the representative firm, firm i, depend on aggregate output, y, and the firm's real price, r_i: $\pi_i = \pi(y, r_i)$, where $\pi_{22} < 0$ (subscripts denote partial derivatives). Let $r^*(y)$ denote the profit-maximizing price as a function of y; note that $r^*(y)$ is characterized by $\pi_2(y, r^*(y)) = 0$.

Assume that output is at some level y_0, and that firm i's real price is $r^*(y_0)$. Now suppose there is a change in the money supply, and suppose that other firms do not change their prices and that aggregate output therefore changes to some new level, y_1.

(a) Explain why firm i's incentive to adjust its price is given by $G = \pi(y_1, r^*(y_1)) - \pi(y_1, r^*(y_0))$.

(b) Use a second-order Taylor approximation of this expression in y_1 around $y_1 = y_0$ to show that $G \simeq -\pi_{22}(y_0, r^*(y_0))[r^{*\prime}(y_0)]^2(y_1 - y_0)^2/2$.

(c) What component of this expression corresponds to the degree of real rigidity? What component corresponds to the degree of insensitivity of the profit function?

6.15. Multiple equilibria with menu costs. (This follows Ball and D. Romer, 1991.) Consider an economy consisting of many imperfectly competitive firms. The profits that a firm loses relative to what it obtains with $p_i = p^*$ are $K(p_i - p^*)^2$, $K > 0$. As usual, $p^* = p + \phi y$ and $y = m - p$. Each firm faces a fixed cost Z of changing its nominal price.

Initially m is 0 and the economy is at its flexible-price equilibrium, which is $y = 0$ and $p = m = 0$. Now suppose m changes to m'.

(a) Suppose that fraction f of firms change their prices. Since the firms that change their prices charge p^* and the firms that do not charge 0, this implies $p = fp^*$. Use this fact to find p, y, and p^* as functions of m' and f.

(b) Plot a firm's incentive to adjust its price, $K(0-p^*)^2 = Kp^{*2}$, as a function of f. Be sure to distinguish the cases $\phi < 1$ and $\phi > 1$.

(c) A firm adjusts its price if the benefit exceeds Z, does not adjust if the benefit is less than Z, and is indifferent if the benefit is exactly Z. Given this, can there be a situation where both adjustment by all firms and adjustment by no firms are equilibria? Can there be a situation where neither adjustment by all firms nor adjustment by no firms is an equilibrium?

6.16. (This follows Diamond, 1982.)[43] Consider an island consisting of N people and many palm trees. Each person is in one of two states, not carrying a coconut and looking for palm trees (state P) or carrying a coconut and looking for other people with coconuts (state C). If a person without a coconut finds a palm tree, he or she can climb the tree and pick a coconut; this has a cost (in utility units) of c. If a person with a coconut meets another person with a coconut, they trade and eat each other's coconuts; this yields $\bar{u}$ units of utility for each of them. (People cannot eat coconuts that they have picked themselves.)

A person looking for coconuts finds palm trees at rate b per unit time. A person carrying a coconut finds trading partners at rate aL per unit time, where L is the total number of people carrying coconuts. a and b are exogenous.

Individuals' discount rate is r. Focus on steady states; that is, assume that L is constant.

(a) Explain why, if everyone in state P climbs a palm tree whenever he or she finds one, then $rV_P = b(V_C - V_P - c)$, where V_P and V_C are the values of being in the two states.

(b) Find the analogous expression for V_C.

(c) Solve for $V_C - V_P$, V_C, and V_P in terms of $r, b, c, \bar{u}, a$, and L.

(d) What is L, still assuming that anyone in state P climbs a palm tree whenever he or she finds one? Assume for simplicity that $aN = 2b$.

(e) For what values of c is it a steady-state equilibrium for anyone in state P to climb a palm tree whenever he or she finds one? (Continue to assume $aN = 2b$.)

(f) For what values of c is it a steady-state equilibrium for no one who finds a tree to climb it? Are there values of c for which there is more than one steady-state equilibrium? If there are multiple equilibria, does one involve higher welfare than the other? Explain intuitively.

---

[43] The solution to this problem requires dynamic programming (see Section 9.4).

Chapter 7
CONSUMPTION

This chapter and the next investigate households' consumption choices and firms' investment decisions. Consumption and investment are important to both growth and fluctuations. With regard to growth, the division of society's resources between consumption and various types of investment—in physical capital, human capital, and research and development—is central to standards of living in the long run. That division is determined by the interaction of households' allocation of their incomes between consumption and saving given the rates of return and other constraints they face, and firms' investment demand given the interest rates and other constraints they face. With regard to fluctuations, consumption and investment make up the vast majority of the demand for goods. Thus if we want to understand how such forces as government purchases, technology, and monetary policy affect aggregate output, we must understand how consumption and investment are determined.

There are two other reasons for studying consumption and investment. First, they introduce some important issues involving financial markets. Financial markets affect the macroeconomy mainly through their impact on consumption and investment. In addition, consumption and investment have important feedback effects on financial markets. We will investigate the interaction between financial markets and consumption and investment both in cases where financial markets function perfectly and in cases where they do not.

Second, much of the most insightful empirical work in macroeconomics over the past 20 years has been concerned with consumption and investment. These two chapters therefore have an unusually intensive empirical focus.

7.1   Consumption under Certainty: The Life-Cycle/Permanent-Income Hypothesis

Assumptions

Although we have already examined aspects of individuals' consumption decisions in our investigations of the Ramsey and Diamond models in Chapter 2 and of real-business-cycle theory in Chapter 4, here we start with a simple case. Consider an individual who lives for T periods whose lifetime utility is

$$U = \sum_{t=1}^{T} u(C_t), \qquad u'(\bullet) > 0, \qquad u''(\bullet) < 0, \tag{7.1}$$

where $u(\bullet)$ is the instantaneous utility function and C_t is consumption in period t. The individual has initial wealth of A_0 and labor incomes of $Y_1, Y_2, \ldots, Y_T$ in the T periods of his or her life; the individual takes these as given. The individual can save or borrow at an exogenous interest rate, subject only to the constraint that any outstanding debt be repaid at the end of his or her life. For simplicity, this interest rate is set to 0.[1] Thus the individual's budget constraint is

$$\sum_{t=1}^{T} C_t \le A_0 + \sum_{t=1}^{T} Y_t. \tag{7.2}$$

Behavior

Since the marginal utility of consumption is always positive, the individual satisfies the budget constraint with equality. The Lagrangian for his or her maximization problem is therefore

$$\mathcal{L} = \sum_{t=1}^{T} u(C_t) + \lambda \left(A_0 + \sum_{t=1}^{T} Y_t - \sum_{t=1}^{T} C_t \right). \tag{7.3}$$

---

[1] Note that we have also assumed that the individual's discount rate is 0 (see [7.1]). Assuming that the interest rate and the discount rate are equal but not necessarily 0 would have almost no effect on the analysis in this section and the next. And assuming that they need not be equal would have only modest effects.

The first-order condition for C_t is

$$u'(C_t) = \lambda. \tag{7.4}$$

Since (7.4) holds in every period, the marginal utility of consumption is constant. And since the level of consumption uniquely determines its marginal utility, this means that consumption must be constant. Thus $C_1 = C_2 = \cdots = C_T$. Substituting this fact into the budget constraint yields

$$C_t = \frac{1}{T}\left(A_0 + \sum_{\tau=1}^{T} Y_\tau\right) \qquad \text{for all } t. \tag{7.5}$$

The term in parentheses is the individual's total lifetime resources. Thus (7.5) states that the individual divides his or her lifetime resources equally among each period of life.

Implications

This analysis implies that the individual's consumption in a given period is determined not by income that period, but by income over his or her entire lifetime. In the terminology of Friedman (1957), the right-hand side of (7.5) is *permanent income,* and the difference between current and permanent income is *transitory income.* Equation (7.5) implies that consumption is determined by permanent income.

To see the importance of the distinction between permanent and transitory income, consider the effect of a windfall gain of amount Z in the first period of life. Although this windfall raises current income by Z, it raises permanent income by only Z/T. Thus if the individual's horizon is fairly long, the windfall's impact on current consumption is small. One implication is that a temporary tax cut may have little impact on consumption; as described in Chapter 6, this appears to be the case in practice.

Our analysis also implies that although the time pattern of income is not important to consumption, it is critical to saving. The individual's saving in period t is the difference between income and consumption:

$$\begin{aligned} S_t &= Y_t - C_t \\ &= \left(Y_t - \frac{1}{T}\sum_{\tau=1}^{T} Y_\tau\right) - \frac{1}{T}A_0, \end{aligned} \tag{7.6}$$

where the second line uses (7.5) to substitute for C_t. Thus saving is high when income is high relative to its average—that is, when transitory income is high. Similarly, when current income is less than permanent income, saving is negative. Thus the individual uses saving and borrowing to smooth the path of consumption. This is the key idea of the life-cycle/permanent-income hypothesis of Modigliani and Brumberg (1954) and Friedman (1957).

What Is Saving?

At a more general level, the basic idea of the life-cycle/permanent-income hypothesis is a simple insight about saving: saving is future consumption. As long as an individual does not save just for the sake of saving, he or she saves to consume in the future. The saving may be used for conventional consumption later in life, or bequeathed to the individual's children for their consumption, or even used to erect monuments to the individual upon his or her death. But as long as the individual does not value saving in itself, the decision about the division of income between consumption and saving is driven by preferences between present and future consumption and information about future consumption prospects.

This observation suggests that many common statements about saving may be incorrect. For example, it is often asserted that poor individuals save a smaller fraction of their incomes than the wealthy do because their incomes are little above the level needed to provide a minimal standard of living. But this claim overlooks the fact that individuals who have trouble obtaining even a low standard of living today may also have trouble obtaining that standard in the future. Thus their saving is likely to be determined by the time pattern of their income, just as it is for the wealthy.

To take another example, consider the common assertion that individuals' concern about their consumption relative to others' tends to raise their consumption as they try to "keep up with the Joneses." Again, this claim fails to recognize what saving is: since saving represents future consumption, saving less implies consuming less in the future, and thus falling further behind the Joneses. Thus one can just as well argue that concern about relative consumption causes individuals to try to catch up with the Joneses in the future, and thus lowers rather than raises current consumption.[2]

Empirical Application: Understanding Estimated Consumption Functions

The traditional Keynesian consumption function posits that consumption is determined by current disposable income. Keynes (1936) argued that "the amount of aggregate consumption mainly depends on the amount of aggregate income," and that this relationship "is a fairly stable function." He claimed further that "it is also obvious that a higher absolute level of income ... will lead, as a rule, to a greater *proportion* of income being saved" (Keynes, 1936, pp. 96–97; emphasis in original).

---

[2] See Abel (1990) and Campbell and Cochrane (1999) for more on how individuals' concern about their consumption relative to others' affects saving once one recognizes that saving represents future consumption.

The importance of the consumption function to Keynes's analysis of fluctuations led many researchers to estimate the relationship between consumption and current income. Contrary to Keynes's claims, these studies did not demonstrate a consistent, stable relationship. Across households at a point in time, the relationship is indeed of the type that Keynes postulated; an example of such a relationship is shown in Panel (a) of Figure 7.1. But within a country over time, aggregate consumption is essentially proportional to aggregate income; that is, one sees a relationship like that in Panel (b) of the figure. Further, the cross-section consumption function differs across groups. For example, the slope of the estimated consumption function is similar for whites and blacks, but the intercept is higher for whites. This is shown in Panel (c) of the figure.

As Friedman (1957) demonstrates, the permanent-income hypothesis provides a straightforward explanation of all of these findings. Suppose that consumption is in fact determined by permanent income: $C = Y^P$. Current income equals the sum of permanent and transitory income: $Y = Y^P + Y^T$. And since transitory income reflects departures of current income from permanent income, in most samples it has a mean near zero and is roughly uncorrelated with permanent income.

Now consider a regression of consumption on current income:

$$C_i = a + bY_i + e_i. \tag{7.7}$$

In a univariate regression, the estimated coefficient on the independent variable is the ratio of the covariance of the independent and dependent variables to the variance of the independent variable. In this case, this implies

$$\hat{b} = \frac{\text{Cov}(Y, C)}{\text{Var}(Y)}$$

$$= \frac{\text{Cov}(Y^P + Y^T, Y^P)}{\text{Var}(Y^P + Y^T)} \tag{7.8}$$

$$= \frac{\text{Var}(Y^P)}{\text{Var}(Y^P) + \text{Var}(Y^T)}.$$

Here the second line uses the facts that current income equals the sum of permanent and transitory income and that consumption equals permanent income, and the last line uses the assumption that permanent and temporary income are uncorrelated. In addition, the estimated constant equals the mean of the dependent variable minus the estimated slope coefficient times the mean of the independent variable. Thus,

$$\hat{a} = \overline{C} - \hat{b}\overline{Y}$$

$$= \overline{Y}^P - \hat{b}(\overline{Y}^P + \overline{Y}^T) \tag{7.9}$$

$$= (1 - \hat{b})\overline{Y}^P,$$

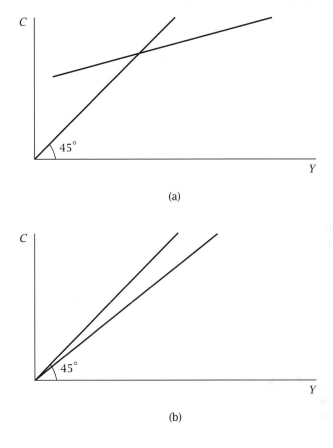

(a)

(b)

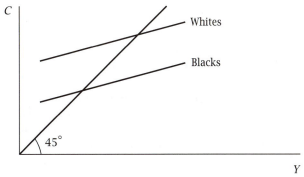

(c)

FIGURE 7.1 Some different forms of the relationship between current income and consumption

where the last line uses the assumption that the mean of transitory income is 0.

Thus the permanent-income hypothesis predicts that the key determinant of the slope of an estimated consumption function, $\hat{b}$, is the relative variation in permanent and transitory income. Intuitively, an increase in current income is associated with an increase in consumption only to the extent that it reflects an increase in permanent income. When the variation in permanent income is much greater than the variation in transitory income, almost all differences in current income reflect differences in permanent income; thus consumption rises nearly one-for-one with current income. But when the variation in permanent income is small relative to the variation in transitory income, little of the variation in current income comes from variation in permanent income, and so consumption rises little with current income.

This analysis can be used to understand the estimated consumption functions in Figure 7.1. Across households, much of the variation in income reflects such factors as unemployment and the fact that households are at different points in their life cycles. As a result, the estimated slope coefficient is substantially less than 1, and the estimated intercept is positive. Over time, in contrast, almost all the variation in aggregate income reflects long-run growth—that is, permanent increases in the economy's resources. Thus the estimated slope coefficient is close to 1, and the estimated intercept is close to 0.[3]

Now consider the differences between blacks and whites. The relative variances of permanent and transitory income are similar in the two groups, and so the estimates of b are similar. But blacks' average incomes are lower than whites'; as a result, the estimate of a for blacks is lower than the estimate for whites (see [7.9]).

To see the intuition for this result, consider a member of each group whose income equals the average income among whites. Since there are many more blacks with permanent incomes below this level than there are with permanent incomes above it, the black's permanent income is much more likely to be less than his or her current income than more. As a result, blacks with this current income have on average lower permanent income; thus on average they consume less than their income. For the white, in contrast, his or her permanent income is about as likely to be more than current income as it is to be less; as a result, whites with this current income on average have the same permanent income, and thus on average they consume their income. In sum, the permanent-income hypothesis attributes

---

[3] In this case, although consumption is approximately proportional to income, the constant of proportionality is less than 1; that is, consumption is on average less than permanent income. As Friedman describes, there are various ways of extending the basic theory to make it consistent with this result. One is to account for turnover among generations and long-run growth: if the young generally save and the old generally dissave, the fact that each generation is wealthier than the previous one implies that the young's saving is greater than the old's dissaving.

the different consumption patterns of blacks and whites to the different average incomes of the two groups, and not to any differences in tastes or culture.

7.2 Consumption under Uncertainty: The Random-Walk Hypothesis

Individual Behavior

We now extend our analysis to account for uncertainty. Continue to assume that both the interest rate and the discount rate are zero. In addition, suppose that the instantaneous utility function, $u(\bullet)$, is quadratic. Thus the individual maximizes

$$E[U] = E\left[\sum_{t=1}^{T}\left(C_t - \frac{a}{2}C_t^2\right)\right], \qquad a > 0. \tag{7.10}$$

We will assume that the individual's wealth is such that consumption is always in the range where marginal utility is positive. As before, the individual must pay off any outstanding debts at the end of life. Thus the budget constraint is again given by equation (7.2), $\sum_{t=1}^{T} C_t \le A_0 + \sum_{t=1}^{T} Y_t$.

To describe the individual's behavior, we use the Euler equation approach that we employed in Chapters 2 and 4. Specifically, suppose that the individual has chosen first-period consumption optimally given the information available, and suppose that he or she will choose consumption in each future period optimally given the information then available. Now consider a reduction in C_1 of dC from the value the individual has chosen and an equal increase in consumption at some future date from the value he or she would have chosen. If the individual is optimizing, a marginal change of this type does not affect expected utility. Since the marginal utility of consumption in period 1 is $1 - aC_1$, the change has a utility cost of $(1 - aC_1) dC$. And since the marginal utility of period-t consumption is $1 - aC_t$, the change has an expected utility benefit of $E_1[1 - aC_t] dC$, where $E_1[\bullet]$ denotes expectations conditional on the information available in period 1. Thus if the individual is optimizing,

$$1 - aC_1 = E_1[1 - aC_t], \qquad \text{for } t = 2, 3, \ldots, T. \tag{7.11}$$

Since $E_1[1 - aC_t]$ equals $1 - aE_1[C_t]$, this implies

$$C_1 = E_1[C_t], \qquad \text{for } t = 2, 3, \ldots, T. \tag{7.12}$$

The individual knows that his or her lifetime consumption will satisfy the budget constraint, (7.2), with equality. Thus the expectations of the two sides of the constraint must be equal:

$$\sum_{t=1}^{T} E_1[C_t] = A_0 + \sum_{t=1}^{T} E_1[Y_t]. \tag{7.13}$$

Equation (7.12) implies that the left-hand side of (7.13) is TC_1. Substituting this into (7.13) and dividing by T yields

$$C_1 = \frac{1}{T} \left(A_0 + \sum_{t=1}^{T} E_1[Y_t] \right). \tag{7.14}$$

That is, the individual consumes $1/T$ of his or her expected lifetime resources.

Implications

Equation (7.12) implies that the expectation as of period 1 of C_2 equals C_1. More generally, reasoning analogous to what we have just done implies that in each period, expected next-period consumption equals current consumption. This implies that changes in consumption are unpredictable. By the definition of expectations, we can write

$$C_t = E_{t-1}[C_t] + e_t, \tag{7.15}$$

where e_t is a variable whose expectation as of period $t-1$ is 0. Thus, since $E_{t-1}[C_t] = C_{t-1}$, we have

$$C_t = C_{t-1} + e_t. \tag{7.16}$$

This is Hall's famous result that the life-cycle/permanent-income hypothesis implies that consumption follows a random walk (Hall, 1978). The intuition for this result is straightforward: if consumption is expected to change, the individual can do a better job of smoothing consumption. Suppose, for example, that consumption is expected to rise. This means that the current marginal utility of consumption is greater than the expected future marginal utility of consumption, and thus that the individual is better off raising current consumption. Thus the individual adjusts his or her current consumption to the point where consumption is not expected to change.

In addition, our analysis can be used to find what determines the change in consumption, e. Consider for concreteness the change from period 1 to period 2. Reasoning parallel to that used to derive (7.14) implies that C_2 equals $1/(T-1)$ of the individual's expected remaining lifetime resources:

$$C_2 = \frac{1}{T-1} \left(A_1 + \sum_{t=2}^{T} E_2[Y_t] \right)$$

$$= \frac{1}{T-1} \left(A_0 + Y_1 - C_1 + \sum_{t=2}^{T} E_2[Y_t] \right), \tag{7.17}$$

where the second line uses the fact that $A_1 = A_0 + Y_1 - C_1$. We can rewrite the expectation as of period 2 of income over the remainder of life, $\sum_{t=2}^{T} E_2[Y_t]$, as the expectation of this quantity as of period 1, $\sum_{t=2}^{T} E_1[Y_t]$, plus the information learned between period 1 and period 2, $\sum_{t=2}^{T} E_2[Y_t] - \sum_{t=2}^{T} E_1[Y_t]$. Thus we can rewrite (7.17) as

$$C_2 = \frac{1}{T-1}\left[A_0 + Y_1 - C_1 + \sum_{t=2}^{T} E_1[Y_t] + \left(\sum_{t=2}^{T} E_2[Y_t] - \sum_{t=2}^{T} E_1[Y_t] \right) \right]. \quad (7.18)$$

From (7.14), $A_0 + Y_1 + \sum_{t=2}^{T} E_1[Y_t]$ equals TC_1. Thus (7.18) becomes

$$C_2 = \frac{1}{T-1}\left[TC_1 - C_1 + \left(\sum_{t=2}^{T} E_2[Y_t] - \sum_{t=2}^{T} E_1[Y_t] \right) \right]$$

$$= C_1 + \frac{1}{T-1}\left(\sum_{t=2}^{T} E_2[Y_t] - \sum_{t=2}^{T} E_1[Y_t] \right). \quad (7.19)$$

Equation (7.19) states that the change in consumption between period 1 and period 2 equals the change in the individual's estimate of his or her lifetime resources divided by the number of periods of life remaining.

Finally, note that the individual's behavior exhibits certainty equivalence: as (7.14) shows, the individual consumes the amount he or she would if his or her future incomes were certain to equal their means; that is, uncertainty about future income has no impact on consumption.

To see the intuition for this certainty-equivalence behavior, consider the Euler equation relating consumption in periods 1 and 2. With a general instantaneous utility function, this condition is

$$u'(C_1) = E_1[u'(C_2)]. \quad (7.20)$$

When utility is quadratic, marginal utility is linear. Thus the expected marginal utility of consumption is the same as the marginal utility of expected consumption. That is, since $E_1[1 - aC_2] = 1 - aE_1[C_2]$, for quadratic utility (7.20) is equivalent to

$$u'(C_1) = u'(E_1[C_2]). \quad (7.21)$$

This implies $C_1 = E_1[C_2]$.

This analysis shows that quadratic utility is the source of certainty-equivalence behavior: if utility is not quadratic, marginal utility is not linear, and so (7.21) does not follow from (7.20). We return to this point in Section 7.6.[4]

---

[4] Although the specific result that the change in consumption has a mean of 0 and is unpredictable (equation [7.16]) depends on the assumption of quadratic utility (and on the assumption that the discount rate and the interest rate are equal), the result that departures of consumption growth from its average value are not predictable arises under more general assumptions. See, for example, Problem 7.3.

7.3   Empirical Application: Two Tests of the Random-Walk Hypothesis

Hall's random-walk result ran strongly counter to existing views about consumption.[5] The traditional view of consumption over the business cycle implies that when output declines, consumption declines but is expected to recover; thus it implies that there are predictable movements in consumption. Hall's extension of the permanent-income hypothesis, in contrast, predicts that when output declines unexpectedly, consumption declines only by the amount of the fall in permanent income; as a result, it is not expected to recover.

Because of this divergence in the predictions of the two views, a great deal of effort has been devoted to testing whether predictable changes in income produce predictable changes in consumption. The hypothesis that consumption responds to predictable income movements is referred to as *excess sensitivity* of consumption (Flavin, 1981).[6]

Campbell and Mankiw's Test Using Aggregate Data

The random-walk hypothesis implies that the change in consumption is unpredictable; thus it implies that no information available at time $t - 1$ can be used to forecast the change in consumption from $t - 1$ to t. Thus one approach to testing the random-walk hypothesis is to regress the change in consumption on variables that are known at $t - 1$. If the random-walk hypothesis is correct, the coefficients on the variables should not differ systematically from 0.

This is the approach that Hall took in his original work. He was unable to reject the hypothesis that lagged values of either income or consumption cannot predict the change in consumption. He did find, however, that lagged stock-price movements have statistically significant predictive power for the change in consumption.

---

[5] Indeed, it is said that when Hall first presented the paper deriving and testing the random-walk result, one prominent macroeconomist told him that he must have been on drugs when he wrote the paper.

[6] The permanent-income hypothesis also makes predictions about how consumption responds to unexpected changes in income. In the model of Section 7.2, for example, the response to news is given by equation (7.19). The hypothesis that consumption responds less than the permanent-income hypothesis predicts to unexpected changes in income is referred to as *excess smoothness* of consumption. Since excess sensitivity concerns expected changes in income and excess smoothness concerns unexpected changes, it is possible for consumption to be excessively sensitive and excessively smooth at the same time. For more on excess smoothness, see Campbell and Deaton (1989); West (1988); Flavin (1993); and Problem 7.4.

The disadvantage of this approach is that the results are hard to interpret. For example, Hall's result that lagged income does not have strong predictive power for consumption could arise not because predictable changes in income do not produce predictable changes in consumption, but because lagged values of income are of little use in predicting income movements. Similarly, it is hard to gauge the importance of the rejection of the random-walk prediction using stock-price data.

Campbell and Mankiw (1989b) therefore use an instrumental-variables approach to test Hall's hypothesis against a specific alternative. The alternative they consider is that some fraction of consumers simply spend their current income, and the remainder behave according to Hall's theory. This alternative implies that the change in consumption from period $t - 1$ to period t equals the change in income between $t - 1$ and t for the first group of consumers, and equals the change in estimated permanent income between $t - 1$ and t for the second group. Thus if we let λ denote the fraction of consumption that is done by consumers in the first group, the change in aggregate consumption is

$$C_t - C_{t-1} = \lambda(Y_t - Y_{t-1}) + (1 - \lambda)e_t$$
$$\equiv \lambda Z_t + v_t,$$

(7.22)

where e_t is the change in consumers' estimate of their permanent income from $t - 1$ to t.

Z_t and v_t are almost surely correlated. Times when income increases greatly are usually also times when households receive favorable news about their total lifetime incomes. But this means that the right-hand-side variable in (7.22) is positively correlated with the error term. Thus estimating (7.22) by ordinary least squares (OLS) leads to estimates of λ that are biased upward.

The solution to correlation between the right-hand-side variable and the error term is to use instrumental variables (IV) rather than OLS. The intuition behind IV estimation is easiest to see using the two-stage least squares interpretation of instrumental variables. What one needs are variables correlated with the right-hand-side variables but uncorrelated with the residual. Once one has such *instruments,* the first-stage regression is a regression of the right-hand-side variable, Z_t, on the instruments. The second-stage regression is then a regression of the left-hand-side variable, $C_t - C_{t-1}$, on the fitted value of Z_t from the first-stage regression, $\hat{Z}_t$. That is, we estimate

$$C_t - C_{t-1} = \lambda\hat{Z}_t + \lambda(Z_t - \hat{Z}_t) + v_t$$
$$\equiv \lambda\hat{Z}_t + \tilde{v}_t.$$

(7.23)

The residual in (7.23), $\tilde{v}_t$, consists of two terms, v_t and $\lambda(Z_t - \hat{Z}_t)$. By assumption, the instruments used to construct $\hat{Z}$ are not systematically correlated with v_t. And since $\hat{Z}$ is the fitted value from a regression, by construction it is uncorrelated with the residual from that regression, $Z - \hat{Z}$. Thus regressing $C_t - C_{t-1}$ on $\hat{Z}$ yields a valid estimate of λ.[7]

The usual problem in using instrumental variables is finding valid instruments: it is often hard to find variables that one can be confident are uncorrelated with the residual. But in cases where the residual reflects new information between $t - 1$ and t, theory tells us that there are many candidate instruments: any variable that is known as of time $t - 1$ is uncorrelated with the residual.

We can now turn to the specifics of Campbell and Mankiw's test. They measure consumption as real purchases of consumer nondurables and services per person, and income as real disposable income per person. The data are quarterly, and the sample period is 1953–1986. They consider various sets of instruments. They find that lagged changes in income have almost no predictive power for future changes. This suggests that Hall's failure to find predictive power of lagged income movements for consumption is not strong evidence against the traditional view of consumption. As a base case, they therefore use lagged values of the change in consumption as instruments. When three lags are used, the estimate of λ is 0.42, with a standard error of 0.16; when five lags are used, the estimate is 0.52, with a standard error of 0.13. Other specifications yield similar results.

Thus Campbell and Mankiw's estimates suggest quantitatively large and statistically significant departures from the predictions of the random-walk model: consumption appears to increase by about fifty cents in response to an anticipated 1-dollar increase in income, and the null hypothesis of no effect is strongly rejected. At the same time, the estimates of λ are far below 1. Thus the results also suggest that the permanent-income hypothesis is important to understanding consumption.[8]

---

[7] The fact that $\hat{Z}$ is based on estimated coefficients causes two complications. First, the uncertainty about the estimated coefficients must be accounted for in finding the standard error of the estimate of λ; this is done in the usual formulas for the standard errors of instrumental-variables estimates. Second, the fact that the first-stage coefficients are estimated introduces some correlation between $\hat{Z}$ and v in the same direction as the correlation between Z and v. This correlation disappears as the sample size becomes large; thus IV is consistent but not unbiased. If the instruments are only moderately correlated with the right-hand-side variable, however, the bias in finite samples can be substantial. See, for example, Nelson and Startz (1990) and Staiger and Stock (1997).

[8] In addition, the instrumental-variables approach has *overidentifying restrictions* that can be tested. If the lagged changes in consumption are valid instruments, they are uncorrelated with v. This implies that once we have extracted all the information in the instruments about income growth, they should have no additional predictive power for the left-hand-side variable: if they do, that means that they are correlated with v, and thus that they are not valid instruments. This implication can be tested by regressing the estimated residuals from (7.22) on the instruments and testing whether the instruments have any explanatory power. Specifically, one can show that under the null hypothesis of valid instruments, the R^2 of this regression times the number of observations is asymptotically distributed χ^2 with degrees of freedom equal to the number of overidentifying restrictions—that is, the number of instruments minus the number of endogenous variables.

In Campbell and Mankiw's case, this TR^2 statistic is distributed χ^2_2 when three lags of

Shea's Test Using Household Data

Testing the random-walk hypothesis with aggregate data has several disadvantages. Most obviously, the number of observations is small. In addition, it is difficult to find variables with much predictive power for changes in income; it is therefore hard to test the key prediction of the random-walk hypothesis that predictable changes in income are not associated with predictable changes in consumption. Finally, the theory concerns individuals' consumption, and additional assumptions are needed for the predictions of the model to apply to aggregate data. Entry and exit of households from the population, for example, can cause the predictions of the theory to fail in the aggregate even if they hold for each household individually.

Because of these considerations, many investigators have examined consumption behavior using data on individual households. Shea (1995) takes particular care to identify predictable changes in income. He focuses on households in the PSID with wage-earners covered by long-term union contracts. For these households, the wage increases and cost-of-living provisions in the contracts cause income growth to have an important predictable component.

Shea constructs a sample of 647 observations where the union contract provides clear information about the household's future earnings. A regression of actual real wage growth on the estimate constructed from the union contract and some control variables produces a coefficient on the constructed measure of 0.86, with a standard error of 0.20. Thus the union contract has important predictive power for changes in earnings.

Shea then regresses consumption growth on this measure of expected wage growth; the permanent-income hypothesis predicts that the coefficient should be 0.[9] The estimated coefficient is in fact 0.89, with a standard error of 0.46. Thus Shea also finds a quantitatively large (though only marginally statistically significant) departure from the random-walk prediction.

Recall that in our analysis in Sections 7.1 and 7.2, we assumed that households can borrow without limit as long as they eventually repay their debts. One reason that consumption might not follow a random walk is that this assumption might fail—that is, that households might face *liquidity constraints*. If households are unable to borrow and their current income

---

the change in consumption are used, and χ_4^2 when five lags are used. The values of the test statistic in the two cases are only 1.83 and 2.94; these are only in the 59th and 43rd percentiles of the relevant χ^2 distributions. Thus the hypothesis that the instruments are valid cannot be rejected.

[9] An alternative would be to follow Campbell and Mankiw's approach and regress consumption growth on actual income growth by instrumental variables, using the constructed wage growth measure as an instrument. Given the almost one-for-one relationship between actual and constructed earnings growth, this approach would probably produce similar results.

is less than their permanent income, their consumption is determined by their current income. In this case, predictable changes in income produce predictable changes in consumption.

Shea tests for liquidity constraints in two ways. First, following Zeldes (1989) and others, he divides the households according to whether they have liquid assets. Households with liquid assets can smooth their consumption by running down these assets rather than by borrowing. Thus if liquidity constraints are the reason that predictable wage changes affect consumption growth, the prediction of the permanent-income hypothesis will fail only among the households with no assets. Shea finds, however, that the estimated effect of expected wage growth on consumption is essentially the same in the two groups.

Second, following Altonji and Siow (1987), Shea splits the low-wealth sample according to whether the expected change in the real wage is positive or negative. Individuals facing expected declines in income need to save rather than borrow to smooth their consumption. Thus if liquidity constraints are important, predictable wage increases produce predictable consumption increases, but predictable wage decreases do not produce predictable consumption decreases.

Shea's findings are the opposite of this. For the households with positive expected income growth, the estimated impact of the expected change in the real wage on consumption growth is 0.06 (with a standard error of 0.79); for the households with negative expected growth, the estimated effect is 2.24 (with a standard error of 0.95). Thus there is no evidence that liquidity constraints are the source of Shea's results.

Campbell and Mankiw's and Shea's findings that consumption responds to predictable changes in income are representative of what other researchers have found. For example, Wilcox (1989), Parker (1999), and Souleles (1999) each identify a feature of government policy that causes predictable income movements. Wilcox focuses on cost-of-living increases for social security recipients; Parker considers the fact that workers do not pay social security taxes once their wage income for the year exceeds a certain level; and Souleles examines income tax refunds. All three authors find that the resulting predictable changes in income are associated with substantial predictable changes in consumption.

7.4   The Interest Rate and Saving

An important issue concerning consumption involves its response to rates of return. For example, many economists have argued that more favorable tax treatment of interest income would increase saving, and thus increase growth. But if consumption is relatively unresponsive to the rate of return, such policies would have little effect. Understanding the impact of rates of return on consumption is thus important.

The Interest Rate and Consumption Growth

We begin by extending the analysis of consumption under certainty in Section 7.1 to allow for a nonzero interest rate. This largely repeats material in Section 2.2; for convenience, however, we quickly repeat that analysis here.

Once we allow for a nonzero interest rate, the individual's budget constraint is that the present value of lifetime consumption not exceed initial wealth plus the present value of lifetime labor income. For the case of a constant interest rate and a lifetime of T periods, this constraint is

$$\sum_{t=1}^{T} \frac{1}{(1+r)^t} C_t \le A_0 + \sum_{t=1}^{T} \frac{1}{(1+r)^t} Y_t, \tag{7.24}$$

where r is the interest rate and where all variables are discounted to period 0.

When we allow for a nonzero interest rate, it is also useful to allow for a nonzero discount rate. In addition, it simplifies the analysis to assume that the instantaneous utility function takes the constant-relative-risk-aversion form used in Chapter 2: $u(C_t) = C_t^{1-\theta}/(1-\theta)$, where θ is the coefficient of relative risk aversion (the inverse of the elasticity of substitution between consumption at different dates). Thus the utility function, (7.1), becomes

$$U = \sum_{t=1}^{T} \frac{1}{(1+\rho)^t} \frac{C_t^{1-\theta}}{1-\theta}, \tag{7.25}$$

where ρ is the discount rate.

Now consider our usual experiment of a decrease in consumption in some period, period t, accompanied by an increase in consumption in the next period by $1+r$ times the amount of the decrease. Optimization requires that a marginal change of this type has no effect on lifetime utility. Since the marginal utilities of consumption in periods t and $t+1$ are $C_t^{-\theta}/(1+\rho)^t$ and $C_{t+1}^{-\theta}/(1+\rho)^{t+1}$, this condition is

$$\frac{1}{(1+\rho)^t} C_t^{-\theta} = (1+r) \frac{1}{(1+\rho)^{t+1}} C_{t+1}^{-\theta}. \tag{7.26}$$

We can rearrange this condition to obtain

$$\frac{C_{t+1}}{C_t} = \left(\frac{1+r}{1+\rho}\right)^{1/\theta}. \tag{7.27}$$

This analysis implies that once we allow for the possibility that the real interest rate and the discount rate are not equal, consumption need not be a random walk: consumption is rising over time if r exceeds ρ and falling if r is less than ρ. In addition, if there are variations in the real interest rate, there are variations in the predictable component of consumption growth. Mankiw (1981), Hansen and Singleton (1983), Hall (1988b),

Campbell and Mankiw (1989b), and others therefore examine how much consumption growth responds to variations in the real interest rate. For the most part they find that it responds relatively little, which suggests that the intertemporal elasticity of substitution is low (that is, that θ is high).

The Interest Rate and Saving in the Two-Period Case

Although an increase in the interest rate causes the path of consumption to be more steeply sloped, it does not necessarily follow that the increase reduces initial consumption and thereby raises saving. The complication is that the change in the interest rate has not only a substitution effect, but also an income effect. Specifically, if the individual is a net saver, the increase in the interest rate allows him or her to attain a higher path of consumption than before.

The qualitative issues can be seen in the case where the individual lives for only two periods. For this case, we can use the standard indifference-curve diagram shown in Figure 7.2. For simplicity, assume the individual has no initial wealth. Thus in (C_1, C_2) space, the individual's budget constraint goes through the point (Y_1, Y_2): the individual can choose to consume his or her income each period. And the slope of the budget constraint is $-(1 + r)$: giving up 1 unit of first-period consumption allows the individual to increase second-period consumption by $1 + r$. When r rises, the budget constraint continues to go through (Y_1, Y_2) but becomes steeper; thus it pivots clockwise around (Y_1, Y_2).

In Panel (a), the individual is initially at the point (Y_1, Y_2); that is, saving is initially 0. In this case the increase in r has no income effect—the individual's initial consumption bundle continues to be on the budget constraint. Thus first-period consumption necessarily falls, and so saving necessarily rises.

In Panel (b), C_1 is initially less than Y_1, and thus saving is positive. In this case the increase in r has a positive income effect—the individual can now afford strictly more than his or her initial bundle. The income effect acts to decrease saving, whereas the substitution effect acts to increase it. The overall effect is ambiguous; in the case shown in the figure, saving does not change.

Finally, in Panel (c) the individual is initially borrowing. In this case both the substitution and income effects reduce first-period consumption, and so saving necessarily rises.

Since the stock of wealth in the economy is positive, individuals are on average savers rather than borrowers. Thus the overall income effect of a rise in the interest rate is positive. An increase in the interest rate thus has two competing effects on overall saving, a positive one through the substitution effect and a negative one through the income effect.

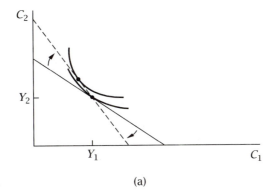

(a)

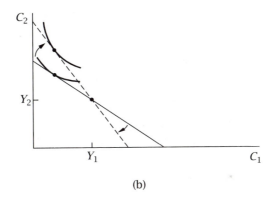

(b)

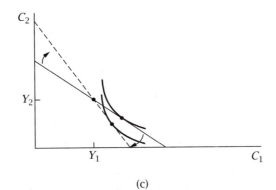

(c)

FIGURE 7.2   The interest rate and consumption choices in the two-period case

Complications

This discussion appears to imply that unless the elasticity of substitution between consumption in different periods is large, increases in the interest rate are unlikely to bring about substantial increases in saving. There are two reasons, however, that the importance of this conclusion is limited.

First, many of the changes we are interested in do not involve just changes in the interest rate. For tax policy, the relevant experiment is usually a change in composition between taxes on interest income and other taxes that leaves government revenue unchanged. As Problem 7.5 shows, such a change has only a substitution effect, and thus necessarily shifts consumption toward the future.

Second, and more subtly, if individuals have long horizons, small changes in saving can accumulate over time into large changes in wealth (Summers, 1981a). To see this, first consider an individual with an infinite horizon and constant labor income. Suppose that the interest rate equals the individual's discount rate. From (7.27), this means that the individual's consumption is constant. The budget constraint then implies that the individual consumes the sum of interest and labor incomes: any higher steady level of consumption implies violating the budget constraint, and any lower level implies failing to satisfy the constraint with equality. That is, the individual maintains his or her initial wealth level regardless of its value: the individual is willing to hold any amount of wealth if $r = \rho$. A similar analysis shows that if $r > \rho$, the individual's wealth grows without bound, and that if $r < \rho$, his or her wealth falls without bound. Thus the long-run supply of capital is perfectly elastic at $r = \rho$.

Summers shows that similar, though less extreme, results hold in the case of long but finite lifetimes. Suppose, for example, that r is slightly larger than ρ, that the intertemporal elasticity of substitution is small, and that labor income is constant. The facts that r exceeds ρ and that the elasticity of substitution is small imply that consumption rises slowly over the individual's lifetime. But with a long lifetime, this means that consumption is much larger at the end of life than at the beginning. But since labor income is constant, this in turn implies that the individual gradually builds up considerable savings over the first part of his or her life and gradually decumulates them over the remainder. As a result, when horizons are finite but long, wealth holdings may be highly responsive to the interest rate in the long run even if the intertemporal elasticity of substitution is small.[10]

---

[10] Carroll (1997) shows, however, that the presence of uncertainty weakens this conclusion.

7.5 Consumption and Risky Assets

Individuals can invest in many assets, almost all of which have uncertain returns. Extending our analysis to account for multiple assets and risk raises some new issues concerning both household behavior and asset markets.

The Conditions for Individual Optimization

Consider our usual experiment of an individual reducing consumption in period t by an infinitesimal amount and using the resulting saving to raise consumption in period $t + 1$. If the individual is optimizing, this change leaves expected utility unchanged regardless of which asset the increased saving is invested in. Thus optimization requires

$$u'(C_t) = \frac{1}{1 + \rho} E_t[(1 + r_{t+1}^i)u'(C_{t+1})] \qquad \text{for all } i, \qquad (7.28)$$

where r^i is the return on asset i. Since the expectation of the product of two variables equals the product of their expectations plus their covariance, we can rewrite this expression as

$$u'(C_t) = \frac{1}{1 + \rho} \{E_t[1 + r_{t+1}^i]E_t[u'(C_{t+1})] + \text{Cov}_t(1 + r_{t+1}^i, u'(C_{t+1}))\} \quad \text{for all } i, \tag{7.29}$$

where $\text{Cov}_t(\bullet)$ is covariance conditional on information available at time t.

If we assume that utility is quadratic, $u(C) = C - aC^2/2$, then the marginal utility of consumption is $1 - aC$. Using this to substitute for the covariance term in (7.29), we obtain

$$u'(C_t) = \frac{1}{1 + \rho} \left\{ E_t[1 + r_{t+1}^i]E_t[u'(C_{t+1})] - a\text{Cov}_t(1 + r_{t+1}^i, C_{t+1}) \right\}. \tag{7.30}$$

Equation (7.30) implies that in deciding whether to hold more of an asset, the individual is not concerned with how risky the asset is: the variance of the asset's return does not appear in (7.30). Intuitively, a marginal increase in holdings of an asset that is risky, but whose risk is not correlated with the overall risk the individual faces, does not increase the variance of the individual's consumption. Thus in evaluating that marginal decision, the individual considers only the asset's expected return.

Equation (7.30) implies that the aspect of riskiness that matters to the decision of whether to hold more of an asset is the relation between the asset's payoff and consumption. Suppose, for example, that the individual is given an opportunity to buy a new asset whose expected return equals the rate of return on a risk-free asset that the individual is already able to buy. If the payoff to the new asset is typically high when the marginal utility of consumption is high (that is, when consumption is low), buying one unit of the asset raises expected utility by more than buying one unit of the risk-free asset does. Thus (since the individual was previously indifferent about buying more of the risk-free asset), the individual can raise his or her expected utility by buying the new asset. As the individual invests more in the asset, his or her consumption comes to depend more on the asset's payoff, and so the covariance between consumption and the asset's return becomes less negative. In the example we are considering, since the asset's expected return equals the risk-free rate, the individual invests in the asset until the covariance of its return with consumption reaches zero.

This discussion implies that hedging risks is crucial to optimal portfolio choices. A steelworker whose future labor income depends on the health of the U.S. steel industry should avoid—or better yet, sell short—assets whose returns are positively correlated with the fortunes of the steel industry, such as shares in U.S. steel companies. Instead the worker should invest in assets whose returns move inversely with the health of the U.S. steel industry, such as foreign steel companies or U.S. aluminum companies.

One implication of this analysis is that individuals should exhibit no particular tendency to hold shares of companies that operate in the individuals' own countries. In fact, because the analysis implies that individuals should avoid assets whose returns are correlated with other sources of risk to their consumption, it implies that their holdings should be skewed against domestic companies. For example, for plausible parameter values it predicts that the typical person in the United States should sell U.S. stocks short (Baxter and Jermann, 1997). In fact, however, individuals' portfolios are very heavily skewed toward domestic companies (French and Poterba, 1991). This pattern is known as *home bias.*

The Consumption CAPM

This discussion takes assets' expected returns as given. But individuals' demands for assets determine these expected returns. If, for example, an asset's payoff is highly correlated with consumption, its price must be driven down to the point where its expected return is high for individuals to hold it.

To see the implications of this observation, suppose that all individuals are the same, and return to the first-order condition in (7.30). Solving this expression for the expected return on the asset yields

$$E_t[1 + r_{t+1}^i] = \frac{1}{E_t[u'(C_{t+1})]}[(1 + \rho)u'(C_t) + a\text{Cov}_t(1 + r_{t+1}^i, C_{t+1})]. \quad (7.31)$$

Equation (7.31) states that the higher the covariance of an asset's payoff with consumption, the higher its expected return must be.

We can simplify (7.31) by considering the return on a risk-free asset. If the payoff to an asset is certain, then the covariance of its payoff with consumption is 0. Thus the risk-free rate, $\bar{r}_{t+1}$, satisfies

$$1 + \bar{r}_{t+1} = \frac{(1 + \rho)u'(C_t)}{E_t[u'(C_{t+1})]}. \tag{7.32}$$

Subtracting (7.32) from (7.31) gives

$$E_t[r^i_{t+1}] - \bar{r}_{t+1} = \frac{a\mathrm{Cov}_t(1 + r^i_{t+1}, C_{t+1})}{E_t[u'(C_{t+1})]}. \tag{7.33}$$

Equation (7.33) states that the expected-return premium that an asset must offer relative to the risk-free rate is proportional to the covariance of its return with consumption.

This model of the determination of expected asset returns is known as the *consumption capital-asset pricing model,* or *consumption CAPM.* The covariance between an asset's return and consumption is known as its *consumption beta.* Thus the central prediction of the consumption CAPM is that the premiums that assets offer are proportional to their consumption betas (Breeden, 1979; see also Merton, 1973, and Rubinstein, 1976).[11]

Empirical Application: The Equity-Premium Puzzle

One of the most important implications of this analysis of assets' expected returns concerns the case where the risky asset is a broad portfolio of stocks. To see the issues involved, it is easiest to return to the Euler equation, (7.28), and to assume that individuals have constant-relative-risk-aversion utility rather than quadratic utility. With this assumption, the Euler equation becomes

$$C_t^{-\theta} = \frac{1}{1 + \rho}E_t[(1 + r^i_{t+1})C_{t+1}^{-\theta}], \tag{7.34}$$

where θ is the coefficient of relative risk aversion. If we divide both sides by $C_t^{-\theta}$ and multiply both sides by $1 + \rho$, this expression becomes

$$1 + \rho = E_t\left[(1 + r^i_{t+1})\frac{C_{t+1}^{-\theta}}{C_t^{-\theta}}\right]. \tag{7.35}$$

Finally, it is convenient to let g^c_{t+1} denote the growth rate of consumption from t to $t+1$, $(C_{t+1}/C_t) - 1$, and to omit the time subscripts. Thus we have

$$E[(1 + r^i)(1 + g^c)^{-\theta}] = 1 + \rho. \tag{7.36}$$

To see the implications of (7.36), we take a second-order Taylor approximation of the left-hand side around $r = g = 0$. Computing the relevant

---

[11] The original CAPM assumes that investors are concerned with the mean and variance of the return on their portfolio rather than the mean and variance of consumption. That version of the model therefore focuses on *market betas*—that is, the covariances of assets' returns with the returns on the market portfolio—and predicts that expected-return premiums are proportional to market betas (Lintner, 1965; Sharpe, 1964).

derivatives yields

$$(1 + r)(1 + g)^{-\theta} \simeq 1 + r - \theta g - \theta g r + \tfrac{1}{2}\theta(\theta + 1)g^2. \tag{7.37}$$

Thus we can rewrite (7.36) as

$$E[r^i] - \theta E[g^c] - \theta\{E[r^i]E[g^c] + \text{Cov}(r^i, g^c)\}$$
$$+ \tfrac{1}{2}\theta(\theta + 1)\{(E[g^c])^2 + \text{Var}(g^c)\} \simeq \rho. \tag{7.38}$$

When the time period involved is short, the $E[r^i]E[g^c]$ and $(E[g^c])^2$ terms are small relative to the others.[12] Omitting these terms and solving the resulting expression for $E[r^i]$ yields

$$E[r^i] \simeq \rho + \theta E[g^c] + \theta \text{Cov}(r^i, g^c) - \tfrac{1}{2}\theta(\theta + 1)\text{Var}(g^c). \tag{7.39}$$

Again, it is helpful to consider a risk-free asset. For such an asset, (7.39) simplifies to

$$\overline{r} \simeq \rho + \theta E[g^c] - \tfrac{1}{2}\theta(\theta + 1)\text{Var}(g^c). \tag{7.40}$$

Subtracting (7.40) from (7.39) yields

$$E[r^i] - \overline{r} \simeq \theta \text{Cov}(r^i, g^c). \tag{7.41}$$

In a famous paper, Mehra and Prescott (1985) show that it is difficult to reconcile observed asset returns with equation (7.41). Mankiw and Zeldes (1991) report a simple calculation that shows the essence of the problem. For the United States during the period 1890–1979 (which is the sample that Mehra and Prescott consider), the difference between the average return on the stock market and the return on short-term government debt—the *equity premium*—is about 6 percentage points. Thus if we take the average return on short-term government debt as an approximation to the average risk-free rate, the quantity $E[r^i] - \overline{r}$ is about 0.06. Over the same period, the standard deviation of the growth of consumption (as measured by real purchases of nondurables and services) is 3.6 percentage points, and the standard deviation of the excess return on the market is 16.7 percentage points; the correlation between these two quantities is 0.40. These figures imply that the covariance of consumption growth and the return on the market is 0.40(0.036)(0.167), or 0.0024.

Equation (7.41) therefore implies that the coefficient of relative risk aversion needed to account for the equity premium is the solution to $0.06 = \theta(0.0024)$, or $\theta = 25$. This is an extraordinary level of risk aversion; it implies, for example, that individuals would rather accept a 17 percent reduction in consumption with certainty than risk a 50-50 chance of a 20 percent reduction. As Mehra and Prescott describe, other evidence suggests that risk aversion is much lower than this. Among other things, such a high degree of aversion to variations in consumption makes it puzzling

---

[12] Indeed, for the continuous-time case, one can derive equation (7.39) without any approximations.

that the average risk-free rate is close to 0 despite the fact that consumption is growing over time.

The large equity premium, particularly when coupled with the low risk-free rate, is thus difficult to reconcile with household optimization. This *equity-premium puzzle* has stimulated a large amount of research, and many explanations for it have been proposed. No clear resolution of the puzzle has been provided, however.[13]

Furthermore, the equity-premium puzzle has become more severe in the period since Mehra and Prescott identified it. From 1979 to 1999, the average equity premium is a staggering 11 percentage points. In addition, consumption growth has become more stable and less correlated with returns: the standard deviation of consumption growth over this period is 1.2 percentage points, the standard deviation of the excess market return is 12.1 percentage points, and the correlation between these two quantities is 0.30. These figures imply a coefficient of relative risk aversion of $0.11/[0.30(0.012)(0.121)]$, or about 240.

The remarkable equity returns over the period since Mehra and Prescott wrote are mainly a phenomenon of the second half of the 1990s. One intriguing possibility is that these returns represent not the exacerbation of the equity-premium puzzle, but its end (see, for example, Glassman and Hassett, 1999). Although this idea may seem counterintuitive, the logic is simple: if the expected rate of return needed to induce investors to hold equities falls, the equities' payouts are discounted at a lower rate, and so the equities' prices rise. Thus a sharp reduction in the ex ante return premium needed for investors to hold stocks produces very high ex post returns during the period the premium is falling. Thereafter, unless there are further declines in the premium, average equity returns are low. It is obviously too soon to know if this story is correct.

7.6 Beyond the Permanent-Income Hypothesis

Background: Buffer-Stock Saving

The permanent-income hypothesis provides appealing explanations of many important features of consumption. For example, it explains why temporary tax cuts appear to have much smaller effects than permanent ones, and it accounts for many features of the relationship between current income and consumption, such as those described in Section 7.1.

---

[13] Proposed explanations include incomplete markets and transactions costs (Mankiw, 1986a; Mankiw and Zeldes, 1991; Heaton and Lucas, 1996; Luttmer, 1999); habit formation (Constantinides, 1990; Campbell and Cochrane, 1999); nonexpected utility (Weil, 1989b; Epstein and Zin, 1991; Bekaert, Hodrick, and Marshall, 1997); and loss aversion (Benartzi and Thaler, 1995). Kocherlakota (1996) provides a survey and argues that the puzzle is still unresolved.

Yet there are also important features of consumption that appear inconsistent with the permanent-income hypothesis. For example, as described in Section 7.3, both macroeconomic and microeconomic evidence suggest that consumption responds to predictable changes in income. And as we just saw, simple models of consumer optimization cannot account for the equity premium.

Indeed, the permanent-income hypothesis fails to explain some central features of consumption behavior. One of the hypothesis's key predictions is that there should be no relation between the expected growth of an individual's income over his or her lifetime and the expected growth of his or her consumption: consumption growth is determined by the real interest rate and the discount rate, not by the time pattern of income.

Carroll and Summers (1991) present extensive evidence that this prediction of the permanent-income hypothesis is incorrect. For example, individuals in countries where income growth is high typically have high rates of consumption growth over their lifetimes, and individuals in slowly growing countries typically have low rates of consumption growth. Similarly, typical lifetime consumption patterns of individuals in different occupations tend to match typical lifetime income patterns in those occupations. Managers and professionals, for example, generally have earnings profiles that rise steeply until middle age and then level off; their consumption profiles follow a similar pattern.

More generally, most households have little wealth (see, for example, Wolff, 1998). Their consumption approximately tracks their income. As a result, as described in Section 7.3, their current income has a large role in the determination of their consumption. Nonetheless, these households have a small amount of saving that they use in the event of sharp falls in income or emergency spending needs. In the terminology of Deaton (1991), most households exhibit *buffer-stock* saving behavior. As a result, a small fraction of households hold the vast majority of wealth.

These failings of the permanent-income hypothesis have motivated a large amount of work on extensions or alternatives to the theory. Three ideas that have received particular attention are precautionary saving, liquidity constraints, and departures from full optimization. The remainder of this section touches on some of the issues raised by these ideas.[14]

Precautionary Saving

Recall that our derivation of the random-walk result in Section 7.2 was based on the assumption that utility is quadratic. Quadratic utility implies, how-

---

[14] Three extensions of the permanent-income hypothesis that we will not discuss are durability of consumption goods, habit formation, and nonexpected utility. For durability, see Mankiw (1982); Caballero (1990, 1993); Eberly (1994); and Problem 7.6. For habit formation, see Deaton (1992, pp. 29–34, 99–100) and Campbell and Cochrane (1999). For nonexpected utility, see Weil (1989b, 1990) and Epstein and Zin (1989, 1991).

ever, that marginal utility reaches zero at some finite level of consumption and then becomes negative. It also implies that the utility cost of a given variance of consumption is independent of the level of consumption. This means that, since the marginal utility of consumption is declining, individuals have increasing absolute risk aversion: the amount of consumption they are willing to give up to avoid a given amount of uncertainty about the level of consumption rises as they become wealthier. These difficulties with quadratic utility suggest that marginal utility falls more slowly as consumption rises; that is, the third derivative of utility is probably positive rather than zero.

To see the effects of a positive third derivative, assume that both the real interest rate and the discount rate are 0, and consider again the Euler equation relating consumption in consecutive periods, equation (7.20): $u'(C_t) = E_t[u'(C_{t+1})]$. As described in Section 7.2, if utility is quadratic, marginal utility is linear, and so $E_t[u'(C_{t+1})]$ equals $u'(E_t[C_{t+1}])$; thus in this case, the Euler equation reduces to $C_t = E_t[C_{t+1}]$. But if $u'''(\bullet)$ is positive, then $u'(C)$ is a convex function of C. Thus in this case $E_t[u'(C_{t+1})]$ exceeds $u'(E_t[C_{t+1}])$. But this means that if C_t and $E_t[C_{t+1}]$ are equal, $E_t[u'(C_{t+1})]$ is greater than $u'(C_t)$, and so a marginal reduction in C_t increases expected utility. Thus the combination of a positive third derivative of the utility function and uncertainty about future income reduces current consumption, and thus raises saving. This saving is known as *precautionary saving* (Leland, 1968).

Panel (a) of Figure 7.3 shows the impact of uncertainty and a positive third derivative of the utility function on the expected marginal utility of consumption. Since $u''(C)$ is negative, $u'(C)$ is decreasing in C. And since $u'''(C)$ is positive, $u'(C)$ declines less rapidly as C rises—that is, $u'(C)$ is convex. If consumption takes on only two possible values, C_A and C_B, each with probability $\frac{1}{2}$, the expected marginal utility of consumption is the average of marginal utility at these two values. In terms of the diagram, this is shown by the midpoint of the line connecting $u'(C_A)$ and $u'(C_B)$. As the diagram shows, the fact that $u'(C)$ is convex implies that this quantity is larger than marginal utility at the average value of consumption, $(C_A + C_B)/2$.

Panel (b) shows the effects of an increase in uncertainty. When the high value of consumption rises, the fact that $u'''(C)$ is positive means that marginal utility falls relatively little; but when the low value falls, the positive third derivative magnifies the rise in marginal utility. As a result, the increase in uncertainty raises expected marginal utility for a given value of expected consumption. Thus the increase in uncertainty raises the incentive to save.

An important question, of course, is whether precautionary saving is quantitatively important. To address this issue, recall that in our analysis of the equity premium we found that the Euler equation for the risk-free asset is $\bar{r} \simeq \rho + \theta E[g^c] - \theta(\theta + 1)\text{Var}(g^c)/2$ (see [7.40]). For the case of $\bar{r} = \rho$, we can rewrite this as

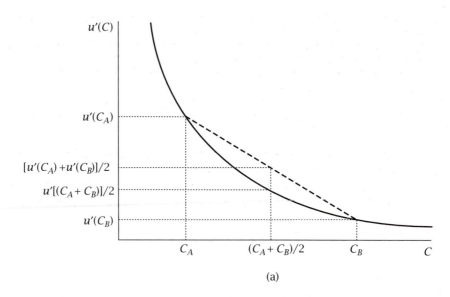

(a)

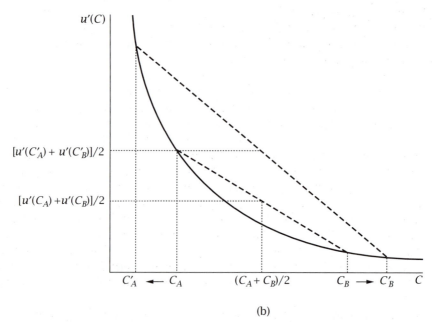

(b)

FIGURE 7.3   The effects of a positive third derivative of the utility function on the expected marginal utility of consumption

$$E[g^c] \simeq \tfrac{1}{2}(\theta + 1)\mathrm{Var}(g^c). \qquad (7.42)$$

Thus the impact of precautionary saving on expected consumption growth depends on the variance of consumption growth and the coefficient of relative risk aversion.[15] If both are substantial, precautionary saving can have a large effect on expected consumption growth. If the coefficient of relative risk aversion is 4 (which is toward the high end of values that are viewed as plausible), and the standard deviation of households' uncertainty about their consumption 1 year ahead is 0.1 (which is consistent with the evidence in Dynan, 1993, and Carroll, 1992), (7.42) implies that precautionary saving raises expected consumption growth by $\frac{1}{2}(4 + 1)(0.1)^2$, or 2.5 percentage points.

This analysis implies that precautionary saving raises expected consumption growth; that is, it decreases current consumption and thus increases saving. But one of the basic features of household behavior we are trying to understand is that most households save very little. Carroll (1992, 1997) argues that the key to understanding this phenomenon is a combination of a precautionary motive for saving and a high discount rate. The high discount rate tends to make households want to have high consumption. All else equal, this would lead them to have negative savings—that is, to be in debt—early in life. But Carroll argues that the precautionary-saving motive is quite strong; indeed, in his formal model, he assumes that the marginal utility of consumption approaches infinity as consumption becomes sufficiently low. As a result, households are unwilling to risk the very low consumption that would occur if they were in debt and their future income turned out to be low. They therefore typically keep a small amount of savings to use in the event of a large fall in income.

Gourinchas and Parker (1999) extend this analysis to the life cycle. They argue that for plausible utility functions and parameter values, most households are mainly buffer-stock savers early in life but begin accumulating savings for retirement once they reach middle age, and that these predictions are supported by the data.[16]

Liquidity Constraints

The permanent-income hypothesis assumes that individuals can borrow at the same interest rate at which they can save as long as they eventually repay their loans. Yet the interest rates that households pay on credit card debt, automobile loans, and other borrowing are often much higher than the

---

[15] For a general utility function, the $\theta + 1$ term is replaced by $-Cu'''(C)/u''(C)$. In analogy to the coefficient of relative risk aversion, $-Cu''(C)/u'(C)$, Kimball (1990) refers to $-Cu'''(C)/u''(C)$ as the coefficient of relative prudence.

[16] The presence of precautionary saving implies that not just expectations of future income but also uncertainty about that income affects consumption. C. Romer (1990), for example, argues that the tremendous uncertainty generated by the stock market crash of 1929 and by the subsequent gyrations of the stock market was a major force behind the sharp fall in consumption spending in 1930, and thus behind the onset of the Great Depression.

rates they obtain on their saving. In addition, some individuals are unable to borrow more at any interest rate.

Liquidity constraints can raise saving in two ways. First, and most obviously, whenever a liquidity constraint is binding, it causes the individual to consume less than he or she otherwise would. Second, as Zeldes (1989) emphasizes, even if the constraints are not currently binding, the fact that they may bind in the future reduces current consumption. Suppose, for example, that there is some chance of low income in the next period. If there are no liquidity constraints, and if income in fact turns out to be low, the individual can borrow to avoid a sharp fall in consumption. If there are liquidity constraints, however, the fall in income causes a large fall in consumption unless the individual has savings. Thus the presence of liquidity constraints causes individuals to save as insurance against the effects of future falls in income.

These points can be seen in a three-period model. To distinguish the effects of liquidity constraints from precautionary saving, assume that the instantaneous utility function is quadratic. In addition, continue to assume that the real interest rate and the discount rate are zero.

Begin by considering the individual's behavior in period 2. Let A_t denote assets at the end of period t. Since the individual lives for only three periods, C_3 equals $A_2 + Y_3$, which in turn equals $A_1 + Y_2 + Y_3 - C_2$. The individual's expected utility over the last two periods of life as a function of his or her choice of C_2 is therefore

$$U = (C_2 - \tfrac{1}{2}aC_2^2) + E_2[(A_1 + Y_2 + Y_3 - C_2) - \tfrac{1}{2}a(A_1 + Y_2 + Y_3 - C_2)^2]. \quad (7.43)$$

The derivative of this expression with respect to C_2 is

$$\frac{\partial U}{\partial C_2} = 1 - aC_2 - (1 - aE_2[A_1 + Y_2 + Y_3 - C_2]) \quad (7.44)$$

$$= a(A_1 + Y_2 + E_2[Y_3] - 2C_2).$$

This expression is positive for $C_2 < (A_1 + Y_2 + E_2[Y_3])/2$, and negative thereafter. Thus, as we know from our earlier analysis, if the liquidity constraint does not bind, the individual chooses $C_2 = (A_1 + Y_2 + E_2[Y_3])/2$. But if it does bind, he or she sets consumption to the maximum attainable level, which is $A_1 + Y_2$. Thus,

$$C_2 = \min\left\{\frac{A_1 + Y_2 + E_2[Y_3]}{2}, A_1 + Y_2\right\}. \quad (7.45)$$

Thus the liquidity constraint reduces current consumption if it is binding.

Now consider the first period. If the liquidity constraint is not binding that period, the individual has the option of marginally raising C_1 and paying for this by reducing C_2. Thus if the individual's assets are not literally zero, the usual Euler equation holds. With the specific assumptions we are making here, this means that C_1 equals the expectation of C_2.

But the fact that the Euler equation holds does not mean that the liquidity constraints do not affect consumption. Equation (7.45) implies that if the probability that the liquidity constraint will bind in the second period is strictly positive, the expectation of C_2 as of period 1 is strictly less than the expectation of $(A_1 + Y_2 + E_2[Y_3])/2$. A_1 is given by $A_0 + Y_1 - C_1$, and the law of iterated projections implies that $E_1[E_2[Y_3]]$ equals $E_1[Y_3]$. Thus,

$$C_1 < \frac{A_0 + Y_1 + E_1[Y_2] + E_1[Y_3] - C_1}{2}. \tag{7.46}$$

Adding $C_1/2$ to both sides of this expression and then dividing by $\frac{3}{2}$ yields

$$C_1 < \frac{A_0 + Y_1 + E_1[Y_2] + E_1[Y_3]}{3}. \tag{7.47}$$

Thus even when the liquidity constraint does not bind currently, the possibility that it will bind in the future reduces consumption.

Finally, if the value of C_1 that satisfies $C_1 = E_1[C_2]$ (given that C_2 is determined by [7.45]) is greater than the individual's period-1 resources, $A_0 + Y_1$, the first-period liquidity constraint is binding; in this case the individual consumes $A_0 + Y_1$.[17]

The case that liquidity constraints can explain buffer-stock saving is similar to the case that precautionary saving can. By themselves, liquidity constraints, like precautionary saving, raise saving. Thus explaining buffer-stock saving on the basis of liquidity constraints again requires appealing to a high discount rate. As before, the high discount rate tends to make households want to have high consumption. But with liquidity constraints, consumption cannot systematically exceed income early in life. Instead, households are constrained, and so consumption follows income.

When there are liquidity constraints, the risks of increases and decreases in income are asymmetric even with quadratic utility; this is why the possibility of future liquidity constraints lowers consumption. Thus liquidity constraints have the potential to explain why even impatient households typically have some savings. Researchers who have examined this issue quantitatively, however, generally find that this effect is not large enough to account for even the small savings we observe. Thus they typically introduce a precautionary-saving motive as well. As we have seen, the positive third derivative of the utility function can cause impatient consumers to normally hold a small amount of savings as protection against drops in income.

Empirical Application: Liquidity Constraints and Aggregate Saving

Jappelli and Pagano (1994) investigate empirically whether cross-country differences in liquidity constraints are important to cross-country differences in aggregate saving rates. They begin by arguing that there are

---

[17] Because both present and future liquidity constraints potentially affect behavior, complete solutions of models with liquidity constraints usually require the use of numerical methods (see, for example, Deaton, 1992, pp. 180–189).

important differences in the extent of liquidity constraints across countries. In Spain and Japan, for example, home purchases generally require down payments of 40 percent of the purchase price, whereas in the United States and France they require 20 percent or less. Similarly, Korea strongly restricts the availability of consumer credit, but the Scandinavian countries do not. Bankruptcy and foreclosure laws also vary greatly. In Belgium and Spain, for example, it takes 2 years or more to foreclose on a mortgage, whereas in Denmark and the Netherlands it takes less than 6 months. Greater legal barriers to foreclosure are likely to discourage lending.

Jappelli and Pagano then ask whether these differences in credit availability are associated with differences in saving rates. They first examine the relationship between the loan-to-value ratio for home purchases (that is, 1 minus the required down payment) and the saving rate. As Figure 7.4 shows, there is a clear negative association. They then add the loan-to-value ratio to a regression of saving rates on measures of government saving, the demographic composition of the population, and income growth. The loan-to-value ratio enters negatively and significantly. In a typical specification, the point estimates imply that an increase in the required down payment of 10 percent of the purchase price is associated with a rise in the saving rate of 2 percent of NNP. They also find that using a measure of the availability of consumer credit in place of the loan-to-value ratio yields similar results. In sum, their evidence suggests that liquidity constraints are important to aggregate saving.[18]

Departures from Complete Optimization

The assumption of costless optimization is a powerful modeling device, and it provides a good first approximation to how individuals respond to many changes. At the same time, it does not provide a perfect description of how people behave. There are well-documented cases in which individuals appear to depart consistently and systematically from the predictions of standard models of utility maximization, and in which those departures are quantitatively important (see, for example, Tversky and Kahneman, 1974, and Loewenstein and Thaler, 1989). This may be the case with choices between consumption and saving. The calculations involved are complex, the time periods are long, and there is a great deal of uncertainty that is difficult to quantify. So instead of attempting to be completely optimizing, individuals may follow rules of thumb in choosing their consumption (Shefrin and Thaler, 1988). Indeed, such rules of thumb may be the rational response to

---

[18] Jappelli and Pagano go on to investigate the relationship between liquidity constraints and aggregate growth. They find that even when they control for investment, liquidity constraints are positively related to growth. Given that the way that liquidity constraints most plausibly affect growth is through their effect on saving (and hence investment), this finding is difficult to interpret.

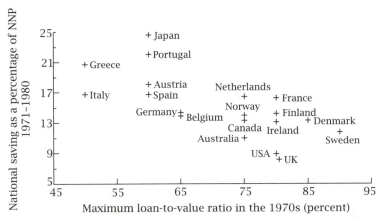

FIGURE 7.4   The loan-to-value ratio for home purchases and the saving rate (from Jappelli and Pagano, 1994; used with permission)

such factors as computation costs and fundamental uncertainty about how future after-tax income is determined. Examples of possible rules of thumb are that it is usually reasonable to spend one's current income and that assets should be dipped into only in exceptional circumstances. Relying on such rules may lead households to use saving and borrowing to smooth short-run income fluctuations; thus they will typically have some savings, and consumption will follow the predictions of the permanent-income hypothesis reasonably well at short horizons. But such behavior may also cause consumption to track income fairly closely over long horizons; thus savings will typically be small.

One specific departure from full optimization that has received considerable attention is time-inconsistent preferences (for example, Laibson, 1997). There is considerable evidence that individuals (and animals as well) are impatient at short horizons but patient at long horizons. This leads to time inconsistency. Consider, for example, choices concerning consumption over a two-week period. When the period is in the distant future—when it is a year away, for instance—individuals typically have little preference for consumption in the first week over consumption in the second. Thus they prefer roughly equal levels of consumption in the two weeks. When the two weeks arrive, however, individuals often want to depart from their earlier plans and have higher consumption in the first week.

It is not clear that time inconsistency, by itself, can explain why consumption responds to predictable changes in income. But it may be part of the explanation. More importantly, time-inconsistent preferences may be essential to understanding many phenomena other than consumption behavior. See, for example, Akerlof (1991) and O'Donoghue and Rabin (1999a, 1999b).

Can the Permanent-Income Hypothesis Be Saved?

Finally, Hubbard, Skinner, and Zeldes (1994, 1995) suggest an explanation of the fact that most households have little wealth that is close in spirit to the permanent-income hypothesis. The key element of their explanation, aside from intertemporal optimization, is the fact that welfare programs provide insurance against very low levels of consumption. For households that face a nonnegligible probability of going on welfare, the presence of welfare discourages saving in two ways: it directly provides insurance against unfavorable realizations of income, and it imposes extremely high implicit tax rates on asset holdings. For households whose income prospects are favorable enough that the possibility of going on welfare is negligible, on the other hand, consumption is determined by conventional intertemporal optimization; thus they exhibit conventional life-cycle saving. Hubbard, Skinner, and Zeldes therefore argue that the different patterns of wealth accumulation of the poor and the rich can be explained without appealing to differences in their preferences.[19]

Problems

7.1. The average income of farmers is less than the average income of nonfarmers, but fluctuates more from year to year. Given this, how does the permanent-income hypothesis predict that estimated consumption functions for farmers and nonfarmers differ?

7.2. The time-averaging problem. (Working, 1960.) Actual data give not consumption at a point in time, but average consumption over an extended period, such as a quarter. This problem asks you to examine the effects of this fact.

Suppose that consumption follows a random walk: $C_t = C_{t-1} + e_t$, where e is white noise. Suppose, however, that the data provide average consumption over two-period intervals; that is, one observes $(C_t + C_{t+1})/2$, $(C_{t+2} + C_{t+3})/2$, and so on.

(a) Find an expression for the change in measured consumption from one two-period interval to the next in terms of the e's.

(b) Is the change in measured consumption uncorrelated with the previous value of the change in measured consumption? In light of this, is measured consumption a random walk?

(c) Given your result in part (a), is the change in consumption from one two-period interval to the next necessarily uncorrelated with anything known

---

[19] Hubbard, Skinner, and Zeldes appeal to a precautionary-saving motive to explain why poor households typically hold some assets when their consumption is above the guaranteed floor; thus they do not claim that the standard permanent-income hypothesis provides a complete explanation of buffer-stock saving. See Carroll (1998) for an alternative view of the consumption behavior of the rich.

as of the first of these two-period intervals? Is it necessarily uncorrelated with anything known as of the two-period interval immediately preceding the first of the two-period intervals?

(*d*) Suppose that measured consumption for a two-period interval is not the average over the interval, but consumption in the second of the two periods. That is, one observes C_{t+1}, C_{t+3}, and so on. In this case, is measured consumption a random walk?

7.3. (This follows Hansen and Singleton, 1983.) Suppose instantaneous utility is of the constant-relative-risk-aversion form, $u(C_t) = C_t^{1-\theta}/(1-\theta)$, $\theta > 0$. Assume that the real interest rate, r, is constant but not necessarily equal to the discount rate, ρ.

(*a*) Find the Euler equation relating C_t to expectations concerning C_{t+1}.

(*b*) Suppose that the log of income is distributed normally, and that as a result the log of C_{t+1} is distributed normally; let σ^2 denote its variance conditional on information available at time t. Rewrite the expression in part (*a*) in terms of $\ln C_t$, $E_t[\ln C_{t+1}]$, σ^2, and the parameters r, ρ, and θ. (Hint: If a variable x is distributed normally with mean μ and variance V, $E[e^x] = e^\mu e^{V/2}$.)

(*c*) Show that if r and σ^2 are constant over time, the result in part (*b*) implies that the log of consumption follows a random walk with drift: $\ln C_{t+1} = a + \ln C_t + u_{t+1}$, where u is white noise.

(*d*) How do changes in each of r and σ^2 affect expected consumption growth, $E_t[\ln C_{t+1} - \ln C_t]$? Interpret the effect of σ^2 on expected consumption growth in light of the discussion of precautionary saving in Section 7.6.

7.4. A framework for investigating excess smoothness. Suppose that C_t equals $[r/(1+r)]\{A_t + \sum_{s=0}^{\infty} E_t[Y_{t+s}]/(1+r)^s\}$, and that $A_{t+1} = (1+r)(A_t + Y_t - C_t)$.

(*a*) Show that these assumptions imply that $E_t[C_{t+1}] = C_t$ (and thus that consumption follows a random walk) and that $\sum_{s=0}^{\infty} E_t[C_{t+s}]/(1+r)^s = A_t + \sum_{s=0}^{\infty} E_t[Y_{t+s}]/(1+r)^s$.

(*b*) Suppose that $\Delta Y_t = \phi \Delta Y_{t-1} + u_t$, where u is white noise. Suppose that Y_t exceeds $E_{t-1}[Y_t]$ by 1 unit (that is, suppose $u_t = 1$). By how much does consumption increase?

(*c*) For the case of $\phi > 0$, which has a larger variance, the innovation in income, u_t, or the innovation in consumption, $C_t - E_{t-1}[C_t]$? Do consumers use saving and borrowing to smooth the path of consumption relative to income in this model? Explain.

7.5. Consider the two-period setup analyzed in Section 7.4. Suppose that the government initially raises revenue only by taxing interest income. Thus the individual's budget constraint is $C_1 + C_2/[1 + (1-\tau)r] \le Y_1 + Y_2/[1 + (1-\tau)r]$, where τ is the tax rate. The government's revenue is 0 in period 1 and $\tau r(Y_1 - C_1^0)$ in period 2, where C_1^0 is the individual's choice of C_1 given this tax rate. Now suppose the government eliminates the taxation of interest income and instead institutes lump-sum taxes of amounts T_1 and T_2 in the two periods; thus the individual's budget constraint is now $C_1 + C_2/(1+r) \le$ $(Y_1 - T_1) + (Y_2 - T_2)/(1+r)$. Assume that Y_1, Y_2, and r are exogenous.

(a) What condition must the new taxes satisfy so that the change does not affect the present value of government revenues?

(b) If the new taxes satisfy the condition in part (a), is the old consumption bundle, (C_1^0, C_2^0), not affordable, just affordable, or affordable with room to spare?

(c) If the new taxes satisfy the condition in part (a), does first-period consumption rise, fall, or stay the same?

7.6. Consumption of durable goods. (Mankiw, 1982.) Suppose that, as in Section 7.2, the instantaneous utility function is quadratic and the interest rate and the discount rate are zero. Suppose, however, that goods are durable; specifically, $C_t = (1 - \delta)C_{t-1} + E_t$, where E_t is purchases in period t and $0 \le \delta < 1$.

(a) Consider a marginal reduction in purchases in period t of dE_t. Find values of dE_{t+1} and dE_{t+2} such that the combined changes in E_t, E_{t+1}, and E_{t+2} leave the present value of spending unchanged (so $dE_t + dE_{t+1} + dE_{t+2} = 0$) and leave C_{t+2} unchanged (so $(1 - \delta)^2 dE_t + (1 - \delta)dE_{t+1} + dE_{t+2} = 0$).

(b) What is the effect of the change in part (a) on C_t and C_{t+1}? What is the effect on expected utility?

(c) What condition must C_t and $E_t[C_{t+1}]$ satisfy for the change in part (a) not to affect expected utility? Does C follow a random walk?

(d) Does E follow a random walk? (Hint: Write $E_t - E_{t-1}$ in terms of $C_t - C_{t-1}$ and $C_{t-1} - C_{t-2}$.) Explain intuitively. If $\delta = 0$, what is the behavior of E?

7.7. Consider a stock that pays dividends of D_t in period t and whose price in period t is P_t. Assume that consumers are risk-neutral and have a discount rate of r; thus they maximize $E[\sum_{t=0}^{\infty} C_t/(1+r)^t]$.

(a) Show that equilibrium requires $P_t = E_t[(D_{t+1} + P_{t+1})/(1+r)]$ (assume that if the stock is sold, this happens after that period's dividends have been paid).

(b) Assume that $\lim_{s \to \infty} E_t[P_{t+s}/(1+r)^s] = 0$ (this is a *no-bubbles* condition; see the next problem). Iterate the expression in part (a) forward to derive an expression for P_t in terms of expectations of future dividends.

7.8. Bubbles. Consider the setup of the previous problem without the assumption that $\lim_{s \to \infty} E_t[P_{t+s}/(1+r)^s] = 0$.

(a) **Deterministic bubbles.** Suppose that P_t equals the expression derived in part (b) of Problem 7.7 plus $(1+r)^t b$, $b > 0$.

(i) Is consumers' first-order condition derived in part (a) of Problem 7.7 still satisfied?

(ii) Can b be negative? (Hint: Consider the strategy of never selling the stock.)

(b) **Bursting bubbles.** (Blanchard, 1979.) Suppose that P_t equals the expression derived in part (b) of Problem 7.7 plus q_t, where q_t equals $(1 + r)q_{t-1}/\alpha$ with probability α and equals 0 with probability $1 - \alpha$.

    (i) Is consumers' first-order condition derived in part (a) of Problem 7.7 still satisfied?

    (ii) If there is a bubble at time t (that is, if $q_t > 0$), what is the probability that the bubble has burst by time $t + s$ (that is, that $q_{t+s} = 0$)? What is the limit of this probability as s approaches infinity?

(c) **Intrinsic bubbles.** (Froot and Obtsfeld, 1991.) Suppose that dividends follow a random walk: $D_t = D_{t-1} + e_t$, where e is white noise.

    (i) In the absence of bubbles, what is the price of the stock in period t?

    (ii) Suppose that P_t equals the expression derived in (i) plus b_t, where $b_t = (1 + r)b_{t-1} + ce_t$, $c > 0$. Is consumers' first-order condition derived in part (a) of Problem 7.7 still satisfied? In what sense do stock prices overreact to changes in dividends?

7.9. The Lucas asset-pricing model. (Lucas, 1978.) Suppose the only assets in the economy are infinitely lived trees. Output equals the fruit of the trees, which is exogenous and cannot be stored; thus $C_t = Y_t$, where Y_t is the exogenously determined output per person and C_t is consumption per person. Assume that initially each consumer owns the same number of trees. Since all consumers are assumed to be the same, this means that, in equilibrium, the behavior of the price of trees must be such that, each period, the representative consumer does not want to either increase or decrease his or her holdings of trees.

Let P_t denote the price of a tree in period t (assume that if the tree is sold, the sale occurs after the existing owner receives that period's output). Finally, assume that the representative consumer maximizes $E[\sum_{t=0}^{\infty} \ln C_t/(1 + \rho)^t]$.

(a) Suppose the representative consumer reduces his or her consumption in period t by an infinitesimal amount, uses the resulting saving to increase his or her holdings of trees, and then sells these additional holdings in period $t + 1$. Find the condition that C_t and expectations involving Y_{t+1}, P_{t+1}, and C_{t+1} must satisfy for this change not to affect expected utility. Solve this condition for P_t in terms of Y_t and expectations involving Y_{t+1}, P_{t+1}, and C_{t+1}.

(b) Assume that $\lim_{s\to\infty} E_t[(P_{t+s}/Y_{t+s})/(1 + \rho)^s] = 0$. Given this assumption, iterate your answer to part (a) forward to solve for P_t. (Hint: Use the fact that $C_{t+s} = Y_{t+s}$ for all s.)

(c) Explain intuitively why an increase in expectations of future dividends does not affect the price of the asset.

(d) Does consumption follow a random walk in this model?

7.10. The equity premium and the concentration of aggregate shocks. (Mankiw, 1986b.) Consider an economy with two possible states, each of which occurs with probability $\frac{1}{2}$. In the good state, each individual's consumption is 1.

In the bad state, fraction λ of the population consumes $1 - (\phi/\lambda)$ and the remainder consumes 1, where $0 < \phi < 1$ and $\phi \leq \lambda \leq 1$. ϕ measures the reduction in average consumption in the bad state, and λ measures how broadly that reduction is shared.

Consider two assets, one that pays off 1 unit in the good state and one that pays off 1 unit in the bad state. Let p denote the relative price of the bad-state asset to the good-state asset.

(a) Consider an individual whose initial holdings of the two assets are zero, and consider the experiment of the individual marginally reducing (that is, selling short) his or her holdings of the good-state asset and using the proceeds to purchase more of the bad-state asset. Derive the condition for this change not to affect the individual's expected utility.

(b) Since consumption in the two states is exogenous and individuals are ex ante identical, p must adjust to the point where it is an equilibrium for individuals' holdings of both assets to be zero. Solve the condition derived in part (a) for this equilibrium value of p in terms of ϕ, λ, $U'(1)$, and $U'(1 - (\phi/\lambda))$.

(c) Find $\partial p/\partial \lambda$.

(d) Show that if utility is quadratic, $\partial p/\partial \lambda = 0$.

(e) Show that if $U'''(\bullet)$ is everywhere positive, $\partial p/\partial \lambda < 0$.

7.11. Time-inconsistent preferences. Consider an individual who lives for three periods. In period 1, his or her objective function is $\ln c_1 + \delta \ln c_2 + \delta \ln c_3$, where $0 < \delta < 1$. In period 2, it is $\ln c_2 + \delta \ln c_3$. (Since the individual's period-3 choice problem is trivial, the period-3 objective function is irrelevant.) The individual has wealth of W and faces a real interest rate of 0.

(a) Find the values of c_1, c_2, and c_3 under the following assumptions about how they are determined:

(i) *Commitment:* The individual chooses c_1, c_2, and c_3 in period 1.

(ii) *No commitment, naivete:* The individual chooses c_1 in period 1 to maximize the period-1 objective function, thinking he or she will also choose c_2 to maximize this objective function. In fact, however, the individual chooses c_2 to maximize the period-2 objective function.

(iii) *No commitment, sophistication:* The individual chooses c_1 in period 1 to maximize the period-1 objective function, realizing that he or she will choose c_2 in period 2 to maximize the period-2 objective function.

(b) (i) Use your answers to parts (a)(i) and (a)(ii) to explain in what sense the individuals' preferences are time-inconsistent.

(ii) Explain intuitively why sophistication does not produce different behavior than naivete.

Chapter **8**
INVESTMENT

This chapter investigates the demand for investment. As described at the beginning of Chapter 7, there are two main reasons for studying investment. First, the combination of firms' investment demand and households' saving supply determines how much of an economy's output is invested; as a result, investment demand is potentially important to the behavior of standards of living over the long run. Second, investment is highly volatile; thus investment demand may be important to short-run fluctuations.

Section 8.1 presents a baseline model of investment where firms face a perfectly elastic supply of capital goods and can adjust their capital stocks costlessly. We will see that this model, even though it is a natural one to consider, provides little insight into actual investment. It implies, for example, that discrete changes in the economic environment (such as discrete changes in interest rates) produce infinite rates of investment or disinvestment.

Sections 8.2 through 8.5 therefore develop and analyze the *q theory* model of investment. The model's key assumption is that firms face costs of adjusting their capital stocks. As a result, the model avoids the unreasonable implications of the baseline case and provides a useful framework for analyzing the effects that expectations and current conditions have on investment.

Sections 8.6 and 8.7 introduce some important extensions of the model: Section 8.6 considers uncertainty and irreversibility, and Section 8.7 investigates financial-market imperfections. Finally, Section 8.8 presents some empirical tests and applications of the models.

8.1 Investment and the Cost of Capital

The Desired Capital Stock

Consider a firm that can rent capital at a price of r_K. The firm's profits at a point in time are given by $\pi(K, X_1, X_2, \ldots, X_n) - r_K K$, where K is the amount of capital the firm rents and the X's are variables that it takes as given.

In the case of a perfectly competitive firm, for example, the X's include the price of the firm's product and the costs of other inputs. $\pi(\bullet)$ is assumed to account for whatever optimization the firm can do on dimensions other than its choice of K. For a competitive firm, for example, $\pi(K, X_1, \ldots, X_n) - r_K K$ gives the firm's profits at the profit-maximizing choices of inputs other than capital given K and the X's. We assume that $\pi_K > 0$ and $\pi_{KK} < 0$, where subscripts denote partial derivatives.

The first-order condition for the profit-maximizing choice of K is

$$\pi_K(K, X_1, \ldots, X_n) = r_K. \tag{8.1}$$

That is, the firm rents capital up to the point where its marginal revenue product equals its rental price.

Equation (8.1) implicitly defines the firm's desired capital stock as a function of r_K and the X's. We can differentiate this condition to find the impact of a change in one of these exogenous variables on the desired capital stock. Consider, for example, a change in the rental price of capital, r_K. By assumption, the X's are exogenous; thus they do not change when r_K changes. K, however, is chosen by the firm. Thus it adjusts so that (8.1) continues to hold. Differentiating both sides of (8.1) with respect to r_K shows that this requires

$$\pi_{KK}(K, X_1, \ldots, X_n) \frac{\partial K(r_K, X_1, \ldots, X_n)}{\partial r_K} = 1. \tag{8.2}$$

Solving this expression for $\partial K / \partial r_K$ yields

$$\frac{\partial K(r_K, X_1, \ldots, X_n)}{\partial r_K} = \frac{1}{\pi_{KK}(K, X_1, \ldots, X_n)}. \tag{8.3}$$

Since π_{KK} is negative, (8.3) implies that K is decreasing in r_K. A similar analysis can be used to find the effects of changes in the X's on K.

The User Cost of Capital

Most capital is not rented but is owned by the firms that use it. Thus there is no clear empirical counterpart of r_K. This difficulty has given rise to a large literature on the *user cost of capital*.

Consider a firm that owns a unit of capital. Suppose the real market price of the capital at time t is $p_K(t)$, and consider the firm's choice between selling the capital and continuing to use it. Keeping the capital has three costs to the firm. First, the firm forgoes the interest it would receive if it sold the capital and saved the proceeds; this has a real cost of $r(t)p_K(t)$ per unit time, where $r(t)$ is the real interest rate. Second, the capital is depreciating; this has a cost of $\delta p_K(t)$ per unit time, where δ is the depreciation rate. And third, the price of the capital may be changing. This increases the cost of using the capital if the price is falling (since the firm obtains less if it waits to sell the capital) and decreases the cost if the price is rising. This has a cost of $-\dot{p}_K(t)$ per unit time. Putting the three components together yields the real user cost of capital:

$$r_K(t) = r(t)p_K(t) + \delta p_K(t) - \dot{p}_K(t)$$

$$= \left[r(t) + \delta - \frac{\dot{p}_K(t)}{p_K(t)} \right] p_K(t).$$

(8.4)

This analysis ignores the existence of taxes. In practice, however, the tax treatments of investment and of capital income have large effects on the user cost of capital. To give an idea of these effects, consider an investment tax credit. Specifically, suppose the firm's income that is subject to the corporate income tax is reduced by fraction f of its investment expenditures; for symmetry, suppose also that its taxable income is increased by fraction f of any receipts from selling capital goods. Such an investment tax credit implies that the effective price of a unit of capital to the firm is $(1 - f\tau)p_K(t)$, where τ is the marginal corporate income tax rate. The user cost of capital is therefore

$$r_K(t) = \left[r(t) + \delta - \frac{\dot{p}_K(t)}{p_K(t)} \right] (1 - f\tau)p_K(t).$$

(8.5)

Thus the investment tax credit reduces the user cost of capital, and hence increases firms' desired capital stocks. One can also investigate the effects of depreciation allowances, the tax treatment of interest, and many other features of the tax code on the user cost of capital and the desired capital stock.[1]

Difficulties with the Baseline Model

This simple model of investment has at least two major failings as a description of actual behavior. The first concerns the impact of changes in the exogenous variables. Our model concerns firms' demand for capital, and it implies that firms' desired capital stocks are smooth functions of the exogenous variables. As a result, a discrete change in one of the exogenous variables leads to a discrete change in the desired capital stock. Suppose, for example, that the Federal Reserve reduces interest rates by a discrete amount; as the analysis above shows, this discretely reduces the cost of capital, r_K. This in turn means that the capital stock that satisfies (8.1) rises discretely.

The problem with this implication is that, since the rate of change of the capital stock equals investment minus depreciation, a discrete change in the capital stock requires an infinite rate of investment. For the economy

---

[1] The seminal paper is Hall and Jorgenson (1967). See also Problems 8.2 and 8.3.

as a whole, however, investment is limited by the economy's output; thus aggregate investment cannot be infinite.

The second problem with the model is that it does not identify any mechanism through which expectations affect investment demand. The model implies that firms equate the current marginal revenue product of capital with its current user cost, without regard to what they expect future marginal revenue products or user costs to be. Yet it is clear that in practice, expectations about demand and costs are central to investment decisions: firms expand their capital stocks when they expect their sales to be growing and the cost of capital to be low, and they contract them when they expect their sales to be falling and the cost of capital to be high.

Thus we need to modify the model if we are to obtain even a remotely reasonable picture of actual investment decisions. The standard theory that does this emphasizes the presence of costs to changing the capital stock. Those adjustment costs come in two forms, internal and external (Mussa, 1977). *Internal adjustment costs* arise when firms face direct costs of changing their capital stocks (Eisner and Strotz, 1963; Lucas, 1967; Gould, 1968). Examples of such costs are the costs of installing the new capital and training workers to operate the new machines. Consider again a discrete cut in interest rates. If the adjustment costs approach infinity as the rate of change of the capital stock approaches infinity, the fall in interest rates causes investment to increase but not to become infinite. As a result, the capital stock moves gradually toward the new desired level.

External adjustment costs arise when each firm, as in our baseline model, faces a perfectly elastic supply of capital, but where the price of capital goods relative to other goods adjusts so that firms do not wish to invest or disinvest at infinite rates (Foley and Sidrauski, 1970). When the supply of capital is not perfectly elastic, a discrete change that increases firms' desired capital stocks bids up the price of capital goods. Under plausible assumptions, the result is that the rental price of capital does not change discontinuously but merely begins to adjust, and that again investment increases but does not become infinite.

8.2   A Model of Investment with Adjustment Costs

We now turn to a model of investment with adjustment costs. For concreteness, the adjustment costs are assumed to be internal; it is straightforward, however, to reinterpret the model as one of external adjustment costs.[2] The model is known as the *q* theory model of investment.

---

[2] See n. 11 and Problem 8.7. The model presented here is developed by Abel (1982); Hayashi (1982); and Summers (1981b).

Assumptions

Consider an industry with N identical firms. A representative firm's real profits at time t, neglecting any costs of acquiring and installing capital, are proportional to its capital stock, $\kappa(t)$, and decreasing in the industry-wide capital stock, $K(t)$; thus they take the form $\pi(K(t))\kappa(t)$, where $\pi'(\bullet) < 0$. The assumption that the firm's profits are proportional to its capital is appropriate if the production function has constant returns to scale, output markets are competitive, and the supply of all factors other than capital is perfectly elastic. Under these assumptions, if one firm has, for example, twice as much capital as another, it employs twice as much of all inputs; as a result, both its revenues and its costs are twice as high as the other's.[3] And the assumption that profits are decreasing in the industry's capital stock is appropriate if the demand curve for the industry's product is downward-sloping.

The key assumption of the model is that firms face costs of adjusting their capital stocks. The adjustment costs are a convex function of the rate of change of the firm's capital stock, $\dot{\kappa}$. Specifically, the adjustment costs, $C(\dot{\kappa})$, satisfy $C(0) = 0$, $C'(0) = 0$, and $C''(\bullet) > 0$. These assumptions imply that it is costly for a firm to increase or decrease its capital stock, and that the marginal adjustment cost is increasing in the size of the adjustment.

The purchase price of capital goods is constant and equal to 1; thus there are only internal adjustment costs. Finally, for simplicity, the depreciation rate is assumed to be 0; thus $\dot{\kappa}(t) = I(t)$, where I is the firm's investment.

A Discrete-Time Version of the Firm's Problem

These assumptions imply that the firm's profits at a point in time are $\pi(K)\kappa - I - C(I)$. The firm maximizes the present value of these profits,

$$\Pi = \int_{t=0}^{\infty} e^{-rt} \left[\pi(K(t))\kappa(t) - I(t) - C(I(t))\right] dt, \tag{8.6}$$

where we assume for simplicity that the real interest rate is constant. Each firm takes the path of the industry-wide capital stock, K, as given, and chooses its investment over time to maximize Π given this path.

To solve the firm's maximization problem, we need to employ the *calculus of variations*. To understand this method, it is helpful to first consider a discrete-time version of the firm's problem.[4] The evolution of the firm's

---

[3] Note that these assumptions imply that in the model of Section 8.1, $\pi(K, X_1, \ldots, X_n)$ takes the form $\tilde{\pi}(X_1, \ldots, X_n)K$, and so the assumption that $\pi_{KK} < 0$ fails. Thus in this case, in the absence of adjustment costs, the firm's demand for capital is not well defined: it is infinite if $\tilde{\pi}(X_1, \ldots, X_n) > 0$, zero if $\tilde{\pi}(X_1, \ldots, X_n) < 0$, and not defined if $\tilde{\pi}(X_1, \ldots, X_n) = 0$.

[4] For more thorough and formal introductions to the calculus of variations, see Kamien and Schwartz (1991); Dixit (1990, Chapter 10); and Obstfeld (1992).

capital stock is now given by $\kappa_{t+1} = \kappa_t + I_t$, and the adjustment costs are given by $C(I_t)$. The firm's objective function is therefore

$$\tilde{\Pi} = \sum_{t=0}^{\infty} \frac{1}{(1+r)^t} \left[\pi(K_t)\kappa_t - I_t - C(I_t) \right]. \tag{8.7}$$

We can think of the firm as choosing its investment and capital stock each period subject to the constraint that they are related by $\kappa_{t+1} = \kappa_t + I_t$ for each t. Since there are infinitely many periods, there are infinitely many constraints. The Lagrangian for the firm's maximization problem is

$$\mathcal{L} = \sum_{t=0}^{\infty} \frac{1}{(1+r)^t} \left[\pi(K_t)\kappa_t - I_t - C(I_t) \right]$$

$$+ \sum_{t=0}^{\infty} \lambda_t (\kappa_t + I_t - \kappa_{t+1}). \tag{8.8}$$

λ_t is the Lagrange multiplier associated with the constraint relating κ_{t+1} and κ_t. It therefore gives the marginal value of relaxing the constraint; that is, it gives the marginal impact of an exogenous increase in κ_{t+1} on the lifetime value of the firm's profits discounted to time 0. If we define $q_t = (1+r)^t \lambda_t$, it follows that q_t shows the value to the firm of an additional unit of capital at time $t+1$ in time-t dollars.[5] With this definition, we can rewrite the Lagrangian as

$$\mathcal{L}' = \sum_{t=0}^{\infty} \frac{1}{(1+r)^t} \left[\pi(K_t)\kappa_t - I_t - C(I_t) + q_t(\kappa_t + I_t - \kappa_{t+1}) \right]. \tag{8.9}$$

The first-order condition for the firm's investment in period t is therefore

$$\frac{1}{(1+r)^t} [-1 - C'(I_t) + q_t] = 0. \tag{8.10}$$

Multiplying both sides by $(1+r)^t$, we obtain

$$1 + C'(I_t) = q_t. \tag{8.11}$$

To interpret this condition, observe that the cost of acquiring a unit of capital equals the purchase price (which is fixed at 1) plus the marginal adjustment cost. Thus (8.11) states that the firm invests to the point where the cost of acquiring capital equals the value of the capital.

Now consider the first-order condition for capital in period t. The term for period t in the Lagrangian, (8.9), involves both κ_t and κ_{t+1}. Thus the capital stock in period t, κ_t, appears in both the term for period t and the term for period $t - 1$. The first-order condition for κ_t is therefore

$$\frac{1}{(1+r)^t} [\pi(K_t) + q_t] - \frac{1}{(1+r)^{t-1}} q_{t-1} = 0. \tag{8.12}$$

---

[5] The awkward fact that λ and q in period t concern the value of capital in period $t + 1$ will disappear when we consider the continuous-time case.

Multiplying this expression by $(1 + r)^t$ and rearranging yields

$$\pi(K_t) = (1 + r)q_{t-1} - q_t. \tag{8.13}$$

If we define $\Delta q_t = q_t - q_{t-1}$, we can rewrite the right-hand side of (8.13) as $(1 + r)(q_t - \Delta q_t) - q_t$, or $rq_t - \Delta q_t - r\Delta q_t$. Thus we have

$$\pi(K_t) = rq_t - \Delta q_t - r\Delta q_t. \tag{8.14}$$

The left-hand side of (8.14) is the marginal revenue product of capital. And the right-hand side is the opportunity cost of a unit of capital. Intuitively, owning a unit of capital for a period requires forgoing rq_t of real interest and involves offsetting capital gains of Δq_t (see [8.4] with the depreciation rate assumed to be zero; in addition, there is an interaction term involving r and Δq that will disappear in the continuous-time case). For the firm to be optimizing, the returns to capital must equal this opportunity cost. This is what is stated by (8.14). This condition is thus analogous to the condition in the model without adjustment costs that the firm rents capital to the point where its marginal revenue product equals its rental price.

The final condition characterizing the firm's behavior concerns what happens as t approaches infinity. Suppose first the firm has a finite horizon, T. For it to be optimizing, the firm cannot have capital holdings at T that have a strictly positive present value: if it did, it could raise the present value of its profits by reducing those capital holdings. Since the present value of the firm's capital at T is $q_T K_T / (1 + r)^T$, this means that this expression cannot be strictly positive. In addition, none of the three ingredients of this expression—q_T, K_T, and $1 + r$—can ever be strictly negative: higher capital can never reduce future profits, negative capital holdings are not possible, and $1 + r$ is positive by assumption. Thus $q_T K_T / (1 + r)^T$ cannot be strictly negative either. Putting these conclusions together gives us

$$\frac{1}{(1 + r)^T} q_T K_T = 0. \tag{8.15}$$

The infinite-horizon analogue of this condition is

$$\lim_{t \to \infty} \frac{1}{(1 + r)^t} q_t K_t = 0. \tag{8.16}$$

Equation (8.16) is known as the *transversality condition*. It states that the value of the firm's capital discounted to time 0 must approach zero. If this condition fails, then, loosely speaking, the firm is holding valuable capital forever, and so it can increase the present value of its profits by reducing its capital stock.[6]

---

[6] See Section 8.4 for more on the interpretation of this condition.

The Continuous-Time Case

We can now consider the case when time is continuous. The firm's profit-maximizing behavior in this case is characterized by three conditions that are analogous to the three conditions that characterize its behavior in discrete time: (8.11), (8.14), and (8.16). Indeed, the optimality conditions for continuous time can be derived by considering the discrete-time problem where the time periods are separated by intervals of length Δt and then taking the limit as Δt approaches zero. We will not use this method, however; instead we will simply describe how to find the optimality conditions, and justify them as necessary by way of analogy to the discrete-time case.

The firm's problem is now to maximize the continuous-time objective function, (8.6), rather than the discrete-time objective function, (8.7). The first step in analyzing this problem is to set up the *current-value Hamiltonian:*

$$H(\kappa(t), I(t)) = \pi(K(t))\kappa(t) - I(t) - C(I(t)) + q(t)I(t). \qquad (8.17)$$

This expression is analogous to the period-t term in the Lagrangian for the discrete-time case with the term in the change in the capital stock omitted (see [8.9]). There is some standard terminology associated with this type of problem. The variable that can be controlled freely (I) is the *control variable;* the variable whose value at any time is determined by past decisions (κ) is the *state variable;* and the shadow value of the state variable (q) is the *costate variable.*

The first condition characterizing the optimum is that the derivative of the Hamiltonian with respect to the control variable at each point in time is zero; this is analogous to the condition in the discrete-time problem that the derivative of the Lagrangian with respect to I for each t is 0. This condition is

$$1 + C'(I(t)) = q(t). \qquad (8.18)$$

This condition is analogous to (8.11) in the discrete-time case.

The second condition is that the derivative of the Hamiltonian with respect to the state variable equals the discount rate times the costate variable minus the derivative of the costate variable with respect to time. In our case, this condition is

$$\pi(K(t)) = rq(t) - \dot{q}(t). \qquad (8.19)$$

This condition is analogous to (8.14) in the discrete-time problem.[7]

---

[7] An alternative approach is to formulate the *present-value Hamiltonian,* $\tilde{H}(\kappa(t), I(t)) = e^{-rt}[\pi(K(t))\kappa(t) - I(t) - C(I(t))] + \lambda(t)I(t)$. This is analogous to using the Lagrangian (8.8) rather than (8.9). With this formulation, (8.19) is replaced by $e^{-rt}\pi(K(t)) = -\dot{\lambda}(t)$. It is straightforward to check that since $q(t) = \lambda(t)e^{rt}$, these two conditions are equivalent.

The final condition is the continuous-time version of the transversality condition. This condition is

$$\lim_{t \to \infty} e^{-rt} q(t) \kappa(t) = 0. \tag{8.20}$$

Equations (8.18), (8.19), and (8.20) characterize the firm's behavior.

Finally, it is useful to note that we can express q, the value of capital, in terms of capital's future marginal revenue products. Equation (8.19) implies

$$q(t) = \int_{\tau=t}^{T} e^{-r(\tau-t)} \pi(K(\tau)) \, d\tau + e^{-r(T-t)} q(T) \tag{8.21}$$

for any $T > t$.[8] One can show that the transversality condition implies that the second term approaches zero as T approaches infinity. Thus we have

$$q(t) = \int_{\tau=t}^{\infty} e^{-r(\tau-t)} \pi(K(\tau)) \, d\tau. \tag{8.22}$$

Expression (8.22) states that the value of a unit of capital at a given time equals the discounted value of its future marginal revenue products.

8.3 Tobin's *q*

Our analysis implies that q summarizes all information about the future that is relevant to a firm's investment decision. q shows how an additional dollar of capital affects the present value of profits. Thus the firm wants to increase its capital stock if q is high and reduce it if q is low; the firm does not need to know anything about the future other than the information that is summarized in q in order to make this decision (see [8.18]).

q has a natural economic interpretation. A unit increase in the firm's capital stock increases the present value of the firm's profits by q, and thus raises the value of the firm by q. Thus q is the market value of a unit of capital. If there is a market for shares in firms, for example, the total value of a firm with one more unit of capital than another firm exceeds the value of the other by q. And since we have assumed that the purchase price of capital is fixed at 1, q is also the ratio of the market value of a unit of capital to its replacement cost. Thus equation (8.18) states that a firm increases its capital stock if the market value of capital exceeds the cost of acquiring it, and that it decreases its capital stock if the market value of the capital is less than the cost of acquiring it.

The ratio of the market value to the replacement cost of capital is known as *Tobin's q* (Tobin, 1969); it is because of this terminology that we used q to denote the value of capital in the previous section. Our analysis implies that

---

[8] To verify that (8.21) follows from (8.19), differentiate (8.21) with respect to t, and then rearrange the resulting expression to obtain (8.19).

what is relevant to investment is *marginal q*—the ratio of the market value of a marginal unit of capital to its replacement cost. Marginal q is likely to be harder to measure than *average q*—the ratio of the total value of the firm to the replacement cost of its total capital stock. Thus it is important to know how marginal q and average q are related.

One can show that in our model, marginal q is less than average q. The reason is that when we assumed that adjustment costs depend only on $\dot{\kappa}$, we implicitly assumed diminishing returns to scale in adjustment costs. Our assumptions imply, for example, that it is more than twice as costly for a firm with 20 units of capital to add 2 more than it is for a firm with 10 units to add 1 more. Because of this assumption of diminishing returns, firms' lifetime profits, Π, rise less than proportionally with their capital stocks, and so marginal q is less than average q.

One can also show that if the model is modified to have constant returns in the adjustment costs, average q and marginal q are equal (Hayashi, 1982).[9] The source of this result is that the constant returns in the costs of adjustment imply that q determines the growth rate of a firm's capital stock. As a result, all firms choose the same growth rate of their capital stocks. Thus if, for example, one firm initially has twice as much capital as another and if both firms optimize, the larger firm will have twice as much capital as the other at every future date. In addition, profits are linear in a firm's capital stock. This implies that the present value of a firm's profits— the value of Π when it chooses the path of its capital stock optimally—is proportional to its initial capital stock. Thus average q and marginal q are equal.

In other models, there are potentially more significant reasons than the degree of returns to scale in adjustment costs that average q may differ from marginal q. If a firm faces a downward-sloping demand curve for its product, for example, doubling its capital stock is likely to less than double the present value of its profits; thus marginal q is less than average q. If the firm owns a large amount of outmoded capital, on the other hand, its marginal q may exceed its average q.

8.4   Analyzing the Model

We will analyze the model using a phase diagram similar to the one we used in Chapter 2 to analyze the Ramsey model. The two variables we will focus on are the aggregate quantity of capital, K, and its value, q. As with k and c

---

[9] Constant returns can be introduced by assuming that the adjustment costs take the form $C(\dot{\kappa}/\kappa)\kappa$, with $C(\bullet)$ having the same properties as before. With this assumption, doubling both $\dot{\kappa}$ and κ doubles the adjustment costs. Changing our model in this way implies that κ affects profits not only directly, but also through its impact on adjustment costs for a given level of investment. As a result, it complicates the analysis. The basic messages are the same, however. See Problem 8.8.

in the Ramsey model, the initial value of one of these variables is given, but the other must be determined: the quantity of capital is something that the industry inherits from the past, but its price adjusts freely in the market.

Recall from the beginning of Section 8.2 that there are N identical firms. Equation (8.18) states that each firm invests to the point where the purchase price of capital plus the marginal adjustment cost equals the value of capital: $1 + C'(I) = q$. Since $C'(I)$ is increasing in I, this condition implies that I is increasing in q. And since $C'(0)$ is 0, it also implies that I is 0 when q is 1. Finally, since q is the same for all firms, all firms choose the same value of I. Thus the rate of change of the aggregate capital stock, $\dot{K}$, is given by the number of firms times the value of I that satisfies (8.18).

Putting this information together, we can write

$$\dot{K}(t) = f(q(t)), \qquad f(1) = 0, \qquad f'(\bullet) > 0, \tag{8.23}$$

where $f(q) \equiv NC'^{-1}(q-1)$. Equation (8.23) implies that K is increasing when $q > 1$, decreasing when $q < 1$, and constant when $q = 1$. This information is summarized in Figure 8.1.

Equation (8.19) states that the marginal revenue product of capital equals its user cost, $rq - \dot{q}$. Rewriting this as an equation for $\dot{q}$ yields

$$\dot{q}(t) = rq(t) - \pi(K(t)). \tag{8.24}$$

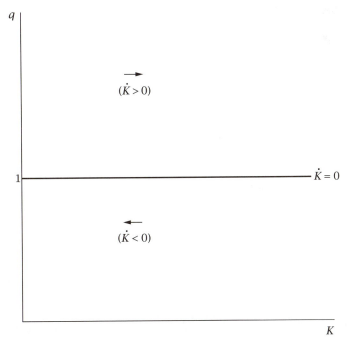

FIGURE 8.1 The dynamics of the capital stock

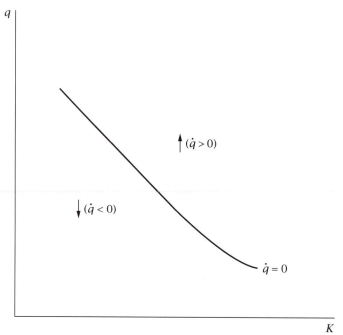

FIGURE 8.2   The dynamics of q

This expression implies that q is constant when $rq = \pi(K)$, or $q = \pi(K)/r$. Since $\pi(K)$ is decreasing in K, the set of points satisfying this condition is downward-sloping in (K, q) space. In addition, (8.24) implies that $\dot{q}$ is increasing in K; thus $\dot{q}$ is positive to the right of the $\dot{q} = 0$ locus and negative to the left. This information is summarized in Figure 8.2.

The Phase Diagram

Figure 8.3 combines the information in Figures 8.1 and 8.2. The diagram shows how K and q must behave to satisfy (8.23) and (8.24) at every point in time given their initial values. Suppose, for example, that K and q begin at Point A. Then, since q is more than 1, firms increase their capital stocks; thus $\dot{K}$ is positive. And since K is high and profits are therefore low, q can be high only if it is expected to rise; thus $\dot{q}$ is also positive. Thus K and q move up and to the right in the diagram.

As in the Ramsey model, the initial level of the capital stock is given. But the level of the other variable—consumption in the Ramsey model, the market value of capital in this model—is free to adjust. Thus its initial level must be determined. As in the Ramsey model, for a given level of K there is a unique level of q that produces a stable path. Specifically, there is a unique level of q such that K and q converge to the point where they are stable (Point E in the diagram). If q starts below this level, the industry

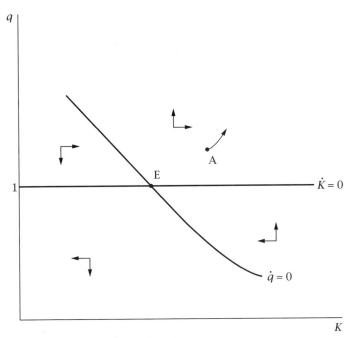

FIGURE 8.3 The phase diagram

eventually crosses into the region where both K and q are falling, and they then continue to fall indefinitely. Similarly, if q starts too high, the industry eventually moves into the region where both K and q are rising and remains there. One can show that the transversality condition fails for these paths, and thus that they can be ruled out.[10]

This discussion suggests why a firm's optimal policy must satisfy the transversality condition. Along the path starting at A, for example, the representative firm is continually building up capital because the value it attaches to the capital is always high. This high value is justified not by large marginal revenue products, but by further increases in the value the firm attaches to the capital (that is, equation [8.19], $\pi(K) = rq - \dot{q}$, holds with a high value of q not because $\pi(K)$ is high, but because $\dot{q}$ is high). But attaching this high and rising value to capital makes sense only if at some point the capital actually makes large contributions to the firm's profits. On the path starting at A, this time never comes. As a result, one can show that the firm can raise the present value of its lifetime profits by lowering the path of its capital holdings. An analogous argument applies to paths where K and q are continually falling.

Thus the unique equilibrium, given the initial value of K, is for q to equal the value that puts the industry on the saddle path, and for K and q to then move along this saddle path to E. This saddle path is shown in Figure 8.4.

---

[10] For formal demonstrations of this, see Abel (1982) and Hayashi (1982).

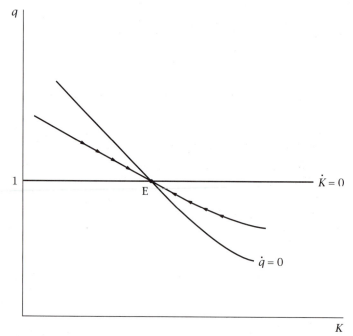

FIGURE 8.4   The saddle path

The long-run equilibrium, Point E, is characterized by $q = 1$ (which implies $\dot{K} = 0$) and $\dot{q} = 0$. The fact that q equals 1 means that the market and replacement values of capital are equal; thus firms have no incentive to increase or decrease their capital stocks. And from (8.19), for $\dot{q}$ to equal 0 when q is 1, the marginal revenue product of capital must equal r. This means that the profits from holding a unit of capital just offset the forgone interest, and thus that investors are content to hold capital without the prospect of either capital gains or losses.[11]

8.5   Implications

The model developed in the previous section can be used to address many issues. This section examines its implications for the effects of changes in output, interest rates, and tax policies.

---

[11] It is straightforward to modify the model to be one of external rather than internal adjustment costs. The key change is to replace the adjustment cost function with a supply curve for new capital goods, $\dot{K} = g(p_K)$, where $g'(\bullet) > 0$ and where p_K is the relative price of capital. With this change, the market value of firms always equals the replacement cost of their capital stocks; the role played by q in the model with internal adjustment costs is played instead by the relative price of capital. See Foley and Sidrauski (1970) and Problem 8.7.

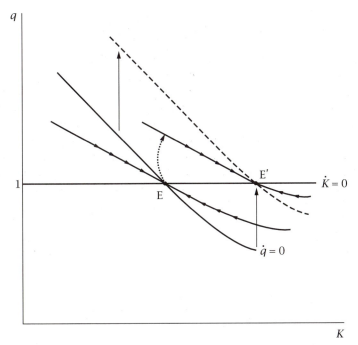

FIGURE 8.5   The effects of a permanent increase in output

The Effects of Output Movements

An increase in aggregate output raises the demand for the industry's product, and thus raises profits for a given capital stock. Thus the natural way to model an increase in aggregate output is as an upward shift of the $\pi(\bullet)$ function.

For concreteness, assume that the industry is initially in long-run equilibrium, and that there is an unanticipated, permanent upward shift of the $\pi(\bullet)$ function. The effects of this change are shown in Figure 8.5. The upward shift of the $\pi(\bullet)$ function shifts the $\dot q = 0$ locus up: since profits are higher for a given capital stock, smaller capital gains are needed for investors to be willing to hold shares in firms (see [8.24]). From our analysis of phase diagrams in Chapter 2, we know what the effects of this change are. q jumps immediately to the point on the new saddle path for the given capital stock; K and q then move down that path to the new long-run equilibrium at Point E′. Since the rate of change of the capital stock is an increasing function of q, this implies that $\dot K$ jumps at the time of the change and then gradually returns to zero. Thus a permanent increase in output leads to a temporary increase in investment.

The intuition behind these responses is straightforward. The increase in output raises the demand for the industry's product. Since the capital stock cannot adjust instantly, existing capital in the industry earns rents, and so its market value rises. The higher market value of capital attracts invest-ment, and so the capital stock begins to rise. As it does so, the industry's output rises, and thus the relative price of its product declines; thus profits and the value of capital fall. The process continues until the value of the capital returns to normal; at this point there are no incentives for further investment.

Now consider an increase in output that is known to be temporary. Specifically, the industry begins in long-run equilibrium. There is then an unexpected upward shift of the profit function; when this happens, it is known that the function will return to its initial position at some later time, T.

The key insight needed to find the effects of this change is that there cannot be an anticipated jump in q. If, for example, there is an anticipated downward jump in q, the owners of shares in firms will suffer capital losses at an infinite rate with certainty at that moment. But that means that no one will hold shares at that moment.

Thus at time T, K and q must be on the saddle path leading back to the initial long-run equilibrium: if they were not, q would have to jump for the industry to get back to its long-run equilibrium. Between the time of the upward shift of the profit function and T, the dynamics of K and q are determined by the temporarily high profit function. Finally, the initial value of K is given, but (since the upward shift of the profit function is unexpected) q can change discretely at the time of the initial shock.

Together, these facts tell us how the industry responds. At the time of the change, q jumps to the point such that, with the dynamics of K and q given by the new profit function, they reach the old saddle path at exactly time T. This is shown in Figure 8.6. q jumps from Point E to Point A at the time of the shock. q and K then move gradually to Point B, arriving there at time T. Finally, they then move up the old saddle path to E.

This analysis has several implications. First, the temporary increase in output raises investment: since output is higher for a period, firms increase their capital stocks to take advantage of this. Second, comparing Figure 8.6 with Figure 8.5 shows that q rises less than it does if the increase in output is permanent; thus, since q determines investment, investment responds less. Intuitively, since it is costly to reverse increases in capital, firms respond less to a rise in profits when they know they will reverse the increases. And third, Figure 8.6 shows that the path of K and q crosses the $\dot{K} = 0$ line before it reaches the old saddle path—that is, before time T. Thus the capital stock begins to decline before output returns to normal. To understand this intuitively, consider the time just before time T. The profit function is just about to return to its initial level; thus firms are about to want to have smaller capital stocks. And since it is costly to adjust the capital stock and since there is only a brief period of high profits left, there is a benefit and almost no cost to beginning the reduction immediately.

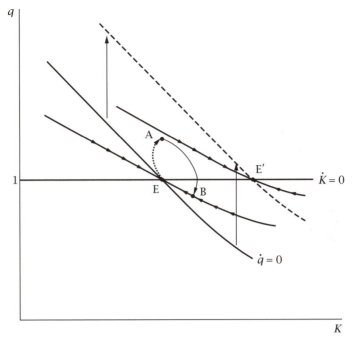

FIGURE 8.6   The effects of a temporary increase in output

These results imply that it is not just current output but its entire path over time that affects investment. The comparison of permanent and temporary output movements shows that investment is higher when output is expected to be higher in the future than when it is not. Thus expectations of high output in the future raise current demand. In addition, as the example of a permanent increase in output shows, investment is higher when output has recently risen than when it has been high for an extended period. This impact of the change in output on the level of investment demand is known as the *accelerator*.

The Effects of Interest-Rate Movements

Recall that the equation of motion for q is $\dot{q} = rq - \pi(K)$ (equation [8.24]). Thus interest-rate movements, like shifts of the profit function, affect investment through their impact on the equation for $\dot{q}$. Their effects are therefore similar to the effects of output movements. A permanent decline in the interest rate, for example, shifts the $\dot{q} = 0$ locus up. In addition, since r multiplies q in the equation for $\dot{q}$, the decline makes the locus steeper. This is shown in Figure 8.7.

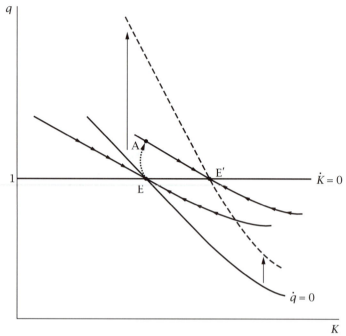

FIGURE 8.7   The effects of a permanent decrease in the interest rate

The figure can be used to analyze the effects of permanent and temporary changes in the interest rate along the lines of our analysis of the effects of permanent and temporary output movements. A permanent fall in the interest rate, for example, causes q to jump to the point on the new saddle path (Point A in the diagram). K and q then move down to the new long-run equilibrium (Point E′). Thus the permanent decline in the interest rate produces a temporary boom in investment as the industry moves to a permanently higher capital stock.

Thus, just as with output, both past and expected future interest rates affect investment. The interest rate in our model, r, is the instantaneous rate of return; thus it corresponds to the short-term interest rate. One implication of this analysis is that the short-term rate does not reflect all the information about interest rates that is relevant for investment. As we will see in greater detail in Section 10.3, long-term interest rates are likely to reflect expectations of future short-term rates. If long-term rates are less than short-term rates, for example, it is likely that investors are expecting short-term rates to fall; if not, they are better off buying a series of short-term bonds than buying a long-term bond, and so no one is willing to hold long-term bonds. Thus, since our model implies that increases in expected future short-term rates reduce investment, it implies that, for a given level of current short-term rates, investment is lower when long-term rates are higher. Thus the model supports the standard view that long-term interest rates are important to investment.

The Effects of Taxes: An Example

A temporary investment tax credit is often proposed as a way to stimulate aggregate demand during recessions. The argument is that an investment tax credit that is known to be temporary gives firms a strong incentive to invest while the credit is in effect. Our model can be used to investigate this argument.

For simplicity, assume that the investment tax credit takes the form of a direct rebate to the firm of fraction θ of the price of capital, and assume that the rebate applies to the purchase price but not to the adjustment costs. When there is a credit of this form, the firm invests as long as the value of the capital plus the rebate exceeds the capital's cost. Thus the first-order condition for current investment, (8.18), becomes

$$q(t) + \theta(t) = 1 + C'(I(t)), \qquad (8.25)$$

where $\theta(t)$ is the credit at time t. The equation for $\dot{q}$, (8.24), is unchanged.

Equation (8.25) implies that the capital stock is constant when $q + \theta = 1$. An investment tax credit of θ therefore shifts the $\dot{K} = 0$ locus down by θ; this is shown in Figure 8.8. If the credit is permanent, q jumps down to the

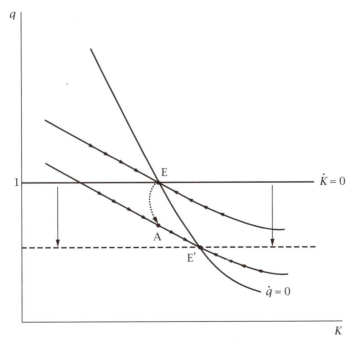

FIGURE 8.8   The effects of a permanent investment tax credit

new saddle path at the time it is announced. Intuitively, because the credit increases investment, it means that the industry's profits (neglecting the credit) will be lower, and thus that existing capital is less valuable. K and q then move along the saddle path to the new long-run equilibrium, which involves higher K and lower q.

Now consider a temporary credit. From our earlier analysis of a temporary change in output, we know that the announcement of the credit causes q to fall to a point where the dynamics of K and q, given the credit, bring them to the old saddle path just as the credit expires. They then move up that saddle path back to the initial long-run equilibrium.

This is shown in Figure 8.9. As the figure shows, q does not fall all the way to its value on the new saddle path; thus the temporary credit reduces q by less than a comparable permanent credit does. The reason is that, because the temporary credit does not lead to a permanent increase in the capital stock, it causes a smaller reduction in the value of existing capital. Now recall that the change in the capital stock, $\dot{K}$, depends on $q + \theta$ (see [8.25]). q is higher under the temporary credit than under the permanent one; thus, just as the informal argument suggests, the temporary credit has a larger effect on investment than the permanent credit does. Finally, note that the figure shows that under the temporary credit, q is rising in

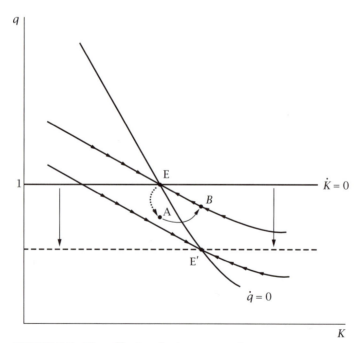

FIGURE 8.9   The effects of a temporary investment tax
             credit

the later part of the period that the credit is in effect. Thus, after a point, the temporary credit leads to a growing investment boom as firms try to invest just before the credit goes out of effect. Under the permanent credit, in contrast, the rate of change of the capital stock declines steadily as the industry moves towards its new long-run equilibrium.

8.6   The Effects of Uncertainty: An Introduction

Our analysis so far assumes that firms are certain about future profitability, interest rates, and tax policies. In practice, they face uncertainty about all of these. This section therefore introduces some of the issues raised by uncertainty.

Uncertainty about Future Profitability

We begin with the case where there is no uncertainty about the path of the interest rate; for simplicity it is assumed to be constant. Thus the uncertainty concerns only future profitability. In the case, the value of 1 unit of capital is given by

$$q(t) = \int_{\tau=t}^{\infty} e^{-r(\tau-t)} E_t[\pi(K(\tau))] d\tau \tag{8.26}$$

(see [8.22]).

This expression can be used to find how q is expected to evolve over time. Since (8.26) holds at all times, it implies that the expectation as of time t of q at some later time, $t + \Delta t$, is given by

$$E_t[q(t + \Delta t)] = E_t\left[\int_{\tau=t+\Delta t}^{\infty} e^{-r[\tau-(t+\Delta t)]} E_{t+\Delta t}[\pi(K(\tau))] d\tau\right]$$

$$= \int_{\tau=t+\Delta t}^{\infty} e^{-r[\tau-(t+\Delta t)]} E_t[\pi(K(\tau))] d\tau, \tag{8.27}$$

where the second line uses the fact that the law of iterated projections implies that $E_t[E_{t+\Delta t}[\pi(K(\tau))]]$ is just $E_t[\pi(K(\tau))]$. Differentiating (8.27) with respect to Δt and evaluating the resulting expression at $\Delta t = 0$ gives us

$$E_t[\dot{q}(t)] = rq(t) - \pi(K(t)). \tag{8.28}$$

Except for the presence of the expectations term, this expression is identical to the equation for $\dot{q}$ in the model with certainty (see [8.24]).

As before, each firm invests to the point where the cost of acquiring new capital equals the market value of capital. Thus equation (8.23), $\dot{K}(t) = f(q(t))$, continues to hold.

Our analysis so far appears to imply that uncertainty has no direct effect on investment: firms invest as long as the value of new capital exceeds the cost of acquiring it, and the value of that capital depends only on its expected payoffs. But this analysis neglects the fact that it is not quite correct to assume that there is exogenous uncertainty about the future values of $\pi(K)$. Since the path of K is determined within the model, what can be taken as exogenous is uncertainty about the position of the $\pi(\bullet)$ function; the combination of that uncertainty and firms' behavior then determines uncertainty about the values of $\pi(K)$.

In one natural baseline case, this subtlety proves to be unimportant: if $\pi(\bullet)$ is linear and $C(\bullet)$ is quadratic and if the uncertainty concerns the intercept of the $\pi(\bullet)$ function, then the uncertainty does not affect investment. That is, one can show that in this case, investment at any time is the same as it is if the future values of the intercept of the $\pi(\bullet)$ function are certain to equal their expected values (see Problems 8.9 and 8.10).

An Example

To see the effects of uncertainty about profitability, consider the following example. Suppose that the assumptions of our baseline case are satisfied, and that initially the $\pi(\bullet)$ function is constant and the industry is in long-run equilibrium. It then becomes known that the government is considering a change in the tax code that would raise the intercept of the $\pi(\bullet)$ function. The proposal will be voted on after time T, and it has a 50 percent chance of passing. There is no other source of uncertainty.

The effects of this development are shown in Figure 8.10. The figure shows the $\dot{K} = 0$ locus and the $\dot{q} = 0$ loci and the saddle paths with the initial $\pi(\bullet)$ function and the potential new, higher function. Given our assumptions, all these loci are straight lines (see Problem 8.9). Initially, K and q are at Point E. After the proposal is voted on, they will move along the appropriate saddle path to the relevant long-run equilibrium (Point E′ if the proposal is passed, E if it is defeated). There cannot be an expected capital gain or loss at the time the proposal is voted on. Thus, since the proposal has a 50 percent chance of passing, q must be midway between the points on the two saddle paths at the time of the vote; that is, it must be on the dotted line in the figure. Finally, before the vote the dynamics of K and q are given by (8.28) and (8.23) with the initial $\pi(\bullet)$ function and no uncertainty about $\dot{q}$.

Thus at the time it becomes known that the government is considering the proposal, q jumps up to the point such that the dynamics of K and q carry them to the dashed line after time T. q then jumps up or down depending on the outcome of the vote, and K and q then converge to the relevant long-run equilibrium.

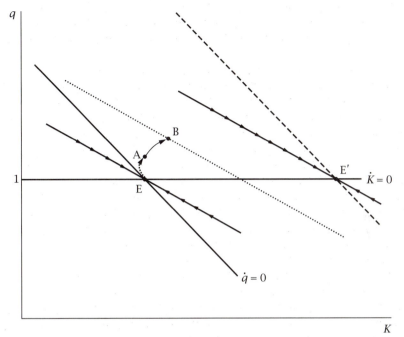

FIGURE 8.10   The effects of uncertainty about future tax policy when adjustment costs are symmetric

Irreversible Investment

If $\pi(\bullet)$ is not linear or $C(\bullet)$ is not quadratic, uncertainty about the $\pi(\bullet)$ function can affect expectations of future values of $\pi(K)$, and thus can affect current investment. Suppose, for example, that it is more costly for firms to reduce their capital stocks than to increase them. Then if $\pi(\bullet)$ shifts up, the industry-wide capital stock will rise rapidly, and so the increase in $\pi(K)$ will be brief; but if $\pi(\bullet)$ shifts down, K will fall only slowly, and so the decrease in $\pi(K)$ will be long-lasting. Thus with asymmetry in adjustment costs, uncertainty about the position of the profit function reduces expectations of future profitability, and thus reduces investment.

This type of asymmetry in adjustment costs means that investment is somewhat *irreversible:* it is easier to increase the capital stock than to reverse the increase. In the phase diagram, irreversibility causes the saddle path to be curved. If K exceeds its long-run equilibrium value, it falls only slowly; thus profits are depressed for an extended period, and so q is much less than 1. If K is less than its long-run equilibrium value, on the other hand, it rises rapidly, and so q is only slightly more than 1.

To see the effects of irreversibility, consider our previous example, but now with the assumption that the costs of adjusting the capital stock are asymmetric. This situation is analyzed in Figure 8.11. As before, at the time the proposal is voted on, q must be midway between the two saddle paths,

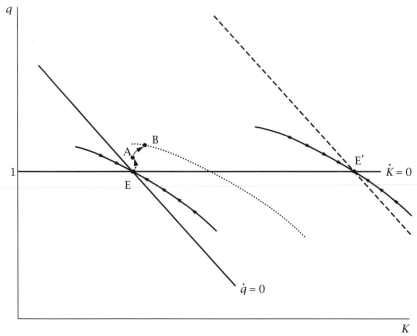

FIGURE 8.11   The effects of uncertainty about future tax policy when adjustment costs are asymmetric

and again the dynamics of K and q before the vote are given by (8.28) and (8.23) with the initial $\pi(\bullet)$ function and no uncertainty about $\dot{q}$.

Thus, as before, when it becomes known that the government is considering the proposal, q jumps up to the point such that the dynamics of K and q carry them to the dashed line after time T. As the figure shows, however, the asymmetry of the adjustment costs causes this jump to be smaller than it is under symmetric costs. Specifically, the fact that it is costly to reduce capital holdings means that if firms build up large capital stocks before the vote and the proposal is then defeated, the fact that it is hard to reverse the increase causes q to be quite low. This acts to reduce the value of capital before the vote, and thus reduces investment. Intuitively, when investment is irreversible, there is an *option value* to waiting rather than investing. If a firm does not invest, it retains the possibility of keeping its capital stock low; if it invests, on the other hand, it commits itself to a high capital stock.

Realistically, adjustment costs are likely to be more complicated than just taking some asymmetric form around $\dot{\kappa} = 0$. For example, the marginal cost of both the first unit of investment and the first unit of disinvestment may be strictly positive (so that $C(\dot{\kappa})$ is not differentiable at $\dot{\kappa} = 0$). In this case, there is a range of values of q around 1 for which the firm leaves its capital stock unchanged. The firm increases its capital only if q exceeds some threshold that is strictly greater than 1, and decreases it only if q is below some threshold that is strictly less than 1 (Abel and Eberly, 1994).

In addition, there may be a fixed cost to undertaking any nonzero amount of investment (so that $C(\dot{\kappa})$ is discontinuous at $\dot{\kappa} = 0$). Such a fixed cost increases the range of values of q for which the firm leaves its capital stock unchanged (again, see Abel and Eberly). In this case, investment is "lumpy": most of the time the firm does not invest at all, but occasionally it invests a large, discrete amount.

A large recent literature investigates the effects of uncertainty, irreversibility, and fixed costs. This work is both theoretical and empirical, and considers these factors' implications not only for investment at the microeconomic level but also for aggregate investment.[12]

Uncertainty about Discount Factors

Firms are uncertain not only about what their future profits will be, but also about how those payoffs will be valued. To see the effects of this uncertainty, suppose the firm is owned by a representative consumer. As we saw in Section 7.5, the consumer values future payoffs not according to a constant interest rate, but according to the marginal utility of consumption. The discounted marginal utility of consumption at time τ, relative to the marginal utility of consumption at t, is $e^{-\rho(\tau-t)}u'(C(\tau))/u'(C(t))$, where ρ is the consumer's discount rate, $u(\bullet)$ is the instantaneous utility function, and C is consumption. Thus our expression for the value of a unit of capital, (8.26), becomes

$$q(t) = \int_{\tau=t}^{\infty} e^{-\rho(\tau-t)} E_t \left[\frac{u'(C(\tau))}{u'(C(t))} \pi(K(\tau)) \right] d\tau. \tag{8.29}$$

As Craine (1989) emphasizes, (8.29) implies that the impact of a project's riskiness on investment in the project depends on the same considerations that determine the impact of assets' riskiness on their values in the consumption CAPM. Idiosyncratic risk—that is, randomness in $\pi(K)$ that is uncorrelated with $u'(C)$—has no impact on the market value of capital, and thus no impact on investment. But uncertainty that is positively correlated with aggregate risk—that is, positive correlation of $\pi(K)$ and C, and thus negative correlation of $\pi(K)$ and $u'(C)$—lowers the value of capital and hence reduces investment. And uncertainty that is negatively correlated with aggregate risk raises investment.

---

[12] Bernanke (1983a) is an important early paper on irreversibility. Recent work includes Abel and Eberly (1994); Dixit and Pindyck (1994); Caballero, Engel, and Haltiwanger (1995); Abel, Dixit, Eberly, and Pindyck (1996); and Cooper, Haltiwanger, and Power (1999). See Caballero (1999) for a survey.

8.7   Financial-Market Imperfections

Introduction

When firms and investors are equally well informed, financial markets function efficiently. Investments are valued according to their expected payoffs and riskiness; as a result, they are undertaken if their value exceeds the cost of acquiring and installing the necessary capital. These are the assumptions underlying our analysis so far. In particular, we have assumed that firms make investments if they raise the present value of profits evaluated using the prevailing economy-wide interest rate; thus we have implicitly assumed that firms can borrow at that interest rate.

In practice, however, firms are much better informed about their investment projects than potential outside investors are. Outside financing must ultimately come from individuals. These individuals usually have little contact with the firm and little expertise concerning the firm's activities. In addition, their stakes in the firm are usually low enough that their incentive to acquire relevant information is small.

Because of these problems, institutions such as banks, mutual funds, and bond-rating agencies that specialize in acquiring and transmitting information play central roles in financial markets. But even they are much less informed than the firms or individuals in whom they are investing their funds. The issuer of a credit card, for example, is usually much less informed than the holder of the card about the holder's financial circumstances and spending habits. In addition, the existence of intermediaries between the ultimate investors and firms means that there is a two-level problem of asymmetric information: there is asymmetric information not just between the intermediaries and the firms, but also between the individuals and the intermediaries (Diamond, 1984).

Asymmetric information creates *agency problems* between investors and firms. Some of the risk in the payoff to investment is usually borne by the investors rather than by the firm; this occurs, for example, in any situation where there is a possibility that the firm may go bankrupt. When this is the case, the firm can change its behavior to take advantage of its superior information. It can only borrow if it knows that its project is particularly risky, for example, or it can choose a high-risk strategy over a low-risk one even if this reduces expected returns. Thus asymmetric information can distort investment choices away from the most efficient projects. In addition, the presence of asymmetric information can lead the investors to expend resources monitoring the firms' activities; thus again it imposes costs.

This section presents a simple model of asymmetric information and the resulting agency problems, and discusses some of their effects. We will find that when there is asymmetric information, investment depends on more than just interest rates and profitability; such factors as investors' ability to monitor firms and firms' ability to finance their investment using internal funds also matter. We will also see that asymmetric information changes how interest rates and profitability affect investment.

Assumptions

An entrepreneur has the opportunity to undertake a project that requires 1 unit of resources. The entrepreneur has wealth of W, which is less than 1; thus he or she must obtain $1 - W$ units of outside financing to undertake the project. If the project is undertaken, it has an expected output of y, which is positive. y is heterogeneous across entrepreneurs and is publicly observable. Actual output can differ from expected output, however; specifically, the actual output of a project with an expected output of y is distributed uniformly on $[0, 2y]$. Since the entrepreneur's wealth is all invested in the project, his or her payment to the outside investors cannot exceed the project's output. This limit on the amount that the entrepreneur can pay to outside investors means that the investors must bear some of the project's risk.

If the entrepreneur does not undertake the project, he or she can invest at the risk-free interest rate, r. The entrepreneur is risk-neutral; thus he or she undertakes the project if the difference between y and the expected payments to the outside investors is greater than $(1 + r)W$.

The outside investors, like the entrepreneur, are risk-neutral and can invest their wealth at the risk-free rate. In addition, the outside investors are competitive; thus in equilibrium their expected rate of return on any financing they provide to entrepreneurs must be r.

The key assumption of the model is that entrepreneurs are better informed than outside investors about their projects' actual output. Specifically, an entrepreneur observes his or her output costlessly; an outside investor, however, must pay a cost c to observe output. c is assumed to be positive; for convenience, it is also assumed to be less than expected output, y.

This type of asymmetric information is known as *costly state verification* (Townsend, 1979). We focus on this type of asymmetric information between entrepreneurs and investors not because it is the most important type in practice, but because it is relatively straightforward to analyze. Other types of information asymmetries, such as asymmetric information about the riskiness of projects or entrepreneurs' actions, have broadly similar effects.

The Equilibrium under Symmetric Information

In the absence of the cost to outside investors of observing the project's output, the equilibrium is straightforward. Entrepreneurs whose projects have an expected payoff that exceeds $1 + r$ obtain financing and undertake their projects; entrepreneurs whose projects have an expected output less than $1 + r$ do not. For the projects that are undertaken, the contract between the entrepreneur and the outside investors provides the investors with expected payments of $(1 - W)(1 + r)$. There are many contracts that do this. One example is a contract that gives to investors the fraction

$(1 - W)(1 + r)/y$ of whatever output turns out to be; since expected output is y, this yields an expected payment of $(1 - W)(1 + r)$. The entrepreneur's expected income is then $y - (1 - W)(1 + r)$, which equals $W(1 + r) + y - (1 + r)$. Since y exceeds $1 + r$ by assumption, this is greater than $W(1 + r)$. Thus the entrepreneur is made better off by undertaking the project.

The Form of the Contract under Asymmetric Information

Let us now reintroduce the assumption that it is costly for outside investors to observe a project's output. In addition, assume that each outsider's wealth is greater than $1 - W$. Thus we can focus on the case where, in equilibrium, each project has only a single outside investor. This allows us to avoid dealing with the complications that arise when there is more than one outside investor who may want to observe a project's output.

Since outside investors are risk-neutral and competitive, an entrepreneur's expected payment to the investor must equal $(1 + r)(1 - W)$ plus the investor's expected spending on verifying output. The entrepreneur's expected income equals the project's expected output, which is exogenous, minus the expected payment to the investor. Thus the optimal contract is the one that minimizes the fraction of the time that the investor verifies output while providing the outside investor with the required rate of return.

Given our assumptions, the contract that accomplishes this takes a simple form. If the payoff to the project exceeds some critical level D, then the entrepreneur pays the investor D and the investor does not verify output. But if the payoff is less than D, the investor pays the verification cost and takes all of output. Thus the contract is a debt contract. The entrepreneur borrows $1 - W$ and promises to pay back D if that is possible. If the entrepreneur's output exceeds the amount that is due, he or she pays off the loan and keeps the surplus. And if the entrepreneur cannot make the required payment, all of his or her resources go to the lender. This payment function is shown in Figure 8.12.

The argument that the optimal contract takes this form has several steps. First, when the investor does not verify output, the payment cannot depend on actual output. To see this, suppose that the payment is supposed to be Q_1 when output is Y_1 and Q_2 when output is Y_2, with $Q_2 > Q_1$, and that the investor does not verify output in either of these cases. Since the investor does not know output, when output is Y_2 the entrepreneur pretends that it is Y_1, and therefore pays Q_1. Thus the contract cannot make the payment when output is Y_2 exceed the payment when it is Y_1.

Second, and similarly, the payment with verification can never exceed the payment without verification, D; otherwise the entrepreneur always pretends that output is not equal to the values of output that yield a payment

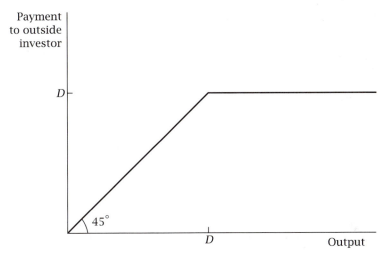

FIGURE 8.12 The form of the optimal payment function

greater than D. In addition, the payment with verification cannot equal D; otherwise it is possible to reduce expected expenditures on verification by not verifying whenever the entrepreneur pays D.

Third, the payment is D whenever output exceeds D. To see this, note that if the payment is ever less than D when output is greater than D, it is possible to increase the investor's expected receipts and reduce expected verification costs by changing the payment to D for these levels of output; as a result, it is possible to construct a more efficient contract.

Fourth, the entrepreneur cannot pay D if output is less than D; thus in these cases the investor must verify output.

Finally, if the payment is less than all of output when output is less than D, increasing the payment in these situations raises the investor's expected receipts without changing expected verification costs. But this means that it is possible to reduce D, and thus to save on verification costs.

Together, these facts imply that the optimal contract is a debt contract.[13]

---

[13] For formal proofs, see Townsend (1979) and Gale and Hellwig (1985). This analysis neglects two subtleties. First, it assumes that verification must be a deterministic function of the state. One can show, however, that a contract that makes verification a random function of the entrepreneur's announcement of output can improve on the contract shown in Figure 8.12 (Bernanke and Gertler, 1989). Second, the analysis assumes that the investor can commit to verification if the entrepreneur announces that output is less than D. For any announced level of output less than D, the investor prefers to receive that amount without verifying than with verifying. But if the investor can decide ex post not to verify, the entrepreneur has an incentive to announce low output. Thus the contract is not *renegotiation-proof*. For simplicity, we ignore these complications.

The Equilibrium Value of D

The next step of the analysis is to determine what value of D is specified in the contract. Investors are risk-neutral and competitive, and the risk-free interest rate is r. Thus the expected payments to the investor, minus his or her expected spending on verification, must equal $1 + r$ times the amount of the loan, $1 - W$. To find the equilibrium value of D, we must therefore determine how the investor's expected receipts net of verification costs vary with D, and then find the value of D that provides the investor with the required expected net receipts.

To find the investor's expected net receipts, suppose first that D is less than the project's maximum possible output, $2y$. In this case, actual output can be either more or less than D. If output is more than D, the investor does not pay the verification cost and receives D. Since output is distributed uniformly on $[0, 2y]$, the probability of this occurring is $(2y - D)/(2y)$. If output is less than D, the investor pays the verification cost and receives all of output. The assumption that output is distributed uniformly implies that the probability of this occurring is $D/(2y)$, and that average output conditional on this event is $D/2$.

If D exceeds $2y$, on the other hand, then output is always less than D. Thus in this case the investor always pays the verification cost and receives all of output. In this case the expected payment is y.

Thus the investor's expected receipts minus verification costs are

$$R(D) = \begin{cases} \dfrac{2y - D}{2y}D + \dfrac{D}{2y}\left(\dfrac{D}{2} - c\right) & \text{if } D \le 2y \\ y - c & \text{if } D > 2y. \end{cases} \tag{8.30}$$

Equation (8.30) implies that when D is less than $2y$, $R'(D)$ equals $1 - [c/(2y)] - [D/(2y)]$. Thus R increases until $D = 2y - c$ and then decreases. The reason that R is eventually decreasing in D is that when D is close to the maximum possible payoff, raising it further mainly means that the investor must verify output more often, and thus reduces his or her expected net receipts. At the maximum, the investor's expected net revenues are $R(2y - c) = [(2y - c)/(2y)]^2 y \equiv R^{\text{MAX}}$. Thus the maximum expected net revenues equal expected output when c is 0, but are less than this when c is greater than 0. Finally, R declines to $y - c$ at $D = 2y$; thereafter further increases in D do not affect $R(D)$. The $R(D)$ function is plotted in Figure 8.13.

Figure 8.14 shows three possible values of the investor's required net revenues, $(1 + r)(1 - W)$. If the required net revenues equal V_1—more generally, if they are less than $y - c$—there is a unique value of D that yields the investor the required net revenues. The contract therefore specifies this value of D. For the case when the required payment equals V_1, the equilibrium value of D is given by D_1 in the figure.

If the required net revenues exceed R^{MAX}—if they equal V_3, for example—there is no value of D that yields the necessary revenues for the investor.

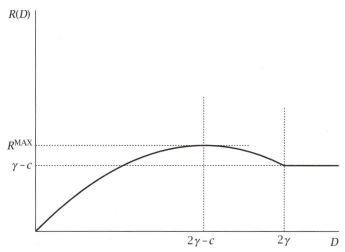

FIGURE 8.13 The investor's expected revenues net of verification costs

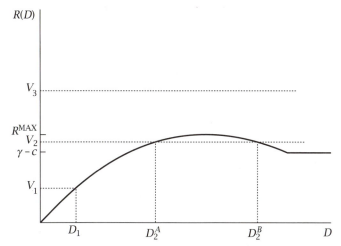

FIGURE 8.14 The determination of the entrepreneur's required payment to the investor

Thus in this situation there is *credit rationing:* investors refuse to lend to the entrepreneur at any interest rate.

Finally, if the required net revenues are between $\gamma - c$ and R^{MAX}, there are two possible values of D. For example, the figure shows that a D of either D_2^A or D_2^B yields $R(D) = V_2$. The higher of these two D's (D_2^B in the figure) is not a competitive equilibrium, however: if an investor is making a loan to an entrepreneur with a required payment of D_2^B, other investors can profitably lend on more favorable terms. Thus competition drives D down to D_2^A. The equilibrium value of D is thus the smaller solution to $R(D) = (1+r)(1-W)$. Expression (8.30) implies that this solution is[14]

$$D^* = 2y - c - \sqrt{(2y-c)^2 - 4y(1+r)(1-W)} \quad \text{for } (1+r)(1-W) \le R^{\text{MAX}}.$$

(8.31)

Equilibrium Investment

The final step of the analysis is to determine when the entrepreneur undertakes the project. Clearly a necessary condition is that he or she can obtain financing at some interest rate. But this is not sufficient: some entrepreneurs who can obtain financing may be better off investing in the safe asset.

An entrepreneur who invests in the safe asset obtains $(1+r)W$. If the entrepreneur instead undertakes the project, his or her expected receipts are expected output, y, minus expected payments to the outside investor. If the entrepreneur can obtain financing, the expected payments to the investor are the opportunity cost of the investor's funds, $(1+r)(1-W)$, plus the investor's expected spending on verification costs. Thus to determine when a project is undertaken, we need to determine these expected verification costs.

These can be found from equation (8.31). The investor verifies when output is less than D^*; this occurs with probability $D^*/(2y)$. Thus expected verification costs are

$$A = \frac{D^*}{2y}c$$

$$= \left[\frac{2y-c}{2y} - \sqrt{\left(\frac{2y-c}{2y}\right)^2 - \frac{(1+r)(1-W)}{y}} \right]c.$$

(8.32)

Straightforward differentiation shows that A is increasing in c and r and decreasing in y and W. We can therefore write

$$A = A(c, r, W, y), \quad A_c > 0, \quad A_r > 0, \quad A_W < 0, \quad A_y < 0. \quad (8.33)$$

The entrepreneur's expected payments to the investor are $(1 + r)(1 - W) + A(c, r, W, y)$. Thus the project is undertaken if $(1 + r)(1 - W) \le R^{\text{MAX}}$

---

[14] Note that the condition for the expression under the square root sign, $(2y - c)^2 - 4y(1 + r)(1 - W)$, to be negative is that $[(2y - c)/(2y)]^2 y < (1 + r)(1 - W)$—that is, that R^{MAX} is less than required net revenues. Thus the case where the expression in (8.31) is not defined corresponds to the case where there is no value of D at which investors are willing to lend.

and if

$$y - (1 + r)(1 - W) - A(c, r, W, y) > (1 + r)W. \qquad (8.34)$$

Although we have derived these results from a particular model of asymmetric information, the basic ideas are general. Suppose, for example, that there is asymmetric information about how much risk the entrepreneur is taking. In such a situation, if the investor bears some of the cost of poor outcomes, the entrepreneur has an incentive to increase the riskiness of his or her activities beyond the point that maximizes the expected return to the project; thus there is *moral hazard*. As a result, asymmetric information again reduces the total expected returns to the entrepreneur and the investor, just as it does in our model of costly state verification. Under plausible assumptions, these agency costs are decreasing in the amount of financing that the entrepreneur can provide (W), increasing in the amount that the investor must be paid for a given amount of financing (r), decreasing in the expected payoff to the project (y), and increasing in the magnitude of the asymmetric information (c when there is costly state verification, and the entrepreneur's ability to take high-risk actions when there is moral hazard).

Similarly, suppose that entrepreneurs are heterogeneous in terms of how risky their projects are, and that risk is not publicly observable—that is, suppose there is *adverse selection*. Then again there are agency costs of outside finance, and again those costs are determined by the same types of considerations as in our model. Thus the qualitative results of this model apply to many other models of asymmetric information in financial markets.

Implications

This model has many implications. As the preceding discussion suggests, most of the major ones arise from financial-market imperfections in general rather than from our specific model. Here we discuss four of the most important.

First, the agency costs arising from asymmetric information raise the cost of external finance, and therefore discourage investment. Under symmetric information, investment occurs in our model if $y > 1 + r$. But when there is asymmetric information, investment occurs only if $y > 1 + r + A(c, r, W, y)$. Thus the agency costs reduce investment at a given safe interest rate.

Second, because financial-market imperfections create agency costs that affect investment, they alter the impact of output and interest-rate movements on investment. Recall from Section 8.5 that when financial markets are perfect, output movements affect investment through their effect on future profitability. Financial-market imperfections create a second channel: because output movements affect firms' current profitability, they affect firms' ability to provide internal finance. In the context of our model, we can think of a fall in current output as lowering entrepreneurs' wealth, W; since a reduction in wealth increases agency costs, the fall in output reduces investment even if the profitability of investment projects (the distribution of the y's) is unchanged.

Similarly, interest-rate movements affect investment not only through the conventional channel, but also through their impact on agency costs: an increase in interest rates raises agency costs and thus discourages invest-ment. Intuitively, an increase in r raises the total amount the entrepreneur must pay the investor. This means that the probability that the investor is unable to make the required payment is higher, and thus that agency costs are higher. Specifically, since the investor's required net revenues are $(1 + r)(1 - W)$, an increase in r of Δr increases these required revenues by $(1 - W)\Delta r$; thus it has the same effect on the required net revenues as a fall in W of $[(1 - W)/(1 + r)]\Delta r$. As a result, as equation (8.32) shows, these two changes have the same effect on agency costs.

In addition, the model implies that the effects of changes in output and interest rates on investment do not all occur through their impact on en-trepreneurs' decisions of whether to borrow at the prevailing interest rate; instead some of the impact comes from changes in the set of entrepreneurs who are able to borrow.

The third implication of our analysis is that many variables that do not affect investment when capital markets are perfect matter when capital mar-kets are imperfect. Entrepreneurs' wealth provides a simple example. Sup-pose that y and W are heterogeneous across entrepreneurs. With perfect financial markets, whether a project is funded depends only on y. Thus the projects that are undertaken are the most productive ones. This is shown in Panel (a) of Figure 8.15. With asymmetric information, in contrast, since W affects the agency costs, whether a project is funded depends on both y and W. Thus a project with a lower expected payoff than another can be funded if the entrepreneur with the less productive project is wealthier. This is shown in Panel (b) of the figure.

The fact that financial-market imperfections cause entrepreneurs' wealth to affect investment implies that these imperfections can magnify the effects of shocks that occur outside the financial system. Declines in output arising from other sources act to reduce entrepreneurs' wealth; these reductions in wealth reduce investment, and thus increase the output declines (Bernanke and Gertler, 1989; Kiyotaki and Moore, 1997).

Two other examples of variables that affect investment only when cap-ital markets are imperfect are average tax rates and idiosyncratic risk. If taxes are added to the model, the average rate (rather than just the marginal rate) affects investment through its impact on firms' ability to use internal finance. And risk, even if it is uncorrelated with consumption, affects in-vestment through its impact on agency costs. Outside finance of a project whose payoff is certain, for example, involves no agency costs, since there is no possibility that the entrepreneur will be unable to repay the investor.

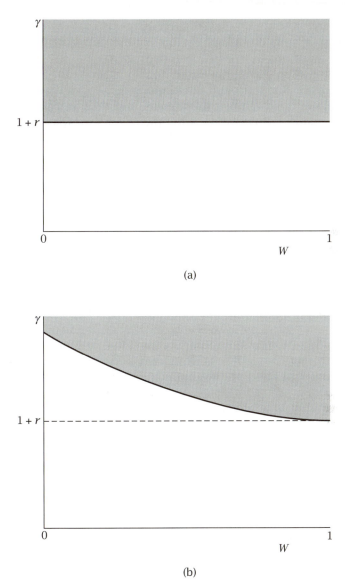

(a)

(b)

FIGURE 8.15 **The determination of the projects that are undertaken under symmetric and asymmetric information**

But, as our model shows, outside finance of a risky project involves agency costs.

Fourth, and potentially most important, our analysis implies that the financial system itself can be important to investment. The model implies that increases in c, the cost of verification, reduce investment. More generally, the existence of agency costs suggests that the efficiency of the financial system in processing information and monitoring borrowers is a potentially important determinant of investment.

This observation has implications for both short-run fluctuations and long-run growth. For short-run fluctuations, it implies that disruptions to the financial system can affect investment, and thus aggregate output. For example, Bernanke (1983b) argues that the collapse of the U.S. banking system in the early 1930s contributed to the severity of the Great Depression by reducing the effectiveness of the financial system in evaluating and funding investment projects. Similarly, many observers argue that an important factor in the 1990–1991 recession in the United States was a "capital crunch" at banks that reduced their ability to make loans. Their argument is that because banks had little capital of their own in this period, they were unusually dependent on external finance; this raised the opportunity cost of funds to them, and thus made them less willing to lend (see, for example, Bernanke and Lown, 1991).

With regard to long-run growth, McKinnon (1973) and others argue that the financial system has important effects on overall investment and on the quality of the investment projects undertaken, and thus on economies' growth over extended periods. Because the development of the financial system may be a by-product, rather than a cause, of growth, this argument is difficult to test. Nonetheless, King and Levine (1993a, 1993b) present some evidence that financial development is important to growth.

8.8 Empirical Applications

The Investment Tax Credit and the Price of Capital Goods

As we saw in Section 8.1, the costs of adjusting the capital stock can be either external or internal to firms. If they are external, they take the form of an increase in the relative price of capital goods when firms' desired capital stocks rise. Since there are data on the relative price of capital goods, it is possible to test for this effect.

Such a test is carried out by Goolsbee (1998). He focuses on how the investment tax credit affects capital-goods prices. His basic specification is

$$\ln P_{it} = b\tau_{it} + c_i' X_{it} + e_{it}, \tag{8.35}$$

where P_{it} is the relative price of capital of type i in year t, τ_{it} is a measure of the investment tax credit's subsidy to the purchase of capital good i in year t (as a percentage of the purchase price), and X_{it} is a vector of control variables whose effects are allowed to vary across the goods. Goolsbee argues that the government may have a tendency to increase the investment tax credit in times, such as recessions, when investment demand is otherwise weak. If this is correct, the estimate of b will tend to understate the true effect of the investment tax credit on capital-goods prices. To address this problem, Goolsbee includes dummy variables for each year in some specifications; when he does this, he is controlling for the variation over time in the overall investment tax credit and focusing only on the differences in the credit across different types of capital.

Goolsbee considers 22 capital goods over the period 1959–1988. His basic regression includes dummy variables for each capital good, a time trend, and macroeconomic controls. This specification yields an estimate of b of 0.17, with a standard error of 0.03. Thus the results provide strong evidence of external adjustment costs. Including dummy variables for each year has little effect: the estimate of b rises to 0.19, and the standard error rises to 0.04.

Goolsbee also examines the variation in the effect of the investment tax credit across capital goods; specifically, he estimates a separate b for each type of capital. He finds that the price responses are large for goods that are purchased almost entirely by firms, such as mining machinery and railroad equipment, and small for goods that are purchased mainly by households, such as personal computers and furniture. Since households are not eligible for the investment tax credit, this suggests that the price effect of the credit is larger when it affects more of the buyers of a good. To investigate this idea further, Goolsbee constructs estimates of the fractions of the purchasers of each good who are eligible for the credit. He then includes in the regression not just the credit, but the product of the credit and his eligibility estimate. If the reason that the credit is associated with increases in the price of capital is through its impact on demand, then under plausible assumptions the association should depend only on this interaction term.

The results provide support for this prediction. The coefficient on the interaction term is quantitatively large and highly statistically significant. The coefficient on the credit term, however, is not zero as the theory predicts, but significantly negative. That is, taken literally, the point estimates imply that a tax subsidy in a sector where no potential users can use the subsidy lowers prices in that sector. In fact, however, in almost every sector most potential users are eligible for the subsidy; thus this anomalous finding may be just an artifact of trying to extrapolate the estimates' implications far outside the range over which they are estimated.

Cash Flow and Investment

Theories of financial-market imperfections imply that internal finance is less costly than external finance. They therefore imply that, for a given level of interest rates, firms with higher profits invest more.

A naive way to test this prediction is to regress investment on measures of the cost of capital and on *cash flow*—loosely speaking, current revenues minus expenses and taxes. Such regressions can use either firm-level data at a point in time or aggregate data over time. In either form, they typically find a strong link between cash flow and investment.

There is a problem with this test, however. The regression does not control for the future profitability of capital, and cash flow is likely to be correlated with future profitability. We saw in Section 8.5, for example, that our model of investment without financial-market imperfections predicts that a rise in output that is not immediately reversed raises investment. The reason is not that higher current output reduces firms' need to rely on outside finance, but that higher future output means that capital is more valuable. A similar relationship is likely to hold across firms at a point in time: firms with high cash flow probably have successful products or low costs, and thus have strong incentives to expand output. Because of this potential correlation between cash flow and current profitability, the regression may show a relationship between cash flow and investment even if financial markets are perfect.

A large literature, begun by Fazzari, Hubbard, and Petersen (1988), addresses this problem by comparing the investment behavior of different types of firms. Specifically, Fazzari, Hubbard, and Petersen's idea is to divide firms into those that are likely to face significant costs of obtaining outside funds and those that are not (see also Hoshi, Kashyap, and Scharfstein, 1991). There is likely to be an association between cash flow and investment among both types of firms even if financial-market imperfections are not important. But the theory that financial-market imperfections have large effects on investment predicts that the association will be stronger among the firms that face greater barriers to external finance. And unless the association between current cash flow and future profitability is for some reason stronger for the firms with less access to financial markets, the view that financial-market imperfections are not important predicts no difference in the cash flow–investment link for the two groups. Thus, Fazzari, Hubbard, and Petersen argue, the difference in the cash flow–investment relationship between the two groups can be used to test for the importance of financial-market imperfections to investment.

The specific way that Fazzari, Hubbard, and Petersen divide their firms is according to their dividend payments as a fraction of income. Firms that pay high dividends can finance additional investment by reducing their dividends. Firms that pay low dividends, in contrast, must rely on external finance.[15]

The basic regression is a pooled time series–cross section regression of investment as a fraction of firms' capital stock on the ratio of cash flow to the capital stock, an estimate of q, and dummy variables for each firm and each year. The regression is estimated separately for the two groups of firms.

---

[15] One complication to this argument is that it may be costly for high-dividend firms to reduce their dividends: there is evidence that reductions in dividends are interpreted by the stock market as a signal of lower future profitability, and that the reductions therefore lower the value of firms' shares. Thus it is possible that the test could fail to find differences between the two groups of firms not because financial-market imperfections are unimportant, but because they are important to both groups.

The sample consists of 422 relatively large U.S. firms over the period 1970–1984. Low-dividend firms are defined as those with ratios of dividends to income consistently under 10 percent, and high-dividend firms are defined as those with dividend-income ratios consistently over 20 percent (Fazzari, Hubbard, and Petersen also consider an intermediate-dividend group).

For the high-dividend firms, the coefficient on cash flow is 0.230, with a standard error of 0.010; for the low-dividend firms, it is 0.461, with a standard error of 0.027. The t-statistic for the hypothesis that the two coefficients are equal is 12.1; thus the hypothesis is overwhelmingly rejected. The point estimates imply that low-dividend firms invest 23 cents more of each extra dollar of cash flow than the high-dividend firms do. Thus even if we interpret the estimate for the high-dividend firms as reflecting only the correlation between cash flow and future profitability, the results still suggest that financial-market imperfections have a large effect on investment by low-dividend firms.

Many authors have used variations on Fazzari, Hubbard, and Petersen's approach. Lamont (1997), for example, compares the investment behavior of the nonoil subsidiaries of oil companies after the collapse in oil prices in 1986 with the investment behavior of comparable companies that are not connected with oil companies. The view that internal finance is cheaper than external finance predicts that a decline in oil prices, by reducing the availability of internal funds, should reduce the subsidiaries' investment; the view that financial-market imperfections are unimportant predicts that it should have no effect. Lamont finds a statistically significant and quantitatively large difference in the behavior of the two groups; the point estimates imply that each dollar of lower income of a parent oil company reduces investment of the company's nonoil subsidiaries by 10 cents. Thus his results suggest that the barriers to outside finance are considerably larger than the barriers to finance between different parts of a company.

Gertler and Gilchrist (1994) carry out a test that is in the same spirit as these but that focuses on the effects of monetary policy (see also Kashyap, Lamont, and Stein, 1994, and Oliner and Rudebusch, 1996). They begin by arguing that small firms are likely to face larger barriers to outside finance than large firms do; for example, the fixed costs associated with issuing publicly traded bonds may be more important for small firms. They then compare the behavior of small and large firms' inventories and sales following moves to tighter monetary policy. Again the results support the importance of imperfect financial markets. Small firms account for a highly disproportionate share of the declines in sales, inventories, and short-term debt following monetary tightening. Indeed, large firms' borrowing increases after a monetary tightening, whereas small firms' borrowing declines sharply.

These papers' findings are representative of the findings in this literature: the bulk of the evidence suggests that financial-market imperfections are important to investment. Precisely what form those imperfections take, and how important they are quantitatively, remain open questions.[16]

---

[16] Recent work by Kaplan and Zingales (1997) challenges much of this literature both

Problems

8.1. Consider a firm that produces output using a Cobb–Douglas combination of capital and labor: $Y = K^{\alpha}L^{1-\alpha}$, $0 < \alpha < 1$. Suppose that the firm's price is fixed in the short run; thus it takes both the price of its product, P, and the quantity, Y, as given. Finally, input markets are competitive; thus the firm takes the wage, W, and the rental price of capital, r_K, as given.

   (*a*) What is the firm's choice of L given P, Y, W, and K?

   (*b*) Given this choice of L, what are profits as a function of P, Y, W, and K?

   (*c*) Find the first-order condition for the profit-maximizing choice of K. Is the second-order condition satisfied?

   (*d*) Solve the first-order condition in part (*c*) for K as a function of P, Y, W, and r_K. How, if at all, do changes in each of these variables affect K?

8.2. Corporations in the United States are allowed to subtract depreciation allowances from their taxable income. The depreciation allowances are based on the purchase price of the capital; a corporation that buys a new capital good at time t can deduct fraction $D(s)$ of the purchase price from its taxable income at time $t + s$. Depreciation allowances often take the form of *straight-line depreciation*: $D(s)$ equals $1/T$ for $s \in [0, T]$, and equals 0 for $s > T$, where T is the *tax life* of the capital good.

   (*a*) Assume straight-line depreciation. If the marginal corporate income tax rate is constant at τ and the interest rate is constant at i, by how much does purchasing a unit of capital at a price of P_K reduce the present value of the firm's corporate tax liabilities as a function of T, τ, i, and P_K? Thus, what is the after-tax price of the capital good to the firm?

   (*b*) Suppose that $i = r + \pi$, and that π increases with no change in r. How does this affect the after-tax price of the capital good to the firm?

8.3. The major feature of the tax code that affects the user cost of capital in the case of owner-occupied housing in the United States is that nominal interest payments are tax-deductible. Thus the after-tax real interest rate relevant to home ownership is $r - \tau i$, where r is the pretax real interest rate, i is the nominal interest rate, and τ is the marginal tax rate. In this case, how does an increase in inflation for a given r affect the user cost of capital and the desired capital stock?

---

theoretically and empirically. Theoretically, these authors argue that the premise of the empirical tests in this literature is flawed. They agree that cash flow will not affect investment for a firm that faces no barriers at all to external finance. But they argue that in considering firms that face costs of outside finance, there is little reason to expect the relationship between investment and cash flow to be stronger for firms for which those costs are greater. Empirically, they argue that the proxies for costs of outside finance used in this literature are flawed and are contradicted by other evidence. Although Kaplan and Zingales's critique is potentially important, to date researchers in this area do not appear either to have refuted their arguments or to have modified their research in light of them. Thus the ultimate importance of Kaplan and Zingales's critique is not yet known. See Fazzari, Hubbard, and Petersen (2000) and Kaplan and Zingales (2000).

8.4. Using the calculus of variations to solve the social planner's problem in the Ramsey model. Consider the social planner's problem that we analyzed in Section 2.4: the planner wants to maximize $\int_{t=0}^{\infty} e^{-\beta t}[c(t)^{1-\theta}/(1-\theta)]\,dt$ subject to $\dot{k}(t) = f(k(t)) - c(t) - (n+g)k(t)$.

(a) What is the current-value Hamiltonian? What variables are the control variable, the state variable, and the costate variable?

(b) Find the three conditions that characterize optimal behavior analogous to equations (8.18), (8.19), and (8.20), in Section 8.2.

(c) Show that the first two conditions in part (b), together with the fact that $f'(k(t)) = r(t)$, imply the Euler equation (equation [2.20]).

(d) Let μ denote the costate variable. Show that $[\dot{\mu}(t)/\mu(t)] - \beta = (n+g) - r(t)$, and thus that $e^{-\beta t}\mu(t)$ is proportional to $e^{-R(t)}e^{(n+g)t}$. Show that this implies that the transversality condition in part (b) holds if and only if the budget constraint, equation (2.15), holds with equality.

8.5. Consider the model of investment in Sections 8.2–8.5. Describe the effects of each of the following changes on the $\dot{K} = 0$ and $\dot{q} = 0$ loci, on K and q at the time of the change, and on their behavior over time. In each case, assume that K and q are initially at their long-run equilibrium values.

(a) A war destroys half of the capital stock.

(b) The government taxes returns from owning firms at rate τ.

(c) The government taxes investment. Specifically, firms pay the government y for each unit of capital they acquire, and receive a subsidy of y for each unit of disinvestment.

8.6. Consider the model of investment in Sections 8.2–8.5. Suppose it becomes known at some date that there will be a one-time capital levy; specifically, capital holders will be taxed an amount equal to fraction f of the value of their capital holdings at some time in the future, time T. Assume the industry is initially in long-run equilibrium. What happens at the time of this news? How do K and q behave between the time of the news and the time the levy is imposed? What happens to K and q at the time of the levy? How do they behave thereafter? (Hint: Is q anticipated to change discontinuously at the time of the levy?)

8.7. A model of the housing market. (This follows Poterba, 1984.) Let H denote the stock of housing, I the rate of investment, p_H the real price of housing, and R the rent. Assume that I is increasing in p_H, so that $I = I(p_H)$, with $I'(\bullet) > 0$, and that $\dot{H} = I - \delta H$. Assume also that the rent is a decreasing function of H: $R = R(H)$, $R'(\bullet) < 0$. Finally, assume that rental income plus capital gains must equal the exogenous required rate of return, r: $(R + \dot{p}_H)/p_H = r$.

(a) Sketch the set of points in (H, p_H) space such that $\dot{H} = 0$. Sketch the set of points such that $\dot{p}_H = 0$.

(b) What are the dynamics of H and p_H in each region of the resulting diagram? Sketch the saddle path.

(c) Suppose the market is initially in long-run equilibrium, and that there is an unexpected permanent increase in r. What happens to H and p_H at the time of the change? How do H, p_H, I, and R behave over time following the change?

(d) Suppose the market is initially in long-run equilibrium, and that it becomes known that there will be a permanent increase in r time T in the future. What happens to H and p_H at the time of the news? How do H, p_H, I, and R behave between the time of the news and the time of the increase? What happens to them when the increase occurs? How do they behave after the increase?

(e) Are adjustment costs internal or external in this model? Explain.

(f) Why is the $\dot{H} = 0$ locus not horizontal in this model?

8.8. Suppose that the costs of adjustment exhibit constant returns in $\dot{\kappa}$ and κ. Specifically, suppose they are given by $C(\dot{\kappa}/\kappa)\kappa$, where $C(0) = 0$, $C'(0) = 0$, $C''(\bullet) > 0$. In addition, suppose capital depreciates at rate δ; thus $\dot{\kappa}(t) = I(t) - \delta\kappa(t)$. Consider the representative firm's maximization problem.

(a) What is the current-value Hamiltonian?

(b) Find the three conditions that characterize optimal behavior analogous to equations (8.18), (8.19), and (8.20), in Section 8.2.

(c) Show that the condition analogous to (8.18) implies that the growth rate of each firm's capital stock, and thus the growth rate of the aggregate capital stock, is determined by q. In (K, q) space, what is the $\dot{K} = 0$ locus?

(d) Substitute your result in part (c) into the condition analogous to (8.19) to express $\dot{q}$ in terms of K and q.

(e) In (K, q) space, what is the slope of the $\dot{q} = 0$ locus at the point where $q = 1$?

8.9. Suppose that $\pi(K) = a - bK$ and $C(I) = \alpha I^2/2$.

(a) What is the $\dot{q} = 0$ locus? What is the long-run equilibrium value of K?

(b) What is the slope of the saddle path? (Hint: Use the approach in Section 2.6.)

8.10. Consider the model of investment under uncertainty with a constant interest rate in Section 8.6. Suppose that, as in Problem 8.9, $\pi(K) = a - bK$ and that $C(I) = \alpha I^2/2$; in addition, suppose that what is uncertain is future values of a. This problem asks you to show that it is an equilibrium for $q(t)$ and $K(t)$ to have the values at each point in time that they would if there were no uncertainty about the path of a. Specifically, let $\hat{q}(t + \tau, t)$ and $\hat{K}(t + \tau, t)$ be the paths q and K would take after time t if $a(t + \tau)$ were certain to equal $E_t[a(t + \tau)]$ for all $\tau \geq 0$.

(a) Show that if $E_t[q(t + \tau)] = \hat{q}(t + \tau, t)$ for all $\tau \geq 0$, then $E_t[K(t + \tau)] = \hat{K}(t + \tau, t)$ for all $\tau \geq 0$.

(b) Use equation (8.26) to show that this implies that if $E_t[q(t + \tau)] = \hat{q}(t + \tau, t)$, then $q(t) = \hat{q}(t, t)$, and thus that $\dot{K}(t) = N[\hat{q}(t, t) - 1]/\alpha$, where N is the number of firms.

8.11. (This follows Bernanke, 1983a, and Dixit and Pindyck, 1994.) Consider a firm that is contemplating undertaking an investment with a cost of I. There are two periods. The investment will pay off π_1 in period 1 and π_2 in period 2. π_1 is certain, but π_2 is uncertain. The firm maximizes expected profits and, for simplicity, the interest rate is zero.

(a) Suppose the firm's only choices are to undertake the investment in period 1 or not to undertake it at all. Under what condition will the firm undertake the investment?

(b) Suppose the firm also has the possibility of undertaking the investment in period 2, after the value of π_2 is known; in this case the investment pays off only π_2. Is it possible for the condition in (a) to be satisfied but for the firm's expected profits to be higher if it does not invest in period 1 than if it does invest?

(c) Define the cost of waiting as π_1, and define the benefit of waiting as $\text{Prob}(\pi_2 < I)E[I - \pi_2 \mid \pi_2 < I]$. Explain why these represent the cost and the benefit of waiting. Show that the difference in the firm's expected profits between not investing in period 1 and investing in period 1 equals the benefit of waiting minus the cost.

8.12. The Modigliani–Miller theorem. (Modigliani and Miller, 1958.) Consider the analysis of the effects of uncertainty about discount factors in Section 8.6. Suppose, however, that the firm finances its investment using a mix of equity and risk-free debt. Specifically, consider the financing of the marginal unit of capital. The firm issues quantity b of bonds; each bond pays 1 unit of output with certainty at time $t + \tau$ for all $\tau \geq 0$. Equity holders are the residual claimant; thus they receive $\pi(K(t + \tau)) - b$ at $t + \tau$ for all $\tau \geq 0$.

(a) Let $P(t)$ denote the value of a unit of debt at t, and $V(t)$ the value of the equity in the marginal unit of capital. Find expressions analogous to (8.29) for $P(t)$ and $V(t)$.

(b) How, if at all, does the division of financing between bonds and equity affect the market value of the claims on the unit of capital, $P(t)b + V(t)$? Explain intuitively.

(c) More generally, suppose the firm finances the investment by issuing n financial instruments. Let $d_i(t + \tau)$ denote the payoff to instrument i at time $t + \tau$; the payoffs satisfy $d_1(t + \tau) + \cdots + d_n(t + \tau) = \pi(K(t + \tau))$, but are otherwise unrestricted. How, if at all, does the total value of the n assets depend on how the total payoff is divided among the assets?

(d) Return to the case of debt and equity finance. Suppose, however, that the firm's profits are taxed at rate θ, and that interest payments are tax-deductible. Thus the payoff to bond holders is the same as before, but the payoff to equity holders at time $t + \tau$ is now $(1 - \theta)[\pi(K(t + \tau)) - b]$. Does the result in part (b) still hold? Explain.

Chapter **9**
UNEMPLOYMENT

9.1 Introduction: Theories of Unemployment

In almost any economy at almost any time, many individuals appear to be unemployed. That is, there are many people who are not working but who say they want to work in jobs like those held by individuals similar to them, at the wages those individuals are earning.

The possibility of unemployment is a central subject of macroeconomics. There are two basic issues. The first concerns the determinants of average unemployment over extended periods. The central questions here are whether this unemployment represents a genuine failure of markets to clear, and if so, what its causes and consequences are. There is a wide range of possible views. At one extreme is the position that unemployment is largely illusory, or the working out of unimportant frictions in the process of matching up workers and jobs. At the other extreme is the view that unemployment is the result of non-Walrasian features of the economy and that it largely represents a waste of resources.

The second issue concerns the cyclical behavior of the labor market. As described in Section 5.6, the real wage appears to be only moderately procyclical. This is consistent with the view that the labor market is Walrasian only if labor supply is quite elastic or if shifts in labor supply play an important role in employment fluctuations. But as we saw in Section 4.10, there is little support for the hypothesis of highly elastic labor supply. And it seems unlikely that shifts in labor supply are central to fluctuations. The remaining possibility is that the labor market is not Walrasian, and that its non-Walrasian features are central to its cyclical behavior. That possibility is the focus of this chapter.

The issue of why shifts in labor demand appear to lead to large movements in employment and only small movements in the real wage is important to all theories of fluctuations. For example, we saw in Chapter 6 that if the real wage is highly procyclical in response to demand shocks, it is essentially impossible for the small barriers to nominal adjustment to generate substantial nominal rigidity. In the face of a decline in aggregate

410

demand, for example, if prices remain fixed the real wage must fall sharply; as a result, each firm has a huge incentive to cut its price and hire labor to produce additional output. If, however, there is some non-Walrasian feature of the labor market that causes the cost of labor to respond little to the overall level of economic activity, then there is some hope for theories of small frictions in nominal adjustment.

This chapter considers various ways in which the labor market may depart from a competitive, textbook market. We investigate both whether these departures can lead to substantial unemployment and whether they can have important effects on the cyclical behavior of employment and the real wage.

If there is unemployment in a Walrasian labor market, unemployed workers immediately bid the wage down until supply and demand are in balance. Theories of unemployment can therefore be classified according to their view of why this mechanism may fail to operate. Concretely, consider an unemployed worker who offers to work for a firm for slightly less than the firm is currently paying, and who is otherwise identical to the firm's current workers. There are at least four possible responses the firm can make to this offer.

First, the firm can say that it does not want to reduce wages. Theories in which there is a cost as well as a benefit to the firm of paying lower wages are known as *efficiency-wage* theories. (The name comes from the idea that higher wages may raise the productivity, or efficiency, of labor.) These theories are the subject of Sections 9.2 through 9.4. Section 9.2 first discusses the possible ways that paying lower wages can harm a firm; it then analyzes a simple model where wages affect productivity but where the reason for that link is not explicitly specified. Section 9.3 considers an important generalization of that model. Finally, Section 9.4 presents a model formalizing one particular view of why paying higher wages can be beneficial. The central idea is that if firms cannot monitor their workers' effort perfectly, they may pay more than market-clearing wages to induce workers not to shirk.

The second possible response the firm can make is that it wishes to cut wages, but that an explicit or implicit agreement with its workers prevents it from doing so.[1] Theories in which bargaining and contracts affect the macroeconomics of the labor market are known as *contracting models.*

Contracting models are the subject of Sections 9.5 through 9.7. Section 9.5 presents some basic models of contracting. Sections 9.6 and 9.7 then investigate what happens when some workers are represented in the bargaining process and others are not. Section 9.6 explores the implications of this distinction between *insiders* and *outsiders* for the cyclical behavior

---

[1] The firm can also be prevented from cutting wages by minimum-wage laws. In most settings, this is relevant only to low-skill workers; thus it does not appear to be central to the macroeconomics of unemployment.

of labor costs and for average unemployment. Section 9.7 investigates its effects on the behavior of unemployment over time.

The third way the firm can respond to the unemployed worker's offer is to say that it does not accept the premise that the unemployed worker is identical to the firm's current employees. That is, heterogeneity among workers and jobs may be an essential feature of the labor market. In this view, to think of the market for labor as a single market, or even as a large number of interconnected markets, is to commit a fundamental error. Instead, according to this view, each worker and each job should be thought of as distinct; as a result, the process of matching up workers and jobs occurs not through markets but through a complex process of search. Models of this type are known as *search models*, or *search and matching models*, or the *flow approach* to labor markets. They are discussed in Section 9.8.

Finally, the firm can accept the worker's offer. That is, it is possible that the market for labor is approximately Walrasian. In this view, measured unemployment consists largely of people who are moving between jobs, or who would like to work at wages higher than those they can in fact obtain. Since the focus of this chapter is on unemployment, we will not develop this idea here. Nonetheless, it is important to keep in mind that this is one view of the labor market.

9.2   A Generic Efficiency-Wage Model

Potential Reasons for Efficiency Wages

The central assumption of efficiency-wage models is that there is a benefit as well as a cost to a firm of paying a higher wage. There are many reasons that this could be the case. Here we describe four of the most important (see Yellen, 1984, and Katz, 1986, for surveys and references).

First, and most simply, a higher wage can increase workers' food consumption, and thereby cause them to be better nourished and more productive. Obviously this possibility is not important in developed economies. Nonetheless, it provides a concrete example of an advantage of paying a higher wage. For that reason, it is often a useful reference point.

Second, a higher wage can increase workers' effort in situations where the firm cannot monitor them perfectly. In a Walrasian labor market, workers are indifferent about losing their jobs, since identical jobs are immediately available. Thus if the only way that firms can punish workers who exert low effort is by firing them, workers in such a labor market have no incentive to exert effort. But if a firm pays more than the market-clearing wage, its jobs are valuable. Thus its workers may choose to exert effort even if there is some chance they will not be caught if they do not. This idea is developed in Section 9.4.

Third, paying a higher wage can improve workers' ability along dimensions the firm cannot observe. Specifically, if higher-ability workers have higher reservation wages, offering a higher wage raises the average quality of the applicant pool, and thus raises the average ability of the workers the firm hires.[2]

Finally, a high wage can build loyalty among workers and hence induce high effort; conversely, a low wage can cause anger and desire for revenge, and thereby lead to shirking or sabotage. Akerlof and Yellen (1990) present extensive evidence that workers' effort is affected by such forces as anger, jealousy, and gratitude. For example, they describe studies showing that workers who believe they are underpaid sometimes perform their work in ways that are harder for them in order to reduce their employers' profits.[3]

Other Compensation Schemes

This discussion implicitly assumes that a firm's financial arrangements with its workers take the form of some wage per unit of time. An important question is whether there are more complicated ways for the firm to compensate its workers that allow it to obtain the benefits of a higher wage less expensively. The nutritional advantages of a higher wage, for example, can be obtained by compensating workers partly in kind (such as by feeding them at work). To give another example, firms can give workers an incentive to exert effort by requiring them to post a bond that they lose if they are caught shirking.

If there are cheaper ways for firms to obtain the benefits of a higher wage, then these benefits lead not to a higher wage but just to complicated compensation policies. Whether the benefits can be obtained in such ways depends on the specific reason that a higher wage is advantageous. We will therefore not attempt a general treatment. The end of Section 9.4 discusses this issue in the context of efficiency-wage theories based on imperfect monitoring of workers' effort. In this section and the next, however, we simply assume that compensation takes the form of a conventional wage, and investigate the effects of efficiency wages under this assumption.

Assumptions

We now turn to a model of efficiency wages. There is a large number, N, of identical competitive firms.[4] The representative firm seeks to maximize its

---

[2] When ability is observable, the firm can pay higher wages to more able workers; thus observable ability differences do not lead to any departures from the Walrasian case.

[3] See Problem 9.5 for a formalization of this idea. Three other potential advantages of a higher wage are that it can reduce turnover (and hence recruitment and training costs, if they are borne by the firm); that it can lower the likelihood that the workers will unionize; and that it can raise the utility of managers who have some ability to pursue objectives other than maximizing profits.

[4] We can think of the number of firms as being determined by the amount of capital in the economy, which is fixed in the short run.

real profits, which are given by

$$\pi = Y - wL, \tag{9.1}$$

where Y is the firm's output, w is the real wage that it pays, and L is the amount of labor it hires.

A firm's output depends both on the number of workers it employs and on their effort. For simplicity we neglect other inputs and assume that labor and effort enter the production function multiplicatively. Thus the representative firm's output is

$$Y = F(eL), \quad F'(\bullet) > 0, \quad F''(\bullet) < 0, \tag{9.2}$$

where e denotes workers' effort. The crucial assumption of efficiency-wage models is that effort depends positively on the wage the firm pays. In this section we consider the simple case (due to Solow, 1979) where the wage is the only determinant of effort. Thus,

$$e = e(w), \quad e'(\bullet) > 0. \tag{9.3}$$

Finally, there are $\bar{L}$ identical workers, each of whom supplies 1 unit of labor inelastically.

Analyzing the Model

The problem facing the representative firm is

$$\max_{L,w} F(e(w)L) - wL. \tag{9.4}$$

If there are unemployed workers, the firm can choose the wage freely. If unemployment is zero, on the other hand, the firm must pay at least the wage paid by other firms.

When the firm is unconstrained, the first-order conditions for L and w are[5]

$$F'(e(w)L)e(w) - w = 0, \tag{9.5}$$

$$F'(e(w)L)Le'(w) - L = 0. \tag{9.6}$$

We can rewrite (9.5) as

$$F'(e(w)L) = \frac{w}{e(w)}. \tag{9.7}$$

Substituting (9.7) into (9.6) and dividing by L yields

$$\frac{we'(w)}{e(w)} = 1. \tag{9.8}$$

---

[5] We assume that the second-order conditions are satisfied.

Equation (9.8) states that at the optimum, the elasticity of effort with respect to the wage is 1. To understand this condition, note that output is a function of the quantity of effective labor, eL. The firm therefore wants to hire effective labor as cheaply as possible. When the firm hires a worker, it obtains $e(w)$ units of effective labor at a cost of w; thus the cost per unit of effective labor is $w/e(w)$. When the elasticity of e with respect to w is 1, a marginal change in w has no effect on this ratio; thus this is the first-order condition for the problem of choosing w to minimize the cost of effective labor. The wage satisfying (9.8) is known as the *efficiency wage*.

Figure 9.1 depicts the choice of w graphically in (w, e) space. The rays coming out from the origin are lines where the ratio of e to w is constant; the ratio is larger on the higher rays. Thus the firm wants to choose w to attain as high a ray as possible. This occurs where the $e(w)$ function is just tangent to one of the rays—that is, where the elasticity of e with respect to w is 1. Panel (a) shows a case where effort is sufficiently responsive to the wage that over some range the firm prefers a higher wage. Panel (b) shows a case where the firm always prefers a lower wage.

Finally, equation (9.7) states that the firm hires workers until the marginal product of effective labor equals its cost. This is analogous to the condition in a standard labor-demand problem that the firm hires labor up to the point where the marginal product equals the wage.

Equations (9.7) and (9.8) describe the behavior of a single firm. Describing the economy-wide equilibrium is straightforward. Let w^* and L^* denote the values of w and L that satisfy (9.7) and (9.8). Since firms are identical, each firm chooses these same values of w and L. Total labor demand is therefore NL^*. If labor supply, $\bar{L}$, exceeds this amount, firms are unconstrained in their choice of w. In this case the wage is w^*, employment is NL^*, and there is unemployment of amount $\bar{L} - NL^*$. If NL^* exceeds $\bar{L}$, on the other hand, firms are constrained. In this case, the wage is bid up to the point where demand and supply are in balance, and there is no unemployment.

Implications

This model shows how efficiency wages can give rise to unemployment. In addition, the model implies that the real wage is unresponsive to demand shifts. Suppose the demand for labor increases. Since the efficiency wage, w^*, is determined entirely by the properties of the effort function, $e(\bullet)$, there is no reason for firms to adjust their wages. Thus the model provides a candidate explanation of why shifts in labor demand lead to large movements in employment and small changes in the real wage. In addition, the fact that the real wage and effort do not change implies that firms' labor costs do not change. As a result, in a model with price-setting firms, the incentive to adjust prices is small.

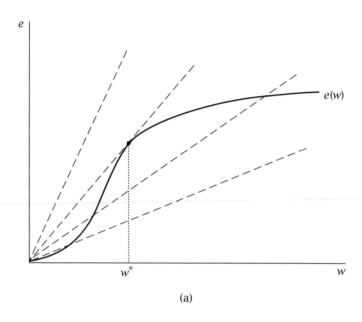

(a)

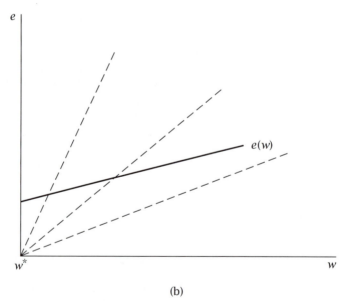

(b)

FIGURE 9.1   The determination of the efficiency wage

Unfortunately, these results are less promising than they may appear. The difficulty is that they apply not just to the short run but to the long run: the model implies that as economic growth shifts the demand for labor outward, the real wage remains unchanged and unemployment trends downward. Eventually, unemployment reaches zero, at which point further increases in demand lead to increases in the real wage. In practice, however, we observe no clear trend in unemployment over extended periods. In other words, the basic fact about the labor market that we need to understand is not just that shifts in labor demand appear to have little impact on the real wage and fall mainly on employment in the short run; it is also that they fall almost entirely on the real wage in the long run. Our model does not explain this pattern.

9.3   A More General Version

Introduction

With many of the potential sources of efficiency wages, the wage is unlikely to be the only determinant of effort. Suppose, for example, that the wage affects effort because firms cannot monitor workers perfectly and workers are concerned about the possibility of losing their jobs if the firm catches them shirking. In such a situation, the cost to a worker of being fired depends not just on the wage the job pays, but also on how easy it is to obtain other jobs and on the wages those jobs pay. Thus workers are likely to exert more effort at a given wage when unemployment is higher, and to exert less effort when the wage paid by other firms is higher. Similar arguments apply to situations where the wage affects effort because of unobserved ability or feelings of gratitude or anger.

Thus a natural generalization of the effort function, (9.3), is

$$e = e(w, w_a, u), \qquad e_1(\bullet) > 0, \qquad e_2(\bullet) < 0, \qquad e_3(\bullet) > 0, \qquad (9.9)$$

where w_a is the wage paid by other firms and u is the unemployment rate, and where subscripts denote partial derivatives.

Each firm is small relative to the economy, and therefore takes w_a and u as given. The representative firm's problem is the same as before, except that w_a and u now affect the effort function. The first-order conditions can therefore be rearranged to obtain

$$F'(e(w, w_a, u)L) = \frac{w}{e(w, w_a, u)}, \qquad (9.10)$$

$$\frac{w e_1(w, w_a, u)}{e(w, w_a, u)} = 1. \qquad (9.11)$$

These conditions are analogous to (9.7) and (9.8) in the simpler version of the model.

Assume that the $e(\bullet)$ function is sufficiently well behaved that there is a unique optimal w for a given w_a and u. Given this assumption, equilibrium requires $w = w_a$; if not, each firm wants to pay a wage different from the prevailing wage. Let w^* and L^* denote the values of w and L satisfying (9.10)–(9.11) with $w = w_a$. As before, if NL^* is less than $\bar{L}$, the equilibrium wage is w^* and there is unemployment of amount $\bar{L} - NL^*$. And if NL^* exceeds $\bar{L}$, the wage is bid up and the labor market clears.

This extended version of the model has promise for accounting for both the absence of any trend in unemployment over the long run and the fact that shifts in labor demand appear to have large effects on unemployment in the short run. This is most easily seen by means of an example.[6]

Example

Suppose effort is given by

$$e = \begin{cases} \left(\dfrac{w - x}{x}\right)^{\beta} & \text{if } w > x \\ 0 & \text{otherwise,} \end{cases} \tag{9.12}$$

$$x = (1 - bu)w_a, \tag{9.13}$$

where $0 < \beta < 1$ and $b > 0$. x is a measure of labor-market conditions. If b equals 1, x is the wage paid at other firms multiplied by the fraction of workers who are employed. If b is less than 1, workers put less weight on unemployment; this could occur if there are unemployment benefits or if workers value leisure. If b is greater than 1, workers put more weight on unemployment; this might occur because workers who lose their jobs face unusually high chances of continued unemployment, or because of risk aversion. Finally, equation (9.12) states that for $w > x$, effort increases less than proportionately with $w - x$.

Differentiation of (9.12) shows that for this functional form, the condition that the elasticity of effort with respect to the wage equals 1 (equation [9.11]) is

$$\beta \frac{w}{[(w - x)/x]^{\beta}} \left(\frac{w - x}{x}\right)^{\beta-1} \frac{1}{x} = 1. \tag{9.14}$$

Straightforward algebra can be used to simplify (9.14) to

$$\begin{aligned} w &= \frac{x}{1 - \beta} \\ &= \frac{1 - bu}{1 - \beta} w_a. \end{aligned} \tag{9.15}$$

For small values of β, $1/(1 - \beta) \simeq 1 + \beta$. Thus (9.15) implies that when β is small, the firm offers a premium of approximately fraction β over the index of labor-market opportunities, x.

---

[6] This example is based on Summers (1988).

Equilibrium requires that the representative firm wants to pay the prevailing wage, or that $w = w_a$. Imposing this condition in (9.15) yields

$$(1 - \beta)w_a = (1 - bu)w_a. \tag{9.16}$$

For this condition to be satisfied, the unemployment rate must be given by

$$u = \frac{\beta}{b} \tag{9.17}$$

$$\equiv u_{EQ}.$$

As equation (9.15) shows, each firm wants to pay more than the prevailing wage if unemployment is less than u_{EQ}, and wants to pay less if unemployment is more than u_{EQ}. Thus equilibrium requires that $u = u_{EQ}$.

Substituting (9.17) and $w = w_a$ into the effort function, (9.12), implies that equilibrium effort is given by

$$e_{EQ} = \left[\frac{w_a - (1 - bu_{EQ})w_a}{(1 - bu_{EQ})w_a} \right]^{\beta}$$

$$= \left[\frac{1 - (1 - \beta)}{1 - \beta} \right]^{\beta} \tag{9.18}$$

$$= \left(\frac{\beta}{1 - \beta} \right)^{\beta}.$$

Finally, the equilibrium wage is determined by the condition that the marginal product of effective labor equals its cost (equation [9.10]): $F'(eL) = w/e$. We can rewrite this condition as $w = eF'(eL)$. Since total employment is $(1 - u_{EQ})\overline{L}$ in equilibrium, each firm must hire $(1 - u_{EQ})\overline{L}/N$ workers. Thus the equilibrium wage is given by

$$w_{EQ} = e_{EQ}F'\left(\frac{e_{EQ}(1 - u_{EQ})\overline{L}}{N} \right). \tag{9.19}$$

Implications

This analysis has three important implications. First, (9.17) implies that equilibrium unemployment depends only on the parameters of the effort function; the production function is irrelevant. Thus an upward trend in the production function does not produce a trend in unemployment.

Second, relatively modest values of β—the elasticity of effort with respect to the premium firms pay over the index of labor-market conditions— can lead to nonnegligible unemployment. For example, either $\beta = 0.06$ and $b = 1$ or $\beta = 0.03$ and $b = 0.5$ imply that equilibrium unemployment is 6 percent. This result is not as strong as it may appear, however: while these parameter values imply a low elasticity of effort with respect to $(w - x)/x$, they also imply that workers exert no effort at all until the wage is quite high. For example, if b is 0.5 and unemployment is at its equilibrium level of 6 percent, effort is zero until a firm's wage reaches 97 percent of the prevailing wage. In that sense, efficiency-wage forces are quite strong for these parameter values.

Third, firms' incentive to adjust wages or prices (or both) in response to changes in aggregate unemployment is likely to be small for reasonable cases. Suppose we embed this model of wages and effort in a model of price-setting firms along the lines of Chapter 6. Consider a situation where the economy is initially in equilibrium, so that $u = u_{EQ}$ and marginal revenue and marginal cost are equal for the representative firm. Now suppose that the money supply falls and firms do not change their nominal wages or prices; as a result, unemployment rises above u_{EQ}. We know from Chapter 6 that small barriers to wage and price adjustment can cause this to be an equilibrium only if the representative firm's incentive to adjust is small.

For concreteness, consider the incentive to adjust wages. Equation (9.15), $w = (1 - bu)w_a/(1 - \beta)$, shows that the cost-minimizing wage is decreasing in the unemployment rate. Thus the firm can reduce its costs, and hence raise its profits, by cutting its wage. The key issue is the size of the gain. Equation (9.12) for effort implies that if the firm leaves its wage equal to the prevailing wage, w_a, its cost per unit of effective labor, w/e, is

$$
\begin{aligned}
C_{\text{FIXED}} &= \frac{w_a}{e(w_a, w_a, u)} \\[2mm]
&= \frac{w_a}{\left(\dfrac{w_a - x}{x}\right)^{\beta}} \\[2mm]
&= \frac{w_a}{\left[\dfrac{w_a - (1 - bu)w_a}{(1 - bu)w_a}\right]^{\beta}} \\[2mm]
&= \left(\frac{1 - bu}{bu}\right)^{\beta} w_a.
\end{aligned}
\tag{9.20}
$$

If the firm changes its wage, on the other hand, it sets it according to (9.15), and thus chooses $w = x/(1 - \beta)$. In this case, the firm's cost per unit of effective labor is

$$
\begin{aligned}
C_{\text{ADJ}} &= \frac{w}{\left(\dfrac{w - x}{x}\right)^{\beta}} \\[2mm]
&= \frac{x/(1 - \beta)}{\left\{\dfrac{[x/(1 - \beta)] - x}{x}\right\}^{\beta}}
\end{aligned}
\tag{9.21}
$$

$$= \frac{x/(1-\beta)}{[\beta/(1-\beta)]^\beta}$$

$$= \frac{1}{\beta^\beta} \frac{1}{(1-\beta)^{1-\beta}} (1-bu)w_a.$$

Suppose that $\beta = 0.06$ and $b = 1$, so that $u_{\text{EQ}} = 6\%$. Suppose, however, that unemployment rises to 9 percent and that other firms do not change their wages. Equations (9.20) and (9.21) imply that this rise lowers C_{FIXED} by 2.6 percent and C_{ADJ} by 3.2 percent. Thus the firm can save only 0.6 percent of costs by cutting its wages. For $\beta = 0.03$ and $b = 0.5$, the declines in C_{FIXED} and C_{ADJ} are 1.3 percent and 1.5 percent; thus in this case the incentive to cut wages is even smaller.[7]

In a competitive labor market, in contrast, the equilibrium wage falls by the percentage fall in employment divided by the elasticity of labor supply. For a 3 percent fall in employment and a labor supply elasticity of 0.2, for example, the equilibrium wage falls by 15 percent. And without endogenous effort, a 15 percent fall in wages translates directly into a 15 percent fall in costs. Firms therefore have an overwhelming incentive to cut wages and prices in this case.[8]

Thus efficiency wages have a potentially large impact on the incentive to adjust wages in the face of fluctuations in aggregate output. As a result, they have the potential to explain why shifts in labor demand mainly affect employment in the short run. Intuitively, in a competitive market firms are initially at a corner solution with respect to wages: firms pay the lowest possible wage at which they can hire workers. Thus wage reductions, if possible, are unambiguously beneficial. With efficiency wages, in contrast, firms are initially at an interior optimum where the marginal benefits and costs of wage cuts are equal.

9.4   The Shapiro–Stiglitz Model

One source of efficiency wages that has received a great deal of attention is the possibility that firms' limited monitoring abilities force them to

---

[7] One can also show that if firms do not change their wages, for reasonable cases their incentive to adjust their prices is also small. If wages are completely flexible, however, the incentive to adjust prices is not small. With u greater than u_{EQ}, each firm wants to pay less than other firms are paying (see [9.15]). Thus if wages are completely flexible, they must fall 0—or, if workers have a positive reservation wage, to this reservation wage. As a result, firms' labor costs are extremely low, and thus their incentive to cut prices and increase output is high. Thus in the absence of any barriers to changing wages, small costs to changing prices are not enough to prevent price adjustment in this model.

[8] In fact, in a competitive labor market, an individual firm's incentive to reduce wages if other firms do not is even larger than the fall in the equilibrium wage. If other firms do not cut wages, some workers are unemployed. Thus the firm can hire workers at an arbitrarily small wage (or at workers' reservation wage).

provide their workers with an incentive to exert effort. This section presents a specific model, due to Shapiro and Stiglitz (1984), of this possibility.[9]

Presenting a formal model of imperfect monitoring serves three purposes. First, it allows us to investigate whether this idea holds up under scrutiny. Second, it permits us to analyze additional questions; for example, only with a formal model can we ask whether government policies can improve welfare. Third, the mathematical tools the model employs are useful in other settings.

Assumptions

The economy consists of a large number of workers, $\bar{L}$, and a large number of firms, N. The workers maximize their expected discounted utilities, and firms maximize their expected discounted profits. The model is set in continuous time. For simplicity, the analysis focuses on steady states.

Consider workers first. The representative worker's lifetime utility is

$$U = \int_{t=0}^{\infty} e^{-\rho t} u(t) \, dt, \qquad \rho > 0. \tag{9.22}$$

$u(t)$ is instantaneous utility at time t, and ρ is the discount rate. Instantaneous utility is

$$u(t) = \begin{cases} w(t) - e(t) & \text{if employed} \\ 0 & \text{if unemployed.} \end{cases} \tag{9.23}$$

w is the wage and e is the worker's effort. There are only two possible effort levels, $e = 0$ and $e = \bar{e}$. Thus at any moment a worker must be in one of three states: employed and exerting effort (denoted E), employed and not exerting effort (denoted S, for shirking), or unemployed (denoted U).

A key ingredient of the model is its assumptions concerning workers' transitions among the three states. First, there is an exogenous rate at which jobs end. Specifically, if a worker begins working in a job at some time, t_0 (and if the worker exerts effort), the probability that the worker is still employed in the job at some later time, t, is

$$P(t) = e^{-b(t-t_0)}, \qquad b > 0. \tag{9.24}$$

(9.24) implies that $P(t+\tau)/P(t)$ equals $e^{-b\tau}$, and thus that it is independent of t: if a worker is employed at some time, the probability that he or she is still employed time τ later is $e^{-b\tau}$ regardless of how long the worker has already been employed. This lack of *time dependence* simplifies the analysis greatly, because it implies that there is no need to keep track of how long

---

[9] Dickens, Katz, Lang, and Summers (1989) document the importance of worker theft and shirking in the United States and argue that these phenomena are essential to understanding the labor market.

workers have been in their jobs. Processes like (9.24) are known as *Poisson processes.*

An equivalent way to describe the process of job breakup is to say that it occurs with probability b per unit time, or to say that the *hazard rate* for job breakup is b. That is, the probability that an employed worker's job ends in the next dt units of time approaches bdt as dt approaches 0. To see that our assumptions imply this, note that (9.24) implies $P'(t) = -bP(t)$.

The second assumption concerning workers' transitions between states is that firms' detection of workers who are shirking is also a Poisson process. Specifically, detection occurs with probability q per unit time. q is exogenous, and detection is independent of job breakups. Workers who are caught shirking are fired. Thus if a worker is employed but shirking, the probability that he or she is still employed time τ later is $e^{-q\tau}$ (the probability that the worker has not been caught and fired) times $e^{-b\tau}$ (the probability that the job has not ended exogenously).

Third, unemployed workers find employment at rate a per unit time. Each worker takes a as given. In the economy as a whole, however, a is determined endogenously. When firms want to hire workers, they choose workers at random out of the pool of unemployed workers. Thus a is determined by the rate at which firms are hiring (which is determined by the number of employed workers and the rate at which jobs end) and the number of unemployed workers. Because workers are identical, the probability of finding a job does not depend on how workers become unemployed or on how long they are unemployed.

Firms' behavior is straightforward. A firm's profits at t are

$$\pi(t) = F(\overline{e}L(t)) - w(t)[L(t) + S(t)], \qquad F'(\bullet) > 0, \qquad F''(\bullet) < 0, \qquad (9.25)$$

where L is the number of employees who are exerting effort and S is the number who are shirking. The problem facing the firm is to set w sufficiently high that its workers do not shirk, and to choose L. Because the firm's decisions at any date affect profits only at that date, there is no need to analyze the present value of profits: the firm chooses w and L at each moment to maximize the instantaneous flow of profits.

The final assumption of the model is $\overline{e}F'(\overline{e}\overline{L}/N) > \overline{e}$, or $F'(\overline{e}\overline{L}/N) > 1$. This condition states that if each firm hires $1/N$ of the labor force, the marginal product of labor exceeds the cost of exerting effort. Thus in the absence of imperfect monitoring, there is full employment.

The Values of E, U, and S

Let V_i denote the "value" of being in state i (for $i = E$, S, and U). That is, V_i is the expected value of discounted lifetime utility from the present moment forward of a worker who is in state i. Because transitions among states are Poisson processes, the V_i's do not depend on how long the worker has been in his or her current state or on his or her prior history. And because we are focusing on steady states, the V_i's are constant over time.

To find V_E, V_S, and V_U, it is not necessary to analyze the various paths the worker may follow over the infinite future. Instead we can use *dynamic programming*. The central idea of dynamic programming is to look at only a brief interval of time and use the V_i's themselves to summarize what occurs after the end of the interval.[10] Consider first a worker who is employed and exerting effort at time 0. Suppose temporarily that time is divided into intervals of length Δt, and that a worker who loses his or her job during one interval cannot begin to look for a new job until the beginning of the next interval. Let $V_E(\Delta t)$ and $V_U(\Delta t)$ denote the values of employment and unemployment as of the beginning of an interval under this assumption. In a moment we will let Δt approach 0. When we do this, the constraint that a worker who loses his or her job during an interval cannot find a new job during the remainder of that interval becomes irrelevant. Thus $V_E(\Delta t)$ will approach V_E.

If a worker is employed in a job paying a wage of w, $V_E(\Delta t)$ is given by

$$V_E(\Delta t) = \int_{t=0}^{\Delta t} e^{-bt} e^{-\rho t}(w - \bar{e}) \, dt + e^{-\rho \Delta t}[e^{-b\Delta t}V_E(\Delta t) + (1 - e^{-b\Delta t})V_U(\Delta t)].$$

(9.26)

The first term of (9.26) reflects utility during the interval $(0, \Delta t)$. The probability that the worker is still employed at time t is e^{-bt}. If the worker is employed, flow utility is $w - \bar{e}$. Discounting this back to time 0 yields an expected contribution to lifetime utility of $e^{-(\rho+b)t}(w - \bar{e})$.[11]

The second term of (9.26) reflects utility after Δt. At time Δt, the worker is employed with probability $e^{-b\Delta t}$, and is unemployed with probability $1 - e^{-b\Delta t}$. Combining these probabilities with the V's and discounting yields the second term.

If we compute the integral in (9.26), we can rewrite the equation as

$$V_E(\Delta t) = \frac{1}{\rho + b}\left(1 - e^{-(\rho+b)\Delta t}\right)(w - \bar{e})$$

(9.27)

$$+ e^{-\rho \Delta t}[e^{-b\Delta t}V_E(\Delta t) + (1 - e^{-b\Delta t})V_U(\Delta t)].$$

Solving this expression for $V_E(\Delta t)$ gives

$$V_E(\Delta t) = \frac{1}{\rho + b}(w - \bar{e}) + \frac{1}{1 - e^{-(\rho+b)\Delta t}}e^{-\rho \Delta t}(1 - e^{-b\Delta t})V_U(\Delta t). \quad (9.28)$$

As described above, V_E equals the limit of $V_E(\Delta t)$ as Δt approaches 0. (Similarly, V_U equals the limit of $V_U(\Delta t)$ as t approaches 0.) To find this limit,

---

[10] If time is discrete rather than continuous, we look one period ahead. See Sargent (1987b) for an introduction to dynamic programming.

[11] Because of the steady-state assumption, if it is optimal for the worker to exert effort initially, it continues to be optimal. Thus we do not have to allow for the possibility of the worker beginning to shirk.

we apply l'Hôpital's rule to (9.28). This yields

$$V_E = \frac{1}{\rho + b}[(w - \bar{e}) + bV_U]. \tag{9.29}$$

Equation (9.29) can also be derived intuitively. Think of an asset that pays dividends at rate $w - \bar{e}$ per unit time when the worker is employed and no dividends when the worker is unemployed; in addition, assume that the asset is being priced by risk-neutral investors with required rate of return ρ. Since the expected present value of lifetime dividends of this asset is the same as the worker's expected present value of lifetime utility, the asset's price must be V_E when the worker is employed and V_U when the worker is unemployed. For the asset to be held, it must provide an expected rate of return of ρ. That is, its dividends per unit time, plus any expected capital gains or losses per unit time, must equal ρV_E. When the worker is employed, dividends per unit time are $w - \bar{e}$, and there is a probability b per unit time of a capital loss of $V_E - V_U$. Thus,

$$\rho V_E = (w - \bar{e}) - b(V_E - V_U). \tag{9.30}$$

Rearranging this expression yields (9.29).

If the worker is shirking, the "dividend" is w per unit time, and the expected capital loss is $(b + q)(V_S - V_U)$ per unit time. Thus reasoning parallel to that used to derive (9.30) implies

$$\rho V_S = w - (b + q)(V_S - V_U). \tag{9.31}$$

Finally, if the worker is unemployed, the dividend is 0 and the expected capital gain (assuming that firms pay sufficiently high wages that employed workers exert effort) is $a(V_E - V_U)$ per unit time.[12] Thus,

$$\rho V_U = a(V_E - V_U). \tag{9.32}$$

The No-Shirking Condition

The firm must pay enough that $V_E \geq V_S$; otherwise its workers exert no effort and produce nothing. At the same time, since effort cannot exceed $\bar{e}$, there is no need to pay any excess over the minimum needed to induce effort. Thus the firm chooses w so that V_E just equals V_S:[13]

$$V_E = V_S. \tag{9.33}$$

Since V_E and V_S must be equal, (9.30) and (9.31) imply

$$(w - \bar{e}) - b(V_E - V_U) = w - (b + q)(V_E - V_U), \tag{9.34}$$

---

[12] Equations (9.31) and (9.32) can also be derived by defining $V_U(\Delta t)$ and $V_S(\Delta t)$ and proceeding along the lines used to derive (9.29).

[13] Since all firms are the same, they choose the same wage. Thus V_E and V_S do not depend on what firm a worker is employed by.

or

$$V_E - V_U = \frac{\bar{e}}{q}. \tag{9.35}$$

Equation (9.35) implies that firms set wages high enough that workers strictly prefer employment to unemployment. Thus workers obtain rents. The size of the premium is increasing in the cost of exerting effort, $\bar{e}$, and decreasing in firms' efficacy in detecting shirkers, q.

The next step is to find what the wage must be for the rent to employment to equal $\bar{e}/q$. Equations (9.30) and (9.32) imply

$$\rho(V_E - V_U) = (w - \bar{e}) - (a + b)(V_E - V_U). \tag{9.36}$$

This expression implies that for $V_E - V_U$ to equal $\bar{e}/q$, the wage must be

$$w = \bar{e} + (a + b + \rho)\frac{\bar{e}}{q}. \tag{9.37}$$

This condition states that the wage needed to induce effort is increasing in the cost of effort ($\bar{e}$), the ease of finding jobs (a), the rate of job breakup (b), and the discount rate (ρ), and is decreasing in the probability that shirkers are detected (q).

It turns out to be more convenient to express the wage needed to prevent shirking in terms of employment per firm, L, rather than the rate at which the unemployed find jobs, a. To substitute for a, we use the fact that, since the economy is in steady state, movements into and out of unemployment must balance. The number of workers becoming unemployed per unit time is N (the number of firms) times L (the number of workers per firm) times b (the rate of job breakup).[14] The number of unemployed workers finding jobs is $\bar{L} - NL$ times a. Equating these two quantities yields

$$a = \frac{NLb}{\bar{L} - NL}. \tag{9.38}$$

Equation (9.38) implies $a + b = \bar{L}b/(\bar{L} - NL)$. Substituting this into (9.37) yields

$$w = \bar{e} + \left(\rho + \frac{\bar{L}}{\bar{L} - NL}b\right)\frac{\bar{e}}{q}. \tag{9.39}$$

Equation (9.39) is the *no-shirking condition*. It shows, as a function of the level of employment, the wage that firms must pay to induce workers to exert effort. When more workers are employed, there are fewer unemployed workers and more workers leaving their jobs; thus it is easier for unemployed workers to find employment. The wage needed to deter shirking is therefore an increasing function of employment. At full employment, unemployed workers find work instantly, and so there is no cost to being fired and thus no wage that can deter shirking. The set of points in (NL, w) space satisfying the no-shirking condition (NSC) is shown in Figure 9.2.

---

[14] We are assuming that the economy is large enough that although the breakup of any individual job is random, aggregate breakups are not.

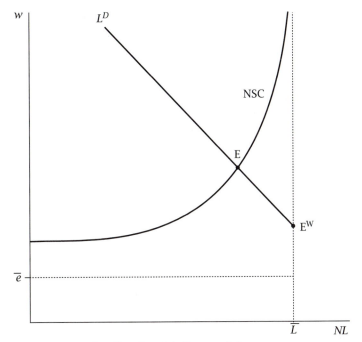

FIGURE 9.2   The Shapiro–Stiglitz model

Closing the Model

Firms hire workers up to the point where the marginal product of labor equals the wage. Equation (9.25) implies that when its workers are exerting effort, a firm's flow profits are $F(\bar{e}L) - wL$. Thus the condition for the marginal product of labor to equal the wage is

$$\bar{e}F'(\bar{e}L) = w. \tag{9.40}$$

The set of points satisfying (9.40) (which is simply a conventional labor demand curve) is also shown in Figure 9.2.

Labor supply is horizontal at $\bar{e}$ up to the number of workers, $\bar{L}$, and then vertical. In the absence of imperfect monitoring, equilibrium occurs at the intersection of labor demand and supply. Our assumption that the marginal product of labor at full employment exceeds the disutility of effort $(F'(\bar{e}L/N) > 1)$ implies that this intersection occurs in the vertical part of the labor supply curve. The Walrasian equilibrium is shown as Point E^W in the diagram.

With imperfect monitoring, equilibrium occurs at the intersection of the labor demand curve (equation [9.40]) and the no-shirking condition (equation [9.39]). This is shown as Point E in the diagram. At the equilibrium, there is unemployment. Unemployed workers strictly prefer to be employed at the prevailing wage and to exert effort, rather than to remain unemployed. Nonetheless, they cannot bid the wage down: firms know that if they hire additional workers at slightly less than the prevailing wage, the workers will prefer shirking to exerting effort. Thus the wage does not fall, and the unemployment remains.

Two examples may help to clarify the workings of the model. First, a rise in q—an increase in the probability per unit time that a shirker is detected—shifts the no-shirking locus down and does not affect the labor demand curve. This is shown in Figure 9.3. Thus the wage falls and employment rises. As q approaches infinity, the probability that a shirker is detected in any finite length of time approaches 1. As a result, the no-shirking wage approaches $\bar{e}$ for any level of employment less than full employment. Thus the economy approaches the Walrasian equilibrium.

Second, if there is no turnover ($b = 0$), unemployed workers are never hired. As a result, the no-shirking wage is independent of the level of employment. From (9.39), the no-shirking wage in this case is $\bar{e} + \rho\bar{e}/q$. Intuitively, the gain from shirking relative to exerting effort is $\bar{e}$ per unit time. The cost is that there is probability q per unit time of becoming permanently unemployed and thereby losing the discounted surplus from the job, which is $(w - \bar{e})/\rho$. Equating the cost and benefit gives $w = \bar{e} + \rho\bar{e}/q$. This case is shown in Figure 9.4.

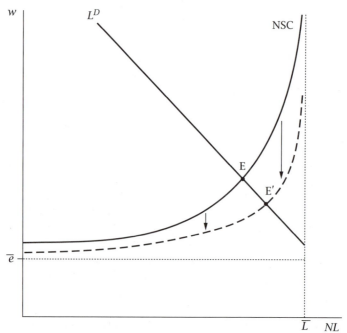

FIGURE 9.3   The effects of a rise in q in the
Shapiro–Stiglitz model

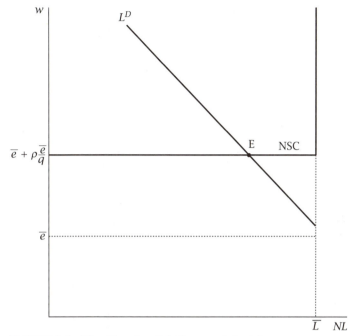

FIGURE 9.4   The Shapiro–Stiglitz model without turnover

Implications

The model implies the existence of equilibrium unemployment and suggests various factors that are likely to influence it. Thus the model has some promise as a candidate explanation of unemployment. Unfortunately, the model is so stylized that it is difficult to determine what level of unemployment it predicts or to use it to derive specific predictions concerning the behavior of unemployment over time.

With regard to short-run fluctuations, consider the impact of a fall in labor demand, shown in Figure 9.5. w and L move down along the no-shirking locus. Since labor supply is perfectly inelastic, employment necessarily responds more than it would without imperfect monitoring. Thus the model suggests one possible reason that wages may respond less to demand-driven output fluctuations than they would if workers were always on their labor supply curves. Again, however, the model is sufficiently stylized that it is difficult to gauge its quantitative implications.[15]

---

[15] This discussion neglects two important issues. First, we have been comparing steady states with different levels of labor demand rather than analyzing the dynamic effects of a change in labor demand. Kimball (1994) analyzes the dynamics of the Shapiro–Stiglitz model. Second, the model has the same problem as the simple efficiency-wage model in Section 9.2: it implies that as technological progress continually shifts the labor demand curve up, unemployment trends down. One promising route to eliminating this counterfactual prediction is to make the cost of exerting effort, $\bar{e}$, endogenous, and to structure the

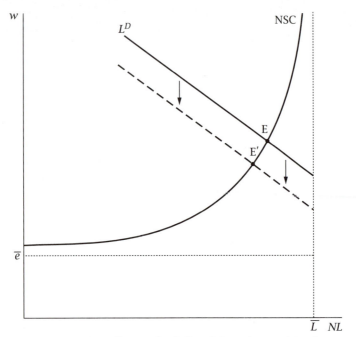

FIGURE 9.5   The effects of a fall in labor demand in the Shapiro–Stiglitz model

Finally, the model implies that the decentralized equilibrium is inefficient. To see this, note that since the marginal product of labor at full employment, $\bar{e}F'(\bar{e}\bar{L}/N)$, exceeds the cost to workers of supplying effort, $\bar{e}$, the first-best allocation is for everyone to be employed and exert effort. Of course, the government cannot bring this about simply by dictating that firms move down the labor demand curve until full employment is reached: this policy causes workers to shirk, and thus results in zero output. But Shapiro and Stiglitz note that wage subsidies financed by lump-sum taxes or profits taxes improve welfare. Such a policy shifts the labor demand curve up, and thus increases the wage and employment along the no-shirking locus. Since the value of the additional output exceeds the opportunity cost of producing it, overall welfare rises. How the gain is divided between workers and firms depends on how the wage subsidies are financed.

---

model so that $\bar{e}$ and output per worker grow at the same rate in the long run. This causes the NSC curve to shift up at the same rate as the labor demand curve in the long run, and thus eliminates the downward trend in unemployment. But with $\bar{e}$ endogenous, one then has to reexamine the short-run effects of a shift in labor demand accounting for any effects through $\bar{e}$.

Extensions

The basic model can be extended in many ways. Here we discuss three.

First, an important question about the labor market is why, given that unemployment appears so harmful to workers, employers use layoffs rather than work-sharing arrangements when they reduce the amount of labor they use. One might expect workers to place sufficient value on reducing the risk of unemployment that they would accept a lower wage to work at a firm that used work-sharing rather than layoffs. Shapiro and Stiglitz's model (modified so that the number of hours employees work can vary) suggests a possible explanation for the puzzling infrequency of work-sharing. A reduction in hours of work lowers the surplus that employees are getting from their jobs. As a result, the wage that the firm has to pay to prevent shirking rises. If the firm lays off some workers, on the other hand, the remaining workers' surplus is unchanged, and so no increase in the wage is needed. Thus the firm may find layoffs preferable to work-sharing even though it subjects its workers to greater risk.

Second, Bulow and Summers (1986) extend the model to include a second type of job where effort can be monitored perfectly. These jobs could be piece-rate jobs where output is observable, for example. Since there is no asymmetric information in this sector, the jobs provide no surplus and are not rationed. Under plausible assumptions, the absence of surplus results in high turnover. The jobs with imperfect monitoring continue to pay more than the market-clearing wage. Thus marginal products in these jobs are higher, and workers, once they obtain such jobs, are reluctant to leave them. If the model is extended further to include groups of workers with different job attachments (different b's), a higher wage is needed to induce effort from workers with less job attachment. As a result, firms with jobs that require monitoring are reluctant to hire workers with low job attachment, and so these workers are disproportionately employed in the low-wage, high-turnover sector. These predictions concerning wage levels, turnover, and occupational segregation fit the stylized facts about *primary* and *secondary* jobs identified by Doeringer and Piore (1971) in their theory of *dual labor markets*.

The third extension is more problematic for the theory. So far, we have assumed that compensation takes the form of conventional wage payments. But, as suggested in the general discussion of potential sources of efficiency wages, more complicated compensation policies can dramatically change the effects of imperfect monitoring. Two examples of such compensation policies are *bonding* and *job selling*. Bonding occurs when firms require each new worker to post a bond that must be forfeited if he or she is caught shirking. By requiring sufficiently large bonds, the firm can induce workers not to shirk even at the market-clearing wage; that is, it can shift the no-shirking locus down until it coincides with the labor supply curve. If firms are able to require bonds, they will do so, and unemployment will be eliminated from the model. Job selling occurs when firms require employees to pay a fee when they are hired. If firms are obtaining payments from new workers, their labor demand is higher for a given wage; thus the wage and employment rise as the economy moves up the no-shirking curve. Again, if firms are able to sell their jobs, they will do so.

Bonding, job selling, and the like may be limited by an absence of perfect capital markets (so that it is difficult for workers to post large bonds, or to pay large fees when they are hired). They may also be limited by workers' fears that the firm may falsely accuse them of shirking and claim the bonds, or dismiss them and keep the job fee. But, as Carmichael (1985) emphasizes, considerations like these will not eliminate these schemes entirely: if workers strictly prefer employment to unemployment, firms can raise their profits by, for example, charging marginally more for jobs. In such situations, jobs are not rationed, but go to those who are willing to pay the most for them. Thus even if these schemes are limited by such factors as imperfect capital markets, they still eliminate unemployment. In short, the absence of job fees and performance bonds is a puzzle for the theory.[16]

Finally, it is important to keep in mind that the Shapiro–Stiglitz model focuses on one particular source of efficiency wages. Its conclusions are not general. For example, suppose firms find high wages attractive because they improve the quality of job applicants on dimensions they cannot observe. Since the attractiveness of a job presumably depends on the overall compensation package, in this case firms have no incentive to adopt schemes such as job selling. Likewise, there is no reason to expect the implications of the Shapiro–Stiglitz model concerning the effects of a shift in labor demand to apply in this case.

As described in Section 9.9, workers' feelings of gratitude, anger, and fairness appear to be important to wage-setting. If these considerations are the reason that the labor market does not clear, again there is no reason to expect the Shapiro–Stiglitz model's implications concerning compensation schemes and the effects of shifts in labor demand to hold. In this case, theory provides little guidance. Generating predictions concerning the determinants of unemployment and the cyclical behavior of the labor market requires more detailed study of the determinants of workers' attitudes and their impact on productivity. Section 9.9 describes some preliminary attempts in this direction.

9.5 Implicit Contracts

The second departure from Walrasian assumptions that we consider in this chapter is the existence of long-term relationships between firms and work-

---

[16] See Shapiro and Stiglitz (1985) and Akerlof and Katz (1989) for further discussion of these issues.

ers. Firms do not hire workers afresh each period. Instead, many jobs involve long-term attachments and considerable firm-specific skills on the part of workers. Akerlof and Main (1981) and Hall (1982), for example, find that the average worker in the United States is in a job that will last about 10 years.

The possibility of long-term relationships implies that the wage does not have to adjust to clear the labor market each period. Workers are content to stay in their current jobs as long as the income streams they expect to obtain are preferable to their outside opportunities; because of their long-term relationships with their employers, their current wages may be relatively unimportant to this comparison. This section and the next two explore the consequences of this observation. This section considers the case where the pool of workers dealing with the firm is fixed; Sections 9.6 and 9.7 investigate the effects of relaxing this assumption.

The Model

Consider a firm dealing with a group of workers. The firm's profits are

$$\pi = AF(L) - wL, \qquad F'(\bullet) > 0, \qquad F''(\bullet) < 0, \tag{9.41}$$

where L is the quantity of labor the firm employs and w is the real wage. A is a factor that shifts the profit function. It could reflect technology (so that a higher value means that the firm can produce more output from a given amount of labor), or economy-wide output (so that a higher value means that the firm can obtain a higher relative price for a given amount of output).

Instead of considering multiple periods, it is easier to consider a single period and assume that A is random. Thus, for example, when workers decide whether to work for the firm, they consider the expected utility they obtain in the single period given the randomness in A, rather than the average utility they obtain over many periods as their income and hours vary in response to fluctuations in A.

The distribution of A is discrete. There are K possible values of A, indexed by i; p_i denotes the probability that $A = A_i$. Thus the firm's expected profits are

$$E[\pi] = \sum_{i=1}^{K} p_i[A_iF(L_i) - w_iL_i], \tag{9.42}$$

where L_i and w_i denote the quantity of labor and the real wage if the realization of A is A_i. The firm maximizes its expected profits; thus it is risk-neutral.

Each worker is assumed to work the same amount. The representative worker's utility is

$$u = U(C) - V(L), \qquad U'(\bullet) > 0, \qquad U''(\bullet) < 0, \qquad V'(\bullet) > 0, \qquad V''(\bullet) > 0, \tag{9.43}$$

where $U(\bullet)$ gives the utility from consumption and $V(\bullet)$ the disutility from working. Since $U''(\bullet)$ is negative, workers are risk-averse.[17]

Workers' consumption, C, is assumed to equal their labor income, wL.[18] That is, workers cannot purchase insurance against employment and wage fluctuations. In a more fully developed model, this might arise because workers are heterogeneous and have private information about their labor-market prospects. In the present model, however, the absence of outside insurance is simply assumed.

Equation (9.43) implies that the representative worker's expected utility is

$$E[u] - \sum_{i=1}^{K} p_i[U(C_l) - V(L_i)]. \tag{9.44}$$

There is some reservation level of expected utility, u_0, that workers must attain to be willing to work for the firm. There is no labor mobility once workers agree to a contract; thus the only constraint on the contract involves the average level of utility it offers, not the level in any individual state.

Wage Contracts

One simple type of contract just specifies a wage and then lets the firm choose employment once A is determined; many actual contracts at least appear to take this form. Under such a contract, unemployment and real wage rigidity arise immediately. A fall in labor demand, for example, causes the firm to reduce employment at the fixed real wage while labor supply does not shift, and thus creates unemployment (or, if all workers work the same amount, underemployment). And the cost of labor does not respond because, by assumption, the real wage is fixed.

But this is not a satisfactory explanation of unemployment and real wage rigidity. The difficulty is that this type of a contract is inefficient (Leontief, 1946; Barro, 1977b; Hall, 1980). Since the wage is fixed and the firm chooses employment taking the wage as given, the marginal product of labor is independent of A. But since employment varies with A, the marginal disutility of working depends on A. Thus the marginal product of labor is generally not equal to the marginal disutility of work, and so it is possible to make both parties to the contract better off. And if labor supply is not very elastic, the inefficiency is large. When labor demand is low, for example, the

---

[17] Because the firm's owners can diversify away firm-specific risk by holding a broad portfolio, the assumption that the firm is risk-neutral is reasonable for firm-specific shocks. For aggregate shocks, however, the assumption that the firm is less risk-averse than the workers is harder to justify. Since the main goal of the theory is to explain the effects of aggregate shocks, this is a weak point of the model. One possibility is that the owners are wealthier than the workers and that risk aversion is declining in wealth.

[18] If there are $\overline{L}$ workers, the representative worker's hours and consumption are in fact $L/\overline{L}$ and $wL/\overline{L}$, and so utility takes the form $\tilde{U}(C/\overline{L}) - \tilde{V}(L/\overline{L})$. To eliminate $\overline{L}$, define $U(C) = \tilde{U}(C/\overline{L})$ and $V(L) = \tilde{V}(L/\overline{L})$.

marginal disutility of work is low, and so the firm and the workers could both be made better off if the workers worked slightly more.

Thus we can appeal to fixed-wage contracts with employment determined at the firm's discretion as a potential explanation of unemployment and real wage rigidity only if we can explain why a firm and its workers would agree to such an arrangement. The remainder of this section shows, however, that our assumptions imply that they will in fact agree to a very different contract. Section 9.6 then suggests a variation on our model that could give rise to something much closer to this type of a contract.

Efficient Contracts

To see how it is possible to improve on a wage contract, suppose the firm offers the workers a contract specifying the wage and hours for each possible realization of A. Since actual contracts do not explicitly specify employment and the wage as functions of the state, such contracts are known as *implicit contracts*.[19]

Recall that the firm must offer the workers at least some minimum level of expected utility, u_0, but is otherwise unconstrained. In addition, since L_i and w_i determine C_i, we can think of the firm's choice variables as L and C in each state rather than as L and w. The Lagrangian for the firm's problem is therefore

$$\mathcal{L} = \sum_{i=1}^{K} p_i[A_iF(L_i) - C_i] + \lambda \left(\left\{ \sum_{i=1}^{K} p_i[U(C_i) - V(L_i)] \right\} - u_0 \right). \tag{9.45}$$

The first-order condition for C_i is

$$-p_i + \lambda p_i U'(C_i) = 0, \tag{9.46}$$

or

$$U'(C_i) = \frac{1}{\lambda}. \tag{9.47}$$

Equation (9.47) implies that the marginal utility of consumption is constant across states, and thus that consumption is constant across states. Thus the risk-neutral firm fully insures the risk-averse workers.

The first-order condition for L_i is

$$p_i A_i F'(L_i) = \lambda p_i V'(L_i). \tag{9.48}$$

Equation (9.47) implies $\lambda = 1/U'(C)$, where C is the constant level of consumption. Substituting this fact into (9.48) and dividing both sides by p_i yields

$$A_i F'(L_i) = \frac{V'(L_i)}{U'(C)}. \tag{9.49}$$

---

[19] The theory of implicit contracts is due to Azariadis (1975); Baily (1974); and Gordon (1974).

Implications

Under efficient contracts, workers' real incomes are constant. Thus the model appears to imply strong real wage rigidity; in fact, because L is higher when A is higher, the model implies that the wage per hour is countercyclical. Unfortunately, however, this result does not help to account for the puzzle that shifts in labor demand appear to result in large changes in employment. The problem is that with long-term contracts, the wage is no longer playing an allocative role. That is, firms do not choose employment taking the wage as given. Rather, the level of employment as a function of the state is specified in the contract. And, from (9.49), this level is the level that equates the marginal product of labor with the marginal disutility of additional hours of work.

As a result, the model implies that the cost to the firm of varying the amount of labor it uses changes greatly with its level of employment. Suppose the firm wants to increase employment marginally in state i. To do this, it must raise workers' compensation to make them no worse off than before. Since the expected utility cost to workers of the change is $p_i V'(L_i)$, C must rise by $p_i V'(L_i)/U'(C)$. Thus the marginal cost to the firm of increasing employment in a given state is proportional to $V'(L_i)$. If labor supply is relatively inelastic, $V'(L_i)$ is sharply increasing in L_i, and so the cost of labor to the firm is much higher when employment is high than when it is low. Thus, for example, embedding this model of contracts in a model of price determination like that of Section 6.8 would not alter the result that relatively inelastic labor supply creates a strong incentive for firms to cut prices and increase employment in recessions, and to raise prices and reduce employment in booms.

In addition to failing to predict relatively acyclical labor costs, the model fails to predict unemployment: as emphasized above, the implicit contract equates the marginal product of labor and the marginal disutility of work. The model does, however, suggest a possible explanation for apparent unemployment. In the efficient contract, workers are not free to choose their labor supply given the wage; instead the wage and employment are simultaneously specified to yield optimal risk-sharing and allocative efficiency. When employment is low, the marginal disutility of work is low and the hourly wage, C/L_i, is high. Thus workers wish that they could work more at the wage the firm is paying. As a result, even though employment and the wage are chosen optimally, workers appear to be constrained in their labor supply.

9.6   Insider-Outsider Models

The analysis in Section 9.5 assumes that the firm is dealing with a fixed pool of workers. In reality, there are two groups of potential workers. The first group—the insiders—are workers who have some connection with the firm at the time of the bargaining, and whose interests are therefore taken into account in the contract. The second group—the outsiders—are workers who have no initial connection with the firm but who may be hired after the contract is set. This distinction may be important for both fluctuations and unemployment.[20]

Insiders and Outsiders and the Cyclical Behavior of Labor Costs

Consider a firm and a set of insiders. The firm and the insiders bargain over the wage and employment as functions of the state. Hours are fixed, so labor input can vary only through changes in the number of workers. The firm's profits are

$$\pi = AF(L_I + L_O) - w_I L_I - w_O L_O, \tag{9.50}$$

where L_I and L_O are the numbers of insiders and outsiders the firm hires, and w_I and w_O are their wages. As before, A is random, taking on the value A_i with probability p_i. The insiders have priority in hiring; thus L_O can be positive only if L_I equals the number of insiders, $\overline{L}_I$.

Oswald (1993) and Gottfries (1992) argue that labor markets have two features that critically affect the problem facing the firm. The first is that, because of normal employment growth and turnover, most of the time the insiders are fully employed and the only hiring decision concerns how many outsiders to hire. Taking this to the extreme, here we assume that L_I always equals $\overline{L}_I$. Since the insiders are always employed, their utility depends only on their wage:

$$u_I = U(w_I), \qquad U'(\bullet) > 0, \qquad U''(\bullet) < 0. \tag{9.51}$$

The second feature of labor markets emphasized by Oswald and Gottfries is that the wages paid to the two types of workers cannot be set independently: in practice, the higher the wage that the firm pays to its existing employees, the more it must pay to its new hires. Again adopting an extreme form for simplicity, we assume that w_O rises one-for-one with w_I:

$$w_O = w_I - c, \qquad c \geq 0. \tag{9.52}$$

Finally, we assume that the insiders have sufficient bargaining power and that the gap between insider and outsider wages (c) is sufficiently small that the firm is always able to hire as many new workers at $w_I - c$ as it wants. Thus the model applies most clearly to a firm that faces a strong union or that must pay a high wage for some other reason.

It is convenient to think of the firm's choice variables as w_I and L_O in each state. w_O is determined by w_I and equation (9.52); L_I is fixed at $\overline{L}_I$. As in the previous section, the firm must provide the insiders with expected

---

[20] Important contributions to the insider-outsider literature include Shaked and Sutton (1984); Solow (1985); Gregory (1986); Lindbeck and Snower (1988); Blanchard and Summers (1986, 1987); Oswald (1993); and Gottfries (1992).

utility of at least u_0. The Lagrangian for the firm's problem is thus

$$\mathcal{L} = \sum_{i=1}^{K} p_i[A_iF(\bar{L}_I + L_{Oi}) - w_{Ii}\bar{L}_I - (w_{Ii} - c)L_{Oi}] + \lambda\left\{\left[\sum_{i=1}^{K} p_iU(w_{Ii})\right] - u_0\right\}.$$

(9.53)

The first-order condition for L_{Oi} is

$$p_i[A_iF'(\bar{L}_I + L_{Oi}) - (w_{Ii} - c)] = 0,$$

(9.54)

or

$$A_iF'(\bar{L}_I + L_{Oi}) = w_{Ii} - c.$$

(9.55)

Equation (9.55) implies that, just as in a conventional labor demand problem, but in sharp contrast to what happens with implicit contracts, employment is chosen to equate the marginal product of labor with the wage. The reason is that outsiders, who are the workers relevant to the marginal employment decision, are not involved in the original bargaining. The insiders and the firm maximize their joint surplus. They therefore agree to hire outsiders up to the point where their marginal product equals the wage they must be paid; the outsiders' preferences are irrelevant to this calculation.

The first-order condition for w_{Ii} is

$$-p_i(\bar{L}_I + L_{Oi}) + \lambda p_iU'(w_{Ii}) = 0.$$

(9.56)

This implies

$$U'(w_{Ii}) = \frac{\bar{L}_I + L_{Oi}}{\lambda}.$$

(9.57)

Since L_{Oi} is higher in good states, (9.57) implies that $U'(w_{Ii})$ is higher. This requires that w_{Ii} is lower—that is, that the wage is countercyclical. Intuitively, the firm and the insiders want to keep the expenses of hiring outsiders down; they therefore lower the wage in states where employment is high. In short, this model implies that the real wage is countercyclical and that it represents the true cost of labor to the firm.

It is easy to think of changes that weaken these results. For example, if there are states in which some insiders are laid off, for those states the contract would equate the marginal product of labor with the opportunity cost of insiders' time rather than with the wage. Similarly, if there is not an unlimited supply of outsiders, this would tend to make the wage increasing rather than decreasing in A. Such changes, however, do not entirely undo the result that insider-outsider considerations reduce the cyclical sensitivity of the marginal cost of labor to firms.

The critical assumption of the model is that the outsiders' and insiders' wages are linked. Without this link, the firm can hire outsiders at the prevailing economy-wide wage. With inelastic labor supply, that wage is low in recessions and high in booms, and so the marginal cost of labor to the firm is highly procyclical.

Unfortunately, the insider-outsider literature has not made a strong case that outsiders' and insiders' wages are linked. Gottfries argues that such a link arises from the facts that the firm must be given some freedom to discharge insiders who are incompetent or shirking and that an excessive gap between insiders' and outsiders' wages would give the firm an incentive to take advantage of this freedom. Blanchard and Summers (1986) argue that the insiders are reluctant to allow the hiring of large numbers of outsiders at a low wage because they realize that, over time, such a policy would result in the outsiders controlling the bargaining process. But it is far from clear that tying insiders' and outsiders' wages is the best way of dealing with these problems. If the economy-wide wage is sometimes far below $w_I - c$, tying the insiders' and outsiders' wages is very costly. The firms and the insiders might therefore be better off if they instead agreed to some limitation on the firm's ability to hire outsiders, or if they charged new hires a fee (and let the fee vary with the gap between w_I and the economy-wide wage). Thus we can conclude only that *if* a link between insiders' and outsiders' wages can be established, insider-outsider considerations have potentially important implications.

Unemployment

If the entire labor market is characterized by insider power, greater insider power reduces employment by raising the wage and causing firms to move up their labor demand curves. Thus in this case the insider-outsider distinction provides a candidate explanation of unemployment.

The more realistic case, however, is for there to be insider power only in part of the labor market, with the rest relatively competitive. But even in this case, insider power can increase average unemployment. When some sectors offer higher wages than others, workers have an incentive to try to obtain jobs in those sectors. New entrants to the labor market are therefore slower to accept jobs in the competitive sector, and workers who have been laid off from the high-wage sector accept longer spells of unemployment before they give up hope of returning to their old jobs.[21]

This reasoning suggests that the contracting considerations investigated in Section 9.5 may also increase average unemployment. In the model analyzed there, the employment of the workers represented in the contracts is efficient. But we ignored the issues of whether such arrangements cover the entire economy, and of how workers come to be represented in such arrangements. If there are two sectors, one with explicit or implicit contracts and one with employment and wages largely determined competitively, and if workers fare better in the contract sector, then again they have an incentive to accept greater unemployment to increase their chances of obtaining these high-quality jobs.

---

[21] See Problems 9.11 through 9.13 for examples of the effects of wage dispersion.

There is relatively little evidence concerning how important these mechanisms are to actual unemployment. Summers (1986b) argues that such *wait unemployment* is central to the determination of average unemployment. He presents evidence both across U.S. states and over time that general measures of wage dispersion and measures of wage differences between "high-quality" and "low-quality" jobs are strongly associated with differences in average unemployment rates. This is precisely what one would expect if workers' efforts to obtain jobs paying more than the market-clearing wage are an important source of unemployment. Thus the limited evidence we have suggests these models may offer a promising route to understanding unemployment.

9.7 Hysteresis

One of the building blocks of the previous model is the assumption that the insiders are always employed. This assumption is likely to fail in some situations, however. Most importantly, if the insiders' bargaining power is sufficiently great, they will set the wage high enough to risk some unemployment: if the insiders are fully employed with certainty, there is a benefit but not a cost to them of raising the wage further. In addition, unusually large negative shocks to labor demand are likely to lead to some unemployment among the insiders.

Variations in employment can give rise to dynamics in the number of insiders. Under many institutional arrangements, workers who become unemployed eventually lose a say in wage-setting; likewise, workers who are hired eventually gain a role in bargaining. Thus a fall in employment caused by a decline in labor demand is likely to reduce the number of insiders, and a rise in employment is likely to increase the number of insiders. These changes in the number of insiders then affect future wage-setting and employment.

These ideas are developed formally by Blanchard and Summers (1986).[22] Blanchard and Summers focus on Europe in the 1980s, where, they argue, the conditions for these effects to be relevant were satisfied: workers had a great deal of power in wage-setting, there were large negative shocks, and the rules and institutions led to some extent to the disenfranchisement from the bargaining process of workers who lost their jobs.

Assumptions

We consider a simplified version of Blanchard and Summers's model. The wage is set unilaterally by the insiders, and employment is chosen by the

---

[22] See also Gregory (1986).

firm. The number of insiders in one period is determined by the previous period's employment; thus

$$N_{It} = L_{t-1}. \tag{9.58}$$

For simplicity, both the insiders and the firm neglect the impact of their decisions on the future number of insiders; thus they maximize their current-period objective functions each period.

The representative firm's profits are

$$\pi_t = A_t L_t^\alpha - w_t L_t, \qquad 0 < \alpha < 1, \tag{9.59}$$

where we assume for simplicity that all workers are paid the same wage, regardless of whether they are insiders.[23] The first-order condition for the firm's choice of employment is

$$\alpha A_t L_t^{\alpha-1} = w_t. \tag{9.60}$$

Solving (9.60) for L yields the labor demand curve,

$$L_t = \left(\frac{1}{\alpha A_t}\right)^{1/(\alpha-1)} w_t^{1/(\alpha-1)} \tag{9.61}$$

$$\equiv C_t w_t^{-\beta}.$$

Shocks to labor demand are modeled by assuming that A is random, which implies that C is random. Specifically, C_t is assumed to take the form

$$C_t = C_t^0 \varepsilon_t, \tag{9.62}$$

where C_t^0 is a component of C_t that is known when workers set the wage and ε_t is an i.i.d. random shock that is determined after w_t is set.

In setting the wage, the insiders face a tradeoff between the expected fraction of the membership that is employed and the wage conditional on being employed. To see the consequences of endogenous changes in the number of insiders in the strongest possible form, assume that the insiders' period-t objective function is the expected fraction of the insiders who are employed times utility conditional on being employed, and that this utility takes the form w_t^b ($0 < b < 1$). Since the insiders are assumed to be hired first and the number of insiders hired cannot exceed the number available, insider employment is the smaller of total employment and the number of insiders. These assumptions imply that the period-t objective function is

$$u_t = E\left[\min\left\{\frac{L_t}{N_{It}}, 1\right\}\right] w_t^b. \tag{9.63}$$

Note that we are implicitly assuming that the unemployed get no utility; the effects of relaxing this assumption are discussed below.

---

[23] Assuming that insiders' and outsiders' wages differ by a constant, as in Section 9.6, has no important implications for the analysis.

Implications

To analyze the model, begin by substituting (9.61) for L_t and (9.62) for C_t into (9.63). This yields

$$u_t = E\left[\min\left\{\frac{C_t^0 \varepsilon_t w_t^{-\beta}}{N_{It}}, 1\right\}\right] w_t^b. \tag{9.64}$$

Next, define $x_t = (C_t^0/N_{It}) w_t^{-\beta}$; x_t is the ratio of employment to the number of insiders if $\varepsilon_t = 1$. With this definition, w_t^b equals $x_t^{-b/\beta}(C_t^0/N_{It})^{b/\beta}$. Thus (9.64) becomes

$$u_t = E[\min\{\varepsilon_t x_t, 1\}] x_t^{-b/\beta} \left(\frac{C_t^0}{N_{It}}\right)^{b/\beta}. \tag{9.65}$$

N_{It}, the number of insiders, and C_t^0, the expected position of labor demand, affect the objective function only multiplicatively. Thus they cannot affect the value of x_t that maximizes the objective function. The insiders therefore choose the same value of x each period. If x^* denotes this optimal value, the definition of x implies that the insiders' choice of w_t is

$$w_t = \left(\frac{N_{It} x^*}{C_t^0}\right)^{-1/\beta}. \tag{9.66}$$

The labor-demand equation, (9.61), then implies that employment is

$$L_t = \varepsilon_t N_{It} x^*. \tag{9.67}$$

Equations (9.66) and (9.67) imply that insiders adjust to changes in labor demand and to the number of insiders (that is, to changes in C^0 and N_I) only by adjusting the wage, and not by altering the probability of employment. Concretely, consider the effects of a low realization of ε. The unexpectedly low level of labor demand causes the firm to hire relatively few workers, and so the number of insiders falls. When the remaining insiders decide on the wage for the following period, they can afford to set a higher wage, since there are fewer of them for the firm to employ. Thus the one-time shock to labor demand—the low value of ε—has a long-lasting effect on employment. With workers' objective function and the firm's profit function taking the specific functional forms we have assumed, the effect is permanent: as (9.67) shows, the fall in employment is passed fully into reduced employment in the following period—and hence in all subsequent periods as well.

Since it is the unpredictable movements in demand—the ε's—that have permanent effects, the model implies that employment is a *random walk with drift*. That is, the change in employment equals a constant term (reflecting the fact that expected employment can be either more or less than N_{It}) plus an unpredictable component. If insiders determine wages only in some sectors, only employment in these sectors behaves this way. But if insiders set wages in virtually all of the labor market, then it is aggregate employment that follows a random walk with drift. Blanchard and Summers argue that this latter prediction accords well with Europe's experience in the 1980s, and that the mechanism outlined here provides a likely explanation.

Extensions

Forward-looking behavior by the insiders and the firm does not alter the central result of the model. The knowledge that this period's hiring affects next period's number of insiders increases the firm's hiring for a given wage (so that workers set lower wages in the future), and moderates the insiders' wage-setting for a given labor demand curve (to ensure that they remain insiders). But changes in the number of insiders still cause shocks to have permanent effects.

Similarly, more complicated rules for insider status lead to more interesting dynamics but do not eliminate the permanent component of employment fluctuations. Suppose, for example, that it takes two periods of unemployment to lose one's position as an insider. Then a negative shock to labor demand does not immediately lead to a higher wage. (Indeed, if the insiders are forward-looking, it leads to a fall in the wage as the unemployed insiders try to keep their insider status.) But a second negative shock leads to a fall in the number of insiders, which has a permanent effect on the paths of the wage and employment. Formally, the wage and employment still have a unit root. One implication of this discussion is that a fall in aggregate demand that is only moderately long—such as the one experienced by the United States in the early 1980s—may not have a permanent effect on unemployment, but an extended one—such as those experienced by many European countries in the same period—may.

Other plausible changes in the model, however, eliminate the strong result that one-time shocks have permanent effects on employment. Suppose, for example, we modify the insiders' objective function, (9.63), to include positive utility in the event of unemployment. Then it is less attractive for the insiders to reduce the wage to increase the probability of employment when the number of insiders is large and the wage is low than it is when the number of insiders is small. Similarly, if the firm has some bargaining power or the outsiders have some weight in the insiders' objective function, the wage does not rise to fully offset reductions in the number of insiders.

Under plausible assumptions, introducing considerations like these causes employment to return gradually to its initial level after a one-time demand shock. Without membership dynamics, however, employment returns immediately to its initial level. Thus making the number of insiders endogenous still has important implications for the dynamics of employment.

Situations where one-time disturbances permanently affect the path of the economy are said to exhibit *hysteresis*. In the context of unemployment, two sources of hysteresis other than the insider-outsider considerations we have been examining have received considerable attention. One is deterioration of skills: workers who are unemployed do not acquire additional on-the-job training, and their existing human capital may decay or become obsolete. As a result, workers who lose their jobs when labor demand falls may have difficulty finding work when demand recovers, particularly if the downturn is extended. The second additional source of hysteresis is through labor-force attachment. Workers who are unemployed for extended periods may adjust their standard of living to the lower level provided by income maintenance programs; in addition, a long period of high unemployment may reduce the social stigma of extended joblessness. Because of these effects, labor supply may be permanently lower when demand returns to normal.

The possibility of hysteresis has received considerable attention in the context of Europe. European unemployment fluctuated around very low levels in the 1950s and 1960s, rose fairly steadily to more than 10 percent from the mid-1970s to the mid-1980s, and has fluctuated around the 10 percent level since then. Thus there is no evidence of a stable natural rate that unemployment returns to after a shock. Loosely speaking, views of European unemployment fall into two camps. One emphasizes shifts in the natural rate as a result of European labor-market institutions. Since most of the major features of those institutions were in place well before the rise in unemployment, this view requires that institutions' effects operate with long lags. For example, because the social stigma of unemployment changes slowly, the impact of generous unemployment benefits on the natural rate may be felt only very gradually. The other view emphasizes hysteresis. In this view, the labor-market institutions converted what would have otherwise been short-lived increases in unemployment into very long-lasting ones through union wage-setting, skill deterioration, and loss of labor-force attachment. For more on these issues, see Bean (1994); Siebert (1997); Ljungvist and Sargent (1998); Ball (1999b); and Blanchard and Wolfers (1999).

9.8   Search and Matching Models

The final departure of the labor market from Walrasian assumptions that we consider is the simple fact that workers and jobs are heterogeneous. In a frictionless labor market, firms are indifferent about losing their workers, since identical workers are costlessly available at the same wage; likewise, workers are indifferent about losing their jobs. These implications do not appear to be accurate descriptions of actual labor markets.

When workers and jobs are highly heterogeneous, the labor market has little resemblance to a Walrasian market. Rather than meeting in centralized markets where employment and wages are determined by the intersections of supply and demand curves, workers and firms meet in a decentralized, one-on-one fashion, and engage in a costly process of trying to match up idiosyncratic preferences, skills, and needs. Since this process is not instantaneous, it results in some unemployment. In addition, it may have implications for how wages and employment respond to shocks.

This section presents a model of firm and worker heterogeneity and the matching process. Because modeling heterogeneity requires abandoning many of our usual tools, even a basic model is relatively complicated. As a result, the model here only introduces some of the issues involved.[24]

The Model

The economy consists of workers and jobs. Workers can be either employed or unemployed, and jobs can be either filled or vacant. The numbers of employed and unemployed workers are denoted E and U, and the numbers of filled and vacant jobs are denoted F and V. Each job can have at most one worker. Thus F and E must be equal. The labor force is fixed at $\bar{L}$; thus $E + U = \bar{L}$. Throughout, we consider only steady states.

The number of jobs is endogenous. Specifically, vacancies can be created or eliminated freely; there is a fixed cost of C per unit time, however, of maintaining a job (either filled or vacant). C can be thought of as reflecting the cost of capital.

The model is set in continuous time. When a worker is employed, he or she produces output at rate A per unit time and is paid a wage of w per unit time. A is exogenous and is assumed to be greater than C; w is determined endogenously. For simplicity, costs of effort and of job search are ignored. Thus a worker's utility per unit time is w if employed and 0 if unemployed. Similarly, profits per unit time from a job are $A - w - C$ if it is filled and $-C$ if it is vacant. Workers' objective function is the expected present discounted value of their lifetime utility; firms' objective function is the expected present discounted value of lifetime profits. The discount rate, r, is exogenous and constant.

The key assumptions of the model concern how workers become employed. Positive levels of unemployment and vacancies can coexist without being immediately eliminated by hiring. Instead, unemployment and vacancies are assumed to yield a flow of new jobs at some rate per unit time:

$$M = M(U, V)$$
$$= KU^{\beta}V^{\gamma}, \qquad 0 \le \beta \le 1, \qquad 0 \le \gamma \le 1. \tag{9.68}$$

The *matching function,* (9.68), proxies for the complicated process of employer recruitment, worker search, and mutual evaluation. It is not assumed to exhibit constant returns to scale. When it exhibits increasing returns ($\beta + \gamma > 1$), there are *thick-market effects*: increasing the level of search makes the matching process operate more effectively, in the sense that it

---

[24] For examples of search and matching models, see Diamond (1982); Pissarides (1985); Mortenson (1986); Howitt (1988); Blanchard and Diamond (1989); Hosios (1990); and Mortenson and Pissarides (1999). The model in this section is closest to Pissarides's.

yields more output (matches) per unit of input (unemployment and vacancies). When the matching function has decreasing returns ($\beta + \gamma < 1$), there are *crowding effects*.

In addition to the flow of new matches, there is turnover in existing jobs. As in the Shapiro-Stiglitz model, jobs end at an exogenous rate b per unit time. Thus the dynamics of the number of employed workers are given by $\dot{E} = M(U,V) - bE$. Since we are focusing on steady states, M and E must satisfy

$$M(U,V) = bE. \tag{9.69}$$

Let a denote the rate per unit time that unemployed workers find jobs, and α the rate per unit time that vacant jobs are filled. a and α are given by

$$a = \frac{M(U,V)}{U}, \tag{9.70}$$

$$\alpha = \frac{M(U,V)}{V}. \tag{9.71}$$

As in the Shapiro-Stiglitz model, we use dynamic programming to describe the values of the various states. The "return" on being employed is a "dividend" of w per unit time minus the probability b per unit time of a "capital loss" of $V_E - V_U$. Thus,

$$rV_E = w - b(V_E - V_U), \tag{9.72}$$

where r is the interest rate (see equation [9.30] for comparison). Similar reasoning implies

$$rV_F = (A - w - C) - b(V_F - V_V), \tag{9.73}$$

$$rV_U = a(V_E - V_U), \tag{9.74}$$

$$rV_V = -C + \alpha(V_F - V_V). \tag{9.75}$$

Two conditions complete the model. First, when an unemployed worker and a firm with a vacancy meet, they must choose a wage. It must be high enough that the worker wants to work in the job, and low enough that the employer wants to hire the worker. Because neither party can find a replacement instantaneously, however, these requirements do not uniquely determine the wage. Instead, there is a range of wages that makes both parties better off than if they had not met. We assume that the worker and the employer set the wage so that each gets the same gain.[25] That is,

$$V_E - V_U = V_F - V_V. \tag{9.76}$$

---

[25] See Problem 9.15 for the implications of alternative assumptions about how the surplus is divided.

Second, as described above, new vacancies can be created and eliminated costlessly. Thus the value of a vacancy must be zero.

Without the frictions, the model is simple. Labor supply is perfectly inelastic at $\bar{L}$, and labor demand is perfectly elastic at $A - C$. Thus, since $A - C > 0$ by assumption, there is full employment at this wage. Shifts in labor demand—changes in A—lead to immediate changes in the wage and leave employment unchanged.

Solving the Model

We solve the model by focusing on two variables, employment (E) and the value of a vacancy (V_V). Our procedure will be to find the value of V_V implied by a given level of employment, and then to impose the free-entry condition that V_V must be 0.

We begin by considering the determination of the wage and the value of a vacancy given a and α. Subtracting (9.74) from (9.72) and rearranging yields

$$V_E - V_U = \frac{w}{a + b + r}.$$ (9.77)

Similarly, (9.73) and (9.75) imply

$$V_F - V_V = \frac{A - w}{\alpha + b + r}.$$ (9.78)

Since our splitting-the-surplus assumption (equation [9.76]) implies that $V_E - V_U$ and $V_F - V_V$ are equal, (9.77) and (9.78) imply

$$\frac{w}{a + b + r} = \frac{A - w}{\alpha + b + r}.$$ (9.79)

Solving this condition for w yields

$$w = \frac{(a + b + r)A}{a + \alpha + 2b + 2r}.$$ (9.80)

Equation (9.80) implies that when a and α are equal, the firm and the worker divide the output from the job equally. When a exceeds α, workers can find new jobs more rapidly than firms can find new employees, and so more than half of the output goes to the worker. When α exceeds a, the reverse occurs.

Recall that we want to focus on the value of a vacancy. Equation (9.75) states that rV_V equals $-C + \alpha(V_F - V_V)$. Expression (9.78) for $V_F - V_V$ therefore gives us

$$rV_V = -C + \alpha\frac{A - w}{\alpha + b + r}.$$ (9.81)

Substituting expression (9.80) for w into this equation yields

$$rV_V = -C + \alpha \frac{A - \dfrac{a+b+r}{a+\alpha+2b+2r}A}{\alpha+b+r} \tag{9.82}$$

$$= -C + \frac{\alpha}{a+\alpha+2b+2r}A.$$

Equation (9.82) expresses rV_V in terms of C, A, r, b, a, and α. a and α, however, are endogenous. Thus the next step is to express them in terms of E. The facts that $a = M(U,V)/U$ (equation [9.70]), that $M = bE$ (equation [9.69]), and that $E + U = \bar{L}$ imply

$$a = \frac{bE}{\bar{L} - E}. \tag{9.83}$$

Similarly, we know from (9.71) that

$$\alpha = \frac{M(U,V)}{V}. \tag{9.84}$$

To express α in terms of E, we therefore need to express $M(U,V)$ and V in terms of E. In steady state, $M(U,V)$ equals bE (see [9.69]). From the matching function, (9.68), this implies $bE = KU^\beta V^\gamma$, or

$$V = \left(\frac{bE}{KU^\beta}\right)^{1/\gamma}$$

$$= \left[\frac{bE}{K(\bar{L} - E)^\beta}\right]^{1/\gamma}. \tag{9.85}$$

Substituting this expression and the fact that $M(U,V)$ equals bE into (9.84) gives us

$$\alpha = \frac{bE}{\left[\dfrac{bE}{K(\bar{L} - E)^\beta}\right]^{1/\gamma}} \tag{9.86}$$

$$= K^{1/\gamma}(bE)^{(\gamma-1)/\gamma}(\bar{L} - E)^{\beta/\gamma}.$$

Equations (9.83) and (9.86) imply that a is increasing in E and that α is decreasing. Thus (9.82) implies that rV_V is a decreasing function of E. As E approaches $\bar{L}$, a approaches infinity and α approaches 0; hence rV_V approaches $-C$. Similarly, as E approaches 0, a approaches 0 and α approaches infinity. Thus in this case rV_V approaches $A - C$, which we have assumed to be positive. This information is summarized in Figure 9.6.

The equilibrium level of employment is determined by the intersection of the rV_V locus with the free-entry condition, which implies $rV_V = 0$. Imposing this condition on (9.82) yields

$$-C + \frac{\alpha(E)}{a(E) + \alpha(E) + 2b + 2r}A = 0, \tag{9.87}$$

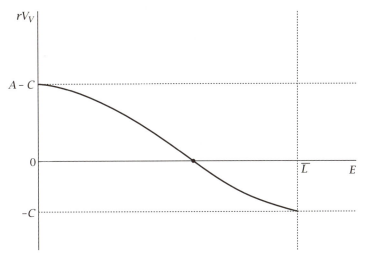

FIGURE 9.6   The determination of equilibrium employment in the search and matching model

where the functions $a(E)$ and $\alpha(E)$ are given by (9.83) and (9.86). This expression implicitly defines E, and thus completes the solution of the model.

The Impact of a Shift in Labor Demand

We now want to ask our usual question of whether the imperfection we are considering—in this case, the absence of a centralized market—affects the cyclical behavior of the labor market. Specifically, we are interested in whether it causes a shift in labor demand to have a larger impact on employment and a smaller impact on the wage than it does in a Walrasian market.

Recall that we do not observe any long-run trend in unemployment. Thus a successful model of the labor market should imply that in response to long-run productivity growth, there is no change in unemployment. In this model, it is natural to model long-run productivity growth as increases of the same proportion in the output from a job (A) and its nonlabor costs (C). From Figure 9.6, it is not immediately clear how such a change affects the point where the rV_V line crosses the horizontal axis. Instead we must examine the equilibrium condition, (9.87). Inspecting this condition shows that if A and C change by the same proportion, the value of E for which the condition holds does not change. Thus the model implies that long-run productivity growth does not affect employment. This means that a and α do not change, and thus that the wage changes by the same proportion as A (see [9.80]). In short, the model's long-run implications are reasonable.

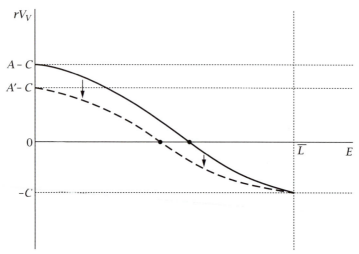

FIGURE 9.7   The effects of a fall in labor demand in the search and matching model

We will model a cyclical change as a shift in A with no change in C. To analyze this change, begin by considering the steady-state effects of a fall in A. From (9.82), this shifts the rV_V locus down. Thus, as Figure 9.7 shows, employment falls. In a Walrasian market, in contrast, employment is unchanged at $\overline{L}$. Intuitively, in the absence of a frictionless market, workers are not costlessly available at the prevailing wage. The decline in A, with C fixed, raises firms' costs of searching for a worker relative to the profits they obtain when they find one. Thus the number of firms—and hence employment—falls.

In addition, the matching function (9.68), together with the fact that $M(U,V)$ equals bE in steady state, implies that steady-state vacancies are $(bE/K)^{1/\gamma}/(\overline{L}-E)^{\beta/\gamma}$. Thus the decline in A and the resulting decrease in the number of firms reduce vacancies. The model therefore implies a negative relation between unemployment and vacancies—a *Beveridge curve*.

The model does not imply substantial wage rigidity, however. From (9.83) and (9.84), the fall in E causes a to fall and α to rise: when unemployment is higher, workers cannot find jobs as easily as before, and firms can fill positions more rapidly. From (9.80), this implies that the wage falls more than proportionately with A.[26]

The dynamics of the transition between the two steady states are also of interest. Since there is no reason for firms whose positions are filled

---

[26] Since $w = A - C$ in the Walrasian market, the same result holds there. Thus it is not clear which case exhibits greater wage adjustment. Nonetheless, simply adding heterogeneity and matching does not appear to generate strong wage rigidity.

to discharge their workers, employment and unemployment do not change discontinuously at the time of the shock. The reduced attractiveness of hiring, in contrast, causes V_V to fall unless some firms exit. Thus there is exit, and hence a discontinuous drop in V. In practice, this could take the form of some firms with openings stopping their attempts to fill them.

With employment and unemployment the same as before but vacancies lower, the flows into unemployment exceed the outflows, and so unemployment rises. Thus the fall in A leads only to a gradual rise in unemployment. Finally, as unemployment rises, the value of a vacancy would rise if vacancies did not change; thus vacancies must rise as unemployment rises. This implies that the initial drop in V exceeds its steady-state response—that is, that there is overshooting.

A temporary change in A leads to smaller employment responses. The value of a filled job is clearly higher when A is temporarily low than when it is permanently low. Thus there is a smaller fall in the number of vacancies, and hence a smaller rise in unemployment. But since the matching process is not instantaneous, unemployment remains above normal for a time after A returns to its initial value. Thus labor-market frictions create a channel that make the effects of a shock more persistent.

In the extreme case of an infinitesimally brief decline in A, V_V and V_U are unaffected. In this case, firms and workers simply share the loss equally by reducing the wage by half the amount that A falls, and there is no impact on employment or unemployment.[27]

In short, although search and matching considerations have interesting implications for the functioning of labor markets, this model of them does not suggest that they crucially change how the impact of cyclical shifts in labor demand are divided between employment and wages. It does suggest, however, that search and matching may be important to the dynamics of fluctuations. In the Walrasian case, the labor market adjusts immediately to a change in A. But we have seen that with frictions, both permanent and temporary changes in A trigger complicated adjustment processes for vacancies, unemployment, and wages.

Unemployment

Search and matching models offer a straightforward explanation for average unemployment: it may be the result of continually matching workers and jobs in a complex and changing economy. Thus, much of observed unemployment may reflect what is traditionally known as *frictional* unemployment.

---

[27] In addition, as first pointed out by Oi (1962), the fact that a firm cannot costlessly replace its workers makes it more reluctant to discharge workers in response to a temporary downturn if the marginal product of labor falls below the disutility of working. This causes frictions and heterogeneity to dampen the response of employment to shocks.

Labor markets are characterized by high rates of turnover. In U.S. manufacturing, for example, more than 3 percent of workers leave their jobs in a typical month. Moreover, many job changes are associated with wage increases, particularly for young workers (Topel and Ward, 1992); thus at least some of the turnover appears to be useful. In addition, there is high turnover of jobs themselves. In U.S. manufacturing, at least 10 percent of existing jobs disappear each year (Davis and Haltiwanger, 1990, 1992). These statistics suggest that a nonnegligible portion of unemployment is a largely inevitable result of the dynamics of the economy and the complexities of the labor market.[28]

Unfortunately, it is difficult to go much beyond this general statement. Existing theoretical models and empirical evidence do not provide any clear way of discriminating between, for example, the hypothesis that search and matching considerations account for one-quarter of average unemployment and the hypothesis that they account for three-quarters. The importance of long-term unemployment in overall unemployment suggests, however, that at least some significant part of unemployment is not frictional. In the United States, although most workers who become unemployed remain so for less than a month, most of the workers who are unemployed at any time will have spells of unemployment that last more than 3 months; and nearly half will have spells that last more than 6 months (Clark and Summers, 1979). And in the European Community in the late 1980s, more than half of unemployed workers had been out of work for more than a year (Bean, 1994). It seems unlikely that search and matching considerations could be the source of most of this long-term unemployment.

A large recent literature moves away from emphasizing average rates of turnover and focuses on cyclical variations in turnover. The finding from this work that has attracted the most attention is that *job destruction* appears to be much more variable than *job creation*. That is, this research suggests that the falls in employment in recessions stem mainly from increases in the loss of existing jobs and only to a small extent from decreases in the creation of new jobs (for example, Blanchard and Diamond, 1990; Davis and Haltiwanger, 1990, 1992, 1999). Foote (1998), however, provides evidence that this finding may hold only in some data sets.

Welfare

Because this economy is not Walrasian, firms' decisions concerning whether to enter have externalities both for workers and for other firms. Entry makes it easier for unemployed workers to find jobs, and increases their bargaining power when they do. But it also makes it harder for other firms to find workers, and decreases their bargaining power when they do.

As a result, there is no presumption that equilibrium unemployment in this economy is efficient. In one natural special case, for example, whether

---

[28] See also the literature on sectoral shocks discussed in Section 4.10.

equilibrium unemployment is inefficiently high or inefficiently low depends on whether y, the exponent on vacancies in the matching function (equation [9.68]), is more or less than $\frac{1}{2}$ (see Problem 9.17).

Such ambiguous welfare effects are characteristic of economies where allocations are determined through one-on-one meetings rather than through centralized markets. In our model, there is only one endogenous decision—firms must decide whether to enter—and hence only one dimension along which the equilibrium can be inefficient. But in practice, participants in such markets have many choices. Workers can decide whether to enter the labor force, how intensively to look for jobs when they are unemployed, where to focus their search, whether to invest in job-specific or general skills when they are employed, whether to look for a different job while they are employed, and so on. Firms face a similar array of decisions. There is no guarantee that the decentralized economy produces an efficient outcome along any of these dimensions. Instead, agents' decisions are likely to have externalities through direct effects on other parties' surplus or through effects on the effectiveness of the matching process, or both (see, for example, Mortenson, 1986).

This analysis implies that there is no reason to suppose that the natural rate of unemployment is optimal. This observation provides no guidance, however, concerning whether observed unemployment is inefficiently high, inefficiently low, or approximately efficient. Determining which of these cases is correct—and whether there are changes in policy that would lead to efficiency-enhancing changes in equilibrium unemployment—is an important open question.

9.9   Empirical Applications

Contracting Effects on Employment

In our analysis of contracts in Section 9.5, we discussed two views of how employment can be determined when the wage is set by bargaining. In the first, a firm and its workers bargain only over the wage, and the firm chooses employment to equate the marginal product of labor with the agreed-upon wage. But, as we saw, this arrangement is inefficient. Thus the second view is that the bargaining determines how both employment and the wage depend on the conditions facing the firm. Since actual contracts do not spell out such arrangements, this view assumes that workers and the firm have some noncontractual understanding that the firm will not treat the cost of labor as being given by the wage. For example, workers are likely to agree to lower wages in future contracts if the firm chooses employment to equate the marginal product of labor with the opportunity cost of workers' time.

Which of these views is correct has important implications. If firms choose employment freely taking the wage as given, evidence that nominal wages are fixed for extended periods provides direct evidence that nominal disturbances have real effects. If the wage is unimportant to employment determination, on the other hand, nominal wage rigidity is unimportant to the effects of nominal shocks.

Bils (1991) proposes a way to test between the two views (see also Card, 1990). If employment is determined efficiently, then it equates the marginal product of labor and the marginal disutility of work at each date. Thus its behavior should not have any systematic relation to the times that firms and workers bargain.[29] A finding that movements in employment are related to the dates of contracts—for example, that employment rises unusually rapidly or slowly just after contracts are signed, or that it is more variable over the life of a contract than from one contract to the next—would therefore be evidence that it is not determined efficiently.

In addition, Bils shows that the alternative view that employment equates the marginal product of labor with the wage makes a specific prediction about how employment movements are likely to be related to the times of contracts. Consider Figure 9.8, which shows the marginal product of labor, the marginal disutility of labor, and a contract wage. In response to a negative shock to labor demand, a firm that views the cost of labor as being given by the contract wage reduces employment a great deal; in terms of the figure, it reduces employment from L_A to L_B. The marginal product of labor now exceeds the opportunity cost of workers' time. Thus when the firm and the workers negotiate a new contract, they will make sure that employment is increased; in terms of the diagram, they will act to raise employment from L_B to L_C. Thus if the wage determines employment (and if shocks to labor demand are the main source of employment fluctuations), changes in employment during contracts should be partly reversed when new contracts are signed.

To test between the predictions of these two views, Bils examines employment fluctuations in U.S. manufacturing industries. Specifically, he focuses on 12 industries that are highly unionized and where there are long-term contracts that are signed at virtually the same time for the vast majority of workers in the industry. He estimates a regression of the form

$$\Delta \ln L_{i,t} = \alpha_i - \phi Z_{i,t} - \theta (\ln L_{i,t-1} - \ln L_{i,t-10}) + \Gamma D_{i,t} + \varepsilon_{i,t}. \qquad (9.88)$$

Here i indexes industries, L is employment, and $D_{i,t}$ is a dummy variable equal to 1 in quarters when a new contract goes into effect in industry i. The key variable is $Z_{i,t}$. If a new contract goes into effect in industry i in quarter t (that is, if $D_{i,t} = 1$), then $Z_{i,t}$ equals the change in log employment in the industry over the life of the previous contract; otherwise, $Z_{i,t}$ is 0. The parameter ϕ therefore measures the extent to which employment changes over the life of a contract are reversed when a new contract is signed. Bils includes $\ln L_{i,t-1} - \ln L_{i,t-10}$ to control for the possibility that employment changes are typically reversed even in the absence of new contracts; he chooses $t - 10$ because the average contract in his sample lasts 10 quarters.

---

[29] This is not precisely correct if there are income effects on the marginal disutility of labor. Bils argues, however, that these effects are unlikely to be important to his test.

Finally, $D_{i,t}$ allows for the possibility of unusual employment growth in the first quarter of a new contract.

Bils's estimates are $\phi = 0.198$ (with a standard error of 0.037), $\theta = 0.016$ (0.012), and $\Gamma = -0.0077$ (0.0045). Thus the results suggest highly significant and quantitatively large movements in employment related to the dates of new contracts: when a new contract is signed, on average 20 percent of the employment changes over the life of the previous contract are immediately reversed.

There is one puzzling feature of Bils's results, however. When a new contract is signed, the most natural way to undo an inefficient employment change during the previous contract is by adjusting the wage. In the case of the fall in labor demand shown in Figure 9.8, for example, the wage should be lowered when the new contract is signed. But Bils finds little relation between how the wage is set in a new contract and the change in employment over the life of the previous contract. In addition, when he looks across industries, he finds essentially no relation between the extent to which employment changes are reversed when a new contract is signed and the extent to which the wage is adjusted.

Bils suggests two possible explanations of this finding. One is that adjustments in compensation mainly take the form of changes to fringe

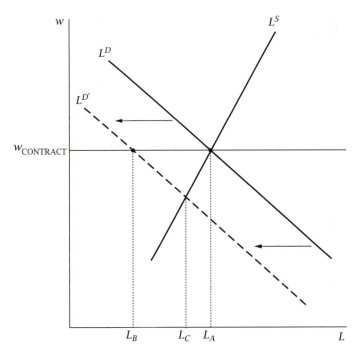

FIGURE 9.8 Employment movements under wage contracts

benefits and other factors that are not captured by his wage measure. The second is that employment determination is more complex than either of the two views we have been considering.

Interindustry Wage Differences

The basic idea of efficiency-wage models is that firms may pay wages above market-clearing levels. If there are reasons for firms to do this, those reasons are unlikely to be equally important everywhere in the economy. Motivated by this observation, Dickens and Katz (1987a) and Krueger and Summers (1988) investigate whether some industries pay systematically higher wages than others.[30]

These authors begin by adding dummy variables for the industries that workers are employed in to conventional wage regressions. A typical specification is

$$\ln w_i = \alpha + \sum_{j=1}^{M} \beta_j X_{ij} + \sum_{k=1}^{N} \gamma_k D_{ik} + \varepsilon_i, \tag{9.89}$$

where w_i is worker i's wage, the X_{ij}'s are worker characteristics (such as age, education, occupation, and so on), and the D_{ik}'s are dummy variables for employment in different industries. In a competitive, frictionless labor market, wages depend only on workers' characteristics and not on what industry they are employed in. Thus if the X's adequately capture workers' characteristics, the coefficients on the industry dummies will be zero.

Dickens and Katz's and Krueger and Summers's basic finding is that the estimated γ_k's are large. Katz and Summers (1989), for example, consider wage differences among U.S. workers in 1984 across *two-digit* industries.[31] Since Katz and Summers consider a sample of more than 100,000 workers, it is not surprising that they find that most of the γ's are highly significant. But they also find that they are quantitatively large. For example, the standard deviation of the estimated γ's (weighted by the sizes of the industries) is 0.15, or 15 percent. Thus wages appear to differ considerably among industries.

Dickens and Katz and Krueger and Summers show that several possible explanations of these wage differences are contradicted by the data. The estimated differences are essentially the same when the sample is restricted to workers not covered by union contracts; thus they do not appear to be

---

[30] See Katz and Summers (1989, pp. 216–247) for a summary of this literature. Groshen (1991) examines wage differences among firms within industries.

[31] Two-digit industries refers to the Standard Industrial Classification (or SIC). One-digit industries are very broad industries, such as durable goods manufacturing, communications, and retail trade. Two-digit industries are narrower classifications within these broad groups; for example, two-digit industries within durable goods manufacturing include furniture and motor vehicles. Three-, four-, and five-digit industries are even finer distinctions.

the result of union bargaining power. The differences are quite stable over time and across countries; thus they are unlikely to reflect transitory adjustments in the labor market (Krueger and Summers, 1987). When broader measures of compensation are used, the estimated differences typically become larger; thus the results do not appear to arise from differences in the mix of wage and nonwage compensation across industries. Finally, there is no evidence that working conditions are worse in the high-wage industries; thus the differences do not appear to be compensating differentials.

There is also some direct evidence that the differences represent genuine rents. Krueger and Summers (1988) and Akerlof, Rose, and Yellen (1988) find that workers in industries with higher estimated wage premiums quit much less often. Krueger and Summers also find that workers who move from one industry to another on average have their wages change by nearly as much as the difference between the estimated wage premiums for the two industries. And Gibbons and Katz (1992) consider workers who lose their jobs because the plants where they are working close. They find that the wage cuts the workers take when they accept new jobs are much higher when the jobs they lost were in higher-wage industries.

Two aspects of the results are more problematic for efficiency-wage theory, however. First, although many competitive explanations of the results are not supported at all by the data, there is one that cannot be readily dismissed. No wage equation can control for all relevant worker characteristics. Thus one possible explanation of the finding of apparent interindustry wage differences is that they reflect unmeasured differences in ability across workers in different industries rather than rents.[32]

To understand this idea, imagine an econometrician studying wage differences among baseball leagues. If the econometrician could only control for the kinds of worker characteristics that studies of interindustry wage differences control for—age, experience, and so on—he or she would find that wages are systematically higher in some leagues than in others: major-league teams pay more than AAA minor-league teams, which pay more than AA minor-league teams, and so on. In addition, quit rates are much lower in the higher-wage leagues, and workers who move from lower-wage to higher-wage leagues experience large wage increases. But there is little doubt that large parts of the wage differences among baseball leagues reflect ability differences rather than rents. Just as an econometrician using Dickens and Katz's and Krueger and Summers's methods to study interleague wage differences in baseball would be led astray, perhaps econometricians studying interindustry wage differences have also been led astray.

Several pieces of evidence support this view. First, if some firms are paying more than the market-clearing wage, they face an excess supply of workers, and so they have some discretion to hire more able workers. Thus it would be surprising if at least some of the estimated wage differences did

---

[32] See, for example, Murphy and Topel (1987b); Hall (1989); and Topel (1989).

not reflect ability differences. Second, higher-wage industries have higher capital-labor ratios, which suggests that they need more skilled workers. Third, workers in higher-wage industries have higher measured ability (in terms of education, experience, and so on); thus it seems likely that they have higher unmeasured ability. Finally, the same patterns of interindustry earnings differences occur, although less strongly, among self-employed workers.

The hypothesis that estimated interindustry wage differences reflect unmeasured ability cannot easily account for all the findings about these differences, however. First, quantitative attempts to estimate how much of the differences can plausibly be due to unmeasured ability generally leave a substantial portion of the differences unaccounted for (see, for example, Katz and Summers, 1989). Second, the unmeasured-ability hypothesis cannot readily explain Gibbons and Katz's findings about the wage cuts of displaced workers. Third, the estimated wage premiums are higher in industries where profits are higher; this is not what the unmeasured-ability hypothesis naturally predicts. Finally, industries that pay higher wages generally do so in all occupations, from janitors to managers; it is not clear that unmeasured ability differences should be so strongly related across occupations. Thus, although the view that interindustry wage differences reflect unmeasured ability is troubling for rent-based explanations of those differences, it does not definitively refute them.

The second aspect of this literature's findings that is not easily accounted for by efficiency-wage theories concerns the characteristics of industries that pay high wages. As described above, higher-wage industries tend to have higher capital-labor ratios, more educated and experienced workers, and higher profits. In addition, they have larger establishments and larger fractions of male and of unionized workers (Dickens and Katz, 1987b). No single efficiency-wage theory predicts all these patterns. As a result, authors who believe that the estimated interindustry wage differences reflect rents tend to resort to complicated explanations of them. Dickens and Katz and Krueger and Summers, for example, appeal to a combination of efficiency-wage theories based on imperfect monitoring, efficiency-wage theories based on workers' perceptions of fairness, and worker power in wage determination.

In sum, the literature on interindustry wage differences has identified an interesting set of regularities that differ greatly from what simple theories of the labor market predict. The reasons for those regularities, however, have not yet been convincingly identified.

Survey Evidence on Wage Rigidity

One of the main reasons we are interested in the labor market is that we would like to understand why falls in labor demand lead firms to reduce employment substantially and cut wages relatively little. This raises a natural question: Why not simply ask individuals responsible for firms' wage and employment policies why they do this?

Asking wage-setters the reasons for their behavior is not a panacea. Most importantly, they may not fully understand the factors underlying their decisions. They may have found successful policies through such means as trial and error, instruction from their predecessors, and observation of other firms' policies. Friedman and Savage (1948) give the analogy of an expert billiard player. Talking to the player is likely to be of little value in predicting how the player will shoot or in understanding the reasons for his or her choices. One would do better computing the optimal shots based on such considerations as the elasticity of the balls, the friction of the table surface, how spin affects the balls' bounces, and so on, even though these factors may not directly enter the player's thinking.

When wage-setters are not completely sure of the reasons for their decisions, small differences in how questions are phrased can be important. For example, economists use the phrases "shirk," "exert less effort," and "be less productive" more or less interchangeably to describe how workers may respond to a wage cut. But these phrases may have quite different connotations to wage-setters.

Despite these difficulties, surveys of wage-setters are potentially useful. If, for example, wage-setters disagree with a theory no matter how it is phrased and find its mechanisms implausible regardless of how they are described, we should be skeptical of the theory's relevance.

Examples of surveys of wage-setters include Blinder and Choi (1990); Campbell and Kamlani (1997); and Bewley (1999). Here we focus on Campbell and Kamlani's. These authors survey compensation managers at roughly 100 of the largest 1000 firms in the United States and at roughly 100 smaller U.S. firms. They ask the managers' views both about various theories of wage rigidity and about the mechanisms underlying the theories. Their central question asks the respondents their views concerning the importance of various possible reasons that "firms normally do not cut wages to the lowest level at which they can find the necessary number of qualified applicants during a recession."

The reason for not cutting wages in a recession that the survey participants view as clearly the most important is, "If your firm were to cut wages, your most productive workers might leave, whereas if you lay off workers, you can lay off the least productive workers." Campbell and Kamlani interpret the respondents' agreement with this statement as support for the importance of adverse selection. Unfortunately, however, this question serves mainly to illustrate the perils of surveys. The difficulty is that the phrasing of the statement presumes that firms know which workers are more productive. Adverse selection can arise, however, only from *unobservable* differences among workers. Thus it seems likely that compensation managers' strong agreement with the statement is due to other reasons.

Other surveys find much less support for the importance of adverse selection. For example, Blinder and Choi ask,

> There are two workers who are being considered for the same job. As far as you can tell, ... both workers are equally well qualified. One of the workers agrees to work for the wage you offer him. The other one says he needs more money to work for you. Based on this difference, do you think one of these workers is likely to be an inherently more productive worker?

All 18 respondents to Blinder and Choi's survey answer this question negatively. But this too is not decisive. For example, the reference to one worker being "inherently more productive" may be sufficiently strong that it biases the results against the adverse-selection hypothesis.

A hypothesis that fares better in surveys is that concern about quits is critical to wage-setting. The fact that the respondents to Campbell and Kamlani's survey agree strongly with the statement that wage cuts may cause highly productive workers to leave supports this view. The respondents also agree strongly with statements that an important reason not to cut wages is that cuts would increase quits and thereby raise recruitment and training costs and cause important losses of firm-specific human capital. Other surveys also find that firms' desire to avoid quits is important to their wage policies.

The impact of concern about quits on wage-setting is very much in the spirit of the Shapiro–Stiglitz model. There is an action under workers' control (shirking in the Shapiro–Stiglitz model, quitting here) that affects the firm. For some reason, the firm's compensation policy does not cause workers to internalize the action's impact on the firm. Thus the firm raises wages to discourage the action. In that sense, the survey evidence supports the Shapiro–Stiglitz model. If we take a narrow view of the model, however, the survey evidence is less favorable: respondents consistently express little sympathy for the idea that imperfect monitoring and effort on the job are important to their decisions about wages.

The other theme of surveys of wage-setters besides the importance of quits is the critical role of fairness considerations. The surveys consistently suggest that workers' morale and perceptions of whether they are being treated appropriately are critical to their productivity. The surveys also suggest that workers have strong views about what actions by the firm are appropriate, and that as a result their sense of satisfaction is precarious.

One important concern about this evidence is that if other forces cause a particular policy to be the equilibrium outcome, and therefore what normally occurs, that policy may come to be viewed as fair. That is, views concerning what is appropriate can be a reflection of the equilibrium outcome rather than an independent cause of it.

This effect may be the source of some of the apparent importance of fairness, but it seems unlikely to be the only one: concerns about fairness seem too strong to be just reflections of other forces. In addition, in some cases fairness considerations appear to push wage-setting in directions one would not otherwise expect. For example, there is evidence that individuals' views about what compensation policies are fair put some weight on equalizing compensation rather than equalizing compensation relative to marginal products. And there is evidence that firms in fact set wages so that they rise less than one-for-one with observable differences in workers' marginal products. Because of this, firms obtain greater surplus from their more productive workers. This provides a more plausible explanation than adverse selection for the survey respondents' strong agreement with Campbell and Kamlani's statement about the advantages of layoffs over wage cuts. To give another example, many researchers, beginning with Kahneman, Knetsch, and Thaler (1986), find that workers view reductions in real wages as highly objectionable if they result from cuts in nominal wages, but as not especially objectionable if they result from increases in nominal wages that are less than the inflation rate.

Finally, although Campbell and Kamlani focus on why firms do not cut wages in recessions, their results probably tell us more about why firms might pay more than market-clearing wages than about the cyclical behavior of wages. The reason is that they do not provide evidence concerning wage-setting in booms. For example, if concern about quits causes firms to pay more than they have to in recessions, it may do the same in booms. Indeed, concern about quits may have a bigger effect on wages in booms than in recessions.

Problems

9.1. Union wage premiums and efficiency wages. (Summers, 1988.) Consider the efficiency-wage model analyzed in equations (9.12)–(9.19). Suppose, however, that fraction f of workers belong to unions that are able to obtain a wage that exceeds the nonunion wage by proportion μ. Thus, $w_u = (1 + \mu)w_n$, where w_u and w_n denote wages in the union and nonunion sectors; and the average wage, w_a, is given by $fw_u + (1-f)w_n$. Nonunion employers continue to set their wages freely; thus (by the same reasoning used to derive [9.15] in the text), $w_n = (1 - bu)w_a/(1 - \beta)$.

(a) Find the equilibrium unemployment rate in terms of β, b, f, and μ.

(b) Suppose $\mu = f = 0.15$.

    (i) What is the equilibrium unemployment rate if $\beta = 0.06$ and $b = 1$? By what proportion is the cost of effective labor higher in the union sector than in the nonunion sector?

    (ii) Repeat part (i) for the case of $\beta = 0.03$ and $b = 0.5$.

9.2. Efficiency wages and bargaining. (Garino and Martin, 1999.) Summers (1988, p. 386) states, "In an efficiency wage environment, firms that are forced to pay their workers premium wages suffer only second-order losses. In almost any plausible bargaining framework, this makes it easier for workers to extract concessions." This problem asks you to investigate this claim. Consider a firm with profits given by $\pi = [(eL)^\alpha/\alpha] - wL, 0 < \alpha < 1$, and a union with objective function $U = (w - x)L$, where x is an index of its workers' outside opportunities. Assume that the firm and the union bargain over the wage, and that the firm then chooses L taking w as given.

(a) Suppose that $e \equiv 1$, so that efficiency-wage considerations are absent.

(*i*) What value of L does the firm choose, given w? What is the resulting level of profits?

(*ii*) Suppose that the firm and the union choose w to maximize $U^\gamma \pi^{1-\gamma}$, where $0 < \gamma < \alpha$ indexes the union's power in the bargaining (this is known as the *Nash bargaining solution*). What level of w do they choose?

(*b*) Suppose that e is given by equation (9.12) in the text: $e = [(w - x)/x]^\beta$ for $w > x$, where $0 < \beta < 1$.

(*i*) What value of L does the firm choose, given w? What is the resulting level of profits?

(*ii*) Suppose that the firm and the union choose w to maximize $U^\gamma \pi^{1-\gamma}$, $0 < \gamma < \alpha$. What level of w do they choose? (Hint: For the case of $\beta = 0$, your answer should simplify to your answer in part [*a*][*ii*].)

(*iii*) Is the proportional impact of workers' bargaining power on wages greater with efficiency wages than without, as Summers implies? Is it greater when efficiency-wage effects, β, are greater?

9.3. Describe how each of the following affect equilibrium employment and the wage in the Shapiro–Stiglitz model:

(*a*) An increase in workers' discount rate, ρ.

(*b*) An increase in the job breakup rate, b.

(*c*) A positive multiplicative shock to the production function (that is, suppose the production function is $AF(L)$, and consider an increase in A).

(*d*) An increase in the size of the labor force, $\bar{L}$.

9.4. Suppose that in the Shapiro–Stiglitz model, unemployed workers are hired according to how long they have been unemployed rather than at random; specifically, suppose that workers who have been unemployed the longest are hired first.

(*a*) Consider a steady state where there is no shirking. Derive an expression for how long it takes a worker who becomes unemployed to get a job as a function of b, L, N, and $\bar{L}$.

(*b*) Let V_U be the value of being a worker who is newly unemployed. Derive an expression for V_U as a function of the time it takes to get a job, workers' discount rate (ρ), and the value of being employed (V_E).

(*c*) Using your answers to parts (*a*) and (*b*), find the no-shirking condition for this version of the model.

(*d*) How, if at all, does the assumption that the longer-term unemployed get priority affect the equilibrium unemployment rate?

9.5. The fair wage-effort hypothesis. (Akerlof and Yellen, 1990.) Suppose there are a large number of firms, N, each with profits given by $F(eL) - wL$, $F'(\bullet) > 0$, $F''(\bullet) < 0$. L is the number of workers the firm hires, w is the wage it pays, and e is workers' effort. Effort is given by $e = \min[w/w^*, 1]$, where w^* is the "fair wage"; that is, if workers are paid less than the fair wage, they reduce their effort in proportion to the shortfall. Assume that there are $\bar{L}$ workers who are willing to work at any positive wage.

(a) If a firm can hire workers at any wage, what value (or range of values) of w minimizes the cost per unit of effective labor, w/e? For the remainder of the problem, assume that if the firm is indifferent over a range of possible wages, it pays the highest value in this range.

(b) Suppose w^* is given by $w^* = \bar{w} + a - bu$, $b > 0$, where u is the unemployment rate and $\bar{w}$ is the average wage paid by the firms in the economy. Assume $b > 0$ and $a/b < 1$.

  (i) Given your answer to part (a) (and the assumption about what firms pay in cases of indifference), what wage does the representative firm pay if it can choose w freely (taking $\bar{w}$ and u as given)?

  (ii) Under what conditions does the equilibrium involve positive unemployment and no constraints on firms' choice of w? (Hint: In this case, equilibrium requires that the representative firm, taking $\bar{w}$ as given, wishes to pay $\bar{w}$.) What is the unemployment rate in this case?

  (iii) Under what conditions is there full employment?

(c) Suppose the representative firm's production function is modified to be $F(Ae_1L_1 + e_2L_2)$, $A > 1$, where L_1 and L_2 are the numbers of high-productivity and low-productivity workers the firm hires. Assume that $e_i = \min[w_i/w_i^*, 1]$, where w_i^* is the fair wage for type-i workers. w_i^* is given by $w_i^* = (\bar{w}_1 + \bar{w}_2)/2 - bu_i$, where $b > 0$, $\bar{w}_i$ is the average wage paid to workers of type i, and u_i is their unemployment rate. Finally, assume there are $\bar{L}$ workers of each type.

  (i) Explain why, given your answer to part (a) (and the assumption about what firms pay in cases of indifference), neither type of worker will be paid less than the fair wage for that type.

  (ii) Explain why w_1 will exceed w_2 by a factor of A.

  (iii) In equilibrium, is there unemployment among high-productivity workers? Explain. (Hint: If u_1 is positive, firms are unconstrained in their choice of w_1.)

  (iv) In equilibrium, is there unemployment among low-productivity workers? Explain.

9.6. Implicit contracts without variable hours. Suppose that each worker must either work a fixed number of hours or be unemployed. Let C_i^E denote the consumption of employed workers in state i and C_i^U the consumption of unemployed workers. The firm's profits in state i are therefore $A_iF(L_i) - [C_i^E L_i + C_i^U(\bar{L} - L_i)]$, where $\bar{L}$ is the number of workers. Similarly, workers' expected utility in state i is $(L_i/\bar{L})[U(C_i^E) - K] + [(\bar{L} - L_i)/\bar{L}]U(C_i^U)$, where $K > 0$ is the disutility of working.

(a) Set up the Lagrangian for the firm's problem of choosing the L_i's, C_i^E's, and C_i^U's to maximize expected profits subject to the constraint that the representative worker's expected utility is u_0.[33]

---

[33] For simplicity, neglect the constraint that L cannot exceed $\bar{L}$. Accounting for this

(b) Find the first-order conditions for L_i, C_i^E, and C_i^U. How, if at all, do C^E and C^U depend on the state? What is the relation between C_i^E and C_i^U?

(c) After A is realized and some workers are chosen to work and others are chosen to be unemployed, which workers are better off?

9.7. Unemployment insurance. (This follows Feldstein, 1976.) Consider a firm with revenues $AF(L)$. A has two possible values, A_B and A_G ($A_B < A_G$), each of which occurs half the time. Workers who are employed when $A = A_G$ and unemployed when $A = A_B$ receive an unemployment insurance benefit of $B > 0$ when $A = A_B$. Workers are risk-neutral; thus the representative worker has an expected utility of $U = (w - K)/2 + \{(L_B/L_G)(w - K) + [(L_G - L_B)/L_G]B\}/2$, where w is the wage (which is assumed without loss of generality to be independent of the state), K is the disutility of working, and L_B and L_G are employment in the two states. The firm's expected profits are $[A_G F(L_G) - wL_G]/2 + [A_B F(L_B) - wL_B - fB(L_G - L_B)]/2$, where f is the fraction of unemployment benefits that are paid by the firm. Assume $0 \le f \le 1$.[34]

(a) Set up the Lagrangian for the firm's problem of choosing w, L_G, and L_B to maximize expected profits subject to the constraint that workers' expected utility is u_0.

(b) Find the first-order conditions for w, L_G, and L_B.

(c) Show that a fall in f (or a rise in B if $f < 1$) reduces L_B.

(d) Show that a fall in f (or a rise in B if $f < 1$) raises L_G.

9.8. Implicit contracts under asymmetric information. (Azariadis and Stiglitz, 1983.) Consider the model of Section 9.5. Suppose, however, that only the firm observes A. In addition, suppose there are only two possible values of A, A_B and A_G ($A_B < A_G$), each occurring with probability $\frac{1}{2}$.

We can think of the contract as specifying w and L as functions of the firm's announcement of the state, and as being subject to the restriction that it is never in the firm's interest to announce a state other than the actual one; formally, the contract must be *incentive-compatible*.

(a) Is the efficient contract under symmetric information derived in Section 9.5 incentive-compatible under asymmetric information? Specifically, if A is A_B, is the firm better off claiming that A is A_G (so that C and L are given by C_G and L_G) rather than that it is A_B? And if A is A_G, is the firm better off claiming it is A_B rather than A_G?

(b) One can show that the constraint that the firm not prefer to claim that the state is bad when it is good is not binding, but that the constraint that it not prefer to claim that the state is good when it is bad is binding. Set up the Lagrangian for the firm's problem of choosing C_G, C_B, L_G, and L_B subject to the constraints that workers' expected utility is u_0 and that the firm is indifferent about which state to announce when A is A_B. Find the first-order conditions for C_G, C_B, L_G, and L_B.

---

constraint, one would find that for A_i above some critical level, L_i would equal $\bar{L}$ rather than be determined by the condition derived in part (b), below.

[34] In the United States, a firm's unemployment insurance taxes only partly account for the extent to which the firm's workers obtain unemployment insurance; that is, the taxes are only partially *experience-rated*. Thus f is between 0 and 1.

(c) Show that the marginal product and the marginal disutility of labor are equated in the bad state—that is, that $A_B F'(L_B) = V'(L_B)/U'(C_B)$.

(d) Show that there is "overemployment" in the good state—that is, that $A_G F'(L_G) < V'(L_G)/U'(C_G)$.

(e) Is this model helpful in understanding the high level of average unemployment? Is it helpful in understanding the large size of employment fluctuations?

9.9. Does worker influence on the wage after shocks to labor demand are realized affect the cyclical characteristics of the labor market?

(a) (This follows McDonald and Solow, 1981.) Consider a union with the objective function $[U(w) - K]L + U(w_u)(N - L)$, $U'(\bullet) > 0$, where N is the number of union members, L is the number who are employed, $K > 0$ is the disutility of working, w is the wage, and w_u is unemployment compensation. The firm's profits are $AL^\alpha/\alpha - wL$, $A > 0$, $0 < \alpha < 1$. The union sets w after A is known, and the firm then chooses L given w and A. (Assume throughout the problem that the constraint that L cannot exceed N is not binding.)

(i) What is the firm's choice of L given w and A?

(ii) Given its knowledge of how the firm will behave, what is the union's choice of w given A? Given this, how does L vary with A?

(b) Given the union's objective function, what is labor supply under spot markets—that is, if the union takes w as given and chooses L to maximize its objective function? How do w and L vary with A under spot markets?

(c) Suppose the union's objective function is $wL - [\sigma/(\sigma+1)]L^{(\sigma+1)/\sigma}$, $\sigma > 0$, instead of the expression in part (a).

(i) How do w and L vary with A under spot markets?

(ii) Redo part (a)(ii) using the modified union objective function. Does assuming that the wage is determined by the union rather than by spot markets affect the elasticities of w and L with respect to A?

9.10. Does worker influence on the wage and employment after shocks to labor demand are realized affect the cyclical characteristics of the labor market?

(a) (This is based on McDonald and Solow, 1981.) Consider a union and a firm with the objective functions assumed in part (a) of Problem 9.9. The union chooses w and L given A, subject to the constraint that the firm's profits must be at least some level, π_0.

(i) Set up the Lagrangian for the union's maximization problem.

(ii) Find the first-order conditions for w and L.

(iii) What role does w play in this model?

(iv) How does L vary with A? Compare your answer with your finding in part (b) of Problem 9.9 concerning how L varies with A under spot markets.

(b) Suppose the union's objective function is given instead by the expression in part (c) of Problem 9.9. Redo parts (i) and (ii) of part (a) using the modified union objective function. Compare how L varies with A with your finding in part $(c)(i)$ of Problem 9.9 concerning how it varies under spot markets.

9.11. The Harris–Todaro model. (Harris and Todaro, 1970.) Suppose there are two sectors. Jobs in the primary sector pay w_p; jobs in the secondary sector pay w_s. Each worker decides which sector to be in. All workers who choose the secondary sector obtain a job. But there are a fixed number, N_p, of primary-sector jobs. These jobs are allocated at random among workers who choose the primary sector. Primary-sector workers who do not get a job are unemployed, and receive an unemployment benefit of b. Workers are risk-neutral, and there is no disutility of working. Thus the expected utility of a primary-sector worker is $qw_p + (1 - q)b$, where q is the probability of a primary-sector worker getting a job. Assume that $b < w_s < w_p$, and that $N_p/\overline{N} < (w_s - b)/(w_p - b)$.

(a) What is equilibrium unemployment as a function of w_p, w_s, N_p, b, and the size of the labor force, $\overline{N}$?

(b) How does an increase in N_p affect unemployment? Explain intuitively why, even though unemployment takes the form of workers waiting for primary-sector jobs, increasing the number of these jobs can increase unemployment.

(c) What are the effects of an increase in the level of unemployment benefits?

9.12. Partial-equilibrium search. Consider a worker searching for a job. Wages, w, have a probability density function across jobs, $f(w)$, that is known to the worker; let $F(w)$ be the associated cumulative distribution function. Each time the worker samples a job from this distribution, he or she incurs a cost of C, where $0 < C < E[w]$. When the worker samples a job, he or she can either accept it (in which case the process ends) or sample another job. The worker maximizes the expected value of $w - nC$, where w is the wage paid in the job the worker eventually accepts and n is the number of jobs the worker ends up sampling.

Let V denote the expected value of $w - n'C$ of a worker who has just rejected a job, where n' is the number of jobs the worker will sample from that point on.

(a) Explain why the worker accepts a job offering $\hat{w}$ if $\hat{w} > V$, and rejects it if $\hat{w} < V$. (A search problem where the worker accepts a job if and only if it pays above some cutoff level is said to exhibit the *reservation-wage property*.)

(b) Explain why V satisfies $V = F(V)V + \int_{w=V}^{\infty} wf(w)\,dw - C$.

(c) Show that an increase in C reduces V.

(d) In this model, does a searcher ever want to accept a job that he or she has previously rejected?

9.13. In the setup described in Problem 9.12, suppose that w is distributed uniformly on $[\mu - a, \mu + a]$ and that $C < \mu$.

(a) Find V in terms of μ, a, and C.

(*b*) How does an increase in *a* affect *V*? Explain intuitively.

9.14. Describe how each of the following affects equilibrium employment in the model of Section 9.8:

(*a*) An increase in the job breakup rate, *b*.

(*b*) An increase in the interest rate, *r*.

(*c*) An increase in the effectiveness of matching, *K*.

9.15. Suppose we replace the assumption in equation (9.76) that the worker and the firm divide the surplus from their relationship equally with the assumption that fraction *f* of the surplus goes to the worker and fraction $1 - f$ goes to the firm: $(1 - f)(V_E - V_U) = f(V_F - V_V)$.

(*a*) How does this change in the model affect the equation implicitly defining *E*, (9.87)?

(*b*) How does a change in *f* affect the equilibrium level of *E*?

9.16. Consider the model of Section 9.8. Suppose the economy is initially in equilibrium, and that *A* then falls permanently. Suppose, however, that entry and exit are ruled out; thus the total number of jobs, $F + V$, remains constant. How do unemployment and vacancies behave over time in response to the fall in *A*?

9.17. The efficiency of the decentralized equilibrium in a search economy. Consider the model of Section 9.8. Let the interest rate, *r*, approach 0, and assume that the firms are owned by the households; thus welfare can be measured as the sum of utility and profits per unit time, which equals $AE - (F + V)C$. Letting *N* denote the total number of jobs, we can therefore write welfare as $W(N) = AE(N) - NC$, where $E(N)$ gives equilibrium employment as a function of *N*.

(*a*) Use the matching function, (9.68), and the steady-state condition, (9.69), to derive an expression for the impact of a change in the number of jobs on employment, $E'(N)$, in terms of $N, \bar{L}, E(N), \gamma$, and β.

(*b*) Substitute your result in part (*a*) into the expression for $W(N)$ to find $W'(N)$ in terms of $N, \bar{L}, E(N), \gamma, \beta$, and *A*.

(*c*) Use (9.82) and the facts that $a = bE/(\bar{L} - E)$ and $\alpha = bE/V$ to find an expression for *C* in terms of $N_{EQ}, \bar{L}, E(N_{EQ})$, and *A*, where N_{EQ} is the number of jobs in the decentralized equilibrium.

(*d*) Use your results in parts (*b*) and (*c*) to show that if $\beta + \gamma = 1$, then $W'(N_{EQ}) > 0$ if $\gamma > \frac{1}{2}$ and $W'(N_{EQ}) < 0$ if $\gamma < \frac{1}{2}$.

(*e*) If γ is $\frac{1}{2}$ but $\beta + \gamma$ is not necessarily 1, what determines the sign of $W'(N_{EQ})$?

Chapter **10**
INFLATION AND MONETARY POLICY

10.1 Introduction

Our final two chapters are devoted to macroeconomic policy. This chapter considers monetary policy, and Chapter 11 considers fiscal policy. We will focus on two main aspects of policy. The first is its short-run conduct: we would like to know how policymakers should act in the face of the various disturbances that impinge on the economy. In most countries today, short-run stabilization is done mainly by monetary rather than fiscal policy. Stabilization policy is therefore addressed in this chapter; specifically, it is the subject of Sections 10.6 and 10.7.

The second central aspect of policy is its long-run performance. Monetary policy often causes high rates of inflation over extended periods, and fiscal policy often causes persistent high budget deficits. In many cases, these inflation rates and budget deficits appear to be higher than is socially optimal. That is, it appears that in at least some circumstances, there is *inflation bias* in monetary policy and *deficit bias* in fiscal policy. The possibility of such biases is a major subject of the next two chapters.

Sections 10.2 and 10.3 begin our analysis of monetary policy by explaining why inflation is almost always the result of rapid growth of the money supply; they also investigate the effects of money growth on inflation, real balances, and interest rates. We then turn to inflation bias. There are two main sets of explanations of how such bias can arise. The first set emphasizes the output-inflation tradeoff. If monetary policy has real effects (or if policymakers believe that it does), policymakers may increase the money supply in an effort to increase output. Theories of how inflation can arise from this tradeoff—particularly theories that emphasize the *dynamic inconsistency* of low-inflation policy—are discussed in Sections 10.4 and 10.5.

The second set of explanations of rapid money growth focuses on *seignorage*—the revenue the government gets from printing money. These theories, which are more relevant to less developed countries than to indus-

468

trialized ones, and which are at the heart of hyperinflations, are the subject of Section 10.8.

All of this analysis presumes that we understand why inflation is costly and how large its costs are. In fact, however, these are difficult issues. Section 10.9 is therefore devoted to the costs of inflation. This section not only describes the various potential costs of inflation, but also attempts to understand the basis for the intense concern about inflation among policy-makers, the business community, and the public.

10.2   Inflation, Money Growth, and Interest Rates

Inflation and Money Growth

The simple diagram from Chapter 5 showing aggregate supply and aggregate demand, which is reproduced as Figure 10.1, provides a framework

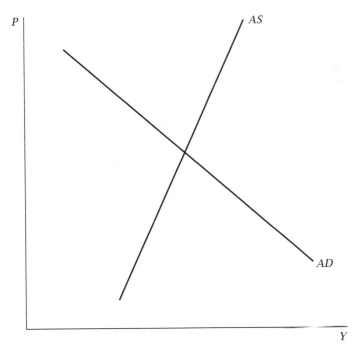

FIGURE 10.1   The aggregate demand and aggregate supply curves

for identifying potential sources of inflation. Since our interest is in prices rather than output, the issue of whether the aggregate supply curve is vertical or merely upward-sloping is not important: in either case, both expansions of aggregate demand and contractions of aggregate supply raise the price level. Thus there are many potential sources of inflation. Negative technology shocks, downward shifts in labor supply, and other factors that shift the aggregate supply curve to the left cause inflation; the same is true of increases in the money stock, downward shifts in money demand, increases in government purchases, and other factors that shift the aggregate demand curve to the right.[1] Since all these types of shocks occur to some extent, there are many factors that affect inflation.

Nonetheless, when it comes to understanding inflation over the longer term, economists typically emphasize just one factor: growth of the money supply. The reason for this emphasis is that no other factor is likely to lead to persistent increases in the price level. Repeated increases in prices require either repeated falls in aggregate supply or repeated rises in aggregate demand. Given technological progress, repeated falls in aggregate supply are unlikely. And although there are many factors that can increase aggregate demand, most are limited in scope. For example, there cannot be repeated large increases in aggregate demand coming from increases in government purchases or reductions in taxes, because there are practical limits on these variables; for instance, we never observe government purchases that are larger than total output, or total taxes that are negative. The money supply, in contrast, can grow at almost any rate, and we observe huge variations in money growth—from large and negative during some deflations to immense and positive during hyperinflations.

To see more clearly why money is crucial to inflation, consider the money market. With the specification of money demand from Chapter 5, the condition for equilibrium in the money market is

$$\frac{M}{P} = L(i, Y), \tag{10.1}$$

where M is the money stock, P the price level, i the nominal interest rate, Y real income, and $L(\bullet)$ the demand for real money balances. This condition implies that the price level is given by

$$P = \frac{M}{L(i, Y)}. \tag{10.2}$$

Conventional estimates of money demand suggest that the income elasticity of money demand is about 1 and the interest elasticity is about -0.2 (see Goldfeld and Sichel, 1990, for example). Thus for the price level to double

---

[1] Many shocks affect both curves. A rise in government purchases, for example, may not only shift the aggregate demand curve, but also move the aggregate supply curve through its impact on labor supply. The overall effect of any shock on the price level depends on how it affects both curves.

over some period of time without a change in the money supply, income must fall roughly in half or the interest rate must rise by a factor of about 32. Alternatively, the demand for real balances at a given interest rate and income must fall in half. All these possibilities are essentially unheard of. In contrast, a doubling of the money supply, either over several years in a moderate inflation or over a few days at the height of a hyperinflation, is not uncommon.

Thus money growth plays a special role in determining inflation not because money affects prices more directly than other factors do, but because empirically variations in money growth account for most of the variation in the growth of aggregate demand. Figure 10.2 provides powerful confirmation of the importance of money growth to inflation. The figure plots average inflation against average money growth for the period 1980–1995 for a sample of 105 countries. There is a clear and strong relationship between the two variables.

Money Growth and Interest Rates

Since money growth is the main determinant of inflation, it is natural to examine its effects in greater detail. As we will see, there are interesting links between the growth of the nominal money stock and the behavior of inflation, real and nominal interest rates, and real balances.

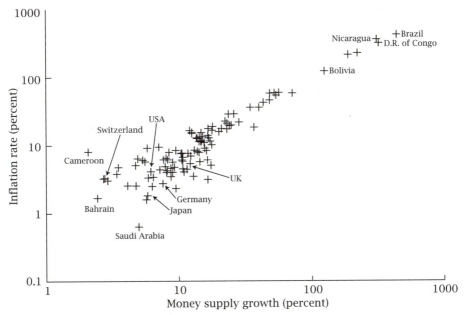

FIGURE 10.2 Money growth and inflation

We begin with the case where prices are completely flexible; this is presumably a good description of the long run. As we know from our analysis of fluctuations, this assumption implies that the money supply does not affect real output or the real interest rate. For simplicity, we assume that these are constant at $\overline{Y}$ and $\overline{r}$, respectively.

By definition, the real interest rate is the difference between the nominal interest rate and expected inflation. That is, $r \equiv i - \pi^e$, or

$$i \equiv r + \pi^e. \tag{10.3}$$

Equation (10.3) is known as the *Fisher identity*.

Using (10.3) and our assumption that r and Y are constant, we can rewrite (10.2) as

$$P = \frac{M}{L(\overline{r} + \pi^e, \overline{Y})}. \tag{10.4}$$

Assume that initially M and P are growing together at some steady rate (so that M/P is constant) and that π^e equals actual inflation. Now suppose that at some time, time t_0, there is a permanent increase in money growth. The resulting path of the money stock is shown in the top panel of Figure 10.3. After the change, since M is growing at a new steady rate and r and Y are constant by assumption, M/P is constant; that is, (10.4) is satisfied with P growing at the same rate as M and with π^e equal to the new rate of money growth.

But what happens at the time of the change? Since the price level rises faster after the change than before, expected inflation jumps up when the change occurs. Thus the nominal interest rate jumps up, and so the quantity of real balances demanded falls discontinuously. Since M does not change discontinuously, it follows that P must jump up at the time of the change. This information is summarized in the remaining panels of Figure 10.3.[2]

This analysis has two messages. First, the change in inflation resulting from the change in money growth is reflected one-for-one in the nominal interest rate. The hypothesis that inflation affects the nominal rate one-for-one is known as the *Fisher effect;* it follows from the Fisher identity and the assumption that inflation does not affect the real rate.

Second, a higher growth rate of the *nominal* money stock reduces the *real* money stock. The rise in money growth increases expected inflation, thereby increasing the nominal interest rate. This increase in the opportunity cost of holding money reduces the quantity of real balances that individuals want to hold. Thus equilibrium requires that P rises more than M does. That is, there must be a period when inflation exceeds the rate of money growth. In our model, this occurs at the moment that money growth increases. In models where prices are not completely flexible or individuals

---

[2] In addition to the path of P described here, there may also be *bubble paths* that satisfy (10.4). Along these paths, P rises at an increasing rate, thereby causing π^e to be rising and the quantity of real balances demanded to be falling. See, for example, Problem 2.20 and Blanchard and Fischer (1989, Chapter 5, Section 3).

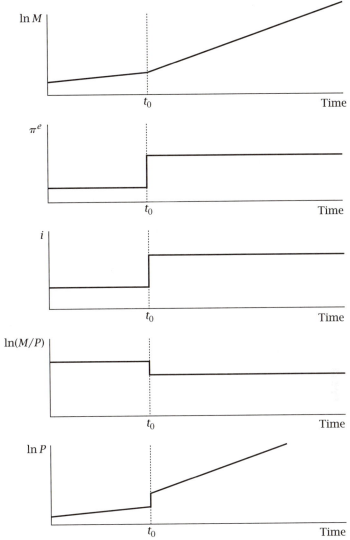

FIGURE 10.3   The effects of an increase in money growth

cannot adjust their real money holdings costlessly, in contrast, it occurs over a longer period.

A corollary is that a reduction in inflation can be accompanied by a temporary period of unusually high money growth. Suppose that policymakers want to reduce inflation and that they do not want the price level to change discontinuously. What path of M is needed to do this? The decline in inflation will reduce expected inflation, and thus lower the nominal interest rate and raise the quantity of real balances demanded. Writing the money market equilibrium condition as $M = PL(i, Y)$, it follows that—since

$L(i, Y)$ increases discontinuously and P does not jump—M must jump up. Of course, to keep inflation low, the money stock must then grow slowly from this higher level.

Thus, the monetary policy that is consistent with a permanent drop in inflation is a sudden upward jump in the money supply, followed by low growth. And, in fact, the clearest examples of declines in inflation—the ends of hyperinflations—are accompanied by spurts of very high money growth that continue for a time after prices have stabilized (Sargent, 1982).[3]

The Case of Incomplete Price Flexibility

In the preceding analysis, an increase in money growth increases nominal interest rates. In practice, however, the immediate effect of a monetary expansion is to lower short-term nominal rates. This negative effect of monetary expansions on nominal rates is known as the *liquidity effect.*

The conventional explanation of the liquidity effect is that monetary expansions reduce real rates. If prices are not completely flexible, an increase in the money stock raises output, which requires a decline in the real interest rate. In terms of the *IS-LM* framework of Chapter 5, the *LM* curve shifts to the right along the downward-sloping *IS* curve. If the decline in the real rate is large enough, it more than offsets the effect of the increase in expected inflation.[4]

If prices are fully flexible in the long run, then the real rate eventually returns to normal following a shift to higher money growth. Thus if the real-rate effect dominates the expected-inflation effect in the short run, the shift depresses the nominal rate in the short run but increases it in the long run. As Friedman (1968) pointed out, this appears to provide an accurate description of the effects of monetary policy in practice. The Federal Reserve's expansionary policies in the late 1960s, for example, seem to have lowered nominal rates for several years but, by generating inflation, to have raised them over the longer term.

10.3   Monetary Policy and the Term Structure of Interest Rates

In many situations, we are interested in the behavior not just of short-term interest rates, but also of long-term rates. To understand how monetary policy affects long-term rates, we must consider the relationship between short-term and long-term rates. The relationship among interest rates over

---

[3] This analysis raises the question of why expected inflation falls when the money supply is exploding. We return to this issue in Section 10.8.

[4] See Problem 10.2. In addition, if inflation is completely unresponsive to monetary policy for any interval of time, then expectations of inflation over that interval do not rise; thus in this case short-term nominal rates necessarily fall.

different horizons is known as the *term structure of interest rates*, and the standard theory of that relationship is known as the *expectations theory of the term structure*. This section describes this theory and considers its implications for the effects of monetary policy.

The Expectations Theory of the Term Structure

Consider the problem of an investor deciding how to invest a dollar over the next n periods; assume for simplicity that there is no uncertainty about future interest rates. Suppose first the investor puts the dollar in an n-period zero-coupon bond (that is, a bond whose entire payoff comes after n periods). If the bond has a continuously compounded return of i_t^n per period, the investor has $\exp(ni_t^n)$ dollars after n periods. Now consider what happens if he or she puts the dollar into a sequence of 1-period bonds paying continuously compounded rates of return of $i_t^1, i_{t+1}^1, \ldots, i_{t+n-1}^1$ over the n periods. In this case, he or she ends up with $\exp(i_t^1 + i_{t+1}^1 + \cdots + i_{t+n-1}^1)$ dollars.

Equilibrium requires that investors are willing to hold both 1-period and n-period bonds. Thus the returns on the investor's two strategies must be the same. This requires

$$i_t^n = \frac{i_t^1 + i_{t+1}^1 + \cdots + i_{t+n-1}^1}{n}. \tag{10.5}$$

That is, the interest rate on the long-term bond must equal the average of the interest rates on short-term bonds over its lifetime.

In this example, since there is no uncertainty, rationality alone implies that the term structure is determined by the path that short-term interest rates will take. With uncertainty, under plausible assumptions expectations concerning future short-term rates continue to play an important role in the determination of the term structure. A typical formulation is

$$i_t^n = \frac{i_t^1 + E_t i_{t+1}^1 + \cdots + E_t i_{t+n-1}^1}{n} + \theta_{nt}, \tag{10.6}$$

where E_t denotes expectations as of period t. With uncertainty, the strategies of buying a single n-period bond and a sequence of 1-period bonds generally involve different risks. Thus rationality does not imply that the expected returns on the two strategies must be equal. This is reflected by the inclusion of θ, the *term premium* to holding the long-term bond, in (10.6).

The expectations theory of the term structure is the hypothesis that changes in the term structure are determined by changes in expectations of future interest rates (rather than by changes in the term premium). Typically, though not always, the expectations are assumed to be rational.[5]

---

[5] See Shiller (1990) for an overview of the study of the term structure.

As described at the end of Section 10.2, even if prices are not completely flexible, a permanent increase in money growth eventually increases the short-term nominal interest rate permanently. Thus even if short-term rates fall for some period, (10.5) implies that interest rates for sufficiently long maturities (that is, for sufficiently large n) immediately rise. Thus our analysis implies that a monetary expansion is likely to reduce short-term rates but increase long-term ones.

Empirical Application: The Response of the Term Structure to Changes in the Federal Reserve's Federal-Funds-Rate Target

In many periods, the Federal Reserve has had a target level of a particular interest rate, the Federal funds rate, and has implemented monetary policy through discrete changes in that target. The Federal funds rate is the interest rate that banks charge one another on one-day loans of reserves; thus it is a very short-term rate. Because changes in the Federal Reserve's target are discrete, it is usually clear what the target is and when it changes. Cook and Hahn (1989) use this fact to investigate monetary policy's impact on interest rates on bonds of different maturities. They focus on the period 1974–1979, which was a time when the Federal Reserve was targeting the funds rate.

Cook and Hahn begin by compiling a record of the changes in the Federal Reserve's target over this period. They examine both the records of the Federal Reserve Bank of New York (which implemented the changes) and the reports of the changes in *The Wall Street Journal*. They find that the *Journal*'s reports are almost always correct; thus it is reasonable to think of the changes in the target reported by the *Journal* as publicly observed.

As Cook and Hahn describe, the actual Federal funds rate moves closely with the Federal Reserve's target. Moreover, it is highly implausible that the Federal Reserve is changing the target in response to factors that would have moved the funds rate in the absence of the policy changes. For example, it is unlikely that, absent the Federal Reserve's actions, the funds rate would move by discrete amounts. In addition, there is often a lag of several days between the Federal Reserve's decision to change the target and the actual change; thus arguing that the Federal Reserve is responding to forces that would have moved the funds rate in any event requires arguing that the Federal Reserve has advance knowledge of those forces.

The close link between the actual funds rate and the Federal Reserve's target thus provides strong evidence that monetary policy affects short-term interest rates. As Cook and Hahn describe, earlier investigations of this issue mainly regressed changes in interest rates over periods of a month or a quarter on changes in the money supply over those periods; the regressions produced no clear evidence of the Federal Reserve's ability to influence interest rates. The reason appears to be that the regressions are complicated by the same types of issues that complicate the money-output regressions discussed in Section 5.5: the money supply is not determined solely by the Federal Reserve, the Federal Reserve adjusts policy in response to information about the economy, and so on.

Cook and Hahn then examine the impact of changes in the Federal Reserve's target on longer-term interest rates. Specifically, they estimate regressions of the form

$$\Delta R_t^i = b_1^i + b_2^i \Delta FF_t + u_t^i, \tag{10.7}$$

where ΔR_t^i is the change in the nominal interest rate on a bond of maturity i on day t, and ΔFF_t is the change in the target Federal funds rate on that day.

Cook and Hahn find, contrary to the predictions of the analysis in the first part of this section, that increases in the Federal-funds-rate target raise nominal interest rates at all horizons. An increase in the target of 100 basis points (that is, 1 percentage point) is associated with increases in the 3-month interest rate of 55 basis points (with a standard error of 6.8 basis points), in the 1-year rate of 50 basis points (5.2), in the 5-year rate of 21 basis points (3.2), and the 20-year rate of 10 basis points (1.8).

The idea that contractionary monetary policy should immediately lower long-term nominal interest rates is intuitive: contractionary policy is likely to raise real interest rates only briefly and is likely to lower inflation over the longer term. Yet, as Cook and Hahn's results show, the evidence does not support this prediction.

One possible explanation of this anomaly is that the Federal Reserve often changes policy on the basis of information that it has concerning future inflation that market participants do not have. As a result, when market participants observe a shift to tighter monetary policy, they do not infer that the Federal Reserve is tougher on inflation than they had previously believed. Rather, they infer that there is unfavorable information about inflation that they were previously not aware of.

C. Romer and D. Romer (2000) test this explanation by examining the inflation forecasts made by commercial forecasts and the Federal Reserve. Because the Federal Reserve's forecasts are made public only after 5 years, the forecasts provide a potential record of information that was known to the Federal Reserve but not to market participants. Romer and Romer ask whether individuals who know the commercial forecast could improve their forecasts if they also had access to the Federal Reserve's. Specifically, they estimate regressions of the form

$$\pi_t = a + b_C \hat{\pi}_t^C + b_F \hat{\pi}_t^F + e_t, \tag{10.8}$$

where π_t is actual inflation and $\hat{\pi}_t^C$ and $\hat{\pi}_t^F$ are the commercial and Federal Reserve forecasts of π_t. Their main interest is in b_F, the coefficient on the Federal Reserve forecast.

For most specifications, the estimates of b_F are close to 1 and overwhelmingly statistically significant. In addition, the estimates of b_C are generally near 0 and highly insignificant. These results suggest that the Federal Reserve has useful information about inflation; indeed, they suggest that the optimal forecasting strategy of someone with access to both forecasts would be to discard the commercial forecast and adopt the Federal Reserve's.

For the Federal Reserve's additional information to explain the increases in long-term rates in response to contractionary policy moves, the moves must reveal some of the Federal Reserve's information. Romer and Romer therefore consider the problem of a market participant trying to infer the Federal Reserve's forecast. To do this, they estimate regressions of the form

$$\hat{\pi}_t^F = \alpha + \beta P_t + \gamma \hat{\pi}_t^C + \varepsilon_t, \tag{10.9}$$

where P is the change in the Federal-funds-rate target. A typical estimate of β is around 0.25: a rise in the funds-rate target of 1 percentage point suggests that the Federal Reserve's inflation forecast is about $\frac{1}{4}$ percentage points higher than one would expect given the commercial forecast. In light of the results about the value of the Federal Reserve forecasts in predicting inflation, this suggests that the rise should increase market participants' expectations of inflation by about this amount; this is more than enough to account for Cook and Hahn's findings. Unfortunately, the estimates of β are not very precise: typically the two-standard-error confidence interval ranges from less than 0 to above 0.5. Thus, although Romer and Romer's results are consistent with the information-revelation explanation of policy actions' impact on long-term interest rates, they do not provide decisive evidence for it.

10.4   The Dynamic Inconsistency of Low-Inflation Monetary Policy

Our analysis thus far suggests that money growth is the key determinant of inflation. Thus to understand what causes high inflation, we need to understand what causes high money growth. For the major industrialized countries, where government revenue from money creation does not appear important, the leading candidate is the existence of a perceived output-inflation tradeoff. If policymakers believe that aggregate demand movements affect real output, they may increase the money supply to try to push output above its normal level. Or, if they are faced with inflation that they believe is too high, they may be reluctant to undergo a recession to reduce it.

Any theory of how an output-inflation tradeoff can lead to inflation must confront the fact that there is no tradeoff in the long run. Since average inflation has no effect on average output, it might seem that the existence of a short-run tradeoff is irrelevant to the determination of average infla-tion. Consider, for example, two monetary policies that differ only because money growth is lower by a constant amount in every situation under one policy than the other. If the public is aware of the difference, there is no reason for output to behave differently under the low-inflation policy than under the high-inflation one.

In a famous paper, however, Kydland and Prescott (1977) show that the inability of policymakers to commit themselves to such a low-inflation pol-icy can give rise to excessive inflation despite the absence of a long-run tradeoff (see also Barro and Gordon, 1983a). Kydland and Prescott's basic observation is that if expected inflation is low, so that the marginal cost of additional inflation is low, policymakers will pursue expansionary policies to push output temporarily above its normal level. But the public's knowl-edge that policymakers have this incentive means that they will not in fact expect low inflation. The end result is that policymakers' ability to pursue discretionary policy results in inflation without any increase in output. This section presents a simple model that formalizes this idea.

Assumptions

Kydland and Prescott consider an economy where aggregate demand dis-turbances have real effects and expectations concerning inflation affect ag-gregate supply. We can capture both of these effects by assuming that ag-gregate supply is given by the Lucas supply curve (see equations [5.38] and [6.21]):

$$y = \bar{y} + b(\pi - \pi^e), \qquad b > 0, \tag{10.10}$$

where y is the log of output and $\bar{y}$ is the log of its flexible-price level.[6] Kydland and Prescott assume that the flexible-price level of output is less than the socially optimal level. This could arise from positive marginal tax rates (so that individuals do not capture the full benefits of additional labor supply) or from imperfect competition (so that firms do not capture the full benefits of additional output). In addition, they assume that inflation above some level is costly, and that the marginal cost of inflation increases as inflation rises. A simple way to capture these assumptions is to make social welfare quadratic in both output and inflation. Thus the policymaker minimizes

$$L = \tfrac{1}{2}(y - y^*)^2 + \tfrac{1}{2}a(\pi - \pi^*)^2, \qquad y^* > \bar{y}, \qquad a > 0. \tag{10.11}$$

---

[6] The assumption that only unexpected inflation matters is not essential. For example, a model along the lines of equation (5.39), in Section 5.4, where core inflation is given by a weighted average of past inflation and expected inflation, has similar implications.

The parameter a reflects the relative importance of output and inflation in social welfare.[7]

Finally, the policymaker controls money growth, which determines the behavior of aggregate demand. Since there is no uncertainty, we can think of the policymaker as choosing inflation directly, subject to the constraint that inflation and output are related by the aggregate supply curve, (10.10).

Analyzing the Model

To see the model's implications, consider two ways that monetary policy and expected inflation could be determined. In the first, the policymaker makes a binding commitment about what inflation will be before expected inflation is determined. Since the commitment is binding, expected inflation equals actual inflation, and so (by [10.10]) output equals its natural rate. Thus the policymaker's problem is to choose π to minimize $(\bar{y} - y^*)^2/2 + a(\pi - \pi^*)^2/2$. The solution is simply $\pi = \pi^*$.

In the second situation, the policymaker chooses inflation taking expectations of inflation as given. This could occur either if expected inflation is determined before money growth is, or if π and π^e are determined simultaneously. Substituting (10.10) into (10.11) implies that the policymaker's problem is

$$\min_{\pi} \tfrac{1}{2}[\bar{y} + b(\pi - \pi^e) - y^*]^2 + \tfrac{1}{2}a(\pi - \pi^*)^2. \tag{10.12}$$

The first-order condition is

$$[\bar{y} + b(\pi - \pi^e) - y^*]b + a(\pi - \pi^*) = 0. \tag{10.13}$$

Solving (10.13) for π yields

$$\pi = \frac{b^2\pi^e + a\pi^* + b(y^* - \bar{y})}{a + b^2}$$

$$= \pi^* + \frac{b}{a + b^2}(y^* - \bar{y}) + \frac{b^2}{a + b^2}(\pi^e - \pi^*). \tag{10.14}$$

Figure 10.4 plots the policymaker's choice of π as a function of π^e. The relationship is upward sloping with a slope less than 1. The figure and

---

[7] Equation (10.9) is intended to reflect not just the policymaker's preferences, but also the representative individual's. The reason that the decentralized equilibrium with flexible prices does not achieve the first-best level of output is that (because of the taxes or imperfect competition) there are positive externalities from higher output. That is, neglecting inflation for the moment, we can think of the representative individual's welfare as depending on his or her own output (or labor supply), y_i, and average economy-wide output, y: $U_i = V(y_i, y)$. The assumption underlying (10.11) is that $\bar{y}$ is the Nash equilibrium (so $V_1(\bar{y}, \bar{y}) = 0$ and $V_{11}(\bar{y}, \bar{y}) < 0$, where subscripts denote partial derivatives), but is less than the social optimum (so $V_2(\bar{y}, \bar{y}) > 0$).

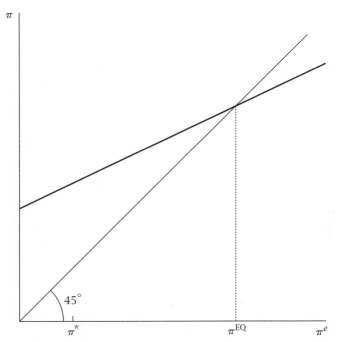

FIGURE 10.4   The determination of inflation in the absence of commitment

equation (10.14) show the policymaker's incentive to pursue expansionary policy. If the public expects the policymaker to choose the optimal rate of inflation, π^*, then the marginal cost of slightly higher inflation is zero, and the marginal benefit of the resulting higher output is positive. Thus in this situation the policymaker chooses an inflation rate greater than π^*.

Since there is no uncertainty, equilibrium requires that expected and actual inflation are equal. As Figure 10.4 shows, there is a unique inflation rate for which this is true. If we impose $\pi = \pi^e$ in (10.14) and then solve for this inflation rate, we obtain

$$\pi^e = \pi^* + \frac{b}{a}(y^* - \overline{y})$$

$$\equiv \pi^{\text{EQ}}.$$

(10.15)

If expected inflation exceeds this level, then actual inflation is less than individuals expect, and thus the economy is not in equilibrium. Similarly, if π^e is less than π^{EQ}, then π exceeds π^e.

Thus the only equilibrium is for π and π^e to equal π^{EQ}, and for y to therefore equal $\overline{y}$. Intuitively, expected inflation rises to the point where the policymaker, taking π^e as given, chooses to set π equal to π^e. In short, all that the policymaker's discretion does is to increase inflation without affecting output.[8]

Discussion

The reason that the ability to choose inflation after expected inflation is determined makes the policymaker worse off is that the policy of announcing that inflation will be π^*, and then producing that inflation rate after expected inflation is determined, is not *dynamically consistent* (equivalently, it is not *subgame-perfect*). If the policymaker announces that inflation will equal π^* and the public forms its expectations accordingly, the policymaker will deviate from the policy once expectations are formed. The public's knowledge that the policymaker will do this causes it to expect inflation greater than π^*; this expected inflation worsens the menu of choices that the policymaker faces.

To see that it is the knowledge that the policymaker has discretion, rather than the discretion itself, that is the source of the problem, consider what happens if the public believes the policymaker can commit but he or she in fact has discretion. In this case, the policymaker can announce that inflation will equal π^* and thereby cause expected inflation to equal π^*. But the policymaker can then set inflation according to (10.14). Since (10.14) is the solution to the problem of minimizing the social loss function given expected inflation, this "reneging" on the commitment raises social welfare.[9]

Dynamic inconsistency arises in many other situations. Policymakers choosing how to tax capital may want to encourage capital accumulation by adopting a low tax rate. Once the capital has been accumulated, however, taxing it is nondistortionary; thus it is optimal for policymakers to tax it at high rates. As a result, the low tax rate is not dynamically consistent.[10] To give another example, policymakers who want individuals to obey a law may want to promise that violators will be punished harshly. Once individuals have decided whether to comply, however, there is no benefit to punishing violators. Thus again the optimal policy is not dynamically consistent.

---

[8] None of these results depend on the use of specific functional forms. With general functional forms, the equilibrium is for expected and actual inflation to rise to the point where the marginal cost of inflation just balances its marginal benefit through higher output. Thus output equals its natural rate and inflation is above the optimal level. The equilibrium if the policymaker can make a binding commitment is still for inflation to equal its optimal level and output to equal its natural rate.

[9] In fact, the policymaker can do even better by announcing that inflation will equal $\pi^* - (y^* - \bar{y})/b$ and then setting $\pi = \pi^*$; this yields $y = y^*$ and $\pi = \pi^*$.

[10] A corollary of this observation is that low-inflation policy can be dynamically inconsistent not because of an output-inflation tradeoff, but because of government debt. Since government debt is denominated in nominal terms, unanticipated inflation is a lump-sum tax on debt holders. As a result, even if monetary shocks do not have real effects, a policy of setting $\pi = \pi^*$ is not dynamically consistent as long as the government has nominally denominated debt (Calvo, 1978b).

10.5   Addressing the Dynamic-Inconsistency Problem

Kydland and Prescott's analysis shows that discretionary monetary policy can give rise to inefficiently high inflation. This naturally raises the question of what can be done to avoid, or at least mitigate, this possibility.

One approach, of course, is to have monetary policy determined by rules rather than discretion. It is important to emphasize, however, that the rules must be binding. Suppose the policymaker just announces that he or she is going to determine monetary policy according to some procedure, such as pegging the exchange rate or making the money stock grow at a constant rate. If the public believes this announcement and therefore expects low inflation, the policymaker can raise social welfare by departing from the announced policy and choosing a higher rate of money growth. Thus the public will not believe the announcement. Only if the monetary authority relinquishes the ability to determine the money supply does a rule solve the problem.

There are two problems, however, with using binding rules to overcome the dynamic-inconsistency problem. One is normative, the other positive. The normative problem is that rules cannot account for completely unexpected circumstances. There is no difficulty in constructing a rule that makes money growth respond to normal economic developments (such as changes in unemployment and movements in indexes of leading indicators). But sometimes there are events that could not plausibly have been expected. In the 1980s, for example, the United States experienced a major stock market crash that caused a severe liquidity crisis, a "capital crunch" that may have significantly affected banks' lending, and a collapse of the relationships between economic activity and many standard measures of the money stock. It is almost inconceivable that a binding rule would have anticipated all these possibilities.

The positive problem with binding rules as the solution to the dynamic-inconsistency problem is that we observe low rates of inflation in many situations (such as the United States in the 1950s and in recent years, and Germany over most of the postwar period) where policy is not made according to fixed rules. Thus there must be ways of alleviating the dynamic-inconsistency problem that do not involve binding commitments.

Because of considerations like these, there has been considerable interest in other ways of dealing with dynamic inconsistency. The two approaches that have received the most attention are reputation and delegation.[11]

---

[11] Two other possibilities are punishment equilibria and incentive contracts. Punishment equilibria (which are often described as models of reputation, but which differ fundamentally from the models considered below) arise in infinite-horizon models. These models typically have multiple equilibria, including ones where inflation stays below the one-time discretionary level (that is, below π^{EQ}). Low inflation is sustained by beliefs that if the policymaker were to choose high inflation, the public would "punish" him or her by expecting

A Model of Reputation

Reputation can be used to address the dynamic-inconsistency problem if policymakers are in office for more than one period and the public is unsure of their characteristics. For example, the public may not know policymakers' preferences between output and inflation or their beliefs about the output-inflation tradeoff, or whether their announcements about future policy are binding. In such situations, policymakers' behavior conveys information about their characteristics, and thus affects the public's expectations of inflation in subsequent periods. Since policymakers face a more favorable menu of output-inflation choices when expected inflation is lower, this gives them an incentive to pursue low-inflation policies.

To see this formally, consider the following model, which is based on Backus and Driffill (1985) and Barro (1986). Policymakers are in office for two periods, and the output-inflation relationship is given by (10.10) each period; thus $y_t = \bar{y} + b(\pi_t - \pi_t^e)$. It simplifies the algebra to assume that social welfare is linear rather than quadratic in output, and that π^* is 0. Thus social welfare in period t is

$$
\begin{aligned}
w_t &= y_t - \bar{y} - \tfrac{1}{2}a\pi_t^2 \\
&= b(\pi_t - \pi_t^e) - \tfrac{1}{2}a\pi_t^2.
\end{aligned}
\tag{10.16}
$$

There are two possible types of policymaker; the public does not know in advance which type it is dealing with. A type-1 policymaker, which occurs with probability p, shares the public's preferences concerning output and inflation. He or she therefore maximizes

$$
W = w_1 + \beta w_2, \qquad 0 < \beta \le 1, \tag{10.17}
$$

where β reflects the importance of the second period in social welfare. A type-2 policymaker, which occurs with probability $1 - p$, cares only about inflation and therefore sets inflation to 0 in both periods.[12]

Analyzing the Model

Since a type-2 policymaker always sets inflation to 0, we focus on the behavior of a type-1 policymaker. In the second period, he or she takes π_2^e

---

high inflation in subsequent periods; the punishments are structured so that the expectations of high inflation would in fact be rational if that situation ever arose. See, for example, Barro and Gordon (1983b); Rogoff (1987); and Problems 10.8–10.10. Incentive contracts are arrangements in which the central banker is penalized (either financially or through loss of prestige) for inflation. In simple models, the appropriate choice of penalties produces the optimal policy (Persson and Tabellini, 1993; Walsh, 1995). The empirical relevance of such contracts is not clear, however.

[12] The key assumption is that the two types have different preferences, not that one type always chooses zero inflation.

as given, and therefore chooses π_2 to maximize $b(\pi_2 - \pi_2^e) - a\pi_2^2/2$. The solution is $\pi_2 = b/a$.

The policymaker's first-period problem is more complicated, because his or her choice of inflation affects expected inflation in the second period. If the policymaker chooses any value of π_1 other than 0, the public learns that it is facing a type-1 policymaker, and therefore expects inflation of b/a in the second period. Conditional on π_1 not equaling 0, the choice of π_1 has no effect on π_2^e. Thus if the policymaker chooses a nonzero first-period inflation rate, he or she chooses it to maximize $b(\pi_1 - \pi_1^e) - a\pi_1^2/2$, and therefore sets $\pi_1 = b/a$. Both π_2^e and π_2 are then equal to b/a, and y_2 equals $\bar{y}$. The value of the objective function for the two periods in this case is thus

$$W_{\text{INF}} = \left[b\left(\frac{b}{a} - \pi_1^e\right) - \frac{1}{2}a\left(\frac{b}{a}\right)^2 \right] - \beta\frac{1}{2}a\left(\frac{b}{a}\right)^2$$

$$= \frac{b^2}{a}\frac{1}{2}(1 - \beta) - b\pi_1^e. \tag{10.18}$$

The type-1 policymaker's other possibility is to set π_1 to 0. It turns out that in equilibrium, he or she may randomize between $\pi_1 = b/a$ and $\pi_1 = 0$. Thus, let q denote the probability that the type-1 policymaker chooses $\pi_1 = 0$. Now consider the public's inference problem if it observes zero inflation. It knows that this means either that the policymaker is a type 2 (which occurs with probability $1 - p$), or that the policymaker is a type 1 but chose zero inflation (which occurs with probability pq). Thus, by Bayes's law, its estimate of the probability that the policymaker is a type 1 is $qp/[(1-p)+qp]$. Its expectation of π_2 is therefore $\{qp/[(1-p)+qp]\}(b/a)$, which is less than b/a.

This analysis implies that the value of the objective function when the policymaker chooses $\pi_1 = 0$ is

$$W_0(q) = b(-\pi_1^e) + \beta\left\{ b\left[\frac{b}{a} - \frac{qp}{(1-p)+qp}\frac{b}{a} \right] - \frac{1}{2}a\left(\frac{b}{a}\right)^2 \right\}.$$

$$= \frac{b^2}{a}\beta\left[\frac{1}{2} - \frac{qp}{(1-p)+qp} \right] - b\pi_1^e. \tag{10.19}$$

Note that $W_0(q)$ is decreasing in q, the probability that the type-1 policy-maker chooses zero inflation in the first period: a higher q implies a higher value of π_2^e if $\pi_1 = 0$, and thus a smaller value to the policymaker of choosing $\pi_1 = 0$.

The equilibrium of the model can take three possible forms. The first possibility occurs if $W_0(0)$ is less than W_{INF}. In this case, even if the type-1 policymaker can cause the public to be certain that it is facing a type-2 policymaker by setting $\pi_1 = 0$, he or she will not want to do so. Thus in this case the type-1 policymaker always chooses $\pi_1 = b/a$. Equations (10.18) and (10.19) imply that $W_0(0)$ is less than W_{INF} when

$$\frac{b^2}{a}\beta\frac{1}{2} - b\pi_1^e < \frac{b^2}{a}\frac{1}{2}(1 - \beta) - b\pi_1^e, \tag{10.20}$$

or simply

$$\beta < \tfrac{1}{2}. \tag{10.21}$$

Thus if the weight on the second period is sufficiently small, the public's uncertainty about the policymaker's type has no effects.

The second possibility arises when $W_0(1)$ is greater than W_{INF}. In this situation, the type-1 policymaker always chooses $\pi_1 = 0$: even if the public learns nothing about the policymaker's type from observing $\pi_1 = 0$, the cost of revealing that he or she is a type 1 is enough to dissuade the policymaker from choosing positive inflation. Equations (10.18) and (10.19) imply that $W_0(1)$ exceeds W_{INF} when

$$\frac{b^2}{a}\beta\left(\frac{1}{2} - p\right) - b\pi_1^e > \frac{b^2}{a}\frac{1}{2}(1 - \beta) - b\pi_1^e. \tag{10.22}$$

This condition simplifies to

$$\beta > \frac{1}{2}\frac{1}{1 - p}. \tag{10.23}$$

The final possibility arises when $W_0(0) > W_{\text{INF}} > W_0(1)$; the preceding analysis implies that this occurs when $\frac{1}{2} < \beta < \frac{1}{2}[1/(1 - p)]$. In this case, type-1 policymakers would choose zero first-period inflation if the public believes they would choose positive inflation, and would choose positive inflation if the public believes they would choose zero inflation. As a result, the economy can be in equilibrium only if the type-1 policymakers sometimes choose positive inflation and sometimes choose zero inflation. Specifically, q must adjust to the point where the type-1 policymakers are indifferent between $\pi_1 = 0$ and $\pi_1 = b/a$. Equating (10.18) and (10.19) and solving for q shows that this requires

$$q = \frac{1 - p}{p}(2\beta - 1) \quad \text{if} \quad \frac{1}{2} < \beta < \frac{1}{2}\frac{1}{1 - p}. \tag{10.24}$$

Discussion

Although this model is highly stylized, the basic idea is simple. The public is unsure about what policies the government will follow in future periods. Under plausible assumptions, the lower the inflation it observes today, the lower its expectations of inflation in future periods. This gives policymakers an incentive to keep inflation low. Because of the simplicity of the central idea, the basic result that uncertainty about policymakers' characteristics reduces inflation is highly robust (see, for example, Vickers, 1986; Cukierman and Meltzer, 1986; Rogoff, 1987; and Problem 10.11).

This analysis implies that the impact of reputation considerations on inflation is greater when policymakers place more weight on future periods. Specifically, q—the probability that a type-1 policymaker chooses $\pi_1 = 0$—is increasing in β for $\frac{1}{2} < \beta < \frac{1}{2}[1/(1-p)]$, and is independent of β elsewhere. Similarly, one can show that the impact of the reputation considerations is greater when there are more periods.

The model also implies that the impact on inflation is greater when there is greater uncertainty about policymakers' characteristics. To see this, consider, for simplicity, the case of $\beta = 1$. If the policymaker's type is publicly observed, the type 1's always set $\pi_1 = b/a$ and the type 2's always set $\pi_1 = 0$. Under imperfect information, however, the type 1's set $\pi_1 = 0$ with probability q. Thus the uncertainty lowers average first-period inflation by $pq(b/a)$. With $\beta = 1$, (10.23) implies that $q = 1$ when $p < \frac{1}{2}$; thus for these values of p, the reduction in average first-period inflation is pb/a. And (10.24) implies that $q = (1 - p)/p$ when $p > \frac{1}{2}$; thus for these values, the reduction is $(1 - p)b/a$. The maximum reduction thus occurs at $p = \frac{1}{2}$, and equals $b/(2a)$. In short, the impact of the reputation considerations is greater when the difference between the two types' preferred inflation rates is larger (that is, when b/a is larger) and when there is greater uncertainty about the policymaker's type (that is, when p is closer to $\frac{1}{2}$).[13]

The idea that reputation considerations cause policymakers to pursue less expansionary policies seems not only theoretically robust, but also realistic. Central bankers appear to be very concerned with establishing reputations as being tough on inflation and as being credible. If the public were certain of policymakers' preferences and beliefs, there would be no reason for this. Only if the public is uncertain and if expectations matter is this concern appropriate.

Delegation

A second way to overcome the dynamic inconsistency of low-inflation monetary policy is to delegate policy to individuals who do not share the public's view about the relative importance of output and inflation. The idea, due to Rogoff (1985), is simple: inflation—and hence expected inflation—is lower when monetary policy is controlled by someone who is known to be especially averse to inflation.

To see how delegation can address the dynamic-inconsistency problem, suppose that the output-inflation relationship and social welfare are given by (10.10) and (10.11); thus $y = \bar{y} + b(\pi - \pi^e)$ and $L = [(y - y^*)^2/2] + [a(\pi - \pi^*)^2/2]$. Suppose, however, that monetary policy is determined by an individual whose objective function is

$$L' = \frac{1}{2}(y - y^*)^2 + \frac{1}{2}a'(\pi - \pi^*)^2, \qquad y^* > \bar{y}, \qquad a' > 0. \qquad (10.25)$$

---

[13] For a general value of $\beta > \frac{1}{2}$, one can show that the maximum effect occurs at $p = (2\beta - 1)/(2\beta)$, and equals $[(2\beta - 1)/(2\beta)](b/a)$. For $\beta < \frac{1}{2}$, there is no effect.

a' may differ from a, the weight that society as a whole places on inflation. Solving the policymaker's maximization problem along the lines of (10.12) implies that his or her choice of π, given π^e, is given by (10.14) with a' in place of a. Thus,

$$\pi = \pi^* + \frac{b}{a' + b^2}(y^* - \overline{y}) + \frac{b^2}{a' + b^2}(\pi^e - \pi^*). \qquad (10.26)$$

Figure 10.5 shows the effects of delegating policy to an individual with a value of a' greater than a. Because the policymaker puts more weight on inflation than before, he or she chooses a lower value of inflation for a given level of expected inflation (at least over the range where $\pi^e \geq \pi^*$); in addition, his or her response function is flatter.

As before, the public knows how inflation is determined. Thus equilibrium again requires that expected and actual inflation are equal. As a result, when we solve for expected inflation, we find that it is given by (10.15) with a' in place of a:

$$\pi^{EQ} = \pi^* + \frac{b}{a'}(y^* - \overline{y}). \qquad (10.27)$$

The equilibrium is for both actual and expected inflation to be given by (10.27), and for output to equal its natural rate.

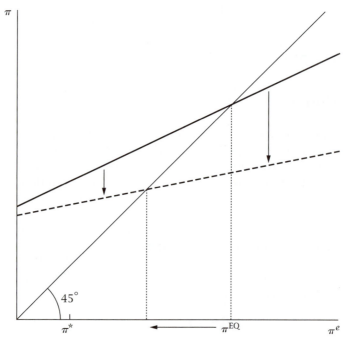

FIGURE 10.5   The effect of delegation to a conservative policymaker on equilibrium inflation

Now consider social welfare, which is higher the lower is $(y - y^*)^2/2 +$ $a(\pi - \pi^*)^2/2$. Output is equal to $\overline{y}$ regardless of a'. But the higher a' is, the closer π is to π^*. Thus the higher a' is, the higher social welfare is. Intuitively, when monetary policy is controlled by someone who cares strongly about inflation, the public realizes that the policymaker has little desire to pursue expansionary policy; the result is that expected inflation is low.

Rogoff extends this analysis to the case where the economy is affected by shocks. Under plausible assumptions, a policymaker whose preferences between output and inflation differ from society's does not respond optimally to shocks. Thus in choosing whom to delegate monetary policy to, there is a tradeoff: choosing someone with a stronger dislike of inflation produces a better performance in terms of average inflation, but a worse one in terms of responses to disturbances. As a result, there is some optimal level of "conservatism" for central bankers.[14]

Again, the idea that societies can address the dynamic-inconsistency problem by letting individuals who particularly dislike inflation control monetary policy appears realistic. In many countries, monetary policy is determined by independent central banks rather than by the central government. And the central government often seeks out individuals who are known to be particularly averse to inflation to run those banks. The result is that those who control monetary policy are often known for being more concerned about inflation than society as a whole, and only rarely for being less concerned.

Empirical Application: Central-Bank Independence and Inflation

Theories that attribute inflation to the dynamic inconsistency of low-inflation monetary policy are difficult to test. The theories suggest that inflation is related to such variables as the costs of inflation, policymakers' ability to commit, their ability to establish reputations, and the extent to which policy is delegated to individuals who particularly dislike inflation. All of these are hard to measure.

One variable that has received considerable attention is the independence of the central bank. Alesina (1988) argues that central-bank independence provides a measure of the delegation of policymaking to conservative policymakers. Intuitively, the greater the independence of the central bank, the greater the government's ability to delegate policy to individuals who especially dislike inflation. Empirically, central-bank independence is generally measured by qualitative indexes based on such factors as how its governor and board are appointed and dismissed, whether there are

---

[14] This idea is developed in Problem 10.12.

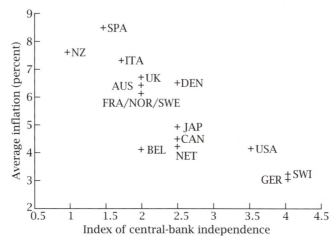

FIGURE 10.6 Central-bank independence and inflation[15]

government representatives on the board, and the government's ability to veto or directly control the bank's decisions.

Investigations of the relation between these measures of independence and inflation find that among industrialized countries, independence and inflation are strongly negatively related (Alesina, 1988; Grilli, Masciandaro, and Tabellini, 1991; Cukierman, Webb, and Neyapti, 1992). Figure 10.6 is representative of the results.

There are three limitations to this finding, however. First, it is not clear that theories of dynamic inconsistency and delegation predict that greater central-bank independence will produce lower inflation. The argument that they do predict this implicitly assumes that both central bankers' and government policymakers' preferences do not vary systematically with central-bank independence. But the delegation hypothesis implies that they will. Suppose, for example, that monetary policy depends on the central bank's and the government's preferences, with the weight on the bank's preferences increasing in its independence. Then when the bank is less independent, government officials should compensate by appointing more inflation-averse individuals to the bank. Similarly, when the government is less able to delegate policy to the bank, voters should elect more inflation-averse governments. These effects will mitigate, and might even offset, the effects of reduced central-bank independence.

Second, the fact that there is a negative relation between central-bank independence and inflation does not mean that the independence is the

---

[15] Figure 10.6, from "Central Bank Independence and Macroeconomic Performance" by Alberto Alesina and Lawrence H. Summers, *Journal of Money, Credit, and Banking*, Vol. 25, No. 2 (May 1993), is reprinted by permission. Copyright 1993 by the Ohio State University Press. All rights reserved.

source of the low inflation. As Posen (1993) observes, countries whose citizens are particularly averse to inflation are likely to try to insulate their
central banks from political pressure. For example, it is widely believed
that Germans especially dislike inflation, perhaps because of the hyperinflation that Germany experienced after World War I. And the institutions
governing Germany's central bank appear to have been created largely because of this desire to avoid inflation. Thus some of Germany's low inflation
is almost surely the result of the general aversion to inflation, rather than
of the independence of its central bank.

Third, even if independence is the source of the low inflation, the mechanism linking the two may not involve dynamic inconsistency. As we will
see shortly, there are other possibilities.[16]

Limitations of Dynamic-Inconsistency Theories of Inflation

Theories based on dynamic inconsistency provide a simple and appealing
explanation of inflation. Unfortunately, it is not clear that their explanation
is important to actual inflation, particularly for the industrialized countries.
There are two problems. First, the importance of forward-looking expectations to aggregate supply, which is central to the dynamic-inconsistency
explanation, is not well established. For example, Canada and New Zealand
took strong measures in the 1990s to make credible commitments to low-
inflation monetary policies. New Zealand, for instance, modified the central
bank's charter to make price stability the sole objective of policy and to
provide for the dismissal of the bank's governor if inflation falls outside
a target range. Yet, contrary to the predictions of dynamic-inconsistency
models, these measures do not appear to have had a major impact on the
output-inflation relationship in these countries (Debelle, 1996). Similarly,
Fuhrer (1997) fails to find any evidence that forward-looking expectations
are important to the behavior of U.S. inflation.

Second, dynamic-inconsistency theories have difficulty accounting for
the time-series variation in inflation. At least in industrialized countries,
high inflation was mainly a phenomenon of the 1970s, not a general characteristic of monetary policy. Yet dynamic-inconsistency theories imply
that high inflation is the result of optimizing behavior by the relevant players given the institutions; thus the theories predict that in the absence of
changes to those institutions, high inflation will remain. This is not what
we observe. In the United States, for example, policymakers were able to

---

[16] In addition, there is no clear relationship between legal measures of central-bank
independence and average inflation among nonindustrialized countries (Cukierman, Webb,
and Neyapti, 1992). Further, the usual measures of independence appear to be biased in
favor of finding a link between independence and low inflation. For example, the measures
put some weight on whether the bank's charter gives low inflation as its principal goal
(Pollard, 1993).

reduce inflation from about 10 percent at the end of the 1970s to under 5 percent just a few years later, and to maintain the lower inflation, without any significant changes in the institutions or rules governing policy. Similarly, in countries such as New Zealand and the United Kingdom, reforms to increase central-bank independence followed rather than preceded major reductions in inflation. Indeed, if one is not willing to interpret the correlation between central-bank independence and inflation as reflecting the effects of dynamic inconsistency and delegation, it is hard to identify any important part of either the time-series or cross-sectional variations in inflation in the industrialized countries that is due to dynamic-inconsistency considerations.

An alternative explanation of the inflation of the 1970s is that it resulted from a belief on the part of many policymakers that there was (or might be) a permanent output-inflation tradeoff (De Long, 1997; Mayer, 1999; Sargent, 1999). In the 1960s and 1970s, many economists and policymakers thought that there was a long-run tradeoff, and that the costs of inflation were low. They therefore believed that the expected benefits of moderate inflation exceeded the costs. Samuelson and Solow (1960), for example, described a downward-sloping Phillips curve as showing "the menu of choices between different degrees of unemployment and price stability," and went on to conclude, "To achieve the nonperfectionist's goal of high enough output to give us no more than 3 percent unemployment, the price index might have to rise by as much as 4 to 5 percent per year."

This view provides an alternative explanation of the link between central-bank independence and low inflation. Individuals who specialize in monetary policy are likely to be more knowledgeable about its effects. They are therefore likely to have more accurate estimates of the benefits and costs of expansionary policy. If incomplete knowledge of those costs and benefits leads to inflationary bias, increasing specialists' role in determining policy is likely to reduce that bias.[17]

10.6 What Can Policy Accomplish?

The discussion in the previous two sections makes it appear that monetary policymakers face a single problem: they must find a way of getting inflation to its optimal level. Actual policymaking is much more complicated. There are two issues. First, it is not clear what the optimal rate of inflation is; this

---

[17] This discussion suggests a possible explanation of the lack of stabilization of the U.S. economy in the decades after World War II and its remarkable stability since the mid-1980s. When policymakers were unsure of the correct model of the economy and the costs of inflation, they repeatedly pursued policies that caused inflation to rise, then induced recessions to reduce it. With the triumph of the natural-rate hypothesis and the emergence of a consensus among policymakers that inflation should be kept low, this boom-bust cycle disappeared (C. Romer, 1999).

issue is addressed in Section 10.9. Second, various disturbances are continually affecting the economy. This section and the next address some of the issues raised by the presence of these shocks. This section examines the question of how much weight policymakers should put on stabilizing output as opposed to other objectives, such as keeping inflation low and predictable. The next section discusses more practical issues concerning the conduct of policy.

A Baseline Case

To address the issue of what monetary policy should aim to accomplish, it is useful to begin with a simple case. Suppose that aggregate supply relates the change in inflation linearly to the departure of the unemployment rate from the natural rate, and that it has no forward-looking element (see equations [5.36]–[5.37]):

$$\pi_t = \pi_{t-1} - \alpha(u_t - \overline{u}) + \varepsilon_t^S, \qquad \alpha > 0, \tag{10.28}$$

where ε_t^S represents supply shocks. In addition, suppose that social welfare depends on unemployment and inflation, and that the dependence on unemployment is linear:

$$W_t = -cu_t - f(\pi_t), \qquad c > 0, \qquad f''(\bullet) > 0. \tag{10.29}$$

This simple model has strong implications for policy. First, the aggregate supply curve, (10.28), implies that policy has no impact on average unemployment unless policymakers are willing to accept ever-increasing (or ever-decreasing) inflation. Equation (10.28) implies that the average change in inflation is determined by average unemployment and average supply shocks. Thus altering average unemployment alters the average change in inflation. But if the average change in inflation is anything other than zero, the level of inflation grows (or falls) without bound.[18]

This result, coupled with the assumption that social welfare is linear in unemployment, implies that policy should put essentially no weight on unemployment. Suppose that policymakers' discount rate is zero, and consider the first-order condition for π_t.[19] The aggregate supply curve, (10.28), implies that raising π_t by a small amount $d\pi$ is associated with a decrease in u_t of $d\pi/\alpha$. Thus the increase changes social welfare by $-f'(\pi)\,d\pi$ through its direct effect, and by $c\,d\pi/\alpha$ through its effect on unemployment. In addition, the increase in current inflation means (for given next-period inflation) higher unemployment next period; this contributes $-c\,d\pi/\alpha$ to social

---

[18] In addition, as described in Chapter 5, if policymakers allow inflation to grow without bound, the aggregate supply curve (10.28) will almost surely break down. This is not relevant to the point made here, however.

[19] We are assuming that policymakers can control inflation perfectly, subject to (10.28).

welfare. Thus the first-order condition for π_t is simply $f'(\pi_t) = 0$: policymakers should keep inflation at its optimal level and pay no attention to unemployment. This is true regardless of the importance of unemployment (that is, regardless of c) and regardless of what supply shocks are buffeting the economy. Intuitively, any change in the path of inflation that does not permanently raise inflation can only rearrange the timing of unemployment, which has no effect on welfare. And with a discount rate of zero, any policy that permanently raises inflation above the optimal level has infinite costs regardless of how small inflation's costs are.

With discounting, one can show that the first-order condition for π_t is

$$\frac{1+\rho}{\rho}f'(\pi_t) = \frac{c}{\alpha}, \tag{10.30}$$

where ρ is policymakers' discount rate.[20] Thus inflation should be set at the level where the cost of a permanent increase in inflation just balances the benefit of the associated one-time decrease in unemployment. Even with discounting, there is little scope for stabilization policy: because the first-order condition does not depend on π_{t-1} or ε_t^S, the optimal policy is to go directly to the inflation rate that satisfies (10.30) regardless of the current state of the economy. If policymakers respond to high inflation by creating an extended recession that brings inflation down to the level satisfying (10.30) only slowly, the total amount of unemployment is no different than it would have been if they had reduced inflation all at once. Thus they have subjected the economy to an extended period of above-normal inflation for no benefit.

This baseline case implies that policymakers should not attempt to stabilize unemployment in the face of supply shocks. It also implies that the benefits of using policy to offset aggregate demand shocks come only from reducing the variability of inflation. The linearity of aggregate supply implies that if policymakers allow demand shocks to cause fluctuations in unemployment and inflation, average unemployment is unaffected; and the linearity of social welfare implies that fluctuations in unemployment do not affect welfare. Thus the only costs of the fluctuations come from the costs of the variation in inflation. If inflation variability has low costs over the relevant range, policymakers should attach little importance to offsetting demand shocks.

Is There a Case for Stabilization Policy?

The key assumptions behind these results are the linearity of the social welfare function, (10.29), and of the aggregate supply curve, (10.28). Thus

---

[20] That is, policymakers maximize $\sum_{t=0}^{\infty}(1+\rho)^{-t}W_t$.

for there to be a substantial benefit to stabilization policy, one of these functions must be significantly nonlinear.[21]

Consider first social welfare. Lucas (1987) shows that in a representative-agent setting, the potential welfare gain from stabilizing consumption around its mean is small. That is, he suggests that social welfare is not sufficiently nonlinear in output for there to be a significant gain from stabilization. His argument is straightforward. Suppose utility takes the constant-relative-risk-aversion form,

$$U(C) = \frac{C^{1-\theta}}{1-\theta}, \qquad \theta > 0, \tag{10.31}$$

where θ is the coefficient of relative risk aversion (see Section 2.1). Since $U''(C) = -\theta C^{-\theta-1}$, a second-order Taylor expansion of $U(\bullet)$ around the mean of consumption implies

$$E[U(C)] \simeq \frac{\overline{C}^{1-\theta}}{1-\theta} - \frac{\theta}{2}\overline{C}^{-\theta-1}\sigma_C^2, \tag{10.32}$$

where $\overline{C}$ and σ_C^2 are the mean and variance of consumption. Thus eliminating consumption variability would raise expected utility by approximately $(\theta/2)\overline{C}^{-\theta-1}\sigma_C^2$. Similarly, doubling consumption variability would lower welfare by approximately that amount.

To translate this into units that can be interpreted, note that the marginal utility of consumption at $\overline{C}$ is $\overline{C}^{-\theta}$. Thus setting σ_C^2 to 0 would raise expected utility by approximately as much as would raising average consumption by $(\theta/2)\overline{C}^{-\theta-1}\sigma_C^2/\overline{C}^{-\theta} = (\theta/2)\overline{C}^{-1}\sigma_C^2$. As a fraction of average consumption, this equals $(\theta/2)\overline{C}^{-1}\sigma_C^2/\overline{C}$, or $(\theta/2)(\sigma_C/\overline{C})^2$.

Lucas argues that a generous estimate of the standard deviation of consumption due to short-run fluctuations is 1.5 percent of its mean, and that a generous estimate of the coefficient of relative risk aversion is 5. Thus, he concludes, an optimistic figure for the maximum possible welfare gain from more successful stabilization policy is equivalent to $(5/2)(0.015)^2$, or 0.06 percent, of average consumption—a very small amount.

At first glance, it appears that Lucas's conclusion rests critically on his assumption that there is a representative agent. Actual recessions do not reduce everyone's consumption by a small amount, but reduce the consumption of a small fraction of the population by a large amount; thus their welfare costs are larger than they would be in a representative-agent setting. Atkeson and Phelan (1994) show, however, that accounting for the dispersion of consumption decreases rather than increases the potential gain from stabilization. Indeed, their analysis suggests a basis for the linear social welfare function, (10.29), where there is no gain at all from

---

[21] For demand shocks, this assumes that the cost of moderate inflation variability is low.

stabilizing unemployment. Suppose that individuals have one level of consumption, C_E, when they are employed, and another level, C_U, when they are unemployed, and suppose that C_E and C_U do not depend on the state of the economy. Since u is the fraction of individuals who are unemployed, average utility from consumption is $uU(C_U) + (1-u)U(C_E)$. Thus expected social welfare from consumption is $E[u]U(C_U) + (1 - E[u])U(C_E)$: social welfare is independent of the variance of unemployment. Intuitively, in this case stabilizing unemployment has no effect on the variance of individuals' consumption; individuals have consumption C_E fraction $1-E[u]$ of the time, and C_U fraction $E[u]$ of the time.

Consumption variability is not the only cost of fluctuations, however. The variability of hours of work may have much larger costs than the variability of consumption. The cyclical variability of hours is much larger than that of consumption; and if labor supply is relatively inelastic, utility may be much more sharply curved in hours than in consumption. Ball and D. Romer (1990) find that as a result, it is possible (though by no means clear-cut) that the cost of fluctuations through hours variability is substantial. Intuitively, the utility benefit of the additional leisure during periods of below-normal output may not nearly offset the utility cost of the reduced consumption, whereas the disutility from the additional hours during booms may nearly offset the benefit of the higher consumption.[22]

It is also possible that individuals are much more risk-averse than Lucas's calculation assumes. Recall from Section 7.5 that stocks earn much higher average returns than bonds. One possible explanation is that individuals dislike risk so much that they require a substantial premium to accept the moderate risk of holding stocks (for example, Kandel and Stambaugh, 1991, and Campbell and Cochrane, 1999). If this is right, the welfare costs of the moderate variability associated with short-run fluctuations could be substantial.

Stabilization policy can also have important indirect benefits. One natural mechanism is through investment: investment may be higher when the economy is more stable. As a result, stabilization policy could raise income substantially over the long run (see, for example, Meltzer, 1988). As Section 8.6 describes, however, the effect of uncertainty on investment is complicated and not necessarily negative. Thus whether stabilization policy has important benefits through this channel is not known.

The issue of nonlinearities in the aggregate supply curve is unsettled. The conventional finding is that a linear specification provides an adequate description of the data over the relevant range (see, for example, Ball and Mankiw, 1995, and Gordon, 1997). Some recent work provides evidence of important nonlinearities, however (Clark, Laxton, and Rose, 1996; De-

---

[22] Just as with the argument for the cost from consumption variability, Ball and Romer's argument concerning the cost from hours variability requires that not all the variation in aggregate hours takes the form of movements between employment and unemployment.

belle and Laxton, 1997; Laxton, Rose, and Tambakis, 1999). These papers suggest that the increase in inflation triggered by a fall in unemployment below the natural rate is larger than the decrease in inflation caused by a comparable rise in unemployment above the natural rate. If this is correct, reducing the variance of unemployment reduces the average increase in inflation and thus makes a lower average unemployment rate feasible. Ball (1994b), on the other hand, argues that there is nonlinearity of the opposite form; this implies that stabilization policy could actually increase average unemployment.

If social welfare or aggregate supply is nonlinear in output, the optimal response to an unfavorable supply shock that raises inflation is to reduce inflation gradually rather than all at once. Thus a supply shock could give rise to an extended period of inflation. At the same time, however, such nonlinearities would also imply that the optimal response to a positive supply shock is to bring inflation back up to its initial level only gradually. Thus although nonlinearities may provide grounds for stabilization policy, they do not provide a simple explanation of high average inflation.

10.7 The Conduct of Policy

Policy actions affect the economy with a lag. In addition, policymakers have imperfect information about the current condition of the economy, about the path the economy would follow if policy did not change, and about what effects a change in policy would have. This naturally raises the issue of how these lags and uncertainties should affect policy.

Targets, Indicators, and Instruments

The traditional analysis of policymaking under uncertainty distinguishes among objectives, instruments, intermediate targets, and indicators of policy.[23] The objectives are the ultimate goals of policy, such as inflation and unemployment. The instruments are the variables that policymakers can control directly, such as open-market operations, reserve requirements, tax rates, and government purchases.

Indicators and intermediate targets fall between the instruments and the objectives. Indicators are variables that provide information about the current or future behavior of the objectives. Some examples are orders for new goods, prices of raw materials, and measures of money and lending. As policymakers obtain new information about the likely behavior of the objectives by observing the indicators, they may adjust the settings of the instruments. Intermediate targets, in contrast, are variables that

---

[23] This analysis was pioneered by Tinbergen (1952).

policymakers choose to focus on in place of the ultimate objectives. The most famous candidate target is the money stock. Many economists have argued that it is better to instruct policymakers to try to keep the growth rate of a measure of the money stock (such as $M1$ or $M2$) as close as possible to some steady, low rate (such as 3 percent per year) rather than to try to maximize some broader objective function (see, for example, Friedman, 1960).

To see how instruments, indicators, targets, and objectives are used in practice, consider the following stylized description of U.S. monetary policy in recent years. The main ultimate objectives of policy are the behavior of unemployment (or real output) and inflation. Policymakers appear to want inflation to be around 2 or 3 percent per year and to avoid large swings in unemployment.[24] Thus, for example, when inflation is above the 2–3 percent range, policymakers have sought to reduce it gradually. Other objectives, such as keeping exchange rates and interest rates moderately stable, also appear to have some weight in the policymakers' objective function.

Over the short term (say, day to day and week to week), the key intermediate target of policy is the Federal funds rate. The Federal Reserve conducts its daily open-market operations to try to keep the funds rate close to its current target level.[25] Although on a day-to-day basis there are noticeable departures of the funds rate from the target, on a weekly or longer-term basis the Federal Reserve usually hits the target quite accurately.

Over the longer term (say, month to month and quarter to quarter), the Federal Reserve does not focus on any single intermediate target. Instead, it adjusts the target level of the funds rate in response to many variables that can provide information about the future paths of real activity and inflation. Unfortunately for policymakers, neither information about real activity nor information about inflation provides a timely guide to how they should conduct policy to best achieve their long-run objectives. In the case of inflation, the difficulty is that inflation seems to respond fairly slowly to departures of output from its natural rate and that there is considerable short-run variability in measured inflation. As a result, if policymakers wait until there is clear evidence that inflation is rising or falling before they adjust policy, the economy is likely to undergo large swings in output and inflation. Real activity, in contrast, can be measured relatively quickly. But it is not possible to determine the natural rate of output with much precision. For example, Staiger, Stock, and Watson (1997) show that a 95 percent confidence interval for the natural rate of unemployment is probably at least 2 percentage points wide. As a result, it is often hard for policymakers to tell whether output is above or below its natural rate. Because of these difficulties, the

---

[24] As the discussion earlier in Section 10.6 suggests, it is not clear that this is what policymakers should in fact be trying to achieve.

[25] Meulendyke (1998) describes the specifics of the Federal Reserve's operating procedures.

Federal Reserve adjusts its target level of the funds rate in response to many variables that can provide information about current and future inflation, real activity, and the natural rate.

Finally, over the longer run (say, a period of several years), the Federal Reserve tries to conduct policy to keep inflation near its long-run objective, and lets real activity vary in whatever way is consistent with this.

The Traditional Argument for Rules

A natural question about indicators and intermediate targets is why policy-makers would ever adopt an intermediate target. It seems that policymakers should take all relevant information into account in their efforts to achieve their ultimate goals. A particular indicator, such as a measure of the money stock, may turn out to be particularly informative; but even then, it appears that there is a cost and no benefit to targeting that variable.

One possible answer involves the dynamic-inconsistency issue, discussed in Sections 10.4 and 10.5: adopting a binding rule about the behavior of an intermediate target can overcome the dynamic-inconsistency problem, and can therefore lead to lower average inflation. But support for money-stock rules and other intermediate targets long predates concern about dynamic inconsistency. Moreover, many proposed ways of adopting intermediate targets do not involve binding commitments, and thus would not solve the problem.

The basis for the traditional argument for instructing policymakers to target some intermediate variable is twofold. Consider for concreteness a money-stock target. The first, and less important, part of the argument for targeting the money stock is that the relation between the money stock and the ultimate objectives of policy is strong enough, and the uncertainty about the effects of departures of the money stock from a path of steady growth large enough, that the potential for improvement over a money-stock rule is small. And since the rule would not be completely binding, in the event of a calamitous breakdown it could be abandoned.

The second, and more important, part of the argument is that instructing policymakers to try to achieve the ultimate goals of policy to the best of their ability may lead to systematic errors in policy. Those potential errors have several sources.

First, policymakers are subject to political pressures. Policymakers outside the Federal Reserve, and the public, may place too much weight on the short-run cost of lower unemployment relative to the long-run cost of higher inflation. This could arise from a higher discount rate than is appropriate, or from a failure to understand how the economy operates. Some evidence for this view is provided by the fact that during periods (such as 1979–1982) when the Federal Reserve has pursued policies that involved very high interest rates, it has not explicitly acknowledged that it was doing so. Instead, policymakers have characterized policy as focusing on some intermediate target (such as *nonborrowed reserves* in 1979–1982) and as not being directly concerned with interest rates.

Second, monetary policymakers may have objectives other than maximizing social welfare, and providing them with only vague instructions about how to conduct policy may increase their ability to pursue those objectives. For example, they may wish to improve the President's chances of being reelected, or to increase seignorage revenues.[26]

Finally, policymakers may genuinely try to maximize social welfare but may nonetheless make systematic errors. Individuals are often overconfident in their judgments (of the state of the economy, or of the likely effects of policy, for example). In addition, they may be reluctant to admit that, given the lags and uncertainties in the effects of policies, the best reaction to a problem may be to do little or nothing. As a result, policy may systematically overreact, easing too much in recessions and thereby causing the subsequent expansions to be too strong, and tightening too much in expansions and thereby causing recessions (see, for example, Friedman, 1960). Similarly, given the suffering associated with unemployment, policymakers may have a tendency to read the evidence about the natural rate optimistically. This can generate an inflationary bias in policy. And, as with the tendency to overreact, it can generate fluctuations. Policymakers may first, out of concern about unemployment and in hopes that the natural rate is low, push unemployment below the natural rate; then, when signs of rising inflation become clear, they may tighten and cause a recession.[27]

Interest-Rate Rules

As just described, traditional proposals for monetary-policy rules were phrased in terms of the money stock. But central banks for the most part conduct policy by adjusting the short-term nominal interest rate in response to various disturbances, using the money stock as just one indicator. Further, in many countries the relationship between the money stock and aggregate demand has broken down in recent years, greatly weakening the case for specifying policy rules in terms of the money stock. These facts have led researchers to consider interest-rate rules.

---

[26] The possibility of the Federal Reserve pursuing objectives other than social welfare (either because of its own preferences or because of political pressures) suggests that fluctuations can arise from political forces rather than exogenous disturbances. For examples of theories of such *political business cycles,* see Nordhaus (1975); Rogoff and Sibert (1988); Harrington (1993); and Alesina, Roubini, and Cohen (1997).

[27] Karamouzis and Lombra (1989) present one piece of evidence of a tendency for over-optimism among policymakers: during the 1970s, the Federal Open Market Committee tended to adopt combinations of interest-rate and money-growth targets that were systematically off the frontier (in the direction of lower money growth and lower interest rates) of possibilities presented by the staff as being feasible.

One important fact to note about interest-rate rules is that, in contrast to money-stock rules, they must be active for the economy to be stable. Suppose, for example, the central bank keeps the nominal interest rate constant. A disturbance to aggregate demand that pushes output above its natural rate causes inflation to rise. With the nominal interest rate fixed, this reduces the real interest rate, which raises output further, which causes inflation to rise even faster, and so on (Friedman, 1968).[28]

Taylor (1993) proposes a simple interest-rate rule. The rule has two elements. The first is for the nominal interest rate to rise more than one-for-one with inflation, so that the real rate increases when inflation rises. The second is for the interest rate to fall when output is below normal and rise when output is above normal. Taylor's proposed rule is linear in inflation and in the percentage departure of output from its natural rate. That is, his rule takes the form

$$i_t - \pi_t = a + b\pi_t + c(\ln Y_t - \ln \overline{Y}_t). \tag{10.33}$$

If we let $\overline{r}_t$ denote the real interest rate that prevails when $Y_t = \overline{Y}_t$ and if we assume that it is constant over time, (10.33) is equivalent to

$$i_t - \pi_t = \overline{r} + b(\pi_t - \pi^*) + c(\ln Y_t - \ln \overline{Y}_t), \tag{10.34}$$

where $\pi^* = (\overline{r} - a)/b$. This way of presenting the rule says that the central bank should raise the real interest rate above its long-run equilibrium level in response to inflation exceeding its target and to output exceeding its natural rate. Interest-rate rules of the form shown in (10.33) and (10.34) are known as *Taylor rules*.

Taylor argues that a rule like (10.34) with $b = c = 0.5$ and $\overline{r} = \pi^* = 2\%$ provides a good description of U.S. monetary policy in the period since the Federal Reserve shifted to a clear policy of trying to adjust interest rates to keep inflation low and the economy fairly stable. Specifically, the interest rate predicted by the rule tracks the actual interest rate well starting around 1985. He also argues that this rule with these parameter values is a good one.

Issues in the Design of Interest-Rate Rules

Recent research has devoted a great deal of attention to trying to construct interest-rate rules that are likely to produce desirable outcomes.[29] Central banks show little interest in actually committing themselves to a rule, or even in mechanically following the dictates of a rule. Thus research in this

---

[28] When expectations are rational and prices are completely flexible, the effects of pegging the nominal interest rate are more complicated. See Sargent and Wallace, 1975, and Blanchard and Fischer, 1989, Section 11.2.

[29] Many of the relevant papers are in Taylor (1999).

area has focused on the question of whether there are prescriptions for how interest rates should be adjusted that can provide valuable guidelines for policymakers.

This research for the most part does not concern itself with dynamic inconsistency. That is, it presumes that for some reason, such as reputation considerations, the central bank can set the interest rate according to a rule without a binding commitment even if the policy prescribed by the rule is not dynamically consistent.

A large number of issues concerning interest-rate rules like Taylor's have been discussed. Here we mention some of the most important. The first is what values the coefficients on inflation and output, b and c, should take. When the coefficients are larger, inflation returns more rapidly to the long-run target and output returns more rapidly to its natural rate after a disturbance. But large coefficients can cause inflation and output to overshoot π^* and $\overline{Y}$. There is also more short-run volatility in interest rates, which may be undesirable.

A second issue is how inflation, output, and the natural rate should be measured. Taylor proposed measuring inflation as average inflation from four quarters ago to the current quarter and output as the current quarter's value. But current inflation and output are not known when the central bank chooses the interest rate. An alternative is to use the measures proposed by Taylor, but with a one-quarter lag. Most analyses suggest that this delay would have little effect on the rule's performance.

A more serious measurement issue concerns the natural rate of output. Most analyses of interest-rate rules assume that the natural rate of output is known. But as described earlier in this section, the natural rate is highly uncertain. This may be important. In particular, Orphanides (2000) considers applying the basic Taylor rule with Taylor's coefficients to the data on inflation and output and estimates of $\overline{Y}$ that were available to policymakers in the 1970s. He finds that the resulting series for the interest rate corresponds fairly well with the actual series. That is, his findings suggest that the inflation of the 1970s was due not to policy being fundamentally different from what it is today, but to policymakers significantly overestimating the economy's natural rate of output, and therefore overstimulating the economy.

Whether Orphanides's conclusion is correct is not clear. The measures from the 1970s that Orphanides interprets as estimates of the natural rate may have been intended as estimates of something more like the economy's maximum capacity. After all, the natural-rate hypothesis had just been proposed and was not yet widely accepted. Nonetheless, Orphanides's findings—and the more general evidence of uncertainty about the natural rate—suggest that an interest-rate rule should put only limited weight on apparent departures of output from its natural rate.

A third issue is whether the rule should be forward-looking. For example, the measures of recent output and inflation in the rule could be replaced with forecasts of these variables over the next several quarters. Using fore-casts would make policy respond more rapidly to new information. But it would make the rules more difficult to understand and might make them less robust to errors in modeling the economy.[30]

A final issue is whether additional variables should be included in the rule. The two additional variables that have received the most attention are the exchange rate and the lagged interest rate. An appreciation of the exchange rate, like a rise in the interest rate, dampens economic activity. Thus it lowers the interest rate needed to generate a given level of aggregate demand. One might therefore want to modify (10.33) to

$$i_t - \pi_t = a + b\pi_t + c(\ln Y_t - \ln \overline{Y}_t) + de_t, \tag{10.35}$$

where e is the real exchange rate (that is, the price of foreign goods in terms of domestic goods). Moving the exchange-rate term over to the right-hand side of this expression gives

$$-de_t + (i_t - \pi_t) = a + b\pi_t + c(\ln Y_t - \ln \overline{Y}_t). \tag{10.36}$$

The left-hand side of (10.36) is referred to as a *monetary conditions index.* It is a linear combination of the real exchange rate and the real interest rate; if the coefficient on the exchange rate, d, is chosen properly, the index shows the overall impact of the exchange rate and the interest rate on ag-gregate demand. Thus (10.36) is a rule for the monetary conditions index as a function of inflation and output.

Including the lagged interest rate may be desirable for several reasons. It can reduce short-run interest-rate volatility and make the rule more robust to errors in estimating the long-run equilibrium real interest rate. In addi-tion, it can cause a given change in the interest rate to have a larger impact on the economy: agents will realize that, for example, a rise in rates im-plies that rates will remain high for an extended period. On the other hand, having interest rates affected by a variable that is not of direct concern to policymakers may produce inefficient outcomes in terms of the variables that policymakers are concerned about.

A Model for Analyzing Policy Rules

To provide a sense of how proposals concerning policy rules can be ana-lyzed, here we examine the simple model considered by Svensson (1997) and Ball (1999a). We will ask whether optimal policy in the model takes the form of a Taylor rule and what the model tells us about the appropriate coefficient values in the optimal rule.

The economy is a textbook economy with two equations, one describing aggregate demand and the other describing aggregate supply. The main

---

[30] For more on the use of forecasts in policymaking, see Bernanke and Woodford (1997) and many of the papers in Taylor (1999).

difference from standard textbook formulations is the inclusion of lags. The aggregate demand equation states that output depends negatively on the previous period's real interest rate. The aggregate supply equation states that the change in inflation depends positively on the previous period's output. Because of this lag structure, a change in the real interest rate has no effect on output until the following period and no effect on inflation until the period after that. This captures the conventional wisdom that policy works with a lag and that it affects output more rapidly than it affects inflation. In addition, lagged output is assumed to enter the aggregate demand equation, and there are disturbances to both aggregate demand and aggregate supply.

Specifically, the aggregate demand equation is

$$y_t = -\beta r_{t-1} + \rho y_{t-1} + \varepsilon_t, \qquad \beta > 0, \qquad 0 < \rho < 1, \qquad (10.37)$$

where the natural rate of output and the long-run real interest rate have been normalized to zero. The aggregate supply equation is

$$\pi_t = \pi_{t-1} + \alpha y_{t-1} + \delta_t, \qquad \alpha > 0. \qquad (10.38)$$

The disturbances, ε and δ, are assumed to be independent of each other and to have mean-zero, i.i.d. distributions.

The central bank chooses r_t after observing ε_t and δ_t. It dislikes variation in both output and inflation; specifically, it minimizes $E[(y-y^*)^2]+\lambda E[\pi^2]$, where λ is a positive parameter showing the relative weight it puts on inflation and y^* is its most preferred level of output; the most preferred level of inflation is normalized to zero for simplicity. Without loss of generality, the analysis considers only rules for the real interest rate that are linear in variables describing the state of the economy.[31]

The model is obviously highly stylized. For example, there are no microeconomic foundations to either the behavior of private agents or the central bank's loss function, and aggregate supply is not at all forward-looking. These features make the model transparent and easy to solve; but they also mean that one cannot draw general conclusions from it.

Analyzing the Model

The first step in analyzing the model is to note that the central bank's choice of r_t has no impact on y_t, π_t, or π_{t+1}. Its first impact is on y_{t+1}, and it is only through y_{t+1} that it affects inflation and output in subsequent periods. Thus one can think of policy as a rule not for r_t, but for the expectation as of period t of y in period $t + 1$. That is, for the moment we will think of the central bank as choosing not r_t, but $-\beta r_t + \rho y_t = E_t[y_{t+1}]$ (see [10.37]).

---

[31] A more formal approach is not to assume linearity and to assume that the central bank minimizes the expected discounted sum of terms of the form $(y_t - y^*)^2 + \lambda \pi_t^2$, and to let the discount rate approach zero. As Svensson shows, this approaches yields the rule derived below.

Now note that the paths of inflation and output beginning in period $t+1$ are determined by $E_t[y_{t+1}]$ (which is determined by the central bank's policy in t), $E_t[\pi_{t+1}]$ (which, as [10.38] shows, the central bank cannot control), and future shocks. Because of this, the optimal policy will make $E_t[y_{t+1}]$ a function of $E_t[\pi_{t+1}]$. Further, the aggregate supply equation, (10.38), implies that the average value of y must be 0 for inflation to be bounded. Thus it is reasonable to guess (and one can show formally) that when $E_t[\pi_{t+1}]$ is 0, the central bank sets $E_t[y_{t+1}]$ to 0. Given the assumption of linearity, this means that the optimal policy takes the form

$$E_t y_{t+1} = -q E_t[\pi_{t+1}], \tag{10.39}$$

where the value of q is to be determined.

To find q, we need to find $E[(y - y^*)^2] + \lambda E[\pi^2]$ as a function of q. We will do this by focusing on the behavior of $E_t[\pi_{t+1}]$. Expression (10.38) applied to period $t + 1$ implies

$$E_t[\pi_{t+1}] = \pi_t + \alpha y_t. \tag{10.40}$$

Equations (10.37) and (10.38) imply that $y_t = E_{t-1}[y_t] + \varepsilon_t$ and $\pi_t = E_{t-1}[\pi_t] + \delta_t$. Substituting these facts into (10.40) yields

$$
\begin{aligned}
E_t[\pi_{t+1}] &= E_{t-1}[\pi_t] + \delta_t + \alpha(E_{t-1}[y_t] + \varepsilon_t) \\
&= E_{t-1}[\pi_t] + \delta_t + \alpha(-q E_{t-1}[\pi_t] + \varepsilon_t) \\
&= (1 - \alpha q) E_{t-1}[\pi_t] + \delta_t + \alpha \varepsilon_t,
\end{aligned}
\tag{10.41}
$$

where the second line uses (10.39) applied to period t.

The shocks, δ_t and ε_t, are uncorrelated with each other and with $E_{t-1}[\pi_t]$. Taking expectations of the squares of both sides of (10.41) therefore yields

$$E[(E_t[\pi_{t+1}])^2] = (1 - \alpha q)^2 E[(E_{t-1}[\pi_t])^2] + \sigma_\delta^2 + \alpha^2 \sigma_\varepsilon^2, \tag{10.42}$$

where σ_δ^2 and σ_ε^2 are the variances of δ and ε.

Given the linear structure of the model and the assumption of i.i.d. disturbances, in the long run the distribution of $E_{t-1}[\pi_t]$ will be constant over time and independent of the economy's initial conditions. That is, in the long run the expectations of $(E_t[\pi_{t+1}])^2$ and of $(E_{t-1}[\pi_t])^2$ are equal. We can therefore solve (10.42) for the long-run expectation of $(E_{t-1}[\pi_t])^2$. This yields

$$
\begin{aligned}
E[(E_{t-1}[\pi_t])^2] &= \frac{\sigma_\delta^2 + \alpha^2 \sigma_\varepsilon^2}{1 - (1 - \alpha q)^2} \\
&= \frac{\sigma_\delta^2 + \alpha^2 \sigma_\varepsilon^2}{\alpha q (2 - \alpha q)}.
\end{aligned}
\tag{10.43}
$$

We are now in a position to find the two components of the central bank's loss function. Equation (10.38) implies that π_t equals $E_{t-1}[\pi_t]$ plus δ_t. Thus

(10.43) implies

$$E[\pi^2] = \frac{\sigma_\delta^2 + \alpha^2 \sigma_\varepsilon^2}{\alpha q (2 - \alpha q)} + \sigma_\delta^2. \tag{10.44}$$

Similarly, (10.37) implies that y_t equals $E_{t-1}[y_t]$ plus ε_t, and from (10.39) we know that $E_{t-1}[y_t] = -qE_{t-1}[\pi_t]$. We also know that the mean of y is zero. Thus,

$$E[(y - y^*)^2] = y^{*2} + q^2 E[(E_{t-1}[\pi_t])^2] + \sigma_\varepsilon^2$$

$$= y^{*2} + \frac{q^2 \sigma_\delta^2 + q^2 \alpha^2 \sigma_\varepsilon^2}{\alpha q (2 - \alpha q)} + \sigma_\varepsilon^2. \tag{10.45}$$

Finding the optimal q is now just a matter of algebra. Expressions (10.44) and (10.45) tell us the value of the central bank's loss function, $E[(y-y^*)^2] + \lambda E[\pi^2]$, as a function of q. The first-order condition for q turns out to be a quadratic. One of the solutions is negative. Since a negative q causes the variances of y and π to be infinite, we can rule out this solution. The remaining solution is

$$q^* = \frac{-\lambda\alpha + \sqrt{\alpha^2 \lambda^2 + 4\lambda}}{2}. \tag{10.46}$$

Discussion

To interpret (10.46), it is helpful to consider its implications for how the optimal q varies with λ, the weight the central bank places on inflation stabilization. The central bank's policy is described by $E_t[y_{t+1}] = -q^* E_t[\pi_{t+1}]$ (see [10.39]). (10.46) implies that as λ approaches 0, q^* approaches 0: the central bank always conducts policy so that $E_t[y_{t+1}]$ is 0. Thus output is white noise around zero. The aggregate supply equation, (10.38), then implies that inflation is a random walk.

Equation (10.46) implies that as λ rises, q^* rises: as the central bank places more weight on inflation stabilization, it induces departures of output from its natural rate to bring inflation back to its optimal level after a departure. One can show that as λ approaches infinity, q^* approaches $1/\alpha$. This corresponds to a policy of bringing inflation back to zero as rapidly as possible after a shock. With q^* equal to $1/\alpha$, $E_t[y_{t+1}]$ equals $-(1/\alpha)E_t[\pi_{t+1}]$. The aggregate supply equation, (10.38), then implies that $E_t[\pi_{t+2}]$ equals 0. Note that as λ approaches infinity, the variance of output does not approach infinity (see [10.45] with $q = 1/\alpha$): even if the central bank cares only about inflation, it wants to keep output close to its natural rate to prevent large movements in inflation.

To see what the central bank's policy rule implies concerning interest rates, recall that the aggregate demand equation, (10.37), implies that

$E_t[y_{t+1}]$ equals $-\beta r_t + \rho y_t$. Thus the statement that $E_t[y_{t+1}]$ equals $-q^* E_t[\pi_{t+1}]$ is equivalent to

$$-\beta r_t + \rho y_t = -q^* E_t[\pi_{t+1}], \qquad (10.47)$$

or

$$r_t = \frac{1}{\beta}(\rho y_t + q^* E_t[\pi_{t+1}]). \qquad (10.48)$$

Now note that the aggregate supply equation, (10.38), implies that $E_t[\pi_{t+1}]$ equals $\pi_t + \alpha y_t$. Substituting this fact into (10.48) yields

$$r_t = \frac{1}{\beta}(\rho y_t + q^* \pi_t + q^* \alpha y_t)$$

$$= \frac{\rho + q^* \alpha}{\beta} y_t + \frac{q^*}{\beta} \pi_t. \qquad (10.49)$$

Equation (10.49) is a Taylor rule: the real interest rate is a linear function of output and inflation, and does not depend on any other variables. Thus the optimal policy in the model takes the form of the Taylor rule.

This analysis implies that not all Taylor rules are optimal. In particular, (10.49) places two restrictions on the coefficients on output and inflation. First, since q^* ranges from 0 to $1/\alpha$ as λ ranges from 0 to infinity, (10.49) implies that the coefficient on y must be between ρ/β and $(1 + \rho)/\beta$ and that the coefficient on π must be between 0 and $1/(\alpha\beta)$. The reason that the coefficient on output must be at least ρ/β is that positive serial correlation in output movements is unambiguously undesirable: it increases the variability of both output and inflation. Thus at the very least, policy should offset the positive serial correlation in output movements that comes from the ρy_{t-1} term in the aggregate demand equation. The reason that the coefficients on y and π cannot be too large is that there is a cost but no benefit to responding to fluctuations so aggressively that $E_t[\pi_{t+2}]$ has the opposite sign from $E_t[\pi_{t+1}]$.

The second restriction that (10.49) places on the Taylor rule is a relation between the two coefficients. Specifically, (10.49) implies that the coefficient on y equals the sum of two terms: ρ/β (which induces interest-rate movements that exactly offset the positive serial correlation in output that would otherwise occur) and α times the coefficient on π. Thus when the coefficient on π is higher, the coefficient on y must be higher. The intuition is that if, for example, the central bank cares a great deal about inflation, it should respond aggressively to movements in both output and inflation to keep inflation under control; responding to one but not the other is inefficient.

Ball argues that both Taylor's proposed coefficients and actual policy-making violate these restrictions. In particular, he argues that actual policy in many countries is not aggressive enough in responding to output movements: the coefficient on y is less than ρ/β. A simple way to see his argument is to observe that our model implies that departures of output from its natural rate should not be positively serially correlated, but that in practice they are. Given how stylized the model is, however, one should not put great weight on this conclusion. The model ignores any costs of variability in the growth rate of output and in interest rates; it neglects the possibility of uncertainty about the natural rate; and it assumes rather than derives the form of the central bank's loss function. Rather, the value of the model lies in showing how one can analyze optimal policymaking and interest-rate rules formally, and in showing some factors that should be considered in policymaking.

Inflation Targeting

In recent years, the central banks of New Zealand, Canada, the United Kingdom, and other countries have adopted *inflation targeting*. Inflation targeting is not a policy of focusing only on inflation. Central banks in inflation-targeting countries, like other central banks, do not just try to control inflation; they also try to mitigate output fluctuations, avoid large swings in interest rates and exchange rates, and keep the financial system stable. Rather, inflation targeting has three main elements. First, and most centrally, there is an explicit target for inflation. The target is typically quite low and is usually specified as a range of a few percentage points. Second, central banks in inflation-targeting countries appear to place more weight than other central banks on the behavior of inflation. And third, there is greater emphasis on making the central bank's policies transparent and central bankers accountable for the policies. Central banks have traditionally been quite secretive in their decision-making and obscure about their objectives. Central banks engaged in inflation targeting, however, devote considerable effort to spelling out their objectives, their reading of economic conditions, and the reasons for their policy actions. This greater explicitness is usually coupled with greater accountability. The extreme case is New Zealand, where the central bank and the government make explicit agreements about the objectives of policy and where the central-bank governor can be dismissed for failing to achieve those objectives.

Svensson and Ball point out that the optimal policies in their model can be interpreted as a type of inflation targeting. To see this, recall that the class of optimal policies in the model takes the form $E_t[y_{t+1}] = -qE_t[\pi_{t+1}]$ with q ranging from 0 to $1/\alpha$. Recall also that $E_{t+1}[\pi_{t+2}]$ is equal to $(1-\alpha q)E_t[\pi_{t+1}] + \delta_{t+1} + \alpha\varepsilon_{t+1}$ (see [10.41]); this means that $E_t[\pi_{t+2}]$ equals $(1 - \alpha q)E_t[\pi_{t+1}]$. Since q is between 0 and $1/\alpha$, $1 - \alpha q$ is between 0 and 1. Thus the class of optimal policies consists of rules for the behavior of expected inflation of the form

$$E_t[\pi_{t+2}] = \phi E_t[\pi_{t+1}], \qquad (10.50)$$

with ϕ between 0 and 1. Thus all optimal policies can be described in terms of a rule purely for the expected behavior of inflation; in that sense, the optimal policies are a form of inflation targeting. Specifically, since $E_t[\pi_{t+1}]$ is beyond policymakers' control, the optimal policies take the form of trying to bring inflation back to the most preferred level (which we have normalized to zero) after a disturbance has pushed it away. Where the policies differ is in the speed that they do this with: the more the central bank cares about inflation (that is, the greater is λ), the faster it undoes changes in inflation (that is, the lower is ϕ).

There are two main views of inflation targeting. The first is that it is merely "conservative window-dressing."[32] In this view, the important changes in monetary policy in countries such as New Zealand and the United Kingdom are that the central bank has decided to aim for lower inflation than in earlier decades and to put greater emphasis on the behavior of inflation. The other features of inflation targeting, such as the formal targets, inflation reports, and so on, are of little importance.

One piece of evidence in support of this view is provided by U.S. monetary policy since the mid-1980s. The Federal Reserve has not adopted anything approaching formal inflation targeting. But its policymakers, like those in inflation-targeting countries, have decided that the central goal of policy should be to keep inflation low and stable. In terms of inflation performance, this "just do it" approach has been as successful as inflation targeting. This suggests that it is policymakers' focus on inflation and not the paraphernalia of inflation targeting that is critical.

The other view is that inflation targeting matters. This view focuses on the trio of credibility, transparency, and accountability. Discussions of credibility argue that the emphasis on hitting the inflation target can affect expected inflation. This can be important in two situations. The first is when inflation targeting is adopted. Typically this is done when inflation is well above the newly adopted target. Thus inflation targeting may reduce expected inflation, and hence lower the output costs of the disinflation needed to get inflation down to the target. This idea is appealing and plausible. But as described in Section 10.5, thus far there is little evidence that it is quantitatively important.

The second situation is where a disturbance moves inflation away from the target. By anchoring expectations at the target level, inflation targeting can reduce the disturbance's impact on expected inflation. Indeed, there is some evidence that shocks to the price level have had little influence on expected inflation under inflation targeting. Since disturbances are both positive and negative, this is not likely to have a large effect on average output. But it can make the economy more stable.

Much of the discussion of transparency and accountability is couched in terms of democratic political philosophy rather than economics: it may

---

[32] This argument is due to Anna Schwartz.

be desirable for its own sake for citizens to understand policymakers' goals and the reasons for their actions, and for policymakers to be accountable for their successes and failures in achieving the policy goals. But there may also be economic benefits to transparency and accountability. Greater transparency is likely to reduce uncertainty, and greater accountability is likely to improve incentives. Perhaps more importantly, greater transparency may improve public understanding of the economy and policy, and thereby lead to better policymaking in the long run. At this point, however, these potential benefits are speculative.[33]

10.8   Seignorage and Inflation

Inflation sometimes reaches extraordinarily high levels. The most extreme cases are *hyperinflations*, which are traditionally defined as periods when inflation exceeds 50 percent per month. Many of the most important hyperinflations occurred in Europe in the aftermaths of World War I and World War II, in Latin America in the 1980s and 1990s, and in the former Soviet Union in the 1990s. The all-time record inflation took place in Hungary between August 1945 and July 1946. During this period, the price level rose by a factor of approximately 10^{27}. In the peak month of the inflation, prices on average tripled daily (Sachs and Larrain, 1993). And many countries experience high inflation that falls short of hyperinflation: there are many cases where inflation was between 100 and 1000 percent per year for extended periods.

The existence of an output-inflation tradeoff cannot plausibly lead to hyperinflations, or even to very high rates of inflation that fall short of hyperinflation. By the time inflation reaches triple digits, the costs of inflation are almost surely large, and the real effects of monetary changes are almost surely small. No reasonable policymaker would choose to subject an economy to such large costs out of a desire to obtain such modest output gains.

The underlying cause of most, if not all, episodes of high inflation and hyperinflation is government's need to obtain seignorage—that is, revenue from printing money (Bresciani-Turroni, 1937; Cagan, 1956). Wars, falls in export prices, tax evasion, and political stalemate frequently leave governments with large budget deficits. And often investors do not have enough confidence that the government will honor its debts to be willing to buy its bonds. Thus the government's only choice is to resort to seignorage.[34]

---

[33] For more on inflation targeting, see Bernanke, Laubach, Mishkin, and Posen (1999).

[34] An important question is how the political process leads to situations that require such large amounts of seignorage. The puzzle is that given the apparent high costs of the resulting inflation, there appear to be alternatives that all parties prefer. This issue is addressed in Section 11.6.

This section therefore investigates the interactions among seignorage needs, money growth, and inflation. We begin by considering a situation where seignorage needs are sustainable, and see how this can lead to high inflation. We then consider what happens when seignorage needs are unsustainable, and see how that can lead to hyperinflation.

The Inflation Rate and Seignorage

As in Section 10.2, assume that real money demand depends negatively on the nominal interest rate and positively on real income (see equation [10.1]):

$$\frac{M}{P} = L(i, Y)$$

$$= L(r + \pi^e, Y), \qquad L_i < 0, \qquad L_Y > 0.$$

(10.51)

Since we are interested in the government's revenue from money creation, M should be interpreted as high-powered money (that is, currency and reserves issued by the government). Thus $L(\bullet)$ is the demand for high-powered money.

For the moment we focus on steady states. It is therefore reasonable to assume that output and the real interest rate are unaffected by the rate of money growth, and that actual inflation and expected inflation are equal. If we neglect output growth for simplicity, then in steady state the quantity of real balances is constant. This implies that inflation equals the rate of money growth. Thus we can rewrite (10.51) as

$$\frac{M}{P} = L(\bar{r} + g_M, \bar{Y}),$$

(10.52)

where $\bar{r}$ and $\bar{Y}$ are the real interest rate and output and where g_M is the rate of money growth, $\dot{M}/M$.

The quantity of real purchases per unit time that the government finances from money creation equals the increase in the nominal money stock per unit time divided by the price level:

$$S = \frac{\dot{M}}{P}$$

$$= \frac{\dot{M}}{M} \frac{M}{P}$$

(10.53)

$$= g_M \frac{M}{P}.$$

Equation (10.53) shows that in steady state, real seignorage equals the growth rate of the money stock times the quantity of real balances. The growth rate of money is equal to the rate at which nominal money holdings lose real value, π. Thus, loosely speaking, seignorage equals the "tax rate" on real balances, π, times the amount being taxed, M/P. For this reason, seignorage revenues are often referred to as *inflation-tax* revenues.[35]

Substituting (10.52) into (10.53) yields

$$S = g_M L(\bar{r} + g_M, \bar{Y}). \qquad (10.54)$$

Equation (10.54) shows that an increase in g_M increases seignorage by raising the rate at which real money holdings are taxed, but decreases it by reducing the tax base. Formally,

$$\frac{dS}{dg_M} = L(\bar{r} + g_M, \bar{Y}) + g_M L_1(\bar{r} + g_M, \bar{Y}), \qquad (10.55)$$

where $L_1(\bullet)$ denotes the derivative of $L(\bullet)$ with respect to its first argument.

The first term of (10.55) is positive and the second is negative. The second term approaches zero as g_M approaches zero (unless $L_1(\bar{r} + g_M, \bar{Y})$ approaches minus infinity as g_M approaches zero). Since $L(\bar{r}, \bar{Y})$ is strictly positive, it follows that dS/dg_M is positive for sufficiently low values of g_M. That is, at low tax rates, seignorage is increasing in the tax rate. It is plausible, however, that as g_M becomes large, the second term eventually dominates; that is, it is reasonable to suppose that when the tax rate becomes extreme, further increases in the rate reduce revenue. The resulting "inflation-tax Laffer curve" is shown in Figure 10.7.

As a concrete example of the relation between inflation and steady-state seignorage, consider the money-demand function proposed by Cagan (1956). Cagan suggests that a good description of money demand, particularly under high inflation, is given by

$$\ln \frac{M}{P} = a - bi + \ln Y, \qquad b > 0. \qquad (10.56)$$

Converting (10.56) from logs to levels and substituting the resulting expression into (10.54) yields

$$S = g_M e^a \bar{Y} e^{-b(\bar{r} + g_M)}$$
$$= C g_M e^{-b g_M}, \qquad (10.57)$$

where $C \equiv e^a \bar{Y} e^{-b\bar{r}}$. The impact of a change in money growth on seignorage is therefore given by

---

[35] Phelps (1973) shows that it is more natural to think of the tax rate on money balances as the nominal interest rate, since the nominal rate is the difference between the cost to agents of holding money (which is the nominal rate itself) and the cost to the government of producing it (which is essentially zero). In our framework, where the real rate is fixed and the nominal rate therefore moves one-for-one with inflation, this distinction is not important.

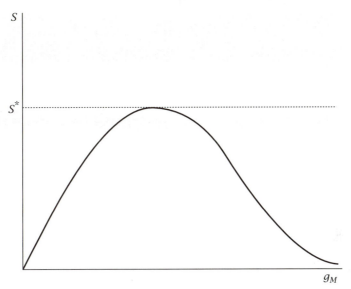

FIGURE 10.7 The inflation-tax Laffer curve

$$\frac{dS}{dg_M} = Ce^{-bg_M} - bCg_M e^{-bg_M}$$

$$= (1 - bg_M)Ce^{-bg_M}.$$

(10.58)

This expression is positive for $g_M < 1/b$ and negative thereafter.

Cagan's estimates suggest that b is between $\frac{1}{3}$ and $\frac{1}{2}$. This implies that the peak of the inflation-tax Laffer curve occurs when g_M is between 2 and 3. This corresponds to a continuously compounded rate of money growth of 200 to 300 percent per year, which implies an increase in the money stock by a factor of between $e^2 \simeq 7.4$ and $e^3 \simeq 20$ per year. Cagan, Sachs and Larrain (1993), and others suggest that for most countries, seignorage at the peak of the Laffer curve is about 10 percent of GDP.

Now consider a government that has some amount of real purchases, G, that it needs to finance with seignorage. Assume that G is less than the maximum feasible amount of seignorage, denoted S^*. Then, as Figure 10.8 shows, there are two rates of money growth that can finance the purchases.[36] With one, inflation is low and real balances are high; with the

---

[36] Figure 10.8 implicitly assumes that the seignorage needs are independent of the inflation rate. This assumption omits an important effect of inflation: because taxes are usually specified in nominal terms and collected with a lag, an increase in inflation typically reduces real tax revenues. As a result, seignorage needs are likely to be greater at higher inflation rates. This *Tanzi* (or *Olivera-Tanzi*) effect does not require any basic change in our analysis; we only have to replace the horizontal line at G with an upward-sloping line. But the effect can be quantitatively significant, and is therefore important to understanding high inflation in practice.

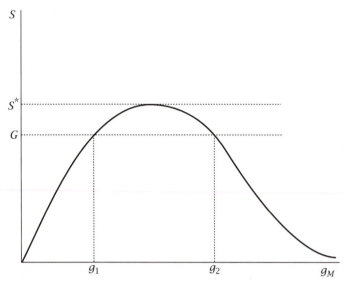

FIGURE 10.8   How seignorage needs determine inflation

other, inflation is high and real balances are low. The high-inflation equilibrium has peculiar comparative-statics properties; for example, a decrease in the government's seignorage needs raises inflation. Since we do not appear to observe such situations in practice, we focus on the low-inflation equilibrium. Thus the rate of money growth—and hence the rate of inflation—is given by g_1.

This analysis provides an explanation of high inflation: it stems from governments' need for seignorage. Suppose, for example, that $b = \frac{1}{3}$ and that seignorage at the peak of the Laffer curve, S^*, is 10 percent of GDP. Since seignorage is maximized when $g_M = 1/b$, (10.57) implies that S^* is Ce^{-1}/b. Thus for S^* to equal 10 percent of GDP when b is $\frac{1}{3}$, C must be about 9 percent of GDP. Straightforward calculations then show that raising 2 percent of GDP from seignorage requires $g_M \simeq 0.24$, raising 5 percent requires $g_M \simeq 0.70$, and raising 8 percent requires $g_M \simeq 1.42$. Thus moderate seignorage needs give rise to substantial inflation, and large seignorage needs produce high inflation.

Seignorage and Hyperinflation

This analysis seems to imply that even governments' need for seignorage cannot account for hyperinflations: if seignorage revenue is maximized at inflation rates of several hundred percent, why do governments ever let inflation go higher? The answer is that the preceding analysis holds only in steady state. If the public does not immediately adjust its money holdings or its expectations of inflation to changes in the economic environment, then in the short run seignorage is always increasing in money growth, and the government can obtain more seignorage than the maximum sustainable amount, S^*. Thus hyperinflations arise when the government's seignorage needs exceed S^* (Cagan, 1956).

Gradual adjustment of money holdings and gradual adjustment of expected inflation have similar implications for the dynamics of inflation. We focus on the case of gradual adjustment of money holdings. Specifically, assume that individuals' desired money holdings are given by the Cagan money-demand function, (10.56). In addition, continue to assume that the real interest rate and output are fixed at $\bar{r}$ and $\bar{Y}$: although both variables are likely to change somewhat over time, the effects of those variations are likely to be small relative to the effects of changes in inflation.

Thus desired real money holdings are

$$m^*(t) = Ce^{-b\pi(t)}. \tag{10.59}$$

The key assumption of the model is that actual money holdings adjust gradually toward desired holdings. Specifically, our assumption is

$$\frac{d \ln m(t)}{dt} = \beta[\ln m^*(t) - \ln m(t)], \tag{10.60}$$

or

$$\frac{\dot{m}(t)}{m(t)} = \beta[\ln C - b\pi(t) - \ln m(t)], \tag{10.61}$$

where we have used (10.59) to substitute for $\ln m^*(t)$. The idea behind this assumption of gradual adjustment is that it is difficult for individuals to adjust their money holdings; for example, they may have made arrangements to make certain types of purchases using money. As a result, they adjust their money holdings toward the desired level only gradually. The specific functional form is chosen for convenience. Finally, β is assumed to be positive but less than $1/b$—that is, adjustment is assumed not to be too rapid.[37]

As before, seignorage equals $\dot{M}/P$, or $(\dot{M}/M)(M/P)$; thus

$$S(t) = g_M(t)m(t). \tag{10.62}$$

Suppose that this economy is initially in steady state with G less than S^*, and that G then increases to a value greater than S^*. If adjustment is

---

[37] The assumption that the change in real money holdings depends only on the current values of m^* and m implies that individuals are not forward-looking. A more appealing assumption, along the lines of the q model of investment in Chapter 8, is that individuals consider the entire future path of inflation in deciding how to adjust their money holdings. This assumption complicates the analysis greatly without changing the implications for most of the issues we are interested in (but see n. 40, below).

instantaneous, there is no equilibrium with positive money holdings. Since S^* is the maximum amount of seignorage the government can obtain when individuals have adjusted their real money holdings to their desired level, the government cannot obtain more than this with instantaneous adjustment. As a result, the only possibility is for money to immediately become worthless and for the government to be unable to obtain the seignorage it needs.

With gradual adjustment, on the other hand, the government can obtain the needed seignorage through increasing money growth and inflation. With rising inflation, real money holdings are falling. But because the adjustment is not immediate, the real money stock exceeds $Ce^{-b\pi}$; as a result (as long as the adjustment is not too rapid), the government is able to obtain more than S^*. But with the real money stock falling, the required rate of money growth is rising. The result is explosive inflation.

To see the dynamics of the economy formally, it is easiest to focus on the dynamics of the real money stock, m. Equation (10.61) gives $\dot{m}/m$ in terms of π and m. Thus to characterize the behavior of m, we need to eliminate π from this equation.

To do this, note that the growth rate of real money, $\dot{m}/m$, equals the growth rate of nominal money, g_M, minus the rate of inflation, π. Rewriting this as an equation for inflation gives us

$$\pi(t) = g_M(t) - \frac{\dot{m}(t)}{m(t)}$$

$$= \frac{G}{m(t)} - \frac{\dot{m}(t)}{m(t)},$$

(10.63)

where the second line uses the fact that $m(t)g_M(t) = G$ (see [10.62]). Substituting this expression into (10.61) yields

$$\frac{\dot{m}(t)}{m(t)} = \beta \left\{ \ln C - b \left[\frac{G}{m(t)} - \frac{\dot{m}(t)}{m(t)} \right] - \ln m(t) \right\}.$$

(10.64)

We can now solve this expression for $\dot{m}(t)/m(t)$; this yields

$$\frac{\dot{m}(t)}{m(t)} = \frac{\beta}{1 - b\beta} \left[\ln C - b\frac{G}{m(t)} - \ln m(t) \right]$$

$$= \frac{\beta}{1 - b\beta} \frac{b}{m(t)} \left[\frac{\ln C - \ln m(t)}{b} m(t) - G \right].$$

(10.65)

Our assumption that G is greater than S^* implies that the expression in brackets is negative for all values of m. To see this, note first that the rate of inflation needed to make desired money holdings equal m is the solution to $Ce^{-b\pi} = m$; taking logs and rearranging the resulting expression shows that this inflation rate is $(\ln C - \ln m)/b$. Next, recall that if real money holdings are steady, seignorage is πm; thus the sustainable level of seignorage asso-

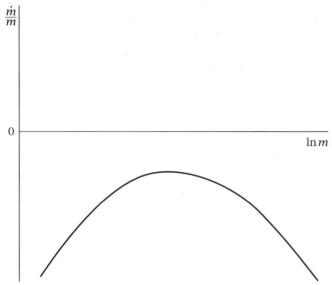

FIGURE 10.9 **The dynamics of the real money stock when seignorage needs are unsustainable**

ciated with real money balances of m is $[(\ln C - \ln m)/b]m$. Finally, recall that S^* is defined as the maximum sustainable level of seignorage. Thus the assumption that S^* is less than G implies that $[(\ln C - \ln m)/b]m$ is less than G for all values of m. But this means that the expression in brackets in (10.65) is negative.

Thus, since $b\beta$ is less than 1, the right-hand side of (10.65) is everywhere negative: regardless of where it starts, the real money stock continually falls. The associated phase diagram is shown in Figure 10.9.[38] With the real money stock continually falling, money growth must be continually rising for the government to obtain the seignorage it needs (see [10.62]). In short, the government can obtain seignorage greater than S^*, but only at the cost of explosive inflation.

This analysis can also be used to understand the dynamics of the real money stock and inflation under gradual adjustment of money holdings when G is less than S^*. Consider the situation depicted in Figure 10.8. Sustainable seignorage, πm^*, equals G if inflation is either g_1 or g_2; it is greater than G if inflation is between g_1 and g_2; and it is less than G otherwise. The resulting dynamics of the real money stock implied by (10.65) for this case are shown in Figure 10.10. The steady state with the higher real money

---

[38] By differentiating (10.65) twice, one can show that $d^2(\dot{m}/m)/(d\ln m)^2 < 0$, and thus that the phase diagram has the shape shown.

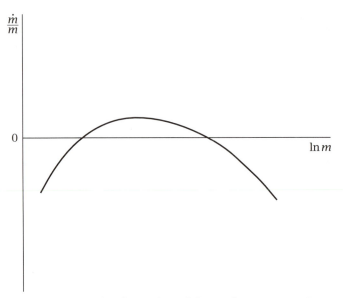

**FIGURE 10.10   The dynamics of the real money stock
when seignorage needs are sustainable**

stock (and thus with the lower inflation rate) is stable, and the steady state
with the lower money stock is unstable.[39]

This analysis of the relation between seignorage and inflation explains
many of the main characteristics of high inflations and hyperinflations.
Most basically, the analysis explains the puzzling fact that inflation often
reaches extremely high levels. The analysis also explains why inflation can
reach some level—empirically, in the triple-digit range—without becoming

---

[39] Recall that this analysis depends on the assumption that $\beta < 1/b$. If this assumption
fails, the denominator of (10.65) is negative. The stability and dynamics of the model are
peculiar in this case. If $G < S^*$, the high-inflation equilibrium is stable and the low-inflation
equilibrium is unstable; if $G > S^*$, $\dot{m} > 0$ everywhere, and thus there is explosive deflation.
And with G in either range, an increase in G leads to a downward jump in inflation (to see
this, note that [10.65] implies that the increase leads to an upward jump in $\dot{m}/m$; from
[10.61], this means that π must jump down).

One interpretation of these results is that it is only because parameter values happen
to fall in a particular range that we do not observe such unusual outcomes in practice. A
more appealing interpretation, however, is that these results suggest that the model omits
important features of actual economies. For example, if there is gradual adjustment of both
real money holdings and expected inflation, then the stability and dynamics of the model are
reasonable regardless of the adjustment speeds. More importantly, Ball (1993) and Cardoso
(1991) argue that the assumption that Y is fixed at $\overline{Y}$ omits crucial features of the dynamics of
high inflations (though not necessarily of hyperinflations). Ball and Cardoso develop models
that combine seignorage-driven monetary policy with the standard Keynesian assumption
that aggregate demand policies can reduce inflation only by temporarily depressing real
output. They show that with this assumption, only the low-inflation steady state is stable.
They then use their models to analyze a variety of aspects of high-inflation economies.

explosive, but that beyond this level it degenerates into hyperinflation. In addition, the model explains the central role of fiscal problems in causing high inflations and hyperinflations, and of fiscal reforms in ending them (Sargent, 1982).

Finally, the central role of seignorage in hyperinflations explains how the hyperinflations can end before money growth stabilizes. As described in Section 10.2, the increased demand for real money balances after hyperinflations end is satisfied by continued rapid growth of the nominal money stock rather than by declines in the price level. But this leaves the question of why the public expects low inflation when there is still rapid money growth. The answer is that the hyperinflations end when fiscal and monetary reforms eliminate either the deficit or the government's ability to use seignorage to finance it, or both. At the end of the German hyperinflation of 1922–1923, for example, Germany's World War I reparations were reduced, and the existing central bank was replaced by a new institution with much greater independence. Because of reforms like these, the public knows that the burst of money growth is only temporary (Sargent, 1982).[40]

10.9   The Costs of Inflation

All the analysis so far in this chapter assumes that inflation is costly, and that policymakers know what those costs are and how they vary with inflation. In fact, however, inflation's costs are not well understood. There is a wide gap between the popular view of inflation and the costs of inflation that economists can identify. Inflation is intensely disliked. In periods when inflation is moderately high in the United States, for example, it is often cited in opinion polls as the most important problem facing the country. It appears to have an important effect on the outcome of Presidential elections, and it is blamed for a wide array of problems. Yet economists have difficulty in identifying substantial costs of inflation.

Easily Identifiable Costs of Inflation

In many models, steady inflation just adds an equal amount to the growth rate of all prices and wages and to the nominal interest rate on all assets; it therefore has no effects on relative prices, real wages, or real interest rates. It is this fact that makes it hard to identify large costs of inflation.

The only exception to the statement that steady inflation has no real effects in simple models is that, since high-powered money's nominal return

---

[40] To incorporate the effects of the knowledge that the money growth is temporary into our formal analysis, we would have to let the change in real money holdings at a given time depend not just on current holdings and current inflation, but on current holdings and the entire expected path of inflation. See n. 37.

is fixed at zero, inflation necessarily reduces its real return. This gives rise to the most easily identified cost of inflation. The increased gap between the rates of return on money and on other assets causes people to exert effort to reduce their holdings of high-powered money; for example, they make smaller and more frequent conversions of other assets into currency. Since high-powered money is essentially costless for the government to produce, these efforts have no social benefit. Thus they represent a cost of inflation.

These socially unproductive efforts to conserve on money holdings can be eliminated if inflation is chosen so that the nominal interest rate—and hence the opportunity cost of holding money—is zero. Since real interest rates are typically modestly positive, this requires slight deflation.[41]

It seems unlikely, however, that this is all there is to the costs of inflation. Most obviously, the *shoe leather* costs associated with a positive nominal interest rate are surely small for almost all inflation rates observed in practice. Even if the price level is doubling each month, money is losing value only at a rate of a few percent per day; thus even in this case individuals will not incur extreme costs to reduce their money holdings.

A second readily identifiable cost of inflation is that nominal prices and wages must be changed more often, or indexing schemes must be adopted. Under natural assumptions about the distribution of relative-price shocks, the frequency of price adjustment is minimized with zero inflation. As Chapter 6 describes, however, the costs of price adjustment and indexation are almost certainly small.

The last cost of inflation that can be easily identified is that it distorts the tax system (see, for example, Feldstein, 1997). In most countries, income from capital gains and interest, and deductions for interest expenses and depreciation, are computed in nominal terms. As a result, inflation can have large effects on incentives for investment and saving. In the United States, the net effect of inflation through these various channels is to raise the effective tax rate on capital income substantially. In addition, inflation can significantly alter the relative attractiveness of different kinds of investment. For example, since the services from owner-occupied housing are generally not taxed and the income generated by ordinary business capital is, even without inflation the tax system encourages investment in owner-occupied housing relative to business capital. The fact that nominal interest payments are deductible from income causes inflation to exacerbate this distortion.

In contrast to the shoe leather and menu costs of inflation, the costs of inflation through tax distortions may be large. Thus it is important for policymakers to account for these effects. At the same time, these distortions are probably not the source of the public's intense dislike of inflation. These costs are quite specific and can be overcome through indexation. Yet the dislike of inflation seems much broader.

---

[41] See, for example, Tolley (1957) and Friedman (1969).

Thus it appears that we must look further to understand the popular view of inflation. There are several ways that inflation may have large costs that are more subtle than the costs just described. Some of the potential costs occur when inflation is anticipated and steady; others arise only if inflation is more variable and less predictable when it is higher.

Other Costs of Steady Inflation

There are at least three ways that steady, anticipated inflation may have large costs. First, because individual prices are not adjusted continuously, even steady inflation causes variations in relative prices as different firms adjust their prices at different times. As a result, inflation increases the departures of relative prices from the values they would have under frictionless price adjustment. Okun (1975) and Carlton (1982) argue informally that this inflation-induced relative-price variability disrupts markets where firms and customers form long-term relationships and prices are not adjusted frequently. For example, it can make it harder for potential customers to decide whether to enter a long-term relationship, or for the parties to a long-term relationship to check the fairness of the price they are trading at by comparing it with other prices. Formal models suggest that inflation can have complicated effects on market structure, long-term relationships, and efficiency (for example, Benabou, 1992, and Tommasi, 1994). This literature has not reached any consensus about the effects of inflation, but it does suggest some ways that inflation may have substantial costs. This literature also suggests that the immense disruptions associated with hyperinflations may just represent extreme versions of the effects of more moderate rates of inflation.

Second, individuals and firms may have trouble accounting for inflation (Modigliani and Cohn, 1979; Hall, 1984). Ten percent annual inflation causes the price level to rise by a factor of 45 in 40 years; even 3 percent inflation causes it to triple over that period. As a result, inflation can cause households and firms, which typically do their financial planning in nominal terms, to make large errors in saving for their retirement, in assessing the real burdens of mortgages, or in making long-term investments.

Finally, steady inflation may be costly not because of any real effects, but simply because people dislike it. People relate to their economic environment in terms of dollar values. They may therefore find large changes in dollar prices and wages disturbing even if the changes have no consequences for their real incomes. In Okun's (1975) analogy, a switch to a policy of reducing the length of the mile by a fixed amount each year might have few effects on real decisions, but might nonetheless cause considerable unhappiness. And indeed, Shiller (1997) reports survey evidence suggesting that people intensely dislike inflation for reasons other than the economic effects catalogued above. Since the ultimate goal of policy is presumably the public's well-being, such effects of inflation represent genuine costs.

Costs of Variable Inflation

Empirically, inflation is more variable and less predictable when it is higher (see, for example, Okun, 1971; Taylor, 1981; and Ball and Cecchetti, 1990). Okun, Ball and Cecchetti, and others argue that the association arises through the effect of inflation on policy. When inflation is low, there is a consensus that it should be kept low, and so inflation is steady and predictable. When inflation is moderate or high, however, there is disagreement about the importance of reducing it; indeed, the costs of slightly greater inflation may appear small. As a result, inflation is variable and difficult to predict.

If this argument is correct, the relationship between the mean and the variance of inflation represents a true effect of the mean on the variance. This implies some potentially important additional costs of inflation. First, since many assets are denominated in nominal terms, unanticipated changes in inflation redistribute wealth. Thus greater inflation variability increases uncertainty and lowers welfare. Second, with debts denominated in nominal terms, increased uncertainty about inflation may make firms and individuals reluctant to undertake investment projects, especially long-term ones.[42] And finally, highly variable inflation (or even higher average inflation alone) can also discourage long-term investment because firms and individuals view it as a symptom of a government that is functioning badly, and that may therefore resort to confiscatory taxation or other polices that are highly detrimental to capital-holders.

Empirically, there is a negative association between inflation and investment, and between inflation and growth (Fischer, 1993; Cukierman, Kalaitzidakis, Summers, and Webb, 1993; Bruno and Easterly, 1998). At this point, however, there is little evidence concerning whether these relationships are causal. It is not difficult to think of reasons that the associations might not represent true effects of inflation. In the short run, negative supply shocks are associated with both higher inflation and lower productivity growth. In the long run, governments that follow policies detrimental to growth— protectionism, large budget deficits, and so on—are likely to also pursue policies that result in inflation (Sala-i-Martin, 1991).

For high inflation rates, one can argue that the issue of whether the association between inflation and growth represents an effect of inflation on growth is of limited relevance. For a country to reduce inflation from

---

[42] If these costs of inflation variability are large, however, there may be large incentives for individuals and firms to write contracts in real rather than nominal terms, or to create markets that allow them to insure against inflation risk. Thus a complete account of large costs of inflation through these channels must explain the absence of these institutions.

very high levels, it is likely to need to adopt a broad range of budgetary and policy reforms. Thus growth is likely to rise, even though it may be the other reforms and not the reductions in inflation that bring it about.[43] In contrast, inflation can be reduced from moderate to low levels without fundamental policy reforms. Thus for moderate and low inflation, the issue of causation is crucial.

Potential Benefits of Inflation

So far we have considered only costs of inflation. But inflation can have benefits as well. Tobin (1972) observes that if it is particularly difficult for firms to cut nominal wages, real wages can make needed adjustments to sector-specific shocks more rapidly when inflation is higher. Summers (1991) notes that since nominal interest rates cannot be negative, low inflation (by causing usual nominal rates to be low) may limit the central bank's ability to stimulate aggregate demand in response to contractionary shocks; Krugman (1998) argues that this limitation was important to Japan's dismal economic performance in the 1990s. And just as inflation above some level can disrupt long-term planning and increase uncertainty, so too can inflation below some level. Given that average inflation has been significantly positive over the last several decades, it is not clear that zero inflation minimizes uncertainty and is least disruptive. Finally, as described above, inflation is a potential source of revenue for the government; under some conditions it is optimal for the government to use this revenue source in addition to more conventional taxes.

In addition, it is possible that the public's aversion to inflation represents not some deep understanding of the costs of inflation that has eluded economists, but a misapprehension. For example, Katona (1976) argues that the public perceives how inflation affects prices but not wages. Thus when inflation rises, individuals attribute only the faster growth of prices to the increase; they therefore incorrectly conclude that it has reduced their standard of living. Alternatively, individuals may dislike inflation just because times of high inflation are also times of low real growth; but if the high inflation is not in fact the source of the low growth, again inflation does not actually make them worse off.

Concluding Comments

As this discussion shows, research has not yet yielded any firm conclusions about the costs of inflation and the optimal rate of inflation. Thus economists and policymakers must rely on their judgment in weighing the

---

[43] This argument is due to Allan Meltzer.

different considerations. Loosely speaking, they fall into two groups. One group views inflation as pernicious, and believes that policy should focus on eliminating inflation and pay virtually no attention to other considerations. Members of this group generally believe that policy should aim for zero inflation or moderate deflation. The other group concludes that extremely low inflation is of little benefit, or perhaps even harmful, and believes that policy should aim to keep average inflation low to moderate but should keep other objectives in mind. The opinions of members of this group about the level of inflation that policy should aim for generally range from a few percent to close to 10 percent.

Problems

10.1. Consider a discrete-time version of the analysis of money growth, inflation, and real balances in Section 10.2. Suppose that money demand is given by $m_t - p_t = c - b(E_t p_{t+1} - p_t)$, where m and p are the logs of the money stock and the price level, and where we are implicitly assuming that output and the real interest rate are constant (see [10.56]).

(a) Solve for p_t in terms of m_t and $E_t p_{t+1}$.

(b) Use the law of iterated projections to express $E_t p_{t+1}$ in terms of $E_t m_{t+1}$ and $E_t p_{t+2}$.

(c) Iterate this process forward to express p_t in terms of m_t, $E_t m_{t+1}$, $E_t m_{t+2}$, ... (Assume that $\lim_{i \to \infty} E_t[\{b/(1+b)\}^i p_{t+i}] = 0$. This is a no-bubbles condition analogous to the one in Problem 7.7.)

(d) Explain intuitively why an increase in $E_t m_{t+i}$ for any $i > 0$ raises p_t.

(e) Suppose expected money growth is constant, so $E_t m_{t+i} = m_t + gi$. Solve for p_t in terms of m_t and g. How does an increase in g affect p_t?

10.2. Consider a discrete-time model where prices are completely unresponsive to unanticipated monetary shocks for one period and completely flexible thereafter. Suppose the IS and LM curves are $y = c - ar$ and $m - p = b + hy - ki$, where y, m, and p are the logs of output, the money supply, and the price level; r is the real interest rate; i is the nominal interest rate; and a, h, and k are positive parameters.

Assume that initially m is constant at some level, which we normalize to zero, and that y is constant at its flexible-price level, which we also normalize to zero. Now suppose that in some period—period 1 for simplicity—the monetary authority shifts unexpectedly to a policy of increasing m by some amount $g > 0$ each period.

(a) What are r, π^e, i, and p before the change in policy?

(b) Once prices have fully adjusted, $\pi^e = g$. Use this fact to find r, i, and p in period 2.

(c) In period 1, what are i, r, p, and the expectation of inflation from period 1 to period 2, $E_1[p_2] - p_1$?

(*d*) What determines whether the short-run effect of the monetary expansion is to raise or lower the nominal interest rate?

10.3. Assume, as in Problem 10.2, that prices are completely unresponsive to unanticipated monetary shocks for one period and completely flexible thereafter. Assume also that $y = c - ar$ and $m - p = b + hy - ki$ hold each period. Suppose, however, that the money supply follows a random walk: $m_t = m_{t-1} + u_t$, where u_t is a mean-zero, serially uncorrelated disturbance.

(*a*) Let E_t denote expectations as of period t. Explain why, for any t, $E_t[E_{t+1}[p_{t+2}] - p_{t+1}] = 0$, and thus why $E_t m_{t+1} - E_t p_{t+1} = b + h\bar{y} - k\bar{r}$.

(*b*) Use the result in part (*a*) to solve for y_t, p_t, i_t, and r_t in terms of m_{t-1} and u_t.

(*c*) Does the Fisher effect hold in this economy? That is, are changes in expected inflation reflected one-for-one in the nominal interest rate?

10.4. Suppose you want to test the hypothesis that the real interest rate is constant, so that all changes in the nominal interest rate reflect changes in expected inflation. Thus your hypothesis is $i_t = r + E_t \pi_{t+1}$.

(*a*) Consider a regression of i_t on a constant and π_{t+1}. Does the hypothesis that the real interest rate is constant make a general prediction about the coefficient on π_{t+1}? Explain. (Hint: For a univariate OLS regression, the coefficient on the right-hand-side variable equals the covariance between the right-hand-side and left-hand-side variables divided by the variance of the right-hand-side variable.)

(*b*) Consider a regression of π_{t+1} on a constant and i_t. Does the hypothesis that the real interest rate is constant make a general prediction about the coefficient on i_t? Explain.

(*c*) Some argue that the hypothesis that the real interest rate is constant implies that nominal interest rates move one-for-one with actual inflation in the long run—that is, that the hypothesis implies that in a regression of i on a constant and the current and many lagged values of π, the sum of the coefficients on the inflation variables will be 1. Is this claim correct? (Hint: Suppose that the behavior of actual inflation is given by $\pi_t = \rho \pi_{t-1} + e_t$, where e is white noise.)

10.5. Policy rules, rational expectations, and regime changes. (See Lucas, 1976, and Sargent, 1983.) Suppose that aggregate supply is given by the Lucas supply curve, $y_t = \bar{y} + b(\pi_t - \pi_t^e)$, $b > 0$, and suppose that monetary policy is determined by $m_t = m_{t-1} + a + \varepsilon_t$, where ε is a white-noise disturbance. Assume that private agents do not know the current values of m_t or ε_t; thus π_t^e is the expectation of $p_t - p_{t-1}$ given $m_{t-1}, \varepsilon_{t-1}, y_{t-1}$, and p_{t-1}. Finally, assume that aggregate demand is given by $y_t = m_t - p_t$.

(*a*) Find y_t in terms of m_{t-1}, m_t, and any other variables or parameters that are relevant.

(*b*) Are m_{t-1} and m_t all one needs to know about monetary policy to find y_t? Explain intuitively.

(c) Suppose that monetary policy is initially determined as above, with $a > 0$, and that the monetary authority then announces that it is switching to a new regime where a is 0. Suppose that private agents believe that the probability that the announcement is true is p. What is y_t in terms of m_{t-1}, m_t, p, $\bar{y}$, b, and the initial value of a?

(d) Using these results, describe how an examination of the money-output relationship might be used to measure the credibility of announcements of regime changes.

10.6. Regime changes and the term structure of interest rates. (See Blanchard, 1984; Mankiw and Miron, 1986; and Mankiw, Miron, and Weil, 1987.) Consider an economy where money is neutral. Specifically, assume that $\pi_t = \Delta m_t$ and that r is constant at zero. Suppose that the money supply is given by $\Delta m_t = k \Delta m_{t-1} + \varepsilon_t$, where ε is a white-noise disturbance.

(a) Assume that the rational-expectations theory of the term structure of interest rates holds (see [10.6]). Specifically, assume that the two-period interest rate is given by $i_t^2 = (i_t^1 + E_t i_{t+1}^1)/2$. i_t^1 denotes the nominal interest rate from t to $t+1$; thus, by the Fisher identity, it equals $r_t + E_t[p_{t+1}] - p_t$.

(i) What is i_t^1 as a function of Δm_t and k? (Assume that Δm_t is known at time t.)

(ii) What is $E_t i_{t+1}^1$ as a function of Δm_t and k?

(iii) What is the relation between i_t^2 and i_t^1; that is, what is i_t^2 as a function of i_t^1 and k?

(iv) How would a change in k affect the relation between i_t^2 and i_t^1? Explain intuitively.

(b) Suppose that the two-period rate includes a time-varying term premium: $i_t^2 = (i_t^1 + E_t i_{t+1}^1)/2 + \theta_t$, where θ is a white-noise disturbance that is independent of ε. Consider the OLS regression $i_{t+1}^1 - i_t^1 = a + b(i_t^2 - i_t^1) + e_{t+1}$.

(i) Under the rational-expectations theory of the term structure (with $\theta_t = 0$ for all t), what value would one expect for b? (Hint: For a univariate OLS regression, the coefficient on the right-hand-side variable equals the covariance between the right-hand-side and left-hand-side variables divided by the variance of the right-hand-side variable.)

(ii) Now suppose that θ has variance σ_θ^2. What value would one expect for b?

(iii) How do changes in k affect your answer to part (ii)? What happens to b as k approaches 1?

10.7. (Fischer and Summers, 1989.) Suppose inflation is determined as in Section 10.4. Suppose the government is able to reduce the costs of inflation; that is, suppose it reduces the parameter a in equation (10.11). Is society made better or worse off by this change? Explain intuitively.

10.8. Solving the dynamic-inconsistency problem through punishment. (Barro and Gordon, 1983b.) Consider a policymaker whose objective function is

$\sum_{t=0}^{\infty} \beta^t (y_t - a\pi_t^2/2)$, where $a > 0$ and $0 < \beta < 1$. y_t is determined by the Lucas supply curve, (10.10), each period. Expected inflation is determined as follows. If π has equaled $\hat{\pi}$ (where $\hat{\pi}$ is a parameter) in all previous periods, then $\pi^e = \hat{\pi}$. If π ever differs from $\hat{\pi}$, then $\pi^e = b/a$ in all subsequent periods.

(a) What is the equilibrium of the model in all subsequent periods if π ever differs from $\hat{\pi}$?

(b) Suppose π has always been equal to $\hat{\pi}$, so $\pi^e = \hat{\pi}$. If the monetary authority chooses to depart from $\pi = \hat{\pi}$, what value of π does it choose? What level of its lifetime objective function does it attain under this strategy? If the monetary authority continues to choose $\pi = \hat{\pi}$ every period, what level of its lifetime objective function does it attain?

(c) For what values of $\hat{\pi}$ does the monetary authority choose $\pi = \hat{\pi}$? Are there values of a, b, and β such that if $\hat{\pi} = 0$, the monetary authority chooses $\pi = 0$?

10.9. Other equilibria in the Barro–Gordon model. Consider the situation described in Problem 10.8. Find the parameter values (if any) for which each of the following is an equilibrium:

(a) **One-period punishment.** π_t^e equals $\hat{\pi}$ if $\pi_{t-1} = \pi_{t-1}^e$ and equals b/a otherwise; $\pi = \hat{\pi}$ each period.

(b) **Severe punishment.** (Abreu, 1988, and Rogoff, 1987.) π_t^e equals $\hat{\pi}$ if $\pi_{t-1} = \pi_{t-1}^e$, equals $\pi_0 > b/a$ if $\pi_{t-1}^e = \hat{\pi}$ and $\pi_{t-1} \neq \hat{\pi}$, and equals b/a otherwise; $\pi = \hat{\pi}$ each period.

(c) **Repeated discretionary equilibrium.** $\pi = \pi^e = b/a$ each period.

10.10. Consider the situation analyzed in Problem 10.8, but assume that there is only some finite number of periods rather than an infinite number. What is the unique equilibrium? (Hint: Reason backward from the last period.)

10.11. More on solving the dynamic-inconsistency problem through reputation. (This is based on Cukierman and Meltzer, 1986.) Consider a policymaker who is in office for two periods and whose objective function is $E[\sum_{t=1}^{2} b(\pi_t - \pi_t^e) + c\pi_t - a\pi_t^2/2]$. The policymaker is chosen randomly from a pool of possible policymakers with differing tastes. Specifically, c is distributed normally over possible policymakers with mean $\bar{c}$ and variance $\sigma_c^2 > 0$. a and b are the same for all possible policymakers.

The policymaker cannot control inflation perfectly. Instead, $\pi_t = \hat{\pi}_t + \varepsilon_t$, where $\hat{\pi}_t$ is chosen by the policymaker (taking π_t^e as given) and where ε_t is normal with mean 0 and variance $\sigma_\varepsilon^2 > 0$. ε_1, ε_2, and c are independent. The public does not observe $\hat{\pi}_t$ and ε_t separately, but only π_t. Similarly, the public does not observe c.

Finally, assume that π_2^e is a linear function of π_1: $\pi_2^e = \alpha + \beta\pi_1$.

(a) What is the policymaker's choice of $\hat{\pi}_2$? What is the resulting expected value of the policymaker's second-period objective function, $b(\pi_2 - \pi_2^e) + c\pi_2 - a\pi_2^2/2$, as a function of π_2^e?

(b) What is the policymaker's choice of $\hat{\pi}_1$ taking α and β as given and accounting for the impact of π_1 on π_2^e?

(c) Assuming rational expectations, what is β? (Hint: Use the signal extraction procedure described in Section 6.2.)

(d) Explain intuitively why the policymaker chooses a lower value of $\hat{\pi}$ in the first period than in the second.

10.12. The tradeoff between low average inflation and flexibility in response to shocks with delegation of control over monetary policy. (Rogoff, 1985.) Suppose that output is given by $y = \bar{y} + b(\pi - \pi^e)$, and that the social welfare function is $yy - a\pi^2/2$, where y is a random variable with mean $\bar{y}$ and variance σ_y^2. π^e is determined before y is observed; the policymaker, however, chooses π after y is known. Suppose policy is made by someone whose objective function is $cyy - a\pi^2/2$.

(a) What is the policymaker's choice of π given π^e, y, and c?

(b) What is π^e?

(c) What is the expected value of the true social welfare function, $yy - a\pi^2/2$?

(d) What value of c maximizes expected social welfare? Interpret your result.

10.13. (a) In the model of reputation analyzed in Section 10.5, is social welfare higher when the policymaker turns out to be a type 1 or a type 2?

(b) In the model of delegation analyzed in Section 10.5, suppose that the policymaker's preferences are believed to be described by (10.25), with $a' > a$, when π^e is determined. Is social welfare higher if these are actually the policymaker's preferences, or if the policymaker's preferences in fact match the social welfare function, (10.11)?

10.14. Money versus interest-rate targeting. (Poole, 1970.) Suppose the economy is described by linear IS and LM curves that are subject to disturbances: $y = c - ai + \varepsilon_{IS}$, $m - p = hy - ki + \varepsilon_{LM}$, where ε_{IS} and ε_{LM} are independent, mean-zero shocks with variances σ_{IS}^2 and σ_{LM}^2, and where a, h, and k are positive. Policymakers want to stabilize output, but they cannot observe y or the shocks, ε_{IS} and ε_{LM}. Assume for simplicity that p is fixed.

(a) Suppose the policymaker fixes i at some level $\bar{i}$. What is the variance of y?

(b) Suppose the policymaker fixes m at some level $\bar{m}$. What is the variance of y?

(c) If there are only LM shocks (so $\sigma_{IS}^2 = 0$), does money targeting or interest-rate targeting lead to a lower variance of y?

(d) If there are only IS shocks (so $\sigma_{LM}^2 = 0$), does money or interest-rate targeting lead to a lower variance of y?

(e) Explain your results in parts (c) and (d) intuitively.

(f) When there are only IS shocks, is there a policy that produces a variance of y that is lower than either money or interest-rate targeting? If so, what policy minimizes the variance of y? If not, why not? (Hint: Consider the LM curve, $m - p = hy - ki$.)

10.15. Uncertainty and policy. (Brainard, 1967.) Suppose output is given by $y = x + (k + \varepsilon_k)z + u$, where z is some policy instrument controlled by the government and k is the expected value of the multiplier for that instrument. ε_k and u are independent, mean-zero disturbances that are unknown when the policymaker chooses z, and that have variances σ_k^2 and σ_u^2. Finally, x is a disturbance that is known when z is chosen. The policymaker wants to minimize $E[(y - y^*)^2]$.

(a) Find $E[(y - y^*)^2]$ as a function of x, k, y^*, σ_k^2, and σ_u^2.

(b) Find the first-order condition for z, and solve for z.

(c) How, if at all, does σ_u^2 affect how policy should respond to shocks (that is, to the realized value of x)? Thus, how does uncertainty about the state of the economy affect the case for "fine-tuning"?

(d) How, if at all, does σ_k^2 affect how policy should respond to shocks (that is, to the realized value of x)? Thus, how does uncertainty about the effects of policy affect the case for "fine-tuning"?

10.16. Growth and seignorage, and an alternative explanation of the inflation-growth relationship. (Friedman, 1971.) Suppose that money demand is given by $\ln(M/P) = a - bi + \ln Y$, and that Y is growing at rate g_Y. What rate of inflation leads to the highest path of seignorage?

10.17. (Cagan, 1956.) Suppose that instead of adjusting their real money holdings gradually toward the desired level, individuals adjust their expectation of inflation gradually toward actual inflation. Thus equations (10.59) and (10.60) are replaced by $m(t) = Ce^{-b\pi^e(t)}$ and $\dot{\pi}^e(t) = \beta[\pi(t) - \pi^e(t)]$, $0 < \beta < 1/b$.

(a) Follow steps analogous to the derivation of (10.65) to find an expression for $\dot{\pi}^e(t)$ as a function of $\pi(t)$.

(b) Sketch the resulting phase diagram for the case of $G > S^*$. What are the dynamics of π^e and m?

(c) Sketch the phase diagram for the case of $G < S^*$.

Chapter **11**
BUDGET DEFICITS AND FISCAL POLICY

In the 1980s and early 1990s, the U.S. federal government ran a large budget deficit every year, with the average deficit exceeding 3 percent of GDP. The deficits began falling sharply in the mid-1990s, and by the end of the 1990s the budget was projected to be in surplus for the next decade. But the projections also implied that U.S. fiscal policy is far from sustainable. There is likely to be a sharp rise in the number of retirees relative to the number of workers in coming decades. In the absence of policy changes, the resulting increases in social security and health care spending are likely to raise the deficit to 10 percent of GDP or more over the coming 50 years (Congressional Budget Office, 1999; Auerbach, 1997). Many other industrialized countries have run persistently large budget deficits in recent decades and face similar long-term budgetary challenges.

These large and persistent budget deficits have generated considerable concern. There is a widespread perception that they reduce growth, and that they could lead to a crisis of some type if they go on too long or become too large.

This chapter studies the sources and effects of budget deficits. Section 11.1 begins by describing the budget constraint a government faces and some accounting issues involving the budget. Section 11.2 lays out a baseline model where the government's choice of whether to finance its purchases through taxes or borrowing has no impact on the economy. Section 11.3 discusses various reasons that this result of *Ricardian equivalence* may fail.

The next several sections consider the sources of budget deficits in settings where Ricardian equivalence fails. Section 11.4 presents the *tax-smoothing* model of deficits. The model's basic idea is that since taxes distort individuals' choices and since those distortions rise more than proportionally with the tax rate, steady moderate tax rates are preferable to alternating periods of high and low tax rates. As we will see, this theory provides an appealing explanation for such phenomena as governments' reliance on deficits to finance wars.

Tax-smoothing does not appear to account for large persistent deficits or for the pursuit of fiscal policies that are unlikely to be sustainable. The presentation therefore turns to the possibility that there is a systematic tendency for the political process to produce excessive deficits. Section 11.5 provides an introduction to the economic analysis of politics. Section 11.6 presents a model where conflict over the composition of government spending can lead to excessive deficits. Section 11.7 considers a model where excessive deficits can result from conflict over how the burden of reducing a deficit is to be divided among different groups.

Finally, Section 11.8 presents some empirical evidence about the sources and effects of deficits, Section 11.9 discusses the costs of deficits, and Section 11.10 presents a simple model of debt crises.[1]

11.1   The Government Budget Constraint

The Basic Budget Constraint

A household's budget constraint is that the present value of its consumption must be less than or equal to its initial wealth plus the present value of its labor income. A government faces an analogous constraint: the present value of its purchases of goods and services must be less than or equal to its initial wealth plus the present value of its tax receipts (net of transfer payments). To express this constraint, let $G(t)$ and $T(t)$ denote the government's real purchases and taxes at time t, and $D(0)$ its initial real debt outstanding. As in Section 2.2, let $R(t)$ denote $\int_{\tau=0}^{t} r(\tau)d\tau$, where $r(\tau)$ is the real interest rate at time τ. Thus the value of a unit of output at time t discounted back to time 0 is $e^{-R(t)}$. With this notation, the government's budget constraint is

$$\int_{t=0}^{\infty} e^{-R(t)} G(t)\, dt \leq -D(0) + \int_{t=0}^{\infty} e^{-R(t)} T(t)\, dt. \tag{11.1}$$

---

[1] The chapter focuses on fiscal policy in the long run. Fiscal policy also has short-run effects on the economy: it can raise or lower output, or counteract disturbances that would otherwise change output. The main macroeconomic issues concerning these short-run effects are similar to those concerning the short-run effects of monetary policy. For example, optimal fiscal policy may be dynamically inconsistent. That is, the fiscal authorities may choose to stimulate aggregate demand once wages and prices are set if expected inflation is low; but the knowledge that they have this incentive will cause price-setters and wage-setters not to expect low inflation. Similarly, the analysis of whether there are significant benefits to stabilization policy applies just as much to fiscal policy as to monetary policy. The most interesting new issues involving the short-run effects of fiscal policy concern the conditions under which changes in taxes and purchases affect aggregate demand. There are cases where tax cuts do not affect aggregate demand at all, and cases where tax cuts and increases in purchases are contractionary rather than expansionary. We will encounter some of the most interesting of these cases in Sections 11.2 and 11.4.

Note that because $D(0)$ represents debt rather than wealth, it enters negatively into the budget constraint.

The government's budget constraint does not prevent it from staying permanently in debt, or even from always increasing the amount of its debt. Recall that the household's budget constraint in the Ramsey model implies that the limit of the present value of its wealth cannot be negative (see Section 2.2). Similarly, the restriction the budget constraint places on the government is that the limit of the present value of its debt cannot be positive. That is, one can show that (11.1) is equivalent to

$$\lim_{s \to \infty} e^{-R(s)} D(s) \leq 0. \tag{11.2}$$

The derivation of (11.2) from (11.1) follows steps analogous to the derivation of (2.10) from (2.6).

If the real interest rate is always positive, a positive but constant value of D—so the government never pays off its debt—satisfies the budget constraint. Likewise, a policy where D is always growing satisfies the budget constraint if the growth rate of D is less than the real interest rate.

The simplest definition of the budget deficit is that it is the rate of change of the stock of debt. The rate of change in the stock of real debt equals the difference between the government's purchases and revenues, plus the real interest on its debt. That is,

$$\dot{D}(t) = [G(t) - T(t)] + r(t)D(t), \tag{11.3}$$

where again $r(t)$ is the real interest rate at t.

The term in brackets on the right-hand side of (11.3) is referred to as the *primary deficit.* Considering the primary rather than the total deficit is often a better way of gauging how fiscal policy at a given time is contributing to the government's budget constraint. For example, we can rewrite the government budget constraint, (11.1), as

$$\int_{t=0}^{\infty} e^{-R(t)} [T(t) - G(t)] dt \geq D(0). \tag{11.4}$$

Expressed this way, the budget constraint states that the government must run primary surpluses large enough in present value to offset its initial debt.

Some Measurement Issues

The government budget constraint involves the present values of the entire paths of purchases and revenues, and not the deficit at a point in time. As a result, conventional measures of either the primary or total deficit can be misleading about how fiscal actions are contributing to the budget constraint. Here we consider three examples.

The first example is inflation's effect on the measured deficit. The change in nominal debt outstanding—that is, the conventionally measured budget deficit—equals the difference between nominal purchases and revenues, plus the nominal interest on the debt. If we let B denote the nominal debt, the nominal deficit is thus

$$\dot{B}(t) = P(t)[G(t) - T(t)] + i(t)P(t)D(t), \tag{11.5}$$

where P is the price level and i is the nominal interest rate. When inflation rises, the nominal interest rate rises for a given real rate. Thus interest payments and the deficit increase. Yet the higher interest payments are just offsetting the fact that the higher inflation is eroding the real value of debt. Nothing involving the behavior of the real stock of debt, and thus nothing involving the government's budget constraint, is affected.

To see this formally, we use the fact that, by definition, the nominal interest rate equals the real rate plus inflation.[2] This allows us to rewrite our expression for the nominal deficit as

$$\dot{B}(t) = P(t)[G(t) - T(t)] + [r(t) + \pi(t)]P(t)D(t)$$
$$= P(t)[\dot{D}(t) + \pi(t)D(t)], \tag{11.6}$$

where the second line uses equation (11.3) for the rate of change in real debt outstanding. Dividing both sides of (11.6) by the price level yields

$$\frac{\dot{B}(t)}{P(t)} = \dot{D}(t) + \pi(t)D(t). \tag{11.7}$$

That is, assuming that the stock of debt is positive, higher inflation raises the conventional measure of the deficit even when it is deflated by the price level.

The second example is the sale of an asset. If the government sells an asset, it increases current revenue and thus reduces the current deficit. But it also forgoes the revenue the asset would have generated in the future. In the natural case where the value of the asset equals the present value of the revenue it will produce, the sale has no effect on the present value of the government's revenue. Thus the sale affects the current deficit but does not affect the budget constraint.

Our third example is an unfunded liability. An unfunded liability is a government commitment to incur expenses in the future that is made without provision for corresponding revenues. In contrast to an asset sale, an unfunded liability affects the budget constraint without affecting the current deficit. If the government sells an asset, the set of policies that satisfy the budget constraint is unchanged. If it incurs an unfunded liability, on the other hand, satisfying the budget constraint requires higher future taxes or lower future purchases.

In industrialized countries, the largest unfunded liabilities are entitlement programs, particularly social security and health insurance. These unfunded liabilities are typically larger than the conventionally measured

---

[2] We neglect uncertainty about inflation for simplicity.

stock of government debt; they are the main reason that fiscal policies in these countries do not appear to be on sustainable paths. Unfunded liabilities are also important to short-term developments. For example, when medical costs rise unexpectedly, the expected present value of the government's future health insurance spending rises. The year-to-year changes in the expected present value of government spending in the United States through this channel often exceed the value of major deficit reduction packages.[3]

The lack of a close relationship between the deficit and the budget constraint implies that the government can satisfy legislative or constitutional rules restricting the deficit without substantive changes. Asset sales and switches from conventional spending programs to unfunded liabilities are just two of the devices it can use to satisfy requirements about the measured deficit without any genuine changes in policies. Others include "off-budget" spending, mandates concerning private-sector spending, unrealistic forecasts, and shifts of spending among different fiscal years.

Despite this fact, the empirical evidence concerning the effects of deficit restrictions, though not clear-cut, suggests that they have genuine effects on government behavior.[4] If this is correct, it suggests that it is costly for governments to use devices that reduce measured deficits without substantive changes.

Ponzi Games

The fact that the government's budget constraint involves not just present values, but present values over the infinite future, introduces another complication: there are cases where the government does not have to satisfy the constraint. An agent's budget constraint is not exogenous, but is determined by the transactions other agents are willing to make. If the economy consists of a finite number of individuals who have not reached satiation, the government does indeed have to satisfy (11.1). If the present value of the government's purchases exceeds the present value of its revenues, the limit of the present value of its debt is strictly positive (see [11.1] and [11.2]). And if there are a finite number of agents, at least one agent must be holding a strictly positive fraction of this debt. This means that the limit of the present value of the agent's wealth is strictly positive; that is, the present value of the agent's spending is strictly less than the present value of his or her after-tax income. This cannot be an equilibrium, because such an agent can obtain higher utility by increasing his or her spending.

If there are infinitely many agents, however, this argument does not apply. Even if the present value of each agent's spending equals the present

---

[3] This observation is due to Laurence Kotlikoff.

[4] Much of the evidence comes from the examination of U.S. states. See Eichengreen (1992); Alt and Lowry (1994); Poterba (1994); Bayoumi, Goldstein, and Woglom (1995); and Bohn and Inman (1995).

value of his or her after-tax income, the present value of the private sector's total spending may be less than the present value of its total after-tax
income. To see this, consider the Diamond overlapping-generations model
of Chapter 2. In that model, each individual saves early in life and dissaves
late in life. As a result, at any time some individuals have saved and not yet
dissaved. Thus the present value of private-sector income up to any date
exceeds the present value of private-sector spending up to that date. If this
difference does not approach zero, the government can take advantage of
this by running a Ponzi scheme. That is, it can issue debt at some date and
roll it over forever.

The specific condition that must be satisfied for the government to be
able to run a Ponzi scheme in the Diamond model is that the equilibrium is
dynamically inefficient, so that the real interest rate is less than the growth
rate of the economy. Consider what happens in such a situation if the government issues a small amount of debt at time 0 and tries to roll it over
indefinitely. That is, each period, when the previous period's debt comes
due, the government just issues new debt to pay the principal and interest
on the old debt. With this policy, the value of the debt outstanding grows at
the real interest rate. Since the growth rate of the economy exceeds the real
interest rate, the ratio of the value of the debt to the size of the economy is
continually falling. Thus there is no reason the government cannot follow
this policy. Yet the policy does not satisfy the conventional budget constraint: because the government is rolling the debt over forever, the value
of the debt discounted to time 0 is constant, and so does not approach zero.

One implication is that debt issue is a possible solution to dynamic inefficiency. By getting individuals to hold some of their savings in the form of
government debt rather than capital, the government can reduce the capital
stock from its inefficiently high level.

The possibility of a government Ponzi scheme is largely a theoretical curiosity, however. In the realistic case where the economy is not dynamically
inefficient, Ponzi games are not feasible, and the government must satisfy
the traditional present-value budget constraint.[5]

11.2 The Ricardian Equivalence Result

We now turn to the effects of the government's choice between taxes and
bonds. A natural starting point is the Ramsey–Cass–Koopmans model of
Chapter 2 with lump-sum taxation, since that model avoids all complications involving market imperfections and heterogeneous households.

---

[5] See O'Connell and Zeldes (1988) for more on these issues. The situation is more
complicated under uncertainty. In an uncertain economy, the realized rate of return on
government debt is sometimes less than the economy's growth rate even when the economy
is not dynamically inefficient. As a result, an attempt to issue debt and roll it over forever
has a positive probability of succeeding. See Bohn (1995) and Ball, Elmendorf, and Mankiw
(1998).

When there are taxes, the representative household's budget constraint is that the present value of its consumption cannot exceed its initial wealth plus the present value of its after-tax labor income. And with no uncertainty or market imperfections, there is no reason for the interest rate the household faces at each point in time to differ from the one the government faces. Thus the household's budget constraint is

$$\int_{t=0}^{\infty} e^{-R(t)} C(t)\, dt \le K(0) + D(0) + \int_{t=0}^{\infty} e^{-R(t)} [W(t) - T(t)]\, dt. \qquad (11.8)$$

Here $C(t)$ is consumption at t, $W(t)$ is labor income, and $T(t)$ is taxes; $K(0)$ and $D(0)$ are the quantities of capital and government bonds at time 0.[6]

Breaking the integral on the right-hand side of (11.8) in two gives us

$$\int_{t=0}^{\infty} e^{-R(t)} C(t) dt \le K(0) + D(0) + \int_{t=0}^{\infty} e^{-R(t)} W(t)\, dt - \int_{t=0}^{\infty} e^{-R(t)} T(t)\, dt.$$
$$(11.9)$$

It is reasonable to assume that the government satisfies its budget constraint, (11.1), with equality. If it did not, its wealth would be growing forever, which does not seem realistic.[7] With that assumption, (11.1) implies that the present value of taxes, $\int_{t=0}^{\infty} e^{-R(t)} T(t)\, dt$, equals initial debt, $D(0)$, plus the present value of government purchases, $\int_{t=0}^{\infty} e^{-R(t)} G(t)\, dt$. Substituting this fact into (11.9) gives us

$$\int_{t=0}^{\infty} e^{-R(t)} C(t)\, dt \le K(0) + \int_{t=0}^{\infty} e^{-R(t)} W(t)\, dt - \int_{t=0}^{\infty} e^{-R(t)} G(t)\, dt. \quad (11.10)$$

Equation (11.10) shows that we can express households' budget constraint in terms of the present value of government purchases without reference to the division of the financing of those purchases at any point in time between taxes and bonds. In addition, it is reasonable to assume that taxes do not enter directly into households' preferences; this is true in any model where utility depends only on such conventional economic goods as consumption, leisure, and so on. Since the path of taxes does not enter either households' budget constraint or their preferences, it does not affect consumption. Likewise, it is government purchases, not taxes, that affect capital accumulation, since investment equals output minus the sum of consumption and government purchases. Thus we have a key result: only the quantity of government purchases, not the division of the financing of those purchases between taxes and bonds, affects the economy.

---

[6] In writing the representative household's budget constraint in this way, we are implicitly normalizing the number of households to 1. With H households, all the terms in (11.8) must be divided by H: the representative household's consumption at t is $1/H$ of total consumption, its initial wealth is $1/H$ of $K(0) + D(0)$, and so on. Multiplying both sides by H then yields (11.8).

[7] Moreover, if the government attempts such a policy, an equilibrium may not exist if its debt is denominated in real terms. See, for example, Aiyagari and Gertler (1985) and Woodford (1995).

The result of the irrelevance of the government's financing decisions is the famous Ricardian equivalence between debt and taxes.[8] The logic of the result is simple. To see it clearly, think of the government giving some amount D of bonds to each household at some date t_1 and planning to retire this debt at a later date t_2; this requires that each household be taxed amount $e^{R(t_2)-R(t_1)}D$ at t_2. Such a policy has two effects on the representative household. First, the household has acquired an asset—the bond—that has present value as of t_1 of D. Second, it has acquired a liability—the future tax obligation—that also has present value as of t_1 of D. Thus the bond does not represent "net wealth" to the household, and it therefore does not affect the household's consumption behavior. In effect, the household simply saves the bond and the interest the bond is accumulating until t_2, at which point it uses the bond and interest to pay the taxes the government is levying to retire the bond.

Traditional economic models, and many informal discussions, assume that a shift from tax to bond finance increases consumption. Traditional analyses of consumption often model consumption as depending just on current disposable income, $Y - T$. With this assumption, a bond-financed tax cut raises consumption. The Ricardian and traditional views of consumption have very different implications for many policy issues. For example, the traditional view implies that the United States's large budget deficits in the 1980s and 1990s increased consumption, and thus reduced capital accumulation and growth. But the Ricardian view implies that they had no effect on consumption or capital accumulation. To give another example, governments often cut taxes during recessions to increase consumption spending. But if Ricardian equivalence holds, these efforts are futile.

11.3   The Ricardian Equivalence Debate

An enormous amount of research has been devoted to trying to determine how much truth there is to Ricardian equivalence. There are, of course, many reasons that Ricardian equivalence does not hold exactly. The important question, however, is whether there are large departures from it.

The Entry of New Households into the Economy

One reason that Ricardian equivalence is likely not to be exactly correct is that there is turnover in the population. When new individuals are entering the economy, some of the future tax burden associated with a bond issue is borne by individuals who are not alive when the bond is issued. As a

---

[8] The name comes from the fact that this idea was first proposed (though ultimately rejected) by David Ricardo. See O'Driscoll (1977).

result, the bond represents net wealth to those who are currently living, and thus affects their behavior. This possibility is illustrated by the Diamond overlapping-generations model.

There are two difficulties with this objection to Ricardian equivalence. First, a series of individuals with finite lifetimes may behave as if they are a single household. In particular, if individuals care about the welfare of their descendants, and if that concern is sufficiently strong that they make positive bequests, the government's financing decisions may again be irrelevant. This result, like the basic Ricardian equivalence result, follows from the logic of budget constraints. Consider the example of a bond issue today repaid by a tax levied several generations in the future. It is possible for the consumption of all the generations involved to remain unchanged. All that is needed is for each generation, beginning with the one alive at the time of the bond issue, to increase its bequest by the size of the bond issue plus the accumulated interest; the generation living at the time of the tax increase can then use those funds to pay the tax levied to retire the bond.

Although this discussion shows that individuals can keep their consumption paths unchanged in response to the bond issue, it does not establish whether they do. The bond issue does provide each generation involved (other than the last) with some possibilities it did not have before. Because government purchases are unchanged, the bond issue is associated with a cut in current taxes. The bond issue therefore increases the lifetime resources available to the individuals then alive. *But the fact that the individuals are already planning to leave positive bequests means that they are at an interior optimum in choosing between their own consumption and that of their descendants.* Thus they do not change their behavior. Only if the requirement that bequests not be negative is a binding constraint—that is, only if bequests are zero—does the bond issue affect consumption. Since we have assumed that this is not the case, the individuals do not change their consumption; instead they pass the bond and the accumulated interest on to the next generation. Those individuals, for the same reason, do the same, and the process continues until the generation that has to retire the debt uses its additional inheritance to do so.

The result that intergenerational links can cause a series of individuals with finite lifetimes to behave as if they are a household with an infinite horizon is due to Barro (1974). It was this insight that started the debate on Ricardian equivalence, and it has led to a large literature on the reasons for bequests and transfers among generations, their extent, and their implications for Ricardian equivalence and many other issues.[9]

The second difficulty with the argument that finite lifetimes cause Ricardian equivalence to fail is more prosaic. As a practical matter, lifetimes are long enough that if the only reason that governments' financing decisions

---

[9] For a few examples, see Bernheim, Shleifer, and Summers (1985); Bernheim and Bagwell (1988); Wilhelm (1996); and Altonji, Hayashi, and Kotlikoff (1997).

matter is because lifetimes are finite, Ricardian equivalence is a good approximation (Poterba and Summers, 1987). For realistic cases, large parts of the present value of the taxes associated with bond issues are levied during the lifetimes of the individuals alive at the time of the issue. For example, Poterba and Summers calculate that most of the burden of retiring the United States's World War II debt was borne by people who were already of working age at the time of the war, and they find that similar results hold for other wartime debt issues. Thus even in the absence of intergenerational links, bonds represent only a small amount of net wealth.

Further, the fact that lifetimes are long means that an increase in wealth has only a modest impact on consumption. For example, if individuals spread out the spending of an unexpected wealth increase equally over the remainder of their lives, an individual with 30 years left to live increases consumption spending in response to a one-dollar increase in wealth only by about three cents.[10] Thus it appears that if Ricardian equivalence fails in a quantitatively important way, it must be for some reason other than an absence of intergenerational links.

Ricardian Equivalence and the Permanent-Income Hypothesis

The issue of whether Ricardian equivalence is a good approximation is closely connected with the issue of whether the permanent-income hypothesis provides a good description of consumption behavior. In the permanent-income model, only a household's lifetime budget constraint affects its behavior; the time path of its after-tax income does not matter. A bond issue today repaid by future taxes affects the path of after-tax income without changing the lifetime budget constraint. Thus if the permanent-income hypothesis describes consumption behavior well, Ricardian equivalence is likely to be a good approximation. But significant departures from the permanent-income hypothesis can lead to significant departures from Ricardian equivalence.

We saw in Chapter 7 that the permanent-income hypothesis in fact fails in important ways: most households have little wealth, and predictable changes in after-tax income lead to predictable changes in consumption. This strongly suggests that Ricardian equivalence fails in a quantitatively important way: if current disposable income has a significant impact on consumption for a given lifetime budget constraint, a tax cut accompanied by an offsetting future tax increase has a significant impact on consumption.

The details of how failures of the permanent-income hypothesis can lead to failures of Ricardian equivalence depend on the sources of the failures.

---

[10] Of course, this is not exactly what an optimizing individual would do. See, for example, Problem 2.5.

Here we consider two possibilities. The first is liquidity constraints. When the government issues a bond to a household to be repaid by higher taxes on the household at a later date, it is in effect borrowing on the household's behalf. If the household already had the option of borrowing at the same interest rate as the government, the policy has no effect on its opportunities, and thus no effect on its behavior. But suppose the household faces a higher interest rate for borrowing than the government does. If the household would borrow at the government interest rate and increase its consumption if that were possible, it will respond to the government's borrowing on its behalf by raising its consumption (see, for example, Tobin, 1980, and Hubbard and Judd, 1986).

This discussion omits a potentially important complication. Liquidity constraints are not exogenous. Instead, they reflect calculations by potential lenders of borrowers' likelihood of repaying their loans. When the government issues bonds today to be repaid by future taxes, households' future liabilities are increased. If lenders do not change the amounts and terms on which they are willing to lend, the chances that their loans will be repaid therefore fall. Thus rational lenders respond to the bond issue by reducing the amounts they lend. Indeed, there are cases where the amount that households can borrow falls one-for-one with government bond issues, so that Ricardian equivalence holds even in the presence of liquidity constraints (Hayashi, 1987; Yotsuzuka, 1987).

This possibility arises only when taxes are lump-sum, however. In realistic cases, bond issues have little impact on the amounts households can borrow. The intuition is that when a borrower fails to repay a loan, it is usually because his or her income turned out to be low. But if taxes are a function of income, this is precisely the case when the borrower's share of the tax liability associated with a bond issue is small. A bond issue is therefore likely to have only a small effect on the borrower's probability of repaying the loan, and hence only a small effect on the amount he or she can borrow (Bernheim, 1987). Thus, if liquidity constraints are the source of important failures of the permanent-income hypothesis, there are likely to be large departures from Ricardian equivalence.

The second possible source of failures of the permanent-income hypothesis we will consider is the combination of a precautionary-saving motive and a high discount rate. Recall from Section 7.6 that this combination can account for buffer-stock saving and the large role of current disposable income in consumption choices. Suppose that these forces are important to consumption, and consider our standard example of a bond issue to be repaid by higher taxes in the future. The impact on consumption again turns out to hinge on the fact that taxes are not lump-sum. With lump-sum taxes, the bond issue has no impact on the household's budget constraint; that is, the present value of the household's lifetime after-tax income in every state of the world is unchanged. As a result, the bond issue does not affect consumption. Intuitively, the household's prime motive for saving in this environment is to avoid low consumption if its future income turns out to be low. With lump-sum taxes, the household's tax liability when income is low is higher by its full share of the taxes needed to pay off the bond. To keep this from reducing its consumption in this situation, the household saves the tax cut.

Since taxes are a function of income, however, in practice the situation is very different. The bond issue causes the household's future tax liabilities to be only slightly higher if its income turns out to be low. That is, the combination of the tax cut today and the higher future taxes raises the present value of the household's lifetime after-tax income in the event that its future income is low, and reduces it in the event that its future income is high. As a result, the household has little incentive to increase its saving. Instead it can indulge its high discount rate and increase its consumption, knowing that its tax liabilities will be high only if its income is high (Barsky, Mankiw, and Zeldes, 1986).

This discussion suggests that there is little reason to expect Ricardian equivalence to provide a good first approximation in practice. The Ricardian equivalence result rests on the permanent-income hypothesis, and the permanent-income hypothesis fails in quantitatively important ways. Nonetheless, because it is so simple and logical, Ricardian equivalence (like the permanent-income hypothesis) is a valuable theoretical baseline.

11.4   Tax-Smoothing

We now turn to the question of what determines the deficit. This section develops a model, due to Barro (1979), in which deficits are chosen optimally. Sections 11.5 through 11.7 consider reasons that deficits might be inefficiently high.

Barro focuses on the government's desire to minimize the distortions associated with obtaining revenue. The distortions created by taxes are likely to increase more than proportionally with the amount of revenue raised. In standard models, for example, a tax has no distortion costs to first order. Thus for low taxes, the distortion costs are approximately proportional to the square of the amount of revenue raised. When distortions rise more than proportionally with taxes, they are on average higher under a policy of variable taxes than under one with steady taxes at the same average level. Thus the desire to minimize distortions provides a reason for the government to smooth the path of taxes over time.

To investigate the implications of this observation, Barro considers an environment where the distortions associated with taxes are the only departure from Ricardian equivalence.[11] The government's problem is then

---

[11] Alternatively, one can consider a setting where there are other departures from Ricardian equivalence but where the government can offset the other effects of its choice between

similar to the problem facing a household in the permanent-income hypothesis. In the permanent-income hypothesis, the household wants to maximize its discounted lifetime utility subject to the constraint that the present value of its lifetime spending not exceed some level. Because there is diminishing marginal utility of consumption, the household chooses a smooth path for consumption. Here, the government wants to minimize the present value of distortions from raising revenue subject to the constraint that the present value of its revenues not be less than some level. Because there are increasing marginal distortion costs of raising revenue, the government chooses a smooth path for taxes. Our analysis of tax-smoothing will therefore parallel our analysis of the permanent-income hypothesis in Sections 7.1 and 7.2. As in those sections, we will first assume that there is certainty and then consider the case of uncertainty.

Tax-Smoothing under Certainty

Consider a discrete-time economy. The paths of output (Y), government purchases (G), and the real interest rate (r) are exogenously given and certain. For simplicity, the real interest rate is constant. There is some initial stock of outstanding government debt, D_0. The government wants to choose the path of taxes (T) to satisfy its budget constraint while minimizing the present value of the costs of the distortions that the taxes create.[12] Following Barro, we will not model the sources of those distortion costs. Instead, we just assume that the distortion costs from raising amount T_t are given by

$$C_t = Y_t f\left(\frac{T_t}{Y_t}\right), \qquad f(0) = 0, \qquad f'(\bullet) > 0, \qquad f''(\bullet) > 0, \qquad (11.11)$$

where C_t is the cost of the distortions in period t. This equation implies that distortions relative to output are a function of taxes relative to output, and that they rise more than proportionally with taxes relative to output. These implications seem reasonable.

The government's problem is to choose the path of taxes to minimize the present value of the distortion costs subject to the requirement that it

---

bond and tax finance. For example, it can use monetary policy to offset any impact on overall economic activity, and tax incentives to offset any impact on the division of output between consumption and investment.

[12] For most of the models in this chapter, it is easiest to define G as government purchases and T as taxes net of transfers. Raising taxes to finance transfers involves distortions, however. Thus for this model, G should be thought of as purchases plus transfers and T as gross taxes. For consistency with the other models in the chapter, however, in the presentation we will neglect transfers and refer to G as government purchases.

satisfy its overall budget constraint. Formally, this problem is

$$\min_{T_0,T_1,\dots} \sum_{t=0}^{\infty} \frac{1}{(1+r)^t} Y_t f\left(\frac{T_t}{Y_t}\right) \tag{11.12}$$

subject to

$$\sum_{t=0}^{\infty} \frac{1}{(1+r)^t} T_t = D_0 + \sum_{t=0}^{\infty} \frac{1}{(1+r)^t} G_t.$$

One can solve the government's problem either by setting up the Lagrangian and proceeding in the standard way, or by using perturbation arguments to find the Euler equation. We will use the second approach. Specifically, consider the government reducing taxes in period t by a small amount ΔT and increasing taxes in the next period by $(1 + r)\Delta T$, with taxes in all other periods unchanged. This change does not affect the present value of its revenues. Thus if the government was initially satisfying its budget constraint, it continues to satisfy it after the change. And if the government's initial policy was optimal, the marginal impact of the change on its objective function must be zero. That is, the marginal benefit (MB) and marginal cost (MC) of the change must be equal.

The benefit of the change is that it reduces distortions in period t. Specifically, equation (11.12) implies that the marginal reduction in the present value of distortions is

$$\begin{aligned} \text{MB} &= \frac{1}{(1+r)^t} Y_t f'\left(\frac{T_t}{Y_t}\right) \frac{1}{Y_t} \Delta T \\ &= \frac{1}{(1+r)^t} f'\left(\frac{T_t}{Y_t}\right) \Delta T. \end{aligned} \tag{11.13}$$

The cost of the change is that it increases distortion in $t + 1$. From (11.12) and the fact that taxes in period $t+1$ rise by $(1+r)\Delta T$, the marginal increase in the present value of distortions is

$$\begin{aligned} \text{MC} &= \frac{1}{(1+r)^{t+1}} Y_{t+1} f'\left(\frac{T_{t+1}}{Y_{t+1}}\right) \frac{1}{Y_{t+1}} (1 + r)\Delta T \\ &= \frac{1}{(1+r)^t} f'\left(\frac{T_{t+1}}{Y_{t+1}}\right) \Delta T. \end{aligned} \tag{11.14}$$

Comparing (11.13) and (11.14) shows that the condition for the marginal benefit and marginal cost to be equal is

$$f'\left(\frac{T_t}{Y_t}\right) = f'\left(\frac{T_{t+1}}{Y_{t+1}}\right). \tag{11.15}$$

This requires

$$\frac{T_t}{Y_t} = \frac{T_{t+1}}{Y_{t+1}}. \tag{11.16}$$

That is, taxes as a share of output—the tax rate—must be constant. As described above, the intuition is that with increasing marginal distortion costs from higher taxes, smooth taxes minimize distortion costs. More precisely, because the marginal distortion cost per unit of revenue raised is increasing in the tax rate, a smooth tax rate minimizes distortion costs.[13]

Tax-Smoothing under Uncertainty

Extending the analysis to allow for uncertainty about the path of government purchases is straightforward. The government's new problem is to minimize the expected present value of the distortions from raising revenue. Its budget constraint is the same as before: the present value of tax revenues must equal initial debt plus the present value of purchases.

We can analyze this problem using a perturbation argument like the one we used for the case of certainty. Consider the government reducing taxes in period t by a small amount ΔT from the value it was planning to choose given its information available at that time. To continue to satisfy its budget constraint, it then increases taxes in period $t + 1$ by $(1 + r)\Delta T$ from whatever value it would have chosen given its information in that period. If the government is optimizing, this change does not affect the expected present value of distortions. Reasoning like that we used to derive expression (11.15) shows that this condition is

$$f'\left(\frac{T_t}{Y_t}\right) = E_t\left[f'\left(\frac{T_{t+1}}{Y_{t+1}}\right)\right], \tag{11.17}$$

where $E_t[\bullet]$ denotes expectations given the information available in period t. This condition states that there cannot be predictable changes in the marginal distortion costs of obtaining revenue.

In the case where the distortion costs, $f(\bullet)$, are quadratic, equation (11.17) simplifies in a natural way. When $f(\bullet)$ is quadratic, $f'(\bullet)$ is linear. Thus, $E_t[f'(T_{t+1}/Y_{t+1})]$ equals $f'(E_t[T_{t+1}/Y_{t+1}])$. Equation (11.17) becomes

$$f'\left(\frac{T_t}{Y_t}\right) = f'\left(E_t\left[\frac{T_{t+1}}{Y_{t+1}}\right]\right), \tag{11.18}$$

which requires

$$\frac{T_t}{Y_t} = E_t\left[\frac{T_{t+1}}{Y_{t+1}}\right]. \tag{11.19}$$

This equation states that there cannot be predictable changes in the tax rate. That is, the tax rate follows a random walk.

---

[13] To find the level of the tax rate, one needs to combine the government's budget constraint in (11.12) with the fact that the tax rate is constant. This calculation shows that the tax rate equals the ratio of the present value of the revenue the government must raise to the present value of output.

Implications

Our motive for studying tax-smoothing was to examine its implications for the behavior of deficits. The model implies that if government purchases as a share of output are a random walk, there will be no deficits: with this behavior of purchases, a balanced-budget policy causes the tax rate to follow a random walk. Thus the model implies that deficits and surpluses arise when the ratio of government purchases to output is expected to change.

The most obvious potential sources of predictable movements in the purchases-to-output ratio are wars and recessions. Military purchases are usually temporarily high during wars. Similarly, government purchases are roughly acyclical, and are thus likely to be temporarily high relative to output in recessions.[14] That is, wars and recessions are times when the expected future ratio of government purchases to output is less than the current ratio. Consistent with the tax-smoothing model, we observe that governments usually run deficits during these times. The literature testing the tax-smoothing model formally finds that the response of deficits to temporary military purchases and cyclical fluctuations is generally consistent with the model's qualitative predictions. Some tests find, however, that the model's specific quantitative predictions are rejected by the data.[15]

Extensions

Lucas and Stokey (1983) observe that the same logic that suggests that governments should smooth taxes suggests that they should issue contingent debt. Expected distortions are lower if government debt has a low real payoff when there is a positive shock to government purchases and a high real payoff when there is a negative shock. With fully contingent debt, the government can equalize tax rates across all possible states, and so the tax rate never changes (Bohn, 1990). This strong implication is obviously incorrect. But Bohn (1988) notes that one way for the government to make its debt have contingent real payoffs is for it to issue nominal debt and follow policies that produce high inflation in response to positive shocks to purchases and low inflation in response to negative shocks. Thus the desire to reduce distortions provides a candidate explanation of governments' use of nominal debt.

The analysis can also be extended to include capital accumulation, so that the path of output is endogenous. If the government can commit to its

---

[14] Also, recall that the relevant variable for the model is in fact not government purchases, but purchases plus transfer payments (see n. 12). Transfers are generally countercyclical, and thus also likely to be temporarily high relative to output in recessions.

[15] Two early papers testing the tax-smoothing model are Barro's original paper (Barro, 1979) and Sahasakul (1986). For more recent tests, see Huang and Lin (1993) and Ghosh (1995), both of which build on the analysis of consumption and saving in Campbell (1987).

policies, a policy of no capital taxation is likely to be optimal or nearly so. Both capital taxes and labor-income taxes distort individuals' labor-leisure choice, since both reduce the overall attractiveness of working. But the capital income tax also distorts individuals' intertemporal choices.[16]

Ex post, a tax on existing capital is not distortionary, and thus is desirable from the standpoint of minimizing distortions. As a result, a policy of no or low capital taxation is not dynamically consistent (Kydland and Prescott, 1977). That is, if the government cannot make binding commitments about future tax policies, it will not be able to follow a policy of no capital taxation. The prediction of optimal tax models with commitment that capital taxes are close to zero is clearly false. Whether this reflects imperfect commitment or something else is not known.

Finally, this analysis suggests another reason for there to be departures from Ricardian equivalence. We have taken the path of government purchases as exogenous. But, realistically, purchases are likely to be affected by their costs and benefits. A bond issue accompanied by a tax cut increases the revenue the government must raise in the future, and therefore implies that future tax rates must be higher. Thus the marginal cost of financing a given path of government purchases is higher. When the government is choosing its purchases by trading off the costs and benefits, it will respond to this change with a mix of higher taxes and lower purchases. The lower government purchases increase households' lifetime resources and therefore increase their current consumption (Bohn, 1992).

Expansionary Fiscal Contractions?

Under the assumptions that give rise to Ricardian equivalence, a tax cut raises expectations of the present value of future tax payments by exactly the amount of the cut. Households' lifetime resources are therefore unaffected, and so their consumption does not change. In the case of endogenous government purchases that we have just discussed, a tax cut raises expectations of future tax payments by less than the amount of the cut, and so consumption rises. This role of expectations raises the possibility that there are situations where an increase in taxes or a reduction in government purchases raises the overall demand for goods and services. Suppose, for example, that for some reason a small tax increase signals that there will be large reductions in future government purchases—and thus large future tax cuts. Then households will respond to the tax increase by raising their estimates of their lifetime resources; as a result, they may raise their consumption. Similarly, a small reduction in current government purchases could signal large future reductions, and therefore cause consumption to rise by more than the fall in government purchases.

---

[16] See Chari and Kehoe (1999) for an analysis of optimal tax policy in a stochastic environment with capital.

Surprisingly, these possibilities are more than just theoretical curiosities. Giavazzi and Pagano (1990) show that fiscal reform packages in Denmark and Ireland in the 1980s caused consumption booms, and they argue that effects operating through expectations were the reason. Similarly, Alesina and Perotti (1997) show that deficit reductions coming from cuts in government employment and transfers are much more likely to be maintained than reductions coming from tax increases, and that, consistent with the importance of expectations, the first type of deficit reduction is often expansionary while the second type usually is not. The United States's deficit reduction policies in 1993 may be another example of an expansionary fiscal contraction.

Work on the possibility of expansionary fiscal contractions has emphasized two channels other than households' beliefs about their lifetime tax liabilities through which expectations can cause fiscal tightenings to raise aggregate demand. The first is through interest rates. Since reductions in government purchases reduce interest rates, expectations of lower future purchases reduce expectations of future interest rates. Similarly, if Ricardian equivalence fails, expectations of higher future taxes reduce expectations of future interest rates. And, as described in Section 8.5, expectations of lower future interest rates raise current investment. They also raise the present value of households' lifetime after-tax incomes, and thus raise current consumption.

The second channel is through the supply side. Lower future taxes imply lower future distortions, and thus higher future income. Further, we will see in Sections 11.9 and 11.10 that a sufficiently high level of government debt can lead to a fiscal crisis, with a range of harmful effects on the economy. Fiscal contractions can lower estimates of the likelihood of a crisis, and thus again raise estimates of future income. And higher estimates of future income are likely to raise current consumption and investment (Bertola and Drazen, 1993; Perotti, 1996, 1999).

11.5 Political-Economy Theories of Budget Deficits

The tax-smoothing hypothesis provides a candidate explanation of variations in budget deficits over time, but not of a systematic tendency toward high deficits. In light of many countries' persistent deficits in the 1980s and 1990s and the evidence that many countries' current fiscal policies are far from sustainable, much recent research has been devoted to possible sources of *deficit bias* in fiscal policy. That is, this work asks whether there are forces that tend to cause fiscal policy to produce deficits that are on average inefficiently high.

Most of this work falls under the heading of *new political economy*. This is the field devoted to applying economic tools to politics. In this line of work, politicians are viewed not as benevolent social planners, but as individuals who maximize their objective functions given the constraints they face and the information they have. Likewise, voters are viewed as neither the idealized citizens of high school civics classes nor the mechanical actors of much of political science, but as rational economic agents.

One strand of new political economy uses economic tools to understand issues that have traditionally been in the domain of political science, such as the behavior of political candidates and voters. The seminal work in this part of the field is Downs (1957); Ordeshook (1986) provides an introduction.

A second strand—and the one we will focus on—is concerned with the importance of political forces for traditional economic issues. Probably the most important question tackled by this work is how the political process can produce inefficient outcomes. Even casual observation suggests that governments are sources of enormous inefficiencies. Officials enrich themselves at a cost to society that vastly exceeds the wealth they accumulate; regulators influence markets using highly distortionary price controls and command-and-control regulations rather than taxes and subsidies; legislatures and officials dole out innumerable favors to individuals and small groups, thereby causing large amounts of resources to be devoted to rent-seeking; high and persistent inflation and budget deficits are common; and so on. But a basic message of economics is that when there are large inefficiencies, there are large incentives to eliminate them. Thus the apparent existence of large inefficiencies resulting from the political process is an important puzzle.

Work in new political economy has proposed several candidate explanations for inefficient political outcomes. Although excessive deficits are surely not the largest inefficiency produced by the political process, many of those candidate explanations have been applied to deficit bias. Indeed, some were developed in that context. Thus we will examine work on possible political sources of deficit bias both for what it tells us about deficits and as a way of providing an introduction to new political economy.

One potential source of inefficient policies is that politicians and voters may not know what the optimal policies are. Individuals have heterogeneous understandings of economics and of the impacts of alternative policies. The fact that some individuals are less well informed than others can cause them to support policies that the best available evidence suggests are inefficient. For example, one reason that support for protectionist policies is so widespread is probably that the idea of comparative advantage is sufficiently subtle that many people do not understand it.

Some features of policy are difficult to understand unless we recognize that voters' and policymakers' knowledge is incomplete. New ideas sometimes influence policy. This can happen only if the ideas were not already universally known. Similarly, the existence of extensive debate about the effects that alternative policies would have makes sense only if individuals' knowledge is heterogeneous.[17]

Buchanan and Wagner (1977) argue that incomplete knowledge is an important source of deficit bias. The benefits of high purchases and low taxes are direct and evident, while the costs—the lower future purchases and higher future taxes that are needed to satisfy the government's budget constraint—are indirect and less obvious. If individuals do not recognize the extent of the costs, there will be a tendency toward excessive deficits. Buchanan and Wagner develop this idea, and argue that the history of views about deficits can explain why limited understanding of deficits' costs did not produce a systematic pattern of high deficits until the 1970s.

D. Romer (1999) considers the implications of heterogeneous understanding for political decisions at a more general level. This paper shows that the view that incomplete understanding relative to the best available knowledge can have a systematic impact on political outcomes is perfectly consistent with the assumption that individuals are rational. It also argues that heterogeneous knowledge provides a simple and parsimonious candidate explanation for a wide range of apparently inefficient political outcomes.

Although limited knowledge may be an important source of excessive deficits, it is not the only one. In some situations, there are policies that would clearly make almost everyone considerably better off. The most obvious examples are hyperinflations. A hyperinflation's costs are large and obvious. Thus it is reasonably clear that a general tax increase or spending reduction that eliminated the need for seignorage, and thereby allowed the government to end the hyperinflation, would make the vast majority of the population better off. Yet hyperinflations often go on for months or years before fiscal policy is changed.

Most work in new political economy does not focus on limited knowledge. This may be because of cases like hyperinflations that are almost surely not due to limited knowledge. Or it may be because models of limited knowledge are not well developed and therefore lack an accepted framework that can be applied to new situations, or because it is difficult to derive specific empirical predictions from the models.

The bulk of work in new political economy focuses instead on the possibility that strategic interactions can cause the policymaking process to produce outcomes that are known to be inefficient. That is, this work considers the possibility that the structure of the policymaking process and

---

[17] It is through ideas that economists' activities as researchers, teachers, and policy advisers affect policy. If observed outcomes, even highly undesirable ones, were the equilibria of interactions of individuals who were fully informed about the consequences of alternative policies, we could hope to observe and understand those outcomes but not to change them. But since the participants do not know all there is to know about policies' consequences, by learning more about them through our research and providing information about them through our teaching and advising, economists can—and sometimes do—change outcomes.

of the economy causes each participant's pursuit of his or her objective to produce inefficiency. The model of the dynamic inconsistency of low-inflation monetary policy we considered in Section 10.4 is an example of such a model. In that model, the fact that policymakers are unable to commit to low inflation, coupled with their incentive to inflate once expected inflation has been determined, leads to inefficient inflation.

In the case of fiscal policy, three main ways that strategic interactions can lead to inefficient deficits have been proposed. First, an elected leader may accumulate an inefficient amount of debt to restrain his or her successor's spending (Persson and Svensson, 1989; Tabellini and Alesina, 1990). A desire to restrain future spending may have been an important motive for Ronald Reagan's high-deficit policies in the 1980s, for example.

Second, disagreement about how to divide the burden of reducing the deficit can cause delay in fiscal reform as each group tries to get others to bear a disproportionate share (Alesina and Drazen, 1991). This mechanism is almost surely relevant to hyperinflations.

Third, deficits can result from elected leaders' attempts to signal their abilities to voters. Voters are likely to have better information about the taxes they pay and the government services they receive than about the government's overall fiscal position. If politicians differ in their ability to provide government services cheaply, this gives them an incentive to choose high spending and low taxes to try to signal that they are especially able (Rogoff, 1990). Depending on how quickly voters learn about the government's true fiscal position, this can lead either to cycles in fiscal policy, with high deficits shortly before elections, or to consistent deficit bias.

A natural variant on this idea is for politicians to differ in their ability to reduce future government spending. Tax-smoothing considerations imply that the optimal level of current taxes is lower (and thus that the deficit is higher) when expected future government spending is lower. Leaders therefore have an incentive to reduce current taxes to signal that they have the ability to identify and eliminate large amounts of wasteful government spending or to restructure programs to deliver the same services at lower cost. This is another possible strategic interpretation of Ronald Reagan's high-deficit policies.[18]

Sections 11.6 and 11.7 present specific models that illustrate the first two potential sources of deficit bias arising from strategic considerations. We will not cover the signaling mechanism, on the grounds that it has received less attention in theoretical and empirical work on deficit bias and that it

---

[18] Rogoff and Sibert (1988) argue that signaling considerations can also cause leaders to pursue policies that produce political business cycles. Signaling may also be important to the microeconomics of government spending. For example, Coate and Morris (1995) argue that signaling considerations may explain why politicians often use inefficient pork-barrel spending rather than straightforward transfers to enrich their friends and allies.

can be modeled using a straightforward application of standard signaling models.[19]

We will see that both models have serious limitations; neither one shows unambiguously that the mechanism it considers gives rise to deficit bias. Thus the purpose of considering the models is not to settle the issue of the sources of deficits. Rather, it is to identify some important issues and open questions concerning the mechanisms the models focus on, and concerning political-economy models more generally.

11.6 Strategic Debt Accumulation

This section investigates a specific mechanism through which strategic considerations can produce inefficiently high deficits. The key idea is that current policymakers realize that future policy may be determined by individuals whose views they disagree with. In particular, it may be determined by individuals who prefer to expend resources in ways the current policymakers view as undesirable. This can cause current policymakers to want to restrain future policymakers' spending. If high levels of government debt reduce government spending, this provides current policymakers with a reason to accumulate debt.

This general idea has been formalized in two ways. Persson and Svensson (1989) consider disagreement about the *level* of government spending: conservative policymakers prefer low spending, and liberal policymakers prefer high spending. Persson and Svensson show that if the conservative policymakers' preference for low spending is strong enough, it causes them to run deficits.[20]

Persson and Svensson's model does not provide a candidate explanation of a general tendency toward deficits. In their model, the same forces that can make conservative policymakers run deficits can cause liberal ones to run surpluses. Tabellini and Alesina (1990) therefore consider disagreement about the *composition* of government spending. Their basic idea is that if each type of policymaker believes that the type of spending the other would undertake is undesirable, both types may have an incentive to accumulate debt.

This section presents Tabellini and Alesina's model and investigates its implications. One advantage of this model is that it goes further than most

---

[19] By focusing on deficit bias, the presentation omits some potential sources of inefficient political outcomes that have been proposed. For example, in a series of papers, Shleifer and Vishny (1992, 1993, 1994) suggest reasons that politicians' pursuit of their self-interest and strategic interactions might give rise to rationing, corruption, and inefficient public employment.

[20] Problem 11.10 develops this idea. It also investigates the possibility that the disagreement can cause conservative policymakers to run surpluses rather than deficits.

political-economy models in building the analysis of political behavior from microeconomic foundations. In many political-economy models, political parties' preferences and probabilities of being in power are exogenous. But in Tabellini and Alesina's analysis, electoral outcomes are derived from assumptions about the preferences and behavior of individual voters. As a result, their model illustrates some of the microeconomic issues that arise in modeling political behavior.

Economic Assumptions

The economy lasts for two periods, 1 and 2. The real interest rate is exogenous and equal to zero. Government spending is devoted to two types of public goods, denoted M and N. For concreteness, we will refer to them as military and nonmilitary goods.

The period-1 policymaker chooses the period-1 levels of the two goods, M_1 and N_1, and how much debt, D, to issue. The period-2 policymaker chooses M_2 and N_2, and must repay any debt issued in the first period.

For the amount of debt issued in the first period to affect what happens in the second, Ricardian equivalence must fail. The literature on strategic debt accumulation has emphasized two sources of failure. In Persson and Svensson's model, the source is the distortionary impact of taxation that is the focus of Barro's analysis of tax-smoothing. A higher level of debt means that the taxes associated with a given level of government purchases are greater. But if taxes are distortionary and the distortions have increasing marginal cost, this means that the marginal cost of a given level of government purchases is greater when the level of debt is greater. As described in Section 11.4, this in turn implies that an optimizing policymaker will choose a lower level of purchases.

The second reason that debt can affect second-period policy is by affecting the economy's wealth. If the issue of debt in period 1 reduces wealth in period 2, it tends to reduce period-2 government purchases. The most plausible way for debt issue to reduce wealth is by increasing consumption. But modeling such an effect through liquidity constraints, a precautionary-saving motive, or some other mechanism is likely to be complicated. Tabellini and Alesina therefore take a shortcut. They assume that private consumption is absent, and that debt represents borrowing from abroad that directly increases period-1 government purchases and reduces the resources available in period 2.

Specifically, the economy's period-1 budget constraint is

$$M_1 + N_1 = W + D, \tag{11.20}$$

where W is the economy's endowment each period and D is the amount of debt the policymaker issues. Since the interest rate is fixed at zero, the period-2 constraint is

$$M_2 + N_2 = W - D. \tag{11.21}$$

The M's and N's are required to be nonnegative. Thus D must satisfy $-W \leq D \leq W$.

A key assumption of the model is that individuals' preferences over the two types of public goods are heterogeneous. Specifically, individual i's objective function is

$$V_i = E\left[\sum_{t=1}^{2} \alpha_i U(M_t) + (1 - \alpha_i) U(N_t)\right], \quad 0 \leq \alpha_i \leq 1, \quad U'(\bullet) > 0, \quad U''(\bullet) < 0,$$
$$\tag{11.22}$$

where α_i is the weight that individual i puts on military relative to nonmilitary goods. That is, all individuals get nonnegative utility from both types of goods, but the relative contributions of the two types to utility differ across individuals.

The model's assumptions imply that debt issue is never desirable. Since the real interest rate equals the discount rate and each individual has diminishing marginal utility, smooth paths of M and N are optimal for all individuals. Debt issue causes spending in period 1 to exceed spending in period 2, and thus violates this requirement. Similar reasoning shows that saving (that is, a negative value of D) is also inefficient.

Political Assumptions

For the period-1 policymaker to have any possible interest in constraining the period-2 policymaker's behavior, there must be some chance that the second policymaker's preferences will differ from the first's. In many political-economy models, this is accomplished by assuming random turnover among political parties with different views. This approach is a useful starting point. But Tabellini and Alesina go slightly deeper: they assume that individuals' preferences are fixed, but that their participation in the political process is random. This makes the period-1 policymaker uncertain about what preferences the period-2 policymaker will have.

To describe the specifics of Tabellini and Alesina's assumptions about how the policymakers' preferences are determined, it is easiest to begin with the second period. Given the choice of military purchases, M_2, nonmilitary purchases are determined by the period-2 budget constraint: $N_2 = (W - D) - M_2$. Thus there is effectively only a single choice variable in period 2, M_2. Individual i's utility in period 2 as a function of M_2 is

$$V_i^2(M_2) = \alpha_i U(M_2) + (1 - \alpha_i) U([W - D] - M_2). \tag{11.23}$$

Since $U''(\bullet)$ is negative, $V_i^{2''}(\bullet)$ is also negative. This means that the individual's preferences over M_2 are *single-peaked*. The individual has some most preferred value of M_2, M_{2i}^*. For any two values of M_2 on the same side of M_{2i}^*, the individual prefers the one closer to M_{2i}^*. If $M_2^A < M_2^B < M_{2i}^*$, for example, the individual prefers M_2^B to M_2^A. Figure 11.1 shows two examples of single-peaked preferences. In Panel (a), the individual's most preferred value is in the interior of the range of feasible values of M_2, $[0, W - D]$. In Panel (b), it is at an extreme.

The facts that there is only a single choice variable and that preferences are single-peaked means that the *median-voter theorem* applies to this situation. This theorem states that when the choice variable is a scalar and preferences are single-peaked, the median of voters' most preferred values of the choice variable wins a two-way contest against any other value of the choice variable. To understand why this occurs, let $M_2^{*\text{MED}}$ denote the median value of M_{2i}^* among period-2 voters. Now consider a referendum in which voters are asked to choose between $M_2^{*\text{MED}}$ and some other value of M_2, M_2^0. For concreteness, suppose M_2^0 is greater than $M_2^{*\text{MED}}$. Since $M_2^{*\text{MED}}$ is the median value of M_{2i}^*, a majority of voters' M_{2i}^*'s are less than or equal to $M_2^{*\text{MED}}$. And since preferences are single-peaked, all these voters prefer

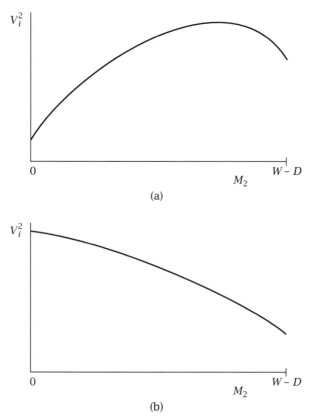

(a)

(b)

FIGURE 11.1 Single-peaked preferences

$M_2^{*\mathrm{MED}}$ to M_2^0. A similar analysis applies to the case when M_2^0 is less than $M_2^{*\mathrm{MED}}$.

Appealing to the median-voter theorem, Tabellini and Alesina assume that the political process leads to $M_2^{*\mathrm{MED}}$ being chosen as the value of M_2. Since M_2^* is a monotonic function of α—a voter with a higher value of α prefers a higher value of M_2—this is equivalent to assuming that M_2 is determined by the preferences of the individual with the median value of α among period-2 voters.

Tabellini and Alesina do not explicitly model the process through which the political process produces this result. Their idea, which is reasonable, is that the logic of the median-voter theorem suggests that $M_2^{*\mathrm{MED}}$ is a more plausible outcome than any other value of M_2. One specific mechanism that would lead to $M_2^{*\mathrm{MED}}$ being chosen is the one outlined by Downs (1957). Suppose that there are two candidates for office, that their objective is to maximize their chances of being elected, and that they can make commitments about the policies they will follow if elected. Suppose also that the distribution of the preferences of the individuals who will vote in period 2 is known before the election takes place. With these assumptions, the only Nash equilibrium is for both candidates to announce that they will choose $M_2 = M_2^{*\mathrm{MED}}$ if elected.[21]

Little would be gained by explicitly modeling the randomness in voter participation and how it induces randomness in voters' median value of M_2^*. For example, these features of the model could easily be derived from assumptions about random costs of voting. Tabellini and Alesina therefore take the distribution of $M_2^{*\mathrm{MED}}$ as exogenous.

Now consider the determination of policy in period 1. There are two complications relative to period 2. First, the set of policy choices is two-dimensional rather than one-dimensional. Specifically, we can think of the period-1 policymaker as choosing M_1 and D, with N_1 determined by the requirement that $M_1 + N_1 = W + D$. Second, in determining their preferences over M_1 and D, individuals must take into account their uncertainty about the period-2 policymaker's preferences. Tabellini and Alesina show, however, that a generalization of the median-voter theorem implies that the combination of M_1 and D preferred by the individual with the median value of α among period-1 voters wins a two-way contest against any other combination. They therefore assume that policy in period 1 is determined by the individual with the median α among period-1 voters.

This completes the description of the model. Although we have developed a general version, we will confine our analysis of the model to two specific cases that together show its main messages. In the first, the only values of α in the population are 0 and 1. In the second, the values of α are strictly between 0 and 1, and $U(\bullet)$ is logarithmic.

---

[21] This result does not hold under other assumptions about candidates' preferences and information. See, for example, Osborne and Slivinski (1996) and Besley and Coate (1997).

Extreme Preferences

We begin with the case where the only types of individuals are ones who would like to spend all resources on military goods and ones who would like to spend all resources on nonmilitary goods. That is, there are only two values of α in the population, 0 and 1.

To solve a dynamic model with a fixed number of periods like this one, it is usually easiest to start with the last period and work backward. Thus we start with the second period. The period-2 median voter's choice problem is trivial: he or she devotes all the available resources to the purpose he or she prefers. Thus if $\alpha_2^{MED} = 1$ (that is, if the majority of the period-2 voters have $\alpha = 1$), $M_2 = W - D$ and $N_2 = 0$. And if $\alpha_2^{MED} = 0$, $M_2 = 0$ and $N_2 = W - D$. Let π denote the probability that $\alpha_2^{MED} = 1$.

Now consider the first period. Suppose first that the period-1 median voter has $\alpha = 1$. Since nonmilitary goods give him or her no utility, he or she purchases only military goods. Thus $M_1 = W + D$ and $N_1 = 0$. The only question concerns the policymaker's choice of D. His or her expected utility as a function of D is

$$U(W + D) + \pi U(W - D) + (1 - \pi)U(0). \tag{11.24}$$

The first term reflects the policymaker's utility from setting $M_1 = W + D$. The remaining two terms show the policymaker's expected period-2 utility. With probability π, policy in period 2 is determined by an individual with $\alpha = 1$. In this case, $M_2 = W - D$, and so the period-1 policymaker obtains utility $U(W - D)$. With probability $1 - \pi$, policy is determined by someone with $\alpha = 0$. In this case $M_2 = 0$, and so the period-1 policymaker obtains utility $U(0)$.

Equation (11.24) implies that the first-order condition for the period-1 policymaker's choice of D is

$$U'(W + D) - \pi U'(W - D) = 0. \tag{11.25}$$

We can rearrange this as

$$\frac{U'(W + D)}{U'(W - D)} = \pi. \tag{11.26}$$

This equation implies that if there is some chance that the period-2 policymaker will not share the period-1 policymaker's preferences (that is, if $\pi < 1$), $U'(W + D)$ must be less than $U'(W - D)$. Since $U''(\bullet)$ is negative, this means that D must be positive. And when π is smaller, the required gap between $U'(W + D)$ and $U'(W - D)$ is greater, and so D is larger. That is, D is decreasing in π.[22]

---

[22] This discussion assumes an interior solution. Recall that D cannot exceed W. If $U'(2W) - \pi U'(0)$ is positive, the period-1 policymaker sets $D = W$ (see [11.25]). Thus in this case the economy's entire second-period endowment is used to pay off debt. One

The analysis of the case where the median voter in period 1 has $\alpha = 0$ is very similar. In this case, $M_1 = 0$ and $N_1 = W + D$, and the first-order condition for D implies

$$\frac{U'(W + D)}{U'(W - D)} = 1 - \pi. \tag{11.27}$$

Here, it is the possibility of the period-2 median voter having $\alpha = 1$ that causes the period-1 policymaker to choose a positive deficit. When this probability is higher (that is, when $1 - \pi$ is lower), the deficit is higher.

Discussion

This analysis shows that as long as π is strictly between 0 and 1, both types of potential period-1 policymaker run a deficit. Further, the deficit is increasing in the probability of a change in preferences from the period-1 policymaker to the period-2 policymaker.

The intuition for these results is straightforward. There is a positive probability that the period-2 policymaker will devote the economy's re-sources to an activity that, in the view of the period-1 policymaker, simply wastes resources. The period-1 policymaker would therefore like to trans-fer resources from period 2 to period 1, where he or she can devote them to the activity he or she views as useful. Borrowing provides a way of doing this.

Thus, disagreement over the composition of government spending can give rise to inefficient budget deficits. One way to describe the inefficiency is to note that if the period-1 policymaker and potential period-2 policymak-ers can make binding agreements about their policies, they will agree to a deficit of zero: since any policy with a nonzero deficit is Pareto-inefficient, a binding agreement among all relevant players always produces no deficit. Thus one reason that deficits arise in the model is that individuals are as-sumed to be unable to make commitments about how they will behave if they are able to set policy in period 2.

Underlying policymakers' inability to make binding agreements about their behavior is individuals' inability to make binding commitments about their voting behavior. Suppose that the period-1 policymaker and a poten-tial period-2 policymaker who prefer different types of purchases are able to make a legally enforceable agreement about what each will do if he or she is the period-2 policymaker. If they make such an agreement, neither will be chosen as the period-2 policymaker: the median period-2 voter will prefer an individual who shares his or her tastes and has not made any commitments to devote resources to both types of goods in period 2.

---

implication is that if π is sufficiently low that $U'(2W) - \pi U'(0)$ is positive, further reductions in π do not affect D.

The assumption that voters cannot make commitments about their behavior is reasonable. But there are other mechanisms that would prevent
inefficient deficits. For example, the election of the period-2 policymaker
could occur before the period-1 policymaker chooses D, and the two policymakers could be permitted to make a binding agreement. Or there could
be a constitutional restriction on deficits.[23] A full explanation of inefficient
deficits would need to account for why such mechanisms are not adopted.

It is also worth noting that Tabellini and Alesina's model does not address some of the basic issues that arise in almost any attempt to use economic tools to model politics. Here we mention two. The first, and more
important, is why individuals participate in the political process at all. As
many authors have observed, it is hard to understand broad political participation on the basis of conventional economic considerations. Most individuals' personal stake in political outcomes is no more than moderate. And
if many individuals participate, each one's chance of affecting the outcome
is extremely small. A typical voter's chance of changing the outcome of a
U.S presidential election, for example, is almost surely well below one in
a million. This means that minuscule costs of participation are enough to
keep broad participation from being an equilibrium (Olson, 1965; see also
Ledyard, 1984, and Palfrey and Rosenthal, 1985).

The usual way of addressing this issue is simply to assume that individuals participate (as in Tabellini and Alesina's model), or to assume that
they get utility from participation (Riker and Ordeshook, 1968, for example). This is a reasonable modeling strategy: it does not make sense to insist
that we have a full understanding of the sources of political participation
before we model the impact of that participation. At the same time, an understanding of why people participate may change the analysis of how they
participate. For example, suppose that a major reason for participation is
that people get utility from being civic-minded, or from expressing their like
or dislike of candidates' positions or actions even if those expressions have
only a trivial chance of affecting the outcome (P. Romer, 1996). If such non-
standard considerations are important to people's decision to participate,
they may also be important to their behavior conditional on participating.
That is, the assumption that people who participate support the outcome
that maximizes their conventionally defined self-interest may be wrong. Yet
this is a basic assumption of Tabellini and Alesina's model (where people
vote for the outcome that maximizes their conventionally defined utility),
and of most other economic models of politics.[24]

The second issue is more specific to Tabellini and Alesina's model. In
their model, individuals' preferences are fixed, and who is chosen as the policymaker may change between the two periods because participation may
change. In practice, changes in individuals' preferences are important to

---

[23] See Problem 11.8 for an analysis of deficit restrictions in the Tabellini–Alesina model.

[24] See Green and Shapiro (1994) for a critique of economic models of voting behavior.

changes in policymakers. In the United States, for example, the main reason that the Democrats did well in 1992, poorly in 1994, and well again in 1996 was not that participation varied, but that swing voters' opinions varied. In analyzing the consequences of changes in policymakers, it matters whether the changes stem from changes in participation or changes in preferences. Suppose, for example, the period-1 policymaker believes that the period-2 policymaker's preferences may differ from his or her own because of new information about the relative merits of the two types of purchases. Then the period-1 policymaker has less interest in restraining the period-2 policymaker's spending. Indeed, the period-1 policymaker may want to transfer resources from period 1 to period 2 so that more spending can be based on the new information.

Logarithmic Utility

We now turn to the second case of Tabellini and Alesina's model that we will consider. Its key feature is that preferences are such that all potential policymakers devote resources to both military and nonmilitary goods. To see the issues clearly, we consider the case where the utility function $U(\bullet)$ is logarithmic. And to ensure that policymakers always devote resources to both types of goods, we assume the median voters' α's are always strictly between 0 and 1.

As before, we begin by considering the second period. The problem of the period-2 median voter is to allocate the available resources, $W - D$, between military and nonmilitary goods to maximize his or her utility. Formally, the problem is

$$\max_{M_2} \alpha_2^{MED} \ln M_2 + (1 - \alpha_2^{MED}) \ln(W - D - M_2), \qquad (11.28)$$

where α_2^{MED} is the period-2 median voter's α. We can solve this problem by finding the first-order condition for M_2, solving it for M_2, and then using the requirement that $N_2 = (W - D) - M_2$ to find N_2. This yields the usual result that with logarithmic preferences, spending on each good is proportional to its weight in the utility function:

$$M_2 = \alpha_2^{MED}(W - D), \qquad (11.29)$$

$$N_2 = (1 - \alpha_2^{MED})(W - D). \qquad (11.30)$$

Now consider period 1. Our main interest is in the period-1 policymaker's choice of D. To find this, it turns out that we do not need to solve the policymaker's full maximization problem. Instead, it is enough to consider the utility the policymaker obtains from the period-2 policymaker's choices for a given value of D and a given realization of α_2^{MED}. Let

$V_1^2(D, \alpha_2^{\text{MED}})$ denote this utility. It is given by

$$V_1^2(D, \alpha_2^{\text{MED}}) = \alpha_1^{\text{MED}} \ln[\alpha_2^{\text{MED}}(W - D)] + (1 - \alpha_1^{\text{MED}}) \ln[(1 - \alpha_2^{\text{MED}})(W - D)],$$

(11.31)

where we have used (11.29) and (11.30) to express M_2 and N_2 in terms of α_2^{MED} and D, and where α_1^{MED} is the period-1 policymaker's α. Note that the values of M_2 and N_2 depend on the period-2 policymaker's preferences (α_2^{MED}), but the weights assigned to them in the period-1 policymaker's utility depend on that policymaker's preferences (α_1^{MED}).

Expanding expression (11.31) and simplifying gives us

$$V_1^2(D, \alpha_2^{\text{MED}}) = \alpha_1^{\text{MED}} \ln(\alpha_2^{\text{MED}}) + \alpha_1^{\text{MED}} \ln(W - D) + (1 - \alpha_1^{\text{MED}}) \ln(1 - \alpha_2^{\text{MED}})$$

$$+ (1 - \alpha_1^{\text{MED}}) \ln(W - D) \qquad (11.32)$$

$$= \alpha_1^{\text{MED}} \ln(\alpha_2^{\text{MED}}) + (1 - \alpha_1^{\text{MED}}) \ln(1 - \alpha_2^{\text{MED}}) + \ln(W - D).$$

Equation (11.32) shows us that the period-2 policymaker's preferences affect the *level* of utility the period-1 policymaker obtains from what happens in period 2, but not the impact of D on that utility. Since the realization of α_2^{MED} does not affect the impact of D on the period-1 policymaker's utility from what will happen in period 2, it cannot affect his or her utility-maximizing choice of D. That is, the period-1 policymaker's choice of D must be independent of the distribution of α_2^{MED}. Since the choice of D is the same for all distributions of α_2^{MED}, we can just look at the case when α_2^{MED} will equal α_1^{MED} with certainty. But we know that in that case, the period-1 policymaker chooses $D = 0$. In short, with logarithmic preferences, there is no deficit bias in Tabellini and Alesina's model.

The intuition for this result is that when all potential policymakers devote resources to both types of goods, there is a disadvantage as well as an advantage to the period-1 policymaker to running a deficit. To understand this, consider what happens if the period-1 policymaker has a high value of α and the period-2 policymaker has a low one. The advantage of a deficit to the period-1 policymaker is that, as before, he or she devotes a large fraction of the resources transferred from period 2 to period 1 to a use that he or she considers more desirable than the main use the period-2 policymaker would put those resources to. That is, the period-1 policymaker devotes most of the resources transferred from period 2 to period 1 to military goods. The disadvantage is that the period-2 policymaker would have devoted some of those resources to military purchases in period 2. Crucially, because the low value of the period-2 policymaker's α causes period-2 military purchases to be low, the marginal utility of those additional military purchases to the period-1 policymaker is high. In the case of logarithmic utility, this advantage and disadvantage of a deficit just balance, and so the period-1 policymaker runs a balanced budget. In the general case, the overall effect can go either way. For example, in the case where the utility function $U(\bullet)$

is more sharply curved than logarithmic, the period-1 policymaker runs a surplus.

This analysis shows that with logarithmic preferences, disagreement over the composition of purchases does not produce deficit bias. Such preferences are a common case to consider. In the case of individuals' preferences concerning government purchases of different kinds of goods, however, we have little idea whether they are a reasonable approximation. As a result, the issue of whether the mechanism identified by Tabellini and Alesina is a significant source of deficit bias remains open.

11.7 Delayed Stabilization

We now turn to the second source of inefficient deficits emphasized in work in new political economy. The basic idea is that when no single individual or interest group controls policy at a given time, interactions among policymakers can produce inefficient deficits. Specifically, inefficient deficits can persist because each policymaker or interest group delays agreeing to fiscal reform in the hope that others will bear a larger portion of the burden.

There are many cases that appear to fit this general idea. Hyperinflations are the clearest example. Given the enormous disruptions hyperinflations create, there is little doubt that there are policies that would make most people considerably better off. Yet reform is often delayed as interest groups struggle over how to divide the burden of the reform. In the hyperinflations after World War I, the struggles were largely over whether higher taxes should be levied on capital or labor. In modern hyperinflations, the struggles are typically over whether the budget deficit will be closed by broad-based tax increases or by reductions in government employment and subsidies.

Another example is U.S. fiscal policy in the 1980s and 1990s. In this period, there was general consensus among policymakers that the budget deficit should be lower. Indeed, there was probably broad agreement that deficit reduction through a mix of broad spending cuts and tax increases was preferable to the status quo. But there was disagreement over the best way to reduce the deficit. As a result, policymakers were unable to agree on any specific set of measures.

The idea that conflict over how the burden of reform will be divided can cause deficits to persist is due to Alesina and Drazen (1991). Their basic idea is that each party in the bargaining may choose to delay to try to get a better deal for itself. By accepting a continuation of the current situation rather than agreeing to immediate reform, a group signals that it is costly for it to accept reform. As a result, choosing to delay may improve the group's expected outcome at the cost of worsening the overall economic situation. The end result can be delayed stabilization even though there are policies that are known to make everyone better off.

There is a natural analogy with labor strikes. Ex post, strikes are inefficient: both sides would have been better off if they had agreed to the eventual settlement without a strike. Yet strikes occur. A leading proposed explanation is that each side is uncertain of the other's situation, and that there is no way for them to convey information to one another costlessly. For example, a statement by management that a proposed settlement would almost surely bankrupt the firm is not credible: if such a statement would get management a better deal, it may make the statement even if it is false. But if management chooses to suffer a strike rather than accept the proposed settlement, this demonstrates that it views the settlement as very costly (for example, Hayes, 1984, and Hart, 1989).

In their model, Alesina and Drazen assume that a fiscal reform must be undertaken, and that the burden of the reform will be distributed asymmetrically between two interest groups. Each group delays agreeing to accept the larger share of the burden in the hope that the other will. The less costly it is for a group to accept the larger share, the sooner it decides that the benefits of conceding outweigh the benefits of continued delay. Formally, Alesina and Drazen consider a *war of attrition*.

We will analyze a version of the variant of Alesina and Drazen's model developed by Hsieh (1998b). Instead of considering a war of attrition, Hsieh considers a bargaining model based on the models used to analyze strikes. One advantage of this approach is that it makes the asymmetry of the burden of reform the outcome of a bargaining process rather than exogenous. A second advantage is that it is simpler than Alesina and Drazen's approach.

Assumptions

There are two groups, which we will refer to as capitalists and workers. The two groups must decide whether to reform fiscal policy and, if so, how to divide the burden of reform. If there is no reform, both groups receive a payoff of zero. If there is reform, capitalists receive pretax income of π and workers receive pretax income of W. However, reform requires that taxes of amount $T > 0$ be levied. We let X denote the amount of taxes paid by capitalists. Thus after-tax incomes under reform are $\pi - X$ for capitalists and $(W - T) + X$ for workers.

A central assumption of the model is that π is random and that its realization is known only to the capitalists. Specifically, it is distributed uniformly on some interval $[A, B]$, where $B \geq A \geq 0$. A is assumed to be nonnegative, and W is assumed to be greater than T. This implies that any choice of X between 0 and A necessarily makes both groups better off than without reform.

We consider a very simple model of the bargaining between the two groups. Workers make a proposal concerning X to the capitalists. If the capitalists accept the proposal, fiscal policy is reformed. If they reject it, there is no reform.[25]

Analyzing the Model

If the capitalists accept the workers' proposal, their payoff is $\pi - X$. If they reject it, their payoff is 0. They therefore accept when $\pi - X > 0$. Thus the probability that the proposal is accepted is the probability that π is greater than X. Since π is distributed uniformly on $[A, B]$, this probability is

$$
P(X) = \begin{cases} 1 & \text{if } X \leq A \\[2mm] \dfrac{B - X}{B - A} & \text{if } A < X < B \\[2mm] 0 & \text{if } X \geq B. \end{cases} \tag{11.33}
$$

The workers receive $(W - T) + X$ if their proposal is accepted and 0 if it is rejected. Their expected payoff, which we denote $V(X)$, therefore equals $P(X)[(W - T) + X]$. Using expression (11.33) for $P(X)$, this is

$$
V(X) = \begin{cases} (W - T) + X & \text{if } X \leq A \\[2mm] \dfrac{(B - X)[(W - T) + X]}{B - A} & \text{if } A < X < B \\[2mm] 0 & \text{if } X \geq B. \end{cases} \tag{11.34}
$$

The workers choose X to maximize their expected payoff. One can see that they will not make a proposal that will be rejected for sure. Such a proposal has an expected payoff of 0, and there are other proposals that have positive expected payoffs. For example, since $W - T$ is positive by assumption, a proposal of $X = 0$—so the workers bear the entire burden of the reform—has a strictly positive payoff. One can also see that there is a cost but no benefit to the workers to reducing their proposed value of X below the lowest level that they know will be accepted for sure.

Thus there are two possibilities. First, the workers may choose a value of X in the interior of $[A, B]$, so that the probability of the capitalists accepting the proposal is strictly between 0 and 1. Second, the workers may make the least generous proposal that they know will be accepted for sure. Since the

---

[25] There are many possible extensions of the bargaining model. In particular, it is natural to consider the possibility that rejection of a proposal delays reform, and therefore imposes costs on both sides, but leaves opportunities for additional proposals. In Hsieh's model, for example, there are two potential rounds of proposals. In many models of strikes, there are infinitely many potential rounds.

capitalists' payoff is $\pi - X$ and the lowest possible value of π is A, this corresponds to a proposal of $X = A$.

To analyze workers' behavior formally, we use equation (11.34) to find the derivative of $V(X)$ with respect to X for $A < X < B$. This yields

$$V'(X) = \frac{[B - (W - T)] - 2X}{B - A} \qquad \text{if } A < X < B. \qquad (11.35)$$

Note that $V''(X)$ is negative over this whole range. Thus if $V'(X)$ is negative at $X = A$, it is negative over all $[A, B]$. In this case, the workers propose $X = A$; that is, they make a proposal that they know will be accepted. Inspection of (11.35) shows that this occurs when $[B - (W - T)] - 2A$ is negative.

The alternative is for $V'(X)$ to be positive at $X = A$. In this case, the optimum is interior to the interval $[A, B]$, and is defined by the condition $V'(X) = 0$. From (11.35), this occurs when $[B - (W - T)] - 2X = 0$.

Thus we have

$$X^* = \begin{cases} A & \text{if } [B - (W - T)] - 2A \le 0 \\ \dfrac{B - (W - T)}{2} & \text{if } [B - (W - T)] - 2A > 0. \end{cases} \qquad (11.36)$$

Equation (11.33) implies that the equilibrium probability that the proposal is accepted is

$$P(X^*) = \begin{cases} 1 & \text{if } [B - (W - T)] - 2A \le 0 \\ \dfrac{B + (W - T)}{2(B - A)} & \text{if } [B - (W - T)] - 2A > 0. \end{cases} \qquad (11.37)$$

Figure 11.2 shows the two possibilities for how workers' expected payoff, V, varies with their proposal, X. The expected payoff always rises one-for-one with X over the range where the proposal is accepted for sure (that is, until $X = A$). And when $X \ge B$, the workers' proposal is rejected for sure, and so their expected payoff is 0. Panel (a) of the figure shows a case where the expected payoff is decreasing over the entire range $[A, B]$, so that the workers propose $X = A$. Panel (b) shows a case where the expected payoff is first increasing and then decreasing over the range $[A, B]$, so that the workers make a proposal strictly within this range.

Discussion

The model's key implication is that $P(X^*)$ can be less than 1: the two sides can fail to agree on a reform package even though there are packages that both sides know are certain to make them both better off. The workers can offer to pay $T - A$ themselves and to have the capitalists pay A, in which case there is reform for sure and both sides are better off than without reform. But if the condition $[B - (W - T)] - 2A > 0$ holds, the workers make a less generous proposal, and thereby run a risk of no agreement being

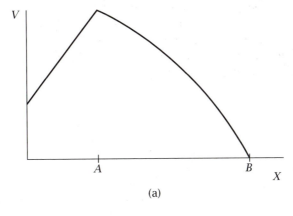

(a)

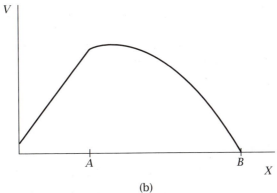

(b)

FIGURE 11.2 Workers' expected payoff as a function of their proposal

reached. Their motive in doing this is to improve their expected outcome at the expense of the capitalists'.

A necessary condition for the possibility of an inefficient outcome is that the workers do not know how much reform matters to capitalists (that is, that they do not know the value of π). To see this, consider what happens as $B - A$, the difference between the highest and lowest possible values of π, approaches 0. The condition for workers to make a proposal that is less than certain of being accepted is $[B-(W-T)]-2A > 0$, or $(B-A)-[(W-T)+A] > 0$. Since $(W - T) + A$ is positive by assumption, this condition fails if $B - A$ is small enough. In this case, the workers propose $X = A$—the highest value of X they are certain the capitalists will accept—and there is reform for sure.[26]

---

[26] One implication of this discussion is that as $B - A$ approaches 0, all the surplus from the reform accrues to the workers. This is an artifact of the assumption that they are able to make a take-it-or-leave-it proposal to the capitalists.

This analysis of delayed stabilization captures the fact that there are situations where policies persist despite the existence of alternatives that appear superior for the relevant parties. At the same time, the model has two important limitations. The first is that it assumes that there are only two types of individuals. Most individuals are not just capitalists or just workers, but receive both capital and labor income. Thus it may not be reasonable to assume that there is bargaining between exogenous groups with strongly opposed interests rather than, for example, a political process that converges quickly to the preferences of the median voter. Certainly Alesina and Drazen and subsequent authors in this literature have not made a compelling case for the division of the population into groups with sharply opposed interests.[27]

The second problem is that this analysis does not actually identify a source of deficit bias. It identifies a source of delay in policy changes of any type. Thus it identifies a reason for an excessive deficit, once it arises, to persist. But it identifies an equally strong reason for an excessive surplus to persist if it arises. By itself, it provides no reason for us to expect deficits to be excessive on average.

One possibility is that other considerations cause the average level of deficits to be excessive, and that the considerations identified by Alesina and Drazen cause inertia in departures of the deficit from its average level. In such a situation, inertia in response to a shock that moves the deficit above its usual level is very costly, since the deficit is too high to start with. Inertia in response to a shock that moves the deficit below its average level, on the other hand, is desirable (and therefore attracts less attention), since the deficit has moved closer to its optimal level.[28]

Finally, Alesina and Drazen's analysis has implications for the role of crises in spurring reform. An old and appealing idea is that a crisis—specifically, a situation where continuation of the status quo would be very harmful—can actually be beneficial by bringing about reforms that would not occur otherwise. In a model like Alesina and Drazen's or Hsieh's, in-

---

[27] One possibility is that there are features of the political process that make political representatives' preferences not cluster around the median voter's, but be more extreme. Another possibility is that individuals' preferences and the set of potential policies are such that the median-voter theorem does not apply, and that this affects efforts to attain reform.

[28] U.S. fiscal policy in 1999–2000 may have fit this pattern. A series of favorable shocks had produced projected surpluses. Although the best available projections suggested that increases in the surpluses were needed for fiscal policy to be sustainable, there was widespread support among policymakers for policy changes that would reduce the surpluses. Disagreement about the specifics of those changes made reaching an agreement difficult, and so no significant policy changes were made. Thus there appears to have been persistence of the departure of the deficit away from a high level.

Tornell and Lane (1999) argue that in poor countries, a fiscal windfall often raises purchases by more than the amount of the windfall, and they present a model that is consistent with this observation. If this is right, it suggests a possible asymmetry in responses to positive and negative fiscal shocks that could help account for deficit bias.

creasing the cost of failing to reform may make the parties alter their behavior in ways that make reform more likely. Whether this effect is strong enough to make the overall effect of a crisis beneficial is not obvious. This issue is investigated by Drazen and Grilli (1993) and by Hsieh, and in Problem 11.12. It turns out that there are indeed cases where a crisis improves expected welfare.

A corollary of this observation is that well-intentioned foreign aid to ease the suffering caused by a crisis can be counterproductive. Aid that increases the incentives for reform, on the other hand, may be more desirable. This idea is investigated by Hsieh and in Problem 11.13.

11.8   Empirical Application: Politics and Deficits in Industrialized Countries

New-political-economy theories of fiscal policy suggest that political institutions and outcomes may be important to budget deficits. Beginning with Roubini and Sachs (1989) and Grilli, Masciandaro, and Tabellini (1991), various researchers have therefore examined the relationship between political variables and deficits. Papers in this area generally do not try to derive sharp predictions from political-economy theories and test them formally. Rather, they try to identify broad patterns or stylized facts in the data and relate them informally to different views of the sources of deficits.

Preliminary Findings

There is considerable variation in the behavior of deficits. In some countries, such as Belgium and Italy, debt-to-GDP ratios rose steadily for extended periods to very high levels. In others, such as Australia and Finland, debt-to-GDP ratios have been consistently low. And other countries display more complicated patterns. In the United States, for example, the debt-to-GDP ratio declined until around 1980, then began a steady, moderate increase until about 1995, and then began to decline again. Finally, debt-to-GDP ratios were falling in most countries until the early 1970s, generally rising from then until the mid-1990s, and generally falling again since then.

This diversity of behavior is modest evidence in favor of political-economy models of deficits. For example, it is hard to believe that economic fundamentals are so different between Belgium and the Netherlands as to warrant a gap of 50 percentage points in their debt-to-GDP ratios. If purely economic forces cannot account for variations in deficits, other forces must be at work. Political forces are one candidate.

Further, Roubini and Sachs (1989) show that the behavior of deficits appears to depart in an important way from tax-smoothing. In every country they consider, the tax-to-GDP ratio has an upward trend, and in most cases the trend is quantitatively and statistically significant. This is what one would expect with deficit bias. The government sets taxes too low relative to what tax-smoothing requires, and as a result starts to accumulate debt. As the debt mounts, the government must raise taxes to satisfy its budget constraint. With continuing deficit bias, the tax rate is always below the value that would be expected to satisfy the budget constraint if it were kept constant, and so there are repeated tax increases. Thus the finding of an upward trend in tax rates also supports political-economy models.

Weak Governments and Budget Deficits

We now turn to results that specifically concern political factors. The central finding of this literature, due to Roubini and Sachs, is that there are systematic differences in the political characteristics of countries that ran large deficits in the decade after the first oil price shocks in 1973 and countries that did not. Countries in the first group had governments that were short-lived and often took the form of multiparty coalitions, while countries in the second group had longer-lived, stronger governments. To test the strength of this pattern, Roubini and Sachs regress the deficit as a share of GDP on a set of economic variables and a political variable measuring how weak the government is (that is, measuring the extent to which policy is not controlled by a single party). The political variable ranges from 0 for a presidential or one-party-majority government to 3 for a minority government. Roubini and Sachs's regression takes the form

$$D_{it} = a + b\text{WEAK}_{it} + c'X_{it} + e_{it}. \tag{11.38}$$

D_{it} is the budget deficit in country i in year t as a share of GDP; WEAK_{it} is the political variable; and X_{it} is a vector of other variables. The data are annual observations for 1960–1986 for each of 15 countries. The resulting estimate of b is 0.4, with a standard error of 0.14. That is, the point estimate suggests that a change in the political variable from 0 to 3 is associated with an increase in the deficit-to-GDP ratio of 1.2 percentage points, which is substantial.[29]

The theory that is most suggestive of the importance of weak governments is Alesina and Drazen's: their model implies that inefficiency arises because no single interest group or party is setting policy. But recall that the model does not imply that weak governments cause high deficits; rather, it implies that weak governments cause persistence of existing deficits or surpluses. This prediction can be tested by including an interaction term between the political variable and the lagged deficit in the regression. That is, one can modify equation (11.38) to

[29] Edin and Ohlsson (1991) and de Haan and Sturm (1994) investigate the robustness of this finding.

$$D_{it} = a + b_1 \text{WEAK}_{it} + b_2 D_{i,t-1} + b_3 D_{i,t-1} \text{WEAK}_{it} + c' X_{it} + e_{it}. \quad (11.39)$$

With this specification, the persistence of the deficit from one year to the next, $\partial D_{it}/\partial D_{i,t-1}$, is $b_2 + b_3 \text{WEAK}_{it}$. Persistence is b_2 under the strongest governments ($\text{WEAK}_{it} = 0$) and $b_2 + 3b_3$ under the weakest ($\text{WEAK}_{it} = 3$). Thus Alesina and Drazen's model predicts $b_3 > 0$.

In estimating a regression with an interaction term, it is almost always important to also include the interacted variables individually. This is done by the inclusion of $b_1 \text{WEAK}_{it}$ and $b_2 D_{i,t-1}$ in (11.39). If $b_2 D_{i,t-1}$ is excluded, for example, the persistence of the deficit is $b_3 \text{WEAK}_{it}$. Thus the specification without $b_2 D_{i,t-1}$ forces persistence to equal 0 when WEAK_{it} equals 0. This is not a reasonable restriction to impose. Further, imposing it can bias the estimate of the main parameter of interest, b_3. For example, suppose that deficits are persistent but that their persistence does not vary with the strength of the government. Thus the truth is $b_2 > 0$ and $b_3 = 0$. In a regression without $b_2 D_{i,t-1}$, the best fit to the data is obtained with a positive value of $\hat{b}_3$, since this at least allows the regression to fit the fact that deficits are persistent under weak governments. Thus in this case the exclusion of $b_2 D_{i,t-1}$ biases the estimate of b_3 up. A similar analysis shows that one should include the $b_1 \text{WEAK}_{it}$ term as well.[30]

When Roubini and Sachs estimate equation (11.39), they obtain an estimate of b_2 of 0.66 (with a standard error of 0.07) and an estimate of b_3 of 0.03 (with a standard error of 0.03). Thus the null hypothesis that the strength of the government has no effect on the persistence of deficits cannot be rejected. More importantly, the point estimate implies that deficits are only slightly more persistent under the weakest governments than under the strongest (0.75 versus 0.66). Thus the results provide little support for a key prediction of Alesina and Drazen's model.

Is the Relationship Causal?

One concern about the finding that weaker governments run larger deficits is the usual one about statistical relationships: the finding may not reflect an impact of government weakness on deficits. Specifically, unfavorable economic and budgetary shocks that we are not able to control for in the regression can lead to both deficits and weak governments.

Two pieces of evidence suggest that this potential problem is not the main source of the correlation between deficits and weak government. First, Grilli, Masciandaro, and Tabellini (1991) find that there is a strong correlation between countries' deficits and whether they have proportional-

---

[30] Note also that when a variable enters a regression both directly and via an interaction term, the coefficient on the variable is no longer the correct measure of its estimated average impact on the dependent variable. In (11.39), for example, the average effect of WEAK on D is not b_1, but $b_1 + b_3 \overline{D}_{i,t-1}$, where $\overline{D}_{i,t-1}$ is the average value of $D_{i,t-1}$. Because of this, the point estimate and confidence interval for $b_1 + b_3 \overline{D}_{i,t-1}$ are likely to be of much greater interest than those for b_1.

representation systems. Countries did not adopt proportional representation in response to unfavorable shocks. And countries with proportional representation have on average weaker governments.

Second, Roubini and Sachs present a *case study* of France around the time of the founding of the Fifth Republic to attempt to determine whether weak government leads to high deficits. A case study is a detailed examination of what in a formal statistical analysis would be just a single data point or a handful of data points. Some case studies consist of little more than descriptions of the behavior of various variables, and are therefore less useful than statistical analysis of those variables. But well-executed case studies can serve two more constructive purposes. First, they can provide ideas for research. In situations where one does not yet have a hypothesis to test, detailed examination of an episode may suggest possibilities. Second, a case study can help to untangle the problems of omitted-variable bias and reverse causation that plague statistical work.

Roubini and Sachs's case study is of the second type. From 1946 to 1958, France had a proportional-representation system, divided and unstable governments, and high deficits. A presidential system was adopted in 1958–1959. After its adoption and de Gaulle's accession to the presidency, deficits fell rapidly and then remained low.

This bare-bones description adds nothing to statistical work. But Roubini and Sachs present several pieces of evidence that suggest that the political variables had large effects on deficits. First, there were no unfavorable shocks large enough to explain the large deficits of the 1950s on the basis of factors other than the political system. France did have unusually large military expenditures in this period because of its involvements in Vietnam and Algeria, but the expenditures were too small to account for a large part of the deficits. Second, there were enormous difficulties in agreeing on budgets in this period. Third, getting a budget passed often required adding large amounts of spending on patronage and local projects. And finally, de Gaulle used his powers under the new constitution to adopt a range of deficit-cutting measures that had failed under the old system or had been viewed as politically impossible. Thus, Roubini and Sachs's additional evidence strongly suggests that the conjunction of weak government and high deficits in the Fourth Republic and of strong government and low deficits in the Fifth Republic reflects an impact of political strength and stability on budgetary outcomes.

Other Findings

The literature has identified two other interesting relationships between political variables and deficits. First, Grilli, Masciandaro, and Tabellini find that average deficits are higher when governments are less durable. Specifically, they find that deficits are much more strongly associated with the frequency of changes in the executive than with the frequency of major changes in government. Roubini and Sachs's case study of France suggests, however, that this association may not be causal. At least in France in the 1950s, changes in governments were often the *result* of failures to agree on a budget. Thus here the additional evidence provided by a case study does not support a causal interpretation of a regression coefficient, but casts doubt on it.

Second, some recent work examines the relation between the institutions of budget-making and deficits. Much of this work views deficits as the result of a *common-pool* problem in government spending. Suppose that government spending is determined by several players, each of whom has particular influence over spending that benefits an interest group that the player is especially concerned about (such as the members of his or her legislative district). In effect, each player gets to choose how much of the economy's overall tax base (the common pool) to exploit to finance spending that particularly benefits him or her. The result is inefficiently high spending (Weingast, Shepsle, and Johnsen, 1981; see also Problem 11.15).

This account has several limitations as a model of deficits. First, it is not clear why the relatively small number of major participants in the budgetary process do not find some way of agreeing on an outcome that avoids this inefficiency. Second, spending that benefits narrow interests is only a small part of total government spending, and thus may not be large enough for the common-pool problem to produce significant bias. And third, in its basic form the model predicts spending bias rather than deficit bias.[31]

Despite these concerns, several papers examine the relationship between budgetary institutions and deficits (see von Hagen and Harden, 1995, and the papers in Poterba and von Hagen, 1999). For example, von Hagen and Harden (1995) construct an index of the extent to which countries' budgetary institutions are hierarchical and transparent. By *hierarchical*, they mean institutions that give the prime minister or finance minister a large role in the process. By *transparent*, they mean institutions that make the official budget more informative about what actual taxes and purchases will be. Neither hierarchy nor transparency provides a clear-cut test of the importance of the common-pool problem. Hierarchical institutions can reduce deficits for the same reasons as strong governments in Alesina and Drazen's model rather than by mitigating the common-pool problem. And transparency appears more likely to counter deficit bias stemming from signaling or imperfect understanding than from the common-pool problem.

von Hagen and Harden find a strong correlation between their index and fiscal outcomes among a sample of 12 European countries. For example, the three countries with the lowest values of the index had average deficit-to-GDP ratios in the 1980s over 10 percent, and average debt-to-GDP ratios of about 100 percent. The three highest-ranked countries had average deficit-to-GDP ratios less than 2 percent and average debt-to-GDP ratios of about 40 percent.

---

[31] On this last point, see Chari and Cole (1993); Velasco (1999); and Problem 11.16.

Conclusion

This line of work has established two main results. First, countries' political characteristics affect their deficits. Second, the political characteristics that appear to matter most are ones that Alesina and Drazen's model suggests lead to delay, such as divided government and division of power in budget-making. The evidence does not support the idea that deficits result from the deliberate decisions of one set of policymakers to leave large debts to their successors to restrain their spending, as in Tabellini and Alesina's model. We do not see large deficits in countries like the United Kingdom, where parties with very different ideologies alternate having strong control of policy. Instead we see them in countries like Belgium and Italy, where there is a succession of coalition and minority governments. This suggests that it is important to understand how division of power can lead to deficits. In particular, we would like to know whether a straightforward variation on Alesina and Drazen's analysis accounts for the link between divided government and deficits, or whether there is some other factor at work.

11.9   The Costs of Deficits

Much of this chapter discusses forces that can give rise to excessive deficits. But it says little about the nature and size of the costs of excessive deficits. This section provides an introduction to this issue.

The costs of deficits, like the costs of inflation, are poorly understood. The reasons are quite different, however. In the case of inflation, the difficulty is that the popular perception is that inflation is very costly, but economists have difficulty identifying channels through which it is likely to have important effects. In the case of deficits, it is not hard to find reasons that they can have significant effects. The difficulty is that the effects are complicated. As a result, it is hard to do welfare analysis in which one can have much confidence.

The first part of this section considers the effects of sustainable deficit policies. The second part discusses the effects of embarking on a policy that cannot be sustained, focusing especially on what can happen if the unsustainable policy ends with a crisis or "hard landing." Section 11.10 presents a simple model of how a crisis can come about.

The Effects of Sustainable Deficits

The most obvious cost of excessive deficits is that they involve a departure from tax-smoothing. If the tax rate is below the level needed for the government's budget constraint to be satisfied in expectation, then the expected future tax rate exceeds the current tax rate. This means that the expected discounted value of the distortion costs from raising revenue is unnecessarily high.

Unless the marginal distortion costs of raising revenue rise sharply with the amount of revenue raised, however, the costs of a moderate period of modestly excessive deficits through this channel are probably small. But this does not mean that departures from tax-smoothing are never important. Some projections suggest that if no changes in U.S. fiscal policy are made over the next few decades, satisfying the government budget constraint solely through tax increases would require average tax rates well over 50 percent. The distortion costs from such a policy would surely be substantial. To give another example, Cooley and Ohanian (1997) argue that Britain's heavy reliance on taxes rather than debt to finance its purchases during World War II—which corresponded to a policy of inefficiently *low* deficits relative to tax-smoothing—had large welfare costs.[32]

Deficits are likely to have larger welfare effects as a result of failures of Ricardian equivalence. Deficits almost surely raise aggregate consumption, and thus lower the economy's future wealth. Unfortunately, obtaining estimates of the resulting welfare effects is very difficult, for three reasons. First, simply obtaining estimates of deficits' impact on the paths of such variables as consumption, capital, foreign asset holdings, and so on requires estimates of the magnitude of departures from Ricardian equivalence. Here we do not have a precise figure. Nonetheless, one can make a rough estimate and proceed. For example, Bernheim (1987) argues that a reasonable estimate is that private saving offsets about half the decline in government saving that results from a switch from tax to deficit finance.

Second, the welfare effects depend on not just the magnitude of the departures from Ricardian equivalence, but also the reasons for the departures. For example, suppose Ricardian equivalence fails because of liquidity constraints. This means that the marginal utility of current consumption is high relative to that of future consumption, and thus that there is a large benefit to greater current consumption. In this case, running a higher deficit than is consistent with tax-smoothing can raise welfare (Hubbard and Judd, 1986). To give another example, suppose Ricardian equivalence fails because consumption is determined partly by rules of thumb. In this case, we cannot use households' consumption choices to infer their preferences. This leaves us with no clear way of evaluating the desirability of alternative paths of consumption.

The third difficulty is that deficits have distribution effects. Since some of the taxes needed to repay new debt fall on future generations, deficits redistribute from future generations to the current one. In addition, to the extent that deficits reduce the capital stock, they depress wages and raise real interest rates, and thus redistribute from workers to capitalists. The

---

[32] However, some of the costs they estimate come from high taxes on capital income rather than departures from tax-smoothing.

fact that deficits do not create Pareto improvements or Pareto deteriorations does not imply that one should have no opinion about their merits. For example, most individuals (including most economists) believe that a policy that benefits many people but involves small costs to a few is desirable, even if the losers are never compensated. In the case of the redistribution from workers to capitalists, the fact that workers are generally poorer than capitalists may be a reason to find the redistribution undesirable. The redistribution from future generations to the current one is more complicated. On one hand, future generations are likely to be better off than the current one; this is likely to make us view the redistribution more favorably. On the other hand, the common view that saving is too low has implicit in it the view that rates of return are high enough to make redistribution from those currently alive to future generations desirable; this suggests that the redistribution from future generations to the current one may be undesirable. For all these reasons, the welfare effects of sustainable deficits are difficult to evaluate.

The Effects of Unsustainable Deficits

Countries often embark on paths for fiscal policy that cannot be sustained. For example, they often pursue policies involving an ever-rising ratio of debt to GDP. By definition, an unsustainable policy cannot continue indefinitely. Thus the fact that the government is following such a policy does not imply that it needs to take deliberate actions to change course. As Herbert Stein once put it, "If something cannot go on forever, it will stop." The difficulty, however, is that the stopping is likely to be sudden and unexpected. Policy is unsustainable when the government is trying to behave in a way that violates its budget constraint. In such a situation, at some point outside developments force it to abandon this attempt. And as we will see in the next section, the forced change is likely to take the form of a crisis rather than a smooth transition. Typically, the crisis involves a sharp contraction in fiscal policy, a large decline in aggregate demand, major repercussions in capital and foreign-exchange markets, and perhaps default on the government's debt.

The possibility of a crisis creates additional costs to deficits. Before we discuss those costs, it is important to note that government default is not in itself a cost. The default is a transfer from bondholders to taxpayers. Typically this means that it is a transfer from wealthier to poorer individuals. Further, to the extent the debt is held by foreigners, the default is a transfer from foreigners to domestic residents. From the point of view of the domestic residents, this is an advantage to default. Finally, default reduces the amount of revenue the government must raise in the future. Since raising revenue involves distortions, this means that default does not just cause transfers, but also improves efficiency.

Nonetheless, there are costs to crises. Some of the most important arise because a crisis is likely to increase the price of foreign goods greatly. When the budget deficit falls sharply, the capital account surplus is likely to fall sharply as well. That is, the economy is likely to move from a situation where foreigners are buying large quantities of the country's assets to one where they are buying few or none. But this means that the trade balance must swing sharply toward surplus. For this to happen, there must be a large depreciation of the real exchange rate. In the Mexican crisis of 1994–1995, for example, the value of the Mexican peso fell roughly in half. And in the East Asian crisis of 1997–1998, the values of many of the affected currencies fell by considerably more.

Such real depreciation reduces welfare through several channels. Because it corresponds to a rise in the real price of foreign goods, it lowers welfare directly. Further, it tends to raise output in export and import-competing sectors and reduce it elsewhere. That is, it is a sectoral shock that induces a reallocation of labor and other inputs among sectors. Since reallocation is not instantaneous, the result is a temporary rise in unemployment and other unused resources. Finally, the depreciation is likely to increase inflation. Because workers purchase some foreign goods, the depreciation raises the cost of living and thus creates upward pressure on wages. In addition, because some inputs are imported, the depreciation raises firms' costs. These effects act to increase inflation. In the terminology of Section 5.4, real depreciation is an unfavorable supply shock.

Some other major costs of crises stem from the fact that they disrupt capital markets. Government default, plummeting asset prices, and falling output are likely to bankrupt many firms and financial intermediaries. In addition, because firms' and intermediaries' debts are often denominated in foreign currencies, real depreciation directly worsens their financial situations and thus further increases bankruptcies. The bankruptcies cause a loss of information and long-term relationships that help direct capital and other resources to their most productive uses. And even when firms and intermediaries are not bankrupted by the crisis, the worsening of their financial positions magnifies the effects of financial-market imperfections.

One effect of these financial-market disruptions is that investment is lower. This effect, however, can be offset by expansionary (or less contractionary) monetary policy. But another effect is that for a given amount of investment, the average quality of projects is lower, since the financial system now allocates capital less effectively. Similarly, output is lower for a given level of employment, since many firms with profitable production opportunities are unable to produce because of bankruptcy or an inability to obtain loans to pay their wages and purchase inputs. Bernanke (1983b) argues that such financial-market disruptions played a large role in the Great Depression. And they appear to have been important in more recent crises as well. In Indonesia in 1998, for example, a large majority of firms were at least technically bankrupt, although many continued to function in some form.

Crises can have other costs as well. Since crises are unexpected, trying to follow an unsustainable policy increases uncertainty. Default and other failures to repay its debts can reduce a government's ability to borrow in

the future.[33] Finally, a crisis can lead to harmful policies, such as broad
trade restrictions, hyperinflation, and very high tax rates on capital.

One way to summarize the effects of a crisis is to note that it typically
leads to a sharp fall in output followed by only a gradual recovery. This
summary, however, overstates the costs of embarking on unsustainable fiscal policy, for two reasons. First, unsustainable fiscal policy is usually not
the only source of a crisis; thus it is not appropriate to attribute the crisis's
full costs to fiscal policy. Second, there may be benefits to the policy before
the crisis. For example, it may lead to real appreciation, with benefits that
are the converse of the costs of real depreciation, and to a period of high
output. Nonetheless, the costs of an attempt to pursue unsustainable fiscal
policy that ends in a crisis are almost surely substantial.

11.10   A Model of Debt Crises

We now turn to a simple model of a government attempting to issue debt.
We focus on the questions of what can cause investors to be unwilling to
buy the debt at any interest rate, and of whether such a crisis is likely to
occur unexpectedly.[34]

Assumptions

Consider a government that has quantity D of debt that it wants investors
to hold for a period. The government offers an *interest factor* of R; that is,
it offers a real interest rate of $R - 1$. It has potential tax revenue of T the
following period. If T exceeds the amount due on the debt, RD, the government pays the debtholders. If T is less than RD, the government defaults.
T is random; its cumulative distribution function, $F(\bullet)$, is continuous.

It is natural to think of the period as one out of a long history. With
this interpretation, we can think of D as the sum of previously issued debt
that is coming due and any new debt the government wants to issue. And
we can think of T as the sum of the tax revenue the government can raise
the following period and the debt it can induce investors to hold then. Our
main goal in examining the model is to determine when the government is
not able to induce investors to purchase its debt. Since we can think of this
as a situation where the government cannot roll over debt that is coming
due, we will interpret this as a crisis.

Two simplifying assumptions make the model tractable. First, default
is all-or-nothing: if the government cannot pay RD, it repudiates the debt

---

[33] Because there is no authority analogous to domestic courts to force borrowers to
repay, there are some important issues specifically related to international borrowing. See
Obstfeld and Rogoff (1996, Chapter 6) for an introduction.

[34] See Calvo (1988) and Cole and Kehoe (2000) for examples of richer models of debt
crises.

entirely. Second, investors are risk-neutral, and the risk-free interest factor, $\overline{R}$, is independent of R and D. These assumptions do not appear critical to the model's main messages.

Analyzing the Model

Equilibrium is described by two equations in the probability of default, denoted π, and the interest factor on government debt, R. Since investors are risk-neutral, the expected payoff from holding government debt must equal the risk-free payoff, $\overline{R}$. Government debt pays R with probability $1 - \pi$ and 0 with probability π. Thus equilibrium requires

$$(1 - \pi)R = \overline{R}. \tag{11.40}$$

For comparison with the second equilibrium condition, it is useful to rearrange this condition as an expression for π as a function of R. This yields

$$\pi = \frac{R - \overline{R}}{R}. \tag{11.41}$$

The locus of points satisfying (11.41) is plotted in (R, π) space in Figure 11.3. When the government is certain to repay (that is, when $\pi = 0$), R equals $\overline{R}$. As the probability of default rises, the interest factor the government must offer rises; thus the locus is upward-sloping. Finally, R approaches infinity as the probability of default approaches 1.

The other equilibrium condition comes from the fact that whether the government defaults is determined by its available revenue relative to the amount due bondholders. Specifically, the government defaults if and only if T is less than RD. Thus the probability of default is the probability that T is less than RD. Since T's distribution function is $F(\bullet)$, we can write this condition as

$$\pi = F(RD). \tag{11.42}$$

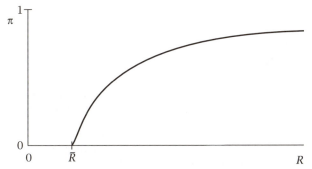

FIGURE 11.3   The condition for investors to be willing to hold government debt

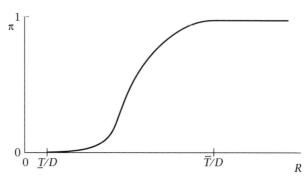

**FIGURE 11.4   The probability of default as a
function of the interest factor**

The set of points satisfying (11.42) is plotted in Figure 11.4. If there are minimum and maximum possible values of T, $\underline{T}$ and $\overline{T}$, the probability of default is 0 for $R < \underline{T}/D$ and 1 for $R > \overline{T}/D$. And if the density function of T is bell-shaped, the distribution function has an S shape like that shown in the figure.

Equilibrium occurs at a point where both (11.41) and (11.42) are satisfied. At such a point, the interest factor on government debt makes investors willing to hold the debt given the probability of default, and the probability of default is the probability that potential tax revenue is insufficient to pay off the debt given the interest factor. In addition to any equilibria satisfying these two conditions, however, there is always an equilibrium where investors are certain the government will not pay off the debt and are therefore unwilling to hold the debt at any interest factor. If investors refuse to hold the debt at any interest factor, the probability of default is 1; and if the probability of default is 1, investors refuse to hold the debt at any interest factor. Loosely speaking, this equilibrium corresponds to the point $R = \infty$, $\pi = 1$ in the diagram. If the government is issuing debt to pay off debt coming due, in this equilibrium the government defaults on that debt.[35]

---

[35] It is straightforward to extend the analysis to the case where default is not all-or-nothing. For example, suppose that when revenue is less than RD, the government pays all of it to debtholders. To analyze the model in this case, define π as the expected fraction of the amount due to investors, RD, that they do not receive. With this definition, the condition for investors to be willing to hold government debt, $(1 - \pi)R = \overline{R}$, is the same as before, and so equation (11.41) holds as before. The expression for the expected fraction of the amount due to investors that they do not receive as a function of the interest factor the government offers is now more complicated than (11.42). It still has the same basic shape in (R, π) space, however: it is 0 for R sufficiently small, upward-sloping, and approaches 1 as R approaches infinity. Because this change in assumptions does not change one curve at all and does not change the other's main features, the model's main messages are unaffected.

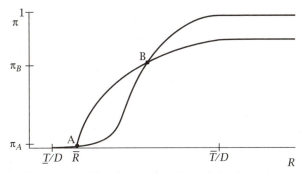

FIGURE 11.5 The determination of the interest factor and the probability of default

Implications

The model has at least four interesting implications. The first is that there is a simple force tending to create multiple equilibria in the probability of default. The higher the probability of default, the higher the interest factor investors demand; but the higher the interest factor investors demand, the higher the probability of default. In terms of the diagram, the fact that the curves showing the equilibrium conditions are both upward-sloping means that they can have multiple intersections.

Figure 11.5 shows one possibility. In this case, there are three equilibria. At Point A, the probability of default is low and the interest factor on government debt is only slightly above the safe interest factor. At Point B, there is a substantial chance of default and the interest factor on the debt is well above the safe factor. Finally, there is the equilibrium where default is certain and investors refuse to hold the government's debt at any interest factor.[36]

Under plausible dynamics, the equilibrium at B is unstable and the other two are stable. Suppose, for example, investors believe the probability of default is slightly below π_B. Then at the interest factor needed to induce them to hold the debt given this belief, the actual probability of default is less than what they conjecture. It is plausible that their estimate of the

---

[36] One natural question is whether the government can avoid the multiplicity by issuing its debt at the lowest equilibrium interest rate. The answer depends on how investors form their expectations of the probability of default. One possibility is that they tentatively assume that the government can successfully issue debt at the interest factor it is offering; they then purchase the debt if the expected return given this assumption at least equals the risk-free return. In this case, the government can issue debt at the lowest interest factor where the two curves intersect. But this is not the only possibility. For example, suppose each investor believes that others believe the government will default for sure, and that others are therefore unwilling to purchase the debt at any interest factor. Then no investor purchases the debt, and so the beliefs prove correct.

probability of default therefore falls, and that this process continues until the equilibrium at Point A is reached. A similar argument suggests that if investors conjecture that the probability of default exceeds π_B, the economy converges to the equilibrium where investors will not hold the debt at any interest factor. Thus there are two stable equilibria. In one, the interest factor and the probability of default are low. In the other, the government cannot get investors to hold its debt at any interest factor, and so it defaults immediately on its outstanding debt. In short, there can be a self-fulfilling element to default.[37]

The second implication is that large differences in fundamentals are not needed for large differences in outcomes. One reason for this is the multiplicity just described: two economies can have the same fundamentals, but one can be in the equilibrium with low R and low π and the other in the equilibrium where investors refuse to buy the debt at any interest factor. A more interesting source of large differences stems from differences in the set of equilibria. Suppose the two curves have the form shown in Figure 11.5, and suppose an economy is in the equilibrium with low R and low π at Point A. A rise in $\overline{R}$ shifts the $\pi = (R - \overline{R})/R$ curve to the right. Similarly, a rise in D shifts the $\pi = F(RD)$ curve to the left. For small enough changes, π and R change smoothly in response to either of these developments. Figure 11.6, for example, shows the effects of a moderate change in $\overline{R}$ from $\overline{R}_0$ to $\overline{R}_1$. The equilibrium with low R and low π changes smoothly from A to A'. But now suppose $\overline{R}$ rises further. If $\overline{R}$ becomes sufficiently large—if it rises to $\overline{R}_2$, for example—the two curves no longer intersect. In this situation, the only equilibrium is the one where investors will not hold the debt. Thus two economies can have similar fundamentals, but in one there is an equilibrium where the government can issue debt at a low interest rate while in the other the only equilibrium is for the government to be unable to issue debt at any interest rate.

Third, the model suggests that default, when it occurs, may always be quite unexpected. That is, it may be that for realistic cases, there is never an equilibrium value of π that is substantial but strictly less than 1. If there is little uncertainty about T, the revenue the government can obtain to pay off the debt, the $\pi = F(RD)$ locus has sharp bends near $\pi = 0$ and $\pi = 1$ like those in Figure 11.6. Since the $\pi = (R - \overline{R})/R$ locus does not bend sharply, in this case the switch to the situation where default is the only equilibrium occurs at a low value of π. That is, there may never be a situation where investors believe the probability of default is substantial but strictly less than 1; as a result, defaults are always a surprise.

The final implication is the most straightforward. Default depends not only on self-fulfilling beliefs, but also on fundamentals. In particular, an

---

[37] Calvo (1988) describes a related reason that expectations of default can be self-fulfilling. If default is costly to the government, the government may choose to default if it must pay a high return but not to default if it must pay a low return.

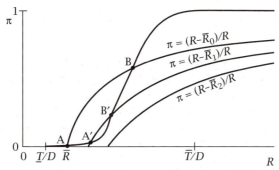

**FIGURE 11.6   The effects of increases in the
safe interest factor**

increase in the amount the government wants to borrow, an increase in the
safe interest factor, and a downward shift in the distribution of potential
revenue all make default more likely. Each of these developments shifts either the $\pi = (R - \bar{R})/R$ locus down or the $\pi = F(RD)$ locus up. As a result,
each development increases π at any stable equilibrium. In addition, each
development can move the economy to a situation where the only equilibrium is the one where there is no interest factor at which investors will hold
the debt. Thus one message of the model is that high debt, a high required
rate of return, and low future revenues all make default more likely.

Multiple Periods

A version of the model with multiple periods raises some interesting additional issues. For instance, suppose the government wants to issue debt for
two periods. The government inherits a stock of debt in period 0, D_0. Let
R_1 denote the interest factor it pays from period 0 to period 1, and R_2 the
interest factor from period 1 to period 2. For simplicity, the government
receives tax revenue only in period 2. Thus it pays off the debt in period
2 if and only if its available revenues, T, exceed the amount due, $R_1 R_2 D_0$.
Finally, since the multiperiod version does not provide important additional
insights into the possibility of multiple equilibria, assume that the equilibrium with the lowest π (and hence the lowest R) is selected when there is
more than one equilibrium.

The most interesting new issues raised by the multiperiod model concern the importance of investors' beliefs, their beliefs about other investors'
beliefs, and so on. The question of when investors can have heterogeneous
beliefs in equilibrium is difficult and important. For this discussion, however, we simply assume that heterogeneous beliefs are possible. Consider
an investor in period 0. In the one-period case with the issue of multiple

equilibria assumed away, the investor's beliefs about others' beliefs are irrelevant to his or her behavior. The investor holds the debt if the interest factor times his or her estimate of the probability that tax revenues will be sufficient to pay off the debt is greater than or equal to the safe interest factor. But in the two-period case, the investor's willingness to hold the debt depends not only on R_1 and the distribution of T, but also on what R_2 will be. This in turn depends on what other investors will believe as of period 1 about the distribution of T. Suppose, for example, that for some R_1, the investor's own beliefs about $F(\bullet)$ imply that if the government offered an R_2 only slightly above the safe factor, the probability of default would be low, so that it would be sensible to hold the debt. Suppose, however, he or she believes that others' beliefs will make them unwilling to hold the debt from period 1 to period 2 at any interest factor. Then the investor believes the government will default in period 1. He or she therefore does not purchase the debt in period 0 despite the fact that his or her own beliefs about fundamentals suggest that the government's policy is reasonable.

Even a belief that there is a small chance that in period 1 others' beliefs will make them unwilling to hold the debt at any interest rate can matter. Such a belief increases the R_1 that investors require to buy the debt in period 0. This raises the amount of debt the government has to roll over in period 1, which reduces the chances that it will be able to do so, which raises R_1 further, and so on. The end result is that the government may not be able to sell its debt in period 0.

With more periods, even more complicated beliefs can matter. For example, if there are three periods rather than two, an investor in period 0 may be unwilling to purchase the debt because he or she believes that in period 1 others may think that in period 2 investors may believe that there is no interest factor that makes it worthwhile for them to hold the debt.

Thus, it is rational for investors to be concerned about others' beliefs about governments' solvency, about others' beliefs about others' beliefs, and so on. Those beliefs affect the government's ability to service its debt and thus the expected return from holding debt. An additional implication is that a change in the debt market, or even a crisis, can be caused by information not about fundamentals, but about beliefs about fundamentals, or about beliefs about beliefs about fundamentals.

Problems

11.1. The stability of fiscal policy. (Blinder and Solow, 1973.) By definition, the budget deficit equals the rate of change of the amount of debt outstanding: $\delta(t) \equiv \dot{D}(t)$. Define $d(t)$ to be the ratio of debt to output: $d(t) = D(t)/Y(t)$. Assume that $Y(t)$ grows at a constant rate $g > 0$.

(a) Suppose that the deficit-to-output ratio is constant: $\delta(t)/Y(t) = a$, where $a > 0$.

  (i) Find an expression for $\dot{d}(t)$ in terms of a, g, and $d(t)$.

(ii) Sketch $\dot{d}(t)$ as a function of $d(t)$. Is this system stable?

(b) Suppose that the ratio of the primary deficit to output is constant and equal to $a > 0$. Thus the total deficit at t, $\delta(t)$, is given by $\delta(t) = aY(t) + r(t)D(t)$, where $r(t)$ is the interest rate at t. Assume that r is an increasing function of the debt-to-output ratio: $r(t) = r(d(t))$, where $r'(\bullet) > 0$, $r''(\bullet) > 0$, $\lim_{d \to -\infty} r(d) < g$, $\lim_{d \to \infty} r(d) > g$.

(i) Find an expression for $\dot{d}(t)$ in terms of a, g, and $d(t)$.

(ii) Sketch $\dot{d}(t)$ as a function of $d(t)$. In the case where a is sufficiently small that $\dot{d}$ is negative for some values of d, what are the stability properties of the system? What about the case where a is sufficiently large that $\dot{d}$ is positive for all values of d?

11.2. Precautionary saving, non-lump-sum taxation, and Ricardian equivalence. (Leland, 1968, and Barsky, Mankiw, and Zeldes, 1986.) Consider an individual who lives for two periods. The individual has no initial wealth and earns labor incomes of amounts Y_1 and Y_2 in the two periods. Y_1 is known, but Y_2 is random; assume for simplicity that $E[Y_2] = Y_1$. The government taxes income at rate τ_1 in period 1 and τ_2 in period 2. The individual can borrow and lend at a fixed interest rate, which for simplicity is assumed to be zero. Thus second-period consumption is $C_2 = (1 - \tau_1)Y_1 - C_1 + (1 - \tau_2)Y_2$. The individual chooses C_1 to maximize expected lifetime utility, $U(C_1) + E[U(C_2)]$.

(a) Find the first-order condition for C_1.

(b) Show that $E[C_2] = C_1$ if Y_2 is not random or if utility is quadratic.

(c) Show that if $U'''(\bullet) > 0$ and Y_2 is random, $E[C_2] > C_1$.

(d) Suppose that the government marginally lowers τ_1 and raises τ_2 by the same amount, so that its expected total revenue, $\tau_1 Y_1 + \tau_2 E[Y_2]$, is unchanged. Implicitly differentiate the first-order condition in part (a) to find an expression for how C_1 responds to this change.

(e) Show that C_1 is unaffected by this change if Y_2 is not random or if utility is quadratic.

(f) Show that C_1 increases in response to this change if $U'''(\bullet) > 0$ and Y_2 is random.

11.3. Consider the Barro tax-smoothing model. Suppose that output, Y, and the real interest rate, r, are constant, and that the level of government debt outstanding at time 0 is 0. Suppose that there will be a temporary war from time 0 to time τ. Thus $G(t)$ equals G_H for $0 \le t \le \tau$, and equals G_L thereafter, where $G_H > G_L$. What are the paths of taxes, $T(t)$, and government debt outstanding, $D(t)$?

11.4. Consider the Barro tax-smoothing model. Suppose there are two possible values of $G(t)$—G_H and G_L—with $G_H > G_L$. Transitions between the two values follow Poisson processes (see Section 9.4). Specifically, if G equals G_H, the probability per unit time that purchases fall to G_L is a; if G equals G_L, the probability per unit time that purchases rise to G_H is b. Suppose also that output, Y, and the real interest rate, r, are constant and that distortion costs are quadratic.

(a) Derive expressions for taxes at a given time as a function of whether G equals G_H or G_L, the amount of debt outstanding, and the exogenous parameters. (Hint: Use dynamic programming, described in Section 9.4, to find an expression for the expected present value of the revenue the government must raise as a function of G, the amount of debt outstanding, and the exogenous parameters.)

(b) Discuss your results. What is the path of taxes during an interval when G equals G_H? Why are taxes not constant during such an interval? What happens to taxes at a moment when G falls to G_L? What is the path of taxes during an interval when G equals G_L?

11.5. If the tax rate follows a random walk (and if the variance of its innovations is bounded from below by a strictly positive number), then with probability 1 it will eventually exceed 100 percent or be negative. Does this observation suggest that the tax-smoothing model with quadratic distortion costs is not useful as either a positive or normative model of fiscal policy, since it has an implication that is both clearly incorrect as a description of the world and clearly undesirable as a prescription for policy? Explain your answer briefly.

11.6. The Condorcet paradox. Suppose there are three voters, 1, 2, and 3, and three possible policies, A, B, and C. Voter 1's preference ordering is A, B, C; voter 2's is B, C, A; and voter 3's is C, A, B. Does any policy win a majority of votes in a two-way contest against each of the alternatives? Explain.

11.7. Consider the Tabellini–Alesina model in the case where α can only take on the values 0 and 1. Suppose that there is some initial level of debt, D_0. How, if at all, does D_0 affect the deficit in period 1?

11.8. Consider the Tabellini–Alesina model in the case where α can only take on the values 0 and 1. Suppose that the amount of debt to be issued, D, is determined before the preferences of the period-1 median voter are known. Specifically, voters vote on D at a time when the probabilities that $\alpha_1^{\text{MED}} = 1$ and that $\alpha_2^{\text{MED}} = 1$ are equal. Let π denote this common value. Assume that the draws of the two median voters are independent.

(a) What is the expected utility of an individual with $\alpha = 1$ as a function of D, π, and W?

(b) What is the first-order condition for this individual's most preferred value of D? What is the associated value of D?

(c) What is the most preferred value of D of an individual with $\alpha = 0$?

(d) Given these results, if voters vote on D before the period-1 median voter is known, what value of D does the median voter prefer?

(e) Explain briefly how, if at all, the question analyzed in part (d) differs from the question of whether individuals will support a balanced-budget requirement if it is proposed before the preferences of the period-1 median voter are known.

11.9. Consider the Tabellini–Alesina model in the case where α can only take on the values 0 and 1. Suppose, however, that there are 3 periods. The period-1 median voter sets policy in periods 1 and 2, but in period 3 a new median voter sets policy. Assume that the period-1 median voter's α is 1, and that the probability that the period-3 median voter's α is 1 is π.

(a) Does $M_1 = M_2$?

(b) Suppose that after choosing purchases in period 1, the period-1 median voter learns that the probability that the period-3 median voter's α will be 1 is not π but π', where $\pi' < \pi$. How does this news affect his or her choice of purchases in period 2?

11.10. **The Persson-Svensson model.** (Persson and Svensson, 1989.) Suppose there are two periods. Government policy will be controlled by different policymakers in the two periods. The objective function of the period-t policymaker is $U + \alpha_t[V(G_1) + V(G_2)]$, where U is citizens' utility from their private consumption; α_t is the weight that the period-t policymaker puts on public consumption; G_t is public consumption in period t; and $V(\bullet)$ satisfies $V'(\bullet) > 0$, $V''(\bullet) < 0$. Private utility, U, is given by $U = W - C(T_1) - C(T_2)$, where W is the endowment; T_t is taxes in period t; and $C(\bullet)$, the cost of raising revenue, satisfies $C'(\bullet) \geq 1$, $C''(\bullet) > 0$. All government debt must be paid off at the end of period 2. This implies $T_2 = G_2 + D$, where $D = G_1 - T_1$ is the amount of government debt issued in period 1 and where the interest rate is assumed to equal 0.

(a) Find the first-order condition for the period-2 policymaker's choice of G_2 given D. (Note: Throughout, assume that the solutions to the policymakers' maximization problems are interior.)

(b) How does a change in D affect G_2?

(c) Think of the period-1 policymaker as choosing G_1 and D. Find the first-order condition for his or her choice of D.

(d) Show that if α_1 is less than α_2, the equilibrium involves inefficiently low taxation in period 1 relative to tax-smoothing (that is, that it has $T_1 < T_2$). Explain intuitively why this occurs.

(e) Does the result in part (d) imply that if α_1 is less than α_2, the period-1 policymaker necessarily runs a deficit? Explain.

11.11. Consider the Alesina–Drazen model. Describe how, if at all, each of the following developments affects workers' proposal and the probability of reform:

(a) A fall in T.

(b) A rise in B.

(c) An equal rise in A and B.

11.12. **Crises and reform.** Consider the model in Section 11.7. Suppose, however, that if there is no reform, workers and capitalists both receive payoffs of $-C$ rather than 0, where $C \geq 0$.

(a) Find expressions analogous to (11.36) and (11.37) for workers' proposal and the probability of reform.

(b) Define social welfare as the sum of the expected payoffs of workers and capitalists. Show that an increase in C can raise this measure of social welfare.

11.13. Conditionality and reform. Consider the model in Section 11.7. Suppose an international agency offers to give the workers and capitalists each an amount $F > 0$ if they agree to reform. Use analysis like that in Problem 11.12 to show that this aid policy unambiguously raises the probability of reform and the social welfare measure defined in part (b) of that problem.

11.14. Status-quo bias. (Fernandez and Rodrik, 1991.) There are two possible policies, A and B. Each individual is either one unit of utility better off under Policy A or one unit worse off. Fraction f of the population knows what its welfare would be under each policy. Of these individuals, fraction α are better off under Policy A and fraction $1 - \alpha$ are worse off. The remaining individuals in the population know only that fraction β of them are better off under Policy A and fraction $1 - \beta$ are worse off.

A decision of whether to adopt the policy not currently in effect is made by majority vote. If the proposal passes, all individuals learn which policy makes them better off; a decision of whether to revert to the original policy is then made by majority vote. Each individual votes for the policy that gives him or her the higher expected utility. But if the proposal to revert to the original policy would be adopted in the event that the proposal to adopt the alternative policy passed, no one votes for the alternative policy. (This assumption can be justified by introducing a small cost of changing policies.)

(a) Find an expression for the fraction of the population that prefers Policy A (as a function of f, α, and β) for the case where fraction $1 - f$ of the population knows only that fraction β of them are better off under Policy A.

(b) Find the analogous expression for the case where all individuals know their welfare under both policies.

(c) Given your answers to parts (a) and (b), can there be cases when whichever policy is initially in effect is retained?

11.15. The common-pool problem in government spending. (Weingast, Shepsle, and Johnsen, 1981.) Suppose the economy consists of $M > 1$ congressional districts. The utility of the representative person living in district i is $E + V(G_i) - C(T)$. E is the endowment, G_i is the level of a local public good in district i, and T is taxes (which are assumed to be the same in all districts). Assume $V'(\bullet) > 0$, $V''(\bullet) < 0$, $C'(\bullet) > 0$, and $C''(\bullet) > 0$. The government budget constraint is $\sum_{i=1}^{M} G_i = MT$. The representative from each district dictates the values of G in his or her district. Each representative maximizes the utility of the representative person living in his or her district.

(a) Find the first-order condition for the value of G_j chosen by the representative from district j, given the values of G_i chosen by the other representatives and the government budget constraint (which implies $T = (\sum_{i=1}^{M} G_i)/M$). (Note: Throughout, assume interior solutions.)

(b) Find the condition for the Nash equilibrium value of G. That is, find the condition for the value of G such that if all other representatives choose that value for their G_i, a given representative wants to choose that value.

(c) Is the Nash equilibrium Pareto-efficient? Explain. What is the intuition for this result?

11.16. Debt as a means of mitigating the common-pool problem. (Chari and Cole, 1993.) Consider the same setup as in Problem 11.15. Suppose, however, that there is an initial level of debt, D. The government budget constraint is therefore $D + \sum_{i=1}^{M} G_i = MT$.

(a) How does an increase in D affect the Nash equilibrium level of G?

(b) Explain intuitively why your results in part (a) and in Problem 11.15 suggest that in a two-period model in which the representatives choose D after the first-period value of G is determined, the representatives would choose $D > 0$.

(c) Do you think that in a two-period model where the representatives choose D before the first-period value of G is determined, the representatives would choose $D > 0$? Explain intuitively.

11.17. Consider the model of crises in Section 11.10, and suppose T is distributed uniformly on some interval $[\mu - X, \mu + X]$, where $X > 0$ and $\mu - X \geq 0$. Describe how, if at all, each of the following developments affects the two curves in (R, π) space that show the determination of R and π:

(a) A rise in μ.

(b) A fall in X.

REFERENCES

A

Abel, Andrew B. 1982. "Dynamic Effects of Permanent and Temporary Tax Policies in a q Model of Investment." *Journal of Monetary Economics* 9 (May): 353–373.

Abel, Andrew B. 1990. "Asset Prices under Habit Formation and Catching Up with the Joneses." *American Economic Review* 80 (May): 38–42.

Abel, Andrew B., Dixit, Avinash K., Eberly, Janice C., and Pindyck, Robert S. 1996. "Options, the Value of Capital, and Investment." *Quarterly Journal of Economics* 111 (August): 753–777.

Abel, Andrew B., and Eberly, Janice C. 1994. "A Unified Model of Investment under Uncertainty." *American Economic Review* 84 (December): 1369–1384.

Abel, Andrew B., Mankiw, N. Gregory, Summers, Lawrence H., and Zeckhauser, Richard J. 1989. "Assessing Dynamic Efficiency: Theory and Evidence." *Review of Economic Studies* 56 (January): 1–20.

Abraham, Katharine G., and Katz, Lawrence F. 1986. "Cyclical Unemployment: Sectoral Shifts or Aggregate Disturbances?" *Journal of Political Economy* 94 (June): 507–522.

Abramovitz, Moses. 1956. "Resource and Output Trends in the United States since 1870." *American Economic Review* 46 (May): 5–23.

Abreu, Dilip. 1988. "On the Theory of Infinitely Repeated Games with Discounting." *Econometrica* 56 (March): 383–396.

Acemoglu, Daron. 1995. "Reward Structures and the Allocation of Talent." *European Economic Review* 39 (January): 17–33.

Acemoglu, Daron, Johnson, Simon, and Robinson, James A. 2000. "The Colonial Origins of Comparative Development." Unpublished paper, Massachusetts Institute of Technology (June).

Acemoglu, Daron, and Robinson, James A. 2000a. "Inefficient Redistribution." Unpublished paper, Massachusetts Institute of Technology (January).

Acemoglu, Daron, and Robinson, James A. 2000b. "Political Losers as a Barrier to Economic Development." *American Economic Review* 90 (May): 126–130.

Acemoglu, Daron, and Scott, Andrew. 1997. "Asymmetric Business Cycles: Theory and Time-Series Evidence." *Journal of Monetary Economics* 40 (December): 501–533.

Aghion, Philippe, and Howitt, Peter. 1992. "A Model of Growth through Creative Destruction." *Econometrica* 60 (March): 323–351.

Aghion, Philippe, and Howitt, Peter. 1998. *Endogenous Growth Theory.* Cambridge, MA: MIT Press.

Aiyagari, S. Rao, Christiano, Lawrence J., and Eichenbaum, Martin. 1992. "The Output, Employment, and Interest Rate Effects of Government Consumption." *Journal of Monetary Economics* 30 (October): 73–86.

Aiyagari, S. Rao, and Gertler, Mark. 1985. "The Backing of Government Bonds and Monetarism." *Journal of Monetary Economics* 16 (July): 19–44.

Akerlof, George A. 1969. "Relative Wages and the Rate of Inflation." *Quarterly Journal of Economics* 83 (August): 353–374.

Akerlof, George A. 1991. "Procrastination and Obedience." *American Economic Review* 81 (May): 1–19.

Akerlof, George A., and Katz, Lawrence F. 1989. "Workers' Trust Funds and the Logic of Wage Profiles." *Quarterly Journal of Economics* 104 (August): 525–536.

Akerlof, George A., and Main, Brian G. M. 1981. "An Experience-Weighted Measure of Employment and Unemployment Durations." *American Economic Review* 71 (December): 1003–1011.

Akerlof, George A., Rose, Andrew K., and Yellen, Janet L. 1988. "Job Switching and Job Satisfaction in the U.S. Labor Market." *Brookings Papers on Economic Activity,* no. 2, 495–582.

Akerlof, George A., and Yellen, Janet L. 1985. "A Near-Rational Model of the Business Cycle, with Wage and Price Inertia." *Quarterly Journal of Economics* 100 (Supplement): 823–838. Reprinted in Mankiw and Romer (1991).

Akerlof, George A., and Yellen, Janet L. 1990. "The Fair Wage-Effort Hypothesis and Unemployment." *Quarterly Journal of Economics* 105 (May): 255–283.

Alesina, Alberto. 1988. "Macroeconomics and Politics." *NBER Macroeconomics Annual* 3: 13–52.

Alesina, Alberto, and Drazen, Allan. 1991. "Why Are Stabilizations Delayed?" *American Economic Review* 81 (December): 1170–1188. Reprinted in Persson and Tabellini (1994).

Alesina, Alberto, and Perotti, Roberto. 1997. "Fiscal Adjustments in OECD Countries: Composition and Macroeconomic Effects." *IMF Staff Papers* 44 (June): 210–248.

Alesina, Alberto, and Roubini, Nouriel, with Cohen, Gerald D. 1997. *Political Cycles and the Macroeconomy.* Cambridge, MA: MIT Press.

Alesina, Alberto, and Summers, Lawrence H. 1993. "Central Bank Independence and Macroeconomic Performance." *Journal of Money, Credit, and Banking* 25 (May): 151–162.

Allais, Maurice. 1947. *Économie et Intérêt.* Paris: Impremerie Nationale.

Alt, James E., and Lowry, Robert C. 1994. "Divided Government, Fiscal Institutions, and Budget Deficits: Evidence from the States." *American Political Science Review* 88 (December): 811–828.

Altonji, Joseph G. 1986. "Intertemporal Substitution in Labor Supply: Evidence from Micro Data." *Journal of Political Economy* 94 (June, Part 2): S176–S215.

Altonji, Joseph G., Hayashi, Fumio, and Kotlikoff, Laurence J. 1997. "Parental Altruism and *Inter Vivos* Transfers: Theory and Evidence." *Journal of Political Economy* 105 (December): 1121–1166.

Altonji, Joseph G., and Siow, Aloysius. 1987. "Testing the Response of Consumption to Income Changes with (Noisy) Panel Data." *Quarterly Journal of Economics* 102 (May): 293–328.

Altug, Sumru. 1989. "Time-to-Build and Aggregate Fluctuations." *International Economic Review* 30 (November): 889–920.

Andersen, Leonall C., and Jordan, Jerry L. 1968. "Monetary and Fiscal Actions: A Test of Their Relative Importance in Economic Stabilization." Federal Reserve Bank of St. Louis *Review* 50 (November): 11–24.

Andolfatto, David. 1996. "Business Cycles and Labor-Market Search." *American Economic Review* 86 (March): 112–132.

Arrow, Kenneth J. 1962. "The Economic Implications of Learning by Doing." *Review of Economic Studies* 29 (June): 155–173. Reprinted in Stiglitz and Uzawa (1969).

Atkeson, Andrew, and Phelan, Christopher. 1994. "Reconsidering the Costs of Business Cycles with Incomplete Markets." *NBER Macroeconomics Annual* 9: 187–207.

Auerbach, Alan J. 1997. "Quantifying the Current U.S. Fiscal Imbalance." *National Tax Journal* 50 (November): 387–398.

Auerbach, Alan J., and Kotlikoff, Laurence J. 1987. *Dynamic Fiscal Policy.* Cambridge: Cambridge University Press.

Azariadis, Costas. 1975. "Implicit Contracts and Underemployment Equilibria." *Journal of Political Economy* 83 (December): 1183–1202.

Azariadis, Costas, and Stiglitz, Joseph E. 1983. "Implicit Contracts and Fixed-Price Equilibria." *Quarterly Journal of Economics* 98 (Supplement): 1–22. Reprinted in Mankiw and Romer (1991).

B

Backus, David, and Driffill, John. 1985. "Inflation and Reputation." *American Economic Review* 75 (June): 530–538.

Backus, David, and Kehoe, Patrick J. 1992. "International Evidence on the Historical Properties of Business Cycles." *American Economic Review* 82 (September): 864–888.

Baily, Martin Neil. 1974. "Wages and Employment under Uncertain Demand." *Review of Economic Studies* 41 (January): 37–50.

Baily, Martin Neil, and Gordon, Robert J. 1988. "The Productivity Slowdown, Measurement Issues, and the Explosion of Computer Power." *Brookings Papers on Economic Activity,* no. 2, 347–420.

Balke, Nathan S., and Gordon, Robert J. 1989. "The Estimation of Prewar Gross National Product: Methodology and New Evidence." *Journal of Political Economy* 97 (February): 38–92.

Ball, Laurence. 1988. "Is Equilibrium Indexation Efficient?" *Quarterly Journal of Economics* 103 (May): 299–311.

Ball, Laurence. 1990. "Intertemporal Substitution and Constraints on Labor Supply: Evidence from Panel Data." *Economic Inquiry* 28 (October): 706–724.

Ball, Laurence. 1991. "The Genesis of Inflation and the Costs of Disinflation." *Journal of Money, Credit, and Banking* 23 (August, Part 2): 439–452.

Ball, Laurence. 1993. "The Dynamics of High Inflation." National Bureau of Economic Research Working Paper No. 4578 (December).

Ball, Laurence. 1994a. "Credible Disinflation with Staggered Price-Setting." *American Economic Review* 84 (March): 282–289.

Ball, Laurence. 1994b. "What Determines the Sacrifice Ratio?" In N. Gregory Mankiw, ed., *Monetary Policy,* 155–182. Chicago: University of Chicago Press.

Ball, Laurence. 1999a. "Aggregate Demand and Long-Term Unemployment." *Brookings Papers on Economic Activity,* no. 2, 189–251.

Ball, Laurence. 1999b. "Efficient Rules for Monetary Policy." *International Finance* 2 (April): 63–83.

Ball, Laurence, and Cecchetti, Stephen G. 1988. "Imperfect Information and Staggered Price Setting." *American Economic Review* 78 (December): 999–1018. Reprinted in Mankiw and Romer (1991).

Ball, Laurence, and Cecchetti, Stephen G. 1990. "Inflation and Uncertainty at Short and Long Horizons." *Brookings Papers on Economic Activity,* no. 1, 215–254.

Ball, Laurence, Elmendorf, Douglas W., and Mankiw, N. Gregory. 1998. "The Deficit Gamble." *Journal of Money, Credit, and Banking* 30 (November): 699–720.

Ball, Laurence, and Mankiw, N. Gregory. 1994. "A Sticky-Price Manifesto." *Carnegie-Rochester Conference Series on Public Policy* 41 (December): 127–151.

Ball, Laurence, and Mankiw, N. Gregory. 1995. "Relative-Price Changes as Aggregate Supply Shocks." *Quarterly Journal of Economics* 110 (February): 161–193.

Ball, Laurence, Mankiw, N. Gregory, and Romer, David. 1988. "The New Keynesian Economics and the Output-Inflation Tradeoff." *Brookings Papers on Economic Activity,* no. 1, 1–65. Reprinted in Mankiw and Romer (1991).

Ball, Laurence, and Romer, David. 1989. "The Equilibrium and Optimal Timing of Price Changes." *Review of Economic Studies* 56 (April): 179–198.

Ball, Laurence, and Romer, David. 1990. "Real Rigidities and the Non-Neutrality of Money." *Review of Economic Studies* 57 (April): 183–203. Reprinted in Mankiw and Romer (1991).

Ball, Laurence, and Romer, David. 1991. "Sticky Prices as Coordination Failure." *American Economic Review* 81 (June): 539–552.

Barro, Robert J. 1972. "A Theory of Monopolistic Price Adjustment." *Review of Economic Studies* 34 (January): 17–26.

Barro, Robert J. 1974. "Are Government Bonds Net Wealth?" *Journal of Political Economy* 82 (November/December): 1095–1117.

Barro, Robert J. 1976. "Rational Expectations and the Role of Monetary Policy." *Journal of Monetary Economics* 2 (January): 1–32.

Barro, Robert J. 1977a. "Unanticipated Money Growth and Unemployment in the United States." *American Economic Review* 67 (March): 101–115.

Barro, Robert J. 1977b. "Long-Term Contracting, Sticky Prices, and Monetary Policy." *Journal of Monetary Economics* 3 (July): 305–316.

Barro, Robert J. 1978. "Unanticipated Money, Output, and the Price Level in the United States." *Journal of Political Economy* 86: 549–580.

Barro, Robert J. 1979. "On the Determination of Public Debt." *Journal of Political Economy* 87 (October): 940–971.

Barro, Robert J. 1986. "Reputation in a Model of Monetary Policy with Incomplete Information." *Journal of Monetary Economics* 17 (January): 3–20. Reprinted in Persson and Tabellini (1994).

Barro, Robert J. 1987. "Government Spending, Interest Rates, Prices, and Budget Deficits in the United Kingdom, 1701–1918." *Journal of Monetary Economics* 20 (September): 221–247.

Barro, Robert J. 1989. "Interest-Rate Targeting." *Journal of Monetary Economics* 23 (January): 3–30.

Barro, Robert J. 1991. "Economic Growth in a Cross Section of Countries." *Quarterly Journal of Economics* 106 (May): 407–443.

Barro, Robert J. 1993. *Macroeconomics,* 4th ed. New York: Wiley.

Barro, Robert J., and Becker, Gary S. 1988. "A Reformulation of the Economic Theory of Fertility." *Quarterly Journal of Economics* 103 (February): 1–25.

Barro, Robert J., and Becker, Gary S. 1989. "Fertility Choice in a Model of Economic Growth." *Econometrica* 57 (March): 481–501.

Barro, Robert J., and Gordon, David B. 1983a. "A Positive Theory of Monetary Policy in a Natural Rate Model." *Journal of Political Economy* 91 (August): 589–610.

Barro, Robert J., and Gordon, David B. 1983b. "Rules, Discretion and Reputation in a Model of Monetary Policy." *Journal of Monetary Economics* 12 (July): 101–121. Reprinted in Persson and Tabellini (1994).

Barro, Robert J., and Grossman, Herschel I. 1971. "A General Disequilibrium Model of Income and Employment." *American Economic Review* 61 (March): 82–93.

Barro, Robert J., Mankiw, N. Gregory, and Sala-i-Martin, Xavier. 1995. "Capital Mobility in Neoclassical Models of Growth." *American Economic Review* 85 (March): 103–115.

Barro, Robert J., and Sala-i-Martin, Xavier. 1991. "Convergence across States and Regions." *Brookings Papers on Economic Activity,* no. 1, 107–182.

Barro, Robert J., and Sala-i-Martin, Xavier. 1992. "Convergence." *Journal of Political Economy* 100 (April): 223–251.

Barro, Robert J., and Sala-i-Martin, Xavier. 1998. *Economic Growth.* Cambridge, MA: MIT Press.

Barsky, Robert B., and Kilian, Lutz. 2000. "A Monetary Explanation of the Great Stagflation of the 1970s." National Bureau of Economic Research Working Paper No. 7547 (February).

Barsky, Robert B., Mankiw, N. Gregory, and Zeldes, Stephen P. 1986. "Ricardian Consumers with Keynesian Propensities." *American Economic Review* 76 (September): 676–691.

Barsky, Robert B., and Miron, Jeffrey A. 1989. "The Seasonal Cycle and the Business Cycle." *Journal of Political Economy* 97 (June): 503–534.

Barth, Marvin J., III, and Ramey, Valerie A. 2000. "The Cost Channel of Monetary Transmission." National Bureau of Economic Research Working Paper No. 7675 (April).

Basu, Susanto. 1995. "Intermediate Goods and Business Cycles: Implications for Productivity and Welfare." *American Economic Review* 85 (June): 512–531.

Basu, Susanto. 1996. "Procyclical Productivity: Increasing Returns or Cyclical Utilization?" *Quarterly Journal of Economics* 111 (August): 719–751.

Basu, Susanto, and Fernald, John G. 1995. "Are Apparent Productivity Spillovers a Figment of Specification Error?" *Journal of Monetary Economics* 36 (August): 165–188.

Basu, Susanto, and Fernald, John G. 1997. "Returns to Scale in U.S. Production: Estimates and Implications." *Journal of Political Economy* 105 (April): 249–283.

Basu, Susanto, and Weil, David N. 1999. "Appropriate Technology and Growth." *Quarterly Journal of Economics* 113 (November): 1025–1054.

Baumol, William. 1986. "Productivity Growth, Convergence, and Welfare." *American Economic Review* 76 (December): 1072–1085.

Baumol, William. 1990. "Entrepreneurship: Productive, Unproductive, and Destructive." *Journal of Political Economy* 98 (October, Part 1): 893–921.

Baxter, Marianne, and Crucini, Mario J. 1993. "Explaining Saving-Investment Correlations." *American Economic Review* 83 (June): 416–436.

Baxter, Marianne, and Jermann, Urban J. 1997. "The International Diversification Puzzle Is Worse than You Think." *American Economic Review* 87 (March): 170–180.

Baxter, Marianne, and King, Robert G. 1993. "Fiscal Policy in General Equilibrium." *American Economic Review* 83 (June): 315–334.

Baxter, Marianne, and Stockman, Alan C. 1989. "Business Cycles and the Exchange-Rate Regime: Some International Evidence." *Journal of Monetary Economics* 23 (May): 377–400.

Bayoumi, Tamim, Goldstein, Morris, and Woglom, Geoffrey. 1995. "Do Credit Markets Discipline Sovereign Borrowers? Evidence from U.S. States." *Journal of Money, Credit, and Banking* 27 (November): 1046–1059.

Bean, Charles R. 1994. "European Unemployment: A Survey." *Journal of Economic Literature* 32 (June): 573–619.

Beaudry, Paul, and Koop, Gary. 1993. "Do Recessions Permanently Change Output?" *Journal of Monetary Economics* 31 (April): 149–163.

Becker, Gary S., Murphy, Kevin M., and Tamura, Robert. 1990. "Human Capital, Fertility, and Economic Growth." *Journal of Political Economy* 98 (October, Part 2): S12–S37.

Bekaert, Geert, Hodrick, Robert J., and Marshall, David A. 1997. "The Implications of First-Order Risk Aversion for Asset Market Risk Premiums." *Journal of Monetary Economics* 40 (September): 3–39.

Benabou, Roland. 1992. "Inflation and Efficiency in Search Markets." *Review of Economic Studies* 59 (April): 299–329.

Benartzi, Shlomo, and Thaler, Richard H. 1995. "Myopic Loss Aversion and the Equity Premium Puzzle." *Quarterly Journal of Economics* 110 (February): 73–92.

Benassy, Jean-Pascal. 1976. "The Disequilibrium Approach to Monopolistic Price Setting and General Monopolistic Equilibrium." *Review of Economic Studies* 43 (January): 69–81.

Benhabib, Jess, and Farmer, Roger E. A. 1999. "Indeterminacy and Sunspots in Macroeconomics." In John B. Taylor and Michael Woodford, eds., *Handbook of Macroeconomics*, 387–448. Amsterdam: Elsevier.

Benhabib, Jess, Rogerson, Richard, and Wright, Randall. 1991. "Homework in Macroeconomics: Household Production and Aggregate Fluctuations." *Journal of Political Economy* 99 (December): 1166–1187.

Bernanke, Ben S. 1983a. "Irreversibility, Uncertainty, and Cyclical Investment." *Quarterly Journal of Economics* 98 (February): 85–106.

Bernanke, Ben S. 1983b. "Nonmonetary Effects of the Financial Crisis in the Propagation of the Great Depression." *American Economic Review* 73 (June): 257–276. Reprinted in Mankiw and Romer (1991).

Bernanke, Ben S. 1986. "Alternative Explanations of the Money-Income Correlation." *Carnegie-Rochester Conference Series on Public Policy* 25 (Autumn): 49–99.

Bernanke, Ben S. 1995. "The Macroeconomics of the Great Depression: A Comparative Approach." *Journal of Money, Credit, and Banking* 27 (February): 1–28.

Bernanke, Ben S., and Blinder, Alan S. 1988. "Credit, Money, and Aggregate Demand." *American Economic Review* 78 (May): 435–439. Reprinted in Mankiw and Romer (1991).

Bernanke, Ben S., and Blinder, Alan S. 1992. "The Federal Funds Rate and the Channels of Monetary Transmission." *American Economic Review* 82 (September): 901–921.

Bernanke, Ben S., and Gertler, Mark. 1989. "Agency Costs, Net Worth, and Business Fluctuations." *American Economic Review* 79 (March): 14–31.

Bernanke, Ben S., and Gertler, Mark. 1990. "Financial Fragility and Economic Performance." *Quarterly Journal of Economics* 105 (February): 87–114.

Bernanke, Ben S., Laubach, Thomas, Mishkin, Frederic S., and Posen, Adam S. 1999. *Inflation Targeting: Lessons from the International Experience.* Princeton, NJ: Princeton University Press.

Bernanke, Ben S., and Lown, Cara S. 1991. "The Credit Crunch." *Brookings Papers on Economic Activity,* no. 2, 205–247.

Bernanke, Ben S., and Mihov, Ilian. 1998. "Measuring Monetary Policy." *Quarterly Journal of Economics* 113 (August): 869–902.

Bernanke, Ben S., and Parkinson, Martin L. 1991. "Procyclical Labor Productivity and Competing Theories of the Business Cycle: Some Evidence from Interwar U.S. Manufacturing Industries." *Journal of Political Economy* 99 (June): 439–459.

Bernanke, Ben S., and Woodford, Michael. 1997. "Inflation Forecasts and Monetary Policy." *Journal of Money, Credit, and Banking* 29 (November, Part 2): 653–684.

Bernheim, B. Douglas. 1987. "Ricardian Equivalence: An Evaluation of Theory and Evidence." *NBER Macroeconomics Annual* 2: 263–304.

Bernheim, B. Douglas, and Bagwell, Kyle. 1988. "Is Everything Neutral?" *Journal of Political Economy* 96 (April): 308–338.

Bernheim, B. Douglas, Shleifer, Andrei, and Summers, Lawrence H. 1985. "The Strategic Bequest Motive." *Journal of Political Economy* 93 (December): 1045–1076.

Bertola, Giuseppe, and Drazen, Allan. 1993. "Trigger Points and Budget Cuts: Explaining the Effects of Fiscal Austerity." *American Economic Review* 83 (March): 11–26.

Besley, Timothy, and Coate, Stephen. 1997. "An Economic Model of Representative Democracy." *Quarterly Journal of Economics* 112 (February): 85–114.

Bewley, Truman. 1999. *Why Wages Don't Fall in a Recession.* Cambridge, MA: Harvard University Press.

Bils, Mark J. 1985. "Real Wages over the Business Cycle: Evidence from Panel Data." *Journal of Political Economy* 93 (August): 666–689.

Bils, Mark J. 1987. "The Cyclical Behavior of Marginal Cost and Price." *American Economic Review* 77 (December): 838–857.

Bils, Mark J. 1991. "Testing for Contracting Effects on Employment." *Quarterly Journal of Economics* 106 (November): 1129–1156.

Bils, Mark J., and Klenow, Peter J. 1998. "Using Consumer Theory to Test Competing Business Cycle Models." *Journal of Political Economy* 106 (April): 233–261.

Bils, Mark J., and Klenow, Peter J. 2000. "Does Schooling Cause Growth?" Unpublished paper, University of Rochester (March). *American Economic Review,* forthcoming.

Black, Fischer. 1974. "Uniqueness of the Price Level in Monetary Growth Models with Rational Expectations." *Journal of Economic Theory* 7 (January): 53–65.

Black, Fischer. 1982. "General Equilibrium and Business Cycles." National Bureau of Economic Research Working Paper No. 950 (August).

Blanchard, Olivier J. 1979. "Speculative Bubbles, Crashes and Rational Expectations." *Economics Letters* 3: 387–389.

Blanchard, Olivier J. 1981. "What Is Left of the Multiplier Accelerator?" *American Economic Review* 71 (May): 150–154.

Blanchard, Olivier J. 1983. "Price Asynchronization and Price Level Inertia." In Rudiger Dornbusch and Mario Henrique Simonsen, eds., *Inflation, Debt, and Indexation,* 3–24. Cambridge, MA: MIT Press. Reprinted in Mankiw and Romer (1991).

Blanchard, Olivier J. 1984. "The Lucas Critique and the Volcker Deflation." *American Economic Review* 74 (May): 211–215.

Blanchard, Olivier J. 1985. "Debts, Deficits, and Finite Horizons." *Journal of Political Economy* 93 (April): 223–247.

Blanchard, Olivier J., and Diamond, Peter A. 1989. "The Beveridge Curve." *Brookings Papers on Economic Activity,* no. 1, 1–60.

Blanchard, Olivier J., and Diamond, Peter A. 1990. "The Cyclical Behavior of the Gross Flows of U.S. Workers." *Brookings Papers on Economic Activity,* no. 2, 85–156.

Blanchard, Olivier J., and Fischer, Stanley. 1989. *Lectures on Macroeconomics.* Cambridge, MA: MIT Press.

Blanchard, Olivier J., and Kiyotaki, Nobuhiro. 1987. "Monopolistic Competition and the Effects of Aggregate Demand." *American Economic Review* 77 (September): 647–666. Reprinted in Mankiw and Romer (1991).

Blanchard, Olivier J., and Summers, Lawrence, H. 1986. "Hysteresis and the European Unemployment Problem." *NBER Macroeconomics Annual* 1: 15–78.

Blanchard, Olivier J., and Watson, Mark W. 1986. "Are Business Cycles All Alike?" In Robert J. Gordon, ed., *The American Business Cycle: Continuity and Change,* 123–156. Chicago: University of Chicago Press.

Blanchard, Olivier J., and Wolfers, Justin. 1999. "The Role of Shocks and Institutions in the Rise of European Unemployment." National Bureau of Economic Research Working Paper No. 7282 (August).

Blank, Rebecca M. 1990. "Why Are Wages Cyclical in the 1970s?" *Journal of Labor Economics* 8 (January, Part 1): 16–47.

Blinder, Alan S. 1998. *Asking about Prices: A New Approach to Understanding Price Stickiness.* New York: Russell Sage Foundation.

Blinder, Alan S., and Choi, Don H. 1990. "A Shred of Evidence on Theories of Wage Stickiness." *Quarterly Journal of Economics* 105 (November): 1003–1015.

Blinder, Alan S., and Fischer, Stanley. 1981. "Inventories, Rational Expectations and the Business Cycle." *Journal of Monetary Economics* 8 (November): 277–304.

Blinder, Alan S., and Solow, Robert M. 1973. "Does Fiscal Policy Matter?" *Journal of Public Economics* 2 (November): 318–337.

Blough, Stephen R. 1992. "The Relationship between Power and Level for Generic Unit Root Tests in Finite Samples." *Applied Econometrics* 7 (July–September): 295–308.

Bohn, Henning. 1988. "Why Do We Have Nominal Government Debt?" *Journal of Monetary Economics* 21 (January): 127–140. Reprinted in Persson and Tabellini (1994).

Bohn, Henning. 1990. "Tax Smoothing with Financial Instruments." *American Economic Review* 80 (December): 1217–1230.

Bohn, Henning. 1992. "Endogenous Government Spending and Ricardian Equivalence." *Economic Journal* 102 (May): 588–597.

Bohn, Henning. 1995. "The Sustainability of Budget Deficits in a Stochastic Economy." *Journal of Money, Credit, and Banking* 27 (February): 257–271.

Bohn, Henning, and Inman, Robert P. 1995. "Constitutional Limits and Public Deficits: Evidence from the U.S. States." *Carnegie-Rochester Conference Series on Public Policy* 45 (December): 13–76.

Borjas, George J. 1987. "Self-Selection and the Earnings of Immigrants." *American Economic Review* 77 (September): 531–553.

Boskin, Michael J., Dulberger, Ellen R., Gordon, Robert J., Griliches, Zvi, and Jorgenson, Dale. 1998. "Consumer Prices, the Consumer Price Index, and the Cost of Living." *Journal of Economic Perspectives* 12 (Winter): 3–26.

Brainard, S. Lael, and Cutler, David M. 1993. "Sectoral Shifts and Cyclical Unemployment Reconsidered." *Quarterly Journal of Economics* 108 (February): 219–243.

Brainard, William. 1967. "Uncertainty and the Effectiveness of Policy." *American Economic Review* 57 (May): 411–425.

Brander, James A., and Taylor, M. Scott. 1998. "The Simple Economics of Easter Island: A Ricardo-Malthus Model of Renewable Resource Use." *American Economic Review* 88 (March): 119–138.

Braun, R. Anton. 1994. "Tax Disturbances and Real Economic Activity in the Postwar United States." *Journal of Monetary Economics* 33 (June): 441–462.

Breeden, Douglas. 1979. "An Intertemporal Asset Pricing Model with Stochastic Consumption and Investment." *Journal of Financial Economics* 7 (September): 265–296.

Bresciani-Turroni, Constantino. 1937. *The Economics of Inflation: A Study of Currency Depreciation in Post-War Germany.* London: Allen and Unwin.

Brock, William. 1975. "A Simple Perfect Foresight Monetary Model." *Journal of Monetary Economics* 1 (April): 133–150.

Bruno, Michael, and Easterly, William. 1998. "Inflation Crises and Long-Run Growth." *Journal of Monetary Economics* 41 (February): 3–26.

Bryant, John. 1983. "A Simple Rational Expectations Keynes-Type Model." *Quarterly Journal of Economics* 98 (August): 525–528. Reprinted in Mankiw and Romer (1991).

Buchanan, James M., and Wagner, Richard E. 1977. *Democracy in Deficit: The Political Legacy of Lord Keynes.* New York: Academic Press.

Bulow, Jeremy, and Summers, Lawrence H. 1986. "A Theory of Dual Labor Markets with Applications to Industrial Policy, Discrimination, and Keynesian Unemployment." *Journal of Labor Economics* 4: 376–414.

Burnside, Craig, and Eichenbaum, Martin. 1996. "Factor-Hoarding and the Propagation of Business-Cycle Shocks." *American Economic Review* 86 (December): 1154–1174.

Burnside, Craig, Eichenbaum, Martin, and Rebelo, Sergio. 1993. "Labor Hoarding and the Business Cycle." *Journal of Political Economy* 101 (April): 245–273.

Burnside, Craig, and Eichenbaum, Martin, and Rebelo, Sergio. 1995. "Capital Utilization and Returns to Scale." *NBER Macroeconomics Annual* 10: 67–110.

C

Caballero, Ricardo J. 1990. "Expenditure on Durable Goods: A Case for Slow Adjustment." *Quarterly Journal of Economics* 105 (August): 727–743.

Caballero, Ricardo J. 1993. "Durable Goods: An Explanation for Their Slow Adjustment." *Journal of Political Economy* 101 (April): 351–384.

Caballero, Ricardo J. 1999. "Aggregate Investment." In John B. Taylor and Michael Woodford, eds., *Handbook of Macroeconomics*, 813–862. Amsterdam: Elsevier.

Caballero, Ricardo J., and Engel, Eduardo M. R. A. 1991. "Dynamic (S, s) Economies." *Econometrica* 59 (November): 1659–1686.

Caballero, Ricardo J., and Engel, Eduardo M. R. A. 1993. "Heterogeneity and Output Fluctuations in a Dynamic Menu-Cost Economy." *Review of Economic Studies* 60 (January): 95–119.

Caballero, Ricardo J., Engel, Eduardo M. R. A., and Haltiwanger, John C. 1995. "Plant-Level Adjustment and Aggregate Investment Dynamics." *Brookings Papers on Economic Activity*, no. 2, 1–54.

Caballero, Ricardo J., and Lyons, Richard K. 1992. "External Effects in U.S. Procyclical Productivity." *Journal of Monetary Economics* 29 (April): 209–225.

Cagan, Philip. 1956. "The Monetary Dynamics of Hyperinflation." In Milton Friedman, ed., *Studies in the Quantity Theory of Money,* 25–117. Chicago: University of Chicago Press.

Calvo, Guillermo. 1978a. "On the Indeterminacy of Interest Rates and Wages with Perfect Foresight." *Journal of Economic Theory* 19 (December): 321–337.

Calvo, Guillermo. 1978b. "On The Time Consistency of Optimal Policy in a Monetary Economy." *Econometrica* 46 (November): 1411–1428. Reprinted in Persson and Tabellini (1994).

Calvo, Guillermo. 1988. "Servicing the Public Debt: The Role of Expectations." *American Economic Review* 78 (September): 647–661. Reprinted in Persson and Tabellini (1994).

Calvo, Guillermo, and Végh, Carlos. 1999. "Inflation Stabilization and BOP Crises in Developing Countries." In John B. Taylor and Michael Woodford, eds., *Handbook of Macroeconomics*, 1531–1614. Amsterdam: Elsevier.

Campbell, Carl M., III, and Kamlani, Kunal S. 1997. "The Reasons for Wage Rigidity: Evidence from a Survey of Firms." *Quarterly Journal of Economics* 112 (August): 759–789.

Campbell, John Y. 1987. "Does Saving Anticipate Declining Labor Income? An Alternative Test of the Permanent Income Hypothesis." *Econometrica* 55 (November): 1249–1273.

Campbell, John Y. 1994. "Inspecting the Mechanism: An Analytical Approach to the Stochastic Growth Model." *Journal of Monetary Economics* 33 (June): 463–506.

Campbell, John Y., and Cochrane, John H. 1999. "By Force of Habit: A Consumption-Based Explanation of Aggregate Stock Market Behavior." *Journal of Political Economy* 107 (April): 205–251.

Campbell, John Y., and Deaton, Angus. 1989. "Why Is Consumption So Smooth?" *Review of Economic Studies* 56 (July): 357–374.

Campbell, John Y., and Mankiw, N. Gregory. 1987. "Are Output Fluctuations Transitory?" *Quarterly Journal of Economics* 102 (November): 857–880.

Campbell, John Y., and Mankiw, N. Gregory. 1989a. "International Evidence on the Persistence of Economic Fluctuations." *Journal of Monetary Economics* 23 (March): 319–333.

Campbell, John Y., and Mankiw, N. Gregory. 1989b. "Consumption, Income, and Interest Rates: Reinterpreting the Time Series Evidence." *NBER Macroeconomics Annual* 4: 185–216.

Campbell, John Y., and Perron, Pierre. 1991. "Pitfalls and Opportunities: What Macroeconomists Should Know about Unit Roots." *NBER Macroeconomics Annual* 6: 141–201.

Caplin, Andrew S., and Leahy, John. 1991. "State-Dependent Pricing and the Dynamics of Money and Output." *Quarterly Journal of Economics* 106 (August): 683–708.

Caplin, Andrew S., and Spulber, Daniel F. 1987. "Menu Costs and the Neutrality of Money." *Quarterly Journal of Economics* 102 (November): 703–725. Reprinted in Mankiw and Romer (1991).

Card, David. 1990. "Unexpected Inflation, Real Wages, and Employment Determination in Union Contracts." *American Economic Review* 80 (September): 669–688.

Card, David. 1991. "Intertemporal Labor Supply: An Assessment." National Bureau of Economic Research Working Paper No. 3602 (January).

Cardoso, Eliana. 1991. "From Inertia to Megainflation: Brazil in the 1980s." In Michael Bruno et al., eds., *Lessons of Economic Stabilization and Its Aftermath,* 143–177. Cambridge, MA: MIT Press.

Carlton, Dennis W. 1982. "The Disruptive Effects of Inflation on the Organization of Markets." In Robert E. Hall, ed., *Inflation: Causes and Effects,* 139–152. Chicago: University of Chicago Press.

Carlton, Dennis W. 1986. "The Rigidity of Prices." *American Economic Review* 76 (September): 637–658. Reprinted in Mankiw and Romer (1991).

Carmichael, Lorne. 1985. "Can Unemployment Be Involuntary? Comment." *American Economic Review* 75 (December): 1213–1214.

Carroll, Christopher D. 1992. "The Buffer-Stock Theory of Saving: Some Macroeconomic Evidence." *Brookings Papers on Economic Activity,* no. 2, 61–156.

Carroll, Christopher D. 1997. "Buffer-Stock Saving and the Life Cycle/Permanent Income Hypothesis." *Quarterly Journal of Economics* 112 (February): 1–55.

Carroll, Christopher D. 1998. "Why Do the Rich Save So Much?" National Bureau of Economic Research Working Paper No. 6549 (May).

Carroll, Christopher D., and Summers, Lawrence H. 1991. "Consumption Growth Parallels Income Growth: Some New Evidence." In B. Douglas Bernheim and John B. Shoven, eds., *National Saving and Economic Performance,* 305–343. Chicago: University of Chicago Press.

Cass, David. 1965. "Optimum Growth in an Aggregative Model of Capital Accumulation." *Review of Economic Studies* 32 (July): 233–240.

Cass, David, and Shell, Karl. 1983. "Do Sunspots Matter?" *Journal of Political Economy* 91 (April): 193–227.

Cecchetti, Stephen G. 1986. "The Frequency of Price Adjustment: A Study of the Newsstand Prices of Magazines." *Journal of Econometrics* 31 (August): 255–274.

Chari, V. V., and Cole, Harold. 1993. "Why Are Representative Democracies Fiscally Irresponsible?" Federal Reserve Bank of Minneapolis Research Department, Staff Report No. 163 (August).

Chari, V. V., and Kehoe, Patrick J. 1999. "Optimal Fiscal and Monetary Policy." In John B. Taylor and Michael Woodford, eds., *Handbook of Macroeconomics,* 1671–1745. Amsterdam: Elsevier.

Chevalier, Judith A., and Scharfstein, David S. 1996. "Capital-Market Imperfections and Countercyclical Markups: Theory and Evidence." *American Economic Review* 86 (September): 703–725.

Chiang, Alpha C. 1984. *Fundamental Methods of Mathematical Economics,* 3d ed. New York: McGraw-Hill.

Cho, Dongchul, and Graham, Stephen. 1996. "The Other Side of Conditional Convergence." *Economics Letters* 50 (February): 285–290.

Cho, Jang-Ok, and Cooley, Thomas F. 1995. "The Business Cycle with Nominal Contracts." *Economic Theory* 6 (June): 13–33.

Cho, Jang-Ok, Cooley, Thomas F., and Phaneuf, Louis. 1997. "The Welfare Cost of Nominal Wage Contracting." *Review of Economic Studies* 64 (July): 465–484.

Christiano, Lawrence J., and Eichenbaum, Martin. 1990. "Unit Roots in Real GNP: Do We Know, and Do We Care?" *Carnegie-Rochester Conference Series on Public Policy* 32 (Spring): 7–61.

Christiano, Lawrence J., and Eichenbaum, Martin. 1992. "Current Real-Business-Cycle Theories and Aggregate Labor-Market Fluctuations." *American Economic Review* 82 (June): 430–450.

Christiano, Lawrence J., Eichenbaum, Martin, and Evans, Charles. 1996. "The Effects of Monetary Policy Shocks: Evidence from the Flow of Funds." *Review of Economics and Statistics* 78 (February): 16–34.

Christiano, Lawrence J., Eichenbaum, Martin, and Evans, Charles. 1997. "Sticky Price and Limited Participation Models: A Comparison." *European Economic Review* 41 (June): 1201–1249.

Christiano, Lawrence J., and Harrison, Sharon G. 1999. "Chaos, Sunspots, and Automatic Stabilizers." *Journal of Monetary Economics* 44 (August): 3–31.

Clark, Kim B., and Summers, Lawrence H. 1979. "Labor Market Dynamics and Unemployment: A Reconsideration." *Brookings Papers on Economic Activity,* no. 1, 13–60.

Clark, Peter, Laxton, Douglas, and Rose, David. 1996. "Asymmetry in the U.S. Output-Inflation Nexus." *IMF Staff Papers* 43 (March): 216–251.

Coate, Stephen, and Morris, Stephen. 1995. "On the Form of Transfers to Special Interests." *Journal of Political Economy* 103 (December): 1210–1235.

Cochrane, John H. 1988. "How Big Is the Random Walk in GNP?" *Journal of Political Economy* 96 (October): 893–920.

Cochrane, John H. 1994. "Permanent and Transitory Components of GNP and Stock Prices." *Quarterly Journal of Economics* 109 (February): 241–265.

Cochrane, John H. 1998. "What Do the VARs Mean? Measuring the Output Effects of Monetary Policy." *Journal of Monetary Economics* 41 (April): 277–300.

Cogley, Timothy. 1990. "International Evidence on the Size of the Random Walk in Output." *Journal of Political Economy* 98 (June): 501–518.

Cogley, Timothy, and Nason, James M. 1995a. "Effects of the Hodrick-Prescott Filter on Trend and Difference Stationary Time Series: Implications for Business Cycle Research." *Journal of Economic Dynamics and Control* 19 (January/February): 253–278.

Cogley, Timothy, and Nason, James M. 1995b. "Output Dynamics in Real-Business-Cycle Models." *American Economic Review* 85 (June): 492–511.

Cole, Harold L., and Kehoe, Timothy J. 2000. "Self-Fulfilling Debt Crises." *Review of Economic Studies* 67 (January): 91–116.

Coleman, Thomas S. 1984. "Essays in Aggregate Labor Market Business Cycle Fluctuations." Ph.D. dissertation, University of Chicago.

Congressional Budget Office. 1999. *The Long-Term Budget Outlook: An Update* (December).

Constantinides, George M. 1990. "Habit Formation: A Resolution of the Equity Premium Puzzle." *Journal of Political Economy* 98 (June): 519–543.

Cook, Timothy, and Hahn, Thomas. 1989. "The Effect of Changes in the Federal Funds Rate Target on Market Interest Rates in the 1970s." *Journal of Monetary Economics* 24 (November): 331-351.

Cooley, Thomas F., and LeRoy, Stephen F. 1985. "Atheoretical Macroeconomics: A Critique." *Journal of Monetary Economics* 16 (November): 283-308.

Cooley, Thomas F., and Ohanian, Lee E. 1991. "The Cyclical Behavior of Prices." *Journal of Monetary Economics* 28 (August): 25-60.

Cooley, Thomas F., and Ohanian, Lee E. 1997. "Postwar British Economic Growth and the Legacy of Keynes." *Journal of Political Economy* 105 (June): 439-472.

Cooper, Russell W., DeJong, Douglas V., Forsythe, Robert, and Ross, Thomas W. 1990. "Selection Criteria in Coordination Games: Some Experimental Results." *American Economic Review* 80 (March): 218-234.

Cooper, Russell W., DeJong, Douglas V., Forsythe, Robert, and Ross, Thomas W. 1992. "Communication in Coordination Games." *Quarterly Journal of Economics* 107 (May): 739-771.

Cooper, Russell W., and Haltiwanger, John. 1996. "Evidence on Macroeconomic Complementarities." *Review of Economics and Statistics* 103 (April): 1106-1117.

Cooper, Russell W., Haltiwanger, John, and Power, Laura. 1999. "Machine Replacement and the Business Cycle: Lumps and Bumps." *American Economic Review* 89 (September): 921-946.

Cooper, Russell W., and John, Andrew. 1988. "Coordinating Coordination Failures in Keynesian Models." *Quarterly Journal of Economics* 103 (August): 441-463. Reprinted in Mankiw and Romer (1991).

Craine, Roger. 1989. "Risky Business: The Allocation of Capital." *Journal of Monetary Economics* 23 (March): 201-218.

Cukierman, Alex, Kalaitzidakis, Pantelis, Summers, Lawrence H., and Webb, Steven B. 1993. "Central Bank Independence, Growth, Investment, and Real Rates." *Carnegie-Rochester Conference Series on Public Policy* 39 (December): 95-140.

Cukierman, Alex, and Meltzer, Allan H. 1986. "A Theory of Ambiguity, Credibility, and Inflation under Discretion and Asymmetric Information." *Econometrica* 54 (September): 1099-1128.

Cukierman, Alex, Webb, Steven B., and Neyapti, Bilin. 1992. "Measuring the Independence of Central Banks and Its Effect on Policy Outcomes." *World Bank Economic Review* 6 (September): 353-398.

D

Danthine, Jean-Pierre, and Donaldson, John B. 1990. "Efficiency Wages and the Business Cycle Puzzle." *European Economic Review* (November): 1275-1301.

Davis, Steven J., and Haltiwanger, John. 1990. "Gross Job Creation and Destruction: Microeconomic Evidence and Macroeconomic Implications." *NBER Macroeconomics Annual* 5: 123-168.

Davis, Steven J., and Haltiwanger, John. 1992. "Gross Job Creation, Gross Job Destruction, and Employment Reallocation." *Quarterly Journal of Economics* 107 (August): 819-863.

Davis, Steven J., and Haltiwanger, John. 1999. "On the Driving Forces behind Cyclical Movements in Employment and Job Reallocation." *American Economic Review* 89 (December): 1234-1258.

Deaton, Angus. 1991. "Saving and Liquidity Constraints." *Econometrica* 59 (September): 1221–1248.

Deaton, Angus. 1992. *Understanding Consumption.* Oxford: Oxford University Press.

Debelle, Guy. 1996. "The Ends of Three Small Inflations: Australia, New Zealand, and Canada." *Canadian Public Policy* 22 (March): 56–78.

Debelle, Guy, and Laxton, Douglas. 1997. "Is the Phillips Curve Really a Curve? Some Evidence for Canada, the United Kingdom, and the United States." *IMF Staff Papers* 44 (June): 249–282.

de Haan, Jakob, and Sturm, Jan-Egbert. 1994. "Political and Institutional Determinants of Fiscal Policy in the European Community." *Public Choice* 80 (July): 157–172.

De Long, J. Bradford. 1988. "Productivity Growth, Convergence, and Welfare: Comment." *American Economic Review* 78 (December): 1138–1154.

De Long, J. Bradford. 1997. "America's Peacetime Inflation: The 1970s." In Christina D. Romer and David H. Romer, eds., *Reducing Inflation: Motivation and Strategy*, 247–276. Chicago: University of Chicago Press.

De Long, J. Bradford, and Shleifer, Andrei. 1993. "Princes and Merchants." *Journal of Law and Economics* 36 (October): 671–702.

De Long, J. Bradford, and Summers, Lawrence H. 1986a. "Are Business Cycles Symmetrical?" In Robert J. Gordon, ed., *The American Business Cycle: Continuity and Change,* 166–179. Chicago: University of Chicago Press.

De Long, J. Bradford, and Summers, Lawrence H. 1986b. "Is Increased Price Flexibility Stabilizing?" *American Economic Review* 76 (December): 1031–1044.

De Long, J. Bradford, and Summers, Lawrence H. 1991. "Equipment Investment and Economic Growth." *Quarterly Journal of Economics* 106 (May): 445–502.

De Long, J. Bradford, and Summers, Lawrence H. 1992. "Equipment Investment and Economic Growth: How Strong Is the Nexus?" *Brookings Papers on Economic Activity,* no. 2, 157–211.

Denison, Edward F. 1967. *Why Growth Rates Differ.* Washington: The Brookings Institution.

Denison, Edward F. 1985. *Trends in American Economic Growth, 1929–1982.* Washington: The Brookings Institution.

Diamond, Douglas W. 1984. "Financial Intermediation and Delegated Monitoring." *Review of Economic Studies* 51 (July): 393–414.

Diamond, Peter A. 1965. "National Debt in a Neoclassical Growth Model." *American Economic Review* 55 (December): 1126–1150.

Diamond, Peter A. 1982. "Aggregate Demand Management in Search Equilibrium." *Journal of Political Economy* 90 (October): 881–894. Reprinted in Mankiw and Romer (1991).

Dickens, William T., Katz, Lawrence F., Lang, Kevin, and Summers, Lawrence H. 1989. "Employee Crime and the Monitoring Puzzle." *Journal of Labor Economics* 7 (July): 331–348.

Dickens, William T., and Katz, Lawrence F. 1987a. "Inter-Industry Wage Differences and Theories of Wage Determination." National Bureau of Economic Research Working Paper No. 2271 (July).

Dickens, William T., and Katz, Lawrence F. 1987b. "Inter-Industry Wage Differences and Industry Characteristics." In Kevin Lang and Jonathan S. Leonard, eds., *Unemployment and the Structure of Labor Markets,* 48–89. Oxford: Basil Blackwell.

Dickey, David A., and Fuller, Wayne A. 1979. "Distribution of the Estimators for Autoregressive Time Series with a Unit Root." *Journal of the American Statistical Association* 74 (June): 427–431.

Dinopoulos, Elias, and Thompson, Peter. 1998. "Schumpeterian Growth without Scale Effects." *Journal of Economic Growth* 3 (December): 313–335.

Dixit, Avinash. 1990. *Optimization in Economic Theory,* 2d ed. Oxford: Oxford University Press.

Dixit, Avinash K., and Pindyck, Robert S. 1994. *Investment under Uncertainty.* Princeton, NJ: Princeton University Press.

Dixit, Avinash, and Stiglitz, Joseph E. 1977. "Monopolistic Competition and Optimum Product Diversity." *American Economic Review* 67 (June): 297–308.

Doeringer, Peter B., and Piore, Michael J. 1971. *Internal Labor Markets and Manpower Analysis.* Lexington, MA: D.C. Heath.

Dolde, Walter. 1979. "Temporary Taxes as Macro-economic Stabilizers." *American Economic Review* 69 (May): 81–85.

Dornbusch, Rudiger. 1976. "Expectations and Exchange Rate Dynamics." *Journal of Political Economy* 84 (December): 1161–1176.

Downs, Anthony. 1957. *An Economic Theory of Democracy.* New York: Harper and Row.

Dowrick, Steve, and Nguyen, Duc-Tho. 1989. "OECD Comparative Economic Growth 1950–85: Catch-up and Convergence." *American Economic Review* 79 (December): 1010–1030.

Drazen, Allan, and Grilli, Vittorio. 1993. "The Benefit of Crises for Economic Reform." *American Economic Review* 83 (June): 598–607.

Dunlop, John T. 1938. "The Movement in Real and Money Wage Rates." *Economic Journal* 48 (September): 413–434.

Durlauf, Steven N. 1993. "Nonergodic Economic Growth." *Review of Economic Studies* 60 (April): 349–366.

Dynan, Karen E. 1993. "How Prudent Are Consumers?" *Journal of Political Economy* 101 (December): 1104–1113.

E

Easterly, William. 1993. "How Much Do Distortions Affect Growth?" *Journal of Monetary Economics* 32 (November): 187–212.

Easterly, William, and Levine, Ross. 1997. "Africa's Growth Tragedy: Policies and Ethnic Divisions." *Quarterly Journal of Economics* 112 (November): 1203–1250.

Eberly, Janice C. 1994. "Adjustment of Consumers' Durables Stocks: Evidence from Automobile Purchases." *Journal of Political Economy* 102 (June): 403–436.

Edin, Per-Anders, and Ohlsson, Henry. 1991. "Political Determinants of Budget Deficits: Coalition Effects versus Minority Effects." *European Economic Review* 35 (December): 1597–1603.

Eichengreen, Barry. 1992. *Should the Maastricht Treaty Be Saved?* Princeton Studies in International Finance, No. 74. Princeton, NJ: Princeton University Press.

Eisner, Robert, and Strotz, Robert H. 1963. "Determinants of Business Fixed Investment." In Commission on Money and Credit, *Impacts of Monetary Policy*, 59–337. Englewood Cliffs, NJ: Prentice-Hall.

Epstein, Larry G., and Zin, Stanley E. 1989. "Substitution, Risk Aversion, and the Temporal Behavior of Consumption and Asset Returns: A Theoretical Framework." *Econometrica* 46 (July): 937–969.

Epstein, Larry G., and Zin, Stanley E. 1991. "Substitution, Risk Aversion, and the Temporal Behavior of Consumption and Asset Returns: An Empirical Analysis." *Journal of Political Economy* 99 (April): 263–286.

Ethier, Wilfred J. 1982. "National and International Returns to Scale in the Modern Theory of International Trade." *American Economic Review* 72 (June): 389–405.

F

Fatás, Antonio. 2000. "Endogenous Growth and Stochastic Trends." *Journal of Monetary Economics* 45 (February): 107–128.

Fazzari, Steven M., Hubbard, R. Glenn, and Petersen, Bruce C. 1988. "Financing Constraints and Corporate Investment." *Brookings Papers on Economic Activity*, no. 1, 141–195.

Fazzari, Steven M., Hubbard, R. Glenn, and Petersen, Bruce C. 2000. "Investment-Cash Flow Sensitivities Are Useful: A Comment on Kaplan and Zingales." *Quarterly Journal of Economics* 115 (May): 695–705.

Feldstein, Martin. 1976. "Temporary Layoffs in the Theory of Unemployment." *Journal of Political Economy* 84 (October): 937–957.

Feldstein, Martin. 1997. "The Costs and Benefits of Going from Low Inflation to Price Stability." In Christina D. Romer and David H. Romer, eds., *Reducing Inflation: Motivation and Strategy*, 123–156. Chicago: University of Chicago Press.

Feldstein, Martin, and Horioka, Charles. 1980. "Domestic Saving and International Capital Flows." *Economic Journal* 90 (June): 314–329.

Fernandez, Raquel, and Rodrik, Dani. 1991. "Resistance to Reform: Status Quo Bias in the Presence of Individual-Specific Uncertainty." *American Economic Review* 71 (December): 1146–1155. Reprinted in Persson and Tabellini (1994).

Fethke, Gary, and Policano, Andrew. 1986. "Will Wage Setters Ever Stagger Decisions?" *Quarterly Journal of Economics* 101 (November): 867–877. Reprinted in Mankiw and Romer (1991).

Fischer, Stanley. 1977a. "Long-Term Contracts, Rational Expectations, and the Optimal Money Supply Rule." *Journal of Political Economy* 85 (February): 191–205. Reprinted in Mankiw and Romer (1991).

Fischer, Stanley. 1977b. "Wage Indexation and Macroeconomic Stability." *Carnegie-Rochester Conference Series on Public Policy* 5: 107–147.

Fischer, Stanley. 1993. "The Role of Macroeconomic Factors in Growth." *Journal of Monetary Economics* 32 (December): 485–512.

Fischer, Stanley, and Summers, Lawrence H. 1989. "Should Governments Learn to Live with Inflation?" *American Economic Review* 79 (May): 382–387.

Fisher, Irving. 1933. "The Debt-Deflation Theory of Great Depressions." *Econometrica* 1 (October): 337–357.

Flavin, Marjorie A. 1981. "The Adjustment of Consumption to Changing Expectations about Future Income." *Journal of Political Economy* 89 (October): 974–1009.

Flavin, Marjorie A. 1993. "The Excess Smoothness of Consumption: Identification and Estimation." *Review of Economic Studies* 60 (July): 651–666.

Fleming, J. Marcus. 1962. "Domestic Financial Policies under Fixed and under Floating Exchange Rates." *IMF Staff Papers* 9 (November): 369–379.

Foley, Duncan K., and Sidrauski, Miguel. 1970. "Portfolio Choice, Investment and Growth." *American Economic Review* 60 (March): 44–63.

Foote, Christopher L. 1998. "Trend Employment Growth and the Bunching of Job Creation and Destruction." *Quarterly Journal of Economics* 113 (August): 809–834.

French, Kenneth R., and Poterba, James M. 1991. "Investor Diversification and International Equity Markets." *American Economic Review* 81 (May): 222–226.

Friedman, Milton. 1953. "The Case for Flexible Exchange Rates." In *Essays in Positive Economics,* 153–203. Chicago: University of Chicago Press.

Friedman, Milton. 1957. *A Theory of the Consumption Function.* Princeton, NJ: Princeton University Press.

Friedman, Milton. 1960. *A Program for Monetary Stability.* New York: Fordham University Press.

Friedman, Milton. 1968. "The Role of Monetary Policy." *American Economic Review* 58 (March): 1–17.

Friedman, Milton. 1969. "The Optimum Quantity of Money." In *The Optimum Quantity of Money and Other Essays,* 1–50. Chicago: Aldine Publishing.

Friedman, Milton. 1971. "Government Revenue from Inflation." *Journal of Political Economy* 79 (July/August): 846–856.

Friedman, Milton, and Savage, L. J. 1948. "The Utility Analysis of Choices Involving Risk." *Journal of Political Economy* 56 (August): 279–304.

Friedman, Milton, and Schwartz, Anna J. 1963. *A Monetary History of the United States, 1867–1960.* Princeton, NJ: Princeton University Press.

Froot, Kenneth A., and Obstfeld, Maurice. 1991. "Intrinsic Bubbles: The Case of Stock Prices." *American Economic Review* 81 (December): 1189–1214.

Fuhrer, Jeffrey C. 1997. "The (Un)Importance of Forward-Looking Behavior in Price Specifications." *Journal of Money, Credit, and Banking* 29 (August): 338–350.

Fuhrer, Jeffrey C., and Moore, George R. 1995. "Inflation Persistence." *Quarterly Journal of Economics* 110 (February): 127–159.

G

Gale, Douglas, and Hellwig, Martin. 1985. "Incentive-Compatible Debt Contracts I: The One-Period Problem." *Review of Economic Studies* 52 (October): 647–663.

Galí, Jordi. 1994. "Monopolistic Competition, Business Cycles, and the Composition of Aggregate Demand." *Journal of Economic Theory* 63 (June): 73–96.

Galor, Oded, and Ryder, Harl E. 1989. "Existence, Uniqueness, and Stability of Equilibria in an Overlapping-Generations Model with Productive Capital." *Journal of Economic Theory* 49 (December): 360–375.

Galor, Oded, and Weil, David N. 1996. "The Gender Gap, Fertility, and Growth." *American Economic Review* 86 (June): 374–387.

Garino, Gaia, and Martin, Christopher. 1999. "Efficiency Wages and Union-Firm Bargaining." Unpublished paper, Brunel University (July).

Geary, Patrick T., and Kennan, John. 1982. "The Employment-Real Wage Relationship: An International Study." *Journal of Political Economy* 90 (August): 854–871.

Genberg, Hans. 1978. "Purchasing Power Parity under Fixed and Flexible Exchange Rates." *Journal of International Economics* 8 (May): 247–276.

Gertler, Mark, and Gilchrist, Simon. 1994. "Monetary Policy, Business Cycles, and the Behavior of Small Manufacturing Firms." *Quarterly Journal of Economics* 109 (May): 309–340.

Ghosh, Atish R. 1995. "Intertemporal Tax-Smoothing and the Government Budget Surplus: Canada and the United States." *Journal of Money, Credit, and Banking* 27 (November, Part 1): 1033–1045.

Giavazzi, Francesco, and Pagano, Marco. 1990. "Can Severe Fiscal Contractions Be Expansionary? Tales of Two Small European Countries." *NBER Macroeconomics Annual* 5: 75–111.

Gibbons, Robert, and Katz, Lawrence. 1992. "Does Unmeasured Ability Explain Inter-Industry Wage Differentials?" *Review of Economic Studies* 59 (July): 515–535.

Glassman, James K., and Hassett, Kevin A. 1999. *Dow 36,000: The New Strategy for Profiting from the Coming Rise in the Stock Market.* New York: Times Business/Random House.

Goldfeld, Stephen M. 1976. "The Case of the Missing Money." *Brookings Papers on Economic Activity,* no. 3, 683–730.

Goldfeld, Stephen M., and Sichel, Daniel E. 1990. "The Demand for Money." In Benjamin M. Friedman and Frank Hahn, eds., *Handbook of Monetary Economics,* vol. 1, 299–356. Amsterdam: Elsevier.

Goolsbee, Austan. 1998. "Investment Tax Incentives, Prices, and the Supply of Capital Goods." *Quarterly Journal of Economics* 113 (February): 121–148.

Gordon, David. 1974. "A Neoclassical Theory of Underemployment." *Economic Inquiry* 12 (December): 432–459.

Gordon, Robert J. 1997. "The Time-Varying NAIRU and Its Implications for Policy." *Journal of Economic Perspectives* 11 (Winter): 11–32.

Gottfries, Nils. 1992. "Insiders, Outsiders, and Nominal Wage Contracts." *Journal of Political Economy* 100 (April): 252–270.

Gould, John P. 1968. "Adjustment Costs in the Theory of Investment of the Firm." *Review of Economic Studies* 35 (January): 47–55.

Gourinchas, Pierre-Olivier, and Parker, Jonathan A. 1999. "Consumption over the Life Cycle." National Bureau of Economic Research Working Paper No. 7271 (July).

Gray, Jo Anna. 1976. "Wage Indexation: A Macroeconomic Approach." *Journal of Monetary Economics* 2 (April): 221–235.

Gray, Jo Anna. 1978. "On Indexation and Contract Length." *Journal of Political Economy* 86 (February): 1–18.

Green, Donald P., and Shapiro, Ian. 1994. *Pathologies of Rational Choice Theory: A Critique of Applications in Political Science.* New Haven, CT: Yale University Press.

Greenwald, Bruce C., and Stiglitz, Joseph E. 1988. "Examining Alternative Macroeconomic Theories." *Brookings Papers on Economic Activity,* no. 1, 207–260.

Greenwald, Bruce C., Stiglitz, Joseph E., and Weiss, Andrew. 1984. "Informational Imperfections in Capital Markets and Macroeconomic Fluctuations." *American Economic Review* 74 (May): 194–199.

Greenwood, Jeremy, and Hercowitz, Zvi. 1991. "The Allocation of Capital and Time over the Business Cycle." *Journal of Political Economy* 99 (December): 1188–1214.

Greenwood, Jeremy, Hercowitz, Zvi, and Huffman, Gregory W. 1988. "Investment, Capacity Utilization, and the Real Business Cycle." *American Economic Review* 78 (June): 402–417.

Greenwood, Jeremy, and Huffman, Gregory W. 1991. "Tax Analysis in a Real-Business-Cycle Model: On Measuring Harberger Triangles and Okun Gaps." *Journal of Monetary Economics* 27 (April): 167–190.

Gregory, R. G. 1986. "Wages Policy and Unemployment in Australia." *Economica* 53 (Supplement): S53–S74.

Griliches, Zvi. 1988. "Productivity Puzzles and R&D: Another Nonexplanation." *Journal of Economic Perspectives* 2 (Fall): 9–21.

Grilli, Vittorio, Masciandaro, Donato, and Tabellini, Guido. 1991. "Political and Monetary Institutions and Public Financial Policies in the Industrial Countries." *Economic Policy* 13 (October): 341–392. Reprinted in Persson and Tabellini (1994).

Groshen, Erica L. 1991. "Sources of Intra-Industry Wage Dispersion: How Much Do Employers Matter?" *Quarterly Journal of Economics* 106 (August): 869–884.

Grossman, Gene M., and Helpman, Elhanan. 1991a. *Innovation and Growth in the Global Economy.* Cambridge, MA: MIT Press.

Grossman, Gene M., and Helpman, Elhanan. 1991b. "Endogenous Product Cycles." *Economic Journal* 101 (September): 1214–1229.

Grossman, Herschel I., and Kim, Minseong. 1995. "Swords or Plowshares? A Theory of the Security of Claims to Property." *Journal of Political Economy* 103 (December): 1275–1288.

Grossman, Herschel I., and Kim, Minseong. 1996. "Inequality, Predation, and Welfare." National Bureau of Economic Research Working Paper No. 5704 (August).

Grossman, Sanford, and Weiss, Laurence. 1983. "A Transactions-Based Model of the Monetary Transmission Mechanism." *American Economic Review* 73 (December): 871–880.

H

Haavelmo, Trygve. 1945. "Multiplier Effects of a Balanced Budget." *Econometrica* 13 (October): 311–318.

Hall, Robert E. 1978. "Stochastic Implications of the Life Cycle-Permanent Income Hypothesis: Theory and Evidence." *Journal of Political Economy* 86 (December): 971–987.

Hall, Robert E. 1980. "Employment Fluctuations and Wage Rigidity." *Brookings Papers on Economic Activity,* no. 1, 91–123.

Hall, Robert E. 1982. "The Importance of Lifetime Jobs in the U.S. Economy." *American Economic Review* 72 (September): 716–724.

Hall, Robert E. 1984. "Monetary Strategy with an Elastic Price Standard." In Federal Reserve Bank of Kansas City, *Price Stability and Public Policy,* 137–159.

Hall, Robert E. 1988a. "The Relation between Price and Marginal Cost in U.S. Industry." *Journal of Political Economy* 96 (October): 921–947.

Hall, Robert E. 1988b. "Intertemporal Substitution in Consumption." *Journal of Political Economy* 96 (April): 339–357.

Hall, Robert E. 1989. "Comment." *Brookings Papers on Economic Activity,* Microeconomics, 276–280.

Hall, Robert E., and Jones, Charles I. 1999. "Why Do Some Countries Produce So Much More Output per Worker than Others?" *Quarterly Journal of Economics* 114 (February): 83–116.

Hall, Robert E., and Jorgenson, Dale W. 1967. "Tax Policy and Investment Behavior." *American Economic Review* 57 (June): 391–414.

Haltiwanger, John, and Waldman, Michael. 1989. "Limited Rationality and Strategic Complements: The Implications for Macroeconomics." *Quarterly Journal of Economics* 104 (August): 463–483.

Hamilton, James. 1994. *Time Series Analysis.* Princeton, NJ: Princeton University Press.

Hansen, Gary D. 1985. "Indivisible Labor and the Business Cycle." *Journal of Monetary Economics* 16 (November): 309–327.

Hansen, Gary D., and Wright, Randall. 1992. "The Labor Market in Real Business Cycle Theory." Federal Reserve Bank of Minneapolis *Quarterly Review* 16 (Spring): 2–12.

Hansen, Lars Peter, and Singleton, Kenneth J. 1983. "Stochastic Consumption, Risk Aversion, and the Temporal Behavior of Asset Returns." *Journal of Political Economy* 91 (April): 249–265.

Harrington, Joseph E., Jr. 1993. "Economic Policy, Economic Performance, and Elections." *American Economic Review* 83 (March): 27–42.

Harris, John R., and Todaro, Michael P. 1970. "Migration, Unemployment and Development: A Two-Sector Analysis." *American Economic Review* 60 (March): 126–142.

Hart, Oliver. 1989. "Bargaining and Strikes." *Quarterly Journal of Economics* 104 (February): 25–43.

Hayashi, Fumio. 1982. "Tobin's Marginal q and Average q: A Neoclassical Interpretation." *Econometrica* 50 (January): 213–224.

Hayashi, Fumio. 1987. "Tests for Liquidity Constraints: A Critical Survey and Some New Observations." In Truman F. Bewley, ed., *Advances in Econometrics*, vol. 2, 91–120. Cambridge: Cambridge University Press.

Hayes, Beth. 1984. "Unions and Strikes with Asymmetric Information." *Journal of Labor Economics* 12 (January): 57–83.

Heaton, John, and Lucas, Deborah J. 1996. "Evaluating the Effects of Incomplete Markets on Risk Sharing and Asset Pricing." *Journal of Political Economy* 104 (June): 443–487.

Hess, Gregory D., and Iwata, Shigeru. 1997. "Asymmetric Persistence of GDP? A Deeper Look at Depth." *Journal of Monetary Economics* 40 (December): 535–554.

Hodrick, Robert J., and Prescott, Edward C. 1997. "Postwar U.S. Business Cycles: An Empirical Investigation." *Journal of Money, Credit, and Banking* 29 (February): 1–16.

Hornstein, Andreas, and Krusell, Per. 1996. "Can Technology Improvements Cause Productivity Slowdowns?" *NBER Macroeconomics Annual* 11: 209–259.

Hoshi, Takeo, Kashyap, Anil, and Scharfstein, David. 1991. "Corporate Structure, Liquidity, and Investment: Evidence from Japanese Industrial Groups." *Quarterly Journal of Economics* 106 (February): 33–60.

Hosios, Arthur J. 1990. "On the Efficiency of Matching and Related Models of Search and Unemployment." *Review of Economic Studies* 57 (April): 279-298.

Howitt, Peter. 1988. "Business Cycles with Costly Search and Recruiting." *Quarterly Journal of Economics* 103 (February): 147-165.

Howitt, Peter. 1999. "Steady Endogenous Growth with Population and R&D Inputs Growing." *Journal of Political Economy* 107 (August): 715-730.

Howitt, Peter, and McAfee, R. Preston. 1988. "Stability of Equilibria with Externalities." *Quarterly Journal of Economics* 103 (May): 261-277.

Hsieh, Chang-Tai. 1998a. "What Explains the Industrial Revolution in East Asia? Evidence from Factor Markets." Unpublished paper, University of California, Berkeley (January).

Hsieh, Chang-Tai. 1998b. "Bargaining over Reform." Unpublished paper, University of California, Berkeley (June). *European Economic Review*, forthcoming.

Huang, Chao-Hsi, and Lin, Kenneth S. 1993. "Deficits, Government Expenditures, and Tax Smoothing in the United States, 1929-1988." *Journal of Monetary Economics* 31 (June): 317-339.

Hubbard, R. Glenn, and Judd, Kenneth L. 1986. "Liquidity Constraints, Fiscal Policy, and Consumption." *Brookings Papers on Economic Activity,* no. 1, 1-50.

Hubbard, R. Glenn, Skinner, Jonathan, and Zeldes, Stephen P. 1994. "The Importance of Precautionary Motives in Explaining Individual and Aggregate Saving." *Carnegie-Rochester Conference Series on Public Policy* 40 (June): 59-125.

Hubbard, R. Glenn, Skinner, Jonathan, and Zeldes, Stephen P. 1995. "Precautionary Saving and Social Insurance." *Journal of Political Economy* 103 (April): 360-399.

I

Inada, Kenichi. 1964. "Some Structural Characteristics of Turnpike Theorems." *Review of Economic Studies* 31 (January): 43-58.

Iwai, Katsuhito. 1981. *Disequilibrium Dynamics: A Theoretical Analysis of Inflation and Unemployment.* New Haven, CT: Yale University Press.

J

Jappelli, Tullio, and Pagano, Marco. 1994. "Saving, Growth, and Liquidity Constraints." *Quarterly Journal of Economics* 109 (February): 83-109.

Jayaratne, Jith, and Strahan, Philip E. 1996. "The Finance-Growth Nexus: Evidence from Bank Branch Deregulation." *Quarterly Journal of Economics* 111 (August): 639-670.

Jones, Charles I. 1995. "Time Series Tests of Endogenous Growth Models." *Quarterly Journal of Economics* 110 (May): 495-525.

Jones, Charles I. 1998. *Introduction to Economic Growth.* New York: W. W. Norton.

Jones, Charles I. 1999a. "Sources of U.S. Economic Growth in a World of Ideas." Unpublished paper, Stanford University (September).

Jones, Charles I. 1999b. "Growth: With or without Scale Effects?" *American Economic Review* 89 (May): 139-144.

Jorgenson, Dale W. 1988. "Productivity and Postwar U.S. Economic Growth." *Journal of Economic Perspectives* 2 (Fall): 23-41.

Jorgenson, Dale W., and Stiroh, Kevin J. 2000. "Raising the Speed Limit: U.S. Economic Growth in the Information Age." Unpublished paper, Harvard University (May). *Brookings Papers on Economic Activity*, forthcoming.

K

Kahneman, Daniel, Knetsch, Jack L., and Thaler, Richard. 1986. "Fairness as a Constraint on Profit Seeking: Entitlements in the Market." *American Economic Review* 76 (September): 728–741.

Kamien, Morton I., and Schwartz, Nancy L. 1991. *Dynamic Optimization: The Calculus of Variations and Optimal Control in Economics and Management,* 2d ed. Amsterdam: Elsevier.

Kandel, Shmuel, and Stambaugh, Robert F. 1991. "Asset Returns and Intertemporal Preferences." *Journal of Monetary Economics* 27 (February): 39–71.

Kaplan, Steven N., and Zingales, Luigi. 1997. "Do Investment-Cash Flow Sensitivities Provide Useful Measures of Financing Constraints?" *Quarterly Journal of Economics* 112 (February): 169–215.

Kaplan, Steven N., and Zingales, Luigi. 2000. "Investment-Cash Flow Sensitivities Are Not Valid Measures of Financing Constraints." *Quarterly Journal of Economics* 115 (May): 707–712.

Karamouzis, Nicholas, and Lombra, Raymond. 1989. "Federal Reserve Policymaking: An Overview and Analysis of the Policy Process." *Carnegie-Rochester Conference Series on Public Policy* 30 (Spring): 7–62.

Kareken, John H., and Solow, Robert M. 1963. "Lags in Monetary Policy." In Commission on Money and Credit, *Stabilization Policy,* 14–96. Englewood Cliffs, NJ: Prentice-Hall.

Kashyap, Anil K. 1995. "Sticky Prices: New Evidence from Retail Catalogs." *Quarterly Journal of Economics* 110 (February): 245–274.

Kashyap, Anil K, Lamont, Owen A., and Stein, Jeremy C. 1994. "Credit Conditions and the Cyclical Behavior of Inventories." *Quarterly Journal of Economics* 109 (August): 565–592.

Kashyap, Anil K, and Stein, Jeremy C. 1994. "Monetary Policy and Bank Lending." In N. Gregory Mankiw, ed., *Monetary Policy,* 221–256. Chicago: University of Chicago Press.

Katona, George. 1976. "The Psychology of Inflation." In Richard T. Curtin, ed., *Surveys of Consumers, 1974–75,* 9–19. Ann Arbor, MI: Institute for Social Research, University of Michigan.

Katz, Lawrence F. 1986. "Efficiency Wage Theories: A Partial Evaluation." *NBER Macroeconomics Annual* 1: 235–276.

Katz, Lawrence F., and Summers, Lawrence H. 1989. "Industry Rents: Evidence and Implications." *Brookings Papers on Economic Activity,* Microeconomics, 209–275.

Keynes, John Maynard. 1936. *The General Theory of Employment, Interest, and Money.* London: Macmillan.

Keynes, John Maynard. 1939. "Relative Movements of Real Wages and Output." *Economic Journal* 49 (March): 34–51.

Kiley, Michael T. 2000. "Endogenous Price Stickiness and Business Cycle Persistence." *Journal of Money, Credit, and Banking* 32 (February): 28–53.

Kimball, Miles S. 1990. "Precautionary Saving in the Small and the Large." *Econometrica* 58 (January): 53–73.

Kimball, Miles S. 1991. "The Quantitative Analytics of the Basic Real Business Cycle Model." Unpublished paper, University of Michigan (November).

Kimball, Miles S. 1994. "Labor-Market Dynamics When Unemployment Is a Worker Discipline Device." *American Economic Review* 84 (September): 1045–1059.

King, Robert G. 1991. "Money and Business Cycles." Unpublished paper, University of Rochester (June).

King, Robert G., and Levine, Ross. 1993a. "Finance and Growth: Schumpeter Might Be Right." *Quarterly Journal of Economics* 108 (August): 717–737.

King, Robert G., and Levine, Ross. 1993b. "Finance, Entrepreneurship, and Growth: Theory and Evidence." *Journal of Monetary Economics* 32 (December): 513–542.

King, Robert G., and Plosser, Charles I. 1984. "Money, Credit, and Prices in a Real Business Cycle." *American Economic Review* 64 (June): 363–380.

King, Robert G., and Rebelo, Sergio T. 1999. "Resuscitating Real Business Cycles." In John B. Taylor and Michael Woodford, eds., *Handbook of Macroeconomics*, 927–1007. Amsterdam: Elsevier.

Kiyotaki, Nobuhiro. 1988. "Multiple Expectational Equilibria under Monopolistic Competition." *Quarterly Journal of Economics* 102 (November): 695–714.

Kiyotaki, Nobuhiro, and Moore, John. 1997. "Credit Cycles." *Journal of Political Economy* 105 (April): 211–248.

Klenow, Peter J., and Rodríguez-Clare, Andrés. 1997. "The Neoclassical Revival in Growth Economics: Has It Gone Too Far?" *NBER Macroeconomics Annual* 12: 73–103.

Knack, Stephen, and Keefer, Philip. 1995. "Institutions and Economic Performance: Cross-Country Tests Using Alternative Institutional Measures." *Economics and Politics* 7 (November): 207–227.

Knack, Stephen, and Keefer, Philip. 1997. "Does Social Capital Have an Economic Payoff? A Cross-Country Investigation." *Quarterly Journal of Economics* 112 (November): 1251–1288.

Kocherlakota, Narayana. 1996. "The Equity Premium: It's Still a Puzzle." *Journal of Economic Literature* 34 (March): 42–71.

Koopmans, Tjalling C. 1965. "On the Concept of Optimal Economic Growth." In *The Economic Approach to Development Planning.* Amsterdam: Elsevier.

Kremer, Michael. 1993. "Population Growth and Technological Change: One Million B.C. to 1990." *Quarterly Journal of Economics* 108 (August): 681–716.

Kreps, David M. 1990. *A Course in Microeconomic Theory.* Princeton, NJ: Princeton University Press.

Krueger, Alan B., and Summers, Lawrence H. 1987. "Reflections on the Inter-Industry Wage Structure." In Kevin Lang and Jonathan S. Leonard, eds., *Unemployment and the Structure of Labor Markets,* 17–47. Oxford: Basil Blackwell.

Krueger, Alan B., and Summers, Lawrence H. 1988. "Efficiency Wages and the Interindustry Wage Structure." *Econometrica* 56 (March): 259–293. Reprinted in Mankiw and Romer (1991).

Krueger, Anne O. 1974. "The Political Economy of the Rent-Seeking Society." *American Economic Review* 64 (June): 291–303.

Krueger, Anne O. 1993. "Virtuous and Vicious Circles in Economic Development." *American Economic Review* 83 (May): 351–355.

Krugman, Paul R. 1979. "A Model of Innovation, Technology Transfer, and the World Distribution of Income." *Journal of Political Economy* 87 (April): 253–266.

Krugman, Paul R. 1991. "Target Zones and Exchange Rate Dynamics." *Quarterly Journal of Economics* 106 (August): 669–682.

Krugman, Paul R. 1998. "It's Baaack: Japan's Slump and the Return of the Liquidity Trap." *Brookings Papers on Economic Activity,* no. 2, 137–205.

Krusell, Per, and Smith, Anthony A., Jr. 1998. "Income and Wealth Heterogeneity in the Macroeconomy." *Journal of Political Economy* 88 (October): 867–896.

Kydland, Finn E., and Prescott, Edward C. 1977. "Rules Rather than Discretion: The Inconsistency of Optimal Plans." *Journal of Political Economy* 85 (June): 473–492. Reprinted in Persson and Tabellini (1994).

Kydland, Finn E., and Prescott, Edward C. 1982. "Time to Build and Aggregate Fluctuations." *Econometrica* 50 (November): 1345–1370.

Kydland, Finn E., and Prescott, Edward C. 1990. "Business Cycles: Real Facts and a Monetary Myth." Federal Reserve Bank of Minneapolis *Quarterly Review* (Spring): 3–18.

L

Laband, David N., and Sophocleus, John P. 1992. "An Estimate of Resource Expenditures on Transfer Activity in the United States." *Quarterly Journal of Economics* 107 (August): 959–983.

Lach, Saul, and Tsiddon, Daniel. 1992. "The Behavior of Prices and Inflation: An Empirical Analysis of Disaggregated Price Data." *Journal of Political Economy* 100 (April): 349–389.

Laibson, David. 1997. "Golden Eggs and Hyperbolic Discounting." *Quarterly Journal of Economics* 112 (May): 443–477.

Lamont, Owen. 1995. "Corporate Debt Overhang and Macroeconomic Expectations." *American Economic Review* 85 (December): 1106–1117.

Lamont, Owen. 1997. "Cash Flow and Investment: Evidence from Internal Capital Markets." *Journal of Finance* 52 (March): 83–109.

La Porta, Rafael, Lopez-de-Silanes, Florencio, Shleifer, Andrei, and Vishny, Robert W. 1997. "Trust in Large Organizations." *American Economic Review* 87 (May): 333–338.

Laxton, Douglas, Rose, David, and Tambakis, Demosthenes. 1999. "The U.S. Phillips Curve: The Case for Asymmetry." *Journal of Economic Dynamics and Control* 23 (September): 1459–1485.

Ledyard, John O. 1984. "The Pure Theory of Large Two-Candidate Elections." *Public Choice* 44: 7–41.

Leeper, Eric M., Sims, Christopher A., and Zha, Tao. 1996. "What Does Monetary Policy Do?" *Brookings Papers on Economic Activity,* no. 2, 1–78.

Leland, Hayne E. 1968. "Saving and Uncertainty: The Precautionary Demand for Saving." *Quarterly Journal of Economics* 82 (August): 465–473.

Leontief, Wassily. 1946. "The Pure Theory of the Guaranteed Annual Wage Contract." *Journal of Political Economy* 54 (February): 76–79.

Levine, Ross, and Zervos, Sara. 1998. "Stock Markets, Banks, and Economic Growth." *American Economic Review* 88 (June): 537–558.

Levy, Daniel, Bergen, Mark, Dutta, Shantanu, and Venable, Robert. 1997. "The Magnitude of Menu Costs: Direct Evidence from Large U.S. Supermarket Chains." *Quarterly Journal of Economics* 112 (August): 791–825.

Lilien, David M. 1982. "Sectoral Shifts and Cyclical Unemployment." *Journal of Political Economy* 90 (August): 777–793.

Lindbeck, Assar, and Snower, Dennis J. 1988. *The Insider-Outsider Theory of Employment and Unemployment.* Cambridge, MA: MIT Press.

Lintner, John. 1965. "The Valuation of Risky Assets and the Selection of Risky Investments in Stock Portfolios and Capital Budgets." *Review of Economics and Statistics* 47 (February): 13–37.

Lipsey, Richard G. 1960. "The Relation between Unemployment and the Rate of Change of Money Wage Rates in the United Kingdom, 1862–1957: A Further Analysis." *Economica* 27 (February): 1–31.

Ljungvist, Lars, and Sargent, Thomas J. 1998. "The European Unemployment Dilemma." *Journal of Political Economy* 108 (June): 514–550.

Loewenstein, George, and Thaler, Richard H. 1989. "Anomalies: Intertemporal Choice." *Journal of Economic Perspectives* 3 (Fall): 181–193.

Long, John B., and Plosser, Charles I. 1983. "Real Business Cycles." *Journal of Political Economy* 91 (February): 39–69.

Lougani, Prakash, Rush, Mark, and Tave, William. 1990. "Stock Market Dispersion and Unemployment." *Journal of Monetary Economics* 25 (June): 367–388.

Lucas, Robert E., Jr. 1967. "Adjustment Costs and the Theory of Supply." *Journal of Political Economy* 75 (August): 321–334.

Lucas, Robert E., Jr. 1972. "Expectations and the Neutrality of Money." *Journal of Economic Theory* 4 (April): 103–124.

Lucas, Robert E., Jr. 1973. "Some International Evidence on Output-Inflation Trade-offs." *American Economic Review* 63 (June): 326–334.

Lucas, Robert E., Jr. 1975. "An Equilibrium Model of the Business Cycle." *Journal of Political Economy* 83 (December): 1113–1144.

Lucas, Robert E., Jr. 1976. "Econometric Policy Evaluation: A Critique." *Carnegie-Rochester Conference Series on Public Policy* 1: 19–46.

Lucas, Robert E., Jr. 1978. "Asset Prices in an Exchange Economy." *Econometrica* 46 (December): 1429–1445.

Lucas, Robert E., Jr. 1987. *Models of Business Cycles.* Oxford: Basil Blackwell.

Lucas, Robert E., Jr. 1988. "On the Mechanics of Economic Development." *Journal of Monetary Economics* 22 (July): 3–42.

Lucas, Robert E., Jr. 1990. "Why Doesn't Capital Flow from Rich to Poor Countries?" *American Economic Review* 80 (May): 92–96.

Lucas, Robert E., Jr., and Prescott, Edward C. 1974. "Equilibrium Search and Employment." *Journal of Economic Theory* 7 (February): 188–209.

Lucas, Robert E., Jr., and Rapping, Leonard. 1969. "Real Wages, Employment and Inflation." *Journal of Political Economy* 77 (September/October): 721–754.

Lucas, Robert E., Jr., and Stokey, Nancy L. 1983. "Optimal Fiscal and Monetary Policy in an Economy without Capital." *Journal of Monetary Economics* 12 (July): 55–93. Reprinted in Persson and Tabellini (1994).

Luttmer, Erzo G. J. 1999. "What Level of Fixed Costs Can Reconcile Consumption and Stock Returns?" *Journal of Political Economy* 107 (October): 969–997.

M

Maddison, Angus. 1982. *Phases of Capitalist Development.* Oxford: Oxford University Press.

Maddison, Angus. 1995. *Monitoring the World Economy: 1820–1992.* Paris: Organization for Economic Cooperation and Development.

Malinvaud, Edmond. 1977. *The Theory of Unemployment Reconsidered.* Oxford: Basil Blackwell.

Malthus, Thomas Robert. 1798. *An Essay on the Principle of Population, as It Affects the Future Improvement of Society.* London: J. Johnson.

Mankiw, N. Gregory. 1981. "The Permanent Income Hypothesis and the Real Interest Rate." *Economics Letters* 7: 307–311.

Mankiw, N. Gregory. 1982. "Hall's Consumption Hypothesis and Durable Goods." *Journal of Monetary Economics* 10 (November): 417–425.

Mankiw, N. Gregory. 1985. "Small Menu Costs and Large Business Cycles: A Macroeconomic Model of Monopoly." *Quarterly Journal of Economics* 100 (May): 529–539. Reprinted in Mankiw and Romer (1991).

Mankiw, N. Gregory. 1986a. "The Allocation of Credit and Financial Collapse." *Quarterly Journal of Economics* 101 (August): 455–470. Reprinted in Mankiw and Romer (1991).

Mankiw, N. Gregory. 1986b. "The Equity Premium and the Concentration of Aggregate Shocks." *Journal of Financial Economics* 17 (September): 211–219.

Mankiw, N. Gregory. 1989. "Real Business Cycles: A New Keynesian Perspective." *Journal of Economic Perspectives* 3 (Summer): 79–90.

Mankiw, N. Gregory, and Miron, Jeffrey A. 1986. "The Changing Behavior of the Term Structure of Interest Rates." *Quarterly Journal of Economics* 101 (May): 211–228.

Mankiw, N. Gregory, Miron, Jeffrey A., and Weil, David N. 1987. "The Adjustment of Expectations to a Change in Regime: A Study of the Founding of the Federal Reserve." *American Economic Review* 77 (June): 358–374.

Mankiw, N. Gregory, and Romer, David, eds. 1991. *New Keynesian Economics.* Cambridge, MA: MIT Press.

Mankiw, N. Gregory, Romer, David, and Weil, David N. 1992. "A Contribution to the Empirics of Economic Growth." *Quarterly Journal of Economics* 107 (May): 407–437.

Mankiw, N. Gregory, and Summers, Lawrence H. 1986. "Money Demand and the Effects of Fiscal Policies." *Journal of Money, Credit, and Banking* 18 (November): 415–429.

Mankiw, N. Gregory, and Zeldes, Stephen P. 1991. "The Consumption of Stockholders and Nonstockholders." *Journal of Financial Economics* 29 (March): 97–112.

Maskin, Eric, and Tirole, Jean. 1988. "A Theory of Dynamic Oligopoly, I: Overview and Quantity Competition with Large Fixed Costs." *Econometrica* 56 (May): 549–570.

Matsuyama, Kiminori. 1991. "Increasing Returns, Industrialization, and Indeterminacy of Equilibrium." *Quarterly Journal of Economics* 106 (May): 617–650.

Mauro, Paolo. 1995. "Corruption and Growth." *Quarterly Journal of Economics* 110 (August): 681–712.

Mayer, Thomas. 1999. *Monetary Policy and the Great Inflation in the United States: The Federal Reserve and the Failure of Macroeconomic Policy, 1965–1979.* Cheltenham, United Kingdom: Edward Elgar.

McCallum, Bennett T. 1989. "Real Business Cycle Models." In Robert J. Barro, ed., *Modern Business Cycle Theory,* 16–50. Cambridge, MA: Harvard University Press.

McCulloch, J. Huston. 1975. "The Monte Carlo Cycle in Economic Activity." *Economic Inquiry* 13 (September): 303–321.

McDonald, Ian M., and Solow, Robert M. 1981. "Wage Bargaining and Employment." *American Economic Review* 71 (December): 896–908. Reprinted in Mankiw and Romer (1991).

McGrattan, Ellen R. 1994. "The Macroeconomic Effects of Distortionary Taxation." *Journal of Monetary Economics* 33 (June): 573–601.

McKinnon, Ronald I. 1973. *Money and Capital in Economic Development.* Washington: The Brookings Institution.

McQueen, Grant, and Thorley, Steven. 1993. "Asymmetric Business Cycle Turning Points." *Journal of Monetary Economics* 31 (June): 341–362.

Meadows, Donella H., Meadows, Dennis L., Randers, Jørgen, and Behrens, William W., III. 1972. *The Limits to Growth.* New York: Universe Books.

Meese, Richard, and Rogoff, Kenneth. 1983. "Empirical Exchange Rate Models of the Seventies: Do They Fit Out of Sample?" *Journal of International Economics* 14 (February): 3–24.

Mehra, Rajnish, and Prescott, Edward C. 1985. "The Equity Premium: A Puzzle." *Journal of Monetary Economics* 15 (March): 145–161.

Meltzer, Allan. 1988. *Keynes's Monetary Theory: A Different Interpretation.* Cambridge: Cambridge University Press.

Mendelsohn, Robert, Nordhaus, William D., and Shaw, Daigee. 1994. "The Impact of Global Warming on Agriculture: A Ricardian Analysis." *American Economic Review* 84 (September): 753–771.

Merton, Robert C. 1973. "An Intertemporal Capital Asset Pricing Model." *Econometrica* 41 (September): 867–887.

Merz, Monika. 1995. "Search in the Labor Market and the Real Business Cycle." *Journal of Monetary Economics* 36 (November): 269–300.

Meulendyke, Ann-Marie. 1998. *U.S. Monetary Policy and Financial Markets.* New York: Federal Reserve Bank of New York.

Miron, Jeffrey A. 1996. *The Economics of Seasonal Cycles.* Cambridge, MA: MIT Press.

Mishkin, Frederic S. 1982. "Does Anticipated Monetary Policy Matter? An Econometric Investigation." *Journal of Political Economy* 90 (February): 22–51.

Mishkin, Frederic S. 1983. *A Rational Expectations Approach to Macroeconometrics: Testing Policy Ineffectiveness and Efficient-Markets Models.* Chicago: University of Chicago Press.

Modigliani, Franco, and Brumberg, Richard. 1954. "Utility Analysis and the Consumption Function: An Interpretation of Cross-Section Data." In Kenneth K. Kurihara, ed., *Post-Keynesian Economics,* 388–436. New Brunswick, NJ: Rutgers University Press.

Modigliani, Franco, and Cohn, Richard A. 1979. "Inflation and the Stock Market." *Financial Analysts Journal* 35 (March/April): 24–44.

Modigliani, Franco, and Miller, Merton H. 1958. "The Cost of Capital, Corporation Finance and the Theory of Investment." *American Economic Review* 48 (June): 261–297.

Moore, Geoffrey H., and Zarnowitz, Victor. 1986. "The Development and Role of the National Bureau of Economic Research's Business Cycle Chronologies." In Robert J. Gordon, ed., *The American Business Cycle: Continuity and Change,* 735–779. Chicago: University of Chicago Press.

Mortenson, Dale T. 1986. "Job Search and Labor Market Analysis." In Orley Ashenfelter and Richard Layard, eds., *Handbook of Labor Economics,* vol. 2, 849–919. Amsterdam: Elsevier.

Mortenson, Dale T., and Pissarides, Christopher A. 1999. "Job Reallocation, Employment Fluctuations and Unemployment." In John B. Taylor and Michael Woodford, eds., *Handbook of Macroeconomics,* 1171–1228. Amsterdam: Elsevier.

Mulligan, Casey B., and Sala-i-Martin, Xavier. 1993. "Transitional Dynamics in Two-Sector Models of Endogenous Growth." *Quarterly Journal of Economics* 108 (August): 739–773.

Mundell, Robert A. 1963. "Inflation and Real Interest." *Journal of Political Economy* 71 (June): 280–283.

Mundell, Robert A. 1968. *International Economics.* New York: Macmillan.

Murphy, Kevin M., Shleifer, Andrei, and Vishny, Robert W. 1989. "Industrialization and the Big Push." *Journal of Political Economy* 97 (October): 1003–1026.

Murphy, Kevin M., Shleifer, Andrei, and Vishny, Robert W. 1991. "The Allocation of Talent: Implications for Growth." *Quarterly Journal of Economics* 106 (May): 503–530.

Murphy, Kevin M., Shleifer, Andrei, and Vishny, Robert W. 1993. "Why Is Rent-Seeking So Costly to Growth?" *American Economic Review* 83 (May): 409–414.

Murphy, Kevin M., and Topel, Robert H. 1987a. "The Evolution of Unemployment in the United States." *NBER Macroeconomics Annual* 2: 11–58.

Murphy, Kevin M., and Topel, Robert H. 1987b. "Unemployment, Risk, and Earnings: Testing for Equalizing Differences in the Labor Market." In Kevin Lang and Jonathan S. Leonard, eds., *Unemployment and the Structure of Labor Markets,* 103–140. Oxford: Basil Blackwell.

Mussa, Michael L. 1977. "External and Internal Adjustment Costs and the Theory of Aggregate and Firm Investment." *Economica* 44 (May): 163–178.

Mussa, Michael L. 1986. "Nominal Exchange Rate Regimes and the Behavior of Real Exchange Rates." *Carnegie-Rochester Conference Series on Public Policy* 25 (Autumn): 117–213.

Muth, John. 1960. "Optimal Properties of Exponentially Weighted Forecasts." *Journal of the American Statistical Association* 55 (June): 290–306.

Muth, John. 1961. "Rational Expectations and the Theory of Price Movements." *Econometrica* 39 (July): 315–334.

N

Nelson, Charles R., and Plosser, Charles I. 1982. "Trends and Random Walks in Macroeconomic Time Series: Some Evidence and Implications." *Journal of Monetary Economics* 10 (September): 139–162.

Nelson, Charles R., and Startz, Richard. 1990. "Some Further Results on the Exact Small Sample Properties of the Instrumental Variable Estimator." *Econometrica* 58 (July): 967–976.

Nordhaus, William D. 1967. "The Optimal Rate and Direction of Technical Change." In Karl Shell, ed., *Essays on the Theory of Optimal Economic Growth,* 53–66. Cambridge, MA: MIT Press.

Nordhaus, William D. 1975. "The Political Business Cycle." *Review of Economic Studies* 42 (April): 169–190.

Nordhaus, William D. 1991. "To Slow or Not to Slow: The Economics of the Greenhouse Effect." *Economic Journal* 101 (July): 920–937.

Nordhaus, William D. 1992. "Lethal Model 2: The Limits to Growth Revisited." *Brookings Papers on Economic Activity*, no. 2, 1–43.

Nordhaus, William D. 1997. "Do Real-Output and Real-Wage Measures Capture Reality? The History of Light Suggests Not." In Timothy F. Bresnahan and Robert J. Gordon, eds., *The Economics of New Goods*, 29–66. Chicago: University of Chicago Press.

North, Douglass C. 1981. *Structure and Change in Economic History.* New York: W. W. Norton.

O

Obstfeld, Maurice. 1986. "Capital Mobility in the World Economy: Theory and Measurement." *Carnegie-Rochester Conference Series on Public Policy* 24 (Spring): 55–104.

Obstfeld, Maurice. 1992. "Dynamic Optimization in Continuous-Time Economic Models (A Guide for the Perplexed)." Unpublished paper, University of California, Berkeley (April). Available at http://elsa.berkeley.edu/~obstfeld/index.html.

Obstfeld, Maurice, and Rogoff, Kenneth. 1996. *Foundations of International Macroeconomics.* Cambridge, MA: MIT Press.

O'Connell, Stephen A., and Zeldes, Stephen P. 1988. "Rational Ponzi Games." *International Economic Review* 29 (August): 431–450.

O'Donoghue, Ted, and Rabin, Matthew. 1999a. "Doing It Now or Later." *American Economic Review* 89 (March): 103–124.

O'Donoghue, Ted, and Rabin, Matthew. 1999b. "Incentives for Procrastinators." *Quarterly Journal of Economics* 114 (August): 739–767.

O'Driscoll, Gerald P., Jr. 1977. "The Ricardian Nonequivalence Theorem." *Journal of Political Economy* 85 (February): 207–210.

Oi, Walter Y. 1962. "Labor as a Quasi-Fixed Factor." *Journal of Political Economy* 70 (December): 538–555.

Okun, Arthur M. 1962. "Potential GNP: Its Measurement and Significance." In *Proceedings of the Business and Economics Statistics Section, American Statistical Association,* 98–103. Washington: American Statistical Association.

Okun, Arthur M. 1971. "The Mirage of Steady Inflation." *Brookings Papers on Economic Activity,* no. 2, 485–498.

Okun, Arthur M. 1975. "Inflation: Its Mechanics and Welfare Costs." *Brookings Papers on Economic Activity,* no. 2, 351–390. Reprinted in Mankiw and Romer (1991).

Oliner, Stephen D., and Rudebusch, Glenn D. 1996. "Monetary Policy and Credit Conditions: Evidence from the Composition of External Finance: Comment." *American Economic Review* 86 (March): 300–309.

Oliner, Stephen D., and Sichel, Daniel E. 2000. "The Resurgence of Growth in the Late 1990s: Is Information Technology the Story?" Federal Reserve Board, Finance and Economics Discussion Series Paper No. 2000-20 (March). *Journal of Economic Perspectives,* forthcoming.

Olson, Mancur, Jr. 1965. *The Logic of Collective Action.* Cambridge, MA: Harvard University Press.

Olson, Mancur, Jr. 1982. *The Rise and Decline of Nations.* New Haven, CT: Yale University Press.

Olson, Mancur, Jr. 1996. "Big Bills Left on the Sidewalk: Why Some Nations Are Rich, and Others Poor." *Journal of Economic Perspectives* 10 (Spring): 3–24.

Ordeshook, Peter C. 1986. *Game Theory and Political Theory: An Introduction.* Cambridge: Cambridge University Press.

Orphanides, Athanasios. 2000. "Activist Stabilization Policy and Inflation: The Taylor Rule in the 1970s." Federal Reserve Board, Finance and Economics Discussion Series Paper No. 2000-13 (February).

Osborne, Martin J., and Slivinski, Al. 1996. "A Model of Political Competition with Citizen-Candidates." *Quarterly Journal of Economics* 111 (February): 65–96.

Oswald, Andrew J. 1993. "Efficient Contracts Are on the Labour Demand Curve: Theory and Facts." *Labour Economics* 1 (June): 85–113.

P

Pagano, Marco. 1989. "Endogenous Market Thinness and Stock Market Volatility." *Review of Economic Studies* 56 (April): 269–288.

Palfrey, Thomas R., and Rosenthal, Howard. 1985. "Voter Participation and Strategic Uncertainty." *American Political Science Review* 79 (March): 62–78.

Parente, Stephen L., and Prescott, Edward C. 1999. "Monopoly Rights: A Barrier to Riches." *American Economic Review* 89 (December): 1216–1233.

Parker, Jonathan. 1999. "The Response of Household Consumption to Predictable Changes in Social Security Taxes." *American Economic Review* 89 (September): 959–973.

Parkin, Michael. 1986. "The Output-Inflation Tradeoff When Prices Are Costly to Change." *Journal of Political Economy* 94 (February): 200–224.

Peretto, Pietro F. 1998. "Technological Change and Population Growth." *Journal of Economic Growth* 4 (December): 283–311.

Perotti, Roberto. 1996. "Fiscal Consolidation in Europe: Composition Matters." *American Economic Review* 86 (May): 105–110.

Perotti, Roberto. 1999. "Fiscal Policy in Good Times and Bad." *Quarterly Journal of Economics* 114 (November): 1399–1436.

Perron, Pierre. 1989. "The Great Crash, the Oil Shock and the Unit Root Hypothesis." *Econometrica* 57 (November): 1361–1401.

Persson, Torsten, and Svensson, Lars E. O. 1989. "Why a Stubborn Conservative Would Run a Deficit: Policy with Time-Inconsistent Preferences." *Quarterly Journal of Economics* 104 (May): 325–345. Reprinted in Persson and Tabellini (1994).

Persson, Torsten, and Tabellini, Guido. 1993. "Designing Institutions for Monetary Stability." *Carnegie-Rochester Conference Series on Public Policy* 39 (December): 53–84. Reprinted in Persson and Tabellini (1994).

Persson, Torsten, and Tabellini, Guido, eds. 1994. *Monetary and Fiscal Policy.* Cambridge, MA: MIT Press.

Phelps, Edmund S. 1966a. *Golden Rules of Economic Growth.* New York: W. W. Norton.

Phelps, Edmund S. 1966b. "Models of Technical Progress and the Golden Rule of Research." *Review of Economic Studies* 33 (April): 133–146.

Phelps, Edmund S. 1968. "Money-Wage Dynamics and Labor Market Equilibrium." *Journal of Political Economy* 76 (July/August, Part 2): 678–711.

Phelps, Edmund S. 1970. "Introduction." In Edmund S. Phelps et al., *Microeconomic Foundations of Employment and Inflation Theory.* New York: W. W. Norton.

Phelps, Edmund S. 1973. "Inflation in the Theory of Public Finance." *Swedish Journal of Economics* 75 (March): 67–82.

Phelps, Edmund S. 1978. "Disinflation without Recession: Adaptive Guideposts and Monetary Policy." *Weltwirtschaftliches Archiv* 114: 783–809.

Phelps, Edmund S., and Taylor, John B. 1977. "Stabilizing Powers of Monetary Policy under Rational Expectations." *Journal of Political Economy* 85 (February): 163–190.

Phillips, A. W. 1958. "The Relationship between Unemployment and the Rate of Change of Money Wages in the United Kingdom, 1861–1957." *Economica* 25 (November): 283–299.

Pigou, A. C. 1943. "The Classical Stationary State." *Economic Journal* 53 (December): 343–351.

Pissarides, Christopher A. 1985. "Short-Run Dynamics of Unemployment, Vacancies, and Real Wages." *American Economic Review* 75 (September): 676–690.

Pollard, Patricia S. 1993. "Central Bank Independence and Economic Performance." Federal Reserve Bank of St. Louis *Review* 75 (July/August): 21–36.

Poole, William. 1970. "Optimal Choice of Monetary Instruments in a Simple Stochastic Macro Model." *Quarterly Journal of Economics* 84 (May): 197–216.

Posen, Adam S. 1993. "Why Central Bank Independence Does Not Cause Low Inflation: There Is No Institutional Fix for Politics." *Finance and the International Economy* 7: 40–65.

Posner, Richard A. 1975. "The Social Costs of Monopoly and Regulation." *Journal of Political Economy* 83 (August): 807–827.

Poterba, James M. 1984. "Tax Subsidies to Owner-Occupied Housing: An Asset-Market Approach." *Quarterly Journal of Economics* 99 (November): 729–752.

Poterba, James M. 1994. "State Responses to Fiscal Crises: The Effects of Budgetary Institutions and Politics." *Journal of Political Economy* 102 (August): 799–821.

Poterba, James M., and Summers, Lawrence H. 1987. "Finite Lifetimes and the Effects of Budget Deficits on National Saving." *Journal of Monetary Economics* 20 (September): 369–391.

Poterba, James M., and von Hagen, Jürgen, eds. 1999. *Fiscal Institutions and Fiscal Performance.* Chicago: University of Chicago Press.

Prescott, Edward C. 1986. "Theory Ahead of Business-Cycle Measurement." *Carnegie-Rochester Conference Series on Public Policy* 25 (Autumn): 11–44.

Pritchett, Lant. 1997. "Divergence, Big Time." *Journal of Economic Perspectives* 11 (Summer): 3–17.

R

Ramsey, F. P. 1928. "A Mathematical Theory of Saving." *Economic Journal* 38 (December): 543–559. Reprinted in Stiglitz and Uzawa (1969).

Ravn, Morton O., and Sola, Martin. 1995. "Stylized Facts and Regime Changes: Are Prices Procyclical?" *Journal of Monetary Economics* 36 (December): 497–526.

Rebelo, Sergio. 1991. "Long-Run Policy Analysis and Long-Run Growth." *Journal of Political Economy* 99 (June): 500–521.

Rebelo, Sergio, and Végh, Carlos. 1995. "Real Effects of Exchange-Rate-Based Stabilization: An Analysis of Competing Theories." *NBER Macroeconomics Annual* 10: 125–174.

Reinganum, Jennifer F. 1989. "The Timing of Innovation: Research, Development, and Diffusion." In Richard Schmalensee and Robert D. Willig, eds., *Handbook of Industrial Organization,* vol. 1, 849–908. Amsterdam: Elsevier.

Riker, William H., and Ordeshook, Peter C. 1968. "A Theory of the Calculus of Voting." *American Political Science Review* 62 (March): 25–42.

Rodríguez, Francisco, and Rodrik, Dani. 1999. "Trade Policy and Economic Growth: A Skeptic's Guide to the Cross-National Evidence." Unpublished paper, Harvard University (April). *NBER Macroeconomics Annual,* forthcoming.

Rogerson, Richard. 1988. "Indivisible Labor, Lotteries and Equilibrium." *Journal of Monetary Economics* 21 (January): 3–16.

Rogerson, Richard, and Wright, Randall. 1988. "Involuntary Unemployment in Economies with Efficient Risk Sharing." *Journal of Monetary Economics* 22 (November): 501–515.

Rogoff, Kenneth. 1985. "The Optimal Degree of Commitment to an Intermediate Monetary Target." *Quarterly Journal of Economics* 100 (November): 1169–1189. Reprinted in Persson and Tabellini (1994).

Rogoff, Kenneth. 1987. "Reputational Constraints on Monetary Policy." *Carnegie-Rochester Conference Series on Public Policy* 26 (Spring): 141–182.

Rogoff, Kenneth. 1990. "Equilibrium Political Budget Cycles." *American Economic Review* 80 (March): 21–36. Reprinted in Persson and Tabellini (1994).

Rogoff, Kenneth, and Sibert, Anne. 1988. "Elections and Macroeconomic Policy Cycles." *Review of Economic Studies* 55 (January): 1–16.

Romer, Christina D. 1986a. "Spurious Volatility in Historical Unemployment Data." *Journal of Political Economy* 94 (February): 1–37.

Romer, Christina D. 1986b. "Is the Stabilization of the Postwar Economy a Figment of the Data?" *American Economic Review* 76 (June): 314–334.

Romer, Christina D. 1989. "The Prewar Business Cycle Reconsidered: New Estimates of Gross National Product, 1869–1908." *Journal of Political Economy* 97 (February): 1–37.

Romer, Christina D. 1990. "The Great Crash and the Onset of the Great Depression." *Quarterly Journal of Economics* 105 (August): 597–624.

Romer, Christina D. 1993. "The Nation in Depression." *Journal of Economic Perspectives* 7 (Spring): 19–39.

Romer, Christina D. 1994. "Remeasuring Business Cycles." *Journal of Economic History* 54 (September): 573–609.

Romer, Christina D. 1999. "Changes in Business Cycles: Evidence and Explanations." *Journal of Economic Perspectives* 13 (Spring): 23–44.

Romer, Christina D., and Romer, David H. 1989. "Does Monetary Policy Matter? A New Test in the Spirit of Friedman and Schwartz." *NBER Macroeconomics Annual* 4: 121–170.

Romer, Christina D., and Romer, David H. 2000. "Federal Reserve Information and the Behavior of Interest Rates." *American Economic Review* 90 (June): 429–457.

Romer, David. 1993. "The New Keynesian Synthesis." *Journal of Economic Perspectives* 7 (Winter): 5–22.

Romer, David. 1999. "Misconceptions and Political Outcomes." Unpublished paper, University of California, Berkeley (March).

Romer, David. 2000. "Keynesian Macroeconomics without the LM Curve." *Journal of Economic Perspectives* 14 (Spring): 149–169.

Romer, Paul M. 1986. "Increasing Returns and Long Run Growth." *Journal of Political Economy* 94 (October): 1002-1037.

Romer, Paul M. 1990. "Endogenous Technological Change." *Journal of Political Economy* 98 (October, Part 2): S71-S102.

Romer, Paul M. 1996. "Preferences, Promises, and the Politics of Entitlement." In Victor R. Fuchs, ed., *Individual and Social Responsibility: Child Care, Education, Medical Care and Long-Term Care in America*, 195-220. Chicago: University of Chicago Press.

Rotemberg, Julio J. 1982. "Sticky Prices in the United States." *Journal of Political Economy* 90 (December): 1187-1211.

Rotemberg, Julio J. 1984. "A Monetary Equilibrium Model with Transactions Costs." *Journal of Political Economy* 92 (February): 41-58.

Rotemberg, Julio J. 1987. "The New Keynesian Microfoundations." *NBER Macroeconomics Annual* 2: 69-104.

Rotemberg, Julio J. 1996. "Price, Output, and Hours: An Empirical Analysis Based on a Sticky Price Model." *Journal of Monetary Economics* 37 (June): 505-533.

Rotemberg, Julio J., and Woodford, Michael. 1996. "Real-Business-Cycle Models and Forecastable Movements in Output, Hours, and Consumption." *American Economic Review* 86 (March): 71-89.

Rotemberg, Julio J., and Woodford, Michael. 1999. "The Cyclical Behavior of Prices and Costs." In John B. Taylor and Michael Woodford, eds., *Handbook of Macroeconomics*, 1052-1135. Amsterdam: Elsevier.

Roubini, Nouriel, and Sachs, Jeffrey D. 1989. "Political and Economic Determinants of Budget Deficits in the Industrial Democracies." *European Economic Review* 33 (May): 903-933.

Rubinstein, Mark. 1976. "The Valuation of Uncertain Income Streams and the Pricing of Options." *Bell Journal of Economics* 7 (Autumn): 407-425.

Rudebusch, Glenn D. 1993. "The Uncertain Unit Root in Real GNP." *American Economic Review* 83 (March): 263-272.

Rudebusch, Glenn D. 1998. "Do Measures of Monetary Policy in a VAR Make Sense?" *International Economic Review* 39 (November): 907-931.

S

Sachs, Jeffrey D., and Larrain, Felipe B. 1993. *Macroeconomics in the Global Economy.* Englewood Cliffs, NJ: Prentice-Hall.

Sachs, Jeffrey D., and Warner, Andrew. 1995. "Economic Reform and the Process of Global Integration." *Brookings Papers on Economic Activity*, no. 1, 1-95.

Sahasakul, Chaipat. 1986. "The U.S. Evidence on Optimal Taxation over Time." *Journal of Monetary Economics* 18 (November): 251-275.

Sala-i-Martin, Xavier. 1991. "Comment." *NBER Macroeconomics Annual* 6: 368-378.

Samuelson, Paul A. 1939. "Interaction between the Multiplier Analysis and the Principle of Acceleration." *Review of Economics and Statistics* 21 (May): 75-78.

Samuelson, Paul A. 1958. "An Exact Consumption-Loan Model of Interest with or without the Social Contrivance of Money." *Journal of Political Economy* 66 (December): 467-482. Reprinted in Stiglitz and Uzawa (1969).

Samuelson, Paul A., and Solow, Robert M. 1960. "Analytical Aspects of Anti-Inflation Policy." *American Economic Review* 50 (May): 177-194.

Sargent, Thomas J. 1976. "The Observational Equivalence of Natural and Unnatural Rate Theories of Macroeconomics." *Journal of Political Economy* 84 (June): 631–640.

Sargent, Thomas J. 1982. "The End of Four Big Inflations." In Robert E. Hall, ed., *Inflation,* 41–98. Chicago: University of Chicago Press.

Sargent, Thomas J. 1983. "Stopping Moderate Inflations: The Methods of Poincare and Thatcher." In Rudiger Dornbusch and Mario Henrique Simonsen, eds., *Inflation, Debt, and Indexation,* 54–96. Cambridge, MA: MIT Press.

Sargent, Thomas J. 1987a. *Macroeconomic Theory,* 2d ed. Boston: Academic Press.

Sargent, Thomas J. 1987b. *Dynamic Macroeconomic Theory.* Cambridge, MA: Harvard University Press.

Sargent, Thomas J. 1999. *The Conquest of American Inflation.* Princeton, NJ: Princeton University Press.

Sargent, Thomas J., and Wallace, Neil. 1975. " 'Rational Expectations,' the Optimal Monetary Instrument, and the Optimal Money Supply Rule." *Journal of Political Economy* 83 (April): 241–254.

Sato, K. 1966. "On the Adjustment Time in Neo-Classical Growth Models." *Review of Economic Studies* 33 (July): 263–268.

Sbordone, Argia M. 1998. "Prices and Unit Labor Costs: A New Test of Price Stickiness." IIES Seminar Paper No. 653 (October).

Shaked, Avner, and Sutton, John. 1984. "Involuntary Unemployment as a Perfect Equilibrium in a Bargaining Model." *Econometrica* 52 (November): 1351–1364.

Shapiro, Carl, and Stiglitz, Joseph E. 1984. "Equilibrium Unemployment as a Worker Discipline Device." *American Economic Review* 74 (June): 433–444. Reprinted in Mankiw and Romer (1991).

Shapiro, Carl, and Stiglitz, Joseph E. 1985. "Can Unemployment Be Involuntary? Reply." *American Economic Review* 75 (December): 1215–1217.

Sharpe, William F. 1964. "Capital Asset Prices: A Theory of Market Equilibrium under Conditions of Risk." *Journal of Finance* 19 (September): 425–442.

Shea, John. 1995. "Union Contracts and the Life-Cycle/Permanent-Income Hypothesis." *American Economic Review* 85 (March): 186–200.

Sheffrin, Steven M. 1988. "Have Economic Fluctuations Been Dampened? A Look at Evidence outside the United States." *Journal of Monetary Economics* 21 (January): 73–83.

Shefrin, Hersh M., and Thaler, Richard H. 1988. "The Behavioral Life-Cycle Hypothesis." *Economic Inquiry* 26 (October): 609–643.

Shell, Karl. 1966. "Toward a Theory of Inventive Activity and Capital Accumulation." *American Economic Review* 56 (May): 62–68.

Shell, Karl. 1967. "A Model of Inventive Activity and Capital Accumulation." In Karl Shell, ed., *Essays on the Theory of Optimal Economic Growth,* 67–85. Cambridge, MA: MIT Press.

Sheshinski, Eytan, and Weiss, Yoram. 1977. "Inflation and Costs of Price Adjustment." *Review of Economic Studies* 44 (June): 287–303.

Shiller, Robert J. 1990. "The Term Structure of Interest Rates." In Benjamin M. Friedman and Frank Hahn, eds., *Handbook of Monetary Economics,* vol. 1, 627–722. Amsterdam: Elsevier.

Shiller, Robert J. 1997. "Why Do People Dislike Inflation?" In Christina D. Romer and David H. Romer, eds., *Reducing Inflation: Motivation and Strategy,* 13–65. Chicago: University of Chicago Press.

Shleifer, Andrei. 1986. "Implementation Cycles." *Journal of Political Economy* 94 (December): 1163–1190. Reprinted in Mankiw and Romer (1991).

Shleifer, Andrei, and Vishny, Robert W. 1992. "Pervasive Shortages under Socialism." *Rand Journal of Economics* 23 (Summer): 237–246.

Shleifer, Andrei, and Vishny, Robert W. 1993. "Corruption." *Quarterly Journal of Economics* 108 (August): 599–617.

Shleifer, Andrei, and Vishny, Robert W. 1994. "Politicians and Firms." *Quarterly Journal of Economics* 109 (November): 995–1025.

Sichel, Daniel E. 1993. "Business Cycle Asymmetry: A Deeper Look." *Economic Inquiry* 31 (April): 224–236.

Siebert, Horst. 1997. "Labor Market Rigidities: At the Root of Unemployment in Europe." *Journal of Economic Perspectives* 11 (Summer): 37–54.

Simon, Carl P., and Blume, Lawrence. 1994. *Mathematics for Economists.* New York: W. W. Norton.

Sims, Christopher A. 1980. "Macroeconomics and Reality." *Econometrica* 48 (January): 1–48.

Sims, Christopher A. 1986. "Are Forecasting Models Usable for Policy Analysis?" Federal Reserve Bank of Minneapolis *Quarterly Review* 10 (Winter): 2–16.

Sims, Christopher A. 1992. "Interpreting the Macroeconomic Time Series Facts: The Effects of Monetary Policy." *European Economic Review* 36 (June): 975–1000.

Solon, Gary, Barsky, Robert, and Parker, Jonathan A. 1994. "Measuring the Cyclicality of Real Wages: How Important Is Composition Bias?" *Quarterly Journal of Economics* 109 (February): 1–25.

Solow, Robert M. 1956. "A Contribution to the Theory of Economic Growth." *Quarterly Journal of Economics* 70 (February): 65–94. Reprinted in Stiglitz and Uzawa (1969).

Solow, Robert M. 1957. "Technical Change and the Aggregate Production Function." *Review of Economics and Statistics* 39: 312–320.

Solow, Robert M. 1960. "Investment and Technical Progress." In Kenneth J. Arrow, Samuel Korbin, and Patrick Suppes, eds., *Mathematical Methods in the Social Sciences 1959,* 89–104. Stanford: Stanford University Press. Reprinted in Stiglitz and Uzawa (1969).

Solow, Robert M. 1979. "Another Possible Source of Wage Stickiness." *Journal of Macroeconomics* 1 (Winter): 79–82.

Solow, Robert M. 1985. "Insiders and Outsiders in Wage Determination." *Scandinavian Journal of Economics* 87: 411–428.

Solow, Robert M., and Stiglitz, Joseph E. 1968. "Output, Employment, and Wages in the Short Run." *Quarterly Journal of Economics* 82 (November): 537–560.

Souleles, Nicholas S. 1999. "The Response of Household Consumption to Income Tax Refunds." *American Economic Review* 89 (September): 947–958.

Staiger, Douglas, and Stock, James H. 1997. "Instrumental Variables Regression with Weak Instruments." *Econometrica* 65 (May): 557–586.

Staiger, Douglas, Stock, James H., and Watson, Mark W. 1997. "How Precise Are Estimates of the Natural Rate of Unemployment?" In Christina D. Romer and David H. Romer, eds., *Reducing Inflation: Motivation and Strategy,* 195–242. Chicago: University of Chicago Press.

Stiglitz, Joseph E. 1979. "Equilibrium in Product Markets with Imperfect Information." *American Economic Review* 69 (May): 339–345.

Stiglitz, Joseph E., and Uzawa, Hirofumi, eds. 1969. *Readings in the Modern Theory of Economic Growth.* Cambridge, MA: MIT Press.

Stockman, Alan C. 1983. "Real Exchange Rates under Alternative Nominal Exchange Rate Systems." *Journal of International Money and Finance* 2 (August): 147–166.

Stokey, Nancy L., and Lucas, Robert E., Jr., with Prescott, Edward C. 1989. *Recursive Methods in Economic Dynamics.* Cambridge, MA: Harvard University Press.

Summers, Lawrence H. 1981a. "Capital Taxation and Accumulation in a Life Cycle Growth Model." *American Economic Review* 71 (September): 533–544.

Summers, Lawrence H. 1981b. "Taxation and Corporate Investment: A *q*-Theory Approach." *Brookings Papers on Economic Activity,* no. 1, 67–127.

Summers, Lawrence H. 1986a. "Some Skeptical Observations on Real Business Cycle Theory." Federal Reserve Bank of Minneapolis *Quarterly Review* 10 (Fall): 23–27.

Summers, Lawrence H. 1986b. "Why Is the Unemployment Rate So Very High Near Full Employment?" *Brookings Papers on Economic Activity,* no. 2, 339–383.

Summers, Lawrence H. 1988. "Relative Wages, Efficiency Wages, and Keynesian Unemployment." *American Economic Review* 78 (May): 383–388.

Summers, Lawrence H. 1991. "How Should Long-Term Monetary Policy Be Determined?" *Journal of Money, Credit, and Banking* 23 (August, Part 2): 625–631.

Summers, Robert, and Heston, Alan. 1991. "The Penn World Table (Mark 5): An Expanded Set of International Comparisons, 1950–1988." *Quarterly Journal of Economics* 106 (May): 327–368.

Svensson, Lars E. O. 1997. "Inflation Forecast Targeting: Implementing and Monitoring Inflation Targets." *European Economic Review* 41 (June): 1111–1146.

Swan, T. W. 1956. "Economic Growth and Capital Accumulation." *Economic Record* 32 (November): 334–361. Reprinted in Stiglitz and Uzawa (1969).

T

Tabellini, Guido, and Alesina, Alberto. 1990. "Voting on the Budget Deficit." *American Economic Review* 80 (March): 37–49. Reprinted in Persson and Tabellini (1994).

Taylor, John B. 1979. "Staggered Wage Setting in a Macro Model." *American Economic Review* 69 (May): 108–113. Reprinted in Mankiw and Romer (1991).

Taylor, John B. 1980. "Aggregate Dynamics and Staggered Contracts." *Journal of Political Economy* 88 (February): 1–23.

Taylor, John B. 1981. "On the Relation between the Variability of Inflation and the Average Inflation Rate." *Carnegie-Rochester Conference Series on Public Policy* 15 (Autumn): 57–86.

Taylor, John B. 1993. "Discretion versus Policy Rules in Practice." *Carnegie-Rochester Conference Series on Public Policy* 39 (December): 195–214.

Taylor, John B. 1998. *Economics,* 2d ed. Boston: Houghton Mifflin.

Taylor, John B., ed. 1999. *Monetary Policy Rules.* Chicago: University of Chicago Press.

Temple, Jonathan, and Johnson, Paul A. 1998. "Social Capability and Economic Growth." *Quarterly Journal of Economics* 113 (August): 965–990.

Tinbergen, Jan. 1952. *On the Theory of Economic Policy.* Amsterdam: Elsevier.

Tobin, James. 1969. "A General Equilibrium Approach to Monetary Theory." *Journal of Money, Credit, and Banking* 1 (February): 15–29.

Tobin, James. 1972. "Inflation and Unemployment." *American Economic Review* 62 (March): 1–18.

Tobin, James. 1980. *Asset Accumulation and Economic Activity.* Chicago: University of Chicago Press.

Tobin, James, and Brainard, William. 1963. "Financial Intermediaries and the Effectiveness of Monetary Control." *American Economic Review* 53 (May): 383–400.

Tolley, George S. 1957. "Providing for the Growth of the Money Supply." *Journal of Political Economy* 65 (December): 465–485.

Tommasi, Mariano. 1994. "The Consequences of Price Instability on Search Markets: Toward Understanding the Effects of Inflation." *American Economic Review* 84 (December): 1385–1396.

Topel, Robert H. 1989. "Comment." *Brookings Papers on Economic Activity,* Microeconomics, 283–288.

Topel, Robert H., and Ward, Michael P. 1992. "Job Mobility and the Careers of Young Men." *Quarterly Journal of Economics* 107 (May): 439–479.

Tornell, Aaron, and Lane, Philip R. 1999. "The Voracity Effect." *American Economic Review* 89 (March): 22–46.

Townsend, Robert M. 1979. "Optimal Contracts and Competitive Markets with Costly State Verification." *Journal of Economic Theory* 21 (October): 265–293.

Tsiddon, Daniel. 1991. "On the Stubbornness of Sticky Prices." *International Economic Review* 32 (February): 69–75.

Tullock, Gordon. 1967. "The Welfare Costs of Tariffs, Monopolies, and Theft." *Western Economic Journal* 5 (June): 224–232.

Tversky, Amos, and Kahneman, Daniel. 1974. "Judgment under Uncertainty: Heuristics and Biases." *Science* 185 (September): 1124–1131.

U

Uzawa, Hirofumi. 1965. "Optimum Technical Change in an Aggregative Model of Economic Growth." *International Economic Review* 6 (January): 12–31.

V

Van Huyck, John B., Battalio, Raymond C., and Beil, Richard O. 1990. "Tacit Coordination Games, Strategic Uncertainty, and Coordination Failure." *American Economic Review* 80 (March): 234–248.

Van Huyck, John B., Battalio, Raymond C., and Beil, Richard O. 1991. "Strategic Uncertainty, Equilibrium Selection, and Coordination Failure in Average Opinion Games." *Quarterly Journal of Economics* 106 (August): 885–910.

Velasco, Andrés. 1999. "A Model of Endogenous Fiscal Deficits and Delayed Fiscal Reforms." In James M. Poterba and Jürgen von Hagen, eds., *Fiscal Institutions and Fiscal Performance,* 37–57. Chicago: University of Chicago Press.

Vickers, John. 1986. "Signalling in a Model of Monetary Policy with Incomplete Information." *Oxford Economic Papers* 38 (November): 443–455.

von Hagen, Jürgen, and Harden, Ian. 1995. "Budget Processes and Commitment to Fiscal Discipline." *European Economic Review* 39 (April): 771–779.

W

Walsh, Carl E. 1995. "Optimal Contracts for Central Bankers." *American Economic Review* 85 (March): 150–167.

Warner, Elizabeth J., and Barsky, Robert B. 1995. "The Timing and Magnitude of Retail Store Markdowns: Evidence from Weekends and Holidays." *Quarterly Journal of Economics* 110 (May): 321–352.

Watson, Mark W. 1986. "Univariate Detrending Methods with Stochastic Trends." *Journal of Monetary Economics* 18 (July): 49–75.

Weil, Philippe. 1989a. "Overlapping Families of Infinitely-Lived Agents." *Journal of Public Economics* 38 (March): 183–198.

Weil, Philippe. 1989b. "The Equity Premium Puzzle and the Risk-Free Rate Puzzle." *Journal of Monetary Economics* 24 (November): 401–421.

Weil, Philippe. 1990. "Nonexpected Utility in Macroeconomics." *Quarterly Journal of Economics* 105 (February): 29–42.

Weingast, Barry, Shepsle, Kenneth, and Johnsen, Christopher. 1981. "The Political Economy of Benefits and Costs: A Neoclassical Approach to Distributive Politics." *Journal of Political Economy* 89 (August): 642–664. Reprinted in Persson and Tabellini (1994).

Weitzman, Martin L. 1974. "Prices vs. Quantities." *Review of Economic Studies* 41 (October): 477–491.

West, Kenneth D. 1988. "The Insensitivity of Consumption to News about Income." *Journal of Monetary Economics* 21 (January): 17–33.

Whelan, Karl. 2000. "Computers, Obsolescence, and Productivity." Federal Reserve Board, Finance and Economics Discussion Series Paper No. 2000-6 (February).

Wilcox, David W. 1989. "Social Security Benefits, Consumption Expenditure, and the Life Cycle Hypothesis." *Journal of Political Economy* 97 (April): 288–304.

Wilhelm, Mark O. 1996. "Bequest Behavior and the Effect of Heirs' Earnings: Testing the Altruistic Model of Bequests." *American Economic Review* 86 (September): 874–892.

Woglom, Geoffrey. 1982. "Underemployment Equilibrium with Rational Expectations." *Quarterly Journal of Economics* 97 (February): 89–107.

Wolff, Edward N. 1998. "Recent Trends in the Size Distribution of Household Wealth." *Journal of Economic Perspectives* 12 (Summer): 131–150.

Woodford, Michael. 1990. "Learning to Believe in Sunspots." *Econometrica* 58 (March): 277–307.

Woodford, Michael. 1991. "Self-Fulfilling Expectations and Fluctuations in Aggregate Demand." In Mankiw and Romer (1991), vol. 2, 77–110.

Woodford, Michael. 1995. "Price-Level Determinacy without Control of a Monetary Aggregate." *Carnegie-Rochester Conference Series on Public Policy* 43 (December): 1–46.

Working, Holbrook. 1960. "A Note on the Correlation of First Differences of Averages in a Random Chain." *Econometrica* 28 (October): 916–918.

Y

Yellen, Janet L. 1984. "Efficiency Wage Models of Unemployment." *American Economic Review* 74 (May): 200–205. Reprinted in Mankiw and Romer (1991).

Yotsuzuka, Toshiki. 1987. "Ricardian Equivalence in the Presence of Capital Market Imperfections." *Journal of Monetary Economics* 20 (September): 411–436.

Young, Alwyn. 1995. "The Tyranny of Numbers: Confronting the Statistical Reality of the East Asian Growth Experience." *Quarterly Journal of Economics* 110 (August): 641–680.

Z

Zeldes, Stephen P. 1989. "Consumption and Liquidity Constraints: An Empirical Investigation." *Journal of Political Economy* 97 (April): 305–346.

NAME INDEX

Abel, Andrew B., 88–89, 333n, 370n, 379n, 391
Abraham, Katherine G., 207n
Abramovitz, Moses, 28
Abreu, Dilip, 527
Acemoglu, Daron, 146, 147, 150, 155, 171n
Aghion, Philippe, 7n, 100, 117, 119
Aiyagari, S. Rao, 173n, 536n
Akerlof, George A., 280, 300n, 361, 413, 432n, 433, 457, 462
Alesina, Alberto, 489–490, 500n, 547, 550–553, 555, 558–562, 566, 568–569, 571–572
Allais, Maurice, 95
Alt, James E., 534n
Altonji, Joseph G., 209, 344, 538n
Altug, Sumru, 202n
Andersen, Leonall C., 252
Andolfatto, David, 210
Arrow, Kenneth J., 120
Atkeson, Andrew, 495
Auerbach, Alan J., 75n, 530
Azariadis, Costas, 435n, 464

Backus, David, 172n, 484
Bagwell, Kyle, 538n
Baily, Martin Neil, 30, 435n
Balke, Nathan S., 171n
Ball, Laurence, 172n, 209, 276, 277–278, 280n, 288, 308, 309, 313–314, 323, 325, 326, 328, 444, 496, 497, 503, 507–508, 518n, 522, 535n
Barro, Robert J., 7n, 35, 73–74, 92, 122n, 127n, 148, 157, 237n, 256n, 275, 276n, 297, 434, 479, 484, 526, 538, 541–542, 545n, 552
Barsky, Robert B., 169n, 239, 247n, 258–260, 308, 541, 583
Barth, Marvin J., III, 257
Basu, Susanto, 149n, 208n, 307, 308n
Battalio, Raymond C., 319–320

Baumol, William, 31–32, 34, 119, 145, 146n
Baxter, Marianne, 173n, 174–175, 206–207, 256, 350
Bayoumi, Tamim, 534n
Bean, Charles R., 444, 452
Beaudry, Paul, 171n, 201n
Becker, Gary S., 127n
Behrens, William W., III, 36n
Beil, Richard O., 319–320
Bekaert, Geert, 353n
Benabou, Roland, 521
Benartzi, Shlomo, 353n
Benassy, Jean-Pascal, 237n
Benhabib, Jess, 207n, 317n
Bergen, Mark, 315–316
Bernanke, Ben S., 171n, 204–205, 208, 223n, 257, 308, 311n, 312n, 391n, 395n, 400, 402, 409, 503n, 510n, 575
Bernheim, B. Douglas, 538n, 540, 573
Bertola, Giuseppe, 547
Besley, Timothy, 555n
Bewley, Truman, 459
Bils, Mark J., 150n, 166, 208n, 239, 258–260, 454–455
Black, Fischer, 96, 173n
Blanchard, Olivier J., 61n, 75n, 185, 213, 214, 257, 269, 280n, 284, 300n, 314, 365, 437n, 439, 440, 443, 444, 445n, 452, 472n, 501n, 526
Blank, Rebecca M., 259
Blinder, Alan S., 223n, 247, 257, 279n, 315, 459–460, 582
Blough, Stephen R., 200n
Blume, Lawrence, 53n, 65n
Bohn, Henning, 534n, 535n, 545, 546
Borjas, George J., 141
Boskin, Michael J., 5n
Brainard, S. Lael, 207n
Brainard, William, 223n, 529

Brander, James A., 43n
Braun, R. Anton, 206
Breeden, Douglas, 351
Bresciani-Turroni, Constantino, 510
Brock, William, 96
Brumberg, Richard, 332
Bruno, Michael, 148, 522
Bryant, John, 319–320
Buchanan, James M., 549
Bulow, Jeremy, 431
Burnside, Craig, 207n, 208n

Caballero, Ricardo J., 208n, 280n, 299n, 308n, 354n, 391n
Cagan, Philip, 510, 512–513, 515, 529
Calvo, Guillermo, 96, 255n, 482n, 576n, 580n
Campbell, Carl M., III, 459, 460, 461
Campbell, John Y., 175, 180, 186, 189n, 190, 193n, 199–201, 206–207, 216, 333n, 340n, 341–342, 343n, 344, 346, 353n, 354n, 459, 496, 545n
Caplin, Andrew S., 280, 297–298, 299, 327
Card, David, 209, 454
Cardoso, Eliana, 518n
Carlton, Dennis W., 315, 521
Carmichael, Lorne, 432
Carroll, Christopher D., 348n, 354, 357, 362
Cass, David, 47, 317n
Cecchetti, Stephen G., 280n, 315, 326, 522
Chari, V. V., 546n, 571n, 587
Chevalier, Judith A., 239, 308
Chiang, Alpha C., 53n
Cho, Dongchul, 159
Cho, Jang-Ok, 210
Choi, Don H., 459–460
Christiano, Lawrence J., 173n, 174, 201n, 202n, 207n, 210, 257, 312
Clark, Kim B., 452
Clark, Peter, 496
Coate, Stephen, 550n, 555n
Cochrane, John H., 201n, 257, 333n, 353n, 354n, 496
Cogley, Timothy, 201n, 202n, 209
Cohen, Gerald D., 500n
Cohn, Richard A., 521
Cole, Harold L., 571n, 576n, 587
Coleman, Thomas S., 259–260

Constantinides, George M., 353n
Cook, Timothy, 256, 476–478
Cooley, Thomas F., 172n, 210, 257, 573
Cooper, Russell W., 308n, 316, 319, 391n
Craine, Roger, 391
Crucini, Mario J., 207n
Cukierman, Alex, 148, 486n, 490, 491n, 522, 527
Cutler, David M., 207n

Danthine, Jean-Pierre, 210
Davis, Steven J., 207n, 452
Deaton, Angus, 340n, 354, 359n
Debelle, Guy, 491, 496–497
de Gaulle, Charles, 570
de Haan, Jakob, 568n
DeJong, Douglas V., 319
De Long, J. Bradford, 31–33, 146n, 147, 149n, 171n, 263, 492
Denison, Edward F., 29, 30
Diamond, Douglas W., 392
Diamond, Peter A., 47, 308n, 319, 329, 445n, 452
Dickens, William T., 422n, 456, 457, 458
Dickey, David A., 198
Dinopoulos, Elias, 114
Dixit, Avinash K., 53n, 61n, 179n, 324, 371n, 391n, 409
Doeringer, Peter B., 431
Dolde, Walter, 275
Donaldson, John B., 210
Dornbusch, Rudiger, 231–232
Downs, Anthony, 548, 555
Dowrick, Steve, 158
Drazen, Allan, 547, 550, 561, 562, 566, 567, 568–569, 571–572
Driffill, John, 484
Dulberger, Ellen R., 5n
Dunlop, John T., 322
Durlauf, Steven N., 319
Dutta, Shantanu, 315–316
Dynan, Karen E., 357

Easterly, William, 147, 148, 522
Eberly, Janice C., 354n, 391
Edin, Per-Anders, 568n
Eichenbaum, Martin, 173n, 174, 201n, 202n, 207n, 208n, 257, 312
Eichengreen, Barry, 534n
Eisner, Robert, 370
Elmendorf, Douglas W., 535n

Engel, Eduardo M. R. A., 280n, 299n, 391n
Epstein, Larry G., 353n, 354n
Ethier, Wilfred J., 161
Evans, Charles, 257, 312

Farmer, Roger E. A., 317n
Fatás, Antonio, 201n
Fazzari, Steven M., 404–405, 406n
Feldstein, Martin, 35, 163, 464, 520
Fernald, John G., 208n, 308n
Fernandez, Raquel, 586
Fethke, Gary, 326
Fischer, Stanley, 61n, 148, 213, 214, 279n, 280, 325, 340n, 472n, 501n, 522, 526
Fisher, Irving, 311n
Flavin, Marjorie A., 340
Fleming, J. Marcus, 227
Foley, Duncan K., 370, 380n
Foote, Christopher L., 452
Forsythe, Robert, 319
French, Kenneth R., 350
Friedman, Milton, 245–246, 247, 251, 254–255, 257, 306n, 332, 334, 336n, 459, 474, 498, 500, 501, 520n, 529
Froot, Kenneth A., 365
Fuhrer, Jeffrey C., 295, 491
Fuller, Wayne A., 198

Gale, Douglas, 395
Galí, Jordi, 319
Galor, Oded, 83n, 127n
Garino, Gaia, 461
Geary, Patrick T., 258
Genberg, Hans, 256
Gertler, Mark, 308, 311n, 312n, 395n, 400, 405, 536n
Ghosh, Atish R., 545n
Giavazzi, Francesco, 547
Gibbons, Robert, 457–458
Gilchrist, Simon, 405
Glassman, James K., 353
Goldfeld, Stephen M., 254n, 470
Goldstein, Morris, 534n
Goolsbee, Austan, 402–403
Gordon, David, 435n
Gordon, David B., 479, 484n, 526
Gordon, Robert J., 5n, 30, 171n, 496
Gottfries, Nils, 437, 439

Gould, John P., 370
Gourinchas, Pierre-Olivier, 357
Graham, Stephen, 159
Gray, Jo Anna, 325
Green, Donald P., 558n
Greenwald, Bruce C., 308, 322n
Greenwood, Jeremy, 206, 207n
Gregory, R. G., 437n, 440n
Griliches, Zvi, 5n, 30
Grilli, Vittorio, 490, 567, 569–570
Groshen, Erica L., 456n
Grossman, Gene M., 100, 117, 164
Grossman, Herschel I., 150, 237n
Grossman, Sanford, 312n

Haavelmo, Trygve, 261
Hahn, Thomas, 256, 476–478
Hall, Robert E., 138–146, 149, 208, 338, 340–341, 345, 369n, 433, 434, 457n, 521
Haltiwanger, John, 207n, 288n, 308n, 391n, 452
Hamilton, James, 258
Hansen, Gary D., 202–203, 206
Hansen, Lars Peter, 345, 363
Harden, Ian, 571
Harrington, Joseph E., Jr., 500n
Harris, John R., 466
Harrison, Sharon G., 210
Hart, Oliver, 562
Hassett, Kevin A., 353
Hayashi, Fumio, 370n, 376, 379n, 538n, 540
Hayes, Beth, 562
Heaton, John, 353n
Hellwig, Martin, 395
Helpman, Elhanan, 100, 117, 164
Hercowitz, Zvi, 207n
Hess, Gregory D., 171n
Heston, Alan, 6n, 139n
Hodrick, Robert J., 202n, 353n
Horioka, Charles, 35, 163
Hornstein, Andreas, 207n
Hoshi, Takeo, 404
Hosios, Arhur J., 445n
Howitt, Peter, 7n, 100, 114, 117, 119, 319, 445n
Hsieh, Chang-Tai, 30, 562, 563n, 566–567

Huang, Chao-Hsi, 545n
Hubbard, R. Glenn, 362, 404–405, 406n, 540, 573
Huffman, Gregory W., 206, 207n

Inada, Kenichi, 11
Inman, Robert P., 534n
Iwai, Katsuhito, 299
Iwata, Shigeru, 171n

Jappelli, Tullio, 148, 359–361
Jayaratne, Jith, 148
Jermann, Urban J., 350
John, Andrew, 316, 319
Johnsen, Christopher, 571, 586
Johnson, Paul A., 146
Johnson, Simon, 146, 147
Jones, Charles I., 7n, 17n, 114–115, 133n, 138–146, 147, 149
Jordan, Jerry, 252
Jorgenson, Dale W., 5n, 30, 369n
Judd, Kenneth L., 540, 573

Kahneman, Daniel, 360, 461
Kalaitzidakis, Pantelis, 148, 522
Kamien, Morton L., 61n, 371n
Kamlani, Kunal S., 459, 460, 461
Kandel, Shmuel, 496
Kaplan, Steven N., 405n, 406n
Karamouzis, Nicholas, 500n
Kareken, John H., 253
Kashyap, Anil K, 223n, 315, 404, 405
Katona, George, 523
Katz, Lawrence F., 207n, 412, 422n, 432n, 456–458
Keefer, Philip, 145–146, 147
Kehoe, Patrick J., 172n, 546n
Kehoe, Timothy J., 576n
Kennan, John, 258
Keynes, John Maynard, 235, 236n, 258, 261, 322, 333–334
Kiley, Michael T., 314
Kilian, Lutz, 247n
Kim, Minseong, 150
Kimball, Miles S., 186n, 194n, 357n, 429n
King, Robert G., 148, 173n, 174–175, 206–207, 210, 253, 402
Kiyotaki, Nobuhiro, 269, 284, 300n, 308, 319, 400

Klenow, Peter J., 138–142, 149, 150n, 166, 208n
Knack, Stephen, 145–146, 147
Knetsch, Jack L., 461
Kocherlakota, Narayana, 353n
Koop, Gary, 171n, 201n
Koopmans, Tjalling C., 47
Kotlikoff, Laurence J., 75n, 534n, 538n
Kremer, Michael, 126–131
Kreps, David M., 53n, 179n
Krueger, Alan B., 456–458
Krueger, Anne O., 144n, 148
Krugman, Paul R., 164, 230n, 523
Krusell, Per, 207n, 210
Kydland, Finn E., 172n, 173n, 201, 207n, 479, 483, 546

Laband, David N., 144n
Lach, Saul, 315
Laibson, David, 361
Lamont, Owen, 319, 405
Lane, Philip R., 566n
Lang, Kevin, 422n
La Porta, Rafael, 147
Larrain, Felipe B., 510, 513
Laubach, Thomas, 510n
Laxton, Douglas, 496–497
Leahy, John, 299, 327
Ledyard, John O., 558
Leeper, Eric M., 257
Leland, Hayne E., 355, 583
Leontief, Wassily, 434
Le Roy, Stephen F., 257
Levine, Ross, 147, 148, 402
Levy, Daniel, 315–316
Lilien, David M., 207
Lin, Kenneth S., 545n
Lindbeck, Assar, 437n
Lintner, John, 351n
Lipsey, Richard G., 245
Ljungvist, Lars, 444
Loewenstein, George, 360
Lombra, Raymond, 500n
Long, John B., 173n, 181n, 207
Lopez-de-Silanes, Florencio, 147
Lougani, Prakash, 207n
Lown, Cara S., 402
Lowry, Robert C., 534n
Lucas, Deborah J., 353n

Lucas, Robert E., Jr., 7, 27, 149n, 165, 178, 183, 207, 266, 270-271, 274, 275, 276n, 277, 279n, 312, 313, 353n, 365, 370, 495-496, 525, 545
Luttmer, Erzo G. J., 353n
Lyons, Richard K., 208n, 308n

Maddison, Angus, 5n, 31, 160
Main, Brian G. M., 433
Malinvaud, Edmond, 237n
Malthus, Thomas Robert, 35-36
Mankiw, N. Gregory, 35, 88-89, 92, 157-158, 172n, 199-201, 208, 261, 277-278, 284, 300n, 312n, 313-314, 323, 341-342, 343n, 344, 345, 346, 352, 353n, 354n, 364, 365, 496, 526, 535n, 541, 583
Marshall, David A., 353n
Martin, Christopher, 461
Martinez, Pedro, 457
Masciandaro, Donato, 490, 567, 569-570
Maskin, Eric, 280n
Matsuyama, Kiminori, 319
Mauro, Paolo, 145-146
Mayer, Thomas, 492
McAfee, R. Preston, 319
McCallum, Bennett T., 181n, 183n
McCulloch, J. Huston, 197
McDonald, Ian M., 465
McGrattan, Ellen R., 206
McKinnon, Ronald I., 402
McQueen, Grant, 171n
Meadows, Dennis L., 36n
Meadows, Donnella H., 36n
Meese, Richard, 227
Mehra, Rajnish, 352-353
Meltzer, Allan H., 486n, 496, 523n, 527
Mendelsohn, Robert, 42
Merton, Robert C., 351
Merz, Monika, 210
Meulendyke, Ann-Marie, 498n
Mihov, Ilian, 257
Miller, Merton, 409
Miron, Jeffrey A., 169n, 526
Mishkin, Frederic S., 276n, 510n
Modigliani, Franco, 332, 409, 521
Moore, Geoffrey H., 168n
Moore, George R., 295

Moore, John, 308, 400
Morris, Stephen, 550n
Mortenson, Dale T., 445n, 453
Mulligan, Casey B., 122n
Mundell, Robert A., 227, 261
Murphy, Kevin M., 119, 127n, 145-146, 150, 207n, 319, 457n
Mussa, Michael L., 256, 370
Muth, John, 271

Nason, James M., 202n, 209
Nelson, Charles R., 197-199, 342n
Neyapti, Bilin, 490, 491n
Nguyen, Duc-Tho, 158
Nordhaus, William D., 5n, 39-40, 42-43, 117, 500n
North, Douglass C., 146n, 147

Obstfeld, Maurice, 35, 61n, 225n, 365, 370n, 576n
O'Connell, Stephen A., 535n
O'Donoghue, Ted, 361
O'Driscoll, Gerald P., Jr., 537n
Ohanian, Lee E., 172n, 573
Ohlsson, Henry, 568n
Oi, Walter Y., 451n
Okun, Arthur M., 172, 521, 522
Oliner, Stephen D., 30, 405
Olson, Mancur., Jr., 145, 146n, 558
Ordeshook, Peter C., 548, 558
Orphanides, Athanasios, 502
Osborne, Martin J., 555n
Oswald, Andrew J., 437

Pagano, Marco, 148, 319, 359-361, 547
Palfrey, Thomas R., 558
Parente, Stephen L., 147
Parker, Jonathan A., 258-260, 344, 357
Parkin, Michael, 300n
Parkinson, Martin L., 204-205, 208
Peretto, Pietro F., 114
Perotti, Roberto, 547
Perron, Pierre, 200n, 201n
Persson, Torsten, 484n, 550-552, 585
Petersen, Bruce C., 404-405, 406n
Phaneuf, Louis, 210
Phelan, Christopher, 495
Phelps, Edmund S., 49n, 100n, 117, 245-247, 251, 266, 280, 512n
Phillips, A. W., 245, 251

Pigou, A. C., 261
Pindyck, Robert S., 391n, 409
Piore, Michael J., 431
Pissarides, Christopher A., 445n
Plosser, Charles I., 173n, 181n,
    197–199, 207, 253
Policano, Andrew, 326
Pollard, Patricia S., 491n
Poole, William, 528
Posen, Adam S., 491, 510n
Posner, Richard A., 144n
Poterba, James M., 350, 407, 534n, 539,
    571
Power, Laura, 391n
Prescott, Edward C., 147, 172n, 173n,
    174, 181n, 183, 201–203, 207,
    352–353, 479, 483, 546
Pritchett, Lant, 7

Rabin, Matthew, 361
Ramey, Valerie, 257
Ramsey, F., 47
Randers, Jørgen, 36n
Rapping, Leonard, 178
Ravn, Morton O., 172n
Reagan, Ronald, 550
Rebelo, Sergio, 149n, 163, 207n, 208n,
    210n, 255n
Reinganum, Jennifer F., 119n
Ricardo, David, 537n
Riker, William H., 558
Robinson, James, 146, 147
Rodríguez, Francisco, 146n
Rodríguez-Clare, Andrés, 138–142, 149
Rodrik, Dani, 146n, 586
Rogerson, Richard, 206, 207n
Rogoff, Kenneth, 225n, 227, 484n,
    486n, 487, 489, 500n, 527, 528,
    550, 576, 589
Rohaly, Jeffrey, 3n
Romer, Christina D., 171, 254–255, 257,
    357n, 477, 492
Romer, David H., 157–158, 222n,
    254–255, 257, 280n, 288, 299n, 302,
    308, 309, 313n, 314, 323, 326, 328,
    477, 496, 549
Romer, Paul M., 100, 112, 113n, 116,
    117, 119, 122, 149n, 162, 558
Rose, Andrew K., 457

Rose, David, 496–497
Rosenthal, Howard, 558
Ross, Thomas W., 319
Rotemberg, Julio J., 172n, 209, 239,
    269, 300n, 308, 312n
Roubini, Nouriel, 500n, 567–571
Rubinstein, Mark, 351
Rudebusch, Glenn D., 201n, 257, 405
Rush, Mark, 207n
Ryder, Harl E., 83n

Sachs, Jeffrey D., 145–147, 510, 513,
    567–571
Sahasakul, Chiapat, 545n
Sala-i-Martin, Xavier, 7n, 35, 92, 122n,
    157, 522
Samuelson, Paul A., 95, 245n, 261, 492
Sargent, Thomas J., 255n, 275, 276,
    295n, 324, 424, 444, 474, 492,
    501n, 519, 525
Sato, K., 45
Savage, L. J., 459
Sbordone, Argia M., 239, 308n
Scharfstein, David S., 239, 308, 404
Schwartz, Anna J., 254–255, 257, 509n
Schwartz, Nancy L., 61n, 371n
Scott, Andrew, 171n
Shaked, Avner, 437
Shapiro, Carl, 422, 430, 432n
Shapiro, Ian, 558n
Shapiro, Matthew, 211n
Sharpe, William F., 351n
Shaw, Daigee, 42
Shea, John, 343, 344
Sheffrin, Steven M., 171n
Shefrin, Hersh M., 360
Shell, Karl, 100n, 117, 317n
Shepsle, Kenneth, 571, 586
Sheshinski, Eytan, 297
Shiller, Robert J., 475n, 521
Shleifer, Andrei, 119, 145–146, 147,
    150, 319, 538n, 551n
Sibert, Anne, 500n, 550n
Sichel, Daniel E., 30, 171n, 470
Sidrauski, Miguel, 348, 358n, 370, 380n
Siebert, Horst, 444
Simon, Carl B., 53n, 65n
Sims, Christopher A., 257–258
Singleton, Kenneth J., 345, 363

Siow, Aloysius, 344
Skinner, Jonathan, 362
Slivinski, Al, 555n
Smith, Adam, 145
Smith, Anthony A., Jr., 210
Snower, Dennis J., 437n
Sola, Martin, 172n
Solon, Gary, 258–260
Solow, Robert M., 7n, 28, 45, 237n,
    245n, 253, 414, 437n, 465, 492, 582
Sophocleus, John P., 144n
Souleles, Nicholas S., 344
Spulber, Daniel F., 280, 297–298
Staiger, Douglas, 249, 342n, 498
Stambaugh, Robert F., 496
Startz, Richard, 342n
Stein, Herbert, 574
Stein, Jeremy C., 223n, 405
Stiglitz, Joseph E., 32n, 237n, 308,
    322n, 324, 422, 430, 432n, 464
Stiroh, Kevin J., 30
Stock, James H., 249, 342n, 498
Stockman, Alan C., 256
Stokey, Nancy L., 183, 545
Strahan, Philip E., 148
Strong, Benjamin, 255, 256
Strotz, Robert H., 370
Sturm, Jan-Egbert, 568n
Summers, Lawrence H., 88–89, 148,
    149n, 171n, 208n, 261, 263, 321,
    348, 354, 370n, 418n, 422n, 431,
    437n, 439, 440, 443, 452, 456–458,
    461, 490n, 522, 523, 526, 538n,
    539, 623
Summers, Robert, 6n, 139n
Sutton, John, 437
Svensson, Lars E. O., 503, 504n, 508,
    550–552, 585
Swan, T. W., 7n

Tabellini, Guido, 55, 484n, 490,
    550–553, 555, 558–561, 567,
    569–570
Tambakis, Demosthenes, 497
Tamura, Robert, 127n
Tave, William, 207n
Taylor, John B., 222n, 280, 501–502,
    503n, 507, 522
Taylor, M. Scott, 43n

Temple, Jonathan, 146
Thaler, Richard H., 353n, 360, 461
Thompson, Peter, 114
Thorley, Steven, 171n
Tinbergen, Jan, 497n
Tirole, Jean, 280n
Tobin, James, 223n, 375, 523, 540
Todaro, Michael P., 466
Tolley, George S., 520n
Tommasi, Mariano, 521
Topel, Robert H., 207n, 452, 457n
Tornell, Aaron, 566n
Townsend, Robert M., 393, 395n
Tsiddon, Daniel, 299, 315
Tullock, Gordon, 144n
Tversky, Amos, 360

Uzawa, Hirofumi, 100n

Van Huyck, John B., 319–320
Végh, Carlos, 255n
Velasco, Andrés, 571n
Venable, Robert, 315–316
Vickers, John, 486n
Vishny, Robert W., 119, 145–146, 147,
    150, 319, 551n
Volcker, Paul, 255
von Hagen, Jürgen, 571

Wagner, Richard E., 549
Waldman, Michael, 288n
Wallace, Neil, 275, 501n
Walsh, Carl E., 484n
Ward, Michael P., 452
Warner, Andrew, 145–147
Warner, Elizabeth J., 239, 308
Watson, Mark W., 201n, 249, 257, 498
Webb, Steven B., 148, 490, 491n, 522
Weil, David N., 127n, 149n, 157, 158,
    526
Weil, Philippe, 75n, 353n, 354n
Weingast, Barry, 571, 586
Weiss, Andrew, 308
Weiss, Laurence, 312n
Weiss, Yoram, 297
Weitzman, Martin L., 42n
West, Kenneth D., 340n
Whelan, Karl, 30
Wilcox, David W., 344
Wilhelm, Mark O., 538n

Woglom, Geoffrey, 308, 534n
Wolfers, Justin, 444
Wolff, Edward N., 354
Woodford, Michael, 209, 239, 308, 317n, 503n, 536n
Working, Holbrook, 362
Wright, Randall, 202–204, 206, 207n

Yellen, Janet L., 300n, 412, 413, 457, 462
Yotsuzuka, Toshiki, 540

Young, Alwyn, 29

Zarnowitz, Victor, 168n
Zeckhauser, Richard J., 88–89
Zeldes, Stephen P., 344, 352, 353n, 358, 362, 535n, 541, 583
Zervos, Sara, 148
Zha, Tao, 257
Zin, Stanley E., 353n, 354n
Zingales, Luigi, 405n, 406n

SUBJECT INDEX

Accelerator, 261, 383
Accountability, 509–510
Adjustment; see Capital adjustment
    costs; Convergence; Price
    adjustment
Adverse selection, 311, 399, 459–460
Agency costs, 399–402
Agency problems, 392
Aggregate demand
    and changes in unemployment, 240
    and exchange rates, 227–229,
        232 234
    and government purchases, 224–225
    and monetary policy rules, 502–508
    in traditional Keynesian models,
        218–225
Aggregate demand curve, 218–219,
    223–224
    downward-sloping, 283–284
    impact of inflation, 242–244,
        469–471, 479–480
    in Lucas model, 268–269
    and output-inflation tradeoff,
        249–251
Aggregate demand externality, 284,
    301–302
Aggregate demand shocks; see also
    Monetary shocks
    anticipated versus unanticipated, 287
    international evidence, 276–278,
        313–314
    long-lasting output effect, 201,
        291–292
    in Lucas model, 267, 313
    measure of, 277–278
    and real wage, 410–411
Aggregate supply, 247–248
    models of, 234–242
    and monetary policy rules, 502–508

Aggregate supply curve, 218–219
    and aggregate price level, 266
    horizontal, 237–238
    and inflation, 242–244, 469–471,
        479–480
    in Keynesian models, 235–236
    long-run, 247–248
    and microeconomic environment, 252
    nonlinear, 496–497
    nonvertical, 234–235
    and output-inflation tradeoff,
        249–251
    and price and wage rigidity, 234–242
    short-run, 247, 251–252
Aghion–Howitt model, 100, 118
Alesina–Drazen model, 561–567,
    585–586
Animal spirits, 317
Asset prices, 364–365
Asset yields, 350–351
Automatic stabilizers, 261
Autoregressive process, 74, 176, 184,
    199

Backshift operator, 293n
Balanced budget multiplier, 261
Balanced growth path
    and constant-relative-risk-aversion
        utility, 48
    convergence to, 30, 156–158
    definition, 16–17
    in Diamond model, 81–82, 86
    and dynamic inefficiency, 88–89
    and golden-rule capital stock, 21–22,
        62–63
    and government purchases, 70
    and level of consumption, 20
    model comparisons, 85
    and natural resources, 38–39
    properties of, 61–62

in Ramsey–Cass–Koopmans model,
61–63
in R&D model, 111–112
in real-business-cycle models,
186–189, 214
speed of convergence to, 25, 68
and transitional dynamics, 124–125
Bargaining; *see* Contracts; Delayed
stabilization; Insider-outsider
models; Unions
Barro–Gordon model, 526–527
Bellman equation, 215
Beveridge curve, 450
Blanchard model, 75n
Bonding, 431–432
Break-even investment, 15–16, 20
Bubble paths, 472n
Bubbles in asset prices, 364–365
Budget deficits
common-pool spending problem,
571, 586–587
costs of, 572–576
and delayed stabilization, 561–571
distribution effects, 573–574
and durability of governments,
570–571
and form of government, 569–570
inefficient, 548, 561–562
measurement issues, 532–534
nominal, 533
political-economy theories of,
547–551
and politics in industrial countries,
567–572
primary, 532
versus taxes, 535–537
through strategic debt accumulation,
551–561
and tax-smoothing, 541–547
variation in behavior of, 567–568
with weak governments, 568–569
Buffer-stock saving, 353–354, 359,
540–541
Business-stealing effect, 118–119

Calculus of variations, 53n, 61n,
371–372
Calibration, 25, 201–203, 211
Capital; *see also* Golden-rule capital
stock; Investment
cost of, 367–370

costs of adjusting, 370, 376, 389
desired, 368–369
and diversion, 142, 155–156
and dynamic inefficiency, 86–88
externalities from, 148–149
and future profitability, 404
and growth, 7–8, 26–27, 62, 85,
107–114, 136, 138–140, 148–149
growth rate of, 65–66, 107–115
human, 132–143, 148–149, 155, 157,
159, 165–166
and knowledge accumulation,
120–122
and Lucas model, 279n
physical *versus* human, 132
rate of return, 27, 30, 44–45, 86–88,
123, 142, 148–149
replacement cost of, 375–376
and Ricardian equivalence, 537
and taxes, 92–93, 386, 482, 545–546
user cost of, 368–369
Capital account, 232, 575
Capital adjustment costs; *see also* q
theory model of investment
asymmetric, 389
external, 370
internal, 370
returns to scale in, 376
Capital asset pricing model (CAPM),
351n
Capital-augmenting technological
progress, 9n, 12n
Capital flows, 27, 30, 34–35, 142–143,
232, 575
Capital goods prices, 402–403
Capital mobility
barriers to, 35, 142
and exchange rate expectations,
226–227
imperfect, 232–234
and interest rates, 232
perfect, 226–230, 231
Capital-output ratio, 9, 26
cross-country differences, 145
and output per worker, 145–146
and predation, 155–156
Caplin-Spulber model, 280, 296–299
Case study, 570
Cash flow, 403–405
Cash-in-advance constraint, 269
Central bank independence, 489–491

Certainty-equivalence behavior, 270, 285–286, 289, 339
Classical dichotomy, 266
Cobb–Douglas function, 11–12, 37, 40–41, 68, 79–80, 155, 181–182
  generalized, 99
  intensive form, 27
  for quantitative analysis, 133
Coefficient of relative prudence, 357n
Coefficient of relative risk aversion, 48, 352, 356–357
Common-pool problem of government spending, 571, 586–587
Communist regimes, 145
Competition, imperfect, 237, 240–242, 281–285, 308, 324–325
Competitive labor market, 236–240
Computer use, 30
Conditional convergence, 157, 159, 167
Condorcet paradox, 584
Constant-relative-risk-aversion (CRRA) utility, 48–49, 91, 351
Constant returns to scale; *see* Returns to scale
Consumer-surplus effect, 118–119
Consumption
  black *versus* white patterns, 334, 336–337
  and bond issues, 538
  certainty-equivalence behavior, 339
  under certainty, 331–336
  and current income, 334–336
  and departures from complete optimization, 360–361
  in Diamond model, 76–78, 86–87
  of durable goods, 170, 354n, 364
  effect of saving rate on path of, 20–22
  and efficiency wages, 412
  excess sensitivity, 340
  excess smoothness, 340n, 363
  and expectations concerning fiscal policy, 546–547
  and fluctuations, 330, 495–496
  and government purchases, 69–71, 194–196
  and income movements, 332–333, 338–344, 354, 363
  interest rates and saving, 345–348
  versus investment, 143–145
  and liquidity constraints, 343–344, 357–360
  in permanent-income model, 539
  and precautionary saving, 354–357
  predictability of, 338, 340
  in Ramsey–Cass–Koopmans model, 48–55, 63–71
  in real-business-cycle models, 176–180, 194–196
  in relation to bond issues, 539–540
  in research and development model, 122–123
  and Ricardian equivalence, 537
  and risky assets, 349–353
  and rule-of-thumb behavior, 360–361, 573
  and taxes, 275
  time-averaging problem, 362–363
  and time-inconsistent preferences, 361, 366
  tradeoff with labor supply, 180
  under uncertainty, 178–180, 337–339, 354–357
  and union contracts, 343
  and utility function, 354n, 355
  variability of, 495–496
  and welfare programs, 362
Consumption beta, 351
Consumption capital asset pricing model, 350–351
Consumption function (Keynes), 70–71, 220, 333–337
Contracting models, 411–412, 432–436, 439–440, 453–456
Contracts
  under asymmetric information, 394–395, 464–465
  debt, 394–395
  efficient, 435–436
  and employment movements, 453–456
  implicit, 432–436, 463–464
  renegotiation-proof, 395n
  setting wages and prices, 280
  and unemployment, 439–440
  without variable hours, 463–464
  wage, 434–435
Control variable, 374

Convergence
  to balanced growth path, 156–158
  conditional, 157, 159, 167
  and cross-country income
      differences, 30–34, 137
  in Diamond model, 81–83
  and measurement error, 32–34
  overall patterns of, 6–7, 24, 159
  in Ramsey model, 68
  regressions, 166–167
  sample selection bias, 31–32
  in Solow model, 24–25, 34–35
  unconditional, 157, 166
Convergence scatter plot, 34
Coordination failures, 316–320
Copyright laws, 116
Core inflation, 249–251
  versus expected inflation, 251–252
Corruption, 142, 144–145, 149, 551n
Costate variable, 374
Costly state verification, 393
Countercyclical markup, 239, 241–242,
      308, 311
Covered interest parity, 231
Credibility, 509–510
Credit rationing, 397
Cross-country income differences; *see*
      Income differences, cross-country
Crowding effects, 446
Culture, 147

Debt contracts, 300, 311, 394–395
Debt crises, 574–582
Debt deflation, 311
Debt-to-GDP ratio, 567, 571, 574
Deficit bias, 468, 547, 566
  from incomplete knowledge, 549
  from strategic considerations,
      550–551
Deficit-to-GDP ratio, 571
Delayed stabilization, 561–567, 585,
      586
Delegation, 487–489, 528
Depreciation, 181–182
Destabilizing price flexibility, 263
Detrending procedure, 202
Diamond model
  assumptions, 75–76
  balanced growth path, 86

bond issues in, 535
capital stock in, 78–79, 87
Cobb–Douglas production, 79–80
consumption in, 86–87
convergence in, 81–83
depreciation in, 94
dynamic inefficiency in, 85–89
dynamics of economy, 78–85
fall in discount rate, 80–81
general case, 83–85
government purchases in, 89–90
household consumption in, 76–78
logarithmic utility, 79–80
versus Ramsey–Cass–Koopmans
      model, 47, 75, 76, 85
saving in, 82–83, 84–85, 535
social security in, 94–95
versus Solow model, 82–83
welfare in, 85–86
Dickey–Fuller unit root test, 198–199
Dictators, 146–147
Differential equations, 65n
Discount rate
  in Diamond model, 80–81
  in Ramsey–Cass–Koopmans model,
      63–68
  in real-business-cycle models, 175
  and real interest rate, 345–346
  under uncertainty, 391
Discrete time, 11n, 371–373, 542
Disequilibrium models, 237n
Disinflation policy, 279n
Distortionary taxation; *see* Taxes,
      distortionary
Diversion, 119–120, 143–145, 148–156,
      166
Dual labor markets, 431
Durable goods, 364
Dynamic efficiency; *see* Dynamic
      inefficiency
Dynamic inconsistency
  and delegation, 487–489
  examples, 482
  limitations of theories, 491–492
  of low-inflation monetary policy, 468,
      478–482
  model of, 479–482
  and policymakers' reputation,
      484–487

and punishment, 526–527
and reputation, 527–528
and rules, 483
Dynamic inefficiency, 85–89, 96, 535
Dynamic programming, 179n, 424, 446
Dynamic stochastic general equilibrium
     models, 211

Economic growth; *see* Growth
     (economic)
Economies of scale; *see* Returns to scale
Education, 134–141, 166, 456, 458
Effective labor demand, 238
Effectiveness of labor, 9, 26, 28, 98
Efficiency wages; *see also*
     Shapiro–Stiglitz model
   and bargaining, 461–462
   and compensation schemes, 413,
     431–432
   definition, 415
   extended model, 417–421
   generic model, 412–417
   and interindustry wage differences,
     456–458
   and Keynesian models of
     fluctuations, 204, 309
   potential reasons for, 412–413
   and unemployment, 415–417
   and union wage premiums, 461
Elasticity of substitution
   intertemporal, 49, 91, 346, 348
   in labor supply, 208–209
   in production, 40–41
Embodied technological progress,
     45–46
Employment movements
   and contracts, 453–456
   cyclical, 258–260
   and government purchases, 194–196
   and insiders, 437–439
   and labor demand movements,
     410–411, 415, 417, 429, 436, 442,
     449–451, 454–455
   in Lucas model, 278
   and no-shirking condition, 426, 430
   random walk with drift, 441–442
   in real-business-cycle models, 206
   and sector-specific shocks, 207
   short-side rule, 263

Entrepreneur-investor contracts,
     394–398
Equity premium, 351–353, 365–366
Ethier production function, 161–162
Euler equation, 54, 69, 71, 76, 77, 337,
     339, 351, 355, 543
European Monetary System, 230n
Excess sensitivity of consumption, 340
Excess smoothness of consumption,
     340n, 353
Exchange rates
   effect of depreciation, 575
   expectations, 226–227, 230–234
   fixed, 227–230, 256
   floating, 227, 229, 230, 232–234, 256
   and interest-rate rules, 503
   and intervention, 262
   nominal, 226, 256
   overshooting, 230–232, 262
   real, 226, 256
   regime, 256
   target band, 230n
   targeted to reduce inflation, 255n
Excludability, 116–117, 119
Expectations-augmented Phillips curve,
     247–252, 272
Expected inflation; *see* Inflation,
     expected
Expenditures
   actual *versus* planned, 219–222
   planned, 224–225, 226, 227–230,
     232–234
Experiments, 319–320
External adjustment costs, 370
Externalities
   aggregate demand, 284, 301–302
   from capital, 148–149
   and income differences across
     countries, 149
   pecuniary, 61n, 118n
   from pollution, 36, 41–43
   from research and development,
     118–119
   thick-market, 308

Factor returns/flows, 142–143
Fair wage-effort hypothesis, 413, 432,
     460, 462–463
Federal funds rate, 257, 476–478, 498

Federal Reserve, 253–258, 279n, 476–478, 498, 500n, 501
Finance
  debt *versus* equity, 409
  internal and external, 403–405
  outside, 400–401
Financial-market imperfections
  and cash flow, 403–405
  and debt crises, 575
  implications of, 399–402
  and long-run growth, 148, 402
  model of, 393–399
  and nominal frictions, 311–312
  and real rigidity, 307–308
  and short-run fluctuations, 307–308, 311–312, 402
  sources of, 392
Firm-specific shocks, 280n
First welfare theorem, 60
Fiscal policy; *see also* Budget deficits; Policymakers
  debt *versus* taxes, 535–541
  deficit bias, 468, 547, 549, 550–551, 566
  in France, 570
  in industrialized countries, 530, 533–534, 567–572
  long- *versus* short-run, 531n
  and monetary policy coordination, 253n
  Ricardian equivalence result, 535–537
  stability of, 582–583
  and unfunded liabilities, 533–534
  in United States, 561, 566n, 573
  unsustainable, 574–576
Fiscal reform
  and aggregate demand, 547
  and bargaining issue, 562
  and conditionality, 586
  crisis-induced, 566–567, 574–575, 585–586
Fischer model, 285–288
  and actual price changes, 315
  versus Caplin–Spulber model, 280, 296
  price adjustment assumption, 280
  versus Taylor model, 280
  with unbalanced price-setting, 326
Fisher effect, 472

Fisher identity, 472
Flexible-price equilibrium, 291–292, 301, 310, 316
Flow approach; *see* Search and matching models
Fluctuations; *see also* Keynesian models; Price adjustment; Real-business-cycle models
  and calibration, 202–203
  and efficiency wages, 415–417, 420–421, 429
  facts about, 168–172
  and financial system, 402
  in Keynesian models, 173–174, 197, 308–309
  from monetary shocks, 209, 252–258
  and multiple sectors, 207
  persistence of, 196–201
  and real-non-Walrasian theories, 174
  real *versus* nominal shocks, 321–322
  in real-business-cycle models, 183–185, 190–196
  seasonal, 169n
  and shifts in labor demand, 410–411
  theories of, 172–174
Frictional unemployment, 451–452
Full-employment output, 247

Game theory, 319–320
General Theory (Keynes), 235, 236, 258, 322
Global warming, 42
Golden-rule capital stock, 21–22
  definition, 20–21
  in Diamond model, 86
  modified, 62
  in Ramsey–Cass–Koopmans model, 62–63
  in Solow model, 21–22
Golden-rule level of education, 137n, 166
Goods market, 235–242, 269–270, 307–308
Government budget constraint, 531–535, 552–553
Government debt; *see* Budget deficits; Fiscal policy; Policymakers
Government default, 574, 576–577, 579–581

Government purchases; *see also* Fiscal
    policy; Tax smoothing
  and aggregate demand, 224–225
  common-pool problem, 571, 586–587
  in Diamond model, 89–90
  and distortionary taxation, 207, 552
  and household budget constraint, 69,
    536–537
  and inflation, 470
  in Keynesian models, 224–225,
    227–229, 234
  predictable movements in, 545
  in Ramsey–Cass–Koopmans model,
    68–74, 93
  in real-business-cycle models,
    185–186, 188, 194–197
  and real interest rate, 72–74
  and wars, 72–74
Great Depression, 171, 203–205, 208,
    357n, 575
Grossman–Helpman model, 100, 118
Growth (economic); *see also* Diamond
    model; Ramsey–Cass–Koopmans
    model; Research and development
    model; Solow model
  basic facts about, 5–7
  central questions of, 26–28, 125–126
  changes in fundamentals, 158–159
  differences in convergence, 30–34,
    156–158
  and environmental issues, 35–43
  and financial system, 148, 402
  and inflation, 148, 522–523, 529
  and kinds of knowledge, 115–116
  and knowledge accumulation, 98,
    103–106
  miracles and disasters, 6, 159–160
  and population growth, 103–104,
    126–132
  and saving rate, 17–19, 121–122
  and scale effects, 114–115
  and seignorage, 529
Growth accounting, 28–30, 46, 138,
    140, 149
Growth disasters, 6, 159–160
Growth drag, 39–40
Growth effect, 18–19
Growth miracles, 6, 159–160
Growth rate, 13, 43

Half-life, 25n
Hamiltonian
  current-value, 374, 407–408
  present-value, 374n
Harris–Todaro model, 466
Harrod-neutral technological progress,
    9
Hazard rate, 423
Hicks-neutral technological progress,
    9n, 12n
Hierarchical institutions, 571
Hodrick–Prescott filter, 202n
Home bias, 350
Households; *see also* Consumption;
    Labor supply
  budget constraint, 50–51, 69, 76,
    77–78, 124, 177, 346, 536
  entry into economy, 47, 75, 537–539
  infinitely lived, 47, 75, 122
Housing, 170, 360, 407–408
Human capital, 132–143, 148–149, 155,
    157, 159, 165–166
Hyperinflation, 474, 510–511, 514–519,
    549, 561
Hysteresis, 440–444

Immigrants, 141
Imperfect competition; *see*
    Competition, imperfect
Implicit contracts, 432–436, 439,
    453–456, 463–465
Implicit differentiation, 22n
Inada conditions, 11, 15–16, 76, 85
Income differences, cross-country
  accounting for, 138–143
  and capital accumulation, 26–27
  and convergence, 6–7, 31–34,
    156–160
  and differences in growth, 156–160
  and effectiveness of labor, 26–28
  growth miracles and disasters, 6,
    159–160
  and human capital, 132
  and knowledge accumulation,
    125–126
  and saving rate, 22–24, 26n
  and social infrastructure, 143–144,
    145–146, 148–149
  and Solow model, 26–28

Indexation, 300, 311, 312, 325
Indicators, in policymaking, 497–499
Indivisible labor, 206
Infinite-horizon model; *see*
    Ramsey–Cass–Koopmans model
Inflation; *see also* Hyperinflation;
    Output-inflation tradeoff; Price
    adjustment
  and central bank independence,
    489–491
  core, 249–251
  costs of, 519–523
  cyclical behavior of, 172
  and delegation, 487–489
  effect on budget deficit, 532–533
  expected *versus* actual, 481
  expected *versus* core, 251–252
  and growth, 148, 522–523, 529
  and interest-rate rules, 501
  limitations of dynamic inconsistency
    theories, 491–492
  from money growth, 469–471
  optimal rate, 523–524
  and output, 274–275
  and owner-occupied housing, 520
  and policymakers' choices, 478–482
  and policymakers' reputation,
    484–487
  potential benefits of, 523
  potential sources of, 470
  and price adjustments, 313–314
  public's view of, 520–521, 523
  and real money balances, 470–471
  and real wage, 245
  and recession, 254–255
  reduced by targeting exchange rates,
    255n
  and seignorage, 510–519
Inflation bias, 468, 500
Inflation inertia, 295–296
Inflation targeting, 508–510
Inflation-tax Laffer curve, 512–513
Inflation-tax revenues, 512
Innovators, 117–120
Insider-outsider models
  assumptions, 436–437
  cyclical behavior of labor costs,
    437–439
  and hysteresis, 440–444

  and unemployment, 439–440
Insiders, 411–412, 437–440
Instantaneous utility function, 48–49,
    167, 206n
Instrumental variables, 255n, 341–342
Instruments, in policymaking, 497–499
Interest-rate parity, 231
Interest-rate rules, 500–503
Interest rates
  and agency costs, 400
  and capital mobility, 230
  and consumption, 345–348
  and expectations, 384, 475–478, 547
  and Federal Reserve policy, 256, 258
  and government purchases, 73–74
  with imperfect capital mobility,
    232–234
  in IS curve, 219–222
  in LM curve, 222–223
  and money growth, 471–474
  nominal
    and change in money growth,
      472–473
    and funds-rate target, 476–478
    as tax rate on money balances, 512n
  real, 49
    and golden-rule capital stock, 88
    and government purchases, 72–74
  and saving, 346–348
  and technology shocks, 191–193
  term structure of, 475–478, 526
  uncertainty about, 387
Interest-rate targeting, 528
Interindustry wage differences,
    456–458
Intermediate target, in policymaking,
    497–498, 499–500
Internal adjustment costs, 370
Intertemporal elasticity of substitution,
    49, 91, 346, 348
Intertemporal first-order condition,
    189–190
Intertemporal substitution in labor
    supply; *see* Labor supply,
    intertemporal substitution in
Intratemporal first-order condition,
    187–189
Inventories, 170, 220, 261, 279n

Investment; *see also q* theory model of
  investment
  actual *versus* breakeven, 15–16, 20
  asymmetric information, 392
  and capital income, 88–89
  and capital-market imperfections,
    311
  and cash flow, 403–405
  versus consumption, 143–145
  and cost of capital, 367–370
  cyclical behavior of, 170, 185, 203
  and financial-market disruptions, 575
  and financial-market imperfections,
    392–402
  and financial system, 400–402
  and fixed costs, 391
  and inflation, 522–523
  irreversible, 389–391
  lumpy, 391
  in machinery, 149n
  and saving rate, 34–35
  and social infrastructure, 143
  and stabilization policy, 496
  and taxes, 92, 163–164, 369, 385–388,
    402–403, 406
  and uncertainty, 88, 387–391, 409
Investment tax credit, 369
  and capital goods prices, 402–403
  permanent or temporary, 385–387
IS curve, 219–222
IS-LM model, 219, 222–223, 224–225,
  225–234, 254, 474
IS-LM-AS model, 254

Job creation and destruction, 452
Job selling, 431–432
Juglar cycles, 169

Keynesian cross, 220–221
Keynesian models
  aggregate demand, 218–225
  aggregate supply, 235–236, 242,
    247–249, 251–252
  consumption function, 70–71, 220,
    333–337
  and core inflation, 251–252
  government budget in, 261
  inflation inertia, 295
  modeling strategy, 210–212, 217,

  252, 306–307, 322–323
  and monetary shocks, 231, 252–258
  versus real-business-cycle models,
    174, 217, 224, 252
  and staggered price adjustment, 279
  theory of fluctuations, 173–174
  vagueness and flexibility, 322–323
Kitchen cycles, 169
Knowledge; *see also* Technology
  excludability, 116–117
  forms of, 115–116
  versus human capital, 133
  lags in diffusion of, 125–126, 164–165
  and market forces, 116
  nonrival, 116, 126
  production function for, 99–100
  worldwide use, 103
Knowledge accumulation; *see also*
      Research and development model
  and allocation of resources, 115–122
  and capital accumulation, 120–122
  and central questions of growth
      theory, 125–126
  determinants of, 115–116
  dynamics of, 101–107
  and endogenous saving, 122–125
  and ever-increasing growth, 105–107
  over human history, 126–132
  and income differences across
      countries, 125–126, 165–165
  and learning-by-doing, 120–125, 163
  scientific research, 117
  and talented individuals, 119–120
Kontratiev cycles, 169
Kuznets cycles, 169
Kydland–Prescott model, 479–483

Labor-augmenting technological
      progress, 9, 12n
Labor market; *see also* Contracts;
      Efficiency wages; Unemployment;
      Wages
  competitive, 236–240
  cyclical behavior, 258–260, 410–411,
      452, 465–466
  dual, 431
  economy-wide, 281n
  non-Walrasian features, 240, 260,
      410–411, 444–445

and real rigidities, 309n
short-side rule, 263
turnover in, 452
Walrasian, 410–412, 444, 450n
Labor supply
  elasticity of, 260, 410
  and elasticity of substitution,
    193–194
  and hours of work, 496
  in imperfect competition model, 282
  inelastic, 303–304
  intertemporal substitution, 177–178,
    208–209
  in real-business-cycle models, 183,
    191
  short-run elasticity, 278
  tradeoff with consumption, 180
  utility function for, 177
Lag operators, 184n, 289, 293–295, 326
Land, 37–41, 127, 129–130
Law of iterated projections, 287, 294n
Layoffs *versus* worksharing, 431
Learning-by-doing, 120–122, 163
Level effect, 18–19
Life-cycle/permanent-income
    hypothesis, 331–337
  alternatives to, 353–362
  and Keynesian consumption function,
    333–337
  and random-walk hypothesis,
    338–339
  and Ricardian equivalence, 539–541
  and taxes, 275
Linear growth models, 107
Liquidity constraints
  and aggregate saving, 359–350
  and buffer-stock saving, 359
  and consumption, 343–344, 357–360
  cross-country differences in, 359–360
  endogenous, 540
  and failure of Ricardian equivalence,
    573
  and non-lump-sum taxes, 540
  and precautionary saving, 358
  and Ricardian equivalence, 540, 573
Liquidity effect, 474
Liquidity trap, 261
LM curve, 222–223, 227
Logarithmic utility, 79–80, 91, 177–178,

    559–561
Log-linear approximation, 186–187, 216
Lognormal distribution, 189n
Long-run aggregate supply curve,
    247–248
Lucas asset-pricing model, 365
Lucas critique, 274–275
Lucas imperfect-information model
  alternative interpretations, 312
  case of perfect information, 267–270
  certainty-equivalence behavior, 270,
    285–286, 289
  difficulties, 278–279
  equilibrium, 272–273
  implications, 274–276
  and monetary policy, 265, 275–276
  versus new Keynesian view, 299–300
  output-inflation tradeoff, 274–278,
    313–314
  producer behavior in, 270–272
  rational expectations assumption,
    271, 279
Lucas–Phelps model; *see* Lucas
    imperfect-information model
Lucas supply curve, 272, 527

Marginal costs, 234, 239, 284, 308,
    311–312
Marginal product of capital, 11, 23, 27,
    88, 123
  private *versus* social, 125
Marginal revenue-marginal cost
    diagram, 301–302, 307–308
Market betas, 351n
Market-oriented regimes, 145
Markup, 239, 241–242, 285n, 308, 311
Markup function, 241
Matching function, 445
Measurement error, 32–34
Median voter theorem, 554–555
Menu costs, 300, 301, 303–304, 306,
    315, 323, 328–329
Method of undetermined coefficients,
    187, 289–291
Mexican crisis of 1994–1995, 575
Models, purpose of, 3–4, 14
Modified golden-rule capital stock, 62
Modigliani–Miller theorem, 409
Monetary conditions index, 503

Monetary policy; *see also* Policymakers
  and central bank independence,
    489–491
  and commitment, 480–481, 482
  and delegation, 487–489, 528
  errors in, 500
  and exchange rate movements, 231,
    503
  and Federal funds rate, 476–478
  and fiscal policy coordination, 253n
  inflationary bias in, 468, 500
  inflation targeting, 508–510
  interest-rate rules, 500–503, 528
  and Lucas model, 265, 275–276
  model for analyzing rules, 503–508
  and natural rate of unemployment,
    246
  and output stabilization, 493–497
  and reputation, 484–487
  and rules, 483, 499–500
  and social welfare, 493–497
  targets, indicators, and instruments,
    497–499
  and term structure of interest rates,
    474–478
  and uncertainty, 529
  and unemployment, 493–494
  in United States, 499–500
  and vector autoregressions, 257–258
Monetary shocks; *see also* Aggregate
    demand shocks
  effects and policies, 257–258
  and fluctuations, 252–258
  long-lasting real effects, 292
  in Lucas model, 267
  natural experiments, 255–256
  observed *versus* unobserved, 275–276
  output movements, 254–255
  and price changes, 284, 309–311
  St. Louis equation, 252–254
  and vector autoregressions, 257–258
Money
  anticipated *versus* unanticipated,
    275–276
  high-powered, 222–223, 253, 312n,
    519–520
  as intermediate target, 497–500
  neutrality of, 297, 299
  and output, 252–258

in overlapping-generations model,
    95–96
  real *versus* nominal, 472–473
  and wealth redistribution, 311–312
Money demand, 222–223, 253, 254,
    276n, 470–471, 511, 512, 515
Money growth
  causes of, 478–479
  and hyperinflation, 515–519
  and inflation, 469–471, 511–512
  and interest rates, 471–474
  and real money balances, 516–518
  and seignorage, 512–513
Money-output regressions, 255n,
    257–258
Monte Carlo experiment, 198–199, 216
Moral hazard, 311, 399
Multiple equilibria, 84–85, 153,
    316–320, 328–329, 483n, 579–580
Multiplier, 222
Multiplier-accelerator, 261
Mundell effect, 261
Mundell-Fleming model, 226–230

Nash equilibrium, 303, 319
National Bureau of Economic Research,
    6n, 168
Natural experiments, 255–256
Natural-rate hypothesis, 245–247, 251,
    502
Natural rate of output, 247, 498, 502
Natural rate of unemployment; *see*
    Unemployment, natural rate of
New growth theory; *see* Human capital;
    Knowledge accumulation;
    Research and development model
New Keynesian economics; *see*
    Keynesian models; Menu costs;
    Price adjustment
Newly industrialized countries, 6,
    29–30
New political economy
  characteristics of, 547–551
  delayed stabilization, 561–567
  political variables and deficits,
    567–572
  strategic debt accumulation, 551–561
Nominal adjustment; *see* Price
    adjustment

Nominal exchange rate, 226, 256
Nonborrowed reserves, 500
Non-lump-sum taxation, 535, 540–541, 583
Non-Walrasian theories, 320–322, 410–411
No-Ponzi-game condition, 51, 52

Observational equivalence, 324–325
Oil prices, 36, 247
Okun's law, 172
Open economy, 225–234
Open-market operations, 498–499
Option value to waiting, 390
Output-inflation tradeoff, 242–252
  and average inflation rate, 313–314
  expectations-augmented Phillips curve, 247–252
  failure of Phillips curve, 246–247
  and hyperinflation, 510–511
  and inflation inertia, 295
  international evidence, 276–278
  in Lucas model, 274–275, 276–278
  and money growth, 478–479
  natural rate hypothesis, 245–247, 251
  permanent, 492
  Phillips curve, 245
Output movements
  and aggregate price level, 266–273
  asymmetries in, 170–171
  and average inflation, 314
  basic facts about, 168–172
  and decline in money stock, 312
  Dickey–Fuller unit root test, 198–199
  driven by real shocks, 183–185, 321–322
  effects of fall in inflation, 295–296
  effects of increase in saving rate, 17–19, 22–24
  and financial-market disruptions, 575
  and government purchases, 194–196, 224, 227–229, 234
  and inflation, 274–275
  and investment, 381–382, 400
  and long-term effects of AD shocks, 291–292
  nonstationary, 197
  persistence of, 196–201
  and policymakers, 498–499

predictable, 209
  in real-business-cycle models, 203–205, 210–212
  serial correlation in, 507
  stabilization of, 493–497
  trend-stationary, 197
  and unemployment fluctuations, 240
  unit root in, 197
Output per worker; see Growth (economic); Income differences, cross-country
Output taxation, 206–207
Outsiders, 411–412, 437–440
Overidentifying restrictions, 342n
Overlapping-generations model, 8, 75n; see also Diamond model; Samuelson overlapping-generations model
Overshooting, 230–232, 262, 451

Panel Study of Income Dynamics, 258–259, 343
Pareto efficiency, 60–61, 86–88, 118n, 319–320, 556, 574
Patent laws, 116
Pecuniary externalities, 61n, 118n
Penn World Tables, 6n, 139
Permanent income hypothesis; see Life-cycle/permanent-income hypothesis
Persson–Svensson model, 551–552, 585
Phase diagram, 16, 57–58, 102–105, 110–113, 376–380
Phillips curve, 245, 492
  expectations-augmented, 247–252, 272
  failure of, 246–247
  and Lucas critique, 274–275
  in United States, 247
Pigou effect, 261
Poisson process, 423
Policymakers
  and aggregate demand shocks, 275–276
  anti-inflationary policy, 255
  commitment, 480, 482
  conservative versus liberal, 551
  credibility, accountability, and transparency, 509–510

delaying stabilization, 561
discretion of, 482
economic stabilization, 287–288
ever-increasing inflation, 250–251
expansionary policies, 244–245
extreme preferences, 556–557
and future spending, 556
incomplete knowledge, 458–459
independent, 489–491
inflation choices, 479–482
inflation targeting, 508–510
known inefficient outcomes, 549–550
in Lucas model, 274–276
monetary policy decision, 478–479
political preferences of, 553–555
political pressures, 499–500
production of inefficient deficits,
     561–562
reasons for accumulating debt, 551
reducing inflation, 491–492
and reputation, 484–487, 527–528
status-quo bias, 586
systematic errors, 500
targets, indicators, and instruments,
     497–499
and unemployment, 493–494
utility function, 559–561
and voter behavior, 557–558
and welfare, 500
Policy rules, 525–526
Political business cycles, 500n, 550n
Political participation, 558
Pollution, 41–43
Ponzi games, 51, 534–535
Population
   and growth rate of knowledge, 106
   and long-run economic growth,
        101–104, 111, 114–115, 121, 127
   versus long-run income growth,
        131–132
   Malthusian condition, 127–130
   specific regions, 129–130
   and technological change, 126–132
   turnover in, 75
Potential output, 247
Precautionary saving, 354–357, 358,
     540–541, 583
Predators, 150–153

Price adjustment
   and aggregate demand, 224, 273,
        287–288, 310
   and average inflation rate, 313–314
   barriers to, 311–316
   in Caplin–Spulber model, 296–299
   and costs of inflation, 521–522
   and destabilizing flexibility, 263
   in Fischer model, 285–288
   and fluctuations, 173–174, 266, 284
   frequency of, 315
   and imperfect competition, 240–242,
        281–285
   incentives for, 301–306
   incomplete, 237, 292
   and interest rates, 474
   in Keynesian models, 265–266
   in labor market, 235–240, 410–411,
        421n
   in Lucas model, 266–279
   and markup, 241–242, 308
   and menu costs, 300–301, 303–304,
        306, 315–316, 328–329
   microeconomic evidence, 315–316
   microeconomic foundations,
        265–266, 279–280, 299–300
   predetermined versus fixed, 280
   in real-business-cycle models,
        173–174, 209
   and real non-Walrasian theories,
        320–322
   Ss policy, 297, 299
   staggered, 279–280, 326
   state-dependent, 299, 327–328
   and supply shocks, 247
   synchronized, 280n, 325–326
   in Taylor model, 288–296
   time-dependent versus
        state-dependent, 280
   unbalanced, 326
Price-level inertia, 295, 296n
Price-setters, 237
   and aggregate demand, 279–280,
        291–292
   and real output, 288
   in Caplin–Spulber model, 296–299
   firms, 301–311
   free to adjust prices, 288

in imperfect-competition model,
281-285
incentive to obtain information, 312
and output, 284-285, 288
in Taylor model, 289
Primary deficit, 532
Primary jobs, 431
Producer behavior
in case of imperfect information,
270-272
in case of perfect information,
267-268
in imperfect competition model, 282
Production function; see also
Cobb-Douglas function
and economic shocks, 173
and growth accounting, 29
for human capital, 134
Inada conditions, 15-16
intensive form, 10-12, 27
and learning by doing, 120-121
in model without capital, 101-103
and natural resources, 37
for new knowledge, 112-113
for single firm, 123, 267
in Solow model, 9-12
and technological progress, 9
for technological progress, 99-101
Productivity growth slowdown, 5, 7, 30
Profitability, uncertainty about,
387-388
Profit function, 304-306
Property rights, 36-39, 116, 120, 126
Punishment equilibria, 483n, 526-527

q (value of capital), 375-376
marginal versus average, 376
q theory model of investment, 370-375
assumptions, 367, 371
firm behavior, 371-375
implications, 380-387
inflation and money holdings, 515n
phase diagram, 376-380
versus Ramsey-Cass-Koopmans
model, 376, 378-389
saddle path in equilibrium, 379-380
and Tobin's q, 375-376
transversality condition, 373, 375,
379

Ramsey-Cass-Koopmans model
assumptions, 47-49
balanced growth path, 61-63
capital taxation in, 92-93
versus Diamond model, 47
dynamics of economy, 55-60
fall in discount rate, 63-68
golden-rule capital stock, 62-63
government purchases in, 68-74, 93
phase diagram, 57-58
versus q theory model of investment,
376, 378-379
quantitative implications, 64-68
and Ricardian equivalence result,
535-537
saddle path, 60
and saving, 62
social planner's problem, 61, 407
versus Solow model, 62
utility function, 48-49
and Walrasian model, 173
welfare in, 60-61
R&D effect, 118
Random walk hypothesis, 337-344
Rational expectations, 230-232, 271,
279, 286-287, 525-526
Reaction function, 316, 319-321
Real-business-cycle models
with additive technology shocks,
213-214
assumptions, 174-176
balanced growth path in, 186-189
calibrating, 201-203, 211
changes in government purchases,
195-196
depreciation in, 181-182, 185
effects of technology shocks,
190-194, 208
extensions, 205-207
finding social optimum, 214-215
and government purchases, 185-186,
188
household behavior, 176-180
indivisible-labor version, 206
intertemporal first-order condition,
189-190
intertemporal substitution in labor
supply, 177-178

intratemporal first-order conditions, 187–189

versus Keynesian model, 173–174, 210–212, 217, 224, 252

labor supply in, 191, 208–209

models growing out of, 210–211

and monetary disturbances, 209

with multiple sectors, 207

nature of fluctuations, 168–172

objections, 208–209

output movements, 183–185

persistence of output fluctuations, 196–201

real wages, 185–186

simplifying assumptions, 180–181

solution of, 181–183, 186–190

with taste shocks, 214

Real-business-cycle-style models, 210–212

Real non-Walrasian theories, 174, 320–322

Real rigidity; *see* Rigidity

Real-wage function, 240, 309

Recessions, 7, 168–172, 254–255, 284, 323, 461, 545; *see also* Fluctuations

Reduced form, 255n

Regime changes, 525–526

Renegotiation-proof contracts, 395n

Rent-seeking, 119–120, 143–145, 148–156, 166

Research and development model; *see also* Knowledge accumulation

assumptions, 99–101

basic scientific research, 117

without capital, 101–107

and cross-country income differences, 125–126

dynamics of knowledge and capital, 107–114

externalities, 118–119

learning by doing, 120–122

opportunities for talented individuals, 119–120

and private incentives, 117–119

production function, 101–103

resource allocation, 115–122

scale effects and growth, 114–115

and worldwide economic growth, 103

Returns to scale

constant, 9–12, 100, 109–110, 122n

diminishing, 100, 120

and entrepreneurial activities, 120

increasing, 100, 122n, 165–166

to knowledge, 109–110

to knowledge production, 100–102, 107

and produced factors, 107, 109–110, 114–115

Ricardian equivalence, 535–541, 546, 552, 573, 583

Rigidity

macroeconomic *versus* microeconomic, 280, 292, 299

nominal, 288

nominal *versus* real, 310–311

real, 288, 304–312, 318–319, 321–322

Risk aversion, 48, 311, 352–353, 355, 434

Risky assets, 349–353

Rival economic goods, 116

Romer model, 100, 118, 162–163

Rule-of-thumb consumption behavior, 360–361, 573

Rules; *see* Monetary policy, and rules

Saddle path, 60, 64–67, 379–380

St. Louis equation, 252–253, 255n

Sample selection bias, 31–32

Samuelson overlapping-generations model, 95–97

Saving; *see also* Consumption

buffer-stock, 353–354

in Diamond model, 82–85

as future consumption, 333

and interest rate, 346–348

and liquidity constraints, 358–360

precautionary, 354–357

in Ramsey–Cass–Koopmans model, 62

Saving rate

and credit availability, 360

in Diamond model, 80

effects of increase, 22–24

endogenous, 8, 47, 122–125

and investment rate, 34–35

level *versus* growth effect, 18–19

and long-run growth, 17–22, 107, 113–114

in real-business-cycle models, 182, 185
in Solow model, 17–22, 135
Scientific research, 117
Search and matching models, 412, 444–453, 467
Seasonal fluctuations, 169n
Secondary jobs, 431
Sector-specific shocks, 207
Seignorage, 468–469, 510–519, 529
Self-fulfilling prophecies, 85, 317
Shapiro–Stiglitz model, 421–432, 460, 462
Shoe leather costs, 520
Short-run aggregate supply curve, 247, 251–252
Short-run fluctuations; *see* Fluctuations
Short-side rule, 263
Signal extraction, 271n
Signal-to-noise ratio, 271n
Simplifying assumptions, 14
Single-peaked preferences, 553–554
Social infrastructure, 143–149, 160
Social security, 94–95, 530, 533
Solow model
  assumptions, 8–14
  balanced growth path, 16–22, 61–62, 135–137
  and central questions of growth theory, 26–28
  and consumption, 20–22
  discrete time version, 94
  dynamics of economy, 14–16
  and effectiveness of labor, 26, 28
  and environmental issues, 35–43
  factor payments, 44–45
  with human capital, 133–138
  long-run growth, 22–23
  microeconomic foundations, 94
  and natural resources, 35–41
  phase diagram, 16
  principle conclusion of, 7–8
  quantitative implications, 22–25
  versus Ramsey–Cass–Koopmans model, 62
  and saving rate, 17–18, 20–22
  simplifications, 13–14
Solow residual, 29, 30, 202, 205, 208

Specialization, gains from, 10
Ss pricing policy, 296–297, 299
Stabilization policy, 276, 287–288, 492–497; *see also* Fiscal policy; Monetary policy
Staggered price adjustment, 279–280, 285–288, 326; *see also* Caplin–Spulber model; Fischer model; Taylor model
Standard Industrial Classification, 456n
State-dependent price adjustment, 280
State variable, 374
Static expectations, 230n, 232–234
Status-quo bias, 586
Stock market crash, 357n, 483
Stock price movements, 340–341, 353
Straight-line depreciation, 406
Strategic debt accumulation, 551–561
Strikes, 562
Structural vector autoregressions, 257
Students, 136–138
Subgame perfection, 482
Sunspots, 85, 317
Supply shocks, 247–248, 493–494, 497, 522
Synchronized price adjustments, 280n, 326

Tabellini–Alesina model, 551–561, 572, 584–585
Talented individuals, 119–120
Tanzi (Olivera–Tanzi) effect, 513n
Target band, 230n
Targets, in policymaking, 497–499
Taste shocks, 214
Taxes
  and capital, 142, 369, 482
  and costs of inflation, 520
  versus deficit spending, 535–537
  distortionary, 206–207, 541–542, 552, 573
  expectations of cuts in, 546–547
  and inflation, 512–513
  and investment, 385–388, 400–401
  lump-sum *versus* non-lump-sum, 535, 540–541, 583
  in q theory model of investment, 385–387
  temporary, 275

Tax-smoothing, 541–547, 583–584
and behavior of deficits, 567–568
excessive deficits as departure from, 572–573
Taylor model, 288–296
and actual price changes, 315
versus Caplin–Spulber model, 280, 298–299
versus Fischer model, 280
and inflation inertia, 295–296
versus new Keynesian view, 299–300
price adjustment assumption, 280
Taylor rule, 501–502, 507
Taylor-series approximation, 24, 25n, 65, 186–187, 351
Technological change
capital-augmenting, 9n, 12n
and computer use, 30
embodied, 45–46
endogenous, 8, 112, 126–127
Harrod-neutral, 9
Hicks-neutral, 9n, 12n
labor-augmenting, 9, 12n
and learning-by-doing, 120–121
and population growth, 126–132
as worldwide phenomenon, 129–130
Technology; *see also* Knowledge; Knowledge accumulation
and cross-country income differences, 125–126, 164–165
and fluctuations, 183–185, 190–194, 196–197, 203–205, 208
in real-business-cycle model, 176
Technology shocks, 183–185, 190–194, 196–197, 203–204, 208, 213–214
Term premium, 475
Term structure of interest rates, 475–476, 526
Thick-market effects, 308, 445–446
Time-averaging problem, 362–363
Time dependence, 422–423
Time-dependent price adjustments, 280
Time-inconsistent preferences, 361, 366
Time-to-build, 207n
Tobin's q, 375–376
Transitory income, 332, 334–336
Transparency, 509–510, 571
Transversality condition, 373, 375, 379
Trend stationarity, 197

Two-stage least squares, 255n

Uncovered interest-rate parity, 231
Underemployment equilibrium, 318
Undershooting, 232
Undetermined coefficients, method of, 187, 289–291
Unemployment; *see also* Shapiro-Stiglitz model
basic macro issues, 410–411
and contracting, 436, 439–440
and efficiency wages, 415–417, 419–420, 427–429
frictional, 451–452
and hysteresis, 440–444
and insider-outsider distinction, 439–440
involuntary, 235
and monetary policy, 493–494
natural rate hypothesis, 245–247
natural rate of, 246, 444, 453, 497, 500
and Okun's law, 172
and output-inflation tradeoff, 242–252
and policymaker errors, 500
search and matching models, 444–453
and sector-specific shocks, 207
in traditional Keynesian models, 234–242
and wage setting, 458–461
Unemployment insurance, 464
Unfunded liability, 533–534
Unions, 454, 461, 465–466
Unit root, 197
User cost of capital, 368–369
Utility
constant-relative-risk-aversion, 48–49, 91, 351
instantaneous, 48–49, 175, 391, 422
logarithmic, 79–80, 91, 177–178, 559–561
nonexpected, 354n
quadratic, 337, 339, 349, 354–355, 358

Value function, 214–215
Vector autoregressions, 257–258
Volcker, Paul, 255

Voters, 548–550, 553–555, 557–558, 584

Wage contracts, 434–435
Wages; *see also* Efficiency wages; Price adjustment; Unemployment
and aggregate demand, 235–236, 410–411
cyclical behavior, 172, 236–242, 258–260, 309–311, 400, 438
in Diamond model, 76
under expansionary policies, 245–247
and fairness, 460–461
and human capital quality, 141
and incentives for price adjustment, 304, 308–309, 410, 415, 421n
incentives to cut, 304n, 420–421
indexation, 300
and inflation, 245, 523
and insiders and outsiders, 437–439
interindustry differences, 456–458
and labor supply, 177–178, 213, 237–240
and liquidity constraints, 344
and long-term relationships with employers, 432–436
in Ramsey–Cass–Koopmans mode, 49–50
in real-business-cycle models, 185–186
rigidity of, 234–242, 309n, 434–435, 458–461
in search and matching models, 446–449
setting, 440–441, 453–456, 459, 460
and shirking, 426
in Solow model, 44–45
staggered adjustment, 279–280
and supply shocks, 247
and technology shocks, 191–193
and unions, 461
Wage stickiness, 240–242
Wait unemployment, 440
Walrasian model, 172–173, 174, 183, 216, 321–322, 450
Walras's law, 222

War of attrition, 562
Wealth redistribution, 311–312, 400, 573–574
Welfare programs, 362
Welfare (social)
and booms and recessions, 7, 83, 284, 493–497
and consumption variability, 495–496
and deficits, 572–576
in Diamond model, 85–86
and inflation, 519–524
and long-run growth, 7
and pollution, 42–43
in Ramsey–Cass–Koopmans model, 60–61
and unemployment, 444, 452–453, 493–494
and variability of hours of work, 496
White-noise disturbances, 176, 184, 274, 277
Workers; *see also* Labor market; Unemployment
abilities of, 412–413, 457–458
bonding, 431–432
heterogeneous, 412, 444–445
and income differences across countries, 138–143
interindustry wage differences, 456–458
job selling, 431–432
labor-force attachment, 444
long-term relationships with employers, 433
and monitoring, 422, 427–428, 431
in search and matching models, 444–453
shirking, 412–413, 417–418, 422n
skills of, 443–444
and students, 136–138
variability of hours, 496
and wage-setting policies, 459–461
Worksharing *versus* layoffs, 431
World War II, 160

Y=AK models, 107